Teach Yourself Borland Delphi in 21 Days

Teach Yourself Borland Delphi in 21 Days

Andrew Wozniewicz
with Namir Shammas

SAMS
PUBLISHING

201 West 103rd Street
Indianapolis, Indiana 46290

To Dorota and Martin

FIRST EDITION

International Standard Book Number: 0-672-30470-8

Library of Congress Catalog Card Number: 95-67653

98 97 96 95 4 3 2 1

Interpretation of the printing code: the rightmost double-digit number is the year of the book's printing; the rightmost single-digit, the number of the book's printing. For example, a printing code of 95-1 shows that the first printing of the book occurred in 1995.

Composed in AGaramond and MCPdigital by Macmillan Computer Publishing

Printed in the United States of America

Trademarks

Publisher
Richard K. Swadley

Acquisitions Manager
Greg Wiegand

Development Manager
Dean Miller

Managing Editor
Cindy Morrow

Acquisitions Editor
Chris Denny

Development Editor
L. Angelique Brittingham

Production Editor
Sean Medlock

Copy Editors
Fran Blauw
Kim Hannel
Chuck Hutchinson
Johnna Van Hoose

Editorial Coordinator
Bill Whitmer

Editorial Assistants
Carol Ackerman
Sharon Cox
Lynette Quinn

Technical Reviewer
Dennis Teague

Marketing Manager
Gregg Bushyeager

Assistant Marketing Manager
Michelle Milner

Cover Designer
Tim Amrhein

Book Designer
Alyssa Yesh

Vice President of Manufacturing and Production
Jeff Valler

Manufacturing Coordinator
Paul Gilchrist

Imprint Manager
Kelly Dobbs

Team Supervisor
Katy Bodenmiller

Support Services Manager
Juli Cook

Support Services Supervisor
Mary Beth Wakefield

Production Analysts
Angela D. Bannan
Dennis Clay Hager
Bobbi Satterfield

Graphics Image Specialists
Becky Beheler
Steve Carlin
Brad Dixon
Teresa Forrester
Jason Hand
Clint Lahnen
Cheri Laughner
Mike Reynolds
Laura Robbins
Dennis Sheehan
Craig Small
Jeff Yesh

Production
Carol Bowers
Georgiana Briggs
Mona Brown
Michael Brumitt
Charlotte Clapp
Mary Ann Cosby
Terrie Deemer
Judy Everly
Donna Harbin
Michael Henry
Aleata Howard
Louisa Klucznik
Ayanna Lacey
Kevin Laseau
Shawn MacDonald
Donna Martin
Steph Mineart
Casey Price
Brian-Kent Proffitt
Susan Springer
Jill Tompkins
Tina Trettin
Susan Van Ness
Mark Walchle
Dennis Wesner
Michelle Worthington

Indexer
Rebecca Mayfield

Overview

Contents

Sams
Learning
Center
SAMS
PUBLISHING

Acknowledgments

I would like to thank the team at Sams Publishing, including Angelique Brittingham, Chris Denny, Sean Medlock, and others, for their guidance and patience. Special thanks to Danny Thorpe of Borland International for an excellent and thorough technical review of this book. To many people around the world who offered questions, inquiries, and encouragement. Last but not least, my warm thanks to Dorota and Martin, who received much less attention than they deserved while I was busily writing.

About the Author

Andrew J. Wozniewicz

Andrew J. Wozniewicz is president and founder of Optimax Development Corporation, a Chicago-based consultancy specializing in Delphi and Windows custom application development, object-oriented analysis, and design. Mr. Wozniewicz has been a consultant since 1987, developing primarily in Pascal, C, and C++. He holds a degree in Computer Science from the University of Waterloo, Ontario, Canada. A speaker at international conferences, an early and vocal advocate of component-based development, he has contributed articles to major computer industry publications. Mr. Wozniewicz can be reached on CompuServe at 75020,3617, and on the Internet at 75020.3617@compuserve.com.

Introduction

Welcome to the exciting world of object-oriented Windows programming with Object Pascal! The audience for this book is primarily the beginner-level programmer. No programming experience, no knowledge of Microsoft Windows programming, nor that of object-oriented techniques is assumed. You are expected to learn all the relevant basics as you proceed through the lessons day by day.

You may also be a more experienced programmer, having acquired your development skills in another environment, in which case you will still likely find a lot of useful information here. This book addresses the issues of programming with Borland Delphi. The emphasis is on the underlying programming language supporting Delphi: Object Pascal. You will see how Object Pascal differs from the language you are familiar with and learn the best way to tame its power.

This book has admittedly ambitious goals. In 21 days it attempts to teach you how to use the Delphi environment, the fundamentals of the Object Pascal programming language, the basics of object-oriented development, and the intricacies of Windows programming, all at once! Let's be realistic here: it is not possible for any single book to cover all the relevant material in all of these areas. The intent here is to give you enough details so that you can quickly get up to speed and start exploring on your own. Overcome the initial frustrations of a new environment as fast as possible; become productive in a matter of days—21 days to be exact!

If you are a beginning programmer, or someone who has never programmed in Windows, you will find plenty of information to get you started, but it would be unrealistic to expect a single book of this size (or of any size!) to teach you everything there is to know about programming in general, programming Windows, object-oriented programming, the Object Pascal language, and the Delphi environment. Delphi is an excellent tool, supporting both the novice and the experienced programmer. There is a lot to learn, and this book gives you the necessary basics. However, it does not make you a true master of the programming craft. It takes some real experience to get there, so start exploring!

Unlike many other programming books, this book has been—for the most part—written by a professional programmer for the benefit of other programmers. Although there is a strong theoretical component in the material covered, the theory is presented with real-life programming problems and their solutions in mind. Everything you'll read about here has been proven in practice.

This book is organized into 21 chapters, or lessons, and you are expected to follow one each day. The exact pace with which you proceed is entirely up to you, however, as it depends on the level of your programming skills and your familiarity with the issues discussed. Feel free to read faster if you already know the material, or take your time if you feel the pace is too aggressive.

Typically, the first time through, you should read this book in the order presented. Later lessons build upon the knowledge gained during the earlier chapters. As you acquire more experience with Delphi's development environment and with the Object Pascal programming language while reading and working your way through the quizzes and exercises, the order in which you read things will become less important. At the beginning, however, you should proceed in order, a day at a time.

Day 1 introduces you to the Delphi programming environment and gives you the opportunity to create your first Object Pascal program. In addition, this lesson gets you started with visual forms, components and their properties, and other practical aspects of developing Windows applications with Delphi.

Day 2 gives you an overview of the fundamental architecture of Delphi programs. You are introduced to the concept of units and shown how to construct complex programs from simpler building blocks.

Day 3 gives you a fast-paced introduction to the world of visual programming. You will see plenty of examples of how quickly you can put Windows applications together visually.

Day 4 is the first lesson in a series of detailed and thorough tutorials in Object Pascal. You start exploring the Delphi programming language by taking a look at variable declarations, constants, and built-in data types.

Day 5 continues the introduction to Object Pascal with the notions of operators and expressions. You are formally introduced to the expression syntax and the various arithmetic, logical, and other operators supported by the language.

Day 6 gives you a thorough understanding of how you can control the logical flow of your programs. The conditional constructs are introduced in this chapter.

Day 7 shows you how to control repetition in your programs by creating loops with Pascal looping constructs.

Day 8 is an overview of the powerful capability Object Pascal gives you to create your own structured and enumerated data types. Creating your own data structures is a very important aspect of a programming language, contributing to its overall expressiveness.

Day 9 introduces subroutines. You learn how to declare and implement Pascal procedures and functions in this chapter.

Day 10 is the first in a series of chapters introducing you to the concepts of object-oriented programming. You encounter the concepts of classes and object instances in this chapter.

Day 11 continues the introduction to object-oriented programming by showing you how to attach subroutines called methods to your objects.

Day 12 gives you examples and explores in more detail the concepts of inheritance and polymorphism, two hallmarks of object-oriented programming.

Day 13 concludes the introduction to object-oriented techniques by showing you how objects and classes can be used to tame the seemingly chaotic world of Windows messages and interactions.

Day 14 concentrates on the error-handling aspects of your applications. This chapter also introduces you to the concepts of run-time-type information, that is, the techniques by which your program obtains and manipulates information about itself.

Day 15 is the final chapter devoted strictly to Object Pascal syntax, reexamining the issues of visibility of identifiers, scope, and the building-block architecture of Delphi programs.

Day 16 introduces you to the nuts and bolts of producing visible output with Delphi. You learn the techniques for drawing, painting, and printing under Windows.

Day 17 gives you an overview of the array of standard Windows controls, such as edit boxes, list boxes, buttons, and so on. You learn how to use the components that Delphi provides to encapsulate the functionality of these standard controls.

Day 18 continues the exploration of built-in Delphi components by giving you a hands-on introduction to standard dialogs and other components.

Day 19 is an exploration of the world of database programming. In this chapter you learn how to create scaleable, relational database applications with Delphi. You are also introduced to some of the fundamentals of database theory, to Delphi components encapsulating the Borland Database Engine (BDE), and to the techniques that make it all work together.

Day 20 is an advanced chapter on creating your own custom components with Delphi. One of the advantages of Delphi is the ability to extend the palette of pre-built components with your own creations, thereby enriching and extending the development environment. This chapter shows you how this is accomplished.

Day 21 teaches you about another extremely important topic, that of Dynamically Linked Libraries (DLLs). You learn how to create your own DLLs with Delphi, and how to use DLLs you and others have created.

A bonus chapter introduces you to the details of exchanging information between two programs via Dynamic Data Exchange (DDE) and the techniques of programming with Windows Object Linking and Embedding (OLE) technology.

As you learn to program in Delphi, keep in mind that you are being introduced to a whole new way of programming. The idea of Rapid Application Development (RAD) is changing the way programs are being developed. Traditionally, linear-structured techniques give way to iterative approaches carried out in a non-linear, highly interactive fashion, where visual prototyping and quick development cycles prevail.

Visual programming has literally reshaped the developer's workbench. Instead of writing our programs using cryptic code, with character-based editors that are controlled by equally cryptic commands typed by hand, we interactively click-and-drop components onto forms, visually place them so that the effect looks appealing, and connect them via short and understandable code snippets.

In the past, developing even the simplest Windows application required a lot of diligent groundwork—carefully setting up the structure for your program, crafting the source code module layout even before a single line of code that actually *did* something was written. You wrote a lot of code inside a very long, flat source-code file, and then you compiled it and tested the results. Delphi changes the paradigm by giving you a head start in the creation of Windows applications. You explore the user interface of your application as you are creating it. You hardly write any code for the routine tasks. Your creativity is saved for truly challenging programming tasks, rather than being wasted on aligning a few controls in a window. Component-based development proves to be the next evolutionary step in the progression of programming techniques.

However, don't let yourself be lured by the promise of easy, visual, component-based development into thinking that programming has become a "click-and-drop" type of activity, where you merely rearrange components on a form and hook them together. Programming in general, and programming in Windows in particular, requires a lot of skill, ingenuity, and creativity. There is no substitute for up-front thinking and designing your application before you jump into coding. What Delphi gives you, in a way no other programming environment has done before, is the power to explore different possibilities and learn from your mistakes before you commit to a particular solution, the power to try out several possibilities and choose the best, and the ease of mind that what you learn during your initial explorations will still be applicable to the final product. Delphi supports you all the way from creating a simple "Hello world" program to developing professional, mission-critical applications. Your skills become scaleable.

You are about to begin a new adventure in the exciting, tempting, and interesting world of object-oriented development in Windows. Good luck in your Object Pascal endeavors. Happy programming!

WEEK 1 AT A GLANCE

M T W R F S

1 2 3 4 5 6 7

During the course of this week, you will learn how easy it is to develop Windows applications with Delphi. At first, you'll get started with the various elements of the integrated Delphi development environment. You'll build your first simple Delphi program on Day 1. You'll also be introduced to the various elements comprising a Delphi project.

Your skills in manipulating the Delphi environment will solidify on Days 2 and 3 as you build a number of example applications, showing you the range of capabilities that Delphi offers.

Finally, Day 4 starts your formal training in Object Pascal, the programming language at the root of Delphi's power. By the end of this week, you will have learned how to build quite sophisticated Object Pascal programs, including constructs like conditional statements, loops, expressions, and other elements.

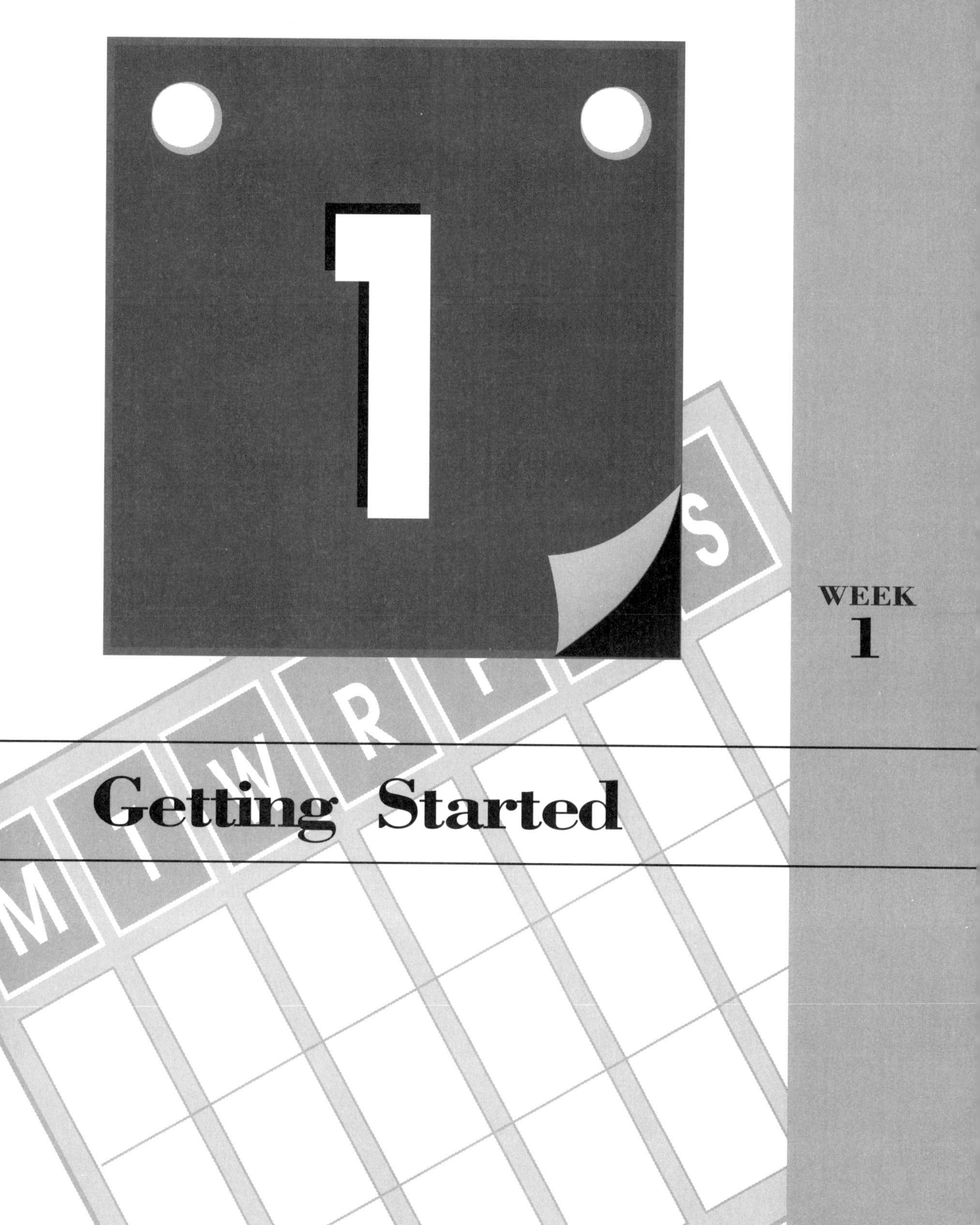

WEEK
1

Getting Started

Welcome to your first day with Delphi! Delphi is an exciting new tool that makes Windows development both productive and fun. Today you learn how to create your very first true Windows program with Delphi. You will

- Become familiar with the various elements of the Delphi interface.
- Learn about components and how you can use them to build Windows programs quickly.
- Learn how to create Delphi forms.
- Learn how to manipulate components that you place on forms.
- Learn about component properties and how to change them at design-time.

Installing and Loading the IDE

In order to benefit from this book, you must have a general knowledge of how to install, run, and manipulate applications in the Microsoft Windows environment. First, you must successfully install Delphi on your machine.

Note: There are two versions of Delphi currently available from Borland. The desktop version, known as Delphi for Windows, includes everything you need to start developing Windows applications right out-of-the-box. The higher-end, client/server edition is targeted as an enterprise-wide development tool. The high-end version includes everything the desktop edition has, plus a number of additional tools specifically designed for client/server database development.

This book's focus is on the basics; it therefore does not make any difference whether you use the low-end, desktop version, or the high-end, client-server edition. Everything you learn about developing Delphi applications here is equally applicable in both environments.

Installing Delphi

How you install Delphi depends on which particular edition you have, and on whether you are installing from a set of disks or from a CD-ROM.

As a general rule, follow the instructions the installation program gives you. Here are the most basic instructions to help you get started with the installation process.

If you are installing from disks, follow these easy steps:

- Start Windows.
- Insert Disk 1 into your A: or B: drive.
- Select Run from the Program Manager's File menu. Program Manager displays the Run dialog box.
- Enter `a:install` (or `b:install`, depending on where you inserted the installation disk) in the Command Line box in the Run dialog box.
- Press the OK button or the Enter key. The Delphi installation program starts running.

These are the steps to install Delphi directly from the CD-ROM:

- Start Windows.
- Insert the CD-ROM into your CD-ROM drive, say drive E:.
- Select Run from the Program Manager's File menu. Program Manager displays the Run dialog box.
- Enter `e:\install\setup.exe` in the Command Line box of the Run dialog box, where `e:` is the designation of your CD-ROM drive.
- Press the OK button or the Enter key. The Delphi installation program starts running.

Follow the instructions that the installation program gives you on the screen. The instructions enable you to install Delphi and some additionally required elements of the computing environment, such as the Borland Database Engine (BDE) components.

The installation program also creates a new Program Manager group with a number of icons representing the different elements of the Delphi environment. The group created by the installation program should appear similar to the one shown in Figure 1.1.

The Delphi icon is the key to starting the *Integrated Development Environment* (IDE). The IDE comprises a number of windows and tools with which you can prototype, design, code, compile, run, and debug your own Windows programs. The reason for calling it "integrated" is that you don't need to leave the development environment during the implementation cycle. All of these tasks can be performed directly from the IDE.

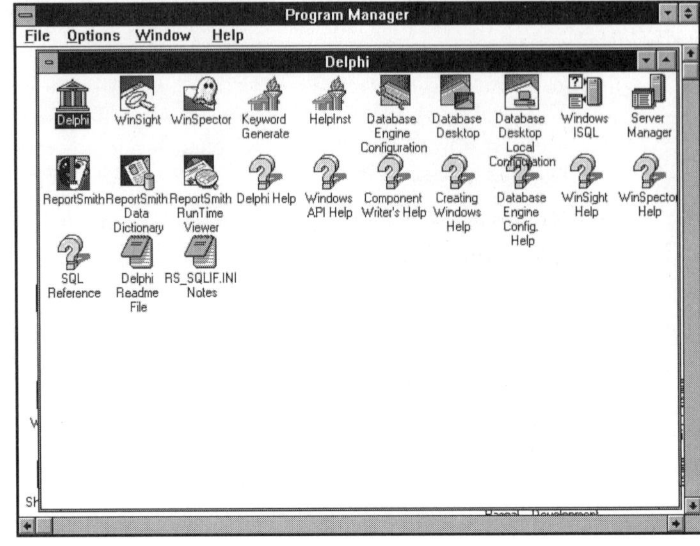

Figure 1.1.
Delphi's Program Manager group.

Starting the Delphi IDE

Double-click the Delphi icon in the "Borland Delphi" Program Manager group to start the Delphi development environment. You should see something similar to what is presented in Figure 1.2 when you start Delphi for the first time.

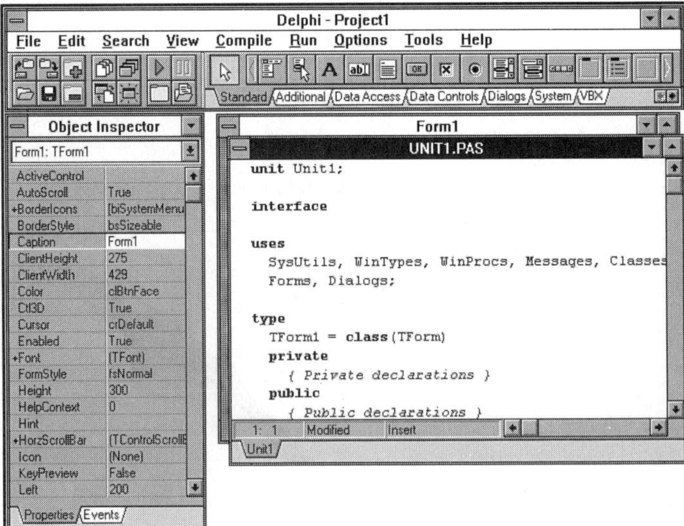

Figure 1.2.
The Delphi Integrated Development Environment (IDE).

Elements of the IDE

The IDE consists of the following elements:

- Main Window
- Object Inspector Window
- Form Designer Window
- Code Editor Window
- Project Manager
- Watch List Window
- Call Stack Window
- Breakpoint List
- Object Browser

Not all of these elements are immediately visible when you start Delphi. The Main Window, Object Inspector, Form Designer, Code Editor, and Project Manager are the ones you will use most often.

Main Window

The main window is placed at the top of your screen. Minimizing the main window also hides all of the other subordinate windows of the Delphi environment (try it now!).

Figure 1.3. shows the Delphi main window in its default configuration.

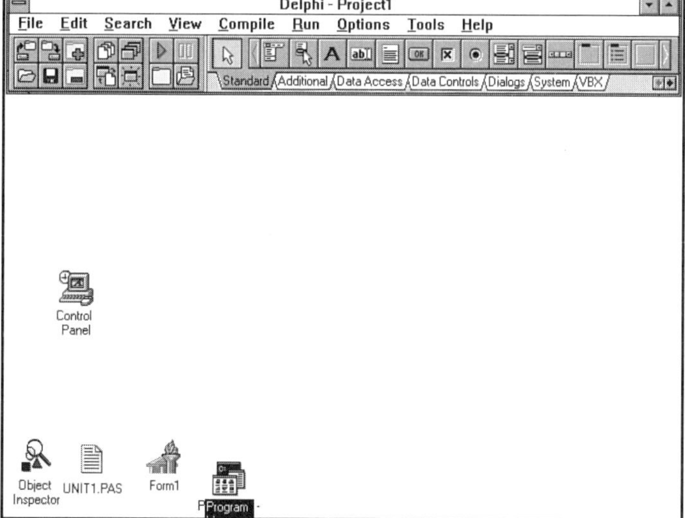

Figure 1.3.
The Delphi main window.

Toolbar

The main window is divided into two distinct areas. The area on the left contains the speed buttons. You press a speed button with the mouse to execute a command; for example, to tell Delphi to open a file, or to copy some selected text to the Clipboard. All of the commands or operations accessible via speed buttons are also accessible through menus.

NEW TERM A *speed button* appears as a small push-button with a picture on it. It is a convenient shortcut for accessing frequently used commands. Click a speed button with the mouse to perform a common action, such as opening a project or file, saving a project, and so on. All of the actions you can perform using speed buttons also can be carried out through the program's menus. The speed buttons simply give faster access to these actions.

The gray area against which all speed buttons rest is known as the *toolbar*. The toolbar is resizeable and customizable. Right-click the toolbar area with your mouse and select Configure from the menu to open the Speedbar Editor. It allows you to customize the contents of the toolbar by dragging speed buttons to and from it.

Component Palette

To the right of the toolbar, a number of little pictures known as *icons* are arranged in a row to form what's known as the Component Palette. As you visually build your programs, you will click on the icon that represents a particular component in the palette to place it on the form. The form is displayed in a separate window below the Component Palette (you will learn about forms shortly). The palette consists of several pages of components marked as Standard, Additional, Graphics, Dialogs, and so on. You can switch component pages by clicking with your mouse on one of the labeled tabs underneath the row of component icons (try it!).

NEW TERM The *Component Palette* is the area to the right of the toolbar. This is one of the hallmarks of Delphi. It contains several tabbed pages full of component icons. Delphi applications are built out of components. The components are represented as small buttons with pictures. You select a component to be placed on an application's form by clicking its icon in the palette.

Form Designer Window

The Form Designer is the blank, gray window captioned `Form1`, covered with regularly arranged dots.

When you first start Delphi, the Form Designer appears below the main Delphi palette. Figure 1.4 shows the initial appearance of the Form Designer. The title of the Form Designer's window, `Form1`, is the default name of the new form that Delphi automatically creates whenever a new project is requested. You will shortly learn how to change that title.

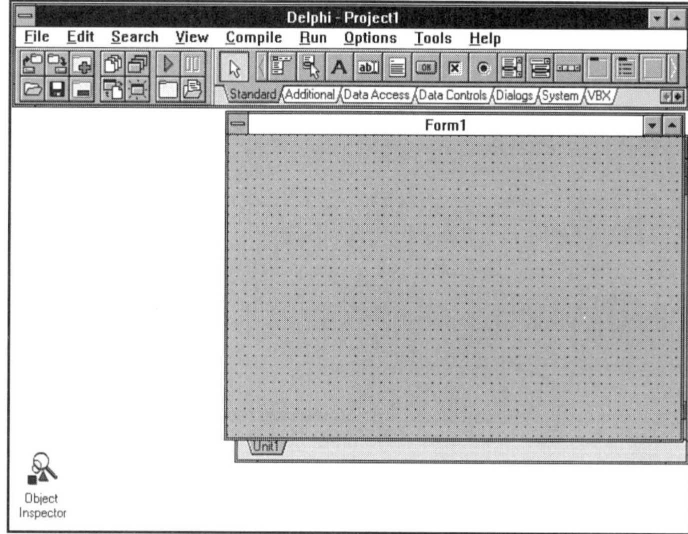

Figure 1.4.
A blank Form Designer window.

NEW TERM *Form* is the term used to describe a program's window—an area of the display where various user-interface components, such as buttons, labels, and edit fields, can be placed. A form contains and owns the components placed on it and provides the framework in which cooperation among the subordinate components is achieved. Practically every Delphi program consists of at least one form.

The Form Designer is where all of your visual programming takes place. You construct your programs by placing components selected from the Component Palette on the form. You will later attach some code to allow these components to communicate and cooperate with one another. The visual design will likely drive the overall development process. Hence the term, visual programming, that is used to describe this particular way of developing programs.

You can resize the Form Designer window like any other standard Windows window by dragging its border with the mouse (try it!). The size preferences you set in this way will be reflected in the final program when you run it; that is, by resizing the form when you are designing it (at *design-time*), you define the initial size of the form when your program is run (at *run-time*).

Even the simplest possible blank form has a number of properties that can be modified. By setting the values of these properties you will be able to customize many aspects of the form's appearance and behavior.

NEW TERM A *property* is a data attribute of a component. You can think of a property as a box storing a single value. For example, the `Width` property of every form stores the horizontal size of the form in terms of the number of individual dots, or *pixels*, across the screen.

You can retrieve the current value of a property, and (typically) set a new value for the property, both when you design a new form and when you run the program. Setting property values at design-time gives them their initial values.

Object Inspector Window

The Object Inspector displays its window along the left edge of the screen. Figure 1.5 shows a sample Object Inspector's window. You will use the Inspector a lot, so now is a good time to familiarize yourself with it.

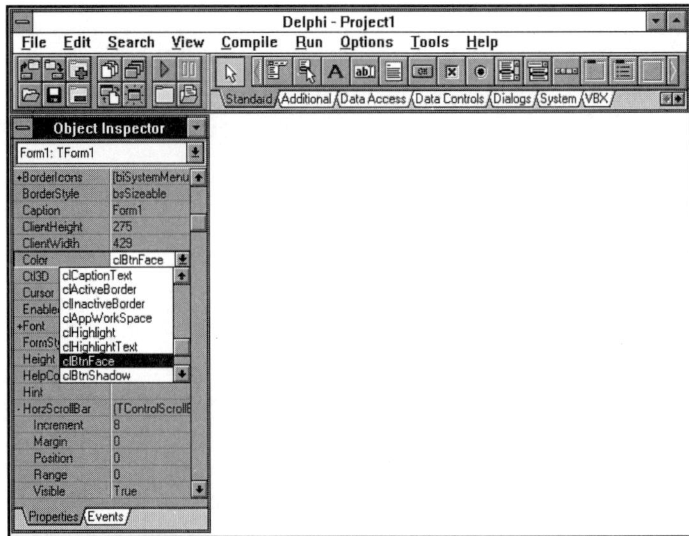

Figure 1.5.
The Object Inspector's window.

Inside the Object Inspector you will find a two-page grid. You can switch the Object Inspector pages by clicking on one of the tabs near the bottom edge of the window, labeled Properties and Events, respectively.

Today, you will concentrate on the form's properties. You will become more familiar with the Events page on Day 2.

The Properties Page

The Object Inspector is intimately tied to the Form Designer. The controls you place inside the Form Designer window can be selected and their properties examined in the Object Inspector.

NEW TERM A *control* is a visual component that can be placed on a form and is typically visible at run-time. Standard Windows controls include labels (static text), edit boxes, pushbuttons, check boxes, radio buttons, list boxes, combo boxes, and scroll bars.

The Properties page of the Object Inspector contains a two-column grid of names on the left and values on the right. Some of those values may appear empty initially. Each row of this grid represents one property of the currently selected component in the Form Designer.

Right now, because you have only a blank form in the Form Designer window, the only properties you are able to see in the Object Inspector are the properties of the form itself.

Note: You can easily obtain more detailed information on any property listed in the Object Inspector by first selecting the property (click on the name of the property inside the Object Inspector's Properties page), and then pressing the F1 key. Delphi displays the help page specific to the property you selected.

Table 1.1 summarizes the properties of a form that are visible inside the Object Inspector. These are called *published* properties, because the component—a form in this case—makes them externally available to the tools like Object Inspector.

Table 1.1. Published form properties visible in the Object Inspector.

Property Name	Description
`Active Control`	Indicates which visual control on the form will initially have the focus when the form is displayed. At run-time, the value of this property indicates which control currently has the focus. Only one control can have focus at any given time.
`AutoScroll`	If `True`, and if there are some controls that do not fit and therefore fall outside of the visible dimensions of the form, the form displays scroll bars and enables you to scroll its contents so that you can bring those invisible or partially visible controls into view.

continues

Table 1.1. continued

Property Name	Description
`BorderIcons`	Capable of holding any combination of the following values: `biSystemMenu`, `biMinimize`, and `biMaximize`. These values determine whether a particular standard Windows border icon is visible on the form. If you double-click the name of the property (in the left-hand column of the Object Inspector), this property expands and enables you to individually determine whether a particular border icon is visible. You can tell that it is an expandable property by the plus sign in front of its name.
`BorderStyle`	Determines the type and behavior of the form's border at run-time. The border can either be resizeable, fixed (non-resizeable), or dialog-like. Changing this property at design-time has no effect on the visual appearance of the Object Inspector's border. The effects are only visible when you run your application.
`Caption`	The text of the form's title bar.
`ClientHeight`	The height of the so-called *client area* of the form, that is, the area within, but not including, the window frame. This is closely related to, and changes along with, the `Height` property.
`ClientWidth`	The width of the client area of the form. This is closely related to, and changes along with, the `Width` property of the form. This is the width of the form minus the width of the frames.
`Color`	The background color of the form. You can either select from a list of predefined values, or—by double-clicking the value side (right-hand column) of the Object Inspector—open the standard Windows Color dialog box, and select a color from there. You can also enter directly an integer value representing the color.
`Ctl3D`	Determines whether the form appears with three-dimensional effects.
`Cursor`	Determines the shape of the image used as the mouse pointer when the mouse passes over an uncovered area of the form. You can select from a predefined list of cursor shapes.
`Enabled`	Determines whether the form allows mouse and keyboard input.
`Font`	A composite (that is, expandable) property that defines the default font characteristics for the form and its controls, such as the face name, point size, text color, and so on. Double-click the name (left) column inside the Object Inspector to expand the `Font`

Property Name	Description
	property and make its subordinate attributes visible and individually accessible. Double-click the value (right) column, or press the "..." button that appears there, to open the standard Windows Font dialog box and to select the font characteristics from there.
`FormStyle`	There are four possible styles for a form: `fsNormal`, `fsMDIChild`, `fsMDIForm`, and `fsStayOnTop`. The value of this property determines the fundamental behavior of the form's window. For example, to use a form as a child window inside an MDI application, you must give it the `fsMDIChild` style. You will learn more about the application architectures on Day 2.
`Height`	The total height of the form, in screen pixels, including any borders and possibly the caption. `Height` is always at least as large as the value of the `ClientHeight` property.
`HelpContext`	A number used to interface to the context-sensitive help system that you might want to build for your application. The value of this property determines which Help page will be displayed when the user presses the F1 key while the form has the focus.
`Hint`	Determines the hint text that can be shown when the mouse passes over the control.
`HorzScrollBar`	A composite (nested) property that determines the characteristics of the form's horizontal scroll bar, if any. As with all nested properties, double-click its name to expand it.
`Icon`	Determines the icon displayed when the form is minimized.
`KeyPreview`	Determines whether the form as a whole gets a chance to "see" a keyboard event (such as a press of a button) first, before the event is passed to the currently active control.
`Left`	The horizontal position (x-coordinate) of the top-left corner of the form expressed in pixels, relative to the screen, starting at zero at the left edge of the screen and increasing as you move right.
`Menu`	Defines the main menu bar for the form.
`Name`	Logical name of the form used to refer to it inside Object Pascal code.
`ObjectMenuItem`	This property is specific to support for Windows OLE (Object Linking and Embedding) functionality. You will have a chance to learn more about OLE in a bonus chapter at the end of the book.

continues

Table 1.1. continued

Property Name	Description
`PixelsPerInch`	Helpful for designing your forms so that they can be displayed on different systems in different screen resolutions without degradation in appearance. Related to the `Scaled` property.
`PopupMenu`	Designates a `PopupMenu` component, if any, to appear if the right mouse button is pressed while the cursor is over the form.
`Position`	Determines the initial position of the form relative to some other anchor point at run-time. For example, the form may be centered on the screen, or may use the default position assigned by Windows. You can select from a list of predefined values.
`PrintScale`	Determines how the form is scaled when you attempt to print it directly.
`Scaled`	Determines whether the form will be scaled according to the value of the `PixelsPerInch` property described previously. This is helpful for designing forms that are independent of the screen resolution at which they are displayed. When `True`, the form will preserve its *aspect ratio*, that is, the horizontal versus the vertical proportions in different screen resolutions.
`ShowHint`	Determines whether helpful hints, that is, the values of the `Hint` property, are displayed to the user when the mouse passes over or rests over a control.
`Tag`	A long-integer value that you can assign for your own purposes. The meaning of this value is up to you.
`Top`	The vertical position (y-coordinate) of the top-left corner of the form expressed in pixels, relative to the screen, starting at the top of the screen and increasing as you move down the screen.
`VertScrollBar`	A composite (nested) property that determines the characteristics of the form's vertical scroll bar, if any.
`Visible`	Determines whether the potentially visible component, a form in this case, actually appears on the screen.
`Width`	The total width of the form, in screen pixels, including any borders. `Width` is always at least equal to the value of `ClientWidth` property.
`WindowMenu`	This is applicable only to so-called MDI frame forms. This property determines which submenu of the main MDI window's menu will be designated as the "window menu," that is, the menu holding an automatic list of the open MDI child windows.

Property Name	Description
`WindowState`	Determines whether the form is initially displayed in its maximized, minimized, or normal (restored) state.

At the top of the Inspector window there is a drop-down list of components. Click the arrow to the right of the list to display the drop-down part of it. Right now, because the current form is blank, only the form itself (`Form1`) is listed. No other components are present on the form yet.

Code Editor Window

Along with the visual design of the user interface of your programs (forms), you also will be developing the underlying program code. The underlying programming language of Delphi is called *Object Pascal*. You will write Object Pascal code using a text editor. Although it is not required to use any particular text editor (you might, in principle, even use the standard Windows Notepad!), you will find that the integrated editor provided by Delphi is well-suited for the task precisely because of its integration with other elements of the environment.

The integrated code editor is also a debugger, allowing you to single-step your program's source code, examine the values of variables and properties at run-time, set breakpoints, and so on.

When you create a new project or run Delphi for the first time, there is a new Object Pascal source file created for you by Delphi in the Code Editor window. This source file is an Object Pascal unit, by default named `Unit1`. You will learn more about Object Pascal source-code units during Day 2 and subsequent lessons.

NEW TERM A *unit* is a high-level building block of an Object Pascal program. Units may contain both data and code. Each unit may export (that is, make available) data and code elements for use by other units. Object Pascal programs are typically built from many units.

Note: The terms *unit* and *module* will be used interchangeably throughout this book and each means a relatively autonomous portion of Object Pascal code, typically contained in a .PAS file, that can be compiled separately from other units/modules.

Many of the units that you will need to build your programs are already provided with Delphi. They are referred to as standard, or built-in, units and include `System`, `WinProcs`, `WinTypes`, `Messages`, `Classes`, and others.

Project Manager

To open the Project Manager window, select Project Manager from the Delphi main window's View menu (press Alt+V, P). You are presented with the list of elements of the currently active project. These elements are units, and forms corresponding to some of those units.

Note: In Delphi you can only have one project open at a time, but a project can consist of a large number of units and forms.

Figure 1.6 shows the Project Manager with an open project listing only one Object Pascal unit and its associated form. Double-clicking with the mouse in the Unit column opens that unit in the code editor. Double-clicking in the Form column opens the corresponding form for visual editing.

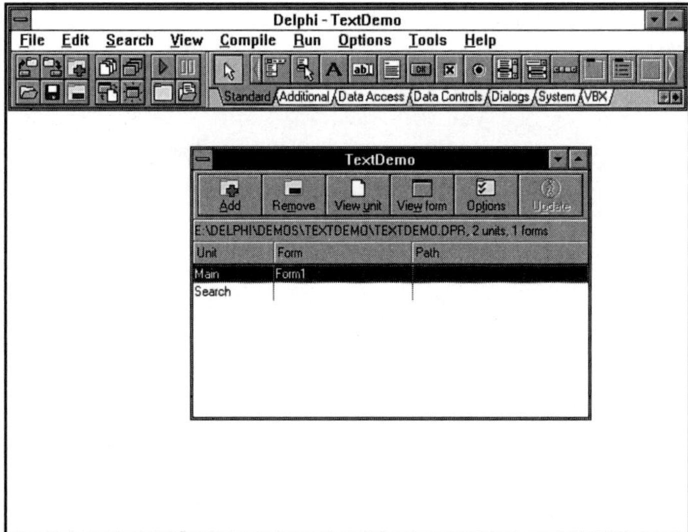

Figure 1.6.
The Project Manager's window.

The Project Manager displays a list consisting of three columns. On the left, the Unit column lists all the Object Pascal modules (units) that belong to the project. Some of these units will have a visual form (window) associated with them. The forms are listed in the next (middle) column, after the unit with which they are associated. The third (right-hand) column shows the directory in which the corresponding Pascal source file resides.

Note: A Delphi form always has a corresponding Object Pascal unit that supports it. On the other hand, a Pascal source-code unit does not have to be associated with any particular form; it can provide services that are potentially available to and shared among all forms.

How to Exit Delphi

With all of the various windows and forms open, you may be wondering: What would I need to do if I wanted to quickly exit the Delphi environment to work with some other program?

To exit Delphi, even if you have a lot of subordinate windows open, simply select Exit from the File menu of the main Delphi window (the one at the top, with the speed buttons and the Component Palette). Alternatively, you can simply press Alt+X at any time when Delphi is running in design mode, but not when your program is running from within the Delphi environment.

Note: When you attempt to exit Delphi after having made some changes to the current project, you will always be asked if you want to save the current project. Don't answer this question mechanically, without thinking. It pays to be careful at this point.

This is your last opportunity to save the project you have modified. You might, however, specifically **not** want to save the project; that is, you might want to revert back to the last version saved on disk. Take your time and actually think of what the implications are when you are asked "Do you want to save?"

Creating a New Project

Now you are ready to create your first programming project with Delphi. You will create the world's simplest Windows program, shown in Figure 1.7: a blank window. Don't discard this example too lightly, though! You will see that the BLANK program is a well-behaved Windows application, with the main window capable of being resized, moved around the screen, minimized, maximized, and so on.

You will also learn how easy it is to change certain aspects of the visual appearance of the BLANK window, such as its color or the title displayed in its caption bar, all without writing any program code whatsoever!

Figure 1.7.
The BLANK example program's window.

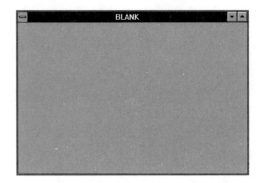

In other words, the BLANK program's main window already has all of the fundamental window behaviors you would expect from any well-behaved Windows program, without your having to write even a single line of source code. Would you be impressed if you realized that accomplishing the same feat during the early days of Windows programming required no less than a few hundred to a thousand lines of C code? Even now, very few development environments can claim to provide this kind of functionality!

The BLANK Program

The very first thing you need to do when you embark on a new programming project is create a new Delphi project. Follow these instructions:

- ☐ Select New Project from the File menu of the main Delphi window (from now on, the phrase "from the File menu of the main Delphi window" will be substituted with simply "from the File menu").

You will see some disk and display activity and will be presented with a blank form, `Form1`, inside the Form Designer's window, as well as a newly generated Object Pascal source-code unit, `Unit1`, which corresponds to the form, in the Code Editor window.

Saving the New Project

Before you do anything else, you should establish a home directory for your new project by saving it so that the Delphi environment knows where to store files it later generates.

1

To save your newly created project, select Save Project from the File menu. At this point, Delphi opens a File dialog box prompting you to first name your Object Pascal form unit appropriately, and then to select the drive and directory where you want the form unit and the form itself stored.

The default name for a form is `Form1`. The default name for its corresponding Object Pascal unit is `Unit1`. These names are assigned by Delphi when you create a new project. You can, however, change any default names Delphi assigns to your own liking.

- ☐ Select Save Project from the File menu. Because this is a new project that you have not had a chance to name yet, a Save Unit As dialog box first appears, enabling you to name the form's unit.
- ☐ Change the default unit name at this point from `Unit1` to something more descriptive. We will call this form file FRMBLANK, so enter **`FRMBLANK`** (you don't have to enter the extension .PAS; it will be added automatically) in the File Name box of the Save Unit1 As dialog box, as shown in Figure 1.8.

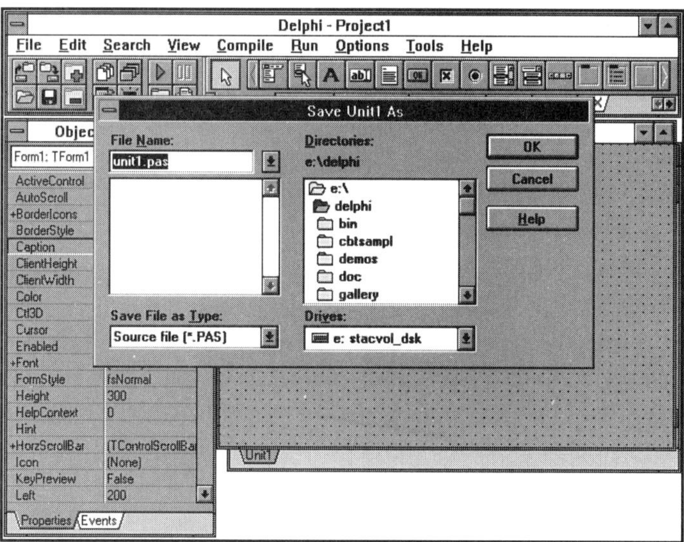

Figure 1.8.
Saving a new form unit.

After naming the form unit file, when you press the OK button of the Save Unit As dialog box, you are again asked to name the project file itself.

- ☐ Enter `BLANK` (no extension) or `BLANK.DPR` in the File Name box of the Save Project As dialog box that appears next, as shown in Figure 1.9.

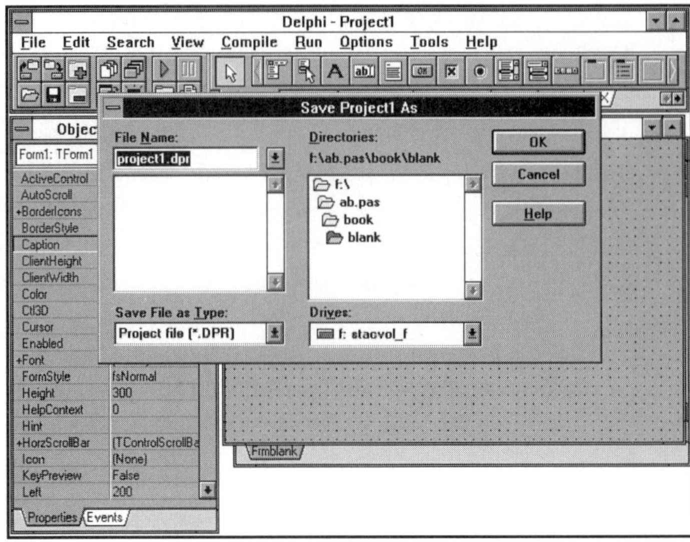

Figure 1.9.
Saving a new project.

Project Files

Delphi creates a number of files when you save a new project. Here is a list of the most important files that you will deal with when creating Delphi projects:

- The main project file.

  This file has the extension .DPR (for "Delphi Project"). It is the main Object Pascal source-code module for the project. There is only one .DPR file for each Delphi project. This file, among other things, lists the names of the other files comprising a Delphi project. It is in a sense equivalent to a makefile (which you may be familiar with from other environments), although it is different from a typical makefile in that it serves as the input to the compiler, not to the `make` utility, and hence is a valid piece of Object Pascal code.

- The form file.

  The form files have the extension .DFM (for "Delphi Form"). These are binary resource files holding the definition of the visual forms as created inside the Form Designer. There may be many forms in a Delphi project, and each form has its own .DFM file (and a corresponding unit's .PAS file; see the following).

- Pascal unit file.

  This file has the extension .PAS and contains the Object Pascal code for the corresponding form or for a stand-alone code module. By default, there is only one such file in the project: the main form's unit. It corresponds to, and provides support for, the main form. As your projects grow, you will be adding more .PAS files with or without associated forms.

- Project options file.

  The extension of .OPT marks a file that contains various Delphi settings that affect the way programs are generated and the way the Delphi IDE operates. There is one such file per project. This is a text file listing options and settings, one per line.

After saving the newly created project, you might want to examine the contents of the directory you specified for the project to verify that indeed all of the required files are present.

Note: The file extension of .PAS is not absolutely required for Object Pascal source files, but is a good naming convention with a long tradition. Whenever you see an extension of .PAS, your expectation should be that you will find source code written in the Pascal programming language inside. It is a good idea to stick to this convention.

DO | **DON'T**

DO change the default name of the project file (`project1.dpr`) and of the form files (`unit1.dfm/unit1.PAS`) to something more meaningful.

DON'T ever use the defaults `Project1` and `Unit1` for the names of the files in your project. After you have accumulated several of those `Unit1`s in different directories, it will be very difficult for you to keep track of what is inside them.

DON'T change one cryptic name, such as `Unit1`, to another equally cryptic and meaningless name such as `MyUnit`. Use meaningful names—something that tells you what is in a file without having to look inside it.

Object Files and Executables

The process of creating a complete Delphi application involves three distinct steps, as follows:

- Creating the visual interface elements, in particular the main form of the program.
- Writing supporting Object Pascal code to perform any needed actions on the form.
- Compiling the Object Pascal source code and the form resources into an executable (.EXE) that can be run as a stand-alone Windows program.

You will be performing these three steps iteratively many times during the course of building a project. You will likely create some elements of the interface, write a little bit of code to connect them to other elements, and quickly compile and test them in a test run. Then you will go back to adding more interface elements and the cycle will repeat itself.

You have already encountered the files created during the first two steps (.PAS, *.DFM, *.DPR, and *.OPT). The third step introduces some new files:

- Compiled unit files. These files have the extension .DCU (for "Delphi Compiled Units") and contain compiled object code of the corresponding unit (.PAS) files. The Delphi compiler creates them when you issue either the Run, Compile, or Build All command from the Run menu. Delphi uses these .DCU files when it creates the final executable (in the phase called *linking*).
- Compiled program files. These files have the extension .EXE. They are stand-alone, compiled Windows programs that can be run from the File Manager or from the Program Manager. They can also be installed inside the Program Manager's groups. Creation of these files is the ultimate goal of the development cycle. These are the Windows programs you are eager to start creating.
- Compiled Dynamic Link Library files. This is the second type of the final executable file that Delphi is capable of creating. The default extension for this type of file is .DLL. They are compiled Windows modules that can be shared among many Windows programs. You will learn more about them on Day 21.

Figure 1.10 illustrates the various files that are usually part of a Delphi project and their relationships to one another.

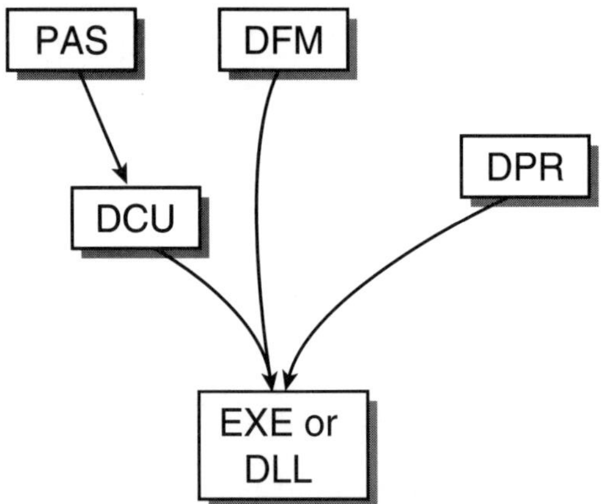

Figure 1.10.
Delphi files and their relationships.

The .EXE and .DLL files that Delphi creates are native Windows executables. They are not only comparable, but often exceed in terms of efficiency the programs created by other professional compilers, most notably C and C++ compilers. Delphi executables are typically smaller than their C/C++ counterparts, too.

Note: Delphi is a true (and very fast) compiler. The .EXE and .DLL files that Delphi creates contain machine-instruction code that requires no further interpreting steps at run-time; they are directly executed by the processor. This is why well-written Delphi-created programs are typically very fast, too.

The BLANK Program's Properties

So far, you have created the main form of the BLANK program. Notice, however, that the caption (title) of the form still says `Form1`. It turns out that you still have some work to do before you can refer to your form by a more meaningful name inside your code.

What you see as the form's title is the `Caption` property. Inside the Object Pascal code, you will refer to the form by its `Name` property.

To change the `Name` of the form, and its `Caption`, follow these steps:

- Click on the Form Editor's window so that it becomes focused. The name of the selected component in the Object Inspector window should be `Form1` already, because you have no other components on the form.
- Find the `Name` property of the selected form in the list of properties that the Object Inspector displays for the form. You might need to use the Object Inspector's scroll bar to bring the `Name` property into view.
- Click on the `Name` property in the left column of the Object Inspector grid, where the name of the property itself (`Name`) is displayed.

The property gets selected, and its corresponding value (currently `Form1`) in the right column of the Object Inspector's property grid gets highlighted. You can now edit and change this value:

- Type in the new value of the `Name` property in the edit box field of the property (right-hand side). Type `FormBlank` and press the Enter key.

Congratulations! You have successfully changed the name of the form. Notice how the form's caption displayed by the Form Editor changed immediately to reflect the new name (`FormBlank`). This is not what we want to appear as the form caption, however. We want the caption to simply say BLANK.

Note: The property of the form that you have changed in the previous step, `Name`, is the logical name you will be using to refer to the form in your Object Pascal code. There is a separate property, `Caption`, that allows you to change the text of the caption independently of the logical name of the form.

Let's change the form's `Caption` property now. Follow these steps:

- ☐ Find the `Caption` property in the Object Inspector (remember, the properties are listed in alphabetical order, sorted by their names).
- ☐ Click on the property grid to activate the property editor for `Caption`.
- ☐ Enter the new caption in the property value column. Type BLANK and press the Enter key.

Notice how the caption on the form itself has changed immediately. Don't forget to save the project now (File|Save project) so that you don't lose these changes should anything go wrong when you run your program.

You are now ready to test the BLANK program.

Running the BLANK Program

- ☐ To run the BLANK program, select Run from the Run menu.

If you don't have a very fast machine, you may notice a half-second delay during which your program is compiled and linked, after which it appears in all of its glory.

BLANK admittedly is a very simple Windows program. (It is simple in Delphi, but equivalent to a few hundred lines of C code, remember?) Keep in mind that you have thus created a stand-alone Windows executable, .exe, that does not require any run-time support beyond just Windows.

What happened when you issued the Run command was that Delphi compiled the source code files comprising your project into linkable, binary object files (.DCU), and then linked them together to form the final executable (.EXE). Finally, because you requested Run, it immediately started the program up for you. All of this was done during the interval between when you selected Run from the menu and when your BLANK program appeared.

You are now running your first Delphi application under Windows. Congratulations!

Note how the Object Inspector's window disappears before the BLANK form shows up when you run the program. Delphi enters a Running mode while your program is active (the word "running" is displayed in the caption of the main Delphi window). During the test run of a Delphi program, the Object Inspector is not normally available. You can still pause the execution or temporarily stop the program, however, by installing a breakpoint in the source code inside the code editor. You can then examine the values of properties and variables when the program is paused, and use other built-in debugging facilities provided by Delphi.

- ☐ While the BLANK program is running, you may want to verify that it indeed behaves as you would expect it to behave. Try resizing the window: Minimize it to an icon and then restore it. Try maximizing it. Finally, use the Close command on its system

menu or double-click the top left-hand corner of its window, at the system menu icon, to terminate it and return Delphi to the design mode.

You could see how BLANK responded to your actions and remember, you have not even written a single line of code, yet you have created functionality equivalent to hundreds of lines of code required in other development environments!

Forms and Components

Forms are at the very foundation of visual programming with Delphi. *Visual programming* means developing programs interactively by visually placing components on forms and manipulating them with interactive, mouse-operated tools to obtain the desired and esthetically pleasing effects.

Writing code in such a scenario comes into play only after a component has been selected visually and placed on the form. This approach to programming is in a stark contrast to the traditional code/compile/debug cycle in which the visual appearance of a program is not fully known until at least the first successful run, sometimes after thousands of lines of code have already been written.

Visual programming offers faster feedback to both the developer and the user. If something does not look right to the user of your program, it is much easier to change it using the interactive tools in the visual environment than it is to re-code it in the traditional fashion.

No wonder the visual programming paradigm has met with such a success in the marketplace. Delphi is the primary example of a visually oriented development tool.

Forms

You have seen how to create a new project with a blank form. Now it's time to make your forms a little more interesting. As mentioned, the key idea of visual programming is selecting and placing components on a form.

The form represents the main application window at run-time, and is a kind of "box" or "package" that holds the components of the application. A *form* is the owner of the components you choose to place on it.

Components

The definition of a component is still not something upon which you'll find many experts agreeing. This term will be used throughout this book in a rather narrow sense. A *component* is simply what Delphi calls one! A Delphi component can be placed on a Delphi form by first being selected from the Component Palette and then being dropped on the form in approximately the place where it should appear. You select components repetitively from the Component Palette pages, and click on the form to place them where you want them to appear. You can rearrange their order and positions on the form, change their size, and adjust their properties with the Object Inspector. This is what the much-touted visual programming approach is all about!

As mentioned, after you have placed a component on a form, you can change the design-time properties of that component using the Object Inspector. Simply select the component on the form by clicking on it and the Object Inspector shows you the properties specific for that component that you can examine and possibly modify.

Component-Based Development

The form itself is a component too. Like other components, it has a number of properties that you can change. It is different from other components in the sense that it is pre-created for you inside the Form Designer. You can never select a form directly from the Component Palette. A form is a very special component that, instead of being dropped on something (what would you drop it on, anyway?), is being created after you select New Form from Delphi's File menu.

All the other components you need you must explicitly select from the Component Palette and place on the form. The form acts as the top-level folder, or *container*, and the owner of all other objects you place there.

Creating Components

The Delphi environment serves a dual purpose as a software-development tool. On one hand, it enables you to build Windows programs from a palette of prefabricated software elements. On the other hand, unlike other environments of its kind, Delphi also enables you to create new, additional components that complement the ones you already have.

You don't need any special or additional tools beyond Delphi itself to create new kinds of software building blocks. You can easily incorporate those new components into the Delphi environment so that they appear on the Component Palette just like the standard components that came with the product. This is a new and exciting kind of development power. You will learn all about it on Day 20. Please be patient.

Changing Form Properties

The BLANK program you created reflects the default values of almost all of its form properties. You have specifically changed only its `Name` and `Caption` properties so far.

Figure 1.11 shows you some of the form's properties as displayed by the Object Inspector.

Notice that the Object Inspector's window is divided into two columns. The left column contains the names of the various properties a form defines. The right column contains values of these properties.

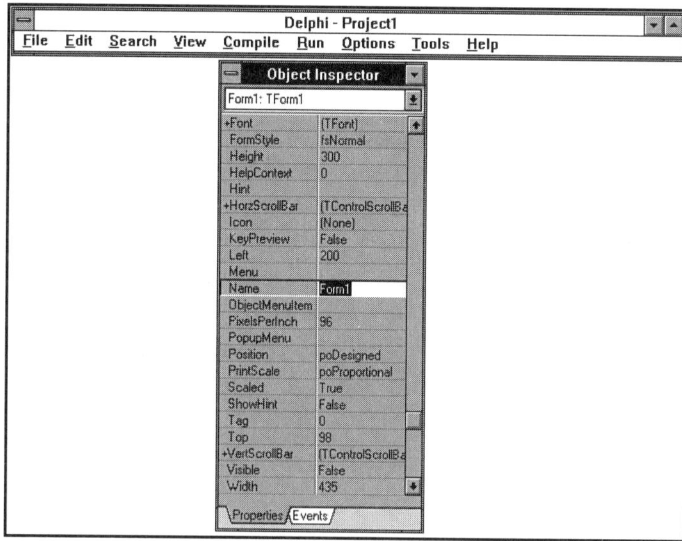

Figure 1.11.
The list of the form's properties as displayed by the Object Inspector.

Feel free to experiment with changing the values of the other form properties as well. For example, you can easily change the background color of the BLANK form.

- ☐ Make sure that the BLANK program is not currently running (Delphi must be in design mode), the Object Inspector window is open, and the form `FormBlank` is selected.
- ☐ Find the `Color` property in the Object Inspector.

Notice that the current value of this property is set to `clBnFace`. `clBnFace`, normally equivalent to `clSilver`, is the default value Delphi assigns to the form's `Color` property.

- ☐ Click the property name and note the little arrow button that appears at the right edge of the Object Inspector's property value field. When you click the arrow button, a list of possible values for the `Color` property unveils.

You can select from the list of predefined color values. Try this—and notice that as you select different values your selections take immediate visual effect on the form.

Being able to select from a predefined list of all possible values comes in handy and greatly reduces the possibility of an error—such as spelling the value incorrectly, for instance. You don't have to remember all of the possible color values; simply select from the list. Table 1.2 lists the predefined values.

Table 1.2. Possible values of the Color property.

Name	Description
clAqua clBlack clBlue clFuchsia clGray clGreen clLime clMaroon clNavy clOlive clPurple clRed clSilver clTeal clWhite clYellow	This set of values refers to the color by its name. You can select one of the 16 standard Windows colors by referring to one of these names.
clActiveBorder clActiveCaption clAppWorkSpace clBackground clBtnFace clBtnShadow clBtnText clCaptionText clGrayText clHighlight clHighlightText clInactiveBorder clInactiveCaption clMenu clMenuText clScrollBar clWindow clWindowFrame clWindowText	This set of color values refers to system colors defined through the Control Panel. Note that one or more of these values may result in the same actual color being displayed. For example, the default Windows color scheme defines `clBtnFace`, `clGrayText`, and `clScrollBar` to be the same as `clSilver`, that is, a light gray shade.

What you see here is an example of interactively setting component properties at design-time. The component in question, in this case, is the form itself. As you design your program, you can enter initial values for the properties of all of the components in your project.

Not only do those values affect the appearance of the program at run-time, but the effects of your changes can be viewed immediately while still in design mode. This is visual programming at its best.

Another important point to notice here is that in addition to being able to select a color from a drop-down list of predefined values, you can use a specialized property editor to change the `Color` characteristic of the form.

When you were entering the new caption for your form, you simply typed in the text. With the `Color` property, not only can you type in the value (for example, `clSilver`) directly, or select from a predefined list of possibilities, but you can double-click the `Color` property value (right-hand side) in the Object Inspector to bring up the standard Windows Color dialog box as the property editor. Figure 1.12 shows the appearance of the Color dialog box.

Figure 1.12.
The `Color` property editor.

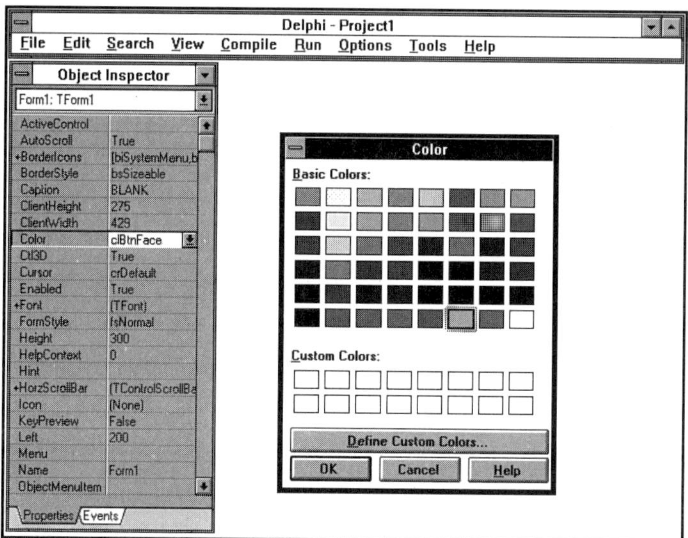

Other kinds of property editors also exist. You have already encountered a custom `Font` property editor. In fact, when you begin writing your own components, you will be able to devise and install your own property editors for these components. You will learn how to create your own components on Day 20.

DO	DON'T

DO experiment. Try different values for the `Color` property. Change the values of other properties. See how they affect the form both at design-time and when you run the program.

DON'T be afraid that you will break something. At this early stage, the worst that can happen is that you will have to reinstall Delphi from scratch. Big deal! Better to make your mistakes now, and perhaps lose only the examples you have been working on, than later, after you have expended considerable effort building your own program.

In general, the button with three dots that shows up next to a property's value gives you access to the property editor installed specifically for the property in question. When you press the button, usually a dialog box pops up to enable you to choose the characteristics of the object you are inspecting.

Note: The values of the various properties you assign at design-time become the initial values of these properties when you run your program.

Nested Properties

The `Font` property you have already encountered is also an example of a so-called *nested* property. Notice a small plus sign next to the name of the property (`+Font`). If you double-click the property name, the `Font` property unfolds (the plus sign turns into a minus sign) and displays lower-level or subordinate properties: `Color`, `Height`, `Name`, `Size`, and `Style`.

Figure 1.13 illustrates this concept by showing you a partially expanded `Font` property.

Notice that the `Font` property's `Style` property is nested in its own right. (You can see that because there is a plus sign in front of it.) When you double-click in the property name column, the `Style` property unfolds, revealing an even lower level of `Font` subproperties that determine the appearance of the font. In this case, the lower-level subproperties consist of a collection of flags: `fsBold`, `fsItalic`, `fsUnderline`, and `fsStrikeOut`.

Figure 1.14 shows the `Font` property fully expanded inside the Object Inspector.

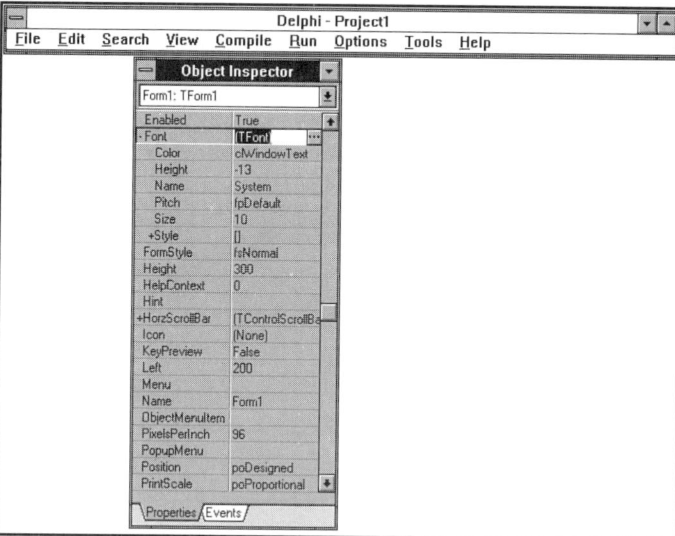

Figure 1.13.
Nested properties: the `Font` *property partially expanded.*

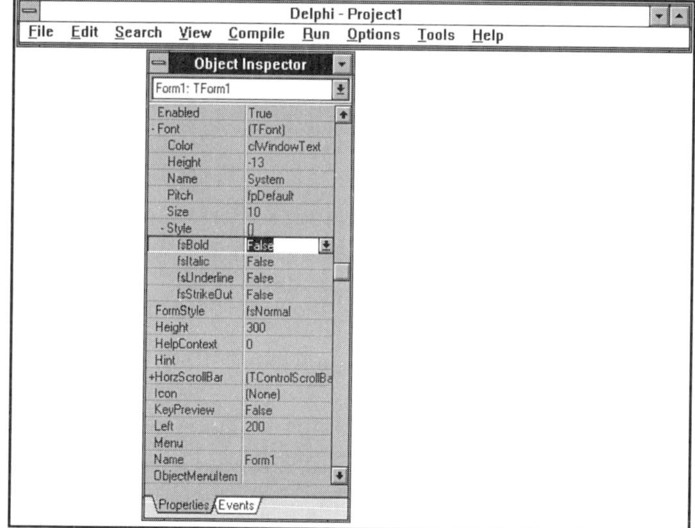

Figure 1.14.
Nested properties: the `Font` *property fully expanded.*

Placing Components on a Form: The HELLO Example

You are now ready for some more hands-on experimentation. There is a time-honored tradition to always begin a tutorial on a new programming language with a `Hello world!`-type of an example, that is, a program that prints nothing but `Hello world!`. Let's pay tribute to this long-standing tradition. Consider how you would enhance the sample BLANK program so that it displays `Hello World!` inside its main form. Let's start with placing a few components on the form.

Follow these steps to place a label and two buttons on the newly created form:

- First create a new project by selecting New Project from the File menu (you may be prompted by Delphi to save your current one first).

Again, a (blank) `Form1` and a `Unit1` are created by Delphi. Save the new project under a meaningful name, such as HELLO.

- Choose Save Project from the File menu and enter FRMHELLO in the File Name of the Save Unit1 As... dialog box. Press the OK button to close the dialog box.
- Type HELLO in the File Name box of the Save Project1 As... dialog box and press the OK button again.
- Change the `Name` property of the form to `FormHello`. Change the `Caption` property of the form to `HELLO`.
- Now, click the tab labeled Standard in the Component Palette (main Delphi window) to bring the standard component page to the forefront, if it is not already visible.
- Click the `Label` component's button shown in Figure 1.15 to select it.

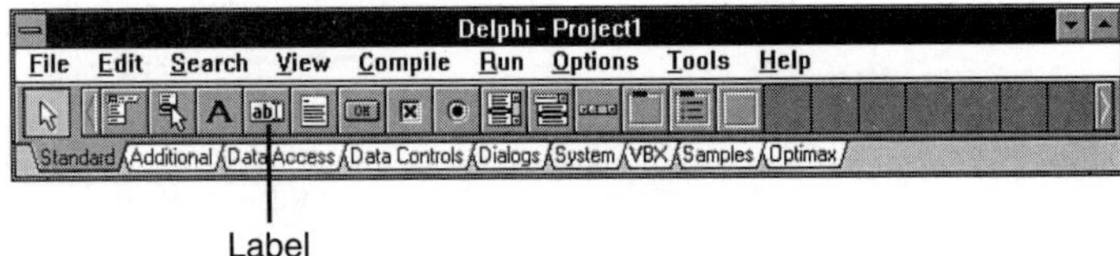

Figure 1.15.
The `Label` component icon on the Component Palette.

- With the `Label` component selected, click the mouse near the left edge of the `FORMSHOW` form. A copy of the `Label` component with the text `Label1` is placed at the position where you clicked the mouse.
- While the `Label1` component is still selected (you can tell this by the small, square handles surrounding the component on the form), change its `Caption` property to `Hello World!`. (Hint: you have to find the `Caption` property in the list of the properties shown by the Object Inspector.)

Note how the component resizes itself on the form automatically as you type the new text.

- From the Standard page of the Component Palette, select the `Button` component shown in Figure 1.16.

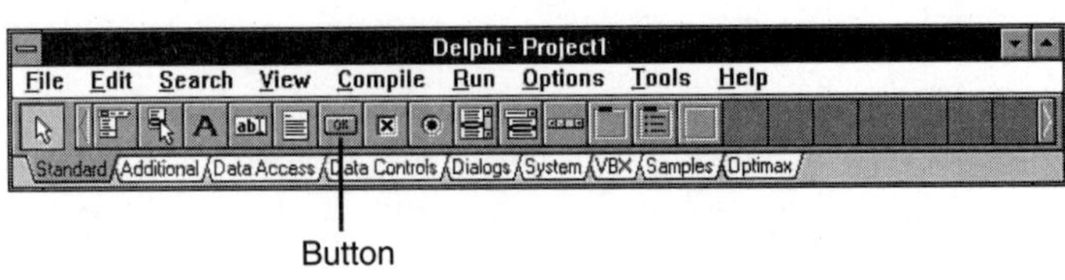

Figure 1.16.
The `Button` component icon on the Component Palette.

- Click on the form underneath the `Hello World!` label to place the new button there.
- Change the `Caption` property of the button from `Button1` to `Close`.
- Now use the same steps as above to place another button on the form, next to the `Close` button. Label it `Unneeded` (`Caption` property, remember?). Don't worry; you will remove this button from the form in one of the next steps.
- Save the project (File|Save Project) and run the program (Run|Run). Your program should display a window similar to the one in Figure 1.17.

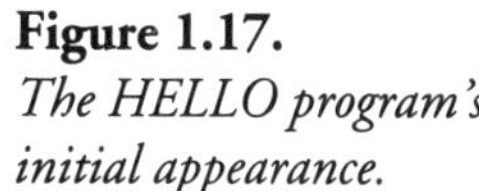

Figure 1.17.
The HELLO program's initial appearance.

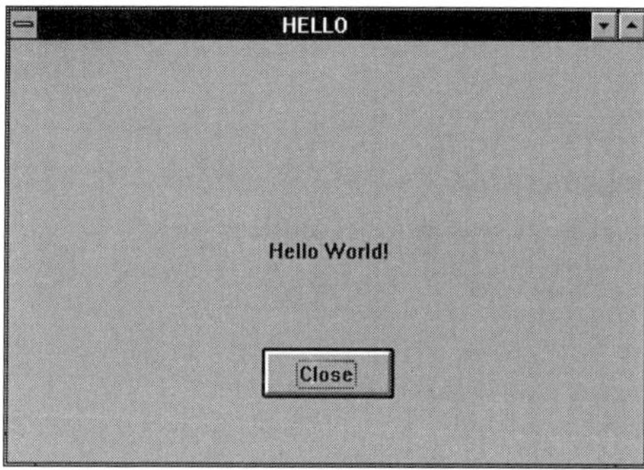

Note: When you attempt to save a new project with the File|Save Project command, remember that you will be giving a name to the form unit first. Do not name the form unit with the name you have in mind for the entire project! If you do that, Delphi will not allow you to save the project file under the same name as the form unit. You will see a message to the effect that a module with that name already exists in the project.

Name the form unit with the name that describes the form itself. Name the project with a more general name reflecting the purpose of the whole project.

Note: About Placing Multiple Components:

If you need to place more than one component of the same kind on a from, rather than clicking back and forth between the Component Palette to select it and the form to place it, select the component from the Component Palette in a "sticky" mode as follows:

> Click on the component tool in the palette *while holding down the Ctrl key*. You can subsequently click on the form several times in succession, placing one copy of the component after another. The component icon remains selected until you explicitly deselect it by clicking the default arrow tool.

Rearranging and Removing Components

Now is the time to improve the visual appearance of the HELLO program.

- ☐ Terminate the trial run of the program.

In the previous step, you placed an Unneeded button on the form for the express purpose of having an opportunity to remove it now.

- ☐ Select the component you would like to delete—in this case the Unneeded button—by clicking it with the mouse. You should see the black, square handles at every corner and on every edge of the component. They tell you that the component is selected.
- ☐ Press the Delete key.

The component is now gone. It's that easy!

Moving the Form Elements

You probably were not esthetically pleased by the haphazard placement of the components on your HELLO form. It is not easy to place a component exactly right the first time. Fortunately, you don't have to.

For a more appealing visual effect, perhaps you would like to see both the label and the remaining Close button horizontally centered within the form.

To interactively move a component around on the form, do the following:

- ☐ Select the component by clicking on it. Do not release the left mouse button, though. Delphi draws a frame around the component you selected.
- ☐ Still holding the left mouse button down, move the mouse pointer around the form. The rectangular frame representing the selected component moves along with it.
- ☐ When you are satisfied with the new placement of the component, release the left mouse button. The component snaps into its new position.
- ☐ Practice moving the two components around the form until you are satisfied with the results.

Note: Moving Groups of Components:

It is possible to move more than one component at a time. Select the first component of the group you would like to move by clicking on it. Hold down the Shift key as you click on subsequent components. You can select any number of components in this way.

After you have selected all the components you want, release the Shift key. Now click on one of the selected components, but do not release the left mouse button. You will be able to drag the entire group around the form as a single entity, and you will see the contours of the controls drawn as you move them so that you can tell their new position even before you release the left mouse button.

To deselect the components, click anywhere inside the form, but not on any of the components in the selected group.

Sometimes you just can't place the component correctly. Your hand trembles and the component seems to always end up off by one pixel from the desired position. Keep in mind that you can place any component on the form at a specific location by directly entering the position attributes: the `Left` and `Top` properties.

Figure 1.18 illustrates the concept of form coordinates and shows you the possible range of coordinates. The coordinates with the highest magnitude that are still visible on the form are `(ClientWidth-1, ClientHeight-1)`.

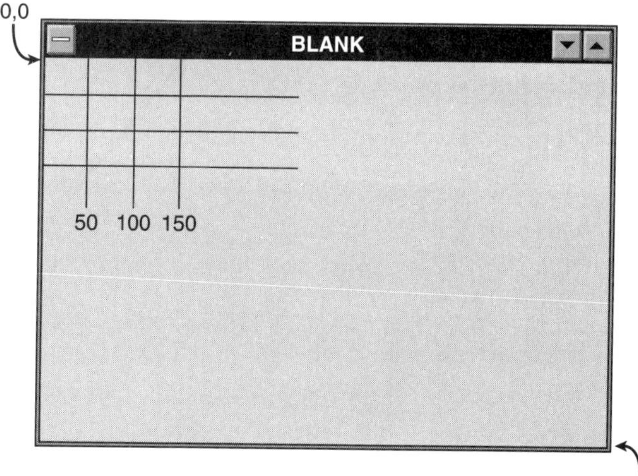

Figure 1.18.
Form coordinates.

If you enter the value `0` (zero) for both the `Top` and `Left` properties, the selected component is placed in the top left-hand corner of the form.

Increasing the value of the `Left` property moves the component across the horizontal dimension of the form, moving it farther and farther to the right. If the `Left` value exceeds the `ClientWidth` property of the form itself, the component will hide beyond the right edge of the form.

Similarly, increasing the value of the `Top` property moves the component farther and farther down until it hides beyond the bottom edge of the form (when its `Top` property has a value greater than the form's `ClientHeight` property).

Try to move the Close button on the form to the coordinates (`Left`=60, `Top`=100) now. Don't forget to press the Enter key each time you type in a new value for one of these properties.

Note: There is a keyboard-only shortcut for moving a component on the form just a few pixels in either the horizontal or vertical directions.

Once the component of interest (or an entire group of components) has been selected, press the Ctrl key and, while still holding it down, press the arrow keys to move the component in the desired direction one pixel at a time.

Aligning Components

Being able to accurately place a component on the form does not quite solve your current problem. You want the `Close` button to be centered within the form, near its bottom edge. Fortunately, there is no need to perform tedious calculations of where the button should fall, given its width and the width of the form.

Follow these steps to automatically center the button within the form:

- ☐ Select the Close button on the form. No other component should be selected at this time.
- ☐ Choose the Align option from the Edit menu. The Alignment dialog box appears as in Figure 1.19.

The last option within the Horizontal group, Center in window, is exactly what you need now.

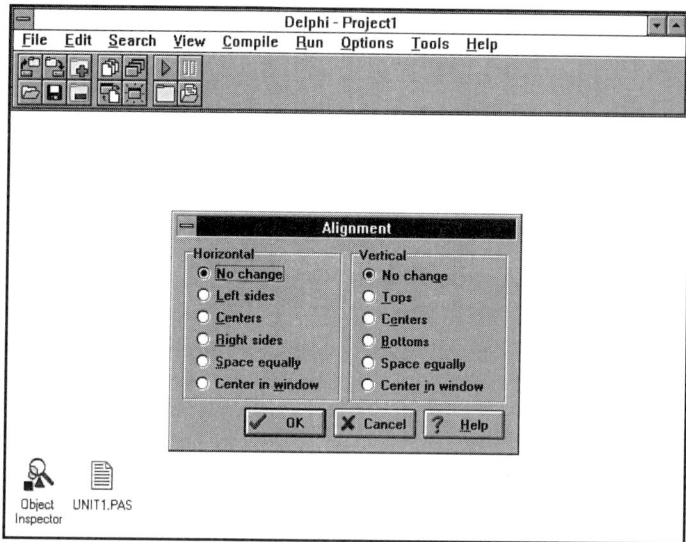

Figure 1.19.
The Alignment dialog box.

- ☐ Check the radio button of the last option on the Horizontal alignment (left-hand) side of the dialog box: Center in window.
- ☐ Press the OK button to close the dialog box.

The Close button is now centered perfectly within the form.

The Alignment dialog box you just used offers a number of options for aligning visual components relative to each other. You will make better use of these options when your forms grow more complex.

- ☐ Follow the same steps as above to center the `Hello World!` label horizontally within the form as well.

Resizing a Component

When you place a new component on the form by simply clicking at the position where you want it, the component assumes its default dimensions as described by its `Width` and `Height` properties. There are several ways to adjust the dimensions of a newly placed component.

- ☐ You can size the component in the process of placing it on the form. Rather than simply clicking on the form to place it after having selected it from the palette, click (but do not release) the left mouse button. You will see a frame that you can size by moving the mouse for as long as you hold down the left mouse button. When you are satisfied with the sizing of the component, release the mouse button.

- The second way of resizing components comes in handy when you need to resize one that's already placed on the form. Click on the component to select it. A set of small, black squares appears on each corner and along each edge of the component. The black squares are referred to as *sizing handles*. You can grab one of those handles with the mouse (by left-clicking on the handle and holding the mouse button down) and move it to resize the component. After you release the mouse button, the component is redrawn in its new size. This is very similar to how you resize windows.

Note: There is a keyboard-only shortcut for sizing a component after it has been placed on the form in increments of a single pixel in either dimension. You can thus fine-tune the `Width` and `Height` of an existing component.

When the component of interest (or an entire group of components) has been selected, press the Shift key and, while still holding it down, press the arrow keys to resize the component in the desired direction one pixel at a time.

Visual versus Non-Visual Components

So far you have seen examples of so-called visual components. These are components that correspond to visual elements of the user interface. For instance, a `Label`, a `Button`, and a `Form` are all visual components. They are all visible to the user when your program is running.

Delphi components do not necessarily have to be visual, however. The non-visual type of component serves other purposes. Examples may include a database, a serial communications port, a printer component, and other application elements that do not appear on the form, but rather perform services and execute actions. They are part of the project, are connected to other components via Object Pascal code, and cooperate with other components at run-time. But they cannot be seen directly by the user.

Even though the non-visual components cannot be seen, you make them part of the project by placing them on the form just as you do with the visual components. At design-time, Delphi shows a small, iconic, graphical representation of the non-visual component on the form. At run-time, the graphical representation is not visible. The component will simply operate inconspicuously in the background rather than being displayed on the form.

Note: Hiding Components:

Even though visual interface components are usually there to be seen and interacted with, you may sometimes find it desirable to temporarily hide a particular component.

> You will learn more about dynamically hiding and un-hiding components in future lessons. For now, you can designate a component as initially hidden or as visible by toggling the value of its `Visible` property. If `Visible` is `True`, the component initially appears on the form. If you set `Visible` to `False`, the component will not appear on the form.

Summary

During today's lesson you learned the following:

- The Delphi Interactive Development Environment (IDE) consists of several windows: Main Window, Code Editor, Form Designer, Object Inspector, Project Manager, and others.
- How to create (File|New project) and save (File|Save project) a new Delphi project.
- The steps involved and the kinds of files needed (.PRJ, .PAS, *.FRM) to create a running program within a Delphi project. First, you need to build the visual form by placing components on its surface. You can then test your form by running the program via the Run|Run command.
- How to create a very simple program (a blank, resizable form, BLANK) without writing any code.
- How to place components listed in the Component Palette on the form.
- How to manipulate components, changing their design-time properties such as size and position on the form.
- How to delete a no-longer-needed component from the form by selecting it and pressing the Delete key.

Q&A

Q True or False? The only language suitable for writing Windows programs is C++. Pascal is for educational and hobbyist use only, not for professionals.

A False, of course. Object Pascal supported by Delphi is an extremely powerful programming language, the latest incarnation of what started as Turbo Pascal about 10 years ago. Object Pascal is an object-oriented programming language like C++. You can write Windows programs of arbitrary complexity with it. Previous versions of the Borland Pascal compiler, prior to Delphi, were used by professionals to write commercial-quality applications. Delphi, being the most powerful of all Pascal compilers to date, will certainly be used by organizations and professionals worldwide to deliver their Windows applications faster and with a lot less effort than what is required using C++.

Q Looking at all of the different windows inside the Delphi environment, I am confused. Is there any simple way of finding one's way through the maze?

A From the View menu, select Project Manager. A list of all Object Pascal units and all visual forms appears. Double-click on a particular unit or form name to bring the appropriate editor to the top and view the entity you selected. It takes a little practice, but after a while you will be able to "find your way through the maze" quite easily.

Q If I am in the middle of doing something in Delphi and need to terminate the session to do something else, how do I get back to where I left off upon my return to Delphi?

A If you save your project before exiting, it is automatically restored for you upon your return to the Delphi IDE. There is no need for any special action on your part.

Q Can I write non-Windows programs with Delphi?

A In a word, no. Delphi is a visual programming tool for building Windows applications. If you want to write programs for character-mode DOS, Delphi is not the right tool.

Q How can I change certain properties of the form when my program is running? For example, I would like to change the background color of the form depending on which button is pressed.

A You need to write some Object Pascal code "behind" the form, so to speak. You will learn the basics of doing that in the next day's lesson.

Workshop

Quiz

1. What filename extension should you use for your Object Pascal units? Projects?
2. How much of a productivity improvement can a skilled Delphi /Object Pascal programmer expect over a C++/Windows programmer?
3. Can existing Turbo Pascal code be used in Delphi programs?
4. How long does it take someone to learn the ins and outs of Windows programming if they use Delphi as their primary development environment?
5. Is it possible to align several visual components on a form at once, without having to resort to individually entering the values for the `Top` and/or `Left` properties?
6. What is the name of the form property corresponding to its visible title?

7. What is the difference/relationship between the name of the form and the name of the form unit?

Exercises

1. Create a variation of the HELLO program that displays its `Hello World!` message in white, centered on a form with a navy blue background.
2. Create another variation of the HELLO program that displays its `Hello World!` message in 18-point Arial font, drawn in bright yellow, centered on a form with a dark red background.
3. Create a program whose main window displays five rows of edit boxes, labeled First Name, Last Name, Street Address, City, and Zip, respectively.

WEEK
1

Programs and Units

by Namir Shammas

This chapter shows you how to build a simple Delphi program and examine the program components of a unit. You will learn how to fine-tune the properties of a visual control as well as how to determine its response to mouse clicks. This chapter will cover the following topics:

- Creating the simple BUTTON example
- Examining the program's code, which is mostly generated by Delphi
- The interface section of a library unit
- The implementation section of a library unit
- The advanced aspects of units

The BUTTON Program

Delphi offers powerful visual programming tools to create programs. In this section you will create a simple program, and in the process learn more about working with Delphi's features. On Day 1 you created the simplest Delphi program, a blank form that only showed you the minimum features of a window. Today you will create a form with a single bit button (this is a button that can be associated with a bitmap image). When you click on the bit button, the program displays a message dialog box. When you click on the OK button of that dialog box, the program closes the form and ends its execution. That's all!

NEW TERM A *bit button* is a button that has a bitmap image (stored in a .BMP file) associated with it.

Creating the Program

To create and run the BUTTON program, perform the following steps:

1. Load Delphi if it is not already loaded.
2. Click on the **File|New Project** option to create a new project.
3. Click on the Additional page tab in the component palette.
4. Click on the bit button, which is the leftmost button in the palette.
5. Move the mouse pointer to the middle of the form window.
6. Hold the left mouse button down and drag the mouse toward the lower left corner of the form. As you drag the mouse, Delphi shows you the outline of the bit button you are drawing. Release the mouse button at your discretion to complete drawing the bit button.
7. Delphi displays a bit button with the default caption of `BitBtn1`, as shown in Figure 2.1.

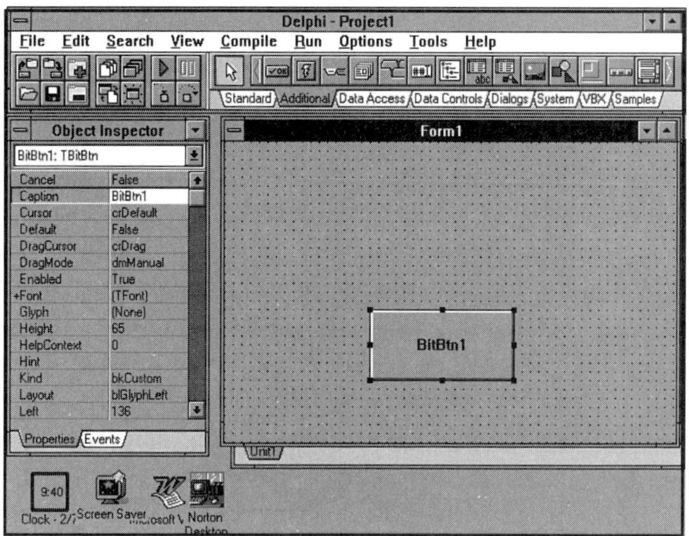

Figure 2.1.
The bit button with its default caption.

8. Click on the Properties page tab in the Object Inspector window.
9. Click on the Caption property, which has the text `BitBtn1`. Delete that text and type in `Close`. When you are finished, press Enter. As you type the new caption, Delphi echoes the new caption on the bit button.
10. Click on the Glyph property whose current value is (None). Delphi displays a small, three-dot button after the current glyph value.
11. Click on the three-dot glyph button. Delphi displays the Picture Editor dialog box, as shown in Figure 2.2.
12. Click on the Load… button to load a .BMP picture. Delphi displays the Load Picture dialog box, which is very similar to the standard Windows Open File dialog box.
13. Select the ARCADE.BMP file from the \WINDOWS directory. You may select any other .BMP file in any other directory. Of course, different .BMP files will display different bitmaps on the button.
14. Click the OK button in the Picture Editor dialog box.
15. Click the Name property in the Object Inspector. The default control name is `BitBtn1`. Delete this name and type in `CloseBtn`.
16. Click the Events page tab in the Object Inspector. Delphi shows you the list of events that *might* be associated with the bit button.
17. Double-click on the `OnClick` event. Delphi displays the UNIT1 window (see Figure 2.3) and places the insertion cursor inside the procedure `Form1.CloseBtnClick`.

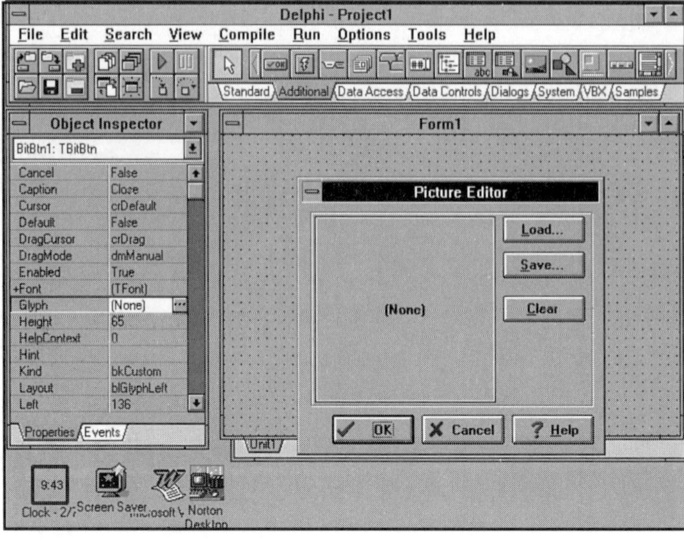

Figure 2.2.
The Picture Editor dialog box.

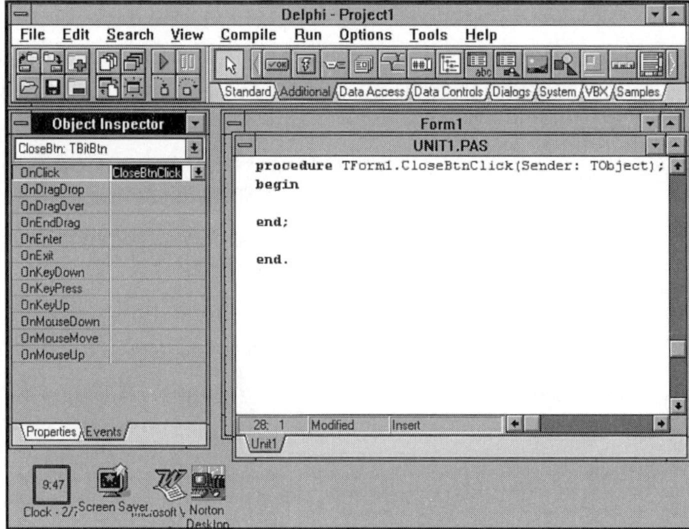

Figure 2.3.
The UNIT1 window.

18. Type in the following two statements:

```
MessageDlg("Close form", mtInformation, [mbOK], 0);
Close;
```

Saving the Project Files

Let's save the project files. First save the unit using the **File | Save File As...** option. Delphi displays a dialog box with the title Save Unit1 As. Select the appropriate subdirectory and then enter the name UBUTTON.PAS in the File Name edit box.

To save the project, select the **File | Save Project As...** option. Delphi displays a dialog box with the title Save Unit1 As. Select the appropriate subdirectory and then enter the name BUTTON.DPR in the File Name edit box.

2

Running the BUTTON Program

To compile and run the BUTTON program, press the F9 function key or select the **Run | Run** option. Delphi compiles, links, and runs the program. If you made an error, Delphi highlights the offending statement and displays an error message. When the program runs, it displays the form with the Close bit button. Click on that button to display the message dialog box, as shown in Figure 2.4. When you click the OK button of the message dialog box, the program closes the form and ends.

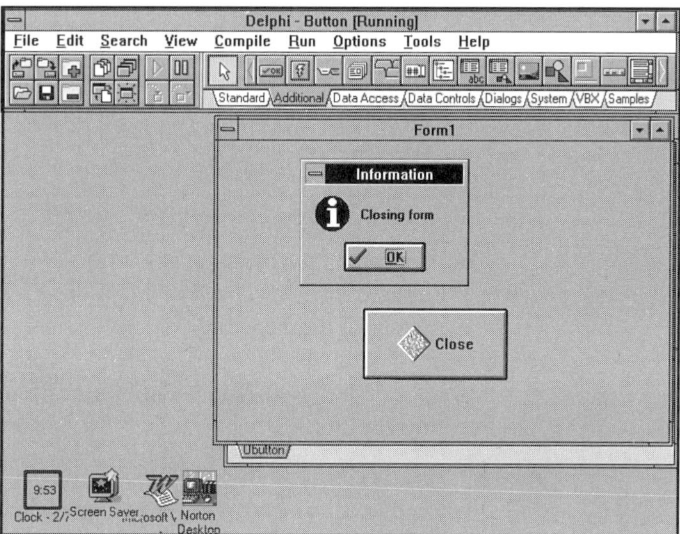

Figure 2.4.
A sample session with the BUTTON program.

Examining the Code

The beauty of programming with Delphi is that it generates the systematic code for you. You need only concentrate on the custom part of the code. Let's examine the code generated by Delphi and see where the two statements you entered fit in.

The Program Code

Every program has a main part that starts executing first. This main part often invokes other, secondary parts to perform the various tasks required. The BUTTON program is no exception. It has a main part and a secondary part. Listing 2.1 shows the main part, which is stored in file BUTTON.DPR. The program is short because it relies on the secondary parts (that is, the units) to perform most of the work. Delphi generated all of the statements in Listing 2.1.

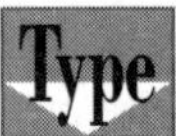

Listing 2.1. Source code for the program BUTTON.DPR.

```
 1:  program Button;
 2:
 3:  uses
 4:    Forms,
 5:    Ubutton in 'UBUTTON.PAS' {Form1};
 6:
 7:  {$R *.RES}
 8:
 9:  begin
10:    Application.CreateForm(TForm1, Form1);
11:    Application.Run;
12:  end.
```

Let's look at the lines of the program in Listing 2.1. Line 1 contains the keyword `program` followed by the name `Button`. The keyword `program` tells the compiler that this is the main part of the program. Line 3 contains the keyword `uses`, which tells the compiler that the main program relies on a set of units that are reusable library modules. Lines 4 and 5 specify the names of the two library units employed. Line 4 specifies the unit `Forms`, which supports the forms. Line 5 specifies the unit `Ubutton` and states that this unit is stored in file UBUTTON.PAS.

Line 7 contains what is called a directive. *Directives* are special instructions to the compiler that are enclosed in comments but start with the `$` sign followed by the directive name. Line 9 contains the keyword `begin`, which specifies the start of the statements of the program. Line 12 contains the keyword `end` (followed by a dot), which tells the compiler that the program statements have ended. The lines between the keywords `begin` and `end` contain the statements of the main programs: Line 10 contains a statement that creates the form and Line 11 contains a statement that runs the program.

The General Syntax of a Program

The Pascal programming language gained popularity because of its support to structured programming. This feature requires that specific program parts appear in a certain order. Here is the general syntax for a Pascal program:

Syntax

The General Program Syntax

```
Program name;

Uses <list of units>;

Const <list of constants>;

Type <list of data user-defined types>;

Var <list of variables>;

<list of functions and/or procedures>

Begin
  <statements>
End.
```

Example:

```
Program Multiply;

Uses WinCrt;

Var i, j : Integer;

Begin
    i := 5;
    j := i * i;
    Writeln(i, ' squared = ', j);
End.
```

Every Pascal program starts with the keyword `program` followed by the program's name. The above syntax shows the keyword `Program` instead of `program`. Does the uppercase P make a difference? The answer is no. Pascal is a case-insensitive language. You can even type `PROGRAM` instead of `Program` and not get an error from the compiler. A Pascal name (also called an *identifier*) must begin with a letter followed by other letters, digits, or the underscore character. The dot character is not part of the name and instead plays special roles in Pascal statements.

The `Uses` keyword lists the names of the library units that are employed by the program. These library units provide important support and operations to the main program.

The `Const` keyword lists the names of constants that are defined in the main program. *Constants* are names that have fixed values.

The `Type` keyword lists the names of the user-defined types that are defined in the main program. Pascal empowers you to define your own data types that represent specific information.

The `Var` keyword lists the names of the variables that are defined in the main program. *Variables* store information that can be updated.

The main program may also define its own set of procedures and functions, which are called in the main `begin-end` block. These procedures and functions (which are sometimes collectively called *routines*) are semi-independent program components. These routines have access to the constants, types, and variables defined in the main program. In addition, the routines can access what the units have to offer.

The `Begin` and `End` keywords define the block of statements that start executing first. There should be at least one statement in this block. Interestingly, the Pascal compiler does not object to a `Begin-End` block that has no statements!

What about comments in Pascal? You can place comments inside pairs of curly braces or sets of `(*` and `*)` characters. The rule to follow is that you must use matching comment-enclosing characters. Thus, the following comment is legal:

```
{ version 1.0 }
```

By contrast, the following comment is **illegal**:

```
{ version 1.0 *)
```

DO	DON'T

DO separate Pascal statements with a semicolon.

DON'T forget that Pascal names are case insensitive.

The Unit Syntax

Pascal uses units to create reusable library modules. These modules empower developers to create code that can be used in different programs without having to retype the code. You can think of a unit as a supplier of constants, data types, variables, and routines. Units empower software developers to create large programs that can be easily maintained and updated. A Pascal unit has a unit heading followed by three parts: the interface, the implementation, and the initialization. The unit heading specifies the unit's name, which appears in the `uses` clauses of other units and programs. The *interface part* (also called *interface section*) tells the compiler which parts of the unit are accessible to the unit's clients (that is, to other units and programs). The *implementation part* (also called the implementation section) contains local declarations and the

detailed implementation of procedures and functions. The *initialization part* contains statements that allow the unit's exported variables to be initialized. Here is the general syntax for the Pascal unit:

Syntax

The General Syntax of a Unit

```
Unit name;

Interface

Uses <list of units>;
Const <list of exported constants>;
Type <list of exported data user-defined types>;
Var <list of exported variables>;
<list of declarations of exported functions
and/or procedures>

Implementation
Uses <list of units>;
Const <list of local constants>;
Type <list of local data user-defined types>;
Var <list of local variables>;
<implementation of functions and/or procedures>

[Begin
    <initializing statements>]
End.
```

Example:

```
Unit Math;

Interface

function Cube(X : Real) : Real;
function OneOver(X : Real) : Real;
function Quadratic(A, B, C, X : Real) : Real;
function Cubic(A, B, C, D, X : Real) : Real;

Implementation

function Cube(X : Real) : Real;
Begin
    Cube := X * X * X;
End;

function OneOver(X : Real) : Real;
Begin
    OneOver := 1 / X;
End;

function Quadratic(A, B, C, X : Real) : Real;
Begin
    Quadratic := (A * X + B) * X + C;
End;
```

```
function Cubic(A, B, C, D, X : Real) : Real;
Begin
    Cubic := ((A * X + B) * X + C) * X + D;
End;

End.
```

If the unit has no initializing code, there is no need to write the `Begin` keyword. Instead, only the final `End` keyword is required. In the next section you will learn about the interface and implementation parts in more detail.

DO	DON'T

DO initialize exported variables using the initialization section.

DON'T place functions or procedures that should not be called by client modules in the interface section.

Form-Supporting Units

Delphi uses Pascal units to support the form. Having been introduced to the general syntax of a unit, let's look at Listing 2.2, which shows the source code for the unit UBUTTON.PAS.

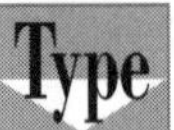

Listing 2.2. Source code for the unit UBUTTON.PAS.

```
unit Ubutton;

interface

uses
  SysUtils, WinTypes, WinProcs, Messages, Classes,
  Graphics, Controls, Forms, Dialogs, StdCtrls, Buttons;

type
  TForm1 = class(TForm)
    CloseBtn: TBitBtn;
    procedure CloseBtnClick(Sender: TObject);
  private
    { Private declarations }
  public
    { Public declarations }
  end;

var
  Form1: TForm1;

implementation

```

```
24:   {$R *.DFM}
25:
26:   procedure TForm1.CloseBtnClick(Sender: TObject);
27:   begin
28:    MessageDlg('Closing form', mtInformation, [mbOK], 0);
29:    Close;
30:   end;
31:
32:   end.
```

Analysis Line 1 contains the unit heading, which defines the unit's name as `Ubutton`. Line 3 starts the interface part, which contains the `uses` and `type` clauses. Lines 5 to 7 list the names of the units used by the unit `Ubutton`. Lines 9 to 17 define the class `TForm1`, which supports the form. (More about classes in the next section.) Line 19 defines the exported variable `Form1` to be of type `TForm1`. The implementation part begins at line 22. This part defines the procedure `TForm1.CloseBtnClick`, which responds to clicking the mouse on the bit button. The contents of lines 28 and 29 should look familiar, because they are the statements that you typed. The statement in line 28 displays the message dialog box. The `Close` statement in line 29 closes the form.

Delphi generated all of the statements in Listing 2.2, except for those in lines 28 and 29. You might inquire about how Delphi came up with the name of the procedure. The answer lies in the declaration of class `TForm1` in lines 10 to 17. Notice that line 12 declares a procedure `CloseBtnClick`. This name is made up of the name of the button, which is `CloseBtn`, and the name of the `Click` event. The definition of the procedure in line 26 uses the name of the owner class `TForm1`, followed by a dot, followed by the name of the procedure. This syntax tells the compiler that the procedure `CloseBtnClick` belongs to the class `TForm1`.

DO	DON'T

DO use Delphi's automatic code-update feature when you alter the name of a control.

DON'T manually edit the name of class fields that represent controls. Also, do not manually edit the names of event-handling methods.

Programs versus Units

After introducing you to the syntax of programs and units, let's take a step back and recap how they relate to each other. Every Pascal application has one and only one main program part (or *module*, if you prefer). The main program may use the exported parts of one or more units. These units may use the exported parts of yet another set of units. Thus an application can be made up of a hierarchy of low-level (that is independent) units, medium-level units, high-level units, and the program part.

DO	DON'T

DO use the divide-and-conquer approach in creating specialized library units. Each unit should be reusable by as many client units and programs as possible.

DON'T add declarations in the main program unless they are very specific to the program.

Programs versus Delphi Projects

Delphi combines the Pascal programming language with visual programming features. To accomplish this combination, Delphi applications use project files that contribute to the application. The following types of files are generated at design-time:

- The .DPR Project file contains Pascal source code for the project's main program file. The .DPR file lists all of the form and unit files in the project, and holds the code that initializes the application. Delphi creates the project file when it is first saved.
- The .PAS unit source (Object Pascal) code. Delphi creates one .PAS file for every form the project contains when the project is first saved. The .PAS file holds all of the declarations and procedures (together with event-handling procedures) for the form.
- The .DFM graphical form files, which are binary files that each contain the design properties of one form contained in the project. Delphi generates a single .DFM file along with the corresponding .PAS file for each form the project contains, when the project is first saved.
- The .OPT project options file is a text file that holds the current settings for Project Options. Delphi generates this file when first saving and updating.
- The .RES compiled resource file, which is a binary file that holds the application icon and separate external resources used by the project.
- The .~DP project backup file, which is generated on the second save of a project and updated on subsequent saves. The .~DP file holds a copy of the .DPR file as it existed before the most recent save.
- The .~PAunit backup file, which holds a copy of a .PAS file as it existed before the most recent save. When you alter a .PAS file, Delphi creates this parallel file on the second project save, or any save of the .PAS unit file after a modification has occurred. It is updated on ensuing saves if you altered the .PAS file.
- The .~DFgraphical form backup. Delphi creates this file when you open a .DFM file as text in the Code Editor, make changes, and then save the .DFM file. The .~DF file contains a binary-format copy of the .DFM file as it existed before the latest save.

- The .DSK desktop settings file, which holds the information about the desktop settings you have designated for the project in the **Options | Environment** options.

The Interface Section

This section looks in more detail at the interface section of a library unit. The *interface section* of a unit specifies what items in the unit are accessible to other units and programs. You can think of these items as exportable. In the following subsections you examine the various parts of a Pascal unit. It is important to point out that most of the subsequent discussion also applies to the main program part in a Pascal application.

The *uses* Clause

The `uses` clause tells the compiler that the unit employs the exportable parts of other units. The `uses` clause lists the supporting units in a comma-delimited list. In Listing 2.2, lines 6 and 7 list 11 units that are used by the `Ubutton` unit.

The *const* Clause

The `const` clause lists the names of identifiers that have fixed values associated with them. These values can be integers, floating-point types, strings, and other predefined or user-defined data types.

Syntax

The General Syntax for Declaring a Constant

```
Const
    constantName  = value;
```

Examples:

```
Const
    MY_MESSAGE = 'Hello there!';
    LANGUAGE = 'Pascal';
    DaysPerWeek = 7;
    HourPerDay = 24;
    Gravity = 98.1;
    SecondPerHour = 60.0 * 60.0;
    SecondPerDay = 24.0 * 60.0 * 60.0;
    BoilingPointF = 212.0; { degrees Fahrenheit }
    BoilingPointC = 100.0; { degrees Celsius }
```

DO | **DON'T**

DO use constants to represent values using names. This approach makes your programs easier to read and easy to update.

DON'T rely on your human memory to decipher what numeric values will mean six months from now!

The *type* Clause

The `type` clause empowers you to declare your own data types. These new data types are either records or classes. A *record* is a collection of fields that represent an item.

Syntax

The General Syntax for Declaring a Record

```
Type
    recordName = Record
        field1 : typeField1;
        field2 : typeField2;
        <other fields>
    end;
```

The declaration of a user-defined record starts by defining the name of the record type. The fields that make up the record definition have predefined data types and/or previously declared record types. Although the names of record types must be unique in a program, the record types can have fields with similar names.

Examples:

```
type
    TDate  = record
        Day, Month, Year : Integer;
    end;
    TDuration = record
        Start, Finish : TDate
    end;
```

The Pascal Class

Delphi allows you to declare classes that play a vital role in creating and managing forms and their controls. You can think of a *class* as a super record that combines fields and methods. The fields describe the state of an object, whereas the method specifies how the object is manipulated.

Syntax

The General Syntax of a Class

```
Type
  TClassName = Class
    public
        <public fields>
        <public methods>
    protected
        <protected fields>
        <protected methods>
    private
        <private fields>
        <private methods>
  end;
```

The class type has three possible sections that control the accessibility of its fields and methods. The *public section* declares fields and methods to have no access restrictions—the class instances and descendant classes can have access to these fields and methods. The *protected section* declares fields and methods to have some access restrictions—the descendant classes can have access to these fields and methods. The *private section* declares fields and methods to have severe access restrictions—they cannot be accessed by class instances or descendant classes.

Example:

```
Type
    TTimeClass = class
        public
            constructor Initialize;
            procedure SetHour(dHour : Integer);
            procedure SetMinute(dMinute : Integer);
            procedure SetSecond(dSecond : Integer);
            function GetHour : Integer;
            function GetMinute : Integer;
            function GetSecond : Integer;
protected
            Hour : Integer;
            Minute : Integer;
            Second : Integer;
    end;
```

The `TTimeClass` declares three protected fields: `Hour`, `Minute`, and `Second`. The class declares methods to initialize, set, and query the protected fields, as well as return the number of seconds since midnight.

The Fields of a Class

The *fields* of a class store the data (or state, if you prefer) that specify the attribute of the class instances. The general rule of thumb is to avoid declaring fields as public, unless a public declaration is more practical. For example, the class `TTimeClass`, declared in the last section, has

2

methods to set and query the protected fields. Because these methods give you full access to the protected fields, you can define a shorter version of class `TTimeClass` as follows:

```
Type
    TTimeClass = class
        public
            Hour : Integer;
            Minute : Integer;
            Second : Integer;

            Initialize;
            function GetSeconds : Integer;
    end;
```

Thus the new version has less overhead because the fields are declared as public.

The Methods of a Class

The *methods* of a class are procedures and functions that manipulate the fields and return results based on the current values of the fields. It is important to point out that the methods of a class have automatic access to all of the fields of the same class. There is no need to pass the fields as parameters. Here is an example of how the code of function `GetSeconds` might look:

```
function TTimeClass.GetSeconds() : Integer;
begin
    GetSeconds := Second + 60 * (Minute +
                              60 * Hour);
end;
```

Notice that the function `GetSeconds` has access to the fields `Second`, `Minute`, and `Hour`. This implementation is valid for either version of class `TTimeClass`.

Classes and Inheritance

The power of using classes comes from the ability to create new classes as descendants of existing ones. Each descendant class inherits the fields and methods of its parent and ancestor classes. You can also declare methods in the new classes that override inherited ones. This feature allows you to avoid being locked into using inherited methods that are not appropriate for the new class. Conceptually, descendant classes refine the behavior of their ancestor classes by introducing new and more specialized behavior.

Syntax

The General Syntax of a Descendant Class

```
Type
  TClassName = Class(TParentClassName)
    public
        <public fields>
        <public methods>
    protected
        <protected fields>
```

```
        <protected methods>
    private
        <private fields>
        <private methods>
end;
```

The above syntax resembles the one for a non-descendant class (also called the *base class*). Notice that the keyword `Class` is followed by the name of the parent class enclosed in parentheses. Here is an example of a descendant class:

```
Type
    TTimeClass = class
        public
            Hour : Integer;
            Minute : Integer;
            Second : Integer;

            Initialize;
            function GetSeconds : Integer;
    end;

    TDateTime = class(TTimeClass)
        public
            Year : Integer;
            Month : Integer;
            Day : Integer;

            Initialize;
            function GetDayNumber : Integer;
    end;
```

The class `TDateTime` is a descendant of class `TTimeClass` and inherits the fields `Hour`, `Minute`, and `Seconds`. The descendant class also inherits the method `GetSeconds`. The class `TDateTime` overrides the inherited method `Initialize` and declares the method `GetDayNumber`.

The *Var* Clause

The `var` clause allows you to declare variables that are exported by the unit. *Variables* are tagged (labeled or named, if you prefer) memory locations that store data. The kind of data stored in a variable depends on the data type associated with that variable.

Syntax

The General Syntax for Declaring a Variable

```
Var
    varName : dataType;
```

You can place multiple variables in a comma-delimited list if these variables have the same data type.

Example:

```
Var
    Second : Integer;
    Hour : Integer;
    Minute : Integer;
    Month, Day, Year : Integer;
    Rate : Real;
    aDate : TDate; { record type }
    Duration : TDuration; { a record type }
    C1, C2, C3 : TComplex; { a record type }
    FirstName, MiddleName, LastName : String;
    OutOfOrder : Boolean;
```

In the case where a variable is of a record type, you access the record fields by using the dot operator. For example, in the case of variable `aDate`, you can access the fields `Day`, `Month`, and `Year` using the expressions `aDate.Day`, `aDate.Month`, and `aDate.Year`, respectively. In the case of the variable `Duration`, you apply the access operator twice: the first time to select either fields `Start` or `Finish`, and the second one to select either fields `Hour`, `Minute`, or `Second`. For example, the expression `Duration.Start.Hour` accesses the starting hour. Another example is `Duration.Finish.Minute`, which accesses the minute of the ending duration.

Class and Objects

Objects are instances of their associated classes. You declare an object in a `var` clause just as with other types of variables. Each object has its own set of class fields and can only access those public fields. Likewise, only the public methods of a class can be applied to an object.

Object-oriented programming (OOP) thinks of manipulating objects in terms of sending them a message. The message tells the object to perform a task. The object searches for a method whose name matches that of the message, and applies that method. Thus, an OOP message specifies *what* to do to an object, whereas a method specifies *how* to manipulate an object. Pascal uses the dot operator to access the public fields of an object and also to send a message to an object. Here is an example of sending an OOP message to a class instance:

```
Var
    DT : TDateTime;
    N : Integer;
Begin
    DT.Initialize;
    N := DT.GetDayNumber
End;
```

The above example sends the messages `Initialize` and `GetDayNumber` to the object `DT` (which is an instance of class `TDateTime`).

The Implementation Section

The *implementation section* contains the detailed implementation of the exported functions and procedures. In addition, the section holds the declarations of local constants, data types, and

variables, as well as the implementation of local functions and procedures. Therefore, the implementation section has access to both exported and local constants, data types, and variables.

The units that support form windows contain the implementation of the event-handling methods. Listing 2.1 offers a simple case where the implementation section defines the procedure `Form1.CloseBtnClick`, which handles the `Click` event for the Close button.

2

The *$R* Directive

The `$R` directive is a resource file directive. The general syntax for this directive is

```
{$R Filename}
```

The `$R` directive specifies the name of the resource file to be included in an application or library. The default extension for the `Filename` parameter is .RES. The filename must be a Windows resource file. If the filename does not contain a directory, the compiler searches for the file first in the directory of the current source, then in the search path.

When you place the `$R` directive in a unit, the resource file name is simply recorded in the resulting unit file; the compiler performs no checks to guarantee that the file exists at compile-time. When you place the `$R` directive in an application or when the library is linked, the resource files specified in all units and in the program or library itself are processed and each resource in each resource file is copied to the .EXE or .DLL file being produced.

Advanced Units

This section looks at two advanced issues that deal with the interdependence of units of each other.

Circular Unit References

Circular unit references take place when you have mutually dependent units. *Mutually dependent units* occur when you put a `uses` clause in the implementation section of a unit, thus concealing the inner details of the unit referenced in the `uses` clause. The referenced unit becomes private and not available to the programs or other units using the unit in which it is referenced.

The compiler flags an error. The compiler accepts a reference to a partially compiled unit in the implementation section of another unit, as long as neither unit's interface section depends upon the other. Therefore, the units follow Pascal's exact rules for the order of declaration. If the interface sections are interdependent, the compiler emits an error indicating a circular unit reference. Mutually dependent units may be advantageous in special cases. If you use them when they are not needed, they can make your program harder to maintain and more susceptible to errors.

Listing 2.3 shows the source code for the program that tests circular unit references.

Listing 2.3. Source code for the program that tests circular unit references.

```
{ Program demonstrates how two circular use of units }

Program CircularUseOfUnits;

Uses
  WinCrt, Display;

Const
  MSG1 = 'Upper left corner of screen';
  MSG2 = 'Way off the screen';
  MSG3 = 'Back to reality';

Begin
  ClrScr;
  { legal output }
  ShowXY(1, 1, MSG1);
  { trigger bad output }
  ShowXY(100, 100, MSG2);
  { legal output }
  ShowXY(81 - Length(MSG3), 15, MSG3);
End.



Unit Display;
{ Contains a basic video display routine }

Interface

procedure ShowXY(X, Y : Integer;
                 Message : String);

Implementation

Uses
  WinCrt, IOError;

Const
  ERRMSG = 'Invalid ShowXY coordinates';

procedure ShowXY(X, Y : Integer;
                 Message : String);
Begin
  If (X in [1..80]) And (Y in [1..25] Then
  Begin
    GoToXY(X, Y);
    Write(Message);
  End
```

```
49:     Else
50:       TellError(ERRMSG);
51:   End;
52:
53:   End.
54:
55:
56:
57:   Unit IOError;
58:   { Contains a simple error-output routine }
59:
60:   Interface
61:
62:   procedure TellError(ErrorMessage : String)
63:
64:   Implementation
65:
66:   Uses
67:     Display;
68:
69:   procedure TellError(ErrorMessage : String);
70:   Begin
71:     ShowXY(1, 25, 'Error: ' + ErrorMessage);
72:   End;
73:
74:   End.
```

Analysis Lines 5 and 6 show the `uses` clause in the main program. This clause states that the main program employs the units `WinCrt` and `Display`. The definition of unit `Display` starts at line 25. The `Uses` clause in lines 35 and 36, which appears in the implementation section, lists units `WinCrt` and `IOError` as units used by unit `Display`. The definition of unit `IOError` starts at line 57. The `Uses` clause in lines 66 and 67, which appears in the implementation section, lists unit `Display` as being used by unit `IOError`. Thus units `Display` and `IOError` refer to each other.

Indirect Unit References

The `uses` clause in a module only requires the name of the units used directly by that module. However, there are many times when a module is directly dependent on another module. To compile a module, the compiler must be able to find all units the module depends upon, either directly or indirectly. When you alter the interface section of a unit, you must recompile all other units that utilize the modified unit. If you invoke the **Compile | Build All** option, the compiler performs the required update. On the other hand, if you only alter code in the implementation or in the initialization part, you need not recompile other units that use the changed unit.

Delphi is able to determine when the interface part of a unit was modified by computing a unit version number when the unit is compiled.

Summary

Today's lesson introduced you to creating a simple Delphi application and to examining the code behind it. You learned about the following topics:

- Creating the simple BUTTON program, which closes a form when you click on a bit button. The chapter showed you how to create the program, customize the properties of the button, and select an event to handle. The text also showed you how to save the project files and run the program.
- Examining the program's code, which is generated by Delphi. You learned about the general syntax of the main program and the library units. The text showed you the source code for the main program and for the form window.
- The interface section of a library unit. The text discussed the `uses`, `const`, `type`, and `var` clauses. You also learned about declaring classes, the class components, descendant classes, and the class instances.
- The implementation section of a library unit. The implementation section contains the detailed implementation of the exported and local routines.
- The advanced aspects of units. Such aspects include circular references of units and indirect unit references.

Q&A

Q Does Pascal use line numbers?

A No. We are using line numbers in the listings in this book only for the sake of reference.

Q What happens if I forget to type the semicolon between statements?

A The compiler tells you that there is an error in the program. You need to add the semicolon to separate statements.

Q Can a program or unit have multiple `const`, `var`, and `type` clauses?

A Yes, Pascal allows this flexible aspect of structured programming.

Q Does the order of declaring constants, types, and variables matter?

A The order of declaring program components matters only in defining the component before using it in another component. For example, you cannot define a variable with a user-defined type that has not been yet declared.

Q What are some of the predefined data types?

A Pascal predefines many data types, such as Byte, Integer, Word (unsigned integer), LongInt, Real (floating-point), String, and Boolean (logical).

Workshop

The Workshop provides quiz questions to help you solidify your understanding of the material covered and exercises to provide you with experience in using what you've learned. Try to understand the quiz and exercise answers before continuing on to the next day's lesson.

Quiz

1. Can a unit call a program?
2. True or False? An object can access directly protected fields.
3. Where is the error in the following code?

```
Type
    Date = record
        Day, Month, Year : Integer
    end;
Var
    complex : Tcomplex;
Type
    TComplex = record
        x, y : Real;
    end;
```

4. What is wrong with the following code?

```
Type
    TClass1 = class
        public
            X, Y, Z : Real;
            procedure InitClass;
            function Calc : Real;
    end;
    TClass2 = class(TClass1)
        public
            S, T, X : Real;
            procedure InitClass);
            function Calc2 : Real;
    end;
```

5. True or False? The variables `MyName` and `MYname` refer to the same piece of information.

6. True or False? The following code is correct:

```
Type
    TClass1 = class
        public
            X, Y, Z : Real;
            procedure InitClass;
            function Calc : Real;
    end;
Var
    C1 : Tclass1;

Type
    TClass2 = class(TClass1)
        public
            S, T, V : Real;
            procedure InitClass;
            function Calc2 : Real;
    end;
Var
    C2 : TClass2;
```

Exercise

1. Modify the BUTTON program such that it displays the message **I am a Pascal Programmer**.
2. Create the program BTN2, which uses a standard button control instead of the bit button. Change the default caption of the button from Button1 to Close. Also, change the default caption of the button from Button1 to CloseBtn. Make the button respond to the Click event and insert the same statements as in program BUTTON.

WEEK 1

Visual Programming Paradigms

by Namir Shammas

This chapter introduces you to the visual programming paradigms. These paradigms guide the way you should view and think of working with a development product like Delphi. You will learn about the following topics:

- The design of forms, which involves drawing visual controls on these forms
- Classes that support visual controls
- Visual components
- Properties of components
- Events that are handled by visual components
- Application architectures

The Form Design

The Microsoft Windows environment uses windows as a basic building block. In fact, even the visual controls, such as the button control, are also windows. Thus, windows are the fundamental *objects* for the Windows user interface. Object-oriented programming purists may not consider Windows a true object-oriented environment. However, Windows does employ some basic notions of windows as objects that interact together and communicate through messages.

Forms are special windows that comprise the foundation of Delphi applications. You can think of a form as a special visual object that may contain other objects, namely, the visual controls. In other words, a form is a kind of *container* window. A form is also an object because it has properties and responds to events just like the controls it contains.

When you start a new project, Delphi brings up a new, empty form. You then add controls to that form to customize it and to specify how the form will interact with the application's end-user. In fact, Delphi allows its applications to have multiple forms. In this case, the application has a main form (the one that is initially opened) and multiple secondary forms that appear in response to the user's actions or to internal actions.

As a window, the form contains the standard window parts such as the control menu, the minimize button, the maximize button, the title bar, and resizable borders.

The following subsections discuss topics related to designing a form.

Design-Time and Run-Time

How flexible is the design of a form? Are the form and control properties cast in stone, so to speak, when a Delphi application starts to run? The answer to the above questions brings good news. Delphi supports a flexible scheme of form design. Customizing a form (while the program is not running) is called *design-time*. Delphi enables you to customize the properties of the form

and controls using the Object Inspector window. This window shows only those properties that can be set while the program is not running. There are additional properties (which vary for each component) that cannot be set at design-time because such initial values are irrelevant or inapplicable. You can set new values for these properties at *run-time* (that is, while the program is running). You also can set new values for design-time properties at run-time.

Placing Components on a Form

Placing components on a form is the fun part of customizing a form. On Day 2 you placed a bit button on a form. Placing other visual components involves basically the same steps as the bit button. The general process is as follows:

1. Select the page tab in the component palette that contains the control you want to paste on the form. If you are not familiar with the location, you can browse through the different sets of components. When you rest the mouse cursor on a component button, in the component palette, Delphi displays the name of that component in a small, yellow window. This feature helps you to become familiar quickly with the various components.
2. Click on the sought component in the currently selected component palette page.
3. Move the mouse over the form.
4. Hold the left mouse button down and drag the mouse down and toward the left. As you drag the mouse, Delphi shows you the outline of the component you are drawing. Release the mouse button at your discretion to complete drawing the component on the form. Each component has its own default image, caption, control name, and other initial values.

Let's apply the above steps to placing a single push-button on a form:

1. Load Delphi if it is not already loaded.
2. Click on File|New Project to create a new project.
3. Click on the Standard page tab in the component palette.
4. Click on the button component, which is the sixth component from the left.
5. Move the mouse over the lower-right part of the form.
6. Hold the left mouse button down and drag the mouse down and toward the left. As you drag the mouse, Delphi shows you the outline of the button you are drawing. Release the mouse button at your discretion to complete drawing the button.
7. Delphi displays a button with the default caption of Button1, as shown in Figure 3.1.

Figure 3.1.
The button with its default caption.

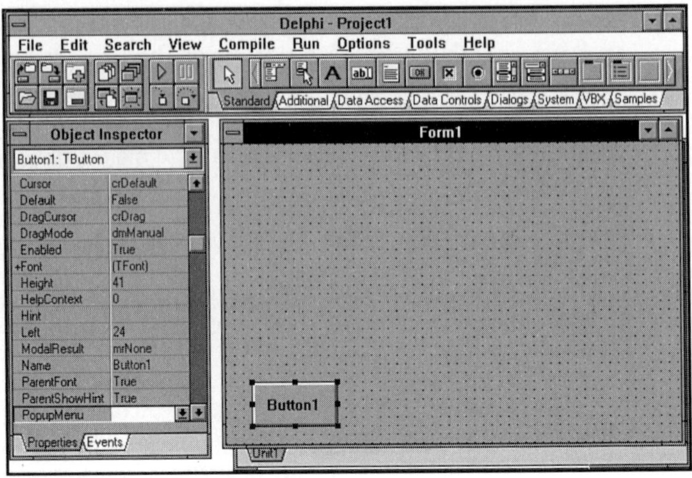

Placing Multiple Controls

To place different controls on a form, repeat the steps outlined in the last subsection. To place several components of the same type in succession, follow these simple steps:

1. Draw the first component in the manner described previously.
2. Select the first component by clicking the mouse on it. Delphi displays the *trackers* (that is the small black squares) on the edges of the control.
3. Press Ctrl-C to copy the component to the Clipboard.
4. Press Ctrl-V to paste a new copy of the component. This copy has the same caption and other properties, but a different component name.
5. Move the copied component to a proper location on the form.
6. Repeat steps 2 to 5 to place the other components.

DO | **DON'T**

DO copy and paste components to easily create a set of components with the same dimensions.

DON'T forget to change the captions of the copied controls.

Let's put these general steps to work by adding three more buttons to the form created in the last subsection. Perform the following steps:

1. Select the button component by clicking the mouse on it.
2. Press Ctrl-C to copy the button control to the Clipboard.

4. Press Ctrl-V to paste a new copy of the button control. This copy also has the caption Button1, but has the control name Button2.
5. Move the copied button control to the right of the first button.
6. Repeat steps 2 to 5 to place two more button controls. Figure 3.2 shows the resulting button controls, which all have the same default caption.

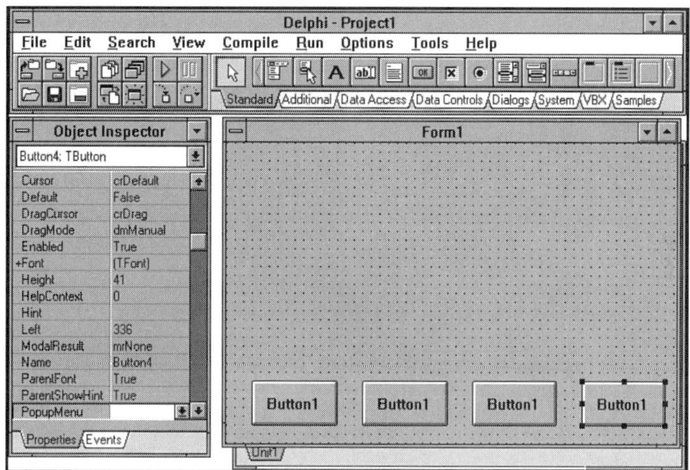

Figure 3.2.
The button controls with the same default caption.

Selecting Multiple Components

Delphi allows you to select multiple components in order to delete, move, and align them. To select multiple components, perform the following steps:

1. Deselect any currently selected component or components by simply clicking on the form itself.
2. Click on the first component to select it. Delphi displays the trackers on that component.
3. While holding down the Shift key, click on the other components you want to select. Delphi displays gray trackers on the selected controls.

To deselect a single component from the set of selected components, click on that component while holding down the Shift key. In fact, clicking the mouse of a component while holding down the Shift key toggles the selected state of that component.

Figure 3.3 shows the four buttons you created earlier after they are selected.

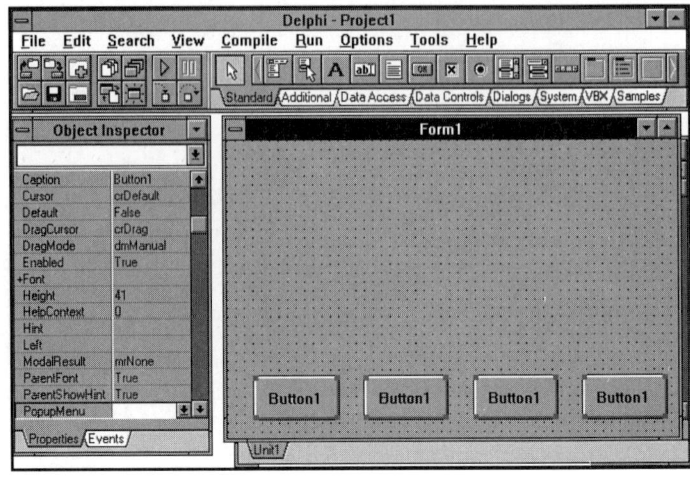

Figure 3.3.
The button controls after being selected.

Removing Components

Delphi permits you to remove components, either one at a time or collectively. To remove a single component, select that component by clicking on it and then pressing the Delete key. To remove multiple components, select the set of components (as described in the last subsection) and then press the Delete key. You can press the Ctrl-Z to undelete the components you just deleted.

Moving Components

You can move components in Delphi either one at a time or collectively. To move a single component, perform the following steps:

1. Select the component by clicking on it with the left mouse button.
2. While the mouse cursor is still over the selected component, hold down the left mouse button. This action prepares the component for the move.
3. Move the mouse (while still holding down the left mouse button) to move the selected component.
4. Release the left mouse button when the component reaches its new location on the form.

To move multiple components, perform the following steps:

1. Select the components as described earlier.
2. Move the mouse cursor over one of the selected components and hold down the left mouse button. This action prepares the components for the move.

3. Move the mouse (while still holding down the left mouse button) to move the selected components.
4. Release the left mouse button when the components reach their new location on the form.

DO	DON'T

DO move a group of selected components to preserve the distance between them.

DON'T forget to release the mouse button after selecting the last component and then hold it down again to move the selected components.

Resizing Components

Delphi enables you to resize only one component at a time. To resize a component, perform the following steps:

1. Select the component by clicking on it with the left mouse button.
2. Move the mouse to a tracker. This action causes the mouse cursor to change shape. The new shape indicates the direction of resizing the component: vertical, horizontal, or diagonal.
3. Hold down the mouse to resize the component.
4. Release the left mouse button when you are done.

Figure 3.4 shows the four buttons after being resized.

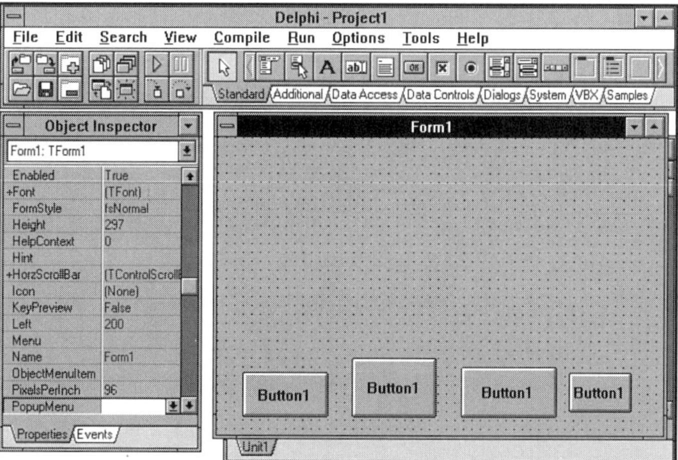

Figure 3.4.
The button controls after being resized.

Aligning the Size of Components

Delphi supports aligning the size of selected components. You need to first select the components whose sizes you want to align. Next, choose Edit | Size... to bring up the Size dialog box, shown in Figure 3.5. This dialog box enables you to resize multiple components to be exactly the same height or width. The Width options modify the horizontal size of the selected components. The Height options align the vertical size. The options for horizontal or vertical sizing are shown in Table 3.1.

Table 3.1. The options for horizontal or vertical sizing.

Option	Description
No Change	Does not change the size of the components.
Shrink To Smallest	Resizes the group of components to the height or width of the smallest selected component.
Grow To Largest	Resizes the group of components to the height or width of the largest selected component.
Width	Sets a custom width for the selected components.
Height	Sets a custom height for the selected components.

Figure 3.5 shows the Size dialog box displaying the buttons before the size alignment but after the Grow To Largest options have been selected for both the vertical and horizontal sizes. Figure 3.6 shows the buttons after the size alignment.

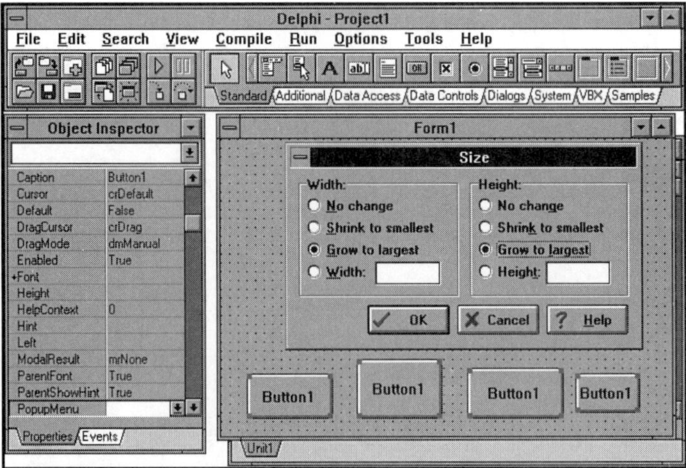

Figure 3.5.
The Size dialog box showing the buttons before the size alignment.

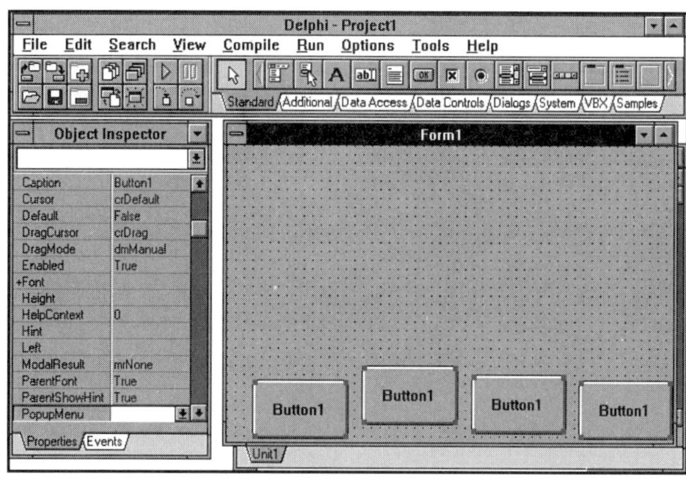

Figure 3.6.
The buttons after the size alignment.

Aligning the Location of Components

Delphi also supports aligning the location of selected components. You need to first select the components whose sizes you want to align. Next, select Edit|Align... to bring up the Align dialog box, shown in Figure 3.7. This dialog box enables you to align the position of multiple components. The Horizontal alignment options align components along their right edges, left edges, or midline. The Vertical alignment options align components along their top edges, bottom edges, or midline. Table 3.2 shows the options for horizontal or vertical alignment.

Table 3.2. The options for horizontal or vertical alignment.

Option	Description
No Change	Does not change the alignment of the component.
Left Sides	Lines up the left edges of the selected components (horizontal only).
Centers	Lines up the centers of the selected components.
Right Sides	Lines up the right edges of the selected components (horizontal only).
Tops	Lines up the top edges of the selected components (vertical only).
Bottoms	Lines up the bottom edges of the selected components (vertical only).
Space Equally	Lines up the selected components equidistant from each other.
Center In Window	Lines up the selected components with the center of the window.

Figure 3.7 shows the Align dialog box displaying the buttons before the position alignment but after the Space Equally and Tops options are selected for the vertical and horizontal locations. Figure 3.8 shows the buttons after the position alignment.

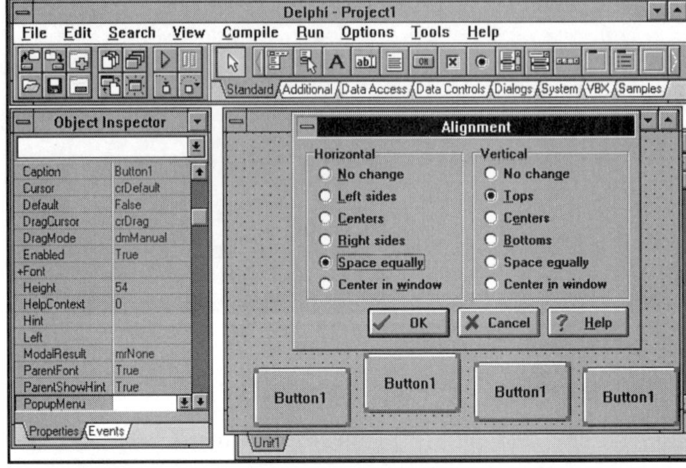

Figure 3.7.
The Align dialog box showing the buttons before the position alignment.

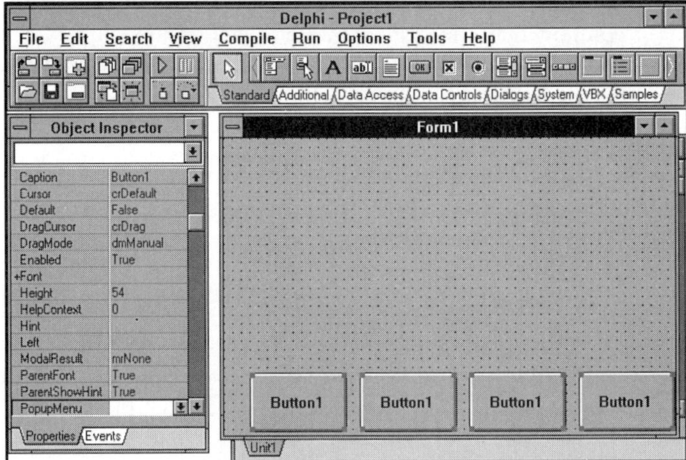

Figure 3.8.
The buttons after the position alignment.

Object Classes

Look at the world around you. It's full of objects, some of which are more animated than others. Each object has specific properties and performs particular tasks (including sitting there and doing nothing). Although each object is unique, objects do fall into categories called *classes*. Thus, although my PC is unique to me, it falls in the class of personal computers, just like your

machine. However, each one of our machines has a different state (that is, DOS version, Windows version, files, directories, and so on) and performs different tasks (writing, accounting, engineering design, or whatever you do with it). However, none of our machines performs any task not defined by the class. In other words, I don't drive my PC like a car. Likewise, none of our machines has properties outside the class of PCs—for example, none of our machines uses internal nuclear power as a source of energy! Each PC is an instance of a class of personal computers. In the next subsections you will learn about the object-oriented aspects of forms and components.

NEW TERM A *class* is a category of objects that share the same properties and operations.

NEW TERM An *object* is a unique instance of class.

Visual versus Object Aspect of Forms

A form and its components are not merely images that are cleverly animated by some code written by a group of programming gurus. Instead, a form and its components are animated objects that have a visual part, a hidden part, and the support of preset behavior. Each form and component has a set of *properties* that determine its behavior and visual appearance. In addition, these objects have the support of *methods* (functions and procedures) that animate them and enable them to interact with other windows.

Classes and Forms

Object-oriented programming offers classes as a very suitable framework for modeling forms and components. Thus, if you think of a form or component as an object, you can regard the kind of form or component as a class. Recall that in Day 2 I introduced you to the general syntax of a class, which encapsulates public, protected, and private fields and methods. Thus the fields of a class that models a form support the properties of that form. Likewise, the methods of a class modeling a form support the operations and event-handling of the form. These aspects of fields and methods also apply to components.

Thus, a class that models a form has fields that determine the visual appearance of the form. In addition, the same class has other fields to keep track of information related to how the form behaves. Moreover, the form-supporting class has methods that determine how the form responds to events as well as performing behind-the-scenes management.

Delphi Classes and Forms

Delphi declares a library of classes that support the form and various components. The class `TForm` supports the minimal form in a Delphi application. When you create a new project,

Delphi automatically declares the class `TForm1`, as a descendant of class `TForm`, to support the project's form. On Day 1, the listing generated by Delphi created the class `TForm1` with no fields and no methods. This meant that class `TForm1` merely inherited the fields and methods of class `TForm`. On Day 2, the BUTTON program used the class `TForm1` with the field `CloseBtn` and the method `CloseBtnClick`.

Listing 3.1 shows the rather impressive declaration of class `TForm`. This declaration should give you a good feel of how non-trivial this class is. The declaration shows many keywords that have not been explained yet. Don't be concerned about them now. The event-handling methods are the procedures that are followed by the keyword `message` and then the name of the Windows message. The properties are those fields that start with the keyword `property`. Of particular interest is line 183, which declares the procedure `Close`. You may recall that in the BUTTON program you typed the statement `Close` inside the procedure `TForm1.CloseBtnClick`. The `Close` statement you typed invoked the procedure `Close`, which is declared in line 183.

Listing 3.1. The declaration of class `TForm`.

```
 1:  TForm = class(TScrollingWinControl)
 2:   private
 3:    FActiveControl: TWinControl;
 4:    FFocusedControl: TWinControl;
 5:    FBorderIcons: TBorderIcons;
 6:    FBorderStyle: TFormBorderStyle;
 7:    FWindowState: TWindowState;
 8:    FShowAction: TShowAction;
 9:    FKeyPreview: Boolean;
10:    FActive: Boolean;
11:    FLastActiveWnd: HWND;
12:    FFormStyle: TFormStyle;
13:    FCanvas: TControlCanvas;
14:    FIcon: TIcon;
15:    FMenu: TMainMenu;
16:    FModalResult: TModalResult;
17:    FDesigner: TDesigner;
18:    FMenuHelp: THelpContext;
19:    FClientHandle: HWND;
20:    FPosition: TPosition;
21:    FTileMode: TTileMode;
22:    FWindowMenu: TMenuItem;
23:    FPixelsPerInch: Integer;
24:    FFormState: TFormState;
25:    FObjectMenuItem: TMenuItem;
26:    FDropTarget: Boolean;
27:    FPrintScale: TPrintScale;
28:    FHelper: TWinOleHelper;
29:    FOnActivate: TNotifyEvent;
30:    FOnClose: TCloseEvent;
31:    FOnCloseQuery: TCloseQueryEvent;
32:    FOnDeactivate: TNotifyEvent;
33:    FOnHide: TNotifyEvent;
34:    FOnPaint: TNotifyEvent;
35:    FOnResize: TNotifyEvent;
```

```
FOnShow: TNotifyEvent;
FOnCreate: TNotifyEvent;
FOnDestroy: TNotifyEvent;
procedure ChangeBorder(CurBorder,
  NewBorder: TFormBorderStyle;
  UpdateWindow: Boolean);
procedure AlignControls(AControl: TControl;
  var Rect: TRect); override;
procedure RefreshMDIMenu;
procedure CloseModal;
function GetActiveMDIChild: TForm;
function GetCanvas: TCanvas;
function GetIconHandle: HICON;
procedure GetNormalBounds;
function GetMDIChildCount: Integer;
function GetMDIChildren(I: Integer): TForm;
function GetPixelsPerInch: Integer;
function GetScaled: Boolean;
function IsColorStored: Boolean;
function IsForm: Boolean;
function IsIconStored: Boolean;
procedure SetActiveControl(Control: TWinControl);
procedure SetBorderIcons(Value: TBorderIcons);
procedure SetBorderStyle(Value: TFormBorderStyle);
procedure SetDesigner(ADesigner: TDesigner);
procedure SetFormStyle(Value: TFormStyle);
procedure SetIcon(Value: TIcon);
procedure SetMenu(Value: TMainMenu);
procedure SetPixelsPerInch(Value: Integer);
procedure SetPosition(Value: TPosition);
procedure SetScaled(Value: Boolean);
procedure SetWindowFocus;
procedure SetWindowMenu(Value: TMenuItem);
procedure SetObjectMenuItem(Value: TMenuItem);
procedure SetWindowState(Value: TWindowState);
procedure MergeMenu(MergeState: Boolean);
procedure WMPaint(var Message: TWMPaint);
  message WM_PAINT;
procedure WMEraseBkgnd(var Message: TWMEraseBkgnd);
  message WM_ERASEBKGND;
procedure WMQueryDragIcon(
  var Message: TWMQueryDragIcon);
  message WM_QUERYDRAGICON;
procedure WMNCCreate(var Message: TWMNCCreate);
  message WM_NCCREATE;
procedure WMDestroy(var Message: TWMNCDestroy);
  message WM_DESTROY;
procedure WMNCDestroy(var Message: TWMNCDestroy);
  message WM_NCDESTROY;
procedure WMCommand(var Message: TWMCommand);
  message WM_COMMAND;
procedure WMInitMenuPopup(
  var Message: TWMInitMenuPopup);
  message WM_INITMENUPOPUP;
procedure WMMenuSelect(var Message: TWMMenuSelect);
  message WM_MENUSELECT;
```

continues

Listing 3.1. continued

```
    procedure WMEnterIdle(var Message: TWMEnterIdle);
      message WM_ENTERIDLE;
    procedure WMActivate(var Message: TWMActivate);
      message WM_ACTIVATE;
    procedure WMSize(var Message: TWMSize);
      message WM_SIZE;
    procedure WMClose(var Message: TWMClose);
      message WM_CLOSE;
    procedure WMQueryEndSession(
      var Message: TWMQueryEndSession);
      message WM_QUERYENDSESSION;
    procedure WMSysCommand(var Message: TWMSysCommand);
      message WM_SYSCOMMAND;
    procedure WMShowWindow(var Message: TWMShowWindow);
      message WM_SHOWWINDOW;
    procedure WMMDIAtivate(var Message: TWMMDIActivate);
      message WM_MDIACTIVATE;
    procedure WMNextDlgCtl(var Message: TWMNextDlgCtl);
      message WM_NEXTDLGCTL;
    procedure WMSetFocus(var Message: TWMSetFocus);
      message WM_SETFOCUS;
    procedure WMKillFocus(var Message: TWMSetFocus);
      message WM_KILLFOCUS;
    procedure WMParentNotify(var Message: TWMParentNotify);
      message WM_PARENTNOTIFY;
    procedure WMEnterMenuLoop(var Message: TMessage);
      message WM_ENTERMENULOOP;
    procedure CMActivate(var Message: TCMActivate);
      message CM_ACTIVATE;
    procedure CMDeactivate(var Message: TCMDeactivate);
      message CM_DEACTIVATE;
    procedure CMDialogKey(var Message: TCMDialogKey);
      message CM_DIALOGKEY;
    procedure CMColorChanged(var Message: TMessage);
      message CM_COLORCHANGED;
    procedure CMCtl3DChanged(var Message: TMessage);
      message CM_CTL3DCHANGED;
    procedure CMFontChanged(var Message: TMessage);
      message CM_FONTCHANGED;
    procedure CMMenuChanged(var Message: TMessage);
      message CM_MENUCHANGED;
    procedure CMShowingChanged(var Message: TMessage);
      message CM_SHOWINGCHANGED;
    procedure CMIconChanged(var Message: TMessage);
      message CM_ICONCHANGED;
    procedure CMRelease(var Message: TMessage);
      message CM_RELEASE;
    procedure CMTextChanged(var Message: TMessage);
      message CM_TEXTCHANGED;
  protected
    procedure Activate; dynamic;
    procedure ActiveChanged; dynamic;
    procedure CreateParams(var Params: TCreateParams);
      override;
    procedure CreateWnd; override;
```

```
    function CreateWindow(ExStyle: LongInt;
      ClassName, WindowName: PChar;
      AStyle: LongInt; AX, AY, AWidth, AHeight: Integer;
      WndParent: HWnd; AMenu: HMenu; Instance: THandle;
      Param: Pointer): HWnd; override;
    procedure Deactivate; dynamic;
    procedure DefaultHandler(var Message); override;
    procedure DestroyWnd; override;
    procedure DestroyWindow(Handle: HWND); override;
    procedure DoHide; dynamic;
    procedure DoShow; dynamic;
    function GetClientRect: TRect; override;
    procedure Notification(AComponent: TComponent;
      Operation: TOperation); override;
    procedure Paint; dynamic;
    procedure PaintWindow(DC: HDC); override;
    procedure PostReadState; override;
    procedure Resize; dynamic;
    procedure ReadState(Reader: TReader); override;
    procedure SetClientSize(const Value: TPoint);
      override;
    procedure SetName(const Value: TComponentName);
      override;
    procedure ValidateRename(AComponent: TComponent;
      const CurName, NewName: string); override;
    procedure VisibleChanging; override;
    procedure WriteState(Writer: TWriter); override;
    procedure WndProc(var Message: TMessage);
      override;
  public
    constructor Create(AOwner: TComponent); override;
    constructor CreateNew(AOwner: TComponent);
    destructor Destroy; override;
    procedure ArrangeIcons;
    procedure Cascade;
    procedure ClearActiveControl(FocusEvents: Boolean);
    procedure Close;
    function CloseQuery: Boolean;
    procedure FocusControl(Control: TWinControl);
    function GetFormImage: TBitmap;
    procedure Hide;
    procedure Next;
    procedure Previous;
    procedure Print;
    procedure Release;
    procedure SetFocus; override;
    function SetFocusedControl(
      Control: TWinControl): Boolean;
    procedure Show;
    function ShowModal: Integer;
    procedure Tile;
    property Active: Boolean read FActive;
    property ActiveMDIChild: TForm read GetActiveMDIChild;
    property Canvas: TCanvas read GetCanvas;
    property ClientHandle: HWND read FClientHandle;
    property Designer: TDesigner read FDesigner
```

continues

Listing 3.1. continued

```
      write SetDesigner;
    property ModalResult: TModalResult read FModalResult
      write FModalResult;
    property MDIChildCount: Integer read GetMDIChildCount;
    property MDIChildren[I:Integer]:TForm read GetMDIChildren;
    property TileMode: TTileMode read FTileMode
      write FTileMode default tbHorizontal;
    property DropTarget: Boolean read FDropTarget
      write FDropTarget;
    property Helper: TWinOleHelper read FHelper
      write FHelper;
  published
    property ActiveControl: TWinControl
      read FActiveControl
      write SetActiveControl
      stored IsForm;
    property AutoScroll stored IsForm;
    property BorderIcons: TBorderIcons read FBorderIcons
      write SetBorderIcons stored IsForm
      default [biSystemMenu, biMinimize, biMaximize];
    property BorderStyle: TFormBorderStyle
      read FBorderStyle
      write SetBorderStyle
      stored IsForm default bsSizeable;
    property Caption stored IsForm;
    property ClientHeight stored False;
    property ClientWidth stored False;
    property Ctl3D default True;
    property Color stored IsColorStored;
    property Enabled;
    property Font;
    property FormStyle: TFormStyle read FFormStyle
      write SetFormStyle
      stored IsForm default fsNormal;
    property HorzScrollBar stored IsForm;
    property Icon: TIcon read FIcon
      write SetIcon stored IsIconStored;
    property KeyPreview: Boolean read FKeyPreview
      write FKeyPreview stored IsForm default False;
    property Menu: TMainMenu read FMenu
      write SetMenu stored IsForm;
    property ObjectMenuItem: TMenuItem
      read FObjectMenuItem
      write SetObjectMenuItem stored IsForm;
    property PixelsPerInch: Integer read GetPixelsPerInch
      write SetPixelsPerInch
      stored IsForm;
    property PopupMenu stored IsForm;
    property Position: TPosition read FPosition
      write SetPosition stored IsForm
      default poDesigned;
    property PrintScale: TPrintScale read FPrintScale
      write FPrintScale stored IsForm
      default poProportional;
```

```
    property Scaled: Boolean read GetScaled
      write SetScaled stored IsForm default True;
    property ShowHint;
    property VertScrollBar stored IsForm;
    property Visible default False;
    property WindowState: TWindowState read FWindowState
      write SetWindowState
      stored IsForm default wsNormal;
    property WindowMenu: TMenuItem read FWindowMenu
      write SetWindowMenu stored IsForm;
    property OnActivate: TNotifyEvent read FOnActivate
      write FOnActivate stored IsForm;
    property OnClick stored IsForm;
    property OnClose: TCloseEvent read FOnClose
      write FOnClose stored IsForm;
    property OnCloseQuery: TCloseQueryEvent
      read FOnCloseQuery
      write FOnCloseQuery stored IsForm;
    property OnCreate: TNotifyEvent read FOnCreate
      write FOnCreate stored IsForm;
    property OnDblClick stored IsForm;
    property OnDestroy: TNotifyEvent read FOnDestroy
      write FOnDestroy stored IsForm;
    property OnDeactivate: TNotifyEvent
      read FOnDeactivate
      write FOnDeactivate stored IsForm;
    property OnDragDrop stored IsForm;
    property OnDragOver stored IsForm;
    property OnHide: TNotifyEvent read FOnHide
      write FOnHide stored IsForm;
    property OnKeyDown stored IsForm;
    property OnKeyPress stored IsForm;
    property OnKeyUp stored IsForm;
    property OnMouseDown stored IsForm;
    property OnMouseMove stored IsForm;
    property OnMouseUp stored IsForm;
    property OnPaint: TNotifyEvent read FOnPaint
      write FOnPaint stored IsForm;
    property OnResize: TNotifyEvent read FOnResize
      write FOnResize stored IsForm;
    property OnShow: TNotifyEvent read FOnShow
      write FOnShow stored IsForm;
  end;
```

Attaching Event-Handling Code

Each form and component has a preset collection of events that the form and component can handle. (The key word here is *can*.) By default, the form and components respond to no preset event. You are responsible for selecting the events to which the form and components respond. In most Delphi applications, the form and each component respond to only a few events. The response depends on the how the form and components interact with the end-user.

To attach an event-handling procedure to a form or a component, perform the following steps:

1. Select the form or component by clicking on it. The Object Inspector displays the properties or events for the currently selected form or component.
2. Click on the Events page tab in the Object Inspector. This window shows the current events that are handled. Initially, there are no handled events and the entries for the various events are empty.
3. Double-click on the entry for the event you want to handle. Delphi responds by inserting the declaration of the related event-handling method in the form class, inserting the empty implementation of the event-handling method, and displaying that method.
4. Type in the statements that make the event-handling method respond to the targeted event. For example, you can type the statement `Close;` to close the form.

The Active Form Example

Let's look at an example in which a form responds to the user clicking on it and also to moving the mouse. The form responds to the event of moving the mouse (while the cursor is over the form) by displaying the current mouse coordinates. The form has a button that closes it and a static text control that displays the current mouse location. The first step in crafting the program involves creating a new project. The subsequent sections discuss placing the various components and providing the form with the sought event-handling methods.

The Button Control

Adding and customizing the button involves the following tasks:

1. Select the button component from the Standard page tab in the component palette.
2. Draw the button in the now-familiar manner.
3. Select the Properties page tab in the Object Inspector.
4. Edit the `Caption` property to replace the default caption with `Close`.
5. Edit the `Name` property to replace the default control name with `CloseBtn`.
6. Select the Events page tab in the Object Inspector.
7. Double-click on the `OnClick` event. When Delphi displays the `Click` event-handling method, enter the statement `Close`.

The Label Control

Adding and customizing the label control involves the following tasks:

1. Select the label component from the Standard page tab in the component palette.

2. Draw the label control at the top-left corner of the form and make it wide enough to type in.
3. Select the Properties page tab in the Object Inspector.
4. Edit the `Caption` property to replace the default caption with `[x,y]`.
5. Edit the `Name` property to replace the default control name with `MouseLbl`.

The Form's Event-Handling Methods

To add the event-handling method for the mouse click, perform the following steps:

1. Select the Events page tab in the Object Inspector.
2. Double-click on the `OnClick` event. When Delphi displays the `Click` event-handling method, enter this statement:

```
MessageDlg('You clicked on the form',
           mtInformation, [mbOK], 0);
```

To add the event-handling method for the mouse movement, double-click on the `OnMouseMove` event. When Delphi displays the `Click` event-handling method, enter the following statement right before the `begin` keyword:

```
var s, bigStr : String;
```

Then enter the following statements right after the `begin` keyword:

```
Str(X, s);
bigStr := '[' + s + ',';
Str(Y, s);
bigStr := bigStr + s + ']';
MouseLbl.Caption := bigStr;
```

Save the unit in file UFORM.PAS and save the project in file FORM.DPR. Listing 3.2 shows the source code for the program file FORM.DPR. Listing 3.3 shows the source code for the UFORM.PAS library unit. The bold lines indicate the statements that you typed in.

Listing 3.2. The source code for the program file FORM.DPR.

```
program Form;

uses
  Forms,
  Uform in 'UFORM.PAS' {Form1};

{$R *.RES}

begin
  Application.CreateForm(TForm1, Form1);
  Application.Run;
end.
```

Listing 3.3. The source code for the UFORM.PAS library unit.

```
unit Uform;

interface

uses
  SysUtils, WinTypes, WinProcs, Messages, Classes,
  Graphics, Controls, Forms, Dialogs, StdCtrls;

type
  TForm1 = class(TForm)
    CloseBtn: TButton;
    MouseLbl: TLabel;
    procedure CloseBtnClick(Sender: TObject);
    procedure FormClick(Sender: TObject);
    procedure FormMouseMove(Sender: TObject;
                Shift: TShiftState;
                X, Y: Integer);
  private
    { Private declarations }
  public
    { Public declarations }
  end;

var
  Form1: TForm1;

implementation

{$R *.DFM}

procedure TForm1.CloseBtnClick(Sender: TObject);
begin
  Close;
end;

procedure TForm1.FormClick(Sender: TObject);
begin
  MessageDlg('You clicked on the form',
             mtInformation, [mbOK], 0);
end;


procedure TForm1.FormMouseMove(Sender: TObject;
                               Shift: TShiftState;
                               X, Y: Integer);

var s, bigStr : String;

begin
  Str(X, s);
  bigStr := '[' + s + ',';
  Str(Y, s);
  bigStr := bigStr + s + ']';
  MouseLbl.Caption := bigStr;
```

```
55:  end;
56:
57:  end.
```

Analysis Lines 13 to 17 show the event-handling methods for the form and the button control. Line 13 contains the method that handles clicking the button control. Line 14 contains the method that responds to clicking on the form. Lines 15 to 17 contain the method that responds to moving the mouse over the form. Lines 31 to 34 hold the implementation of the method `CloseBtnClick`. Lines 36 to 40 contain the implementation of the method `FormClick`. Lines 43 to 55 hold the implementation of the method `FormMouseMove`. Notice that all of the implementations of all the methods qualify the method with the name of the owner class, `TForm1`.

Method Declarations

The form class declares the methods it uses to handle events and perform auxiliary support. Lines 13 to 17 in Listing 3.3 contain the declaration of the event-handling methods. These methods are Pascal procedures. Delphi generated the declarations of the event-handling methods in lines 13 to 17. If you need to manually add auxiliary methods to the form class, you need to insert the declarations of these methods inside the form class declaration. In the case of auxiliary methods, you may insert them in the private or protected section in the class declaration.

Method Parameters

Frequently a function or procedure requires its caller to supply it with information to process. Event-handling methods are no exception. Regarding the code for the event-handling methods generated by Delphi, these methods come with a preset list of parameters. For example, the event-handling method `CloseBtnClick` (line 13 in Listing 3.3) has a single parameter, named `Sender`. This parameter has the general object type `TObject`. The argument (that is, the value supplied by the routine which in turn calls the method) of parameter `Sender` provides the method with basic data as to who sent the event. You need not always use the information passed by parameter `Sender` unless you want to know who sent the mouse-click event.

Lines 15 to 17 in Listing 3.3 show the parameters of method `FormMouseMove`. These parameters are `Sender`, `Shift`, `X`, and `Y`. The parameter `Shift` reports the shift state of the mouse buttons and the keyboard. The parameter allows you to determine if the left, middle, or right mouse buttons were held down, and if the Ctrl, Shift, and Alt keys were held down. The parameters `X` and `Y` supply the mouse location when the mouse movement event occurs.

Method Implementations

Delphi generates only the skeleton code for the implementation of event-handling methods. You are responsible for entering the code that determines the response of the methods.

Line 33 provides the `Close` statement, which makes up the response of the event-handling method `TForm1.CloseBtnClick`. Notice that the response does not use the data passed to the parameter `Sender`.

Lines 38 and 39 provides the `MessageDlg` statement, which makes up the response of the event-handling method `TForm1.FormClick`. Notice, once more, that the response does not use the data passed to the parameter `Sender`.

Lines 47 and 50 to 54 offer the code that supports the response of the method `TForm1.FormMouseMove`. Line 47 declares two local variables, `s` and `bigStr`, that have the `String` type. Lines 50 to 54 provide the statements that display the current mouse location. Notice that these statements do use the data passed to the parameters `X` and `Y`. The statements form a string that has the text image of the mouse coordinates and assigns that string to the caption of the label control.

DO	DON'T

DO insert the number and kind of statements required to support the response of the event-handling method.

DON'T forget that you are not obligated to use the values passed by the parameters of the event-handling method.

Components

Components are the controls that you place on the form. Most of the Delphi components are visual and provide the required user-interface of the form. Components enable the form to display and obtain data from the user and to perform specific tasks.

The next subsections present the various kinds of components as they are grouped in the component palette.

DO	DON'T

DO familiarize yourself with the various components by placing them on a form, viewing their properties, and viewing their events.

DON'T forget that the component palette also includes VBX (Visual Basic) and Samples components. These are bonus components included with Delphi under license from third-party software developers.

The Standard Components

Figure 3.9 shows the components in the Standard page tab of the component palette. In brief, these components are

- The MainMenu component. This component accesses the Menu Designer, which allows you create menus for a form.
- The PopupMenu component. This component furnishes a form or other component with a menu that appears independently of any main menu in the form, typically when the user right-clicks.
- The Label component. This component displays text that the user cannot edit, for example, to display a name for other components that do not possess their own captions.
- The EditBox component. This component allows the user to read or write a single line of text.
- The Memo component. This component supplies a section for text editing. The Memo component can read multiple lines of text, whether entered by the user or by the program.
- The Button component. This component provides visual buttons that the users can choose, typically by clicking the mouse on them, to carry out commands.
- The CheckBox component. This component offers Yes/No or True/False options to the end-user, especially when more than one choice is available from a set of choices.
- The RadioButton component. This component encapsulates the standard Windows option button. The radio button offers Yes/No or True/False options to the user. Only a single radio button can be chosen at a time within the form or within other container-type component.
- The ListBox component. This component displays a scrollable list of items from which the end-user can select. The end-user cannot directly alter the items in the list box.
- The ComboBox component. This component combines the operations of a list box and an edit box. The combo box permits the end-user to choose from a preset list of items or to enter his/her own text.
- The ScrollBar component. This component offers a way to alter which portion of a list or form is visible, or to move through a range by increments.
- The GroupBox component. This component resembles the Panel and ScrollBox components, and acts as a container for other components within your form. The group box gathers related components, such as radio buttons or check boxes, allowing the components to be handled as a single logical unit.

- The RadioGroup component. This component is a container that specializes in grouping radio buttons.
- The Panel component. This component is a container, similar to the GroupBox or the ScrollBox components. The Panel contains the properties Alignment, Bevel, and Hint that easily support status lines and tool bars in a form.

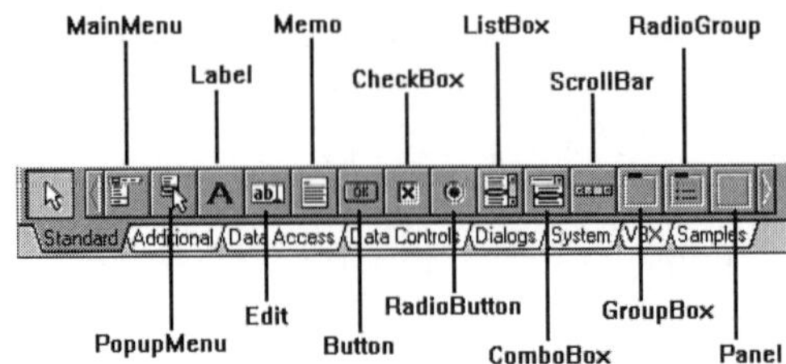

Figure 3.9.
The components in the Standard page tab of the component palette.

The Additional Components

Figure 3.10 shows the components in the Additional page tab of the component palette. In brief, these components are

- The BitMapButton component. This component allows you to customize a command button. The bitmap button enables you to display a glyph.
- The SpeedButton component. This component enables you to group several buttons whose shift states are interrelated at run-time.
- The TabSet component. This component supports tabs on which you can click. You may utilize the TabSet component together with the Notebook component to create a multi-page dialog box or editor.
- The Notebook component. This component generates a single form that contains multiple pages, each of which can hold its own components. The TabSet component, which adds a tab to every page, enables the end-user to move between the notebook pages at run-time.
- The TabbedNotebook component. This component generates a Notebook component that already has tabbed pages built in.
- The MaskEdit component. This component offers an edit component that can be customized to request that the user key in only valid characters.
- The Outline component. This component permits you to display a hierarchical relationship between related data. A node represents every item of the hierarchical grouping. Moreover, each node may have subordinate items.
- The StringGrid component. This component displays strings in column and row format. Thus, a *string grid* is a spreadsheet of text.

- The DrawGrid component. This component displays data in column-and-row format.
- The Image component. This component imports a graphical image into a form. Delphi supports the bitmap (.BMP), metafile (.WMF), and icon (.ICO) picture formats. The component also has a mechanism to register file readers/writers for other formats.
- The Shape component. This component displays graphical shapes on a form.
- The Bevel component. This component lays a raised or lowered line on a form. The Bevel component places a beveled line near related components.
- The Header component. This component creates another component with resizable sections that display the text you designate. For example, use the Header component as column headings with a grid component.
- The ScrollBox component. This component combines a container area, similar to a panel component, with vertical and horizontal scroll bars. You can utilize a scroll box to set the scrollable subarea of the form.

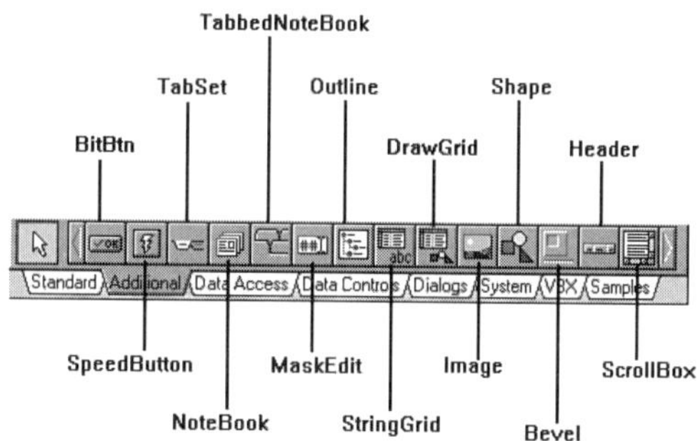

Figure 3.10.
The components in the Additional page tab of the component palette.

The Data Access Components

Figure 3.11 shows the components in the Data Access page tab of the component palette. In brief, these components are

- The DataSource component. This component originates an association between the database table you are viewing and its depiction in any of the Delphi data-aware components. You may establish several queries against the viewed table, and either utilize multiple Query components or multiple DataSource components to shift between the different queries displayed in the data-aware components in a form.
- The Table component. This component shows a table from a local or remote database. The DataSet Designer enables you to configure the table. You may view the table by utilizing any of the Delphi data-aware components.

- The StoreProc component. This component enables Delphi applications to execute server-stored procedures.
- The Database component. This component supplies user ID and password security, transaction control, and persistent connections when connecting to a database.
- The BatchMove component. This component carries out batch operations on groups, records, or datasets.
- The Report Component. This component is an interface to Borland's ReportSmith application.

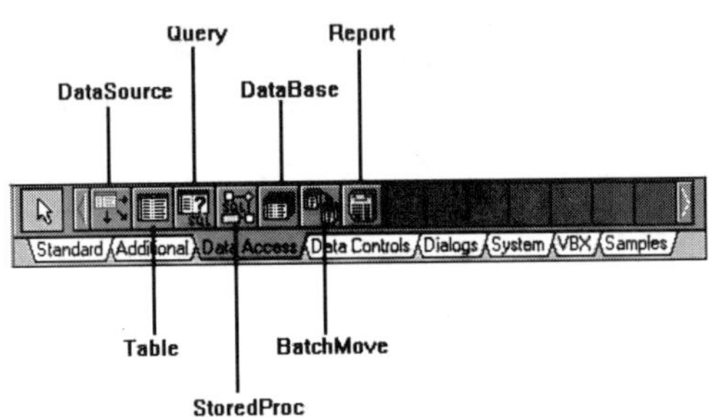

Figure 3.11.
The components in the Data Access page tab of the component palette.

The Data Controls Components

Figure 3.12 shows the components in the Data Controls page tab of the component palette. In brief, these components are

- The DBGrid component. This component displays the data in a table or in a Query component in a grid on a form.
- The DBNavigator component. This component works in conjunction with any of the Delphi data-aware components, such as the DBGrid, to traverse the records in a table or a query, and to carry out operations such as inserting records and posting transactions.
- The DBText component. This component displays the constituents of a field in the current record of a table or a query. The end-user cannot modify the data displayed in a DBText.
- The DBEdit component. This component reads or writes a single line of data into a field of a table or a query.
- The DBMemo component. This component allows the end-user to view and alter the contents of a multi-line field in a table or a query.
- The DBImage component. This component displays a graphical image in a field of a table or query. Delphi supports the bitmap (.BMP), metafile (.WMF), and icon (.ICO) picture formats.

- The DBListBox component. This component supplies a list box that displays the contents of a field in a table or a query.
- The DBComboBox component. This component combines the operations of a DBList box and a DBEdit box, enabling the end-user to choose from a predefined list or to key in new text.
- The DBCheckBox component. This component supports a check box that can read the contents of a field in a table or a query.
- The DBRadioGroup component. This component offers a collection of option buttons whose values can be checked against the values in a database field. Delphi automatically chooses the radio button whose text string matches the current field in the database.
- The DBLookupList component. This component is a data-aware list box that "looks up" a value in a lookup table.
- The DBLookupCombo component. This component is a data-aware combo box that "looks up" a value in a lookup table.

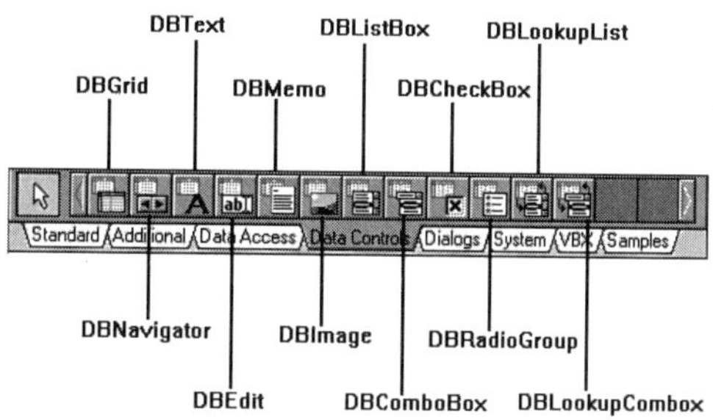

Figure 3.12.
The components in the Data Controls page tab of the component palette.

The Dialogs Components

Figure 3.13 shows the components in the Dialogs page tab of the component palette. In brief, these components are

- The OpenDialog component. This component creates a common Windows Open dialog box that allows the end-user to select the name of a file to open.
- The SaveDialog component. This component produces a common Windows Save dialog box that allows the end-user to select the name of a file to save.
- The FontDialog component. This component creates a common Windows Font dialog box that allows the end-user to select the font at run-time for any component that possesses a Font property.

- The ColorDialog component. This component yields a Color dialog box that allows the end-user to select the color at run-time for any component that possesses a Color property.
- The PrintDialog component. This component brings up a common Windows printer dialog box with which the end-user may interact to carry out printing tasks. When the user chooses the Setup button from within the printer dialog box, the Windows Printer Setup dialog box appears.
- The PrinterSetupDialog component. This component displays the common Windows Printer Setup dialog box in an application at run-time.
- The FindDialog component. This component creates a common Windows Replace dialog box (yes, it's Replace because Windows uses the Replace dialog box for searching *and* replacing text) with the replace text edit box hidden. This dialog box allows you to enter the information required for searching text.
- The ReplaceDialog component. This component creates a common Windows Replace dialog box. This dialog box allows you to enter the information required for searching text.

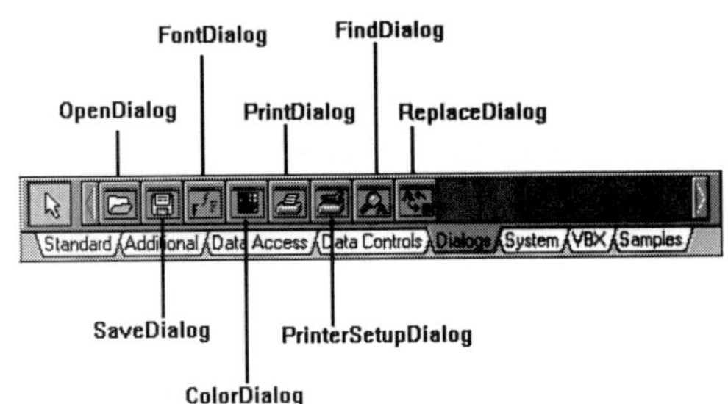

Figure 3.13.
The components in the Dialogs page tab of the component palette.

The System Components

Figure 3.14 shows the components in the System page tab of the component palette. In brief, these components are

- The Timer component. This invisible component triggers an event, either one time or repeatedly, after a measured interval.
- The PaintBox component. This component provides a way of confining the drawing of shapes on a form to the specific rectangular area encompassed by the paint box.
- The FileListBox component. This component displays filenames in the current directory and supports the selection of one or more filenames.
- The DirectoryListBox component. This component enables the run-time selection of a directory on the current drive, or on the drive selected in an associated drive combo box.

- The DriveCombo component. This component enables the run-time selection of a local or network drive.
- The FilterComboBox component. This component determines the type of files accessible to the end-user for selection in a FileListBox component.
- The MediaPlayer component. This component provides an application with the capability to play a CD-ROM player, a VCR, a MIDI sequencer, a sound card, or a digital video.
- The OleContainer component. This component offers an application the capability to link and embed objects from an OLE server. Activating an object inside the OLE container causes the control to transfer to the OLE server application, so the end-user can access all the operations of the server application from within the OLE container application.
- The DdeClientConv component. This invisible component provides an application with the ability to establish a *Dynamic Data Exchange* (DDE) conversation with another application. When this component appears on a form, the application becomes a DDE client. This component works in conjunction with the DdeClientItem component to establish an application as a complete DDE client.
- The DdeClientItem component. This invisible component defines the item of a DDE conversation. Use this component in conjunction with a DdeClientConv component to make an application a DDE client.
- The DdeServerConv component. This invisible component provides an application with the capability to establish a DDE conversation with another application. Putting this component on a form establishes the application as a DDE server. This component works in conjunction with the DdeServerItem component to make your application a complete DDE server.
- The DdeServerItem component. This invisible component defines the topic of a DDE conversation with another application. This component works in conjunction with the DdeServerConv component to make an application a DDE server.

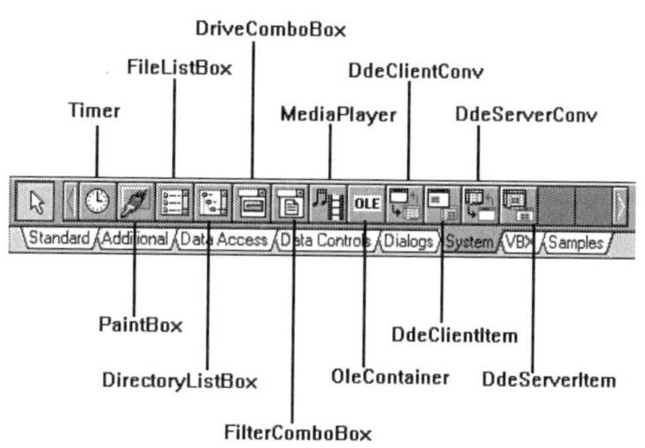

Figure 3.14.
The components in the System page tab of the component palette.

The Component Class Library

Delphi provides you with a rich set of classes to support the various components. Table 3.3 shows the partial list of all controls in the *Visual Component Library* (VCL). The table includes both windowed controls and non-windowed controls.

Table 3.3. The partial list of component classes in the Visual Component Library.

Class	Component
`TBevel`	Bevel
`TBitBtn`	BitMap button
`TButton`	Button
`TCheckBox`	CheckBox
`TComboBox`	ComboBox
`TDBCheckBox`	DBCheckBox
`TDBComboBox`	DBComboBox
`TDBEdit`	DBEditBox
`TDBGrid`	DBGrid
`TDBImage`	DBImage
`TDBText`	DBText
`TDBListBox`	DBListBox
`TDBMemo`	DBMemo
`TDBNavigator`	DBNavigator
`TDBRadioGroup`	DBRadioGroup
`TDirectoryListBox`	DirectoryListBox
`TDrawGrid`	GridControl
`TDriveComboBox`	DriveComboBox
`TEdit`	EditBox
`TFileListBox`	FileListBox
`TFilterComboBox`	FilterComboBox
`TForm`	Form
`TGroupBox`	GroupBox
`THeader`	Header
`TImage`	ImageControl

Class	Component
TLabel	Label
TListBox	ListBox
TMainMenu	MainMenu
TMediaPlayer	MediaPlayer
TMemo	Memo
TMenu	Menu
TMenuItem	MenuItem
TNotebook	Notebook
TOLEContainer	OLEContainer
TOutline	Outline
TPanel	Panel
TPopupMenu	PopupMenu
TRadioButton	RadioButton
TScrollBar	ScrollBar
TShape	Shape
TSpeedButton	SpeedButton
TStringGrid	TextGrid
TTabSet	TabSet

3

Non-Windowed Controls

Non-windowed controls are controls that

- Cannot hold other controls
- Cannot obtain focus while an application is running
- Do not have a window handle

Table 3.4 lists all non-windowed components in the Visual Component Library.

Table 3.4. The list of non-windowed component classes.

Class	Component
TBevel	Bevel
TDBImage	DBImage

continues

Table 3.4. continued

Class	Component
`TDBText`	DBText
`TImage`	Image
`TLabel`	Label
`TShape`	Shape

Non-Visual Controls

Non-visual controls are controls that

- Appear on the form at design-time
- May not appear at all during run-time
- May control or manage other visual aspects of the application, such as common dialogs

Table 3.5 lists the non-visual components in the Visual Component Library.

Table 3.5. The list of component classes.

Class	Component
`TColorDialog`	ColorDialogBox
`TDdeClientConv`	DdeClientConv
`TDdeClientItem`	DdeClientItem
`TDdeServerConv`	DdeServerConv
`TDdeServerItem`	DdeServerItem
`TFindDialog`	FindDialog
`TFontDialog`	FontDialog
`TOpenDialog`	OpenDialog
`TPrintDialog`	PrintDialog
`TPrinterSetupDialog`	PrinterSetupDialog
`TReplaceDialog`	ReplaceDialog
`TSaveDialog`	FileSaveDialog
`TTimer`	Timer

Properties of Components

As mentioned earlier in this chapter, Delphi uses classes to support the form and components. The hierarchy of classes that supports the form and components uses fields to keep track of the attributes of the form and components. Delphi supports a special syntax that uses the keyword `property` to indicate that a field represents a property that might appear in the Object Inspector. (The key words here are *might appear*.) To make those properties appear in the Object Inspector, Delphi uses a special syntax. This syntax involves the `published` clause, which appears in the class declaration. The `published` clause tells Delphi which properties to actually display in the Object Inspector. Thus, the above scheme enables you to control which properties to display when working with a hierarchy of classes that model various controls. If you turn back to Listing 3.1 you will find examples of fields declared as properties in lines 198 through 212. The same listing shows the published section in line 214. This section includes more properties, shown in lines 215 through 298.

The next subsections discuss working with properties of the form and components.

Role of Properties

Properties serve two main purposes. First, they determine how the form or components appear. Second, properties determine how a form or components behave.

Setting Properties at Design-Time

Delphi enables you to view and alter the properties of a form or component at design-time. The form and components come with factory settings, so to speak. Most of these settings are adequate for the average use, but you still need to customize some of them. For example, the caption and control name are among the properties you will edit most frequently. When you edit the visual-related property of a form or component, Delphi promptly updates the visual appearance of the form or component. Some properties, such as the `Boolean Visible` property, have no effect on the appearance of the component at design-time.

There are several types of properties, based on the nature of their values. The next subsections discuss the property types.

Simple Properties

Simple properties are those whose values are integers and strings. For example, the properties `Left` and `Top` take integer values that define the location of the upper-left corner of a form or component. Other examples are the `Caption` and `Name` properties, which accept strings. Changing the settings for simple properties is very straightforward. You click on the setting, type in the new value, and press Enter. Figure 3.15 shows a sample session with a Delphi project in which the `Caption` property is selected to edit its setting.

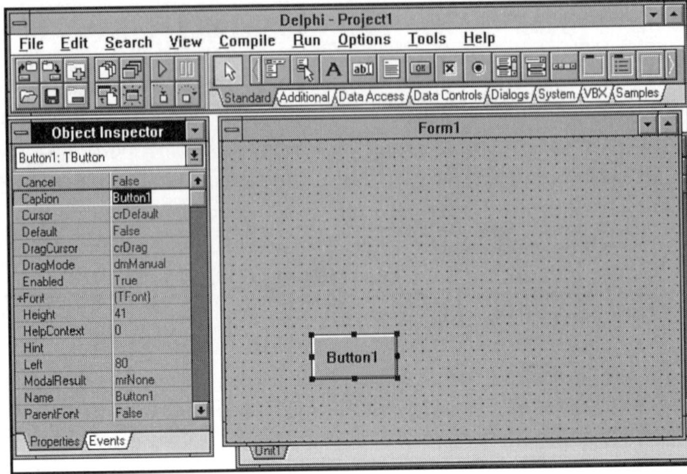

Figure 3.15.
A sample session with a Delphi project in which the `Caption` *property is selected to edit its setting.*

Enumerated Selection Properties

This type of property supports a predefined set of values. The simplest example is `Boolean`-type properties. These properties have settings that are either `True` or `False`. When you click on the setting of a `Boolean`-type property, the Object Inspector displays a small down-arrow button. Clicking on this button invokes a drop-down list of enumerated values. In the case of a `Boolean`-type property, you have only the `False` and `True` values. Other properties that offer enumerated selection typically have longer lists. To select a new setting, simply click on a value in the drop-down list. Figure 3.16 shows a sample session with a Delphi project in which the `Boolean`-type `Visible` property is selected to edit its setting.

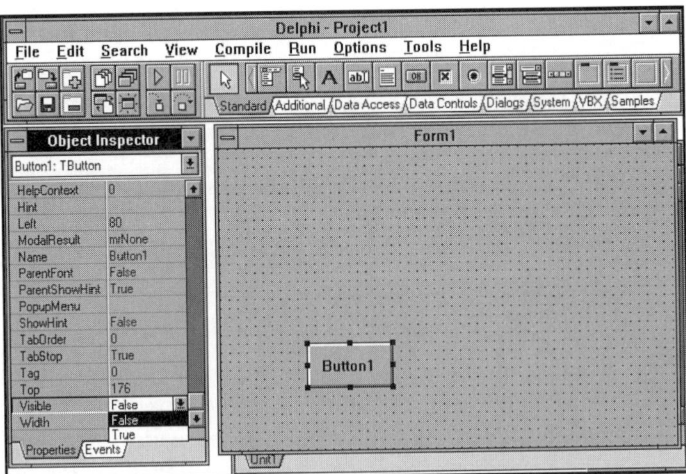

Figure 3.16.
A sample session with a Delphi project in which the `Boolean`*-type* `Visible` *property is selected to edit its setting.*

Nested Properties

This type of property supports nested values (or objects, if you prefer). The Object Inspector places a plus sign to the left of the name of each nested property. To view the settings of a nested property, double-click on that property. Delphi expands the nested property in an outline format and displays the settings. Some nested properties have settings that are themselves nested properties. For example, the `Font` property of a form has the Style setting as a nested property.

There are two kinds of nested properties: sets and combined values. The Object Inspector displays sets inside square brackets. If the set is empty, it appears as [ ]. The settings for a set-type nested property are typically Boolean values. Figure 3.17 shows the set-type `Style` property with its `Boolean` settings.

Figure 3.17.
The set-type `Style` property with its Boolean settings.

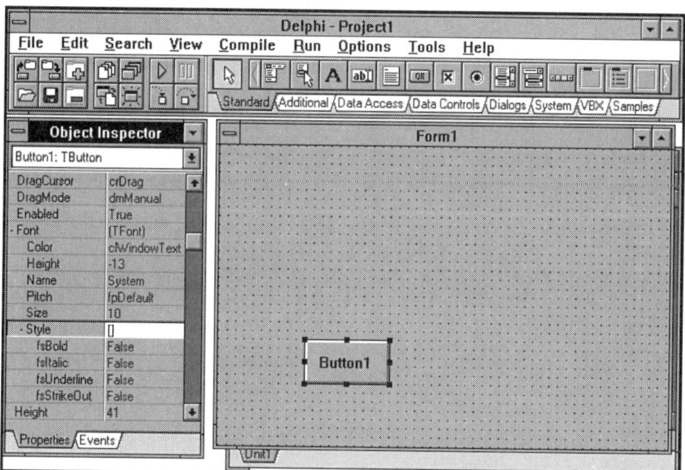

The Object Inspector displays combined values as a collection of settings that have different data types. You can edit these settings one at a time. Some properties, such as the `Font` property, cause the Object Inspector to display a three-dot button in the setting box. When you click on this button, the Object Inspector invokes a dialog box that allows you to easily select a different value. The `Font` property is a good example. Clicking on the three-dot button of a font setting invokes the Font dialog box, shown in Figure 3.18.

DO | **DON'T**

DO use dialog box, when available, to quickly and easily change the settings of nested properties.

DON'T forget that you can expand and contract a nested property by double-clicking on the property name.

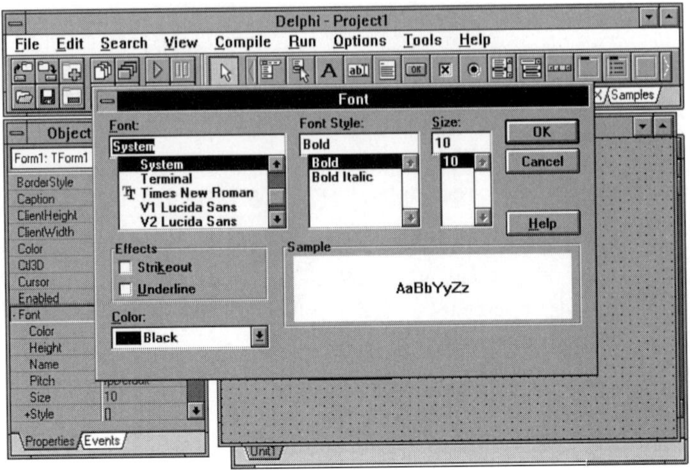

Figure 3.18.
The Font dialog box.

Events

Let's have a quick quiz! What is the main difference between DOS and Windows applications? The answer is that DOS programs are typically linear—they run in a specific sequence. By contrast, Windows applications (including Delphi programs) are event driven. A Windows program is able to manage many alternate actions that you may take. Windows translates these actions, such a clicking the mouse button, invoking a menu option, and pressing a key, into events. The Windows program then deals with that event. This strategy allows Windows programs to deal with an event that can be generated by different actions.

The next subsections discuss trapping and handling events in Delphi applications.

Events Associated with Components

The form and each component have a preset collection of events that can be handled. These events respond to common actions taken by the end-user. By default, Delphi has standard event handlers associating events with a form or component. Your explicit association of an event with a form or component is part of customizing the form or component.

The Events page tab in the Object Inspector lists the events that are and can be handled by the currently selected form or component. The events that are handled have entries in their settings.

DO	DON'T

DO use your own name for an event-handling method to avoid ending up with a much longer default name. Make the name include the component and handled event for the sake of clarity and improved readibility.

DON'T shy away from using the default name of the event-handling method, unless the name is rather long.

Trapping Events

You can trap the events shown in the Object Inspector by specifying the event-handling method. Delphi supports two ways to select the latter method:

- Double-clicking on the event's setting. Delphi then inserts the default name of the event-handling method. In the majority of cases, the default name is adequate.
- Typing in the name of the event-handling method and then pressing Enter.

Either technique causes Delphi to perform the following tasks:

- Inserts the name of the event-handling method in the declaration of the form class.
- Inserts the skeleton code for the implementation of the event-handling method.
- Places the insertion cursor inside the `begin-end` block of the event-handling method.

You already learned about selecting the event to trap in the BUTTON program of Day 2 and in the form program in this chapter.

Handling Events

Handling an event that you trap involves placing the appropriate statements in the event-handling methods. Refer back to Listing 3.3, which shows three event-handling methods. The method `TForm1.CloseBtnClick` has only the `Close` statement on line 33. Likewise, the method `TForm1.FormClick` has only the `MessageDlg` statement in lines 38 and 39. By contrast, the method `TForm1.FormMouseMove` uses five statements (in lines 50 to 54) to offer the required response.

Application Architectures

Delphi supports creating applications that employ multiple forms. This section looks at the various kinds of forms, how to use them, and when to invoke them. Keep in mind that each Delphi application has a main form that initially appears when the program starts running.

Dialog Boxes

Dialog boxes are special windows that, as the name might suggest, exchange information with the end-user. Dialog boxes display and/or obtain data. There are two kinds of dialog boxes: modal and modeless. *Modal* dialog boxes must be closed before you can access any pre-existing window that belongs to the application. The reason for this restriction is that modal dialog boxes typically deal with critical data that must be addressed before you can proceed with the program. Modeless dialog boxes, on the other hand, enable you to access pre-existing program windows. The reason for this flexibility is that modeless dialog boxes do not handle critical data. In addition, keeping a modeless dialog box is sometimes very convenient. For example, consider the Find dialog box, used to search for text in a text editor. It is more convenient to have the Find dialog box remain visible so that you can easily search for other text occurrences.

NEW TERM A *modal* dialog box requires that you close it before you can access pre-existing program windows.

NEW TERM A *modeless* dialog enables you to access pre-existing program windows.

Forms as Modal Dialog Boxes

Delphi enables you to create secondary forms and use them as modal dialog boxes. The process of using a form as a dialog box is simple. The next program, `FrmDlg1`, demonstrates this feature. The program `FrmDlg1` has two forms: the main form and the secondary form, which acts as a modal dialog box. The main form has a button with the caption `Close`. When you click on this button, the program invokes the modal dialog box form that has the text Good Bye! and the button OK. When you click on the OK button, you close the modal form as well as the main form, and end the program. Let's look at the steps involved in customizing each form.

The Main Form

The main form has a single button control, as shown in Figure 3.19. Perform the following steps to customize the main form and its controls:

1. Select the Standard page tab of the component palette.
2. Draw a button control on the lower part of the main form.
3. Set the `Caption` property of the button to `Close`.
4. Set the `Name` property of the button to `CloseBtn`.
5. Set the caption of the form to `Main Form`.
4. Save the unit for the main form in file UFORM11.PAS.

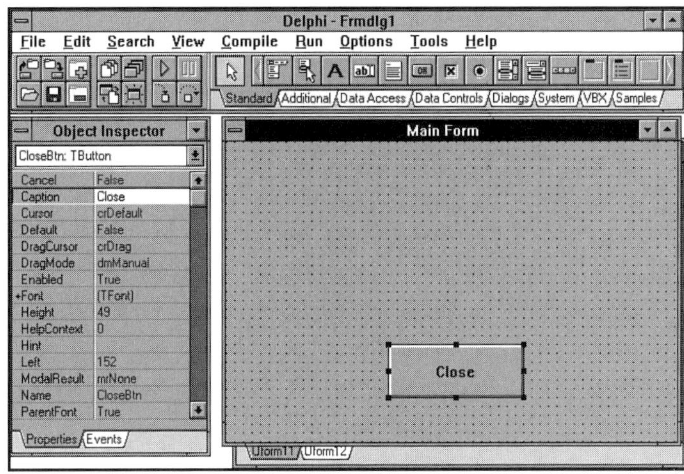

Figure 3.19.
The main form of program `Frmdlg1`.

The Secondary Form

Create the secondary form using by selecting File|New Form. Delphi displays the Browse Gallery dialog box (see Figure 3.20). This dialog box enables you to select from different kinds of forms. The default selection is the blank form, which is the item you want. Click on the OK button of the dialog box. The secondary form has a label and a single button control, as shown in Figure 3.21. Perform the following steps to customize the secondary form and its controls:

1. Select the secondary form.
2. Draw a button control on the lower part of the main form.
3. Set the `Caption` property of the button to `OK`.
4. Set the `Name` property of the button to `OKBtn`.
5. Draw a label in the middle of the form.
6. Set the `Caption` property of the label to `Good Bye!`.
7. Set the `Name` property of the label to `ByeLbl`.
8. Double-click on the nested `Font` property.
9. Set the `Size` property to 24.
10. Select the secondary form by clicking on it.
11. Set the `Caption` property of the form to Modal Dialog Form.
12. Set the `Color` property to `clYellow` to select the yellow color.
13. Set the `BorderStyle` property to `bsDialog`.
14. Save the unit for the secondary form in file UFORM12.PAS.
15. Save the project in file FORMDLG1.DPR.

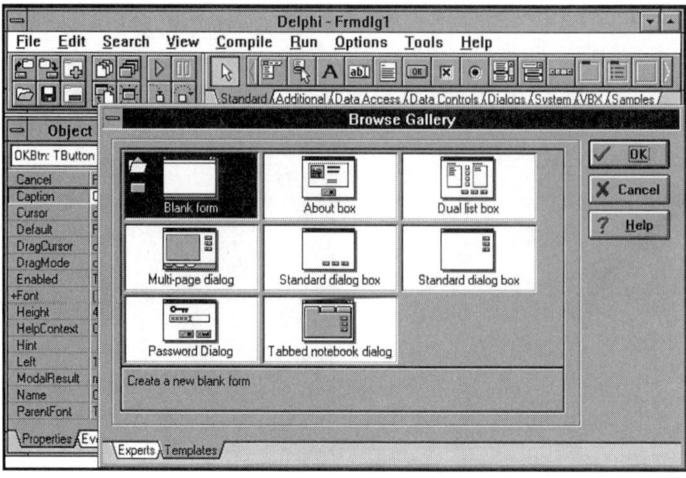

Figure 3.20.
The Browse Gallery dialog box.

Figure 3.21.
The secondary form of program `Frmdlg1`.

Adding Event-Handling Methods

You need to add event-handling methods to the button control on the main and secondary forms. Each button should handle the mouse-click event. For each form, first select that form, then select its button. Next, click on the Events page tab in the Object Inspector and click on the setting of the `OnClick` event. Listing 3.4 shows the source code for the UFORM11.PAS unit. The bold lines show the manually inserted code. Notice that the `uses` clause lists the name of the unit `Uform12`. This declaration is needed to allow the main form bring up the secondary form by accessing the variable `Form2`. This variable, which is exported by unit `Uform12`, is an instance of class `TForm2` and supports the secondary form. Listing 3.5 shows the source code for the UFORM12.PAS unit. The bold line (see line 29) contains the statement you need to insert for the `TForm2.ClickOKBtn` method.

Listing 3.4. The source code for the UFORM11.PAS unit.

```
unit Uform11;

interface

uses
  SysUtils, WinTypes, WinProcs, Messages, Classes,
  Graphics, Controls, Forms, Dialogs, StdCtrls,
{ manually inserted unit name }
  Uform12;

type
  TForm1 = class(TForm)
    CloseBtn: TButton;
    procedure CloseBtnClick(Sender: TObject);
  private
    { Private declarations }
  public
    { Public declarations }
  end;

var
  Form1: TForm1;

implementation

{$R *.DFM}

procedure TForm1.CloseBtnClick(Sender: TObject);
begin
  Form2.ShowModal;
  Close;
end;

end.
```

Listing 3.5. The source code for the UFORM12.PAS unit.

```
unit Uform12;

interface

uses
  SysUtils, WinTypes, WinProcs, Messages, Classes,
  Graphics, Controls, Forms, Dialogs, StdCtrls;

type
  TForm2 = class(TForm)
    OKBtn: TButton;
    ByeLbl: TLabel;
    procedure OKBtnClick(Sender: TObject);
  private
    { Private declarations }
```

continues

Listing 3.5. continued

```
16:     public
17:       { Public declarations }
18:     end;
19:
20:   var
21:     Form2: TForm2;
22:
23:   implementation
24:
25:   {$R *.DFM}
26:
27:   procedure TForm2.OKBtnClick(Sender: TObject);
28:   begin
29:     Close;
30:   end;
31:
32:   end.
```

Analysis Listing 3.4 shows the source code for unit `Uform11`, which supports the main form. Notice how the event-handling method `TForm1.CloseBtnClick` invokes the secondary form as a dialog box. The statement in line 30 sends the OOP message `ShowModal` to the object `Form2` (which represents the secondary form). This OOP message causes the form to invoke the inherited method `ShowModal`, which displays the form as a modal dialog box. It's important to point out here that setting the `BorderStyle` property of the secondary form to `bsDialog` provides the secondary form with appearance of a dialog box. The program execution resumes to the `Close` statement in line 30 only after you close the secondary form. Closing the secondary form occurs when you click the OK button. Line 29 in Listing 3.5 contains the `Close` statement, which closes the modal dialog form.

Forms as Modeless Dialogs

Delphi allows you to create secondary forms and use them as modeless dialog boxes. The next program demonstrates this feature. The program `FrmDlg2` has two forms: the main form and the secondary form, which acts as a modeless dialog box. The main form has two buttons with the captions `Close` and `Show Form`. When you click on the latter button, the program invokes the modeless dialog box form, which has the text `Good Bye!` and the button OK. When you click on the OK button you close the modeless form. When you click on the Close button in the main form you close the main form, close the modeless dialog form (if it is opened), and end the program. Let's look at the steps involved in customizing each form.

The Main Form

The main form has a single button control, as shown in Figure 3.22. Perform the following steps to customize the main form and its controls:

1. Select the Standard page tab of the component palette.
2. Draw a button control on the lower-left part of the main form.
3. Set the `Caption` property of the button to `Close`.
4. Set the `Name` property of the button to `CloseBtn`.
5. Draw another button control on the lower part of the main form.
6. Set the `Caption` property of the new button to `Show Form`.
7. Set the `Name` property of the new button to `ShowFormBtn`.
8. Select the form and set the caption to Main Form.
9. Save the unit for the main form in file UFORM21.PAS.

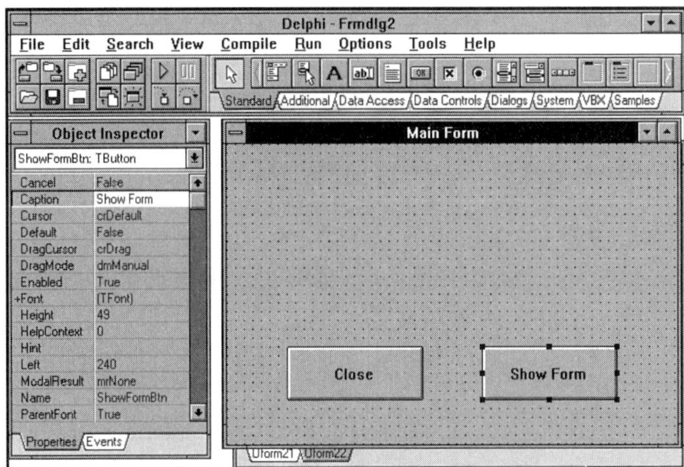

Figure 3.22.
The main form of program `Frmdlg2`.

The Secondary Form

Create the secondary form using the File | New Form option. Delphi displays the Browse Gallery dialog box. Select the default form by clicking on the OK button of the dialog box. The secondary form has a label and a single button control. Perform the following steps to customize the secondary form and its controls:

1. Select the secondary form.
2. Draw a button control on the lower part of the main form.
3. Set the `Caption` property of the button to OK.
4. Set the `Name` property of the button to `OKBtn`.
5. Draw a label in the middle of the form.
6. Set the `Caption` property of the label to `Good Bye!`.

7. Set the `Name` property of the label to `ByeLbl`.
8. Double-click on the nested `Font` property.
9. Set the `Size` property to 24.
10. Select the secondary form by clicking on it.
11. Set the `Caption` property of the form to Modeless Dialog Form.
12. Set the `Color` property to `clYellow` to select the yellow color.
13. Set the `BorderStyle` property to `bsDialog`.
14. Save the unit for the secondary form in file UFORM22.PAS.
15. Save the project in file FORMDLG2.DPR.

Adding Event-Handling Methods

You need to add event-handling methods to the button controls on the main and secondary forms. All buttons handle the mouse-click event. Listing 3.6 shows the source code for the UFORM21.PAS unit. The bold lines show the manually inserted code. Listing 3.7 shows the source code for the UFORM22.PAS unit. The bold line (see line 29) contains the statement you need to insert for the `TForm2.ClickOKBtn` method.

Listing 3.6. The source code for the UFORM21.PAS unit.

```
unit Uform21;

interface

uses
  SysUtils, WinTypes, WinProcs, Messages, Classes,
  Graphics, Controls, Forms, Dialogs, StdCtrls,
{ manually inserted unit name }
  Uform22;

type
  TForm1 = class(TForm)
    CloseBtn: TButton;
    ShowFormBtn: TButton;
    procedure ShowFormBtnClick(Sender: TObject);
    procedure CloseBtnClick(Sender: TObject);
  private
    { Private declarations }
  public
    { Public declarations }
  end;

var
  Form1: TForm1;

```

```
implementation

{$R *.DFM}

procedure TForm1.ShowFormBtnClick(Sender: TObject);
begin
  Form2.Show;
end;

procedure TForm1.CloseBtnClick(Sender: TObject);
begin
  Close;
end;

end.
```


Listing 3.7. The source code for the UFORM22.PAS unit.

```
unit Uform22;

interface

uses
  SysUtils, WinTypes, WinProcs, Messages, Classes,
  Graphics, Controls, Forms, Dialogs, StdCtrls;

type
  TForm2 = class(TForm)
    OKBtn: TButton;
    ByeLbl: TLabel;
    procedure OKBtnClick(Sender: TObject);
  private
    { Private declarations }
  public
    { Public declarations }
  end;

var
  Form2: TForm2;

implementation

{$R *.DFM}

procedure TForm2.OKBtnClick(Sender: TObject);
begin
  Close;
end;

end.
```

Analysis

Listing 3.6 shows the source code for unit `Uform21`, which supports the main form. Notice how the event-handling method `TForm1.CloseBtnClick` invokes the secondary form as a dialog box. The statement in line 32 sends the OOP message `Show` to the object `Form2` (which represents the secondary form). This OOP message causes the form to invoke the inherited method `Show`, which displays the form as a modeless dialog box. Again, setting the `BorderStyle` property of the secondary form to `bsDialog` provides the secondary form with the appearance of a dialog box. Line 37 contains the `Close` statement in a separate event-handling method. If line 32 were followed by the `Close` statement, the application would bring up the modeless dialog box form and then promptly close that form along with the main form. Line 29 in Listing 3.7 contains the `Close` statement, which closes the modal dialog box form.

Modal Dialog Boxes

Delphi offers classes that support dialog boxes. This section shows you how a form invokes a modal dialog box supported by a dialog box class. The next program demonstrates invoking such a dialog box. The program `Dlg1` has two forms: the main form and the dialog box form, which acts as a modal dialog box. The main form has a button with the caption `Close`. When you click on this button, the program invokes the modal dialog box, which has the text `Good Bye!`, the button OK, and the button Cancel. When you click on the OK button, you close the modal form as well as the main form, and end the program. When you click on the Cancel button, you only close the dialog box. Let's look at the steps involved in customizing each form.

The Main Form

The main form has a single button control, similar to the `Frmdlg1` program. Perform the following steps to customize the main form and its controls:

1. Select the Standard page tab of the component palette.
2. Draw a button control on the lower part of the main form.
3. Set the `Caption` property of the button to `Close`.
4. Set the `Name` property of the button to `CloseBtn`.
5. Set the caption of the form to `Main Form`.
4. Save the unit for the main form in file UDLG11.PAS.

The Secondary Form

Create the secondary form using the File | New Form option. Delphi displays the Browse Gallery dialog box. Select the standard dialog box, which is located in the middle of the Browse Gallery dialog box. Click on the OK button of the dialog box. The dialog box form should have a label and two button controls, as shown in Figure 3.23. Initially, the dialog box has the OK, Cancel, and Help buttons. Perform the following steps to customize the secondary form and its controls:

1. Select the secondary form.
2. Delete the Help button.
3. Draw a label in the middle of the dialog box.
4. Set the `Caption` property of the label to `Good Bye!`.
5. Set the `Name` property of the label to `ByeLbl`.
6. Double-click on the nested `Font` property.
7. Set the `Size` property to 20.
8. Save the unit for the secondary form in file UDLG12.PAS.
9. Save the project in file DLG1.DPR.

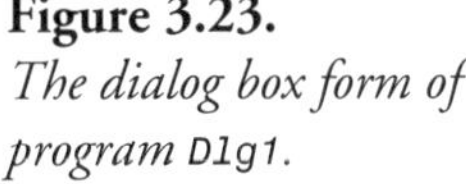

Figure 3.23.
The dialog box form of program `Dlg1`.

Adding Event-Handling Methods

You need to add event-handling methods to the button control on the main and dialog box forms. Each button should handle the mouse-click event. Listing 3.8 shows the source code for the UDLG11.PAS unit. The bold lines show the manually inserted code. Notice that the `uses` clause lists the name of the unit `Udlg12`. This declaration is needed to enable the main form to bring up the dialog box form by accessing the variable `BtnBottomDlg`. This variable, which is exported by unit `Udlg12`, is an instance of class `TBtnBottomDlg` and supports the dialog box form. Listing 3.9 shows the source code for the UDLG12.PAS unit. The bold line contains the statement you need to insert for the methods `TBtnBottomDlg.OKBtnClick` and `TBtnBottomDlg.CancelBtnClick`.

Listing 3.8. The source code for the UDLG11.PAS unit.

```
unit Udlg11;

interface

uses
  SysUtils, WinTypes, WinProcs, Messages, Classes,
  Graphics, Controls, Forms, Dialogs, StdCtrls,
  { manually inserted unit name }
  Udlg12;

type
  TForm1 = class(TForm)
    Button1: TButton;
    procedure Button1Click(Sender: TObject);
  private
    { Private declarations }
  public
    { Public declarations }
  end;

var
  Form1: TForm1;

implementation

{$R *.DFM}

procedure TForm1.Button1Click(Sender: TObject);
begin
  if BtnBottomDlg.ShowModal = mrOK then
    Close;
end;

end.
```

Listing 3.9. The source code for the UDLG12.PAS unit.

```
unit Udlg12;

interface

uses WinTypes, WinProcs, Classes, Graphics, Forms,
  Controls, Buttons, StdCtrls, ExtCtrls;

type
  TBtnBottomDlg = class(TForm)
    OKBtn: TBitBtn;
    CancelBtn: TBitBtn;
    Bevel1: TBevel;
    ByeLbl: TLabel;
    procedure OKBtnClick(Sender: TObject);
    procedure CancelBtnClick(Sender: TObject);
```

```
16:     private
17:       { Private declarations }
18:     public
19:       { Public declarations }
20:     end;
21:
22:   var
23:     BtnBottomDlg: TBtnBottomDlg;
24:
25:   implementation
26:
27:   {$R *.DFM}
28:
29:   procedure TBtnBottomDlg.OKBtnClick(Sender: TObject);
30:   begin
31:     ModalResult := mrOK;
32:   end;
33:
34:   procedure TBtnBottomDlg.CancelBtnClick(Sender: TObject);
35:   begin
36:     ModalResult := mrCancel;
37:   end;
38:
39:   end.
```

Analysis Listing 3.8 shows the source code for unit `Udlg11`, which supports the main form. Notice how the event-handling method `TForm1.CloseBtnClick` invokes the dialog box in the statement at line 30. This statement sends the OOP message `ShowModal` to the object `BtnBottomDlg` (which represents the dialog box form). This OOP message causes the form to invoke the inherited method `ShowModal`, which displays the form as a modal dialog box. The OOP message is located in an `if` statement that compares the result of the message with the predefined constant `mrOK`. This comparison determines if the user clicked the OK button. If this condition is true, the program execution resumes in line 31. This line has the `Close` statement that closes the main form.

Listing 3.9 contains two event-handling methods. The method `TBtnBottomDlg.OKBtnClick` assigns the predefined constant `mrOK` to the property `ModalResult` (line 31). This property passes its setting to the method `ShowModal`. Notice that the event-handling method has no dialog box-closing statement. The method `TBtnBottomDlg.CancelBtnClick` assigns the predefined constant `mrCancel` to the property `ModalResult` (line 36).

MDI Forms

Delphi supports the creation of Windows applications that support *MDI* (Multiple Document Interface) parent and child windows. The Windows Program Manager, the Windows File Manager, and most Windows text editors use the MDI windows to allow you to view multiple documents. Each MDI-compliant application has a parent MDI window (or form, in the case of Delphi applications) and MDI child windows. The MDI parent is responsible for managing the MDI child windows. Windows supports operations to tile and cascade MDI child windows, and to arrange iconic MDI child windows. The topic of managing MDI windows is beyond the level of this chapter.

Summary

Today's lesson discussed the basic aspects of visual programming. You learned about the following topics:

- The design of forms, which involves drawing visual controls on these forms. The chapter discussed inserting, selecting, moving, deleting, and resizing components.
- The classes that support visual controls by offering fields to store properties and methods to respond to events.
- The visual components, which include the Standard, Additional, Data Access, Data Control, Dialog Boxes, and System. The text briefly introduced you to each of the components.
- The properties of components and how to set them for the various kinds of properties. The chapter showed you that there are simple, enumerated, and nested properties.
- The events that can be handled by visual components. The text discussed how to trap and handle events for the form and components.
- The application architectures, which include using multiple forms, using forms as dialog boxes, using dialog box forms, and the MDI forms.

Q&A

Q Does Delphi reset the control name of components when you cut and paste them?

A Yes, it does. Therefore, make sure you restore the name of the first component if you changed it before the cut-and-paste operation.

Q What are the standard buttons in a dialog box?

A The standard buttons in a dialog box are the OK and Cancel buttons. The Help button is typically placed in a dialog box to offer on-line help.

Q What is the main difference between using a form as a dialog box and using a dialog box window?

A The form and the dialog box are supported by distinct classes. The class that supports the dialog box offers operations which respond to clicking the OK and Cancel buttons.

Q Can I draw, in one swoop, multiple components on a form?

A No, you can't. However, pasting previously copied components offers a rapid way to draw similar components.

Q Does the order of creating the components on a form matter?

A The order of creating components matters in the sequence of selecting the next component (when applied to that component) using the Tab key. This is called the *tab order* of components. To edit the tab order, select Edit|Tab Order... to bring up the Edit Tab Order dialog box. This dialog box allows you to move any component up or down in the tab order.

Workshop

The Workshop provides quiz questions to help you solidify your understanding of the material covered and exercises to provide you with experience in using what you've learned. Try to understand the quiz and exercise answers before continuing on to the next day's lesson.

Quiz

1. True or False? The Object Inspector window displays all of the properties of the selected component at design-time.
2. True or False? You can resize, move, and delete a group of selected components.
3. True or False? Delphi generates a form class (whose default name is `TForm1`) as a descendant of class `TForm`.
4. True or False? The data passed by the parameters of an event-handling method is not always relevant to what you intend to do.
5. What page tab in the component palette contains the Color dialog box component?
6. What component allows you to either select from a list or enter a new item?
7. True or False? Within the same group, radio buttons are mutually exclusive.
8. What component combines the effects of the Notebook and Tab Set components?

Exercise

1. Create the program dlg2, which is the version of dlg1 that supports a modeless dialog box. Perform the following steps:
2. Save file UDLG11.PAS as UDLG21.PAS.
3. Save file UDLG12.PAS as UDLG22.PAS.

4. Save the project file as DLG2.DPR.
5. Add the Show Form button to the main form.
6. Edit the event-handling methods for the buttons on both forms.

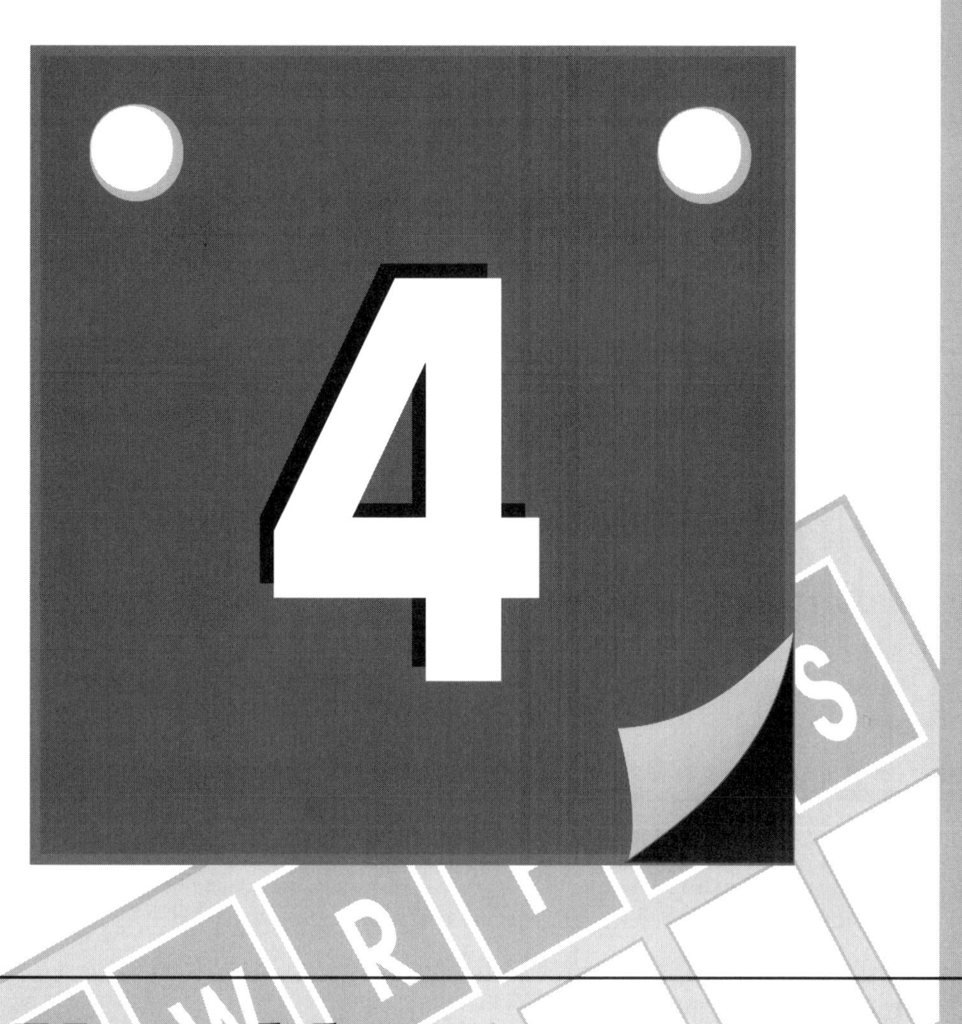

WEEK 1

4

Variables, Constants, and Primitive Types

Constants and variables are two types of data elements that your Object Pascal programs are continuously manipulating. Today's lesson will introduce you to these important programming concepts. You will learn:

- What constants are and how to declare them.
- What variables are and how to declare them.
- How to assign new values to variables through an assignment statement.
- The built-in Object Pascal types: Integers, Reals, and Character-Based.
- What typed-constants are, and how to declare and use them.

Constants

If you find yourself using the same numeric quantity over and over again in your program, or a particular string of text occurs in several places, it is probably time to consider turning the repeating quantity into a constant.

NEW TERM *Constants* are names for fixed quantities that you tend to reference repetitively in your programs. A constant allows you to refer to these quantities by name, rather than by their possibly cryptic value.

The key to understanding constants is that they are just that: constants. Their value does not, and in fact cannot, change during the execution of a program.

Why Use Constants?

Using constants makes your programs more readable and easier to maintain. Declaring a constant allows you to use the constant's meaningful symbolic name whenever the constant's value is needed.

Consider the difference between `NumberOfPassengers` and 234. The label acts as a reminder of what the meaning of 234 is.

Using constants, you can give meaningful names to well-known mathematical, physical, and other quantities (`pi`, `Avogadro`, etc.) rather than having to recall their specific numerical values every time they are needed.

Very often, quantities specific to your program, such as the dimensions of a display window or the number of entries in a list box, benefit from being turned into named constants even if they do not represent well-known universal quantities. Your program becomes *parametrized* through

their use. This means that the aspects of it that might change, should you decide to go to a different screen resolution or add another entry to the list, are easily accessible and require changing in only one place.

It is a lot more convenient and less error-prone to change a single, appropriately named constant, like `Pi`, than to go hunting within your program for all occurrences of 3.1415926536. (Or was it 3.1415926535? Or did you misquote only some of the occurrences, which makes finding them even harder?)

Declaring Constants

Syntax

In Object Pascal, you declare constants in a constant-declaration block (**`const`** block) using the **`const`** keyword. The general syntax for a constant-declaration block is:

```
const
ConstantName1 = ConstantValue1;
ConstantName2 = ConstantValue2;
...
ConstantNameN = ConstantValueN;
```

Examples:

```
const
  Pi                 = 3.1415926536;
  NumberOfEmployees  = 17;
  HourlyRate         = 75;
  PageHeader         = 'Employee Table';
 ReportTitle         = 'Monthly Report';
```

The keyword **`const`** begins the constant-declaration block. Following the keyword are the constant declarations. Each declaration consists of a name, an equal sign, and the constant's value. Each declaration is terminated by a semicolon. There may be one or more constant declarations per block. Multiple blocks can appear throughout the program.

Note: The equal sign (=) in the **`const`** declaration is an indication of equality or equivalence. Do not confuse this usage of the equal sign with the Pascal assignment operator `:=` (colon+equal sign), which you will encounter later in today's lesson.

The first three lines of the example in the preceding syntax box introduce numeric constants suitable for calculations. The fourth and the fifth ones, `PageHeader` and `ReportTitle`, are string constants suitable for printing out or displaying. You will learn more about strings on Day 8. For now, notice that Pascal strings are enclosed in single quotes. Everything between a pair of single quotes, including blanks, is considered a part of the string.

Note: It is a generally a good idea to put the keyword **const** on a separate line so that it stands out. The following is also legal, however:

```
const DaysInAYear = 365;
```

Use whichever style results in better readability of code in a given situation. Also, if some or all of the declaration's elements are especially long, keep in mind that individual declaration statements may each span several lines:

```
const
  ReportPageHeader =
    'Shareholders Meeting Report';
  ReportTitle
    = 'Annual Shareholders Meeting';
```

Feel free to break the lines up so that your code is as readable as possible.

Constant Expressions

Sometimes the value of a constant is not a simple number, but a result of a calculation on other constants. You can build constants from other constants by applying the standard operations. For example:

```
const
  SecondsInAMinute = 60;
  MinutesInAnHour  = 60;
  SecondsInAnHour  =
    SecondsInAMinute*MinutesInAnHour;
  SecondsInADay    = 24*SecondsInAnHour;
```

As you can see, you can combine the numeric values on the value side of the constant declaration (to the right of the equal sign) with symbolic names of other constants that were previously defined, using standard operators specific to the type of the constant you are defining.

For example, if you wish to define a numeric constant, you can use the common numeric operators, such as + (add), - (subtract), * (multiply), and so on to combine several existing constants and form a new one.

The only caveat is that whatever symbolic name you use to the right of the equal sign must have been previously defined, either earlier within the same block of code or in some other block that is "visible" from the current point. You will learn about visibility rules on Day 11.

Of course, you could have declared `SecondsInADay` as:

```
const SecondsInADay = 86400;
```

But the earlier example of this constant being explicitly calculated from other constants was a better approach for two reasons: first, the calculation showed the relationship between seconds, minutes, and hours, thereby making your program more self-documenting (otherwise, the reader of the program might wonder where the number 86400 came from); second, it allowed the computer to do the calculation, rather than forcing you to calculate the number by hand, thereby making it less prone to error (if the computer can do it, don't do it yourself!)

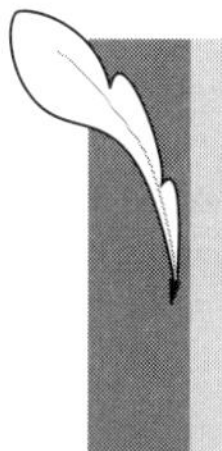

Note: You cannot change the value of a constant at run-time. Like its name suggests, a constant's value is determined at compile-time.

A constant has no location or address. It is merely a convenient way to label repetitively referenced quantities of data.

There is no performance penalty for using constants, even with expressions. Constants are fully evaluated at compile-time and the results of the evaluation inserted into the resulting executable code by the compiler.

Variables

NEW TERM A *variable* is a named data entity of a specified, predetermined type, potentially holding a value of the specific type in a unique location in the computer's memory.

A variable is just a box that possibly holds useful values. More technically, it is a location in memory with a unique name given by the programmer, where values can be stored into and retrieved from. The type of a variable determines the kinds of values you can store in it.

A variable has these four important characteristics:

- Name—The name identifies the variable, that is, gives you a way to reference the unique location in memory that the variable occupies. You don't need to worry about the machine addresses and memory organization. You need to concern yourself only with the meaningful name that you yourself have chosen with care.
- Type—The type determines what kinds of values are possible, or legal, for the variable. It also determines the operations that are available on the values of the variable.
- Value—The value is whatever information is currently stored in the memory location occupied by the variable. At the machine level, this is just zeros and ones. The meaning of this value is given by its type. For instance, the same pattern of zeros and ones may represent a character A, a numeric value 65, or the 66th element of some abstract user-declared type.
- Location in Memory—The location in memory is referred to as the variable's unique "memory address." You rarely, if ever, need to concern yourself with the actual memory address of a variable. The whole point of having a named variable in the first place is so you can refer to it by its meaningful name. The compiler takes care of the drudgery of translating a symbolic name to an actual machine address.

Figure 4.1 illustrates the concept of a variable. Notice the relationship of a variable to its declared type. The actual values come from a predefined set of possible values, known as type. The variable can participate in operations explicitly allowed for that particular type.

Before variables can be used, that is, before you can store or retrieve any values to or from them, they must be declared. The declaration tells the compiler how big a chunk of memory to reserve for each variable.

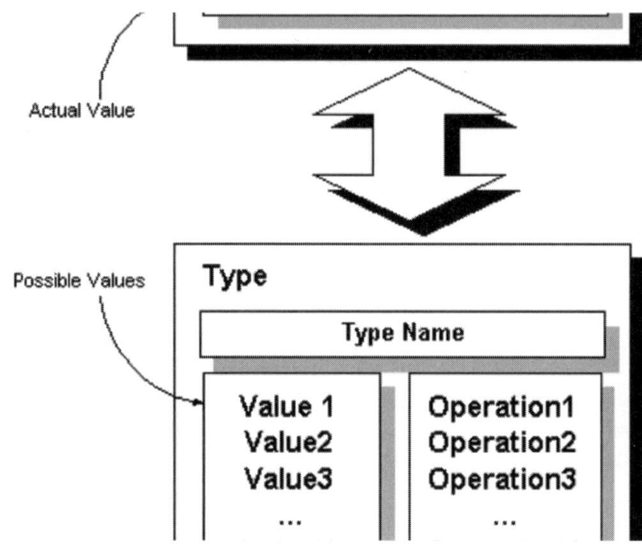

Figure 4.1.
The concept of a variable.

Declaring Variables

In Object Pascal, you declare variables in a variable declaration block (**var** block) using the **var** keyword. The general syntax of a variable declaration block is:

Syntax

```
var
  Name11,
  Name12,
  ...
  Name1N: Type1;
  Name21,
  Name22,
  ..
  Name2N: Type2;
  ...
  NameN1,
  NameN2,
  ..
  NameNN: TypeN;
Examples:
var
  Temperature: Integer;
  Humidity,
```

```
Pressure    : Byte;
FirstName,
LastName    : String;
```

The keyword **var** begins the variable declaration block. Following the keyword are the variable declarations. Each declaration consists of a name, a colon, and the type of the variable. Each declaration is terminated by a semicolon. There may be one or more variable declarations per block. Multiple blocks can appear throughout the program.

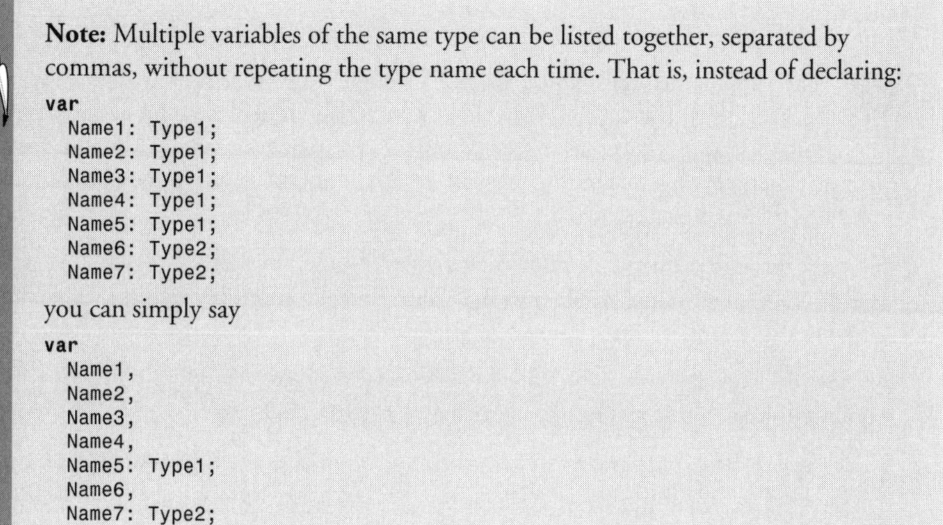

Note: Multiple variables of the same type can be listed together, separated by commas, without repeating the type name each time. That is, instead of declaring:

```
var
  Name1: Type1;
  Name2: Type1;
  Name3: Type1;
  Name4: Type1;
  Name5: Type1;
  Name6: Type2;
  Name7: Type2;
```

you can simply say

```
var
  Name1,
  Name2,
  Name3,
  Name4,
  Name5: Type1;
  Name6,
  Name7: Type2;
```

Note: It is a good idea to put the keyword **var** on a separate line so that it stands out, but the following is also legal:

```
var AnInteger: Integer;
```

Individual variable declaration statements, like constant declarations, may each span several lines:

```
var
  BuildingTemperature:
    LongInt;
  AverageHumidity:
    TAverageHumidityMeasure;
```

Again, use your judgment and apply the style that looks best. Remember that one of the goals of software development is to produce programs that can be shown to and read by others, not just programs that merely work correctly. (As if the latter were not difficult enough!)

Following are some more examples of variable declarations.

Listing 4.1. A variable declaration block.

```
1: var
  2:    Price       : Integer;
  3:    HoursWorked,
  4:    Salary      : Byte;
  5:    NationalDebt: LongInt;
  6:    Percentage  : Real;
  7:    Title       : String;
```

The variable declarations on lines 2 through 7 use predeclared types: `Integer`, `Byte`, `LongInt`, `Real`, and `String`. You will learn more about the Pascal predeclared types later in today's lesson. Right now, observe how the type name is used in a variable declaration: it appears after the colon that terminates a list of variables of the same type being declared together, and it is followed by a semicolon.

Lines 2 through 5 introduce numeric variables. Numeric variables of type `Integer`, `Byte`, or `LongInt` are used to store whole (non-fractional, integer) numbers such as 0, 1, 17, 23, etc. for use in calculations.

Line 6 declares a `Real` variable called `Percentage`, capable of holding numbers with decimal points, also known as real numbers, such as 3.14, 1.0, -0.9, etc.

The last line, line 7, declares a variable called `Title`, which is a string variable capable of holding a character-string value, such as `'Aardvark'`, `'United States and Canada'`, or `'Annual Report'`.

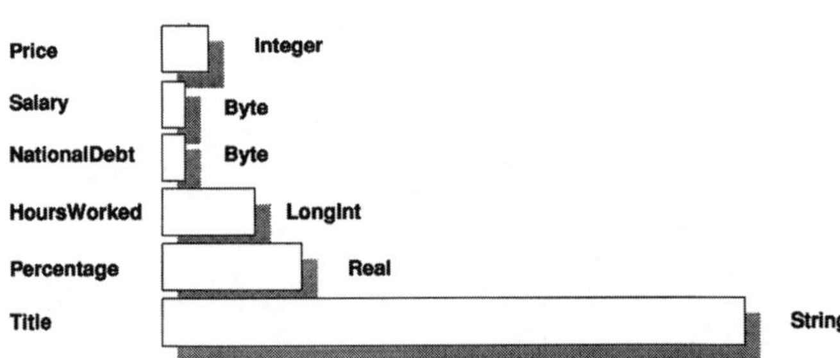

Figure 4.2.
A variable declaration block's memory layout.

Figure 4.2 illustrates the memory "layout" created by the previous declarations. The variables can be treated as "boxes." Notice that, depending on the type of the variable, the size of the "box" (that is, the amount of memory it occupies) will vary. The largest of these variables, the string variable `Title`, occupies 256 bytes, while the smallest, `HoursWorked` and `Salary`, occupy a single byte each.

NEW TERM A *bit*, also known as binary digit, is the smallest chunk of information possible. A bit can have a value of either 0 or 1. To represent numbers larger than 1, bits are strung together to form larger entities: bytes. All computer information is stored as sequences of bits that form bytes.

NEW TERM A *byte* is a measure of memory size, or capacity, capable of holding 8 bits of information. It is the smallest chunk of memory that you can identify and access directly. Consequently, the smallest variable you can declare in your program occupies at least one byte.

Note: A byte is 8 bits; that is, the largest number a byte-sized integer variable can hold is 8 bits large, 11111111 in binary. This is equivalent to 255 in decimal notation. In other words, the largest number a `Byte` variable can represent is 255 decimal.

Note: Memory capacities are usually expressed in units deriving from the word *byte*. In particular, 1024 bytes is a *kilobyte*, abbreviated as KB or K; 1024 kilobytes, or 1024K, is a *megabyte*, abbreviated as MB or M. Notice that the higher-order quantities are multiples of 1024 of the lower-order ones. The "magic" number 1024 is the number 2 raised to the 10th power; simply a number with a convenient binary representation.

When you declare a variable, the compiler sets aside an appropriate amount of memory to accommodate it. The area of memory the compiler sets aside is not initialized with any particular value. In other words, the value of a freshly declared variable is undefined. This is very important, especially if you have programmed in other languages, like BASIC, that automatically pre-initialize variables.

Let me say it again: the value of a Pascal variable is *undefined* until and unless you explicitly assign it a particular value.

Quite frankly, I don't know of any programmer who, at least once, did not forget to explicitly initialize a variable. The results of forgetting to initialize may be unpleasant at best and quite outright disastrous at worst. The incorrect (or garbage) value of a variable may be used in calculations, or may control program behavior; it may be used in decision-making constructs to control the flow of execution of a program.

In any case, you always want to guarantee that the value a variable holds is what you expect it to hold, not a random value.

Note: Initializing variables explicitly and as soon as they are declared is a very important habit to get into. Searching for many hours for a mysterious program error, only to find out it was caused because you didn't initialize a variable, is very frustrating and really unnecessary.

The Assignment Statement

In order to explicitly assign a value to a variable, you must write an assignment statement.

Syntax

Assignment Statement

The general form of the assignment statement is:

```
VariableName := Value;
```

or

```
Variable1Name := Variable2Name;
```

Examples:

```
Temperature:= 10;
Salary     := 1999.99;
 FirstName  := 'Andrew';
Code       := 'A';

Count      := PreviousCount;
TempToday  := TempYesterday;
```

The := is the *assignment operator*. The assignment statement causes the value on the right of the assignment operator to be assigned to the variable on the left of the operator. In other words, the value specified on the right gets stored in, or written to, the memory location designated by the variable name on the left.

DO	DON'T

DO use an assignment operator when setting values of variables. An assignment operator requires a variable on the left and a value or expression on the right.

DON'T confuse the assignment operator (:=) with the equal sign (=), which is used in constant declarations, among other places. An equal sign in a declaration is merely a synonym for "is" and does not result in any program code or explicit action. An assignment, on the other hand, means "gets assigned" and results in an action being performed at run-time.

The value to the right of the assignment operator may be a literal constant (a number), or another variable's name. In the latter case, the value initially stored in the variable listed to the right of the operator gets copied to the variable listed to the left.

Object Pascal is a strongly typed language. This means that the compiler prevents you from inadvertently trying to assign an integer to a string variable, or a number to a Boolean one. Therefore, it does make a difference what types of values are expected on both sides of the assignment statement.

NEW TERM Two variables are said to be *assignment compatible* if the value of the first can be assigned to the second.

Classification of Types

Object Pascal defines a number of built-in or primitive data types, called standard data types. You are primarily interested in the simple types for numeric and character manipulation in today's lesson, as opposed to structured, non-simple types you will learn about later.

NEW TERM *Data* is a general term that describes the raw information that computers manipulate. At the lowest logical level, data is simply a sequence of bits ("binary digits"): zeros and ones. Higher-level languages, such as Object Pascal, allow you to treat data in a more abstract way, disregarding the details of implementation and physical storage. The notion of data type is thus introduced, which gives meaning to the raw computer bits.

NEW TERM A *data type* is a set of values together with all the operations that may be performed on those values. When a variable is defined, a unique type is associated with it. That is, the variable can contain values from only the particular, restricted set known as its type, and can only participate in operations allowed by the type.

You should know right away that one of Pascal's strengths is that it also provides facilities for creating arbitrarily complex structured data types. By structuring and combining the existing types in a variety of ways, new types can be created.

Although in general, data types can be very complex and sophisticated, at the elementary level they are always built from the simple, built-in types.

There are three kinds of simple types in Object Pascal:

- Ordinal types, whose values are really whole numbers, sometimes in disguise.
- Real types, whose values are almost arbitrary numbers, both whole numbers and fractional ones.
- Pointer types, which deal with addresses to entities in computer memory.

NEW TERM An *ordinal* is a general name denoting a data type that comprises a finite and ordered set of values. Ordinals map onto whole numbers 0, 1, 2, 3, and so on.

Note: Each ordinal type has a minimum and maximum value. Each value of an ordinal type, except the first, has a predecessor, and each value, except the last, has a successor.

The name for the group comes from the fact that the values in an ordinal type can be arranged in ascending order, from the smallest to the largest.

Ordinals play an important role by acting as indices, counters, and selectors in various programming constructs.

NEW TERM A *real* is a type whose values form a subset of real numbers. Standard floating-point representation of a real number consists of the mantissa (the significant digits) and the exponent (the magnitude), assuming base 2 notation.

For example, the number 130 in decimal may be represented as 0.13×10^3, where 0.13 is the mantissa and 10^3 is the base—in this case 10—raised to the power of 3—the exponent. Computers use a similar method, except that the number 2 is used instead of 10 as the base for representation.

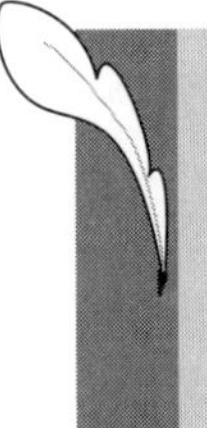

Note: Using the standard *floating-point notation* with a fixed number of binary digits encoding the mantissa and the exponent, computers can represent only a limited set of the real value continuum. Not only is the entire range of numbers limited (this is true of any representation of numbers on a computer), but within the covered range, there are "holes" of quantities that cannot be represented accurately on a digital computer.

The representation of real numbers on a computer is indeed very limited, and you have to be careful when you are using these imperfect representations to perform precise calculations. Here's a piece of advice: stick with integers whenever possible.

Figure 4.3 visually illustrates the classification of Object Pascal primitive types.

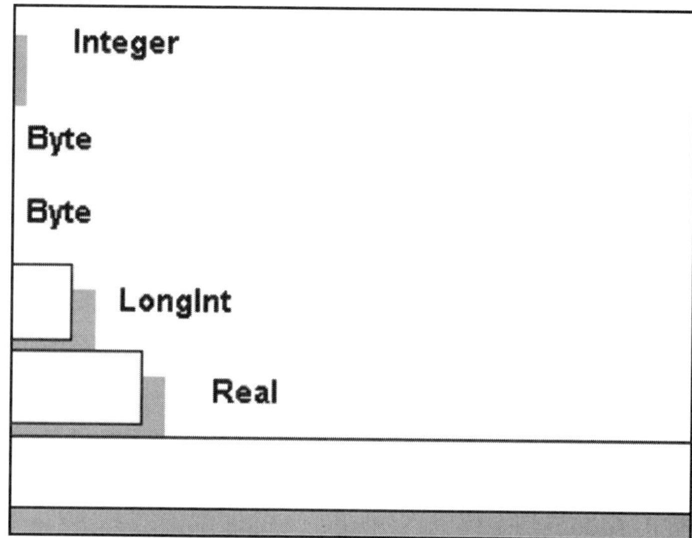

Figure 4.3.
Classification of Object Pascal primitive types.

Exploring the Primitive Data Types

The concepts of data and data types are two of the most fundamental programming notions. Let's look at each of the most common primitive types in order.

Object Pascal provides a number of predefined primitive types for you to use in variable declarations:

- Integers
- Booleans
- Reals
- Characters
- Strings

Integer Types

Integers are used to represent whole numbers that you can use in arithmetic calculations. The various integer types differ in the amount of memory they occupy and, consequently, in the range of values they can represent. Table 4.1 illustrates the Object Pascal built-in integer types.

Table 4.1. Built-in integer types.

Type	Range	Size in Bytes	Status
`ShortInt`	-128–127	1	Signed
`Integer`	-32768–32767	2	Signed
`LongInt`	-2147483648–2147483647	4	Signed
`Byte`	0–255	1	Unsigned
`Word`	0–65535	2	Unsigned

Using Integers

Listing 4.2 shows examples of integer declarations and of using integers in assignments and simple arithmetic expressions.

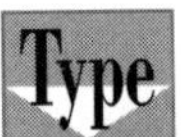

Listing 4.2. Source code for the program INT1.PRJ.

```
program Int1;

{
Demonstrates integers illustrating the usage of integers
and some simple integer operations.
}
uses
  WinCrt;

var
  Celsius,
  Kelvin,
  Fahrenheit: Integer;
begin
  Celsius    := 100;
  Kelvin     := 273 + Celsius;
  Fahrenheit := (9*Celsius) div 5 + 32;
  WriteLn('Water boils at ',Celsius,' C');
  WriteLn('      ...or at ',Kelvin,' K');
  WriteLn('  .. .which is ',Fahrenheit,' F');
  WriteLn('Press Alt-F4 to close window...');
end.
```

The program in Listing 4.2 generates the following output:

```
Water boils at 100 C
      ...or at 373 K
   ...which is 212 F
Press Alt-F4 to close window...
```

The program in Listing 4.2 declares three integer variables, `Celsius`, `Kelvin`, and `Fahrenheit`, on lines 10 through 13. Line 16 initializes the variable `Celsius` with the value 100, which happens to be the boiling point for water in degrees Celsius.

Line 17 calculates the equivalent temperature on the Kelvin scale. The variable `Kelvin` gets assigned the result of the calculation `273 + Celsius`; that is, 273 is added to the value stored in the variable `Celsius`, and the result is placed in the variable `Kelvin`.

The corresponding temperature in degrees Fahrenheit is calculated on line 18 and assigned to the variable `Fahrenheit`.

Lines 20 through 22 simply display the values of the three variables. Line 23 provides a clue to the user of the program on what to do next.

Lines 7 and 8 make the `WinCrt` display services available to the program.

Boolean Types

Boolean types represent logical quantities. There are several Boolean types that differ in the size of their representation in memory.

The generic type `Boolean` is the preferred choice for logical variables, taking up the least possible amount of memory. The possible values for a `Boolean` variable are `True` or `False`.

The remaining Boolean types enable you to explicitly specify the size of the memory representation for the variables of the respective types. Their function is identical to that of the default Boolean type: representing the logical value of `True` and `False`.

The size-specific Boolean types are provided mostly for compatibility with the low-level Windows environment. Typically, you will not have a specific need for any of them unless you end up dealing with the low-level interfaces to Windows.

Table 4.2 lists all the Object Pascal Boolean types.

Table 4.2. Built-in Boolean types.

Type	Range	Size in Bytes
`Boolean`	Preferred 1-byte Boolean.	1
`ByteBool`	Byte-sized Boolean.	1
`WordBool`	Word-sized Boolean.	2
`LongBool`	Double-word-sized Boolean.	4

Using Booleans

Let's take a look at an example program illustrating how to declare and use Boolean variables.

Listing 4.3. Source code for the program BOOL1.PRJ.

```
 1: program Bool1;
 2:
 3: {
 4: Program illustrating the use of
 5: boolean-type variables.
 6: }
 7:
 8: uses
 9:   WinCrt;
10:
11: var
12:   AFlag,
13:   Flag1   : Boolean;
14:   Proceed : Boolean;
15:
16: begin
17:   AFlag   := True;
18:   Flag1   := not AFlag;
19:   Proceed := AFlag and Flag1;
20:
21:   WriteLn('  AFlag is ',AFlag);
22:   WriteLn('  Flag1 is ',Flag1);
23:   WriteLn('Proceed is ',Proceed);
24:
25:   WriteLn('Press Alt-F4 to close window...');
26: end.
```

Here is the output generated by the program in Listing 4.3:

```
  Aflag is TRUE
  Flag1 is FALSE
Proceed is FALSE
Press Alt-F4 to close window...
```

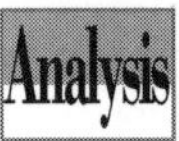

The program in Listing 4.3 declares three `Boolean` variables on lines 11 through 14. `AFlag` and `Flag1` are declared together. `Proceed` is declared in a separate clause.

`AFlag` variable is assigned the value `True` on line 17. On line 18, the variable `Flag1` is assigned the logically opposite value of that stored in the variable `AFlag`. The expression `not AFlag` means "take the value of `AFlag` and negate or flip it." On line 19, the `Boolean` expression `AFlag and Flag1` means "Take the value of `AFlag` and combine it with the value of `Flag1` using the Boolean **and** operator." The result of this expression is a Boolean value that gets assigned to the variable `Proceed`.

Finally, lines 21 through 23 print out the results, and line 25 outputs the friendly reminder on what to do next.

Real/Floating-Point Numbers

Real types are used to represent real-valued numbers, such as numbers with decimal fractions. Real-number types also exist in various sizes and flavors, each with its specific range of values. Table 4.3 illustrates the Object Pascal built-in real types.

Table 4.3. Built-in real types.

Type	Range	Size in Bytes	Decimal Point
`Real`	$\pm 2.9\times10^{-39}–1.7\times10^{38}$	6	Floating
`Single`	$\pm 1.5\times10^{-45}–3.4\times10^{38}$	4	Floating
`Double`	$\pm 5.0\times10^{-324}–1.7\times10^{308}$	8	Floating
`Extended`	$\pm 3.4\times10^{-4932}–1.1\times10^{4932}$	10	Floating
`Comp`	$-2^{63}–2^{63-1}$	8	Fixed

Note: The `Comp` type is really a misnomer. Comp is simply a 64-bit integer. It is listed here together with all the floating-point types because it happens to be implemented using the same floating-point facilities (for example, the math coprocessor) as the real types. Conceptually, however, it really is a whole number.

Using Reals

The declaration and usage of real-type variables are no different than those of other types. An example is found in Listing 4.4. Please keep in mind that this example illustrates the usage of real-typed variables and uses real numbers, despite the fact that it deals with monetary quantities. In most cases, you would want to use sufficiently large integers to represent amounts of money. The reason, of course, is the imprecision with which floating-point calculations are performed. To maintain absolute precision in monetary calculations, use integers to represent the amounts in cents, for example.

Listing 4.4. Source code for the program FLOAT1.PRJ.

```
program Float1;

{
Illustrates the use of floating-point
variables and some operations on
real numbers.
}

```

continues

Listing 4.4. continued

```
 9: {$N+}
10:
11: uses
12:   WinCrt;
13:
14: const
15:   DefaultDaily = 300.00;
16:
17: var
18:   Hourly   : Real;
19:   Daily,
20:   Monthly : Single;
21:   Annually: Double;
22:
23: begin
24:   Daily     := DefaultDaily;
25:   Hourly    := Daily/8;
26:   Monthly   := 20*Daily;
27:   Annually := Monthly*12;
28:
29:   WriteLn('If your daily fee is $',
30:     Daily, '...');
31:   WriteLn('...then your hourly rate is $',
32:     Hourly, '...');
33:   WriteLn('...and you earn $',
34:     Monthly, ' per month...');
35:   WriteLn('...or $',
36:     Annually, ' annually.');
37: end.
```

The program in Listing 4.4 generates the following output:

```
If your daily fee is $ 3.00000000000000E+0002...
...then your hourly rate is $ 3.75000000000000E+0001...
...and you earn $ 6.00000000000000E+0003 per month...
...or $ 7.20000000000000E+0004 annually.
```

The program in Listing 4.4 calculates the hourly rate, the monthly salary, and the annual salary, based on a given daily rate.

Line 9 contains the compiler directive `{$N+}`, which instructs the compiler to enable the floating-point calculations.

NEW TERM A *compiler directive* is a command that is issued to the compiler by embedding it in the compilable code as a special comment. The directive configures the compiler options for the specific project, or part of it.

Note: Compiler options may be specified in one of two ways: either in the IDE, by setting appropriate Project Options in the Compiler page, or inside the code, by embedding compiler directives as special kinds of comments in the code.

A compiler directive in the code is a comment, the first character of which is a dollar sign, such as:

```
{$N+}
```

There are numerous compiler directives supported by the Delphi compiler, controlling everything from error-handling and the embedding of debug information, to code generation and linking, to run-time behavior. For more information about specific compiler directives, search for all entries starting with the dollar sign, such as `$A`, `$B`, `$C`, in the online help.

Lines 17 through 21 declare a few floating-point variables. Lines 14 and 15 define a floating-point constant `DefaultDaily`, which is a kind of global program "parameter" used as the basis for the calculation. The constant is used on line 24, where its value gets assigned to the variable `Daily`.

Once the variable `Daily` is initialized, the calculations can start. On line 25, the hourly rate is calculated by dividing the daily rate by 8. The result of the calculation is assigned to the `Real` variable `Hourly`. Line 26 calculates the monthly salary by multiplying the daily rate by 20.

On line 27, the resulting annual salary is calculated from the basis of the monthly salary and is assigned to the variable `Annually`.

Lines 29 through 36 print out the results.

If you run the program in Listing 4.4, you will notice that its output doesn't look particularly appealing. This is because the floating-point values by default are printed in a scientific notation, with both the mantissa (the significant digits) and the exponent (the number by which the significant digits are to be multiplied) output with a large number of digits of precision.

To improve on the appearance of the output produced by the program in Listing 4.4, change lines 29 through 36 as follows:

```
29.  WriteLn('If your daily fee is $',
30.    Daily:1:2, '...');
31.  WriteLn('...then your hourly rate is $',
32.    Hourly:1:2, '...');
33.  WriteLn('...and you earn $',
34.    Monthly:1:2,' per month...');
35.  WriteLn('...or $',
36.    Annually:1:2, ' annually.');
```

The output for the improved version of the Float1 program, originally implemented in Listing 4.4, follows:

```
If your daily fee is $300.00...
...then your hourly rate is $37.50...
...and you earn $6000.00 per month...
...or $72000.00 annually.
```

The changes you made to lines 29 through 36 affect the way the values of the floating-point variables are displayed. In each case, you added

```
:1:2
```

after each variable name inside the `WriteLn` statements. The `:1:2` is a format specification telling the compiler to right-justify the output in a field at least one character wide, and to provide two digits of precision after the decimal point.

Character-Based Types

Character-based types consist of the character-type `Char` itself and another type that allows you to string a whole bunch of individual characters together to form a piece of text, appropriately called `String`.

The *Char* Type

The variables of type `Char` are capable of holding one and only one character. You will notice that character values are enclosed in single quotes, such as `'a'`, `'b'`, `'c'`, `'D'`, `'E'`, etc.

A `Char` variable occupies a single byte in memory. Thus, there are 256 possible character values. Some of these values do not have printable representations. Some have special meaning, such as Tab or Line-Feed.

Note: There is no real difference between a character (`Char`) value and a numeric (`Byte`) value, as far as their internal machine representation is concerned. In fact, the only difference is how these values are interpreted at run-time: you use characters to display text and numbers in calculations.

The strong typing of the Pascal language requires you to commit a byte-sized variable to be either a `Byte` (or a `SmallInt`) or a `Char`. There are occasions, however, when you want to express a character in terms of its numeric (or ASCII) value, and/or the opposite: to perform some calculations on a character's ASCII value.

A convenient notation exists in Object Pascal to represent non-printable or otherwise special characters using their ASCII values. To represent a character with an ASCII value of 32 decimal (blank space), you can write:

`#32`

This is entirely equivalent to:

`' '`

In general,

`#ASCIIValue`

allows you to represent any character from `#0` (decimal ASCII number 0) to `#255` (decimal ASCII number 255), including the number sign (`#`) itself, which is `#35` in this notation.

You can use either the standard single-quote notation or the number-sign notation for all printable character values. Whenever you need to represent a special, non-printable character, it is convenient to use the number sign+ASCII value notation exclusively.

Using Characters

The example below illustrates how to declare and assign different values to character variables:

Listing 4.5. Program CHAR1.PRJ.

```
program Char1;

{
Demonstrates the use of character variables.
}

uses
  WinCrt;

var
  Alpha: Char;
  Beta : Char;

begin
  Alpha := 'a';
  WriteLn('Alpha = ',Alpha);
  Beta := 'B';
  WriteLn('Beta  = ',Beta);
  Alpha := Beta;
  WriteLn('Alpha = ',Alpha);
  WriteLn('Beta  = ',Beta);
  WriteLn('Press Alt+F4 to close window...');
end.
```

Here is the output generated by the program in Listing 4.5:

```
Alpha = a
Beta  = B
Alpha = B
Beta  = B
Press Alt-F4 to close window...
```

The program in Listing 4.5 declares two character variables, `Alpha` and `Beta`, on lines 10 through 12. The `Alpha` variable is assigned a value of lowercase *a* on line 15 and is then immediately printed out on line 16. Similarly, the variable `Beta` gets a value of uppercase *B* on line 17 and is printed out on line 18.

Line 19 assigns the value stored in variable `Beta` (you now know it to be the uppercase *B*) to the variable `Alpha`. From that point on, both `Alpha` and `Beta` variables contain the same values. This is indeed verified by the two subsequent `WriteLn` statements on lines 20 and 21, which output the values of `Alpha` and `Beta`, respectively, one after the other.

Line 22 displays the hint for the user, as usual.

Strings

Strings, which are essentially sequences (or arrays) of characters, are a bit more complex.

Syntax

Declaring String Variables

The general syntax for declaring string variables is:

```
var
  VariableName: String;
```

or

```
var
  VariableName: String[LengthSpecifier];
```

Examples:

```
var
  FirstName  : String[30];
  LastName   : String[40];
  ShortString: String[2];
  LongString : String[255];
  AnotherLong: String;
```

A `String` data type declaration creates a variable that is capable of holding arbitrary sequences of up to 255 characters in length.

When you declare a `String` variable, the compiler sets aside just enough memory to accommodate strings of up to 255 characters. However, you have the power to define exactly how much memory you would like the compiler to allocate for your strings by specifying the allowable number of characters, up to the maximum of 255 characters per string. The choice you make

will limit the maximum length of a literal string you can assign to the declared variable, but it will also help conserve precious memory.

The string length specification comes after the word `String`, and is enclosed in square brackets.

In many cases, you can declare all your strings simply as `String` and not worry about the details. Notice, however, that it becomes extremely wasteful of memory if you deal with a lot of relatively short strings most of the time. For example, if your program manipulates short string fragments of, say, no more than 25 characters, declaring them as `String` will waste at least 230 bytes *for every such declaration.* The allocated memory space is never used.

This is not a problem for small, tutorial-type programs, but it becomes more of an issue for the production-quality, complex Windows applications you will likely build later. This is when you need to examine your assumptions about the lengths of the strings you are declaring and try not to reserve more space for them than is necessary.

Using Strings

The following example illustrates how several strings of different lengths are used in assignment statements and expressions:

Listing 4.6. Program STR1.PRJ.

```
program Str1;

{
Illustrates strings and
simple string operations.
}

uses
  WinCrt;

var
  FirstName,
  Title     : String[25];
  LastName  : String[40];
  Buffer    : String;
  MidInitial: Char;

begin
  FirstName := 'Andrew ';
  MidInitial := 'J';
  LastName  := ' Wozniewicz';
  Title     := 'Teach Yourself Delphi';
  Buffer    :=
    FirstName + MidInitial + LastName;
  LastName  := '';

  WriteLn('Title    = "',Title,'"');
  WriteLn('Author   = "',Buffer,'"');
  WriteLn('LastName = "',LastName,'"');
  WriteLn('Press Alt+F4 to close window...');
end.
```

The program in Listing 4.6 generates the following output:

```
Title    = "Teach Yourself Delphi"
Author   = "Andrew J Wozniewicz"
LastName = ""
Press Alt+F4 to close window...
```

Lines 11 through 16 comprise a variable declaration block. Lines 18 through 31, the main program block, provide examples of using the declared strings.

Several string variables are defined within the variable declaration block. `FirstName` and `Title` are defined as strings with a maximum length of 25 characters. `LastName` has a maximum length of 40 characters. Since the `Buffer` variable is declared on line 7 simply as `String`, it is equivalent to `String[255]`, which gives it the maximum possible capacity for a Pascal string: 255 characters.

In addition to the strings, the character variable `MidInitial` is defined on line 16. You will see on line 24 how you can mix character and string variables in one expression.

`FirstName` is assigned the value `'Andrew '` on line 19, `LastName` gets the value `' Wozniewicz'` on line 21, and `Title` gets assigned `'Teach Yourself Delphi'` on line 22. Notice the additional blank characters at the end of `FirstName` and at the beginning of `LastName`. These blanks make the effect of concatenating (or gluing) the strings together more visually appealing.

In all cases of the assignment statements on lines 19 through 22, the length of the string assigned to the variable is less than the declared maximum length: the literal value fits nicely into the variable. (What do you think happens when you try to assign a string value that does not fit? See the Q&A section at the end of today's lesson.) The character variable `MidInitial` is initialized on line 20 with the character value `'J'`.

By now you have probably noticed that there is really no discernible difference between the way you express a string of length one and a character. In both cases, the literal contents are enclosed inside single quotes. This is because the two types of variables can be freely mixed in string expressions. Lines 23 and 24 contain an assignment statement. A value of the expression `FirstName + MidInitial + LastName` gets assigned to the variable `Buffer`.

The expression on line 24 means "Take the value of `MidInitial`, copy it, appending to the end of the value of `FirstName`, and then take the value of `LastName` and copy it, appending to the previous two." The plus sign (+), occurring twice in the expression, is called the string *concatenation operator*. It actually glues the two strings together.

Line 25 assigns the value of an empty string to `LastName`. After this statement, the `LastName` becomes cleared, or empty. Note that the `Buffer` variable still contains the value `'Andrew J Wozniewicz'`. You have not explicitly cleared that variable.

Lines 27 through 29 print out the values of `Title`, `Buffer`, and `LastName`, respectively, each on its own line. The values on the printout are enclosed in double quotes. See the Q&A section for a tip on how to put it in single quotes.

NEW TERM An *empty string* is a string of length zero; that is, one containing no meaningful characters. Empty strings are used to clear values of string variables. An empty string is denoted by a pair of single quotes with nothing between them (''). A variable to which an empty string has been assigned still occupies the same declared area of memory: it does not disappear.

Advanced Variables and Constants

You are now going to look at some more advanced but nevertheless important concepts related to variables and constants.

Assignment Compatibility

Generally, you cannot assign a value of one type to a variable of a different type. I have already mentioned that the types on both sides of the assignment statement must be the same. This is the result of the strong type checking Pascal provides for your protection. However, there are circumstances when assigning a value of one type will clearly not cause any problems. Consider the following example:

Listing 4.7. Program ASSIGN1.PRJ.

```
 1: program Assign1;
 2: var
 3:   Small  : SmallInt;
 4:   Normal : Integer;
 5:   Long   : LongInt;
 6: begin
 7:   Small  := 7;
 8:   Normal := Small;
 9:   Long   := Small;
10:   Long   := 30000;
11:   Normal := Long;
12: end.
```

The program in Listing 4.7 has no output.

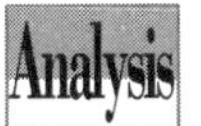

The three variables declared on lines 3 through 5 are each of a different integer type. The assignment statement on line 7 initializes the `Small` variable with the value `7`. The assignment statement on line 8 copies the value stored in `Small` to the `Normal` variable. Note that `Normal` (declared as `Integer`) is of a different type than `Small` (declared as `SmallInt`), yet there is no harm in performing the assignment. Similarly, on line 9, `Long` (declared as `LongInt`) gets assigned the value in `Small` (a `ShortInt`).

Line 11 illustrates the opposite situation: a value of `30000` stored in the variable `Long` gets assigned to `Normal`. This is still OK, because `30000` is small enough to fit into an `Integer` variable. But it would create problems if you tried to assign a number outside the bounds of a regular `Integer`.

If you replace the `30000` on line 10 above with something like `70000`, you will get a run-time error when you try to run the program (given the standard compiler configuration) . The reason for the error is that the number, although within a valid range for a `LongInt`, no longer fits within the storage allocated for an `Integer`.

Naming Variables and Constants

A few words are in order here on how you should name your variables and constants when you declare them. One fundamental truth is that names do matter. Choose variable names, and all other identifiers, carefully.

NEW TERM An *identifier* is simply a symbolic name denoting a constant, a variable, a data type, a procedure or function, a label, etc. An identifier must begin with a letter, followed by any combination and number of letters, digits, and/or underscore characters. The only limitation here is that only the first 63 characters are significant, that is, meaningful to the compiler. This should be more than sufficient for all your needs.

A Pascal identifier is not case-sensitive: corresponding upper- and lowercase letters are equivalent.

Certain identifiers called predeclared identifiers are available automatically. Examples of predeclared identifiers include `SizeOf`, `High`, `Low`, `Sin`, `Cos`, etc.

Give identifiers meaningful names. Name them something that tells the reader of your program as much about the intended usage of the entity you are naming as possible. Names like `X`, `Y`, `Z`, `K`, `L`, `N`, etc. are definitely out. Names like `AChFoo`, `NrFilToProc`, or even `Number`, `Count`, and `Maximum`, are out too, because they are either cryptic or they don't tell nearly enough about the entity they represent. (Count of *what*?!?) The name must fully describe the variable or constant. Names like `NumberOfEmployees`, `TotalSalary`, `CurrentDate`, `LinesPerPage`, etc. are in. They explain what the variable or constant means.

Typed Constants

I have already warned you about the dangers of leaving the variables you declare uninitialized. Wouldn't it be nice to be able to initialize a variable with a specific value right at the time of declaration so that the initialization was easier to spot and track down?

Indeed, Object Pascal provides a way to do something like that, except that it confusingly calls the preinitialized variables "typed constants"!

NEW TERM A *typed constant* is not a constant at all! It is a globally allocated variable, preinitialized with a particular value given at compile-time.

Typed constants are declared in much the same way ordinary constants are, which can cause a lot of confusion, especially among beginning Pascal programmers. Typed constants are used like ordinary variables, not like constants. You can use them on the left side of an assignment statement, something you cannot do with ordinary constants.

Syntax

Declaring Typed Constants

Typed constants are declared in typed-constant declaration blocks (t-**const** blocks). The general syntax for declaring typed constants (as opposed to simply: constants) is:

```
const
  Name1: Type1 = Value1;
  Name2: Type2 = Value2;
 ...
  NameN: TypeN = ValueN;
```

Examples:

```
const
  WindowWidth   : Integer  = 640;
  WindowHeight  : Integer = 480;
  ReportTitle   : String[14] = 'Monthly Report';
  DampingFactor: Real = 0.789;
  ValidPassword: Boolean = False;
```

4

The keyword **const** begins the typed-constant declaration block (t-**const** block). From the compiler's standpoint, there is no difference in appearance between a true constant declaration block and a typed-constant declaration block. Both begin with the same keyword, **const**, and typed-constant declarations can be mixed freely with true constant declarations in the same block.

However, I do advise you to always make a clear distinction between the two types of constants in your programs, and to always declare them in their own separate blocks to highlight the fundamental difference between the two constructs.

Following the **const** keyword are the typed-constant declarations. Each declaration consists of a name, a colon, a type name identifier, the equal sign, and the initial value of an appropriate type. Each declaration is terminated by a semicolon. There may be one or more declarations per block. As was the case with true constants, multiple typed-constant declaration blocks can appear throughout the program.

NEW TERM A *typed constant* is called a constant for historical reasons of compatibility with Borland Turbo Pascal.

This somewhat confusing tradition was not changed in Delphi, and typed-constants, alias preinitialized variables, are declared in a **const** block.

Do not be misled: If an apparent constant contains a type declaration, it is actually a variable! Unlike true constants, typed constants can have values assigned to them during the program's execution. They occupy a location in memory and have a certain size at that location.

Summary

Here is what you have learned during today's lesson:

- Constants are declared within constant-declaration blocks. A constant-declaration block starts with the Pascal reserved word **`const`**.
- Named constants are just convenient labels to denote fixed quantities referenced within a program. You cannot change the value of a constant at run-time. Named constants do not increase the memory requirements of programs that use them, as opposed to the corresponding requirements of programs that incorporate these quantities literally inside the code. Do use named constants!
- Variables are named boxes in which values may be stored and retrieved. The value of a variable can be changed at run-time through an assignment statement. Variables occupy space in memory. The space they occupy, given their type and the precise location at which they are stored, is determined by the compiler.
- A variable declaration block is where you define variables. An individual variable declaration specifies its name and type. A variable declaration block starts with the reserved word **`var`**.
- Assignment statements are used to write values to variables. Assignment statements use the assignment operator `:=`. The two sides of an assignment statement must be type-compatible with each other. Moreover, the left side must designate a variable, that is, a "box" capable of holding values. You cannot assign a value to a constant, for example.
- Object Pascal provides a number of primitive or built-in types that can be used to declare variables. These include integer types (`ShortInt`, `Integer`, `LongInt`; `Byte`, `Word`), logical types (`Boolean`, `ByteBool`, `WordBool`, `LongBool`), real types (`Real`, `Single`, `Double`, `Extended`; `Comp`), and character-based types (`Char`, `String`).
- You can declare string variables of different sizes that are capable of accommodating up to the specified number of characters. The maximum length of a Pascal `String` is 255 characters.
- You should take special care when naming variables and constants. A variable name should be meaningful and understandable. It should convey the understanding of how a variable or constant is used and what it is used for.
- Typed constants are really variables in disguise. They are preinitialized with the specified values, but their values, like those of ordinary variables, can be changed at run-time through an assignment statement. Typed constants are declared with the keyword **`const`**, but they behave like variables at run-time.

Q&A

Q I would like to declare a convenient, meaningfully named constant to use throughout my code, but one of the quantities required for the proper calculation of that constant is not initially known and must be entered by the user as soon as the program starts (and never again). After this, the constant's value never changes. How can I declare my constant to do this?

A You can't do what you are trying to accomplish with constants. The quantity you are trying to calculate requires user input and therefore must be calculated at run-time. In other words, you need a variable, not a constant. Even if the variable's value changes only once during the life of a program, it does change. Remember, a constant cannot change its value. (Unless it is a so-called typed constant, which you now know is really a pre-initialized variable!)

Q What is wrong with the following variable declaration block?

```
var FirstName,
  Title     : String[25]
  LastName  : String[40]
  Buffer    : String
  MidInitial: Char;
```

A The three lines with the `Title`, `LastName`, and `Buffer` declarations lack terminating semicolons. In Object Pascal, there must be semicolon separating one statement from the next. This variable declaration block consists of four statements, only the last of which is terminated with a semicolon.

Q What happens if I assign a long literal string to a string variable declared with an insufficient number of characters? For example, what if I want to assign the string `'Annual Report'` to a variable `Title` declared as `var Title: String[5]`? Will the variable expand to accommodate the longer string value?

A No, the variable will not expand. A Pascal variable, once declared, maintains its properties throughout its life. In this example, the string is automatically truncated and only its first five characters are copied to the variable. The result is `'Annua'`, which is probably not what you want. It is important to allow sufficient room for the variable's text.

Q I would like to print a string of characters, including a pair of embedded single quotes. Since single quotes are used to delimit strings (and characters) in Pascal, how do I embed a single quote into the actual string?

A There are a number of ways to accomplish this. One way is to use the `#ASCII` (number sign+ASCII value) notation you learned in today's lesson to make the single quote a part of the string. The ASCII value of a single quote is 39 (decimal). Hence, you can define a string with embedded single quotes like this:

```
const
  QuotedString = 'This is a '#39'quoted'#39' string.';
```

When you print this `QuotedString` with the statement `WriteLn(QuotedString);`, the output will look like this:

```
This is a 'quoted' string.
```

Another, simpler method involves repeating the single quote character within the string:

```
const QuotedString =
   'This is a ''quoted'' string.';
```

Please note that the word *quoted* is enclosed in two pairs of single quotes, not a single pair of double quotes.

Workshop

The Workshop provides quiz questions to help you solidify your understanding of the material covered and exercises to provide you with experience in using what you've learned. Try to understand the quiz and exercise answers before going to the next day's lesson. Answers are provided in the appendix at the end of this book.

Quiz

1. What's wrong with the following code?

```
var
  I: Integer;
  L: Long;
begin
  L := 32768;
  I := L;
end.
```

2. Which of the following identifiers are valid variable names? Which of them are invalid, and why?

```
_TotalCount
1994Totals
AmountInUS$
Today'sDate
NumberOfHoursMinutesAndSecondsSinceMidnight
a
PageNo___
```

Exercises

1. Modify the program INT1.PRJ in Listing 4.1 so that the temperature in degrees Celsius is calculated from the temperature in degrees Fahrenheit, instead of the other way around.
2. Modify the program FLOAT1.PRJ in Listing 4.3 so that a) the `Daily` amount is calculated from the fixed constant `DefaultHourly` and b) the annual amount is based directly on the `Daily` rate.

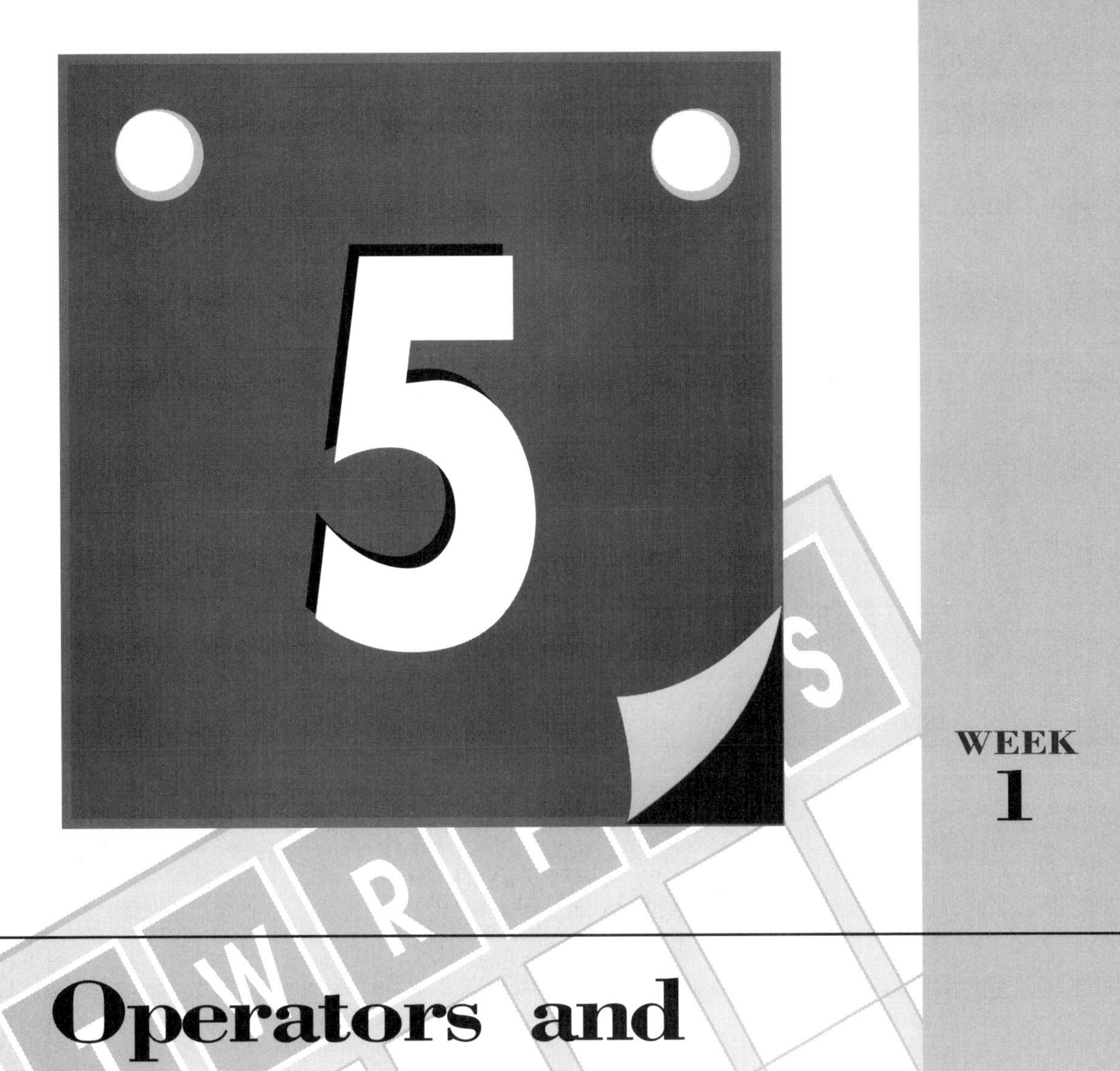

WEEK
1

Operators and Expressions

Yesterday's lesson introduced you to the notions of variables, constants, and Pascal primitive types. Today you will learn the rules of how to combine different variables and constants to form expressions. You will also work through a brief introduction to functions.

In particular, you will learn the following:

- The arithmetic operators in Object Pascal
- The logical operators and their truth tables
- The relational, or comparison, operators supported by Object Pascal
- The rules for evaluating Pascal expressions
- The mysteries of the arithmetic overflow

Operators versus Types

In yesterday's lesson you learned about several built-in types supported by Object Pascal right out of the box. The concept of a data type encompasses a list, or a set, of possible values together with the list of legal operations that can be performed on those values.

Take the type `Integer` as an example. `Integer` represents a set of integral quantities that can be positive, negative, or zero. The particular representation of an integer that is available in Delphi/Object Pascal is a fixed-size 16-bit entity, which means that the set of possible values an `Integer` variable can take ranges from 0000000000000000 to 1111111111111111 in binary format, including all the possible combinations of a mixture of up to 16 zeros and ones together.

These binary numbers can mean different things depending on the convention you use to interpret them. One thing about them is certain, however: there is a limited, albeit fairly large, number of them. A mathematician would say that the set of all values for an `Integer` is finite. The actual `Integer` type consists of 2^{16} (two to the sixteenth power), or 65,536 possible values.

By convention, about half of these possible values are treated as negative numbers, and the remainder as positive. Hence, the `Integer` type consists of a set of integral quantities representing numbers ranging from -32768 to +32767, with zero about halfway in between.

What about operations that can be performed on these values? Object Pascal supports most of the common arithmetic operations that you would want to be able to perform on `Integer` values. The standard operators include

- Addition (+)
- Subtraction (-)
- Multiplication (*)
- Division (/)

Integer Overflows

One important consideration is that some of the operators listed in the previous section behave slightly differently, on occasion, than you would expect based on what you know about adding, subtracting, multiplying, and dividing whole numbers in arithmetic.

First of all, remember that—unlike in pure math—there is a maximum `Integer` value that can be represented with an `Integer` variable. For positive quantities, that maximum value is +32767. Since this value is so fundamental, it even has its own name: `MaxInt`.

NEW TERM `MaxInt` is a pre-defined Object Pascal constant denoting the maximum value that can be represented by an `Integer` variable, and equal to 32767 on a 16-bit system (Windows 3.1 and Delphi are both 16-bit systems).

Considering there is a maximum value, what happens when you add two really large integers together, such that their sum is larger than `MaxInt`? What happens is called an *overflow*.

NEW TERM An *overflow* is a condition occurring at run-time when the result of an arithmetic expression exceeds the maximum allowable (absolute) value for a given data type.

Example Integer Overflow

You are now going to create a simple Delphi program that will illustrate the concept of an arithmetic overflow.

- ☐ Create a new project by selecting New project from the File menu.
- ☐ Save the new project in a newly created directory dedicated to it under the name OVRFLOW.DPR. Name the main form-unit of the project FRMFLOW.PAS.

You have created the simplest possible form-based project in Delphi. The main form contains no controls and is completely blank.

- ☐ With `Form1: TForm1` selected inside the Object Inspector window, click on the Events tab to display the list of events supported by the form.
- ☐ Double-click the Value column (right-hand side) of the `OnCreate` form event to generate an event handler shell.

Delphi responds by creating an empty `TForm1.FormCreate` procedure, as follows:

```
procedure TForm1.FormCreate(Sender: TObject);
begin

end;
```

- Enter the following code inside the newly created `FormCreate` handler:

```
procedure TForm1.FormCreate(Sender: TObject);
var
  i, j: Integer;
begin
  i := 32767;
  j := 1;
  i := i + j;
end;
```

That is, declare a pair of local `Integer` variables `i` and `j` and enter the three lines of code between the **begin** and the **end** of the `FormCreate` handler, as shown in the script.

The code you have just entered will create an overflow error when you attempt to run the program, provided that the overflow-checking compiler option is turned on.

Among the options you can set for the Delphi compiler is an overflow-checking option which, when enabled, allows the generation of code that specifically detects arithmetic overflow errors and alerts the user if such an error occurs at run-time. Otherwise, the overflow errors pass unnoticed.

First, you will examine what happens when you allow an overflow to occur. You will run the example program with the overflow checking compiler option set to "off".

- Select Project from the Delphi Options menu.

Delphi responds by opening the Project Options dialog box.

- Click the Compiler tab at the bottom of the dialog box to reveal the compiler options page.

The Compiler Project Options page with the default settings is shown in Figure 5.1.

Figure 5.1.
The Compiler page of the Project Options dialog box.

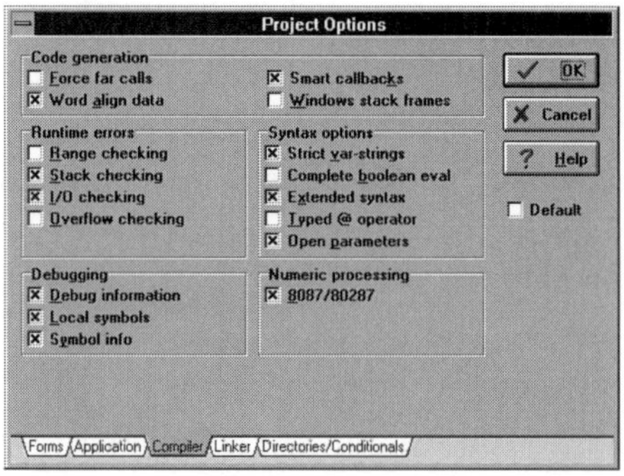

☐ Make sure that the overflow-checking box is unchecked inside the dialog box before you press the OK button.

You are now going to make use of some of the debugging facilities of Delphi's integrated environment.

☐ Place a breakpoint on the last line, just before the terminating **end**, inside the `FormCreate` event handler.

To create a breakpoint, click close to the left edge of the Code Editor window, on the line where you want to place the breakpoint.

A red Stop icon will appear next to the source line on which a breakpoint has been installed. You can toggle the breakpoint by clicking with the mouse, again, to the left of the source code line.

☐ After you have installed the breakpoint, run the program.

Delphi will start the application, hiding the Object Inspector and the Form Designer windows. You can tell that your application is running under the control of the internal Delphi debugger by the annotation in the caption of the main Delphi window. The caption will say something like

```
Delphi - Ovrflow (Running)
```

The application will almost immediately stop at the breakpoint you have created, on the source-code line that says

```
i := i + j;
```

You can now examine the values of the variables `i` and `j` just before the arithmetic expression `i := i + j` is executed.

☐ Place the editor's blinking cursor on the line just before the breakpoint, so that the cursor is immediately to the left of the `j`.

☐ Press Ctrl-F4 to examine the value of the variable `j`.

As expected, the Evaluate/Modify dialog box that is displayed shows the variable `j` to have the value of 1 (one).

☐ Press the Cancel button inside the Evaluate/Modify dialog box to close it.

☐ Examine the value of the variable `i` in a similar way, placing the editor's cursor near the `i` on the first line right after the **begin**, and pressing the Ctrl-F4 key combination.

Again, not surprisingly, you will discover the variable `i` to have the value of 32767. This is precisely what has been assigned to it explicitly.

Now you are ready to perform the calculation on the line with the breakpoint.

- ☐ Press the F8 key once to execute just that single line of code.
- ☐ Examine the value of the variable `j` after the assignment of the sum `i + j`.

You will undoubtedly be surprised to discover that the result of adding 1 to 32767 equals -32768! You have thus experienced an arithmetic overflow.

- ☐ Close the main form of the sample application to terminate it and return to design mode.

Explaining Overflows

The somewhat mysterious result of the calculation in the example above is easily explained when you consider the implications of the way `Integers` are represented at the machine level.

Without delving into the details of binary representations of numbers here, it suffices to say that the representation used by the computer lends itself to treating `Integer` type as a "ring" of values, as shown in Figure 5.2.

Figure 5.2.
The "ring" of `Integers`.

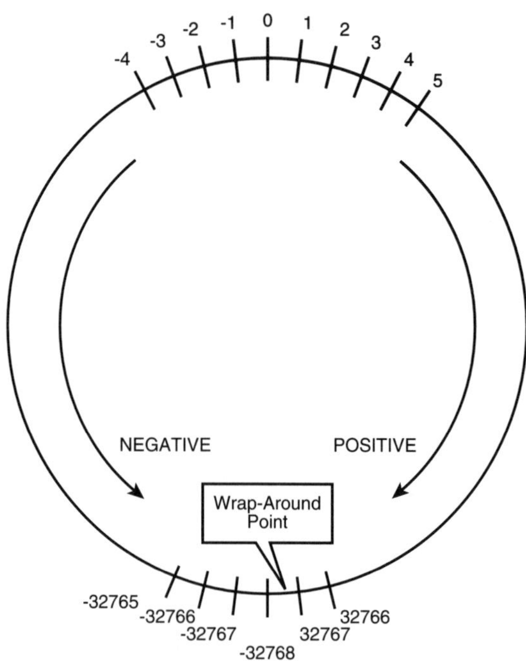

From the perspective of an operation such as addition or multiplication, `Integers` are a closed ring of values. The result of adding an `Integer` to another is always an `Integer`. Adding two positive `Integers` together has the effect of moving in the clockwise direction along the ring of

integers. An overflow condition occurs when, as a result of a calculation, you pass the wrap-around point shown in Figure 5.2, between +32767 and -32768.

The same holds for subtraction. You can verify, using a similar example to the one you just saw, that the result of the calculation -32768–1 is not -32769 as you would expect, but +32767, if you have overflow checking turned off.

Needless to say, multiplication is no different either. If you multiply +256 by +128, the result you expect would be +32768. Because both operands are positive numbers, the result should, at the minimum, be positive, right? Try it with overflow checking disabled, and you will see that the result is actually -32768. Again, the ring representation of `Integers` helps you understand what happened: The result is one more than the maximum positive `Integer` value; hence the wrap-around point is crossed in the clockwise direction, resulting in an overflow and a numerically incorrect value.

Does all that mean that we are forever banned from performing calculations on numbers larger than 32767, or `MaxInt`? Of course not.

The solution to the problem of adding 1 to 32767 is in using a larger entity when necessary, such as a 32-bit `LongInt` capable of representing a much broader—but still finite—range of numbers. The corresponding ring for the `LongInt` type shown in Figure 5.3 encompasses a much broader range, but the same considerations apply as for the 16-bit integers. Try to add 1 to the maximum value of a `LongInt`, called `MaxLongInt`, incidentally, and you will get an overflow.

5

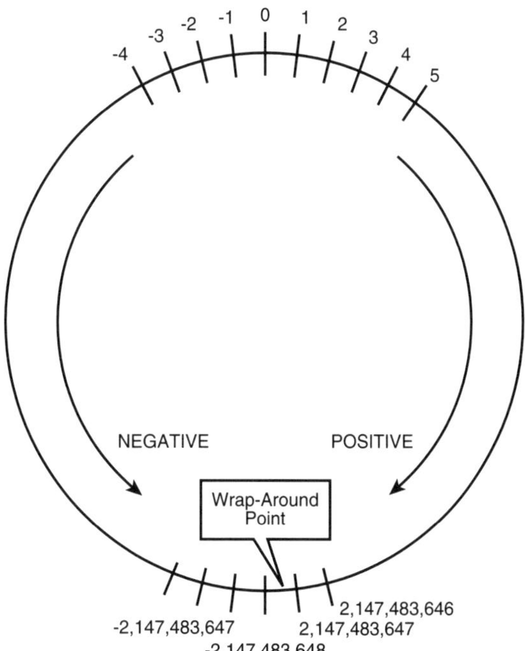

Figure 5.3.
The ring of `LongInts`*.*

The moral of the story about overflows is that you have to be careful when choosing data types for your variables, and when using those variables inside expressions.

Also, no matter what kind of data type you use for a particular numeric variable, there will always be quantities that cannot be represented by that variable.

Division versus Integer Division

Let us now return to the list of operations that the `Integer` type allows. You have already seen that the set of `Integer` values is closed under the operations of addition, subtraction, and multiplication. This means that a result of any of these three operations is of type `Integer` itself.

No such luck with the division operator (`/`). The result of dividing one integral quantity by another, as you know, *might* be, but does not have to be, an integer at all. For example, dividing 27 by 3 yields an integral result, but dividing 27 by 2 does not. In general, a result of dividing one integer by another is an integer by exception rather than as a rule.

Consequently, the division operator in Object Pascal behaves differently than the three other arithmetic operators. The result of a division in Object Pascal is a real number, even though both of its operands can be integers and even though it might seem that the result could be an integer too.

For example, dividing 27 by 3 gives you the result 9.0, which happens to be a whole number, but which is represented in one of the floating-point formats you learned about in yesterday's lesson.

Hence, you can say that the type `Integer` is not closed under the division operator; a result of the division of two integers is not an integer. You cannot assign the result of a division directly to an integer variable, for example, since the strong type-checking rules of Pascal will not let you do it. This is understandable after you realize that integers and real numbers are represented in very different ways at the machine level, and it would make absolutely no sense to assign a real value to an integer variable.

Because standard division of two integers throws you out of the integer realm, there are some additional operators that Object Pascal provides for `Integer` variables to enable you to perform calculations such as division without ever leaving the universe of integers.

One such operator is called the *integer division* operator, denoted by the reserved word **`div`**. Both operands to the **`div`** operator, and the result of the integer division are integers.

An integer division takes two `Integer` operands and returns an `Integer` value, which is the integral part of the arithmetic division. Conceptually, the **`div`** operator performs the division and then throws away the fractional part of the result.

For example, if the result of dividing 27 by 2 being 13 is sufficiently accurate for your purposes, you can use the integer division rather than the regular division operator.

Surprisingly, you will discover that the results of integer divisions are sufficiently accurate for many purposes, not the least of them being the coordinate calculations for screen-display purposes. In fact, Windows itself doesn't use floating-point (real valued) arithmetic to calculate the positions and sizes of various objects. It is all done with integers, mostly for efficiency reasons.

The result of a **`div`** operation effectively tells us how many times one number goes into another, in terms of whole numbers. The calculation is very useful and appears in many contexts.

The advantages of using integers whenever possible boil down to the following considerations:

- Arithmetic operations performed on integers are a lot faster, in some cases up to 1000 times faster than the corresponding operations performed on floating-point representations of real-valued numbers.
- Integer representations of numbers are more compact (take less space) than the corresponding floating-point representations. This is particularly important when a large number of numeric quantities must be manipulated and stored.
- The results of `Integer` calculations, being integers themselves, are always accurate. Floating-point representations, while capable of holding a much broader range of possible values, are limited in their accuracy. Calculations performed on floating-point values accumulate round-off errors that can affect the overall outcome of a complex computation. The problem is that the inaccuracies of floating-point calculations are much harder to control than the inaccuracies of performing arithmetic on integers only.
- Last but not least, as a final argument in favor of integers over reals, the infamous bug inside the floating-point calculation unit of the Pentium processor has once again proven how fragile software based on floating-point arithmetic can be. Early Pentiums would produce incorrect results in some cases of a floating-point division, a testimony to the almost unmanageable complexity hidden behind calculating real values on digital (inherently integer-based) computers.

The conclusion you are expected to draw from all this is that integer calculations are a virtue, and that floating-point or real-valued calculations are to be avoided if at all possible.

Granted, there are uses for floating-point number representations, such as in science, but most everyday applications, including most financial calculations that should remain absolutely accurate, would benefit from focusing on integer computations.

Division by Zero

A very important issue that you have to keep in mind when dealing with division, both of the regular and integer kind, is the anomaly of attempting to divide by zero.

Mathematically, the result of a division by zero is undefined. It is not 1, nor 0. If anything, it could be infinity, but most machines do not handle representing infinity very well (remember, a set of possible values for a variable can be very large but is finite). This uneasiness about dividing by zero is reflected in the design of nearly all computers in that attempting to do so results in a typically serious error condition generated by the arithmetic circuitry of the computer's processor. The fact is that dividing by zero is not safe and will typically cause an abnormal termination of your program.

In general, in the programs you write, you must avoid upsetting the processor by an attempt to divide by zero. There are many ways of guarding against the division-by-zero errors in your code, not the least of which are exception handling mechanisms about which you will learn on day 14, and conditional statements, which you will encounter in the next day's lesson.

For now, just keep in mind that attempting to divide by zero is to be avoided.

Additional Integer Operators

One additional operator is provided by Object Pascal for your convenience in using integers, and that is the modulus operator, or **mod**. The **mod** operator complements the **div** operator introduced in the previous section in that it returns the remainder of dividing one integer number into another.

For example, if you divide 27 by 2, the real value is 13.5, but the integer result—the result of the integer division—would be 13, with the remainder of 1.

Hence the result of taking 27 modulus 13 is 1, or as a Pascal expression,

```
27 mod 13 = 1
```

The **mod** operator yields the integer remainder after dividing two integers. It is not concerned with how many times one number goes into another, but rather in what's left after you perform the division.

Strictly speaking, the **mod** operator is not needed because its effect can be accomplished by using other operators as follows:

```
X mod Y = X - (X div Y)*Y
```

This leads us to another observation: The second operand in the modulus operation must not be zero, since this will ultimately result in an attempt to divide by zero and severely upset the processor, as described before.

Arithmetic Expressions and Operators

To recapitulate what has been said about the integer expressions, and to generalize to other numeric types, Object Pascal defines a number of arithmetic operators. You have already seen

arithmetic expressions and operators in earlier examples. Now is the time for a more formal treatment of these program elements.

Table 5.1 lists all the operators applicable to arithmetic expressions.

Table 5.1. Arithmetic operators.

Operation	Meaning	Result
`-a`	Sign negation	A number of the same magnitude as the operand, but of opposite sign.
`a + b`	Addition	Arithmetic sum of the two operands.
`a - b`	Subtraction	The arithmetic difference between `a` and `b`.
`a*b`	Multiplication	The product of multiplying `a` through `b`.
`a/b`	Division	The quotient, or result of dividing `a` by `b` (`b` must not be zero). Always a real number.
`a div b`	Integer division	The integer result of dividing `a` by `b`, with any fractional part discarded. The operand `b` must not be zero.
`a mod b`	Modulus	The integer remainder after dividing `a` by `b`. The operand `b` must not be zero.

Most of the operators listed in Table 5.1 can be applied with integers, real numbers, or a mixture of both. The only exceptions, as you know already, are the operators: **`div`** and **`mod`**, which require both their operands to be integers.

The types of operands determine the type of the result of an arithmetic expression, and hence the type of the variable to which the result of the expression might be assigned.

As a general rule, if both operands are integers, the result of applying an arithmetic operator is also an integer. If any of the operands is a real number, the result is a real number as well. The only exception is the division operator (`/`), the result of which is always a real number regardless of the types of operands.

Three of the arithmetic operators: `/` (division), **`div`** (integer division), and **`mod`** (modulus) require that their second operand be non-zero, otherwise a run-time error (an *exception*) occurs.

Free-Form Calculator Example

You are now about to build an example program that will illustrate the usage of the arithmetic operators. Your goal is a bit more ambitious than merely entering a few arithmetic expressions, however. You will use the arithmetic expressions you have learned here, but in the context of a full-blown, form-based Delphi application. Consequently, you will be using some of the Delphi features blindly to some extent, because you have not yet been formally introduced to object classes, subroutines, or object properties, to name a few examples.

Just follow the steps described below and you will end up building a simple, free-form calculator program, even if some of the steps might not have been thoroughly explained just yet. The idea is to get you into the routine of building typical Delphi applications. You will gain an understanding of the details later, when you are a little better versed in the Object Pascal language and the intricacies of the development environment.

Creating the Calculator Example

The program you are about to build is a free-form arithmetic calculator. The *free-form* in this context means that the calculator will accept the data as a free-form text entry, inside an edit box, rather than as a series of push-button clicks.

The drawback to using the free-form entry for your calculator at this point is that, to make it a robust application that does not break easily under different conditions, it would normally require performing data validation on the input. For example, one would have to make sure that what the user entered was indeed a valid number. Since the task of data validation seems to require the use of more advanced language constructs than you are currently prepared to handle, you are going to assume the best-case scenario: the user entering only valid integers, within a reasonable range. An assumption like this is clearly unacceptable for a release-quality program but will serve you well for the purposes of this example.

- ☐ Create a new subdirectory where you will store this project's files. Name it FCALC.
- ☐ Start a new, blank project by selecting New project from the Delphi File menu.
- ☐ Save the new project in the newly created directory under the name FCALC.DPR, naming the unit supporting the main form of the application (`Unit1` by default) as FCALC1.PAS.

You have now created a new, blank project located in the FCALC subdirectory. The main form of the application, `Form1` by default, will be the calculator's main window. You are now going to place some controls on the form.

Visually Designing the Calculator

The visual placement of the controls you are going to be dropping onto the form is best illustrated with a drawing. Refer to Figure 5.4 for visual clues as to how to position the various controls on the form relative to each other. It is not important that you create a copy that looks exactly like the screen illustrated, but it is important that all the controls that are supposed to be on the form are indeed there.

Figure 5.4.
The Free-Form Calculator's main form.

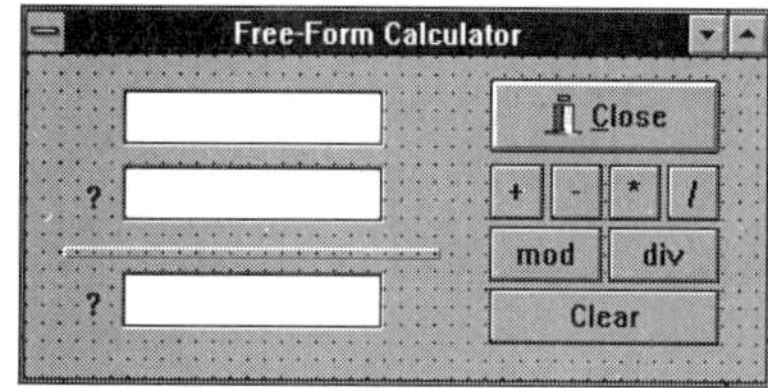

- ☐ Change the `BorderStyle` property of the Calculator's form to `bsSingle`.
- ☐ Change the `Caption` property of the form to `Free-Form Calculator`.
- ☐ From the Standard page of the Component Palette, select the `Edit` component and place an instance of it on the form. The component will be named `Edit1` by Delphi.
- ☐ Rename the `Edit1` component you placed on the form in the previous step to `EditOperand1`.
- ☐ Repeat the previous two steps, placing two additional `Edit` components on the form below the original `EditOperand1`. Name the two new edit boxes `EditOperand2` and `EditResult`, respectively.
- ☐ Select all three `Edit` components together by holding down the Shift key and clicking each of the three edit boxes in succession. The selection of multiple components will be indicated by Delphi with a set of small, gray rectangles (*selection handles*) around each of the selected components.
- ☐ With the three edit boxes selected, click in the right-hand column of the `Text` property inside the Object Inspector and clear the value of the property so that it becomes blank.

The text of all three selected edit boxes is thereby cleared at once.

- ☐ With the three edit boxes still selected, select Align... from the main Delphi Edit menu.

The Alignment dialog box opens.

- ☐ Check the Left sides radio button inside the Horizontal group to make sure that the left sides of the edit boxes are horizontally aligned. Press the OK button to close the dialog box.
- ☐ Select the `EditResult` edit box on the form and, inside the Object Inspector, change the `ReadOnly` property of the box to `True`.

The result of the calculation is something that the calculator will display inside the edit box, and it is therefore advisable to make sure that the user will not interfere with the result displayed by the program. Otherwise the user might assume that he or she is allowed to enter something in the result box and that some additional functionality is associated with it.

- Change the color of the text to be displayed inside the `EditResult` box by adjusting the `Font` property of the `EditResult` component as described in the following steps.

> **Note:** Changing the color of the text will further give the user a hint that the result edit box is different in its function from the other two operand boxes.

- To change the color of the text, double-click the value side (right-hand side) of the `Font` property of the `EditResult` inside the Object Inspector. You can also click the ellipsis button next to the property value, which appears when you select the property.

A standard Windows Font dialog box appears that allows you to change other attributes of the font as well.

- Right now, you are only changing the color, so feel free to select, say, `Red` from the Color drop-down list in the lower left-hand corner of the dialog box, and close the dialog box by pressing the OK button.

Continue the design of the user interface for the Free-Form Calculator program by placing a Close button on the form, so that it is easy to dismiss the calculator's window at run-time.

- Click on the `BitBtn` component on the Additional page of the Component Palette and place an instance of a `BitBtn` on the form.
- Change the `Kind` property of the newly placed `BitBtn1` to `bkClose`.
- Rename the `BitBtn1` component to `BitBtnClose`.

By changing the `Kind` property of the `BitBtnClose` to `bkClose`, you have ensured that the button's action, upon the user's clicking it, will be to close the entire form. This is the default behavior of a Close button, and you don't need to write any code to support it.

You are now going to place a number of buttons on the form, one for each of the calculator's functions (operations).

- On the Additional page of the Component Palette, click the `SpeedButton` component's icon while holding down the Ctrl key.

The `SpeedButton` component's icon will get selected in a persistent mode, allowing you to place several components of the same kind on the form without each time having to explicitly select the component's icon from the palette. Not only will the component's icon button on the palette look pushed-down, but it will also display a rectangle consisting of dots around the icon to indicate a persistent, or *sticky*, mode of operation.

- You can now go ahead and place seven copies of the `SpeedButton` component on the form one-by-one, clicking approximately where you want them placed. Remember you can always rearrange them later, so don't try to be very accurate at the moment.

The `SpeedButtons` you just placed on the form will be named `SpeedButton1` through `SpeedButton7` by Delphi.

Don't forget to *unload* your mouse cursor; that is, to release the persistently selected `SpeedButton` component on the Component Palette.

- Click the leftmost button on the Component Palette, the one with an arrow icon resembling a standard mouse cursor, to return to the normal mode of operation in which the mouse cursor selects components on the form, rather than placing even more copies of `SpeedButtons`.

The `SpeedButtons` you have placed on the form are capable of displaying arbitrary pictures, called bitmaps.

NEW TERM A *glyph* is the bitmap, or picture, displayed inside a `SpeedButton`, or some other component, determining its visual appearance.

You can customize the appearance of `SpeedButtons` to your liking by supplying appropriate Windows bitmap (.bmp) files for their glyphs. This is very useful for creating modern-looking toolbars, for example.

For the purposes of this sample calculator program, however, you will simply provide default, character-based glyphs for these buttons.

- Select the top-left button, `SpeedButton1`, in the group of `SpeedButtons` you placed on the form.
- Change the `Caption` property of `SpeedButton1` to `+` (the plus sign) and change its `Name` property to BtnAdd.
- Now select each of the remaining `SpeedButtons` in succession and change their `Caption` properties to the corresponding operation's symbol and their names according to the Table 5.1.

Refer back to Figure 5.4 to see what other operations your calculator needs to support. Table 5.2 summarizes the functions of the Free-Form Calculator program. There is a corresponding `SpeedButton` on the form for each of these calculator functions.

Table 5.2. The Free-Form Calculator's function keys.

Symbol for the SpeedButton	Button Name	Operation
+	BtnPlus	Addition
-	BtnMinus	Subtraction

continues

Table 5.2. continued

Symbol for the SpeedButton	Button Name	Operation
`*`	`BtnMultiply`	Multiplication
`/`	`BtnDivide`	Regular, floating-point division
`mod`	`BtnMod`	Remainder
`div`	`BtnDiv`	Integer division
`Clear`	`BtnClear`	Clear the entry fields of the calculator

You have now created most of the calculator's visual interface. What remains are a couple of minor details, such as some labels.

- ☐ From the Standard page of the Component Palette, select the `Label` component and place two instances of it on the form, in front of the `EditOperand2` and `EditResult` edit boxes, respectively.
- ☐ Rename the label in front of the `EditOperand2` from `Label1` to `LabelOperator` and change its `Caption` property to `?`, a single question mark.
- ☐ Rename the label in front of the `EditResult` box from `Label2` to `LabelResult` and change its `Caption` property to a single question mark.

The question marks displayed by these labels signify the fact that the calculator does not display any valid calculation at the moment. The labels will change dynamically at run-time, based on what the user chooses to do.

- ☐ As the final touch for the user interface of the calculator program, place a `Bevel` component from the Additional page of the Component palette on the form to set the result of the calculation apart from the operands.
- ☐ Change the `Style` property of the newly placed `Bevel1` component to `bsRaised`. You might also need to adjust its `Height` property so that the result looks visually appealing on your screen. The value of 5, for example, should be acceptable.

You have now completed the first major step in the development of the sample calculator program: the visual interface design. You are now ready to provide the desired behavior to the application.

Entering Code for the Calculator Example

If you attempt to run the calculator program now, it should compile and run successfully, but it will not do anything. There are no actions associated with any of the calculator buttons, beyond the Close button that has a default action of closing the form ingrained in its definition.

To provide actions for the events such as the user pressing a button, you need to write Object Pascal code.

Supporting Addition

It is time to add the support for addition to your calculator program.

- Double-click on the `BtnPlus` inside the Form Designer's window.

Delphi responds by creating a default event handler for the button. As usually is the case, you will see some activity inside the Code Editor window, which will be brought to the forefront, and will see the cursor being placed on a line between a **begin** and an **end** pair of Pascal keywords inside a newly generated block of code that looks like the following:

```
procedure TForm1.BtnAddClick(Sender: TObject);
begin

end;
```

The space between the **begin** and the **end** is where you enter your custom code to respond to the event, a button-click event in this case.

Ideally, what you want to do now would be to tell the calculator to take whatever is currently in the edit box for the first operand, add it to the contents of the second operand's edit box, and place the result inside the result box.

Things are not so simple, however, and there is some additional business that needs to be taken care of first. The problem is that there is no easy way of obtaining the value of the contents of an edit box in a form suitable for performing arithmetic calculations. Remember that you need to perform addition on integers. The contents of the edit box, however, although presumably numeric in nature, is merely a string of characters, that is, a different data type. You need a way of converting back and forth between a `String` representation of a number, suitable for display, and its numeric representation, as an `Integer`-type variable, suitable for performing arithmetic calculations.

You can accomplish the conversion by calling one of the standard functions provided for this purpose in the `SysUtils` unit:

- `StrToInt` takes a `String` parameter and returns its numeric equivalent; for example, `StrToInt('123')` takes a `String` argument `'123'` and returns `123`, a `LongInt` assignment -compatible with `Integer`.
- `IntToStr` takes a numeric integral value as its argument and returns the `String` representation of the number, for example, `IntToStr(789)` taking an `Integer` constant `789` as its argument returns the `String` with the value of `'789'`.
- `FloatToStr` takes a numeric real (floating-point) value as its argument and returns its `String` representation; for example, `FloatToStr(2.10)` returns the `String` `'2.10000000000'`.

The `StrToInt` function allows you to take the contents of an operand edit box, which is accessible as the `Text` property of a respective `Edit` component, and convert it to an `Integer` suitable for calculations. For example, to obtain the numeric value of the first operand, invoke `StrToInt` as follows:

```
StrToInt(EditOperand1.Text)
```

You are now ready to fill the interior of the `BtnAddClick` event handler with code.

In this case, to perform the necessary conversions, you will introduce some temporary variables to store the intermediate values after the conversions.

☐ Insert the following code between the **begin** and the **end** of the `BtnAddClick` event handler:

```
Op1 := StrToInt(EditOperand1.Text);
Op2 := StrToInt(EditOperand2.Text);
Result := Op1 + Op2;
ResultStr := IntToStr(Result);
EditResult.Text := ResultStr;
```

This code accomplishes the actions necessary to perform the addition of the two operands the user has entered and to display the result.

Before you can meaningfully analyze the purpose of the code, observe that it introduces a few new variable names. In order for this to work, these variables must have been declared and their data types known in advance. Also observe that the sole purpose for the existence of these variables is to allow the conversions, and consequently the calculation, inside the `BtnAddClick` subroutine to take place. These are temporary variables because they have no role or meaning outside of the subroutine. A convenient place to declare temporary variables is within the subroutine itself, so that they are only available within that subroutine.

☐ Insert the following variable-declaration block before the **begin** keyword of the `BtnAddClick` subroutine, and after the subroutine header, that is, after the line with

```
procedure TForm1.BtnAddClick(Sender: TObject);
```

insert:

```
var
  Op1,
  Op2,
  Result: Integer;
  ResultStr: String;
```

The code you have just entered reserves room for three `Integer` variables, `Op1`, `Op2`, and `Result`, whose purpose is to store the numeric values of the first and second operands, and of the result of the calculation, respectively. After the calculation has been performed, the numeric result is converted back to a `String` value so it can be sent to the `EditResult` component. The conversion subroutine `IntToStr` stores its result in a temporary variable `ResultStr` of type `String`.

The complete code for the `BtnAddClick` subroutine is as follows:

```
 1: procedure TForm1.BtnAddClick(Sender: TObject);
 2: var
 3:   Op1,
 4:   Op2,
 5:   Result: Integer;
 6:   ResultStr: String;
 7: begin
 8:   Op1 := StrToInt(EditOperand1.Text);
 9:   Op2 := StrToInt(EditOperand2.Text);
10:   Result := Op1 + Op2;
11:   ResultStr := IntToStr(Result);
12:   EditResult.Text := ResultStr;
13: end;
```

Lines 2 through 6 of the `BtnAddClick` subroutine of the `TForm1` form declare the temporary variables for conversions between numeric and string representations.

Line 8 converts the string value of the first operand to a number and stores the result in the `Op1` `Integer` variable.

Similarly, line 9 converts the string value of the second operand and stores the result in the `Op2` `Integer` variable.

Line 10 is where the calculation is actually done. This line is the official purpose of the exercise: It shows you how to use the addition operator to add two `Integer`s together, but you learned a lot more in the process of creating the scaffolding that supports the addition.

Once the variable `Result` on line 10 receives the result of the addition, line 11 converts it back to a string-representation stored inside the `ResultStr` variable.

Finally, line 12 causes the Result edit box to display the string representation of the sum of the two operands by assigning the value of the `ResultStr` to the `EditResult`'s `Text` property.

The code you have just entered for the plus-button event handler, `BtnAddClick`, accomplishes its goal, that is, it calculates the sum of the operands and displays the result. You have to realize, however, that this code is unnecessarily verbose. The only reason to introduce all of the temporary variables in the process was to illustrate exactly what was happening. In reality, you don't need any of the temporary variables at all! The purpose of the routine can be accomplished in a single, although somewhat long, statement.

First, observe what happens on lines 8, 9, and 10 of the `BtnAddClick` subroutine. The string values of operands are converted to integers so that the calculation on line 10 can be performed. You can replace the three statements on lines 8 through 10 with a single one that performs both the conversion and the calculation:

```
Result :=
  StrToInt(EditOperand1.Text) +
  StrToInt(EditOperand2.Text);
```

Now observe that line 11 becomes redundant if you replace line 12 with the following:

```
EditResult.Text := IntToStr(Result);
```

Here the intermediate step of assigning to the temporary variable is omitted, and both the conversion and the assignment are done in a single step.

What you are left with right now is two statements instead of five:

```
begin
  Result :=
    StrToInt(EditOperand1.Text) +
    StrToInt(EditOperand2.Text);
  EditResult.Text := IntToStr(Result);
end;
```

The last step of the simplification process is to eliminate the remaining temporary variable, `Result`.

Note that in general, whenever you have a pair of expressions of the form

```
  A := Something;
  B := A;
```

you can simply reduce them to a single expression

```
  B := Something;
```

eliminating `A` from consideration.

Similarly, whenever you have

```
  A := F(Something);
  B := A;
```

you can convert it to

```
  B := F(Something);
```

Accordingly, the final step of the simplification of the `BtnAddClick` subroutine is to eliminate the `Result` variable as follows:

```
  EditResult.Text :=
    IntToStr( StrToInt(EditOperand1.Text) +
      StrToInt(EditOperand2.Text) );
```

This example is meant to show you how you can streamline your code by eliminating unnecessary temporary variables and assignments. On the other hand, you have to realize that such streamlining can sometimes result in code that is harder to read and understand.

You have to bear this in mind and decide in each case whether the simplification of the code is not offset by the corresponding difficulty in understanding it later. Sometimes, in fact, it is a good idea to do quite the opposite—that is, to introduce a temporary variable to specifically make the code more readable and understandable.

Supporting Subtraction and Multiplication

The event handler responsible for handling the minus-button click event is very similar to what you have developed for the plus button. The only difference is the arithmetic operator: Instead of the addition operator, you use the subtraction operator.

- [ ] Double-click on the `BtnSubtract` inside the Form Designer's window.

Delphi responds again by creating a default event handler for the button. The newly generated block of code looks like the following:

```
procedure TForm1.BtnSubtractClick(Sender: TObject);
begin

end;
```

- [ ] As before, fill in the `BtnSubtractClick` subroutine with code as follows:

```
procedure TForm1.BtnSubtractClick(Sender: Tobject);
begin
  EditResult.Text :=
    IntToStr( StrToInt(EditOperand1.Text) -
      StrToInt(EditOperand2.Text) );
end;
```

Analogously, the finished event-handler subroutine for the multiplication button will look like the following:

```
procedure TForm1.BtnMultiplyClick(Sender: TObject);
begin
  EditResult.Text :=
    IntToStr( StrToInt(EditOperand1.Text) *
      StrToInt(EditOperand2.Text) );
end;
```

- [ ] Enter the code for the `BtnMultiplyClick` event handler according to the example.

Supporting Division

Your calculator is expected to support two types of division: the integer division operating on whole numbers only, and the regular division that yields a real-valued result.

The code for integer division is straightforward after you have dealt with the addition, subtraction, and multiplication:

```
procedure TForm1.BtnDivClick(Sender: TObject);
begin
  EditResult.Text :=
    IntToStr( StrToInt(EditOperand1.Text) div
      StrToInt(EditOperand2.Text) );
end;
```

While you are at it, feel free to enter the supporting code for the modulus operation, that is, to obtain the remainder of the division of the first operand by the second:

```
procedure TForm1.BtnModClick(Sender: TObject);
begin
  EditResult.Text :=
    IntToStr( StrToInt(EditOperand1.Text) mod
      StrToInt(EditOperand2.Text) );
end;
```

Now, the code supporting the regular division must be different in that the result of dividing an integer by another is no longer an integer. Consequently, you cannot use the `IntToStr` conversion to obtain the final string representation of the result, but must use `FloatToStr` instead. Other than that, the code for the division event handler looks similar to all the other event handlers:

```
procedure TForm1.BtnDivideClick(Sender: TObject);
begin
  EditResult.Text :=
    FloatToStr( StrToInt(EditOperand1.Text) /
      StrToInt(EditOperand2.Text) );
end;
```

At this point, your calculator supports all of the arithmetic operators. You can verify that it works by running it and entering a few numbers for the operands. When you click a function button, the result shows up in the result box.

Enhancing the Calculator

As it stands, the calculator is still not very user-friendly. You still need to provide the code to support the Clear button, and to dynamically change the question-mark labels to be more meaningful.

- ☐ Double-click on the Clear button (`BtnClear` component) inside the Form Designer's window.
- ☐ Enter the following code inside the newly generated event handler:

```
procedure TForm1.BtnClearClick(Sender: TObject);
begin
  EditOperand1.Text := '';
  EditOperand2.Text := '';
  EditResult.Text := '';
  LabelOperator.Caption := '?';
  LabelResult.Caption := '?';
end;
```

The code you have just entered clears the `Text` of the operand edit boxes, and of the result edit box, and sets the `Caption` property of the labels to the question-mark symbol. This has the effect of clearing the calculator's display.

The `LabelOperator` is supposed to indicate which of the calculator's operations was invoked last. To make it work, you need to set the value of the Caption property of the label to the symbol of the operator.

☐ Add the following code inside the `BtnAddClick` event handler:

```
LabelOperator.Caption := BtnAdd.Caption;
labelResult.Caption := '=';
```

The code you have entered will ensure that whenever the plus-button is pressed, the plus-symbol will appear as the operator label. Also, whenever the result edit box shows a valid result of a calculation, the result label changes to the equal-sign.

☐ Enter a pair of statements similar to those you just used for each of the six calculator function handlers.

For example, the integer division event handler, after you make the change, will look like the following:

```
procedure TForm1.BtnDivClick(Sender: TObject);
begin
  EditResult.Text :=
    IntToStr( StrToInt(EditOperand1.Text) div
      StrToInt(EditOperand2.Text) );
  LabelOperator.Caption := BtnDiv.Caption;
  LabelResult.Caption := '=';
end;
```

Note that at run-time, once you perform a calculation, and then go back and change the value of one of the operands, the old result still shows in the result window. Since this can be confusing to the user who might be unaware of when the result is valid and when it is not, you will provide a facility to clear the result box automatically whenever one of the operands changes.

☐ As the final step in the process of creation of the Free-Form Calculator program, click on the first operand's edit box (`EditOperand1` component) inside the Form Designer to select it.

☐ Switch the Object Inspector to the Events page by clicking on the Events tab at the bottom.

A list of events that can be generated by the edit box appears. The first of these events is called `OnChange` and is generated every time the contents of the edit box changes. This is what you need now.

- Double-click the Value column (right-hand side) of the `OnChange` event to generate a skeleton for the event handler. The generated event handler will be named `EditOperand1Change` after the component to which it is initially attached.
- Because you will use the same event handler for both operands, change its name to a somewhat more generic `OperandChange`.
- Enter the following code inside the `TForm1.OperandChange` handler:

```
procedure TForm1.OperandChange(Sender: TObject);
begin
  EditResult.Text := '';
  LabelOperator.Caption := '?';
  LabelResult.Caption :=  '?';
end;
```

The code you have entered performs the same function as the code for the Clear button handler, except for clearing the operands.

Running the Free-Form Calculator

You are ready to try the Free-Form Calculator. Keep in mind that it has not been designed to work with anything other than integers and that it does not validate what the user enters as operands, assuming that whatever has been entered is a valid integer number.

The finished look of the Free-Form Calculator appears in Figure 5.5.

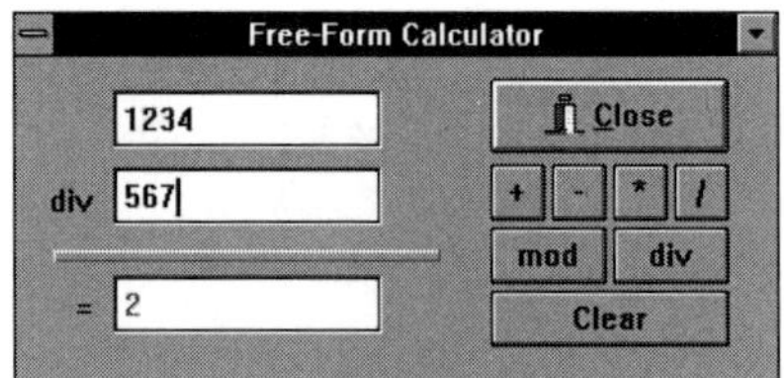

Figure 5.5.
Running the Free-Form Calculator example.

This concludes our discussion of the arithmetic operators and expressions.

Logical Expressions and Operators

Logical operators participate in Boolean expressions, that is, ones that yield either a `True` or a `False` as a result. The results of Boolean expressions are either assigned to Boolean variables, or participate in controlling the program flow. The latter use—something you will learn in tomorrow's lesson—is particularly important to a programmer because it allows you to control the flow of a program's execution based on various conditions.

Table 5.3 summarizes the logical operators supported by Object Pascal.

Table 5.3. Object Pascal's logical operators.

Operator	Meaning	Result
`not` a	Negation	Logical negation. `True` becomes `False`, and vice versa.
a `and` b	Logical AND	`True` only if both operands are `True`.
a `or` b	Logical OR	`True` unless both operands are `False`.
a `xor` b	Exclusive-OR	`True` only if the operands have opposite truth-values, that is, either `True-False`, or `False`, `True`, but not `True-True`, nor `False-False`.

The logical operators perform their actions according to their specific truth tables, which are different for each of the operators. These tables define the meaning for the standard logical operations. Figures 5.6 through 5.8 illustrate how the standard logical operators work.

Note that the negation operator (**`not`**) requires only a single operand. The other logical operators take two operands and combine their values according to the appropriate truth table. For example, the result of applying the **`and`** operator to join two expressions is `False` when one of the expressions is `False`. Joining two expressions with the **`or`** operator results in a `True` value unless both of the participating expressions are simultaneously `False`.

Figure 5.6.
The truth table for the **`and`** *operator.*

AND	True	False
True	True	False
False	False	False

Figure 5.7.
The truth table for the **`or`** *operator.*

OR	True	False
True	True	True
False	True	False

Figure 5.8.
The truth table for the **not** *operator.*

NOT	
True	False
False	True

Relational Expressions and Operators

Relational operators are closely coupled with the logical ones. Both kinds of operators are often mixed within a single Boolean expression. The relational operators are effectively concerned with comparing results of subordinate, usually arithmetic, expressions, yielding a Boolean result overall. They are the *comparison operators.*

NEW TERM A *relational* operator is an operator that takes two operands on both sides and evaluates to a Boolean value, either `False` or `True`.

The operands on either side of a relational operator might be expressions of arbitrary complexity, or simple variables or constants, as the case may be. The important consideration is that whatever appears on one side of a relational operator must be compatible with what appears on the other side. It is certainly meaningful to compare an `Integer` with another `Integer`, or a `String` with another `String`, or even an `Integer` with a `LongInt`. Just as it does not make sense, however, to compare apples with oranges, so it does not make sense to compare an `Integer` with a `String`.

Some examples of relational expressions include

```
Index < Count
Count >= 7
Divisor <> 0

'ABC' < 'BCD'
```

Because the ultimate result of a relational expression is Boolean, the results of many relational sub-expressions can be combined by using the logical operators to form a more complex logical expression.

For example, the expression

```
(Index < Count) and (Count >= 7)
```

will be `True` provided that the value of the variable `Index` is strictly less than the value of `Count`, and simultaneously provided that `Count` is greater or equal to seven.

Table 5.4 illustrates the Object Pascal relational operators.

Table 5.4. Object Pascal relational operators.

Operator	Meaning/ example
`=`	"Equal"/ `2 = 1 + 1`.
`<>`	"Not equal"/ `2 <> 3`.
`<`	"Less than"/ `3 < 7`.
`>`	"Greater than"/ `5 > 2`.
`<=`	"Less than or equal to"/ `2 <= 2 + x`.
`>=`	"Greater than or equal to"/ `2 > = 1 + i`.

Speaking of number comparisons, there is something you need to know about comparing floating-point values. This again confirms that you have to be very careful when you're using real-valued expressions.

The point is that the floating-point calculations accumulate round-off errors, and comparing them directly can yield surprising results.

Consider the following example:

```
var
  a,
  b: Real;
  Result: Boolean;
begin
  a := (1/123456789.123456789);
  a := a*123456789.123456789;
  b := 1.0;
  Result := (a = b);
end;
```

What do you think the result of a comparison `a = b`, that is, the value of the `Result` variable, would be at this point? Common sense would indicate that the comparison would yield `True`, since the variable a should be exactly equal to `1`. The result of the comparison however turns out to be `False` because the calculations performed on a caused it to assume a value very, very close to 1.0, but not *exactly* equal to 1.0. Some precision was lost in the calculation.

Warning: Never compare two floating-point values for equality directly. The result may be surprising (that is, incorrect), because of the cumulative error in the floating-point calculations.

Rather than comparing real values directly, you should be checking whether the value of interest is close enough to the value you are comparing it against. Instead of comparing

```
r = s
```

you should make the degree of precision that is required explicit, by comparing against a known constant:

```
(s - r) <= 0.00001
```

For example, consider the following:

```
var
  a,
  b: Real;
  Result: Boolean;
begin
  a := (1/123456789.123456789);
  a := a*123456789.123456789;
  b := 1.0;
  Result := (b - a) < 0.00001;
end;
```

At the end of this code-block, unlike in the previous example, the `Result` variable is `True`, because instead of comparing `a` to `b` directly, you are comparing the difference between `a` and `b` to a predefined, very small value: the interval of precision, or 0.00001 in this case. The answer you get from the comparison is, yes, the values are close enough, given a precision of five digits after the decimal point.

Operator Precedence and Evaluation Rules

Table 5.5 illustrates the rules of operator precedence in Object Pascal.

Table 5.5. Operator precedence in Object Pascal.

Operator	Comments
`not`	Highest priority. Boolean negation.
`*`	
`/`	
`div`	
`mod`	

Operator	Comments
`and`	Next-to-highest priority. “Multiplying” operators, including arithmetic multiplication, division, integer division, modulus, and the Boolean **`and`** operator.
`+`	
`-`	
`or`	Next-to-lowest priority. “Adding” operators, including arithmetic addition, subtraction, and the Boolean **`or`** operator.
`=`	
`<>`	
`<`	
`<=`	
`>=`	
`>`	Lowest priority. All relational, or “comparison,” operators.

In expressions containing more than one operator at the same priority level, the expression is evaluated left-to-right.

In expressions containing more than one operator, in which some operators have higher precedence than others, the sub-expressions involving the highest-priority operators are evaluated first, then their results are combined with the lower priority operators.

The operators in Object Pascal generally follow the customary rules for operator precedence found in other programming languages and in mathematics. There are some important differences with other programming languages, however. If you ever programmed in some other language before, you will discover that the order of evaluation of logical (Boolean) sub-expressions versus relational sub-expressions is reversed in comparison. You therefore need to parenthesize around the relational sub-expressions to be able to combine them into a more complex `Boolean` expression.

Note: One of the quirks that Object Pascal inherited from standard ANSI/ISO Pascal is that the relational operators have lower priority than do Boolean ones.

This results in the requirement that relational sub-expressions *must* be enclosed in parentheses if there is even a single logical operator joining two relational sub-expressions.

For example, the expression

```
(x > -2.5) and (x < 1.75) or (y >= 100)
```

must be parenthesized around its three relational components to satisfy the compiler precedence rules.

Summary

Today you have learned the basics of the Object Pascal operators. In particular, you have learned the following:

- The signed integer types, `Integer` and `LongInt`, form closed rings of values with respect to most arithmetic operations.
- The regular division operator is a floating-point operation that breaks the integer rings.
- An overflow can occur as a result of integer operations of addition, subtraction, and multiplication. An overflow typically signifies an error condition.
- The division by zero, a mathematically undefined operation, throws the processor into an error condition, raising an exception in your Delphi application.
- A set of `Boolean` and relational operators allows you to build arbitrarily complex logical expressions.
- The evaluation priority rules for Pascal operators are slightly different than in most other programming languages. In particular, relational operators have lower priority than the Boolean and arithmetic operators. When comparing numbers, you must enclose the relational sub-expressions inside parentheses.
- You can parenthesize sub-expressions to change the order of evaluation of expressions.

Q&A

Q How do I avoid the divide-by-zero errors?

A There are many ways to guard against these common errors. No matter which way you choose, please choose one. There is no excuse for a supposedly production-quality program to be generating divide-by-zero exceptions. The simplest way to ensure that you never divide by zero is to precede any division by a simple check for the divisor being zero. You will learn how to construct tests with **if**-statements in the tomorrow's lesson. Another way of guarding against the divide-by-zero errors surfacing to the user of your application is to set-up an exception trapping mechanism. You will learn about exceptions on Day 14.

Q Is it possible to write financial applications without using the floating-point variables and operations?

A Yes, most financial applications would benefit greatly, both in speed and accuracy, from performing all calculations on integers. The `LongInt` type is capable of representing only the amount $21,474,836.47, but larger representations such as 64-bit, or even 128-bit, can be constructed for the purposes of financial calculations as classes. Also keep in mind that the built-in type `Comp` is really a 64-bit integer, except that it requires the use of the floating-point facilities (a math-coprocessor or a floating-point emulation library).

Workshop

The Workshop provides quiz questions to help you solidify your understanding of the material covered and exercises to provide you with experience in using what you've learned. Try to understand the quiz and exercise answers before continuing on to the next day's lesson. Answers are provided in Appendix B at the end of this book.

5

Quiz

1. What is the value of each of the following arithmetic expressions?

   (a) `2 + 3*4 - 5 mod 2`

   (b) `7 - 15 div 3`

   (c) `15/3`

   (d) (15/3) mod 3

2. Assuming A = True, B = False, and C = True, what is the value of each of the following logical expressions?

   (a) `A or B and C`

   (b) `A xor B xor C`

   (c) `not (A or B)`

   (c) `not A or not (B and C)`

3. Assuming that X = 2, Y = 1, and Z = 0, to what do the following complex expressions evaluate?

   (a) `(21 < 9) or (X <= Y)`

   (b) `((X + Y) >= 3) and not ((Y mod 2) = 0)`

Exercises

1. Change the overflow example from today's lesson to illustrate a `LongInt` overflow. Hint: the maximum positive value that can be stored in a `LongInt`, called `MaxLongInt`, is 2,147,483,647.
2. Expand the sample calculator you have developed during the course of today's lesson to handle larger than `Integer` quantities. In other words, convert the `Integer` calculator example to a `LongInt` calculator.

WEEK 1

Controlling the Program Flow

Your programs would be limited in functionality and capabilities if all you could do to them were to merely execute a flat, linear sequence of statements, one after another.

Today's lesson introduces you to the important concept of controlling the flow of execution of programs, which changes the decidedly boring and simple linear sequence into a range of alternate paths of execution that are dynamically selected based on various run-time conditions.

In today's lesson you learn about the following topics related to conditional execution and alternate program paths:

- Program control structures in general
- The **`if-then`** and **`if-then-else`** statements
- The **`case`** statement

You also learn how to use two of the standard Delphi components together on a form as you build the example program. The components you encounter in today's lesson include the following:

- Notebook
- TabSet

Before you delve into the intricacies of controlling program execution logic, let's make a general observation about the issue of compound statements.

Compound Statements

NEW TERM A *compound statement* is a block of Pascal statements enclosed in a **`begin`** and **`end`** pair of keywords.

The general observation that you should remember is: You can substitute a **`begin-end`** block of statements for a single statement. Today's lesson explicitly illustrates several variations of the same statement (the **`if`** statement) to help you to learn the general rule.

You should know the following formal "rule of substitution," however:

Note: Whenever a single statement can be used in an expression, you can insert in its place a block of statements enclosed in a **`begin-end`** pair of keywords.

For example, you can use

```
begin
  Statement1;
  Statement2;
  Statement3;
  ...
  StatementN;
end;
```

whenever

```
AStatement;
```

is expected. This powerful feature of the Pascal language enables you to compose arbitrarily complex statements from the relatively few syntactical constructs or language building blocks.

Control Structures

The Pascal language supports two general categories of control structures:

- Conditional constructs
- Looping structures

Boolean expressions of the form you learned on Day 5 are the key to understanding the control of the program flow. Typically, it is desirable for a program to take a different course of action depending on a value of a Boolean conditional expression that effectively acts as a switch selecting different paths of execution.

Two conditional control constructs, also called *decision-making structures*, are provided by the Object Pascal language and are available in Delphi:

- The **`if`** statement
- The **`case`** statement

Both of these constructs depend on evaluating expressions.

In addition to the conditional control structures is a group of program constructs called *repetition structures*, or *loops*. Looping structures use conditional expressions to control repetition of an action or of a set of actions.

The Pascal language supports the following three looping structures:

- The **`while`** loop
- The **`repeat`** loop
- The **`for`** loop

Today's lesson concentrates on the conditional control structures. You learn more about loops on Day 7.

The *if* Statement

The **if** statement, also called a *conditional* or *selection statement*, selects one of two possible courses of action, depending on the value of a conditional, or Boolean, expression. An **if** statement belongs in executable blocks of statements, that is, between a **begin** and an **end** pair of keywords.

Simple *if* Statement

An **if** statement starts with the reserved word **if**, followed by a Boolean expression, and then followed by the keyword **then**. There are several possibilities of what may follow the **then** keyword.

Syntax

Simple *if* Statement

The syntax for a single-alternative **if** statement that performs a single statement only if the Boolean condition is True is as follows:

```
if ConditionIsTrue then
  DoSomething;
```

Example:

```
if Total < 123 then
  PrintReport;
```

In the simplest case, a single Pascal statement followed by a semicolon appears after the **then** keyword. This example is a single-alternative, simple **if** statement.

Figure 6.1 illustrates the building-block structure of the **if-then** statement.

The statement after **then** is executed only if the condition is True. If the conditional expression after the **if** keyword yields False, nothing inside the **if-then** statement gets executed, and the program control jumps to the next statement following the **if** statement.

Multi-Statement *if* Statement

In a more complex case than the one in the preceding section, multiple statements may need to be executed if the selection condition is True. In this situation, you enclose the set of multiple statements to be executed within a **begin-end** block.

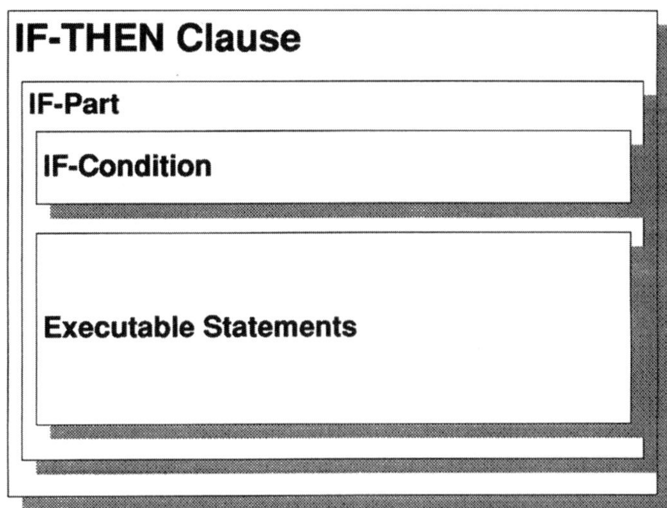

Figure 6.1.
The structure of the **`if-then`** *statement.*

Syntax

Multi-Statement *if* Statement

The syntax for a single-alternative **`if`** statement that performs multiple statements when the Boolean condition is `True` is as follows:

```
if ConditionIsTrue then
  begin
    DoSomething1;
    DoSomething2;
    ...
  end;
```

Example:

```
if Temperature < 10 then
  begin
    TurnHeaterOn;
    TurnVentillationOff;
    NotifyOperator;
  end;
```

Again, if the condition returns `False` at run-time, none of the statements within the block executes, and the execution control simply falls through to the next statement after the **`if`** statement.

Simple *if-then-else* Statement

A simple **`if-then-else`** statement offers a two-way selection. A single statement is executed if the Boolean **`if`** condition is `True`; otherwise, if the conditional expression yields `False`, another statement in the **else** part is executed. An **if-then-else** statement guarantees that one of the statements (the **if** or the **else** part) is executed no matter what the result of the condition evaluation is.

Syntax

Simple *if-then-else* Statement

Here is the general syntax for an **if-then-else** statement that does something if the Boolean condition is `True`; otherwise, it performs some other action.

```
if ConditionIsTrue then
  DoSomething
else
  DoSomethingElse;
```

Example:

```
if (NumberOfPages > 20) then
  DisplayProgressBox
else
  UpdateStatusLine;
```

Figure 6.2 illustrates the building-block structure of the **if-then-else** statement.

Warning: There is never a semicolon before the **else** in an **if-then-else** statement.

Compound *if-then*, Simple *else* Statement

Syntax

Compound *if-then*, Simple *else* Statement

Here is the syntax for an **if-then-else** statement that performs multiple statements when the Boolean condition is `True`; otherwise, it performs a single statement.

```
if ConditionIsTrue then
  begin
    DoSomething1;
    DoSomething2;
    ...
  end
else
  DoSomething3;
```

Example:

```
if PageNumber < PageCount then
  begin
    PageNumber := PageNumber + 1;
    LineNumber := 0;
..end
```

```
else
  ReportNumber := ReportNumber + 1;
```

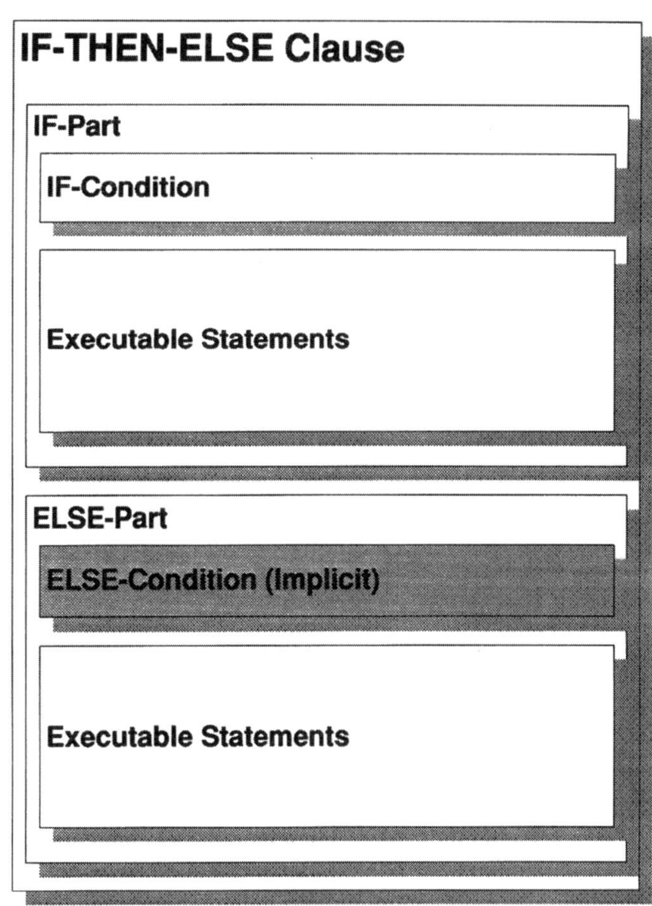

Figure 6.2.
The structure of the ***if-then-else*** *statement.*

6

To perform a number of statements together (but only if the condition is `True`) or otherwise to perform a single statement, you can write a multi-statement **`if-then`** with a simple **`else`** statement. Again, one of the parts of the **`if-then-else`** statement is guaranteed to execute: **`then`** executes if the condition evaluates to `True`; otherwise, **`else`** executes.

Simple *if-then*, Compound *else* Statement

To perform a single statement when the **`if`** condition is `True`, or to perform a block of multiple statements, you can write a simple **`if-then`**, multi-statement **`else`** statement. It is simply another variation on the theme of **`if`** statements. By now, you should know that whenever a single statement is allowed, you can write a block of multiple statements enclosed within a **begin** and an **end**.

Syntax

Simple *if-then*, Multi-Statement *else* Statement

Here is the syntax of an **if-then-else** statement that executes a single statement when the Boolean condition is True; otherwise, it performs a block of multiple statements.

```
if ConditionIsTrue then
  DoSomething3
else begin
  DoSomething1;
  DoSomething2;
  ...
end;
```

Example:

```
if LineNumber <= 55 then
  LineNumber := LineNumber + 1
else begin
  LineNumber := 0;
  NextPage;
end;
```

Compound *if-then-else* Statement

The most general of the **if** statements, a compound **if-then-else** statement, allows for two **begin-end** blocks as the execution alternatives. Again, exactly one of those alternatives is guaranteed to execute regardless of the condition. If the condition is True, the block of statements after the **then** keyword is executed. Otherwise, if the condition evaluates to False, the block of statements after the **else** keyword is executed.

Syntax

Multi-Statement *if-then-else* Statement

Here is the syntax of an **if-then-else** statement that performs multiple statements when the condition is True; otherwise, it performs a different set of multiple statements.

```
if ConditionIsTrue then
  begin
    DoSomething1;
    DoSomething2;
    ...
    DoSomethingN;
  end
else
  begin
    DoSomethingElse1;
    DoSomethingElse2;
    ...
```

```
    DoSomethingElseM;
  end;
```

Example:

```
if LineCount > 55 then
  begin
    LineCount := 0;
    PageCount := PageCount + 1;
    PrintPageFooter;
    NewPage;
  end
else
  begin
    LineCount := LineCount + 1;
    PrintLine;
    NewLine;
  end;
```

Note: Never use a semicolon before the **`then`** keyword after the conditional expression or before the **`else`** keyword. A semicolon is a delimiter rather than a terminator in Pascal: it delimits consecutive statements rather than terminating each of them. In other words, a semicolon is required whenever two statements need to be separated to distinguish one from the other. A semicolon does not have to terminate every statement.

In summary, an **`if`** statement is executed such that the logical expression in the **`if`** condition is evaluated first. If the value of the expression is `True`, the part after **`then`** is executed; otherwise, the part after **`else`**, if any, is executed. Either or both of the **`then`** and **`else`** parts may consist of a single statement or a group of statements within a **`begin`** and an **`end`**.

Nesting of *if*s

An **`if`** statement can be nested to an arbitrary level. Listing 6.1 provides an example.

Listing 6.1. A nested `if-then-else` statement.

```
begin
  if PageNumber > 1 then
    if (PageNumber mod 2) <> 0 then
      OddNonFirstPage
    else
      EvenPage
  else
    FirstPage;
end
```

The example in Listing 6.1 illustrates two **`if`** statements. The outer **`if-then-else`** statement begins on line 2 and ends on line 8. The inner **`if-then-else`** begins on line 3 and ends on line 6. The inner **`if`** statement is executed only if the outer **`if`** statement's condition, `PageNumber > 1`, on line 2 is `True`.

When `PageNumber` is greater than 1, the inner statement is allowed to test for its condition on line 3, which is `(PageNumber mod 2) <> 0`, that is, whether `PageNumber` is an odd integer. If `PageNumber` is odd (remember that it cannot be 1 at this point because it has already been ruled out by the outer **`if`** statement), the statement `OddNonFirstPage` on line 4 is executed. If `PageNumber` is even, the `EvenPage` statement on line 6 executes.

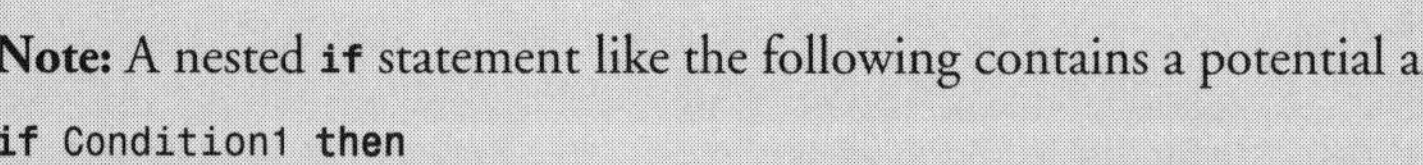

Note: A nested **`if`** statement like the following contains a potential ambiguity:

```
if Condition1 then
  if Condition2 then
    Statement1
  else
    Statement2;
```

It is not clear (other than by way of indentation, which is irrelevant as far as the compiler is concerned) which of the two **`if`** statements is the "owner" of the **`else`** statement. Will `Statement2` execute whenever `Condition1` is `True`, or will it execute when both `Condition1` is `True` and `Condition2` is `False`?

The ambiguity is resolved by the compiler, which treats the preceding example as equivalent to the following:

```
if Condition1 then
 begin
    if Condition2 then
      Statement1
    else
      Statement2;
  end;
```

In other words, the hanging **`else`** clause belongs to the most recently "opened" **`if`** statement that does not yet have an **`else`** part. `Statement2` executes only if both hold: `Condition1` is `True` and `Condition2` resolves to `False`.

Note: Even though **`if`** statements can be nested to an arbitrary level, it is a good idea to keep the nesting to a minimum because, even with careful indentation, it gets hard to figure out to which **`if`** statements the various **`then`** and **`else`** parts belong.

As a rule, never nest more than one level deep. You can always use procedures and functions—something you have been informally using so far and will learn about more formally on Day 9—to flatten the nesting level of a complex `if` statement.

The BUTTON1 Example Program

The BUTTON1 example program illustrates how to use an `if` statement. Figure 6.3 shows how the example program should look on-screen.

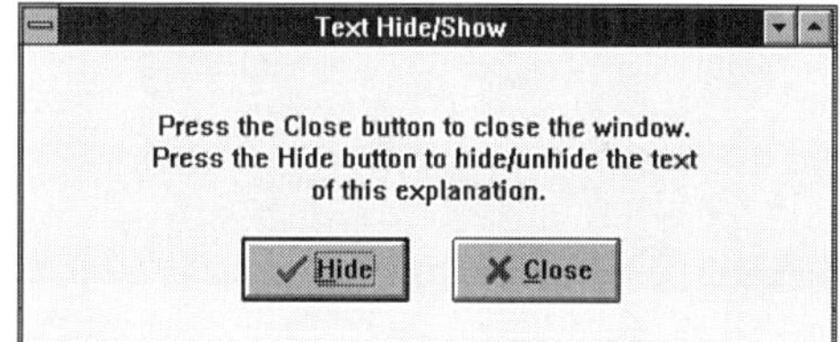

Figure 6.3.
The BUTTON1 example program.

Interactively Creating the BUTTON1 Example Program

To build this simple example, follow these visual construction steps:

1. Create a new project with a blank form.
2. Save the form unit of the project as BUTTON1F.PAS and the project file as BUTTON1.PRJ.
3. Click on the Additional page of the Component Palette.
4. Place two `BitBtn` components on the form, near its bottom edge. They become `BitBtn1` and `BitBtn2`. Change the `Name` property of the buttons to `BtnToggle` and `BtnClose`, respectively.
5. Change the `BtnToggle`'s `Kind` property to `bkOK` and its `Caption` property to `&Hide`.
6. Change the `BtnClose`'s `Kind` property to `bkCancel` and its `Caption` property to `&Close`.
7. From the Standard page of the Component Palette, place a Label component on the form above the buttons. The component is automatically named `Label1`.
8. Change the `Name` property of `Label1` to `LblHint`.
9. Change the `LblHint`'s `AutoSize` property to `False`, and its `Alignment` to `alCenter`.
10. Resize the `LblHint` component on the form so that it fills most of the form's real estate above the buttons.

11. Change the LblHint's `Caption` property to the following user-hint text:
    `Press the Close button to close the window. Press the other button to hide/unhide the text of this explanation.`

Table 6.1 summarizes the component properties of the BUTTON1 example form.

Table 6.1. The properties table for the BUTTON1 program.

Component & Type	Property	Setting
Form	Name	FrmHideShow
	ActiveControl	BtnToggle
	Left	200
	Top	79
	Caption	'Text Hide/Show'
	Color	clYellow
Label	Name	LblHint
	Left	68
	Top	32
	Width	293
	Height	55
	Alignment	taCenter
	AutoSize	False
	WordWrap	True
	Caption	'Press the Close button to close the window. Press the other button to hide/unhide the text of this explanation.'
Hide/Show Button	Name	BtnToggle
	Left	113
	Top	96
	Width	89
	Height	33
	TabOrder	0

Component & Type	Property	Setting
	Kind	bkOk
	Caption	'Hide'
	Default	True
	ModalResult	mrOK
	OnClick	BtnToggleClick
Close Button	Name	BtnClose
	Left	227
	Top	96
	Width	89
	Height	33
	TabOrder	1
	Kind	bkCancel
	Cancel	True
	Caption	'Close'
	ModalResult	mrCancel
	OnClick	BtnCloseClick

Writing Code for the BUTTON1 Example

Here's how to write code for the BUTTON1 example:

1. Double-click the Close button.

   Delphi responds by creating a skeleton for the `BtnCloseClick` event handler. The code editor is brought to the foreground, and the cursor is placed inside the **`begin-end`** pair.

2. Enter the following code inside the `BitBtn2Click` event handler:

   ```
   Close;
   ```

   When you run it, the form closes and the entire program terminates whenever you click the Close button.

3. Click the Form Designer window to bring the form back to the foreground; then double-click the BtnToggle button.

   Delphi responds by creating a skeleton for the `BtnToggleClick` event handler. The code editor is once again brought to the foreground and the cursor is placed inside the **`begin-end`** pair.

4. When in the code editor, enter the following code inside the `BtnToggleClick` event handler generated by Delphi:

```
if Label1.Visible then
  begin
    Label1.Visible := False;
    BitBtn1.Caption := '&Show';
  end
else
  begin
    Label1.Visible := True;
    BitBtn1.Caption := '&Hide';
  end;
```

The preceding code is executed in response to your clicking the BtnToggle button. Clicking the BtnToggle button at run-time toggles the visibility of the user-hint text `LblHint`. The toggling effect is accomplished with an **`if`** statement.

The **`if`** condition checks whether the `LblHint` component is currently visible by evaluating its `Visible` property. If the label is visible, the **`if-then`** clause is executed, thus changing the visibility to `False`, which hides the text. At this time, the caption of the Hide button (`BtnToggle` component) is changed to `'&Show'`.

If the label is already invisible, the **`else`** clause is executed, which changes the `Visible` property of the `LblHint` component to `True` and then changes the `Caption` of the Show button (`BtnToggle` component) to `'&Hide'`.

Running the BUTTON1 Program

Here's how to run the BUTTON1 program:

1. Remember to save the project before running the program.
2. Compile and run the program.
3. Click the Hide button and watch it change to a Show button as the user-hint text disappears. The change is the effect of the **`if-then`** clause of the **`if-then-else`** statement inside the `BtnToggleClick` event handler.
4. Click on the Show button and witness the user-hint text reappear. The reappearing text is the **`if`** statement's **`else`** part at work.
5. To exit the program, click on the Close button.

The *case* Statement

The need for a more concise conditional expression becomes more apparent when you consider selecting not between two but among many alternatives—a multiple-choice selection.

Consider the following nested **if** statement:

```
if Command = 1 then
  DoCommand1
else if Command = 2 then
  DoCommand2
else if Command = 3 then
  DoCommand3
else if Command = 4 then
  DoCommand4
else if Command = 5 then
  DoCommand5;
```

You can simplify the preceding multi-way conditional statement using a **case** construct.

The **case** statement, which is the second form of a conditional control structure available in Object Pascal, selects one of many possible courses of action, depending on the value of a selector expression. A **case** statement appears, similarly to the **if** statement, within executable blocks of statements (between a **begin** and an **end**).

Syntax

Syntax of the *case* Statement

The general syntax of the **case** statement is as follows:

```
case SelectorExpression of
  Value11,
  Value12,
  ...
  Value1N: Statement1;
  Value21,
  Value22,
  ..
  Value2M: Statement2;
  ...
  else
    DefaultStatement1;
    DefaultStatement2;
    ...
    DefaultStatementN;
end;
```

Example:

```
  case ch of
    'a',
    'b',
```

```
    'c': ProcessABC;
    'd',
    'e': begin
           ProcessDandE;
           ProcessDandEFurther;
         end;
    else
        PerformDefaultProcessing;
        MoreDefaultProcessing;
  end;
```

There are numerous specific variations of this general pattern depending on the type of the value list part, complexity of statements within the conditional branches, and the existence or nonexistence of the default clause. Some of these variations are discussed in separate syntax boxes later in this chapter.

A **case** statement starts with a reserved word **case**, followed by the **case** selector, and then followed by the keyword **of**. A **case** selector is an expression yielding an ordinal result—effectively an integer.

The **case** statement is terminated with the reserved word **end**. Inside the **case-end** block, after the **of** keyword, a list of conditionally executed branches is given.

Each branch in a **case** statement starts with a value list. The **case** selector expression can resolve to this list of specific values. Each of the elements of the value list must be a constant whose value is known at compile-time. You cannot place references to variables inside a value list of a **case** branch. The individual values inside a value list are separated with commas, and the value list terminates with a colon.

An executable statement appears after the colon. You know by now that whenever a single statement is expected in an expression, you can substitute a **begin-end** block with zero, one, or more statements inside.

A special branch, called the *default branch*, can be included in a **case** statement. It is introduced with the reserved word **else**. The **else** clause inside a **case** statement guarantees that all possible cases are accounted for; that is, at least one of the branches inside the **case** statement fires no matter what the value of the selector expression is.

Multiple executable statements can appear inside the **else-end** clause of the **case** statement without a need to enclose them within a **begin-end** pair of keywords.

The high-level building-block structure of a **case** statement is illustrated in Figure 6.4.

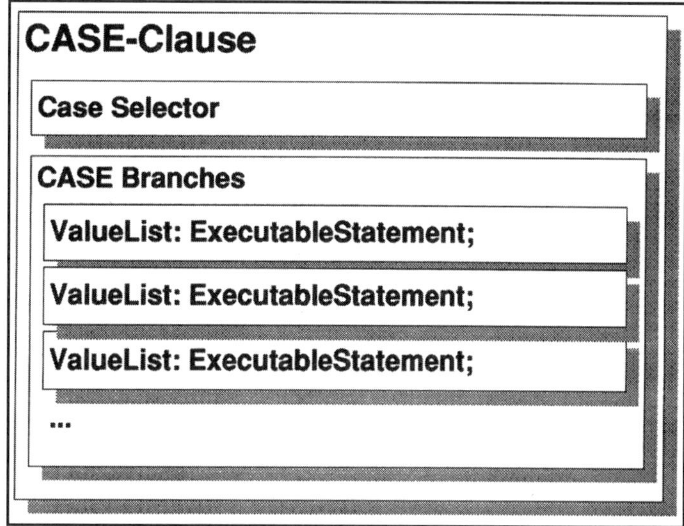

Figure 6.4.
The structure of the `case` *statement.*

Using *case* Statements

A **`case`** statement, like the **`if`** statement, belongs in the executable block portion of a Pascal module—that is, between a **`begin`** and an **`end`** pair of keywords. A **`case`** statement is executed so that the selector expression is evaluated first. Depending on the value of the selector, one of the branches may be taken. Nothing inside the **`case`** statement is executed if the selector expression yields a value for which there is no corresponding branch inside, and no default **`else`** branch.

As an example, the simplified multi-way conditional statement from earlier in this chapter, expressed as a **`case`** statement, looks like the following:

```
case Command of
  1: DoCommand1;
  2: DoCommand2;
  3: DoCoammnd3;
  4: DoCommand4;
end;
```

6

The preceding is a much simpler expression than the original multi-way **`if`** statement for a number of reasons. First, there are fewer keywords to type. Second, the **`case`** statement is "visually cleaner" and easier to maintain. Third, you don't have to worry about the semicolon delimiter rules because *every* branch inside the **`case`** statement is terminated with a semicolon. Fourth, a **`case`** statement is easier to maintain because all you have to do to add another branch is insert a new line. Finally, this expression makes it easier to see which values of the selector expression correspond to which branch being executed; that means fewer possibilities for errors along the road when you need to maintain your code.

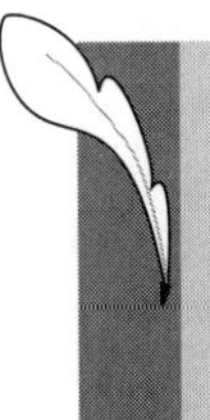

Note: After a particular branch of a **case** statement is executed, the control of execution jumps to the first statement following the **case** block after the **end**, thereby terminating the **case** statement.

This behavior is different from that of the `switch` statement in C/C++. For example, where the control of execution falls sequentially through all the branches until it encounters a `break` statement or the end of the `switch`.

In a Pascal **case** statement, the branches are mutually exclusive: only one can be taken at a time.

Variations of *case* Statements

In the following sections, you examine some of the numerous flavors of **case** statements in more detail.

Simple *case* Statement

Syntax

The general form of a simple **case** statement is as follows:

```
case Condition of
  Value1: Statement1;
  Value2: Statement2;
  ...
  ValueN: StatementN;
end;
```

Example:

```
case Ch of
  'A': HandleValueA;
  'B': HandleValueB;
  'C': HandleValueC;
end;
```

A simple **case** statement has the following characteristics:

- Each value list consists of a single value.
- Each conditional branch consists of a single statement.
- No "default" or **else** clause exists within the **case** block.

Because no **else** clause exists, if the selector expression resolves to a value not explicitly listed in front of one of the conditional branches, nothing inside the **case** statement is executed, and the program control falls through to the next statement immediately following the **case** statement.

Syntax

case Statement with Multi-Statement, Single-Value Branches

The syntax for a **case** statement with single-value but multiple-statement branches is as follows:

```
case Condition of
  Value1:
    begin
      Statement1_1;
      Statement1_2;
      ...
      Statement1_N;
    end;
  Value2:
    begin
      Statement2_1;
      Statement2_2;
      ...
      Statement2_N;
    end;

  ...

  ValueN:
    begin
      Statement1_1;
      Statement1_2;
      ...
      Statement1_N;
    end;
end;
```

Example:

```
case message of
  WM_CREATE:
    begin
      RetrieveDeviceContext;
      RetrieveTextMetrics;
      AllocateMemory;
    end;
  WM_DESTROY:
    begin
      ReleaseDeviceContext;
      ReleaseMemory;
    end;
  WM_PAINT:
    begin
```

```
      DrawLines;
      DrawRectangles;
    end;
end;
```

The preceding syntax again illustrates how you can easily turn a single statement in a Pascal syntax expression into a multi-statement block.

A **case** statement with multi-statement, single-value branches has the following characteristics:

- Each value list consists of a single value.
- Each conditional branch consists of a block of multiple statements enclosed in a **begin-end** pair of keywords.
- No default or **else** clause exists within the **case** block.

You can intermix multiple-statement branches with single-statement branches, but doing so is not recommended. A **case** statement in which all branches are of the same kind is more readable and therefore easier to maintain than one with a mixture of many different kinds of branches.

Note: Avoid multi-statement **case** branches whenever possible. It is always better for the sake of your program's readability to turn the executable statements in each multi-statement branch into a stand-alone procedure (you learn about procedures on Day 9), which you then can call as a single statement inside the **case** branch.

Long **case** statements in which each branch is a large block of potentially complex code are inherently harder to read because the logic of the **case** switch is not readily apparent. It is the conditional switch that's important in a **case** statement from the logical program organization's standpoint.

DO | **DON'T**

DO avoid the temptation to put a lot of code inside **case** branches. You end up putting even more there as you add new functionality to, maintain, and enhance your program, thus reducing the readability of the **case** statement.

DON'T be afraid of creating a new procedure for every branch of a **case** statement.

DO put multiple-statement **case** branches into procedures of their own.

DON'T clutter your **case** statements with a lot of executable code; delegate to subroutines instead.

Syntax

case Statement with Default *else* Clause

The default clause within a **case** statement is introduced with the reserved word **else**.

The syntax for a simple **case** statement with a default **else** clause is as follows:

```
case Selector of
  Value1: Statement1;
  Value2: Statement2;
  ...
  ValueN: StatementN;
  else    DefaultStatement;
end;
```

Example:

```
case Integer of
  1:   I := I + 1;
  2:   I := I - 1;
  3:   I := I*2;
  else I := 0;
end;
```

A simple **case** statement with a default **else** clause has the following characteristics:

- Each value list consists of a single ordinal value.
- Each conditional branch consists of a single statement.
- A default **else** clause appears within the **case** block, which catches all unaccounted for values of the selector.

The only difference with the simple **case** statement is the default clause introduced by the keyword **else**. The default clause ensures that at least one branch executes, no matter to what value the selector expression resolves. The **else** clause effectively catches all possible values of the selector expression that were not specifically accounted for in one of the specific value branches.

Syntax

case Statement with Multi-Valued Branches

The syntax for a **case** statement in which each branch can be entered based on more than one value of the selector expression is as follows:

```
case Condition of
  Value1_1,
  Value1_2,
   ...
  Value1_N: Statement1;
  Value2_1,
   ...
  Value2_N: Statement2;
  ...
```

```
  ValueN_1,
  ...
  ValueN_N: StatementN;
end;
```

Example:

```
case Ch of
  'a','A': ProcessSelectionA;
  'b','B': ProcessSelectionB;
  'c','C': ProcessSelectionC;
end;
```

A **case** statement with multi-valued branches has the following characteristics:

- Each value list consists of one or more values, separated from each other with commas.
- Each conditional branch consists of a single statement or a block of statements enclosed within a **begin-end** pair of keywords.
- There may be, but does not necessarily have to be, a default or **else** clause within the **case** block.

Note: You cannot use strings as **case** value list elements. The values in a value list must be ordinals, which effectively means that they must be equivalent to integers or must directly map to integers.

You can use individual characters, rather than entire strings, because the type `Char` is an ordinal type: characters implicitly have equivalent integer (ASCII) values associated with them. Strings, as sequences of characters, don't.

In a multi-valued **case** branch, the executable statements of the branch are fired if any one of the elements on the value list of that branch matches the result of the selector expression. This is effectively a shorthand for writing a number of single-valued branches with the exact same executable statement on each of them.

Note: A particular value list value can appear only once inside the entire **case** statement. It is an error to have the same value appear multiple times or in value lists of more than one conditional **case** branch.

Syntax

case Statement with Range-Valued Branches

The syntax for a **case** statement in which each branch can be entered based on a range of values of the selector expression is as follows:

```
case Condition of
  Value1Start..Value1End:
    Statement1;
  Value2Start...Value2End:
    Statement2;
  ...
  ValueNStart..ValueNEnd:
    StatementN;
end;
```

Example:

```
case Ch of
  'a'..'z': ProcessLowerCaseLetter;
  'A'..'Z': ProcessUpperCaseLetter;
  '0'..'9': ProcessDigit;
end;
```

A **case** statement in which each value list is defined as a range instead of being given explicitly is useful when the list of values is so large that it becomes impractical to specify all of them individually.

A **case** statement with range-valued branches has the following characteristics:

- Each value list consists of one or more ranges, separated from each other with commas. Individual values can appear also, intermixed with contiguous ranges, and separated with commas from other elements.
- Each conditional branch consists of either a single statement or a **begin-end** block of multiple statements.
- There may be, but does not have to be, a default or **else** clause within the **case** block.

Range of Scalar Values

The syntax for a contiguous range of scalar values is as follows:

```
StartingValue..EndingValue
```

Examples

```
'A'..'Z'
1..100
```

You specify a contiguous range of scalar values for the purposes of building a value list in a **case** block by listing the first value in the range, followed by two periods, and then followed by the ending value in the range.

Note: You can express a noncontiguous range of scalar values as a series of contiguous ranges. You can also list individual values explicitly, separating them from each other with commas. Finally, you can mix and match combinations of ranges and explicit values, separating one from another with a comma.

For example, the range of characters defined as

```
'A'..'E','P','X'..'Z'
```

includes the first five and the last three letters of the alphabet, all uppercase, plus the uppercase letter *P*. The equivalent value list explicitly specifying all the characters in such a noncontiguous range is as follows:

```
'A','B','C','D','E','P','X','Y','Z'
```

Summary of *case* Statements

As you can see from the examples in the preceding sections, many variations of the Pascal **`case`** statement are available to you. Here you have looked at only some of the possible flavors. The simple **`case`** statement is by far the most common one, but you will undoubtedly encounter a great deal of variation in the real world. Sooner or later, you will also want to construct some of the more esoteric variants in your own programs.

Table 6.2 illustrates the criteria that you might use to classify the numerous flavors of **`case`** statements.

Table 6.2. `case` statement classification criteria.

Classification Criterion	Variations
Value List Format	single value
	multiple explicit values
	ranges
	combined ranges and explicit values
Branch Statements	single
	multiple, within **`begin-end`**
Default Clause	no default clause
	a default **`else`** clause

Figure 6.5 illustrates the taxonomy of Pascal **`case`** statements based on the criteria from Table 6.2.

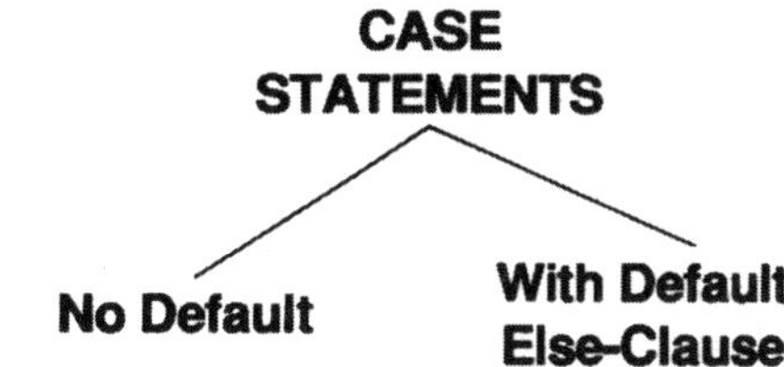

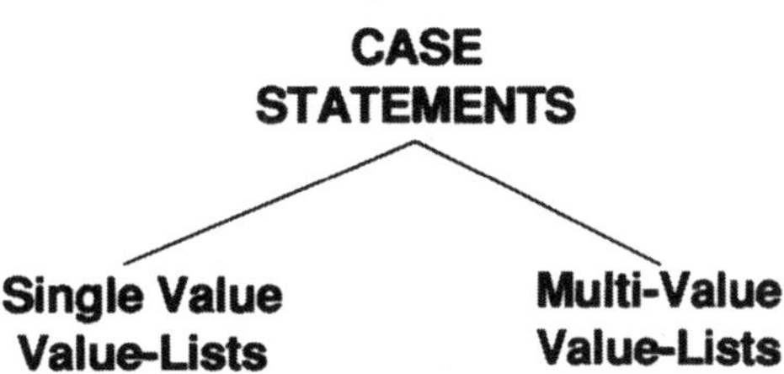

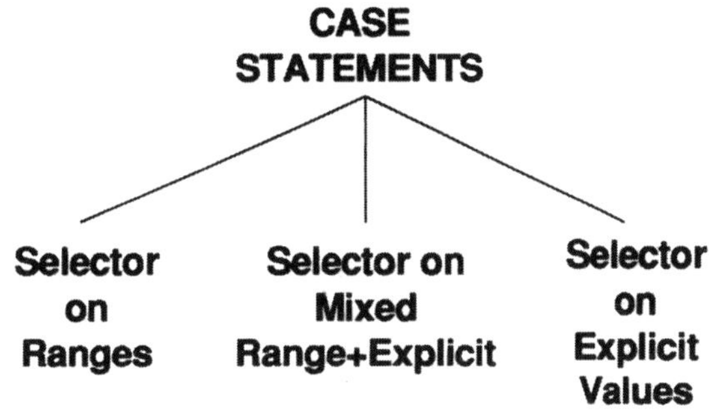

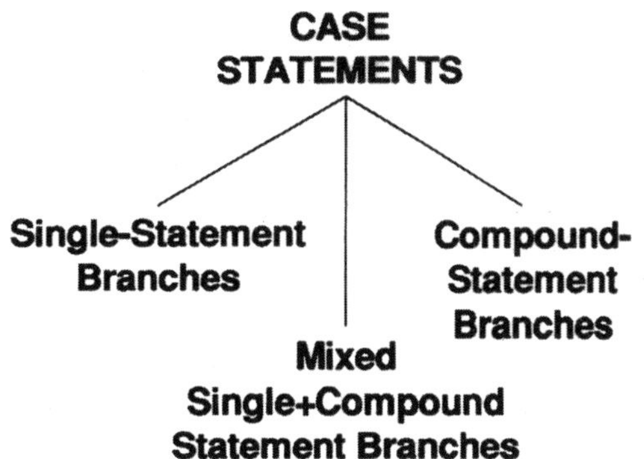

Figure 6.5.
The taxonomy of Pascal case statements.

CASE1 Example Program

You are now going to build a rather complex yet relatively easy-to-create program that, in its first incarnation, illustrates the concepts of using **case** statements discussed here. It also introduces you to some standard Delphi components and shows you a way of hooking components together so that they cooperate smoothly.

The idea behind the CASE1 Yearbook program presented here is simple: to provide a way of entering itemized information on a month-by-month basis. The program can serve as a starting point to building systems as diverse as to-do planners, expense-tracking and reporting systems, appointment calendars, budget and project planners, daily organizers, and so on.

The main form of the CASE1 program is shown in Figure 6.6. Keep in mind that the program presented in today's lesson is not the final product. You have a great deal more to learn about programming in Delphi, and you will find that some of the implementation details change as you learn new programming techniques.

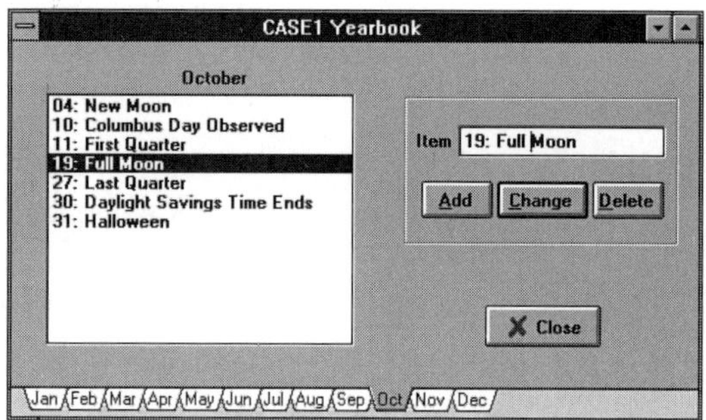

Figure 6.6.
The CASE1 example program's main form.

Visually Developing the CASE1 Program

Here's how to develop the CASE1 program:

1. Create a new project with a blank main form.
2. Save the newly created form unit file in a directory devoted to the CASE1 project under the name MAIN.PAS and the project file as CASE1.PRJ. (From the File menu in Delphi, choose Save Project.)
3. Click in the Form Designer window to select the entire form. In the Object Inspector's component list combo box, `Form1` should be visible.
4. Change the `Caption` property of the form to `CASE1 Yearbook` and the `Name` property of the form to `FormMain`.
5. Place a Notebook component on the form. First, select the Additional page on the Component Palette using the labeled tabs, click the Notebook component icon to select it, and then click on the form at approximately the position where you would like to place it.

Defining the Notebook

Here's how to define the Notebook:

1. With `Notebook1` on the form still selected, select the `Pages` property in the Object Inspector. Double-click on the right of the Pages property name, or click the small button with three dots next to the field to activate the Notebook Editor. The Notebook Editor window, looking like the one in Figure 6.7, pops up.

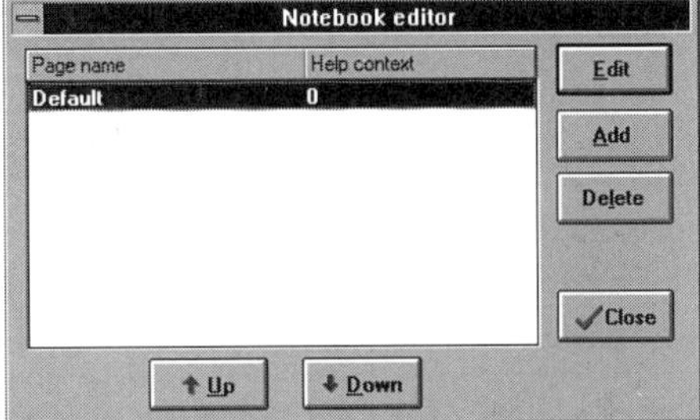

Figure 6.7.
The Notebook Editor—a custom property editor for Notebooks.

   By default, only one page is defined in the Notebook; it is appropriately called `Default`.

2. Select the Default page in the Notebook Editor, and click on the Edit button. The Edit Page dialog box, looking like the one shown in Figure 6.8, pops up.

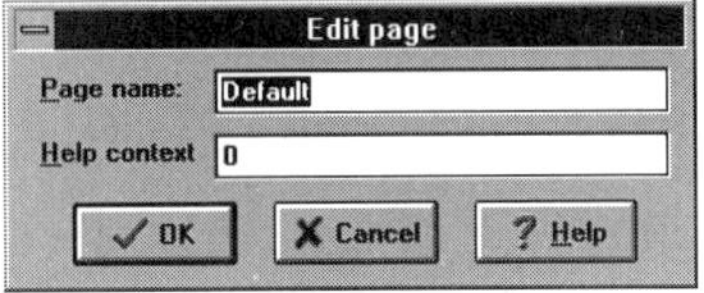

Figure 6.8.
The Edit Page dialog box of the Notebook Editor.

3. Change the `Page name` inside the Edit Page dialog to **`Jan`**. Don't worry about the help context number at this point; simply leave it at 0.
4. Click on the OK button to save the changes to the page properties.
5. Now click on the Add button inside the Notebook Editor to add a new page.

   A blank Page Editor appears this time, enabling you to enter a new page name. Enter **`Feb`**, leaving the help context number at 0.

6. Repeat the preceding step for the remaining pages for the year. Call them **`Mar`**, **`Apr`**, **`May`**, **`Jun`**, **`Jul`**, **`Aug`**, **`Sep`**, **`Oct`**, **`Nov`**, and **`Dec`**, respectively.
7. After you finish adding pages to the Notebook, choose the Close button. The Notebook Editor then closes.

Adding a TabSet

Here's how to add a TabSet:

1. Add a TabSet component to your form in the Form Designer by selecting it from the Additional page of the Component Palette and clicking on the form just below the Notebook you previously placed there.
2. Change the `Alignment` property of the `TabSet1` to `alBottom`. The `TabSet1` component then snaps to the bottom of the form's frame.

Notice that, because you have not defined any tabs yet, the `TabSet1` component you just placed on the form is an empty, light-gray-colored rectangle.

In general, it is possible for you to select the `Tabs` property of the TabSet at this stage, activate the corresponding property editor, and then enter the tab labels that correspond to the Notebook pages. Keep in mind, however, that doing so increases the possibility of creating discrepancies between the TabSet labels and the Notebook pages.

On this project, rather than define the TabSet labels explicitly, you instead synchronize the two components programmatically later. For now, you don't need to worry about the TabSet being empty.

Defining Notebook's Contents

Here's how to define the Notebook's contents:

1. Select the `Notebook1` component in the Form Designer. Make sure that its `ActivePage` property in the Object Inspector is set to `Jan`. If it is not, select the Jan page by clicking on the drop-down arrow button next to the property value field, and select `Jan` from the list.
2. Drop a label component from the Standard page of the Component Palette on top of the Notebook in the Form Designer.
3. Change the `Name` property of the newly placed label from `Label1` to `LblJan` and its `Caption` property to `January`.
4. Drop a `ListBox` component below the label but still on top of the Notebook page. Change its name from `ListBox1` to `LstJan`.
5. In the Form Designer, select the `Notebook1` as a whole again. Switch the `ActivePage` property to `Feb`. All of the components inside the Notebook should disappear, and you should again see a blank Notebook page.
6. Repeat the preceding steps for the February page; that is, drop a label and name it `LblFeb`; also drop a `ListBox` and name it `LstFeb`.
7. Change the `LblFeb`'s `Caption` property to `February`.

Because this process is getting a bit tedious, you are now going to use another, faster method to place the components on the remaining pages of the Notebook. What you are essentially trying to accomplish here is a way of copying the same set of components onto every Notebook page. Instead of adding the components individually from the Palette, you copy all of them from one Notebook page to the next.

1. Select the two components from the Feb page by holding down the Shift key while you click both of the components one by one.
2. After you select both of them, choose Copy from Delphi's Edit menu.

   Choosing Copy places the selected group of components onto the Windows Clipboard.
3. Select the `Notebook1` again. Change the `ActivePage` property to `Mar`.

   The Feb page components disappear, and the blank Mar page appears.
4. With `Notebook1` still selected on the form, choose Paste from Delphi's Edit menu.

   The components you copied from the Feb page are then pasted into the Mar page.
5. Click outside the Notebook but inside the Form Designer window to deselect the newly pasted components as a group.
6. Select the label property and change its name to `LblMar` and its `Caption` to `March`.
7. Select the `ListBox` and change its `Name` property to `LstMar`.
8. Don't forget to save the project frequently. From the File menu, choose Save Project.

You are now done defining the contents of the Notebook. Now is the time to ensure that

- Tabs are visible in the TabSet component at run-time
- The Notebook pages are synchronized with tabs so that the appropriate month's page shows up when you select a particular tab

Synchronizing Tabs with Notebooks

The issue of synchronizing the Notebook pages with the current state of a TabSet component will undoubtedly arise frequently in your programming endeavors. Notebooks and TabSets are natural complements of each other, and you will often place them both, as a cooperating pair, on your forms.

As it stands, not only is the CASE1 program's TabSet not synchronized with the Notebook, but it is also missing its tabs. Now you are going to rectify both of these problems.

1. Select the `TabSet1` component in the Form Designer.
2. Click the Events page tab in the Object Inspector.

   The Events page then appears in the Object Inspector.

3. Double-click the right-hand column next to the `OnClick` event property.

   Delphi creates the `TabSet1Click` method in the code editor and brings the editor to the front so that you can add to the contents of the method.

4. Inside the newly generated `TabSet1Click`, enter the following code:

   ```
   Notebook1.PageIndex := TabSet1.TabIndex;
   ```

   This code assigns the value of the `TabIndex` property of `TabSet1` to the `PageIndex` property of `Notebook1`. This is all you need to do to synchronize the Notebook page with the TabSet's current tab at run-time.

Now, whenever the user clicks on a tab inside the `TabSet1` control to select it, the action results in the Notebook switching to the corresponding page.

You still need to set the initial conditions so that tabs are available in the TabSet, however, and so that the TabSet is initially synchronized with the Notebook when the program starts. Follow these steps:

1. Click on the free area of the form inside the Form Designer to select the form itself, or select `FormMain` directly in the drop-down combo box at the top of the Object Inspector's window.

Note: You can press the Esc key repetitively inside the Form Designer to select the parent or container of the currently selected component. After you press Esc a sufficient number of times, the ultimate parent of all the form's components, the form itself, is selected.

2. Click the `Events` tab inside the Object Inspector to select the Events page.

3. Double-click in the blank area in the right-hand column to the right of the `OnCreate` event name.

   Another method, `TFormMain.FormCreate`, is generated for you.

4. Enter the following two lines of code inside the newly generated procedure in the Code Editor window:

   ```
   TabSet1.Tabs := Notebook1.Pages;
    TabSet1.TabIndex := NoteBook1.PageIndex;
   ```

   The first line of code here copies the contents of the `Notebook1` `Pages` property into the `TabSet1` `Tabs` property. This is all you need to do to ensure that the actual tab labels of the `TabSet1` component exactly correspond to the names you have given to the `Notebook1` pages.

The second line of code you entered here ensures that no matter which page you selected at design time as the `ActivePage` of the `Notebook1`, the corresponding tab inside `TabSet1` is selected also.

It is now up to you to decide which month inside the Notebook you want to have selected initially. You can control that selection by setting the `ActivePage` property of the `Notebook1` inside the Object Inspector. Regardless of the design choice you make, the preceding code always ensures that the `TabSet1` initially displays properly when you run the program.

The three lines of code you have entered so far are all that you need to ensure synchronization between the Notebook and the TabSet components. Note that this technique will also work even if you later decide to add or delete Notebook pages: the corresponding TabSet is updated automatically.

Adding More Controls to the Form

Now is the time to start controlling the contents of the 12 "monthly" list boxes you have placed inside the Notebook.

1. Drop a `GroupBox` component from the Standard page of the Delphi Component Palette onto the form, outside the area occupied by the Notebook.

   Delphi names the box `GroupBox1` as it is being placed on the form.
2. Drop an Edit control from the Standard Palette page inside the `GroupBox1` group box. Change its `Name` property to `EditItem`, and set its `Text` property to blank.
3. Drop a `Label` control from the same Palette page in front of the `EditItem` control, also inside the group box. Change the label's `Caption` property to `Item:`.

   Now you are going to add three buttons in a row inside the group box already containing the label and the edit box.
4. While holding down the Shift key, click on the button icon on the Standard page of the Component Palette.

   In addition to the component icon's button looking "pressed," a dotted focus-like rectangle appears around the icon, indicating a special mode for the mouse cursor. In this special mode, you can place several components in succession without having to explicitly select the desired component from the Palette each time.
5. Release the Shift button. Click three times, one by one, inside the group box on the form.

   Each time you click, a button is deposited on the form. Don't worry about visual placement of these buttons or about their proper alignment at this point. You can always adjust these visual characteristics later.

   Notice that the button component icon on the Palette is not automatically deselected.

6. After your third click, stop. Your mouse cursor is still loaded, but you don't need any more buttons. You have to explicitly deselect the currently active component by clicking the leftmost arrow icon on the Delphi Component Palette. Your mouse will again work as a regular pointing device.
7. Deselect the button component now.

You have thus placed three buttons in a row inside the group box on your form. Delphi names the buttons `Button1`, `Button2`, and `Button3`. Change their properties now as follows:

1. Change the `Name` of `Button1` to `BtnAdd` and its `Caption` to `&Add`.
2. Change the `Name` of `Button2` to `BtnChange` and its `Caption` property to `&Change`.
3. Change the `Name` of `Button3` to `BtnDelete` and its `Caption` to `&Delete`.

As the final step of designing the visual appearance of the main form, follow these steps:

1. Drop a `BitBtn` component on a free area of the form outside both the Notebook and the group box.
2. Change the `Name` property of the just added `BitBtn1` to `BtnClose`, its `Kind` property to `bkCancel`, and its `Caption` to `Close`.

   Your form should now appear inside the Form Designer approximately as shown in Figure 6.9.

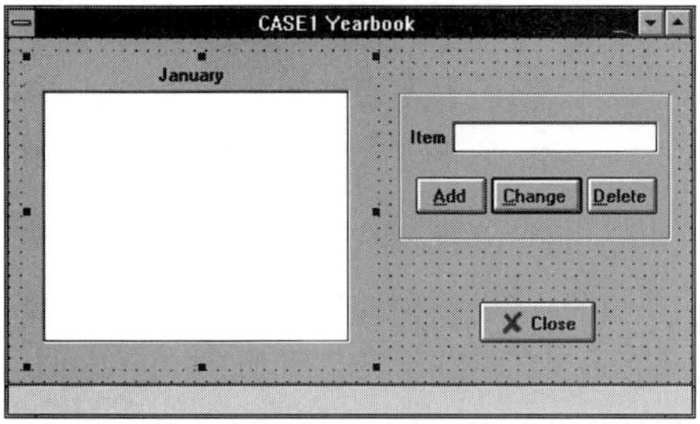

Figure 6.9.
The completed main form of the CASE1 example program, as shown inside the Form Designer.

Adding Close Button Behavior

Here's how to add functionality to the Close button:

1. Double-click the most recently added BtnClose button inside the Form Designer to generate an `OnClick` event handler, which Delphi calls `FormMain.BtnCloseDblClick`.
2. Inside the code editor, between the **begin** and the **end** of the `BtnCloseDblClick` event handler, enter the following line:

```
Close;
```

This code adds specific behavior to the form; namely, when the user clicks on the Close button, the form closes and the program terminates.

Adding the *OnClick* Event Handler for the Add Button

Here's how to add an event handler for the Add button:

1. Double-click the Add button (`BtnAdd`) on the form.
2. Enter the code shown in Listing 6.2 inside the generated `TFormMain.BtnAddClick` event-handler method.

Listing 6.2. `OnClick` event handler for the Add button.

```
1: procedure TFormMain.BtnAddClick(Sender: TObject);
 2: begin
 3:   if EditItem.Text <> '' then begin
 4:     case (Notebook1.PageIndex+1) of
 5:       1:  LstJan.Items.Add(EditItem.Text);
 6:       2:  LstFeb.Items.Add(EditItem.Text);
 7:       3:  LstMar.Items.Add(EditItem.Text);
 8:       4:  LstApr.Items.Add(EditItem.Text);
 9:       5:  LstMay.Items.Add(EditItem.Text);
10:       6:  LstJun.Items.Add(EditItem.Text);
11:       7:  LstJul.Items.Add(EditItem.Text);
12:       8:  LstAug.Items.Add(EditItem.Text);
13:       9:  LstSep.Items.Add(EditItem.Text);
14:       10: LstOct.Items.Add(EditItem.Text);
15:       11: LstNov.Items.Add(EditItem.Text);
16:       12: LstDec.Items.Add(EditItem.Text);
17:     end;
18:     EditItem.Text := '';
19:   end;
20: end;
```

The code you entered inside the `BtnAddClick` subroutine, shown in Listing 6.2, causes the contents of the `EditItem` edit box—a character string—to be added to the list box inside the particular `Notebook1` page that is currently active and visible.

Only lines 1, 2, and 20 of Listing 6.2 are automatically generated by Delphi when you double-click the Add button. You must enter lines 3 through 19 yourself.

Inside the **`begin-end`** block of the `BtnAddClick` procedure are two conditional selection constructs, one nested in the other. Line 3 begins an **`if`** statement, whose scope—enclosed inside a **`begin-end`** pair—reaches the end of the procedure on line 19.

The **`if`** condition tests whether the `Text` property of the `EditItem` is not an empty string (shown on line 3 as a pair of apostrophes or two single quotation marks, not one double quotation mark character) or, in other words, the **`if`** condition evaluates to `True` if something is inside the `EditItem` edit box.

If the user enters something in the edit box, the contents of the **if-then** clause—a 12-way **case** selection statement spanning lines 4 through 17—are executed. This statement is the **case** statement that is meant to illustrate today's lesson.

The purpose of the **case** statement starting on line 4 is to select the appropriate list box control, one of the 12 list boxes inside the `Notebook1`. Once the proper list box is identified, the string contained in the `EditItem`'s `Text` property is added to it.

The **case** selector expression on line 4 retrieves the index of the currently selected page of the `Notebook1` component. The Notebook page indexes are zero-based; that is, the first page has an index of zero; the next, one; and so on. Because months in a year are more commonly numbered starting with one, 1 is added to the Notebook page index to make the **case** statement branches more understandable.

Inside the **case** statement are 12 executable branches indexed by the 12 possible values of the selector. You don't need a catchall **else** clause because the Notebook has only 12 pages and you don't expect any value outside the range 1–12 for the **case** selector. Each branch of the **case** statement represents an action, only one of which is triggered by the user's clicking on the Add button.

Each executable branch of the **case** statement is a long expression essentially inserting the string value stored inside the edit box into the appropriate list box. Which list box it is depends on the value of the **case** selector expression, which in turn depends on which is the currently active Notebook page.

Now look at one of the almost identical branch statements:

```
LstMar.Items.Add(EditItem.Text);
```

You can break out the preceding statement into its individual pieces as follows:

Expression	*Meaning*
`LstMar.Items`	Identifies the list of items of interest.
`.Add`	The action to be performed on it.
`(`	A list of parameters for the action begins.
`EditItem.Text`	The parameter for the action.
`)`	End of list of parameters.
`;`	End of the entire statement.

Table 6.3 explains each of the pieces of this statement one by one.

Table 6.3. The syntactic elements of the statement on line 7 of Listing 6.2.

Element	Description
`LstMar`	This element identifies the specific list box, the `LstMar` box contained on the March page of the Notebook.
.	The period separates the object you are referring to (`LstMar` list box) from the name of one of its properties you want to gain access to—`Items` property.
`Items`	This element is the name of the property of the `LstMar` list box that you need to access. This property of the list box is a collection of strings.
.	The period separates the name of the object you are referring to—the `Items` collection of a list box—from the following method name.
`Add`	This element is the name of the method, or action, you want to have invoked on the object identified before the dot—the collection of `Items`. The action handler takes one string parameter.
(	The left parenthesis opens a list of parameters that you want to pass to the `Add` action handler. In this case, there is only one parameter: `EditItem.Text`.
`EditItem`	The `EditItem` is the name of the component from which you want to read the `Text` value.
.	The dot separates the name of the object you are referring to—the `EditItem` component in this case—from the name of its property you want to access.
`Text`	`Text` is the name of the property of `EditItem` that you are interested in here. The `Text` property contains whatever was entered in the edit box.
)	The right parenthesis closes the parameter list for the `Add` method/action.
;	The semicolon terminates this branch of the **`case`** statement.

You have now finished constructing the example CASE1 program.

Note that the Change and Delete buttons currently have no functionality; no code is attached to either of these buttons. The lack of code is deliberate at this point because you need to learn additional Object Pascal techniques to make these buttons work. You will enhance this program later and add the missing functionality for those buttons.

Running the Example Program

Finally, here's how to run the example program:

1. Make sure you save the project before attempting to run it.
2. Run the program and verify for yourself that the tab labels indeed show up as expected and, when you select a different tab, the Notebook switches to the corresponding page.

   The synchronization of the Notebook pages with the tabs is the effect of the `OnClick` handler of the `TabSet1` component: the `TabSet1Click` method of the main form.
3. Enter some text in the Item edit field, and then click on the Add button.

   The text then goes to the currently active list box as expected. This behavior is the result of the magic of the Add button's `OnClick` event handler: the `BtnAddClick` method of the main form.
4. To terminate the program, click on the Close button.

   The code inside the `OnClick` event handler for the `BtnClose` button component is executed, closing the main form and thereby terminating the program.

Advanced Cases

A **`case`** statement is a powerful and convenient programming construct, but it has both strengths and limitations. It is important to know the limitations when you are considering using **`case`** statements in your programs.

Ordinals and Types

The selector expression in a **`case`** statement must evaluate to an ordinal type. Therefore, you cannot use real numbers, strings, or any other structured data type in value lists of **`case`** statements.

The selector expression must evaluate to a set of values that can be arranged in order from the smallest to the largest, and these values must map one to one onto ordinary integers.

Strings and *case* Statements

Sooner or later, you will run into a situation in which you might want to use a string as a selector value for a multi-way selection statement.

Consider, for example, an old-fashioned command-line interface, still useful even in the age of graphical displays. Commands are read in the form of character strings, and actions are performed based on the command input. Because strings are more complex than ordinal data

types, you cannot use a **case** statement to directly dispatch an action based on the command the user enters. One workaround is to use a set of cascading **if** statements, as follows:

```
if Command='DIR' then
  PerformDIRCommand
else if Command='COPY' then
  PerformCOPYCommand
else if Command='CHDIR' then
  PerformCHDIRCommand
else ...
```

A possible drawback of such an approach is that the literal command strings are deeply embedded in the code, making the program harder to maintain and change.

Another approach often used in such a situation is converting the strings to an ordinal data type, such as the `Integer` type, by means of a string-lookup table. Every time a user enters a command, the table is searched for a matching string, and an ordinal value is returned. The ordinal value can then be used to index a regular **case** statement.

Summary

Today's lesson introduced you to the Object Pascal conditional control structures. You learned about the following:

- Compound statements enclosed within a **begin** and an **end** can be substituted for a simple statement inside any executable block.
- **if-then** and **if-then-else** statements are used to control the path of program execution.
- A **case** statement is a generic switch allowing for multi-way selection of execution paths.
- **if** statements are controlled by conditional Boolean expressions.
- Unlike **if** statements, **case** statements are controlled by ordinal type expressions.
- A cascading **if** statement can be used in place of a **case** statement for string-based selection.
- Notebook components can be easily coupled to a TabSet to provide the functionality of multi-page tabbed forms.

Q&A

Q What is the best order in which to structure if-then-else statements? Should the if-then clause or the else part contain error-handling?

A Get into the habit of writing the normal execution path first. Think: "This is what is going to happen most of the time." Only then, after you have covered the nominal cases, think about exceptions and error conditions.

Q What are the rules of indentation for `if-then-else` statements?

A One thing you should keep in mind is that you are writing your programs for at least two distinct audiences. You write your programs first and foremost for people to read, even if it means just yourself. That's why you need indentation: to make the logical structures in your programs easily recognizable. The other audience is the computer on which the program will be run. The rules of indentation are for people, not for the computer. The Pascal compiler does not care how you indented your **`if`** statement. Having said that, the typical indentation for the various flavors of **`if`** and **`case`** statements is shown in their respective syntax boxes throughout today's lesson.

Q What is the best order in which to put branches inside a `case` statement?

A First of all, keep in mind that this issue is really a minor optimization issue. Don't even think of optimizations like this before your program is done; you are wasting your efforts.

The order of the branches affects the execution of **`case`** statements in two ways. First, the branch conditions near the top of the **`case`** statement are evaluated more often than those near the end. It is therefore a good idea for performance reasons to move to the top the branches that are likely to fire most often. Second, Delphi Pascal is capable of optimizing the **`case`** statements so that the number of calculations being performed for the **`case`** branches is minimized. Therefore, the value lists must be given in properly sorted, ascending order.

Do keep in mind, however, that you should not worry about this issue until late in the development process; you need to experiment in a real-life setting to find out the ordering of branches that gives you best results. Besides, **`case`** statements usually are not the constructs that you want to optimize first. Loops, about which you learn in tomorrow's lesson, are.

Q I am confused about the Pascal delimiter rules! When should and when shouldn't I put the semicolon after a statement?

A As a general rule, always put in a semicolon. Use it as a statement terminator most of the time, and put it after every statement.

You don't put in the semicolon just before the **`else`** keyword inside **`if`** statements specifically. Don't put it after expressions, such as Boolean conditions or **`case`**-selector statements.

Many beginner Pascal programmers worry about making sure that they don't have a semicolon just before the **`end`** in a compound statement. They worry unnecessarily. Just because you don't have to place a semicolon there does not mean that you should

not do so. Doing so makes it easier to maintain your code later. If you simply put the semicolon after every statement whenever possible, when you later insert new statements after that, you don't need to remember about adding the missing semicolon.

Workshop

The Workshop provides quiz questions to help you solidify your understanding of the material covered and exercises to provide you with experience in using what you've learned. Try to understand the quiz and exercise answers before continuing on to the next day's lesson. Answers are provided in an appendix at the end of this book.

Quiz

1. True or False? You can use numbers only as selectors in **case** statements.
2. What's wrong with the following **if-then-else** construct?

```
if NumberOfHours > 37.5 then
  AmountEarned :=
    (NumberOfHours - 37.5)*HourlyRate*1.5 +
    37.5*HourlyRate;
else
  AmountEarned := NumberOfHours*HourlyRate;
```

3. True or False? All possible values of the selector expression must be listed inside the **case** statement.
4. True or False? A multi-valued branch in a **case** statement can contain zero, one, or multiple statements.
5. True or False? All values in a **case** statement must be unique. None may be repeated in more than one branch.

6

Exercises

1. Write a Delphi program that reads user input and displays (1) `'CHARACTER'` if the letter entered is a lowercase character, (2) `'CAPITAL'` if the character entered is a capital letter, and (3) `'DIGIT'` if the character entered is in the range `0`–`9`.
2. Write a Delphi program for payroll calculation. The main form provides two edit boxes: one for entering the number of hours worked and the other for the hourly rate. The program should compute and display the amount earned. Any of the overtime hours in excess of 37.5 should be computed at 1.5 times the normal hourly rate.

Loops

Creating loops is one of the most important aspects of programming. Dull, repetitive tasks are best left for computers to do, and looping structures enable you to tell the machine how to do them.

In today's lesson, you learn about the following topics related to loops:

- The characteristics of all looping structures
- The **`while-do`** loop construct
- The **`repeat-until`** loop construct
- The **`for-to-do`** and **`for-downto-do`** counted loops
- Advanced custom-looping structures
- How to break out of a loop
- How to skip some loop iterations

In addition, this lesson briefly covers array structures and text file input/output—both important elements of a programmer's tool set.

Loop Theory

Looping structures allow for repeated execution of blocks of statements. Repetition is one of the most commonly used constructs, yet one of the most complex aspects of programming. The need to repeat a set of actions arises frequently, and Object Pascal provides no fewer than three different control constructs that deal with repetition: **`while`**, **`repeat`**, and **`for`** loops.

As you will see later in today's lesson, it is also possible to extend the built-in custom looping constructs with *ad hoc* created substitutes, with somewhat different characteristics.

NEW TERM *Loop* is a term used informally to describe a programming structure that causes the program to execute a block of code repeatedly.

All looping constructs have certain characteristics in common. The issues that you must deal with in any kind of loop are as follows:

- Loop condition
- Loop initialization
- Loop increment
- Loop termination
- Loop body

The *loop condition* is the controlling factor for the repetition: the condition determines whether to continue iteration through the loop or whether to terminate the loop. The condition is evaluated on every iteration. Different kinds of loops differ in details as to when the condition is evaluated: either at the very beginning of every iteration (`while` and `for` loops), at the end (`repeat` loop), or somewhere in the middle (custom loops). If the condition still holds, another loop iteration is performed. If the condition no longer holds, the loop is terminated.

Before the loop condition can be evaluated, the loop has to be initialized. You have to ensure that the loop behaves as expected, and doing so requires initializing any iteration counters, exit conditions, and so on, to ensure that the loop behaves predictably.

Every time through the loop, something must happen: a value of a data item must be either incremented, decremented, or otherwise modified; an event must be triggered, and so on; otherwise, the loop condition never changes its value and the loop never terminates. Typically, an integer loop counter variable is maintained and incremented every time through the loop, but other variations are possible. The important point is that *something* must be done inside it to ensure that the loop will terminate.

The fact that you need to ensure that the loop will terminate does not necessarily mean that you must know in advance, before the program is executed, how many times the loop is to iterate. Often you will not know the number of iterations in advance, because the loop condition will depend on some value or values computed at run-time. You have to make sure, however, that when executed, the loop has a way of terminating in every possible case.

Finally, the whole purpose of setting up a loop in the first place is to perform some actions repetitively. The executable statements that are to be performed by the loop are called the *loop body*.

NEW TERM An *infinite loop* is a loop that never terminates: it just keeps iterating. Typically, an infinite loop is an indication of a programming error. Infinite loops often manifest themselves in such a way that the computer *hangs*: it stops responding to the user input and appears to do nothing. Remember always to ensure that every loop you create in your program is guaranteed to terminate at some point.

The *while* Loop

The `while` loop is one of the most versatile programming constructs. You can set it up to emulate many other constructs, including all other standard Pascal loops. It is the preferred kind of loop. You should use it "by default" and take advantage of the other looping constructs only when you have a good reason to do so.

The *while* Loop's Syntax

A **while** loop is one of the most versatile programming tools—definitely a must-know for every programmer.

Syntax

while Loop

The general syntax for a **while** loop is as follows:

```
while ConditionIsTrue do
  Statement;
```

Example:

```
while PageNo < MaxPages do
  PrintPage(PageNo);
```

Syntax

Multi-Statement *while* Loop

The syntax for a **while** loop containing multiple statements is as follows:

```
while ConditionIsTrue do
  begin
    Statement1;
    Statement2;
    ...
    StatementN;
  end;
```

Example:

```
while not EndOfFile(CustomerFile) do
  begin
    UpdateCustomerInfo(CustomerFile);
    PrintCustomerReport(CustomerFile);
    NextRecord(CustomerFile);
  end;
```

A **while** loop starts with the Pascal reserved word **while**. After you give the **while** keyword, you give the loop conditional expression. The expression can be any Boolean expression, including

- A simple Boolean variable or function (you learn more about functions on Day 9). For example,

  ```
  while Continue do ...
  ```

- A relational expression. For example,

  ```
  while (PageNo > 10) do ...
  ```

- A combination of lower-level Boolean expressions joined with **or** or **and** operators. For example,

  ```
  while (PageNo > 0) and (PageNo <= MaxPages) do ...
  ```

Following the Boolean loop condition is the Pascal reserved word **do**. The **while-do** expression constitutes the loop's header.

The loop contents, also called the *body* of the loop, which may be either a single executable statement or a block of statements enclosed within a **begin-end** pair, follow after the header.

The structure of a **while-do** loop is illustrated in Figure 7.1.

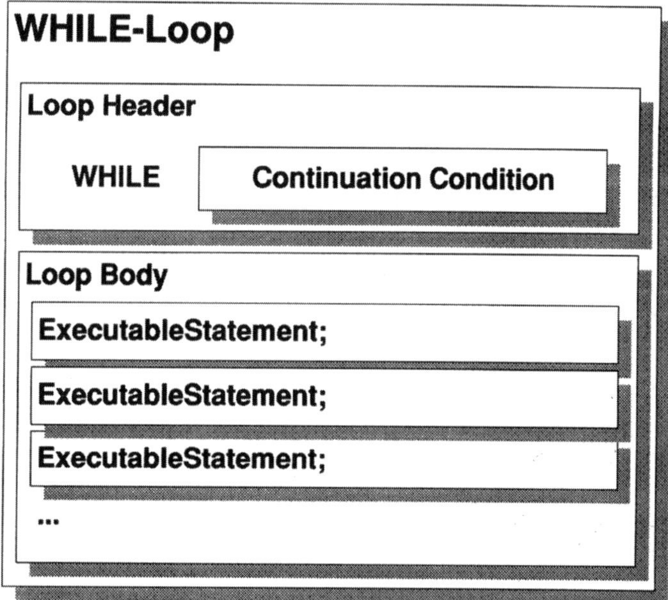

Figure 7.1.
The structure of a `while-do` *loop.*

Using *while* Loops

A **while** loop, like all other looping constructs, belongs in the executable section of a block—that is, between a **begin** and an **end** pair of keywords.

When the program's execution control arrives at the loop's header, the loop condition is evaluated. If the loop condition is True, the statement or statements inside the loop are executed next. If the loop condition is False, the control of execution falls through to the next statement following the loop.

7

Every time, before the loop body is executed, the loop condition is evaluated, and a decision is made whether to continue iterating or whether to terminate the loop.

Notice that the condition of a **while** loop is evaluated at the beginning of every iteration. Consequently, it is possible for a **while** loop not to iterate through its contents at all, if the loop condition evaluates to False at the beginning, before the loop ever executes.

A **while** loop does not have to "know" in advance how many iterations it will execute. The loop condition is tested once at the beginning of every iteration, and the loop may continue until it is finished; that is, while there is no error, as long as the user wants to continue to perform an action, while there are still more customer records to process, and so on.

Reading Text Files

To better understand the concept, you build a sample application, WHILE1, which demonstrates one of the most common uses of **while** loops: reading a text file line by line.

A `File`, in general, and a `Text` file, in particular, are built-in Object Pascal data types in addition to the ones already introduced on Day 4.

NEW TERM A *file* is an external data entity, typically residing on disk.

NEW TERM A *File* is a Pascal type, instances of which can be associated with an external file entity. Once the association is made and the file is said to be opened, the data it contains can be processed inside your Pascal programs by referring to the open file variable.

NEW TERM A *text file* is a special kind of file, containing readable text. A text file consists of sequences of characters, divided into lines.

NEW TERM A *Text* data type is a Pascal type referring to text files on disk. To be able to process, or read and write text files inside your Delphi programs, you can associate them with variables of type `Text`.

NEW TERM A *binary file* is any other kind of file that is not specifically text. A binary file may contain an arbitrary sequence of data elements of any kind. Binary files are associated with variables of type `File`.

You should be familiar with the idea of a text file by now, because any Pascal source code file is a text file. You probably have edited plain text files with Windows Notepad or a similar editor before, too.

So that you can access a text file from your Delphi programs, you need to open the file first. Opening files has traditionally been a two-step process in Pascal:

1. You need to call the `Assign` standard procedure with the `Text` file variable and the operating system filename as its parameters. For example,

   ```
   Assign(ATextFile,'while1.pas');
   ```

   "assigns" the external file `'while1.pas'` to the file variable called `ATextFile`.

   Calling a procedure means simply listing its name inside the executable statement block. *Passing parameters* means listing the values of the parameters inside parentheses after the procedure name. You learn more about these concepts on Day 9.

2. This step depends on what you need to do with the file. You can basically do three things with a text file:

   a. Read from it

   b. Write to it

   c. Append to it

   You have to decide what you're going to do at the time you are opening the file: once it is open, it is available exclusively for one of these three operations, and you cannot change its mode on the fly.

   Nothing, of course, prevents you from first opening a text file for reading, closing it after you read from it, and then reopening it for writing or appending, but these modes of operation on text files are mutually exclusive.

2a. To open a text file for reading, you call the `Reset` standard procedure, passing it the file variable you assigned in the preceding step. For example,

   ```
   Reset(ATextFile);
   ```

   opens the `ATextFile` variable for reading.

   There is also a concept of position within a file when you read from it. Upon a `Reset`, the file variable points at the beginning of the file.

2b. To open a text file for writing, you call the `Rewrite` standard procedure, passing it the file variable you assigned in step 1. For example,

   ```
   Rewrite(ATextFile);
   ```

   prepares the file `ATextFile` for subsequent writing.

   Be forewarned that calling `Rewrite` has potentially destructive effects: if the file referred to by the file variable exists, its contents are wiped out, or *truncated*, and the resulting file has the length of zero bytes, ready to be written to. `Rewrite` does not warn you in any way if the file already exists.

2c. To open a text file for appending, you call the `Append` standard procedure, passing it the file variable you assigned in step 1. For example,

   ```
   Append(ATextFile);
   ```

prepares the file ATextFile for subsequent writing in such a way that new text is appended at the end of any existing lines.

Calling Append is clearly not as invasive as calling Rewrite. With Append, the original contents of the file are preserved. New text lines are successively added to the end of the file. Remember that using Append just keeps growing the file. You may easily run out of available disk space if you just keep appending to a transaction log or a similar file!

After you have successfully opened a text file, you need to add a corresponding Close statement to close it after you are done with it. For example,

```
Close(ATextFile);
```

closes the file you have previously opened with an Assign+Reset or an Assign+Rewrite pair.

Note: It is always a good idea to write the Close statement as soon as you finish writing Assign and Reset, or Assign and Rewrite. Always think in pairs: if something is opened, you must close it. Also, keep the opening and closing of a file to within a single **begin-end** block so that the file's life span is clearly visible in one screenful of code.

So far, you have taken steps to open a text file and ensure that it closes properly. Now is the time to do something with it. The most typical operation you would want to do with a text file is to read its entire contents into memory, sequentially, line by line; do some processing on the text; and write it back to the same or a different text file.

A **while** loop becomes indispensable at this point. Here is a fragment of code that iterates through all lines in a text file ATextFile, reading them one by one into a String variable ATextLine:

```
while not Eof(ATextFile) do
  begin
    ReadLn(ATextFile,ATextLine);
    {Do something to the text line here.}
  end;
```

The loop condition on the first line says:

```
not Eof(ATextFile)
```

This line is a call to another file-related standard, built-in routine: a Boolean function Eof, which tests for the end-of-file condition. Remember, you need to ensure that the **while** loop terminates at some point. In this case, the loop terminates whenever the Eof function returns True; that is, you are at the end of file and there is nothing more to read from it. The **not** operator reverses the `Eof` result so that it can serve as the continuation condition for the loop: you keep reading the file but you never reach the end.

You may also recall that you need to ensure that something is done inside the loop to change the loop-continuation condition eventually; otherwise, the loop will never terminate.

In this case, the call to `ReadLn` does the trick, and you don't need to do anything special. The statement

```
ReadLn(ATextFile,ATextLine);
```

reads the current line from the text file `ATextFile` into the supplied `String` variable `ATextLine`, moving the position within the file to the next line, if any. *Moving the position* eventually ensures that the end-of-file condition becomes True.

`ReadLn` is yet another built-in routine whose purpose is to read a single line of text from the text file referenced by `ReadLn`'s first parameter (`ATextFile`, in this case). `ReadLn` not only reads the line of text into the variable specified as its second parameter, but also moves the position within the file so that it points to the next, as yet unread, line of text. This way, by repetitively calling `ReadLn` on a text file, you can step through all the lines one by one and read their contents into your program.

Note: Text lines in a file on disk are typically each terminated with a Carriage Return+Line Feed (CR-LF) sequence of characters. This sequence is often called a *hard break*. The Carriage Return (CR) character has the ASCII value of 13 decimal; the Line Feed (LF) is ASCII character number 10 decimal. When you read a line of text with `ReadLn`, only the characters up to but *not* including the terminating hard break are read into the supplied string variable. The file position, however, is moved to the beginning of the next text line, that is, past the terminating CR-LF pair.

Listing 7.1 illustrates the typical sequence of steps you need to take to read a text file from disk.

Listing 7.1. Steps required to read a text file from disk into memory.

```
var
  ATextFile: Text;
  ATextLine,
  AFileName: String;
begin
  AFileName := 'file.txt';
  Assign(ATextFile,AFileName);
  Reset(ATextFile);
  while not Eof(ATextFile) do begin
```

continues

Listing 7.1. continued

```
10:     ReadLn(ATextFile,ATextLine);
11:     {
12:     Store the newly read text line away
13:     for further processing.
14:     }
15:   end;
16:   Close(ATextFile);
17:   {Process the entire file.}
18: end;
```

The code in Listing 7.1 declares several variables on lines 1 through 4. The `ATextFile` variable is of type `Text` and is associated with an external text file. `ATextLine` is a string buffer that is used to store the line of text most recently read from the file. `AFileName` is an auxiliary variable that stores the name of the external file you want to access.

On line 6, `'file.txt'` is assigned to the `AFileName` variable. This hard-coded name can be changed at compile-time but not at run-time. You soon see how you can let the user decide dynamically which file he or she wants to open.

Lines 7 and 8 contain the classic pair of `Assign`+`Reset` calls, which open the file for reading. Lines 9 through 15 contain a **`while`** loop, where the contents of the file are read one line at a time. In particular, the `ReadLn` statement on line 10 reads a single line of text from the file and updates the file position to the beginning of the next line. Every time through the loop, the loop condition is determined on line 9. The loop continues iterating as long as there are more text lines to read, that is, as long as the `Eof` condition is False.

Lines 11 through 14 contain a comment that, in a real program, you would replace with code to save the current value of the `ATextLine` variable, which is overwritten with a new value every time through the loop.

Once the loop exits, at the end-of-file, line 16 closes the file. Line 17 contains a comment that is a placeholder for code that would execute to process the contents of the file.

File Browser Example

Now you are ready for a real-life example of a **`while`** loop. Figure 7.2 shows a File Browser program you are going to build.

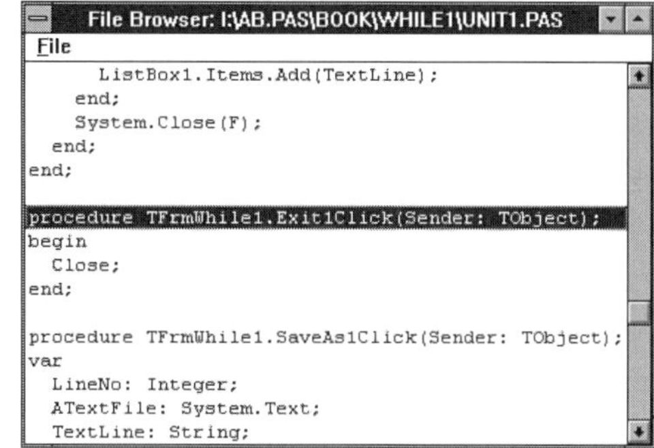

Figure 7.2.
The File Browser Program (WHILE1.EXE).

The File Browser program is capable of reading text files and displaying their contents inside its window. You can "browse" these files by moving the highlight bar. The file contents are displayed in a list box, with each list box item representing a line of text.

Creating the File Browser Program (WHILE1.PRJ)

Here are the steps to create the File Browser program:

1. Create a new project with a blank form.
2. Save the project under the name WHILE1.PRJ.
3. Place the following components on the form: `ListBox`, `OpenDialog`, and `MainMenu`.

   The completed form should look like the one shown in Figure 7.3.

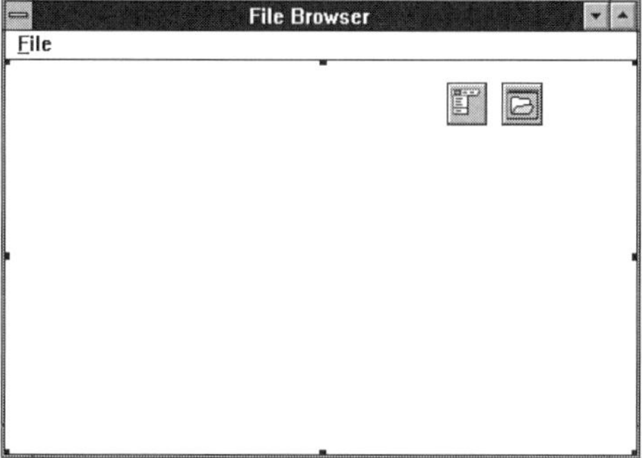

Figure 7.3.
The main form of the File Browser program, as shown in the Form Designer.

4. Set the properties of the form and its components according to Table 7.1.

Table 7.1. The properties table of UNIT1.FRM, the main form of the WHILE1 File Browser program.

Component & Type	Property	Setting
Main Form	**Name**	**FrmWhile1**
	ActiveControl	`ListBox1`
	Caption	`'File' Browser'`
	Height	`300`
	Width	`435`
	Menu	`MainMenu1`
List Box	**Name**	**ListBox1**
	Align	`alClient`
	BorderStyle	`bsNone`
	IntegralHeight	`False`
Open Dialog	**Name**	**OpenDialog1**
	Filter	`'Pascal source (*.pas,*.prj)¦*.pas;*.prj¦Text (*.txt)¦*.txt¦All files (*.*)¦*.*'`
Main Menu	**Name**	**MainMenu1**
	Items	`&File`
		`&Open…`
		`-`
		`E&xit`

Most of the properties described in Table 7.1 you can input directly. Select the appropriate component by clicking on it in the Form Designer; then enter the properties inside the Object Inspector's grid.

The main menu is slightly different in that regard. You can double-click on the main menu component icon in the Form Designer. The Menu Designer, a custom property editor for MainMenu components, is activated and you can construct a menu. Initially, you are presented with an empty main menu.

Type the `Caption` for the first (and for this program, the only) main menu item: **`&File`**; then press Enter. A submenu is then created, and the highlight bar is positioned on the first empty line of the submenu. Type **`&Open...`**; then press Enter.

To put a dividing line in the submenu, enter a single dash (`-`) as the menu item's `Caption`. Complete the submenu by creating a third menu item, with the caption **`E&xit`**, and then close the Menu Designer window.

The newly created menu appears on your form as a functional menu "prop," in addition to the main menu component icon representing the component at design-time. Every time you select an option from the menu in the Form Designer, an appropriate `OnClick` event handler is generated inside the Code Editor window.

Entering the Code of the File Browser Program

Follow these steps to enter the code of the File Browser program:

1. Create an `OnClick` event handler for the Exit menu item by selecting Exit from the File menu "prop" in the Form Designer.

   Delphi responds by bringing the code editor to the front and generating the shell for the procedure method `TFrmWhile1.Exit1Click`.
2. Enter the following single line of code for the `Exit1Click` method:

   ```
   Close;
   ```

   The call to the `Close` method of the form closes the main form window and terminates the program.
3. Create an `OnClick` event handler for the Open menu item by selecting Open from the main menu "prop" in the Form Designer.

   Delphi responds by bringing the code editor to the front and generating the shell for the procedure method `TFrmWhile1.Open1Click`.
4. Enter the code for the `Open1Click` method as shown in Listing 7.2.
5. Remember to save the project before running it.

Listing 7.2. `OnClick` event handler for the Open menu item of the WHILE1 File Browser program.

```
procedure TFrmWhile1.Open1Click(Sender: TObject);
var
  ATextFile: System.Text;
  TextLine: String;
begin
  if OpenDialog1.Execute then begin
    ListBox1.Clear;
    Caption := 'File Browser: ' + OpenDialog1.FileName;
    Assign(ATextFile,OpenDialog1.FileName);
    Reset(ATextFile);
    while not Eof(ATextFile) do begin
      ReadLn(ATextFile,TextLine);
      ListBox1.Items.Add(TextLine);
    end;
    System.Close(ATextFile);
  end;
end;
```

Listing 7.2 is the event handler for the `OnClick` event triggered by selecting Open from the File menu. This event handler comprises most of the File Browser example's functionality.

First, `OpenDialog1` is executed on line 6. `OpenDialog1` is a component you added to the form in the Form Designer, which encapsulates the standard Windows Open File dialog box. Executing the dialog enables the user to select a file to view. The name of the selected file, if any, is available in the `FileName` property of the `OpenDialog1`.

Once the `OpenDialog1.Execute` is done, one of two things could have happened: either the user selected a file and clicked on OK, or he or she clicked on the Cancel button in the Open File dialog box.

The **`if`** statement on line 6 tests which of the two possible outcomes actually occurred. If `OpenDialog1.Execute` evaluates to False, the Cancel button was clicked and the program does nothing. The execution simply falls through to the **`end`** on line 17, at which point the `OnClick` handler method terminates.

If `OpenDialog1.Execute` on line 6 evaluates to True, the code inside the **`begin-end`** block on lines 6 through 16 executes.

Line 7 clears the contents of the list box. At first, no file is loaded in the list box, so this statement really does nothing, but subsequently, when the user opens another file, the one already in the browser has to be purged before the new one can be loaded. The statement

```
ListBox1.Clear
```

accomplishes just that.

It is customary in Windows applications to show the name of the currently open file inside the window's caption. Line 8 updates the caption to reflect the name of the currently selected file. The file name is taken directly from the `OpenDialog1` component's `FileName` property and appended to a prefix `'File Browser: '`.

Lines 9 through 15 contain what you should immediately recognize as the standard algorithm for reading a text file. The `Assign` on line 9 and the `Reset` on line 10 open the external file, specified by the `FileName` property of `OpenDialog1`, as a file variable called `ATextFile`.

The `ATextFile` variable is declared on line 3. Notice a peculiarity in this declaration, however. Instead of simply declaring

```
ATextFile: Text;
```

a `System.` prefix is added to the type name. Why? It turns out that the form already contains a property called `Text`. Because the `OnClick` handler is a method of the form, a conflict occurs between the name of the property and the predeclared type name `Text`. To resolve the conflict, you must qualify the file type name with `System.` to say

```
System.Text;
```

This detail is minor, and you may be wondering how you were supposed to know such little things. You would have received some help from the compiler, which would have complained if you had left out the `System.` from the variable's declaration.

The message generated by the compiler, `Error in type`, is not as informative as you might have wanted, however. Consequently, you should always keep in mind that conflicts are possible whenever you want to deal with the standard file type `Text`. Whenever the `Text` name has been used for something else (and it is a very popular name), a clash is imminent. Simply remember to always prefix your `Text` file declarations with `System.` whenever you need to refer to the file type.

The same rule applies to the `Close` statement on line 15. Notice that you have already entered a `Close` statement in the `OnClick` method for the Exit menu item, where the `Close` referred to the form: you were invoking one of the form's methods.

This time, `Close` should refer to a file, not to the form, and it is crucial that you prefix it with `System`. Otherwise, the compiler insists on removing the parameter; if you simply enter **`Close`**, the compiler assumes the `TForm1.Close` method, which has no parameters. You learn more about visibility of names in future lessons, but it pays to learn now that you have to be careful about which entity a particular name refers to. Whenever you're in doubt, prefix the name in question with the name of the unit it is declared in, plus a period. All the built-in entities reside in a unit called `System`. A number of other pre-defined units, such as `SysUtils`, `Classes`, `Forms`, and so on, are also provided. You can use these in your programs and prefix the identifiers they make available with the respective name of the unit.

The file variable declared on line 3 of Listing 7.2 exists only within this particular procedure block. The file is opened, processed, and closed inside a single, short method. This approach is preferred for handling files in Windows; you should not keep files open for prolonged periods of time. Close them as soon as practically possible.

Lines 11 through 14 contain the **`while`** loop that reads the contents of the selected file—the main purpose of this exercise. At the start of each iteration, the loop tests for the end-of-file condition. When end-of-file has been reached, the loop terminates. Otherwise, yet another line is read into the `TextLine` variable, on line 12. The `TextLine` variable was declared on line 4 as a generic `String`.

Line 13 illustrates how to dynamically add a new item into a list box: by calling the `Add` method of the list box component's `Items` property, you have added `ListBox1` visually to the form in the Form Designer. Now you can refer to the `Items` component of the `ListBox1`, which contains the list of string items currently contained within the list box.

The `Add` method accepts a string parameter, and `TextLine` is passed to it each time a new text line has been read from the file.

In the 17 lines of code in Listing 17.2, you have learned how to open and process a text file, how to use a **while** loop, and how to add items to a list box; and you have provided the functionality for a generic File Browser program.

Running the File Browser Program

Here's how to run the new File Browser program:

1. Execute the WHILE1 program.
2. From the File menu, select Open. The Open File standard dialog then appears. After you select a particular file and click on OK, the file is loaded and displayed inside the list box.
3. From the File menu, select Exit to terminate the program.

The *repeat* Loop

The **repeat** loop comes in handy when you need to iterate through the loop at least once but possibly many times.

You may recall from a previous section that the **while** loop might not ever be executed if the loop condition evaluates to False initially. The condition is evaluated before any of the statements inside the loop are executed.

The **repeat** loop evaluates its condition at the end of the series of statements comprising the loop's contents. It is therefore executed at least once, even if the condition evaluates to False the first time.

The *repeat* Loop's Syntax

Syntax

repeat Loop

The general syntax for a **repeat** loop is as follows:

```
repeat
  Statement1;
  Statement2;
  ...
  StatementN;
until ConditionIsFalse;
```

Example:

```
repeat
  ch := ReadKey;
  ConvertToUpperCase(ch);
until Ch=#27;
```

A **repeat** loop starts with the Pascal reserved word **repeat**. The statements that are to be repetitively executed immediately follow the keyword. The loop spans the statements between the **repeat** and the matching **until** keyword. The **until** keyword is followed by the loop condition, which can be an arbitrary Boolean expression.

Notice that, unlike with most other Pascal constructs, the **repeat** statement's syntax does not differ for the case of a single statement and for the case of multiple statements. You don't need a **begin-end** block to designate the statements inside the loop. The **repeat-until** block is multi-statement by its very nature. However, you don't *have* to include multiple statements inside the **repeat-until** loop. A single statement works as well, or even no statements at all.

The loop condition given at the end of the loop, after the word **until**, can be anything that evaluates to a Boolean value, just as was the case with the **while-do** loops.

Note: A **repeat-until** loop always executes at least once. A **while-do** loop may never execute its body. This is why it is preferable to use a **while** loop to process text files. You should never assume that there is at least one line in a file; a text file can be empty! Executing a `ReadLn` statement when there is nothing to read results in a program error.

It is interesting to note that the condition on a **repeat-until** loop is the reverse of the condition on an equivalent **while-do** loop. For example, you can expect the following loop to run 10 iterations:

```
PageNo := 1;
repeat
  <Statements>;
  PageNo := PageNo + 1;
until (PageNo > 10);
```

The preceding loop terminates when the `PageNo` variable reaches the value of 11, after 10 iterations. Compare that with the following loop, which looks similar but in fact does nothing:

```
PageNo := 1;
while (PageNo > 10) do
  begin
    <Statements>;
    PageNo := PageNo + 1;
  end;
```

The preceding loop never executes because the loop condition is False on entry. To achieve the equivalent behavior to the initial **repeat** loop with a **while-do** statement instead, you have to reverse the loop condition, as follows:

```
PageNo := 1;
while (PageNo <= 10) do
  begin
    <Statements>;
    PageNo := PageNo + 1;
  end;
```

The preceding **while** loop runs for 10 iterations, as required.

> **Note:** The loop conditions on **while-do** and equivalent **repeat-until** loops are reversed. Keep that rule in mind when you're converting one type of loop to the other.
>
> The **until** condition is a termination clause ("terminate as soon as condition turns True"), and the **while** condition is a continuation clause ("continue while condition is True").

The structure of a **repeat-until** loop is illustrated in Figure 7.4.

Figure 7.4.
The structure of a **repeat** *loop.*

REPEAT-Loop
Loop Body
ExecutableStatement;
ExecutableStatement;
ExecutableStatement;
...
Loop Signature
UNTIL
Termination Condition

Using *repeat* Loops

A **repeat** loop, just like the other executable statements you have learned so far, belongs in the executable section of a block, that is, between a **begin** and an **end** pair of keywords.

After the program execution control first passes the **repeat** keyword, the statement or statements inside the loop are executed in order. When the execution reaches the **until** part, the loop condition is evaluated, and a determination is made whether to continue the loop for another iteration or whether to exit. If the loop conditional expression is True, the **until** condition is satisfied, and the control of execution falls through to the next statement following the loop. If the **until** expression evaluates to False, another iteration is executed.

The *for* Loop

Both the **while-do** and **repeat-until** looping constructs allow for a great deal of flexibility in terms of setting up the loop conditions and ensuring termination. You can use them when you don't know the number of repetitions initially. They can execute as long as their looping conditions for continuation are satisfied. The exact number of iterations might only become apparent after executing the loop several times.

Note: Although the exact number of iterations through a **while-do** or a **repeat-until** loop might not be known as the loop begins to execute, you still have to ensure that it is guaranteed to terminate. Not knowing the exact number of iterations does not preclude knowing whether the loop will terminate ultimately. You might not know how many iterations it will take, but you can, and in fact must, ensure that the loop will eventually terminate.

You use the **for** loop when you know the number of iterations in advance. You must know exactly how many times you need to execute the **for** loop before it starts.

The *for* Loop's Syntax

A **for** loop is a counted loop. A counter variable keeps track of the number of iterations through the loop. The **for** loop iterates from the starting value of the counter until a desired ending value is reached. There are two kinds of **for** loops, depending on whether the counter is being decremented or incremented every time through the loop.

Syntax

Incrementing *for* Loop

The general syntax for an incrementing **for** loop is as follows:

```
for LoopCounter := StartValue to EndValue do
  Statement;
```

The syntax for a multi-statement, *incrementing* **for** loop is as follows:

```
for LoopCounter := StartValue to EndValue do
  begin
    Statement1;
    Statement2;
    ...
    StatementN;
  end;
```

The `StartValue` must be less than or equal to the `EndValue`; otherwise, the loop never executes. The `LoopCounter` is incremented by one every time through the loop.

Examples:

```
for PageNo := 1 to 10 do
  PrintPage;
```

```
for ClientCounter := 0 to ClientCount -1 do
  begin
    PrintClientStatement;
    PrintSummaryInfo;
    ArchiveClientAccount;
  end;
```

Syntax

Decrementing *for* Loop

The following is the general syntax for a decrementing **`for`** loop:

```
for LoopCounter := StartValue downto EndValue do
  Statement;
```

The syntax for a multi-statement, *decrementing* **`for`** loop is as follows:

```
for LoopCounter := StartValue downto EndValue do
  begin
    Statement1;
    Statement2;
    ...
    StatementN;
  end;
```

The `StartValue` must be greater than or equal to the `EndValue`; otherwise, the loop never executes. The `LoopCounter` is decremented by one on every iteration.

Examples:

```
for RecordIndex := TransactionCount downto 1 do
  ProcessTransaction;
```

```
for LineNumber := 55 downto 0 do
  begin
    DrawLine;
    PaintBitmap;
    HighlightKeywords;
  end;
```

A **for** loop is introduced by the Pascal reserved word **for**. Following the **for** is an assignment statement initializing the value of the loop counter. The variable on the left-hand side of the assignment is the loop counter. It may be an arbitrary ordinal variable, typically of the Integer type. (You learn about other types of ordinal variables in tomorrow's lesson.) On the right-hand side of the assignment is an expression computing the initial value of the loop counter.

The loop counter variable is an ordinary variable. It can have an arbitrary name. The only restriction is that the loop counter must have been declared, like any other variable, and that it must have been declared locally, in the same scope as the **for** loop.

The initial value that you assign to the loop counter can be anything as long as it is assignment-compatible with the type of the loop counter variable. The simplest case, of course, is a hard-coded constant value. For instance, if the loop counter is an integer variable declared as

```
var
  Index: Integer;
```

the following assignment initializes it to 1 upon the loop initialization:

```
for Index := 1 to ...
```

Instead of the hard-coded value, an arbitrary expression is possible, as usual. For example, the starting value for the loop counter may have already been computed and stored in another compatible variable called StartIndex. In this case, the assignment

```
for Index := StartIndex to ...
```

initializes the loop counter Index with whatever the value of the StartIndex was at the time.

Following the loop counter initialization is a keyword **to** or **downto**, depending on whether you want an incrementing or a decrementing loop, respectively.

Following the keyword is the final value for the loop counter. The final value can be given as a hard-coded constant or as another variable, or indeed as an arbitrary expression compatible with the loop counter variable's type.

The Pascal reserved word **do** follows the final value declaration. After the **do** are the statement or statements to be executed repetitively. If more than one statement is inside the loop, the whole body of the **for** loop is enclosed in a **begin-end** block.

The structure of a Pascal **for** loop is illustrated in Figure 7.5.

Figure 7.5.
The structure of a `for` *loop.*

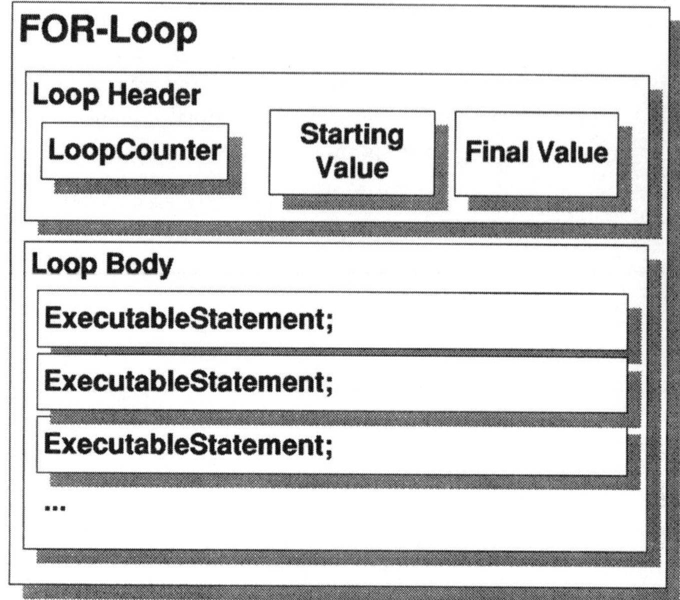

Using *for* Loops

A **`for`** loop, like all other looping constructs, belongs in the executable section of a block, that is, between a **`begin`** and an **`end`** pair of keywords.

A **`for`** loop is executed according to the following sequence of steps:

1. The expressions for the initial value and the final value of the loop counter are evaluated. Note that these expressions are evaluated once, even before the **`for`** loop executes the first time.
2. The loop counter is assigned the starting value.
3. A test is made whether the current value of the loop counter falls between the starting and the final value as computed in step 1. If the loop counter's value falls outside the starting and final value, the loop terminates and the execution falls through to the next statement following the loop.
4. If the test in step 3 determines that the loop counter is still within the starting-final value bounds, the loop body is executed.
5. When all the statements inside the loop have been executed, the loop counter is incremented (in a **`for-to`** loop) or decremented (in a **`for-downto`** loop) by one.
6. The control of execution jumps back to the **`for`** clause and step 3 is repeated.

Note: If the starting value of the loop counter variable is greater than the ending value in a **`for-to`** loop, the loop body is never executed.

Similarly, if the starting value is less than the final value in a **`for-downto`** loop, the loop never executes.

Warning: Do not attempt to change the value of the **`for`** loop counter variable inside the loop. The compiler lets you do it, but, because the loop counter variable is automatically incremented or decremented, changing its value in addition to that may lead to some hard-to-find bugs in your programs. Treat the loop counter variable as read-only.

Warning: According to the Object Pascal rules, the value of the loop counter variable after the loop has completed is undefined! Your code should never rely on a particular behavior of a **`for`** loop counter. After the loop has terminated, consider the contents of the counter variable to be uninitialized garbage. This is important, as the particular implementation of this behavior may change in the future, for example, to accommodate the needs of code-optimization.

In summary, the **`for`** loop requires you to supply the following:

- A loop counter variable
- A starting value for the loop counter variable
- A final value for the loop counter variable
- A direction in which to count (**`to`** or **`downto`**)
- A statement or statements to iterate (the body of the loop)

7

DO	DON'T

DO mentally step through all your loops to ensure that they are executed the expected number of times and that they always terminate.

DON'T explicitly change the value of the **`for`** loop counter to force it to terminate. Use a **`while`** loop instead.

DO | **DON'T**

DO think of a loop as a "black-box," one whose internals you are not meant to see. Make sure that the control logic of the loop is easily understandable from outside.

DON'T use a `for` loop for complex activities requiring re-evaluating loop counters or exit conditions on-the-fly. Use `while` or `repeat` loops instead.

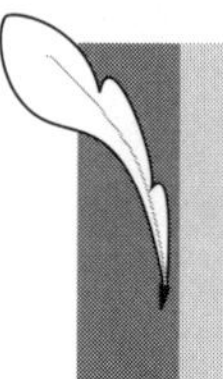

Note: The Pascal `for` loop does not (unfortunately) have a `step` part found in many other programming languages that would allow incrementing or decrementing by a value other than one. The loop counter is *always* incremented or decremented by one.

If you want the loop counter to be "stepped" through by a value other than one, do not use a `for` loop; use a `while` loop with an explicit counter-increment/decrement operation inside instead.

Loops versus Arrays

As you build the example program, you need to know about another important and closely related programming concept: arrays. This overview is brief, however. You learn more about arrays in tomorrow's lesson. Right now, you need to understand the basic concepts to be able to extend the File Browser example program.

An *array* is an example of a structured data type in Pascal. An array consists of a fixed number of components that are all of the same type. Each component of an array can be accessed explicitly by using indices into the array.

NEW TERM An *index* into an array is an ordinal expression placed inside square brackets; for example, `[1]`, `[I+1]`, and so on.

You have been using arrays even without knowing it. A standard `String` type, in its multitude of sizes, is a special kind of array: an array of characters with some additional information about the actual length of the string. You learn more about the internals of strings in tomorrow's lesson.

The important concept to know about arrays is the concept of an index, or subscript, into the array. You can access an individual element of an array by using an index expression in square brackets. For example,

```
Items[3]
```

accesses the element at index 3 of an array called `Items`. Similarly,

```
Items[ItemNo]
```

accesses an element of the array `Items` at an index specified by the contents of the variable `ItemNo`. `ItemNo` must be an ordinal-type variable.

Arrays are particularly closely related to **`for`** loops. Often you need to iterate through all the elements in an array with a known number of elements. A **`for`** loop is a natural choice for this kind of task. For example, the following **`for`** loop iterates through elements from 1 to 100 of the `Integer` array `Items` and sets the value of each element to be equal to its position in the array. Each element of the `Items` array is assumed to be an `Integer`.

```
for Index := 1 to 100 do
  Items[Index] := Index;
```

The expression `Items[Index]` gives access to an element at the position given by `Index`. `Index` is the loop counter and is automatically incremented by one after every iteration. Each element accessed through the `Items[Index]` expression is assigned the value of `Index`. As a result, the element of `Index` at, say, position 52 is assigned the value of 52.

Writing Text Files

You have already learned how to read text files line by line. The reverse process—writing a text file back to disk a line at a time—is similar.

Before you can write to a text file, you must first open it. To open a text file for writing, you need to call the `Assign` standard procedure, followed by the call to the `Rewrite` standard procedure, as follows:

```
Assign(ATextFile,'filename.txt');
Rewrite(ATextFile);
```

`ATextFile` is assumed to be a variable of type `Text`—`System.Text`, that is.

Once the file is open, it can be written to, a line at a time, using the standard procedure `WriteLn`, as follows:

```
WriteLn(ATextFile,ATextLine);
```

Again, `ATextFile` is assumed to be a variable of type `Text`, and `ATextLine` is a `String` variable containing text to be written to the file.

Listing 7.3 illustrates the typical sequence of events when writing to a text file on disk.

Listing 7.3. Steps required to write to a text file on disk.

```
 1: var
 2:   ATextFile: Text;
 3:   ATextLine,
 4:   AFileName: String;
 5: begin
 6:   AFileName := 'file.txt';
 7:   Assign(ATextFile,AFileName);
 8:   Rewrite(ATextFile);
 9:   for LineNo := 1 to LineCount begin
10:     ATextLine := GetLine(LineNo);
11:     WriteLn(ATextFile,ATextLine);
12:   end;
13:   Close(ATextFile);
14: end;
```

The code in Listing 7.3 declares several variables on lines 1 through 4. In particular, the `ATextFile` variable is of type `Text` and is associated with the external text file to be written to. `ATextLine` is a string buffer that stores the line of text just before writing it to the file. `AFileName` is an auxiliary variable that stores the name of the external file you want to access.

On line 6, the literal string `'file.txt'` is assigned to the `AFileName` variable. This hard-coded name can be changed at compile-time but not at run-time. You already know how to let the user choose the file he or she wants to open, using the `OpenDialog` component. A similar `SaveDialog` component allows the selection of the target filename, as you will soon see.

Lines 7 and 8 contain the classic pair of `Assign+Rewrite` calls, which open the file for writing. If the file with the specified name already exists, it is truncated to zero length.

Lines 9 through 12 contain a **`for`** loop that iterates through all the lines to be written to the file. The file's text, broken down into lines, is typically stored internally by the program.

On line 10 inside the **`for`** loop, the string variable `ATextLine` is assigned a new value each time through the loop. In this example, this assignment is accomplished by calling a `GetLine` function, with the current line number as the parameter. In reality, this line is likely to be replaced by a statement specific to the internal structure of text-line storage inside the program.

The `WriteLn` statement on line 11 is the place where the line of text stored inside the `ATextLine` variable is actually written to the file. Lines are appended to the end of the file, and the `WriteLn` procedure automatically updates the file position.

The loop control mechanism is set up on line 9. Because you use a **`for`** loop, you must give both starting and ending loop counter values. The `LineNo` variable serves as the loop counter. The starting value assigned to `LineNo` is one, the starting line number. The final value is obtained by calling a `LineCount` routine in this case, but in reality you replace this with some other, specific way of determining how many lines there are to write.

After all lines are written and the **for** loop exits, the call to the built-in `Close` routine terminates the processing and ensures that all of the data is actually written to the file.

File Browser Example Continued

Now you're ready to enhance the File Browser program you developed earlier in today's lesson to enable its new feature of saving text files under arbitrary names. You use a **for** loop to iterate through the contents of the list box. The list box contains the text lines to be saved to the file.

Enhancing the Visual Appearance of the File Browser

To enhance the appearance of the File Browser, follow these steps:

1. Open the project file WHILE1.PRJ you created earlier in today's lesson.
2. Add a `SaveDialog` component from the Dialogs page on the Delphi Component Palette to the form.
3. Change the `Filter` property of the newly added dialog—`SaveDialog1`—to be the same as that of the `OpenDialog1`. Click on the `OpenDialog1` to select it, hold down Shift, and click on the `SaveDialog1` component. Then click on the `Filter` property in the Object Inspector and press Enter. Both dialogs should now have the same filter property value.
4. Add a Save As... item to the File menu.

   First, double-click on the `MainMenu1` component in the Form Designer to activate the Menu Editor. Inside the Menu Editor, click on the separator line between the Open and the Exit options. Press Insert. Enter **`Save &As...`** in the `Caption` property of the newly created menu item. Close the Menu Editor. You can now verify by clicking on the main menu prop in the Form Designer that the Save As... menu item indeed appears inside the File menu.
5. Click the Save As... item inside the File menu in the Form Designer. Delphi then generates the skeleton `OnClick` handler method in the Code Editor window.
6. Fill in the `TFrmWhile1.SaveAs1Click` method, as shown in Listing 7.4.

Listing 7.4. `OnClick` event handler for the Save As menu item of the WHILE1 File Browser program.

```
procedure TFrmWhile1.SaveAs1Click(Sender: TObject);
var
  LineNo: Integer;
  ATextFile: System.Text;
  TextLine: String;
begin
```

continues

Listing 7.4. continued

```
 7:    if SaveDialog1.Execute then begin
 8:      Assign(ATextFile,SaveDialog1.FileName);
 9:      Rewrite(ATextFile);
10:      for LineNo := 0 to ListBox1.Items.Count-1 do
11:        begin
12:          TextLine := ListBox1.Items[LineNo];
13:          WriteLn(ATextFile,TextLine);
14:        end;
15:      System.Close(ATextFile);
16:    end;
17:  end;
```

Listing 7.4 shows the code for the `OnClick` event handler responding to the user choosing Save As... from the File menu. This method is similar in its structure to the Open handler you developed earlier in today's lesson.

The `SaveDialog1.Execute` expression on line 7 activates the standard Windows Save As... file dialog box. If this expression evaluates to True—that is, the user clicked on the OK button in the dialog box—the **`if`** condition is satisfied, and the code inside the **`if`** statement is executed.

On lines 8 and 9, the file is opened for writing. If the file does not exist, the `Rewrite` statement creates it. After the file is opened, the **`for`** loop on lines 10 through 14 writes the text lines out to it. Notice how the loop counter variable, `LineNo`, is iterated from zero to one less than the number of items in the list box. Starting at zero is necessary because the list box lines are accessed through a zero-based index.

In the expression on line 12

```
TextLine := ListBox1.Items[LineNo];
```

your newly acquired understanding of arrays becomes useful. The `ListBox1` component has an `Items` property which, for all intents and purposes, is an array of strings. You previously added these strings with the `Add` method of the `ListBox1` component when loading a file. You can gain access to an individual element of this array by using the array subscript expression in square brackets.

Line 12 assigns the value of the element of the `Items` array at position `[LineNo]`.

The loop on line 10 runs exactly the number of iterations needed to write all the strings in the list box back to the file. The expression

```
ListBox1.Items.Count
```

retrieves the actual number of items in the list box and provides the final value for the loop counter so that the loop is guaranteed to terminate after exactly this many iterations, minus one.

After the loop has finished, the `System.Close` routine is called to close the file and to ensure that it is physically written to the disk.

Running the Enhanced File Browser

After you enter the `SaveAs1Click` method from the preceding section, do the following:

1. Run the program.
2. Load a text file using the same steps you used previously.
3. From the File menu, select "Save As." Inside the dialog box that appears, select a different name for the target file, preferably one that does not yet exist.

Figure 7.6 illustrates the appearance of the enhanced File Browser program.

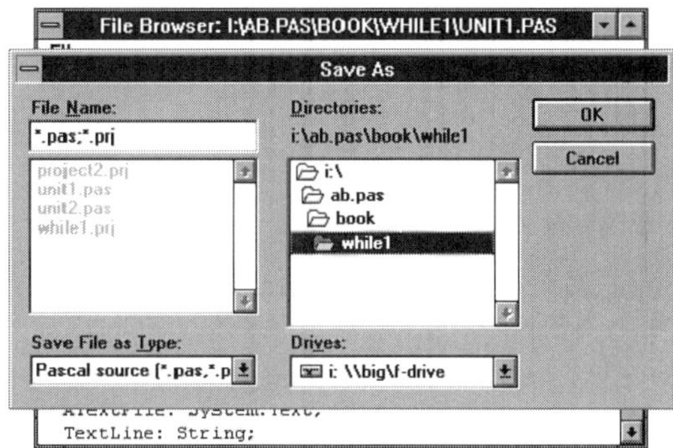

Figure 7.6.
The File Browser program with the Save As feature.

4. Click on the OK button.

   The file currently in the browser is saved under the new name. You can verify the name by reloading the newly saved file back into the browser; it should be identical to the one you had originally.
5. From the File menu, select Exit to exit the program.

Advanced Loop Topics

This section gives you additional skills to enable you to build loops of arbitrary complexity and with characteristics not necessarily supported by the standard looping constructs: **`while-do`**, **`repeat-until`**, **`for-to-do`**, and **`for-downto-do`**.

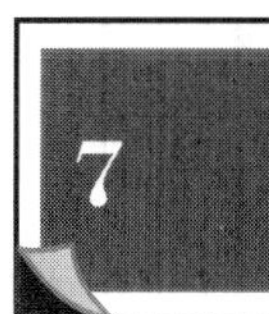

Note: The three standard looping constructs are sufficient for most occasions. Use the advanced techniques described in this section cautiously.

Custom Loops

You saw that the loop condition is evaluated either at the beginning (**while** and **for** loops) or at the end of the looping block (**repeat** loops). You also can construct loops whose condition is effectively evaluated at an arbitrary position within the loop.

If the loop condition is tested somewhere in the middle of the loop, the part of the loop before the test is executed at least once, and the part after the test may not be executed at all.

You can create custom loops in Object Pascal by first creating an endless or infinite loop and then making use of a predefined `Break` procedure to exit the loop at an appropriate time. The technique does not create a truly infinite loop. It is still your responsibility to ensure that the loop will terminate. This technique merely shifts the responsibility for testing the loop condition and possibly exiting the loop onto you, the programmer.

Creating Infinite Loops

The easiest way to create an infinite loop, one that you can use to program custom loops, is to use a standard looping construct and ensure that the looping condition never evaluates in such a way that the loop terminates.

Warning: Do not enter the following example code directly. These examples create truly infinite loops, the effect of which is hanging your machine. Read this section in its entirety before attempting to set up an infinite loop.

The following is an infinite **while** loop (don't try this, your machine will "hang"!):

```
while True do begin
  executable statements
end;
```

You construct an infinite **repeat** loop similarly (don't do it just yet!):

```
repeat
  executable statements
until False;
```

Loop-with-Break Construct

The infinite loops introduced in the preceding section provide the foundation for the ultimately flexible *Loop-with-Break* construct:

Syntax

Custom Loop-with-Break

The general syntax for creating arbitrary custom loops is as follows:

```
while True do begin
  Statements Before The Test
if ConditionIsTrue then
  Break;
  Statements After The Test
end;
```

Example:

```
while True do begin
  GetNextClient;
  ComputeClientData;
  if Total >= Threshold then
    Break;
  ProcessClientData;
  PrintClientReport;
end;
```

The first two statements inside the loop are always executed, like in a **repeat** loop. The last two statements may never be executed, like in a **while** loop.

You create a Loop-with-Break construct by setting up an infinite **while-do** or **repeat-until** loop and inserting a test for breaking out of the loop (the loop condition for termination) somewhere inside the loop. If the test evaluates to True, a standard, predeclared `Break` procedure is called and the loop terminates. The execution of the program jumps to the first statement after the loop.

The loop exit condition is tested on every iteration. The statements before the test are thus guaranteed to execute at least once. The statements inside the loop after the test might never be executed. This way, the custom loop construct combines the advantages of both a **while-do** and a **repeat-until** loop.

DO	DON'T

DO put all the exit condition tests in one place inside a custom loop.

DON'T use a custom loop with a `Break` statement when a standard one will do.

DO make sure that the loop control is easy to follow and understand. Use comments when in doubt.

DON'T use the `Break` statement inside standard counted loops (**for** loops). It makes them harder to understand later.

DO simplify your loops.

DON'T create loops with a large number of statements inside. Use subroutines to reduce the "weight" of a loop.

Figure 7.7 illustrates the structure of a generic loop with a custom exit condition.

Figure 7.7.
The structure of a custom loop.

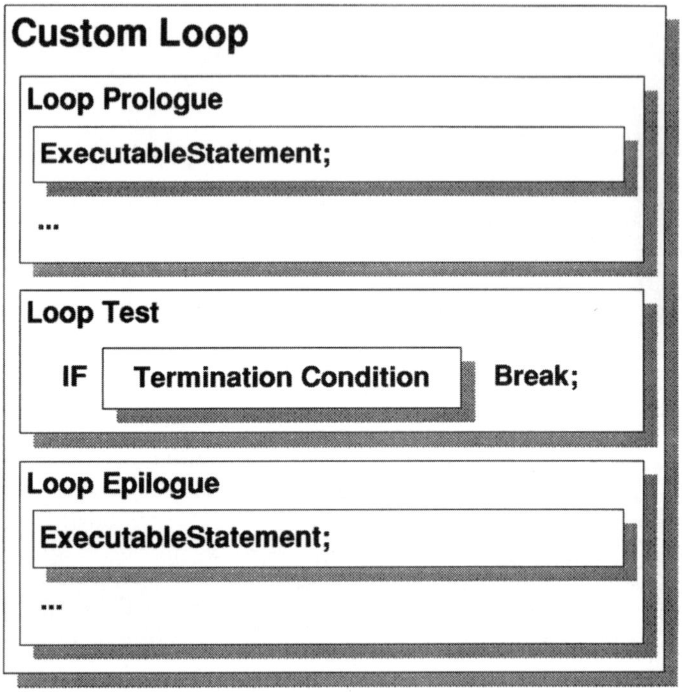

Custom Loop

Loop Prologue

ExecutableStatement;

...

Loop Test

IF Termination Condition Break;

Loop Epilogue

ExecutableStatement;

...

Skipping Loop Iterations

Object Pascal offers another way of controlling the execution of loops: the `Continue` statement.

`Continue`, like `Break`, is a standard, predeclared procedure. Any number of `Continue` statements can appear inside a loop. Whenever a `Continue` is encountered, the program skips the rest of the statements in the loop, returns to the loop's beginning, and starts another iteration, if allowed by the loop condition.

A call to the `Continue` statement is typically combined with a conditional **`if`** clause, testing whether to skip the remaining statements of the loop.

For example, the loop

```
while PageNumber < TotalPages do begin
  ReadClientRecord;
  if ClientCity <> 'Chicago' then
    Continue;
  PrintClientReport;
end;
```

prints the client report (the actual printing is done inside `PrintClientReport` and is of no concern to us here) for every client residing in Chicago, skipping the printing step for residents of all other cities. The `Continue` statement is executed every time `ClientCity` is not equal to `'Chicago'`. The `PrintClientReport` is skipped in each such case.

Summary

Today's lesson discussed looping constructs. You learned the following:

- A **`while-do`** loop tests its condition at the beginning of every iteration. As a consequence, the loop body may never execute. It is suitable for general-purpose loops, in which the number of iterations may not be known beforehand. The loop condition tests whether to continue.
- A **`repeat-until`** loop tests its condition at the end of every iteration. Hence, the loop body executes at least once. The loop condition tests whether to terminate the loop.
- A **`for-to-do`** loop requires an explicit counter that is initialized on entry. The loop runs a predefined number of iterations, until the final value for the counter is reached. The counter is incremented every time through the loop, logically at the end of the loop.
- A **`for-downto-do`** loop is like the **`for-to-do`** loop, except that the counter is decremented at the end of every iteration.
- A custom loop can be composed of an infinite **`while-do`** or **`repeat-until`** loop, and an explicit loop termination test. The loop test is an **`if-then`** statement, which executes the `Break` procedure when its condition is satisfied. A custom loop can test its condition at an arbitrary position within the loop. The loop body statements before the condition are guaranteed to execute at least once, as in a **`repeat`** loop. The statements after the loop condition may not execute at all, as in a **`while`** loop.

Q&A

Q Can I use a `Real` variable as the `for` loop counter?

A No, you cannot use `Reals` as **`for`** loop counters. The counter variable in a **`for`** loop must be of an ordinal type. Therefore, it must map one to one onto integers. `Real` is not an ordinal type, so you cannot use it in this context.

Q Can I have loops inside other loops?

A Yes, loops can be nested to arbitrary levels. You see an example of loop nesting in a later lesson. In general, however, you want to minimize the situations in which deep nesting of loops is necessary. Nested loops can be very inefficient. Use nested loops only when you have to—that is, when there is no other solution.

Q Can loops overlap?

A No. Loops cannot overlap. They must be properly nested in each other or be completely disjointed. Treat a loop like an indivisible black box, a true building block. Although, internally, a loop can contain other statements, on the outside you must treat it as an indivisible whole, a box. Just as you cannot overlap boxes, but you can pack a smaller box inside a larger one, so you can embed an inner loop inside an outer one but cannot interweave the beginning and ending of their blocks.

Q Can I nest a `repeat` loop inside a `while` loop, and vice versa?

A Yes, you can nest any type of loop inside any other type, provided that you do not attempt to overlap the loops.

Workshop

Quiz

1. What is wrong with the following loop?

```
while (Total < Max) and (Sum <= Max) and (Sum < Total) do
Statement1;
```

2. What is wrong with the following loop?

```
while (Sum <= Total) or (Total > Sum) do
  Statement2;
```

3. What is the minimum number of repetitions that a **`while-do`** loop can iterate through?
4. What is the minimum number of repetitions that a **`repeat-until`** loop must iterate through?
5. What is the maximum number of repetitions that a **`for`** loop can iterate through?

Exercises

1. Write a Delphi program with the main form containing a list box and a Go button. When the user clicks the Go button, the program should fill the list box with the strings consisting of the consecutive letters of the alphabet. For example, the first three strings would be `'A','B','C'`.
2. Write a simple Delphi program that counts the number of lines in an arbitrary text file.

WEEK 1 IN REVIEW

1 2 3 4 5 6 7

Congratulations! You have completed the first week of training in Delphi programming under Windows. During the course of this week, you have been introduced to a number of important features of the Delphi environment:

- You know how to operate the Form Designer, Object Inspector, Code Editor, and other elements of Delphi's Integrated Development Environment.
- You understand the various files comprising a Delphi project: .dpr, .dfm, .pas, and so on.
- You know the difference between a program and a unit and how various units contribute to create a full-featured application.
- You've learned how to make one unit's interface visible to another.
- You have explored the visual programming paradigm by creating several example programs illustrating various visual programming techniques.
- You have learned how to declare variables and constants using the **var**- and **const**-block declaration syntax.

Week 1 in Review

- You've discovered a way of assigning values to variables, using the assignment statement.
- You've learned how to perform arithmetic and Boolean calculations in Object Pascal and how to store the results of these calculations inside variables of built-in types.
- You know how to construct complex, even nested, **`if-then-else`**-statements and **`case`**-statements in order to control the flow of logic in an Object Pascal program.
- You've learned the syntax and usage of the Pascal looping constructs: **`while-do`**, **`repeat-until`**, and **`for-do`**.

The next week will continue the introduction to the Object Pascal language.

WEEK 2 AT A GLANCE

8

9

10

11

12

13

14

During the course of the second week, you will complete the overview of the Object Pascal programming language by examining ways of structuring programs as collections of subroutines. You'll also learn how to define your own data types and thereby extend the range of types available to your programs.

The main impact of this week's lessons is undoubtedly the introduction to object-oriented programming in Object Pascal. You'll learn about classes and instances and how to combine code and data together to form objects. You'll discover the meaning of terms like virtual methods, polymorphism, inheritance, and encapsulation. Finally, you'll learn about the Visual Component Library, the built-in framework of classes and components upon which you'll build your Delphi applications.

At the end of the week you'll be introduced to some of the more esoteric issues of object-oriented programming, including issues related to programming under Windows, programming with exceptions, and using the Object Pascal built-in run-time type information (RTTI) to your advantage.

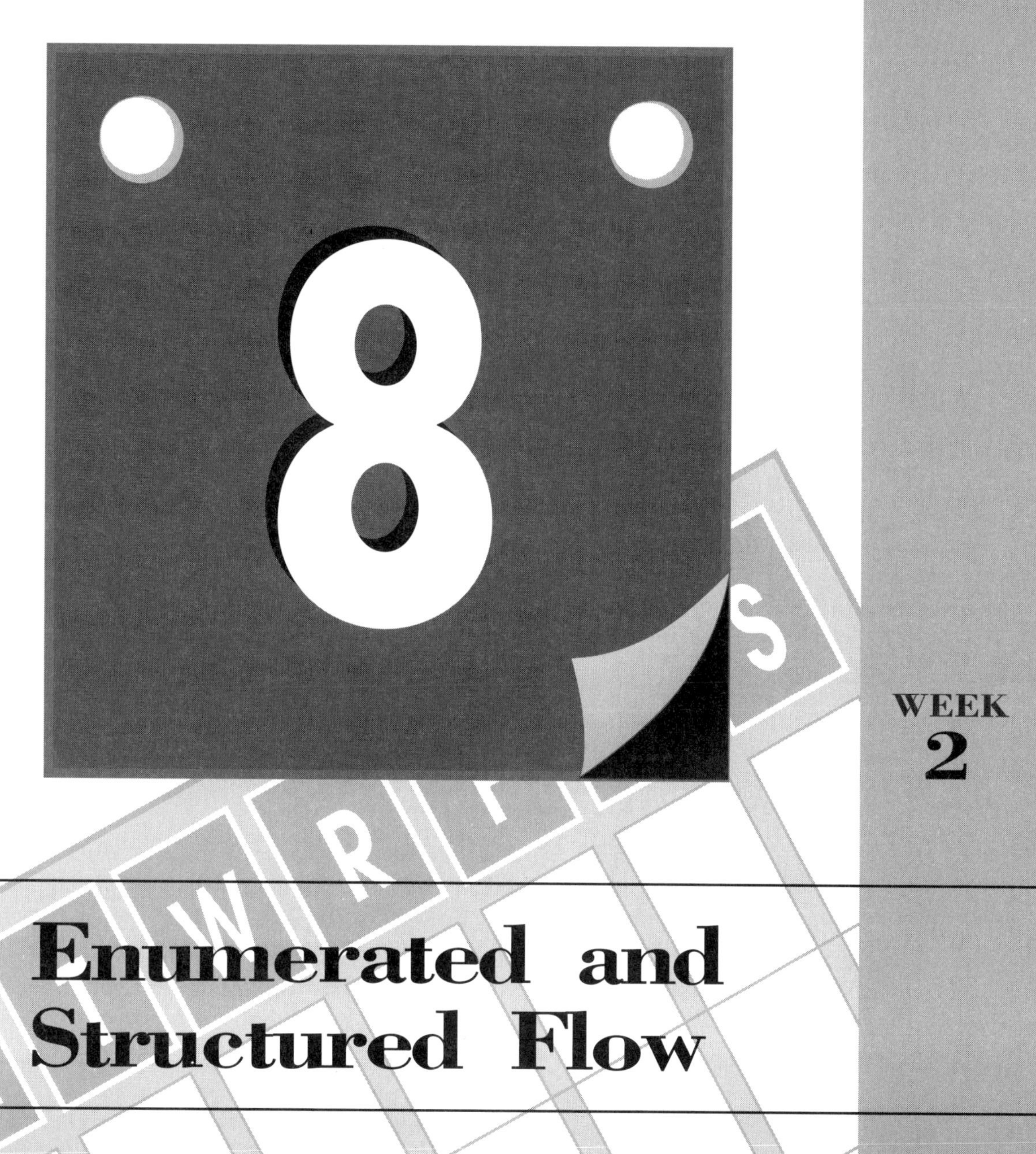

WEEK 2

Enumerated and Structured Flow

You learned about Object Pascal's simple data types, including `Integer`, `Real`, `Boolean`, and `Char`, on Day 4. Object Pascal offers a number of additional *structured* types. You have already made extensive use of one of them: the `String` type. Today you will learn more about other built-in data types. Moreover, after today's lesson you will be able to extend the Object Pascal environment by deriving your own data types from the built-in ones.

Keep in mind that this lesson is long and packed with a lot of theoretical material that will help you gain better understanding of the Object Pascal language. Please allow sufficient time to work your way through this lesson. In it you will learn the following:

- How to extend the Object Pascal language by declaring your own user-defined types.
- How to declare and use subrange types.
- How to define and use enumerated types.
- How to define and use arrays of one, two, or more dimensions.
- The internal structure of Pascal strings and the standard string-manipulation routines available to you.
- How to declare and use Pascal sets.
- How to pack related information into convenient structures called records.

User-Defined Types

A truly powerful programming language must allow for the creation of new data types in addition to the built-in types provided at the outset. Object Pascal fully supports the creation of almost arbitrarily complex and sophisticated data types.

NEW TERM A *user-defined* type is a data type designed and created by the programmer to supplement and extend the built-in set of data types provided by the language. The newly created data type may be specific to a particular programming problem, or to an entire class of problems.

The concept of user-defined types makes the language more powerful and expressive. User-defined types make your programs more readable and easier to maintain. By using new types, you can represent both the programming problem you are facing and its solution in a way that is much easier to follow and understand. As an additional benefit, user-defined types permit the compiler to perform better error-checking of your code, and to generate more efficient code.

For example, rather than expressing a value of a particular variable as `3`, which does not give the reader or compiler of your program any clues as to what this particular number represents, you can define a special type and write `Tuesday` instead of `3`. Doesn't the meaning of the variable immediately become clearer?

The reason for introducing a special type representing weekdays goes beyond readability, however. After all, you could introduce meaningful names with numeric constants, such as

```
const
  Sunday  = 0;
  Monday  = 1;
  Tuesday = 2;
```

The advantage of defining a special type is that the compiler can ensure that you will never assign an inappropriate value to a variable that is meant to store only weekday values. With days defined as numeric constant, there is nothing to prevent you from assigning `8` (or `134`!) to a `WeekDay` variable.

As you may recall, Pascal is a strongly typed language. This means that the compiler can catch a lot of common programming errors (such as those resulting from attempting to assign inappropriate values to variables) as syntax errors at compile-time, rather than letting you discover them later, at run-time. The latter kind of bugs, discovered at run-time, a much more difficult to track down than those the compiler catches for you. You should always use the power of Pascal's type-checking to your advantage and let the compiler verify the correctness of your programs as much as possible, rather than waiting for your users to do so. This is accomplished by declaring appropriate user-defined types.

Type Declarations

Object Pascal makes it very easy to define new data types. You can quickly build new types appropriate to the problem at hand. The entire notion of object-oriented programming, which you will learn during the course of this week, is based on the ability to extend and derive new data types.

New data types are declared in *Type-Declaration Blocks* (**type**-blocks).

Syntax

Type-Declaration Block

The general syntax for declaring a new data type inside a Type-Declaration Block is as follows:

```
type
  TypeName = <Type Definition>;
  Type2Name = <Type definition>;
  ...
```

Examples:

```
type
  ArrayIndex         = Integer;
  PositiveInteger    = 1..32767;
  NonNegativeInteger = 0..32767;
  ShortString        = String[15];
  TRecordNumber      = LongInt;
```

A Type-Declaration Block consists of one or more type declarations, usually one per line, and begins with the reserved word **type**.

Individual Type Declarations begin with the type name, which is a Pascal identifier, followed by an equal sign. A Type Definition follows the equal sign. The individual Type Declaration is always terminated by a semicolon. Of course, any **type**-declaration blocks are entirely optional; they need not be present in a program if you do not declare any new types. You will, however, discover that Pascal's power of type-extensibility will compel you to define many new types as you develop more complex programs. New types make it easier to understand your programs.

There may be (arbitrarily) many Type Declarations within a single **type**-block. The entire **type**-block belongs in the declarations section of a Pascal source-code block.

There might be many **type**-blocks within a single declaration section, interspersed with other declaration-blocks, such as **var**-, **const**-, and subroutine-declaration blocks. Each **type**-block begins with the reserved word **type** and ends implicitly whenever some other block is introduced with another keyword.

The simplicity of the type-declaration syntax box hides the fact that the `<Type Definition>` portion may be very complex. There is no simple rule for how the individual type definitions might look. You will learn a number of ways of defining new types during the course of today's lesson.

Note: Any user-defined type must be declared in terms of more primitive, simpler types. Ultimately, every Pascal type is some combination of the primitive, built-in types you learned on Day 4.

A Pascal type is either *simple* or *structured*. The difference between the two groups of data types stems from whether the type's values are composed of more primitive values, in which case the type is said to be *structured*, or whether the type's values cannot be further subdivided into more primitive Pascal types, in which case the type is *simple*.

Note: A type declaration does not take any memory *per se*, does not reserve any storage space, nor does it impact the program at run-time in any way. It is merely a static recipe for a variable. To actually make use of a type declaration, you need to declare variables of that type.

Subranges

Subrange types are examples of user-defined, simple, ordinal types that are directly derived from existing ordinal types, called *base* types. A subrange essentially narrows down the choices of values otherwise available to its base type, and allows you to define a type that is a subset of an existing ordinal type.

8

NEW TERM A *subrange* type is a subset of values of an ordinal data type, called *base* type. The subrange is specified by listing its first and last values. All operations available on the values of the base type are also available in the subrange.

Subranges use the same ordering as their base types.

Syntax

Subrange Type Definition

The syntax for declaring a subrange type is as follows:

```
type
  SubrangeTypeName = FirstValue..LastValue;
```

Examples:

```
type
  NonNegativeIntegers = 0..32767;
  Digits = '0'..'9';
  LowerCaseChars = 'a'..'z';
```

A subrange is defined after the type definition's equal sign by having its first value listed, followed by two periods and the last value. Both listed values must be constants chosen from the same base ordinal type.

The base type of a subrange can be any ordinal type, including the built-in ordinal types, as well as user-defined enumerated types you will learn about shortly. In practice, subranges of one of the integer types, and those of the `Char` type, are very useful and commonly defined.

Note: Since a subrange is defined in terms of its first and last values, all subranges are single, contiguous blocks or ranges. You cannot exclude a particular value from a base type by defining a subrange consisting of two (or more) contiguous block of values. For example, you cannot define a subrange type consisting of "all integers except zero".

Enumerated Types

Enumerated types are another example of simple, user-defined, ordinal types. Enumerated types are used extensively by the standard Delphi components, for example.

Enumerated Type Syntax

Enumerated types are declared by listing all their values within parentheses, separated by commas.

Syntax

Enumerated Type Declaration

The general syntax for declaring enumerated types is

```
type
  TypeName = (Value1, Value2, Value3, ..., ValueN);
```

Examples:

```
type
  WeekDays = (Monday, Tuesday, Wednesday, Thursday, Friday, Saturday, Sunday);
  Colors = (Red, Green, Blue);
  Shapes = (Square, Rectangle, Circle, Ellipse, Triangle);
```

A declaration of an enumerated type follows the general pattern for type declarations, with the type name being followed by the equal sign and the details of the declaration afterward.

In this case, the type definition consists of the values of an enumerated type being explicitly listed within the parentheses, separated by commas. These values are user-defined names, or identifiers, following the general rules for Pascal identifiers. Each identifier can only appear once within the list, and may not conflict with any other identifier defined within the same module.

Note: You can define up to 255 items maximum per enumerated type.

Ordering of Enumerated Values

An enumerated type is an example of an ordinal type. Each value listed within parentheses corresponds to an ordinal integer number. The order in which the values are listed within the type definition determines the associated ordinal values.

For example, given the enumerated type definition

```
type
  Months = (January, February, March, April, May, June,
    July, August, September, October, November, December);
```

the value of `January` corresponds to the ordinal value of 0, `February` to 1, `March` to 2, and so on, up to the value of `December`, which corresponds to 11.

Because the enumerated types correspond to ordinal values, you can use them anywhere an ordinal is expected. This applies to loop counters in particular. For example, you can use the `Months` type to run a loop through all 12 months as follows:

```
var
  Month: Months;
begin
  ...
  for Month := January to December do
    {perform the loop's function}
  ...
end;
```

Note: The ordinal values of an enumerated type are *zero-based*, that is, the first value in the definition list always corresponds to zero.

Since all ordinal types define an implicit ordering of their elements, you can use the same relational operators you learned on Day 5 to determine which of the two values of the same enumerated type is "greater", that is, which follows the other in the enumeration order.

For example, the following are all `True` for the enumerated type `Months` defined above:

```
January  < December
February < March
February > January
October >= March
October <= November
```

Very often you will be interested in what value is a direct predecessor to, or a direct successor of a given enumerated value.

- You can determine what value follows another in a given enumerated (or in general, ordinal) type by using a standard function `Succ`; for example, `Succ(May)` returns `June`, given the `Months` declaration.
- To determine what value precedes another in an ordinal type, such as an enumerated type, use the standard function `Pred`; for example, `Pred(May)` returns `April`.

Converting Between Enumerated and Ordinal Values

You can convert the enumerated value to its ordinal number by using the `Ord` standard function as follows:

```
var
  OrdValue: Integer;
begin
  OrdValue := Ord(November);
end;
```

Assuming that `November` comes from the `Months` definition above, the resulting value of the `OrdValue Integer` variable will be 10, the zero-based ordinal index of `November` within the `Months` definition.

To convert in the opposite direction (from an ordinal number to the enumerated value), you have to use a typecast.

NEW TERM *Typecasting* means telling the compiler to treat a value of one type as if it were a value of another type. Typecasting is a way of circumventing the strong type-checking mechanism of Object Pascal. Typecasting makes sense only in some specific circumstances, whenever a particular value already is of a type similar to the desired one. The compiler will not allow you to easily typecast to a type considerably different from the original, for example, one resulting in a variable of a different size.

To cast a value into a different type, enclose it in parentheses and prefix it with the new type name as follows:

```
NewTypeName(OldTypeValue)
```

For example:

```
var
  W: Word;
  I: Integer;
begin
  I := Integer(W);
end;
```

For example, the following code assigns the value of `November` to a `Months`-variable `ThisMonth` by using an integer constant 10—the ordinal number of `November` within the `Months` definition:

```
var
  ThisMonth: Months;
begin
  ThisMonth := Months(10);
end;
```

The expression `Months(10)` in this code means "take the integer constant value 10 and treat it as if it were one of the `Months` values, the one at ordinal position 10." The typecast was necessary

here, because the strong type-checking rules of Pascal would have prevented a direct assignment, such as

```
ThisMonth := 10;
```

because the `ThisMonth` variable was defined as a `Months` variable and cannot be assigned an `Integer` value.

Arrays

Arrays are examples of structured data types. You have already encountered arrays on Day 7 when you learned how to iterate through array elements using loops. Today you will explore the topic of arrays in more depth.

NEW TERM An *array* is an in-memory data structure consisting of a sequence of values, all of which are of the same type.

The elements of an array are arranged sequentially in a contiguous area in memory. Arrays can be one-, two-, three-, and in general, many-dimensional.

One-Dimensional Arrays

A *one-dimensional* array is essentially a collection of identical elements, arranged in one row. The elements are of the same type, but might, of course, differ in value.

Figure 8.1 illustrates the concept of a one-dimensional array, also known as a *vector*.

[0]	[1]	[2]	[3]	[4]	[5]	[6]	[7]	[8]	[9]
23	17	42	13	7	2	0	10	0	12

Figure 8.1.
The concept of a single-dimensional array.

Syntax

Declaring One-Dimensional Array Types

The following is the general syntax for declaring one-dimensional array types:

```
type
  ArrayTypeName = array [IndexDefinition] of AnotherType;
```

Examples:

```
type
  MonthlyAmounts: array[1..12] of Real;
  TestResults: array[Boolean] of Byte;
```

Array types are defined within **type** blocks by following the equal sign in the type definition by a pair of the reserved word **array**, followed by an index definition in square brackets, followed by the reserved word **of**, in turn followed by the type declaration for the array elements.

Any defined type can be used as the type for the array elements, but all of the array elements must be of the same type.

The *index definition* in the array declaration specifies a range of values for the array index. The index definition is either an in-line (explicit) declaration of an ordinal type or uses an ordinal type identifier.

- A typical index declaration directly defines an ordinal subrange by specifying the starting value for the index, and its ending value.

For example, the following declaration defines a 10 element array of integers whose index runs from 1 to 10:

```
type
  TIntegers10 = array[1..10] of Integer;
```

The expression `1..10` in this declaration directly defines a subrange of integers from 1 to 10.

- You can use a subrange type identifier directly inside the index definition instead of an explicitly defined subrange.

For example, the following definition uses a subrange of integers to define a 24-element array of real numbers:

```
type
  Hours = 1..24;
  THourlyActivity = array[Hours] of Real;
```

- You can also use an enumerated and any ordinal type in its entirety to define the range for an array index.

For example, the following declaration uses a previously defined enumerated type to create a 12-element array of `Real`-values.

```
type
  Months = (January, February, March, April, May, June,
    July, August, September, October, November, December);

  MonthlyIncome = array[Months] of Real;
```

This declaration of the `MonthlyIncome` array uses the entire range of the enumerated type `Months` for its index. The declaration of `MonthlyIncome` means a 12-element array of `Real`-numbers, which are accessed using an index from the `Months` enumerated type.

Similarly,

```
  CharCodeTable = array[Char] of Byte;
```

defines a 256-element array ranging over all possible character values numbered from 0 to 255.

Two-Dimensional Arrays

A *two-dimensional* array, or a *matrix*, is an extension of the one-dimensional vector concept. You can think of it as an ordered list of one-dimensional vectors, each of the same size and type, forming the rows; that is, you treat them as vectors whose individual elements are vectors themselves. After all, *any* defined type can be used for the element type—even another array type.

In other words, a matrix consists of a rectangular arrangement of rows and columns of elements of the same type—the base type of the array.

Figure 8.2 illustrates the concept of a two-dimensional array.

Figure 8.2.
The concept of a two-dimensional array.

	[0]	[1]	[2]	[3]	[4]	[5]	[6]	[7]	[8]	[9]
[1]	1	2	3	4	5	6	7	8	9	10
[2]	2	4	6	8	10	12	14	16	18	20
[3]	3	6	9	12	15	18	21	24	27	30
[4]	4	8	12	16	20	24	28	32	36	40
[5]	5	10	15	20	25	30	35	40	45	50

Syntax

Declaring Two-Dimensional Array Types

The following is the general syntax for declaring two-dimensional array types:

```
type
  ArrayTypeName = array [Index1Definition, Index2Definition] of AnotherType;
```

Examples:

```
type
  MonthlyAmounts: array[1..12,Income..Expense] of Real;
  TestResults: array[1..5,Boolean] of Byte;
```

Two-dimensional arrays are declared just like one-dimensional arrays, except that there are two index definitions inside the square brackets after the reserved word **array**, corresponding to the two dimensions of the array.

Each of the index definitions is independent from all the others, and may be of different type, as long as the expression resolves to an ordinal type.

For example, the following two-dimensional array MoneyFlow is defined as a 3×12 matrix of LongInts:

```
type
  FlowType = (Expense, Income, Transfer);
  MonthType = (January, February, March, April, May, June,
    July, August, September, October, November, December);

  MoneyFlow = array[FlowType,MonthType] of LongInt;
```

This declaration of `MoneyFlow` makes use of two enumerated types, `FlowType` and `MonthType`, to declare the ranges of index values for each of its two dimensions. The structure of the resulting array is shown in Figure 8.3.

Figure 8.3.
The structure of the `MoneyFlow` *array.*

[Expense]	[Income]	[Transfer]	
1200	1435	327	[January]
780	651	344	[February]
923	720	506	[March]
1004	1123	98	[April]
1002	1234	24	[May]
1234	1111	0	[June]
1328	1789	57	[July]
1349	1820	10	[August]
1351	1050	27	[September]
1510	2030	128	[October]
1890	2134	900	[November]
2037	2017	750	[December]

The individual elements of this array are accessed by specifying an appropriate index in each of the two dimensions. For example, given the variable declaration

```
var
  TheMoneyFlow: MoneyFlow;
```

the expression

```
TheMoneyFlow[Expense,March]
```

accesses the element in the first column of the third row of the array, or—using ordinal equivalents of the enumerated values—the element at position [0, 2].

Notice that when referring to the array elements, the indices are matched according to their position inside the square brackets. The expression

```
TheMoneyFlow[March,Expense]
```

would have been flagged by the compiler as an error, because the first index of the `MoneyFlow` array was declared as being of type `FlowType`. The `March` value is not one of the `FlowType` values.

Notational Conventions

Since two-dimensional arrays can be treated as arrays of arrays, the following two forms of array declaration are equivalent:

```
array[1..N] of array [1..M] of <Type>
```

and

```
array[1..N, 1..M] of <Type>
```

Whereas the first form makes the relationships between arrays and their elements more explicit, the second form is an often-preferred shorthand notation. The two are exactly equivalent as far as the compiler is concerned but may not be equivalent from the programmer's perspective.

Consider a two-dimensional array named `Matrix` or, in other words, a table consisting of rows and columns of entities of a type denoted as `<Type>`, with the number of rows given by `NumRows`, and the number of columns given by `NumColumns`. In a two-dimensional matrix representation

```
Matrix: array[1..NumRows, 1..NumColumns] of <Type>;
```

there is no way to specify the array elements in terms of the entire rows or columns.

On the other hand, its representation as an array of rows of arrays:

```
Matrix: array[1..NumRows] of array [1..NumColumns] of <Type>;
```

allows you to refer to the entire row as follows:

```
Matrix[N]
```

where `N` is an arbitrary number within the range `1..NumRows`.

The individual elements can still be referred to as both

```
Matrix[M][N]
```

and

```
Matrix[M,N]
```

Three-Dimensional Arrays

You are now well-equipped to tackle the concept of three-dimensional arrays. A three-dimensional array can be visualized as a three-dimensional cubicle partitioned into a mesh of individual cells, each of the same type and size.

Figure 8.4 illustrates the concept of a three-dimensional array.

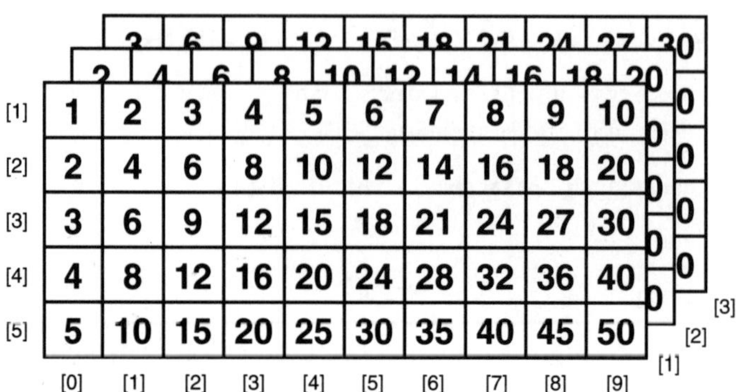

Figure 8.4.
The concept of a three-dimensional array.

Syntax

Declaring Three-Dimensional Array Types

The following is the general syntax for declaring three-dimensional array types:

```
type
  ArrayTypeName = array [Index1Definition, Index2Definition, Index3Definition] of
➥BaseType;
```

Examples:

```
type
  MonthlySales: array[1..12,Regions,Products] of Real;
  TestResults: array[1..5,Boolean,1..100] of Byte;
```

The declaration of a three-dimensional array is again almost identical to its lower-dimensional counterparts, the only difference being one additional index definition within the square brackets.

You can access the individual elements of the array by using expressions of the form

```
ArrayName[Index1,Index2,Index3]
```

where `Index1`, `Index2`, and `Index3` are each an expression evaluating to a value of the respective index type. In other words, each such index expression results in a particular value belonging to the type of the respective index. After evaluating all three index expressions, a unique point in a three-dimensional space, that is a unique array element, is found.

A simple example of a three-dimensional array follows:

```
type
  Array3D = array[1..10,1..10,1..10] of Byte.
```

The example declaration of `Array3D` above declares a 1000-element, cube-shaped 10×10×10 array of `Byte`-sized cells. In this simple example, all index values are identically declared as implicit (nameless) subranges `1..10`, making it possible to access the individual array elements as follows:

```
1: var
2:   AnArray3D: Array3D;
3: begin
4:   AnArray3D[1,1,1] := 0;
5:   AnArray3D[7,5,2] := AnArray3D[2,5,7];
6:   AnArray3D[3,3,3] := 1;
7: end;
```

This variable declaration creates a variable of the type `Array3D`. Memory is thus reserved for the 1000 elements of the array variable with the structure defined by the `Array3D` type declaration.

The executable statements within the begin-end block on lines 4 through 6 assign specific values to some array elements. The expression on the right-hand side of the assignment operator on line 5 of the code uses the value of an element `[2,5,7]` of the array to be assigned to another element in the same array: that at position `[7,5,2]`.

Multi-Dimensional Arrays

The reason for explicitly spelling out the details of one-, two-, and three-dimensional arrays was that these three classes of arrays represent the majority of arrays you will ever encounter in practical applications.

For the rare occasions when more than three dimensions are called for, Object Pascal lets you declare arrays with an arbitrary number of dimensions.

Syntax

Declaring Multi-Dimensional Array Types

The following is the general syntax for declaring array type with an arbitrary number of dimensions:

```
type
  ArrayTypeName = array [Index1Definition, Index2Definition, ..., IndexNDefinition]
➥of AnotherType;
```

Examples:

```
type
  MonthlyAmounts: array[1..12,1..3,Boolean,-1..1] of Real;
  TemperatureGrid: array[1..100,1..100,1..100,-1..1] of Byte;
```

The generic array-type definition allows for an arbitrary number of dimensions indexed by arbitrary ordinal type expressions.

Note: Object Pascal imposes no restrictions on the dimensionality of the arrays. You can declare as many dimensions (that is, provide as many independent index definitions) as needed. There is, however, a restriction on the total size of the array, and indeed on the total size of any single data structure, that can be defined. Due to the segmented architecture of 16-bit Windows (such as Windows 3.1), the total size of a single, contiguous data structure in Delphi cannot exceed 64KB.

For example, if you try to declare

```
A: array[1..100000] of Integer;
```

the compiler rejects this declaration with an error "Data structure too large". This is because one hundred thousand integers take up 100000 × 2 = 200000 bytes, or roughly 195KB.

On the other hand

```
B: array[1..10000] of Integer;
```

is still OK, as it only takes 10000 × 2 = 20000 bytes, or about 19.5KB.

Using Arrays

Individual elements of an array can be accessed via their *index*, also known as *subscript.*

Syntax

Accessing Array Elements

Following is the syntax for referring to a particular array element:

```
ArrayName[Index1, Index2, Index3, ..., IndexN]
```

`Index1` through `IndexN` in this statement are arbitrary ordinal type expressions.

Examples:

```
Count[3]
MonthlySales[January]
Occurrence['A']
Temperature[1,3]
Node[23,7,False]
```

The individual elements of an array are accessed by specifying the array name and an index (or a set of valid indices) inside a pair of square brackets. You can both access a particular array component's value, or assign a new value to it, in this way.

When you are accessing array elements inside your executable code, the array index may be an arbitrary arithmetic expression resulting in a whole number, or an expression that results in an ordinal value, as long as its value is compatible with the specified index type and within the indicated index limits.

8

Merely declaring an array type does not create an actual instance of the array. You already know that you need to declare a variable to actually reserve memory space for it. This also applies for arrays and the array elements.

An array element is a variable just like any other variable of the array base type. Instead, however, of having to directly refer to the variable by name to be able to access it, you use the array name and an index expression within square brackets, uniquely defining the element within the array.

For example, the following two variable declarations are equivalent in the sense that both of them create five distinct `Integer` variables. The first form of the declaration is

```
var
  Number1,
  Number2,
  Number3,
  Number4,
  Number5: Integer;
```

Given the above declaration, you would refer to an individual variable by its name, such as

```
begin
  Number1 := 0;
  Number2 := 23;
  Number5 := -17;
end;
```

The second form of the same declaration is an array declaration:

```
var
  Number: array[1..5] of Integer;
```

Given this more compact but equivalent declaration, you would refer to the individual `Integer` elements of the array as follows:

```
begin
  Number[1] := 0;
  Number[2] := 23;
  Number[5] := -17;
end;
```

As you can see, the two methods are very similar in the way the individual variables/elements are used, but the array notation is more compact in terms of its declaration.

Another advantage of the array notation is its ability to support iteration more easily. You might recall from Day 7 that you can set up a **`for`** loop running through all of the elements in the array. You might also recall from an earlier lesson that all variables should be initialized before they can be used; this certainly applies to arrays as well.

The initialization requirement can be quite a chore to fulfill if there is a large number of variables of the same type to which you need to assign an initial value. The array notation allows for a much more compact way of handling initialization.

In particular, instead of writing

```
begin
  Number1 := 0;
  Number2 := 0;
  Number3 := 0;
  Number4 := 0;
  Number5 := 0;
end;
```

to initialize the five integer variables to zero, you could write

```
begin
  for Indcx :- 1 to 5 do
    Number[Index] := 0;
end;
```

if they were declared as an array instead.

Note: Each component of an array must be initialized—or otherwise assigned a value—separately because each individual element is equivalent to a separate variable of the same type as the base array type.

The only exception to this rule is when you need to copy the contents of an array to another array of the same type. You can accomplish this in a single step by a simple assignment statement of the form

```
Array1 := Array2;
```

Remember that both `Array1` and `Array2` must be of the same type, that is, they must match in the base type, the number of dimensions, and their respective size in each of these dimensions.

You will appreciate the compactness and simplicity of the array notation even more when the number of otherwise identical variables you have to deal with grows to tens, or hundreds, or beyond. Initializing 100 individually named variables "by hand" would be a tedious undertaking indeed.

As indicated in the previous Note, two arrays of the same type can be used in a single assignment statement. For example, given the declarations

```
type
  ArrInteger10: array[1..10] of Integer;
var
  A, B: ArrInteger10;
```

one can copy all element values of the array B into the corresponding elements of array A as follows:

```
begin
  A := B;
end;
```

This notation is a lot more compact than the equivalent

```
begin
  A[1]  := B[1];
  A[2]  := B[2];
  A[3]  := B[3];
  ...
  A[9]  := B[9];
  A[10] := B10];
end;
```

or even

```
var
  Index: Integer;
begin
  for Index := 1 to 10 do
    A[Index] := B[Index];
end;
```

Another important point about using arrays is that their elements can be accessed in an arbitrary order. It is not necessary, although by using a **`for`** loop it becomes quite natural, to access the array elements in sequence. You can access or change any value in an array at any time when the array variable is visible. Arrays are thus said to be *random access* (as opposed to *sequential access*).

Strings

After you understand the structure of the array type, character strings should be no problem. Pascal `String`s *are* themselves arrays in disguise.

Anatomy of a String

Object Pascal supports character string types, that is, structured types representing sequences of characters. String types are really special kinds of character arrays.

Note: Object Pascal provides support for two inherently different string types: Pascal `String`s and null-terminated C strings. Pascal `String`s are a native type of up to 255 characters in length. C strings, also known as null-terminated strings, are simply character arrays of up to 64K in length.

The need for C strings arises when programming directly to the Windows *API* (Application Programming Interface, the arcane "traditional" way of programming

Windows). The built-in Pascal `Strings` are easier to program with, and for most purposes sufficient to represent sequences of characters. This book therefore concentrates on this native type with only an honorable mention of null-terminated strings.

You have already learned on Day 4 that to define a string type you can use the reserved word **`String`** and, optionally, indicate the maximum allowable length for the string by specifying the maximum index within square brackets. The index is specified by a byte-sized constant in the range 1..255. The default length of a string, when no specific length is given in the type declaration, is 255.

Consider the following example:

```
type
  TFileName = String[12];
  TWindowCaption = String[80];
```

The above **`type`**-block defines two string types: `TFileName`, of maximum length 12 characters, and `TWindowCaption`, of maximum length 80.

Given the above declarations, you can now declare instances of these string types in a Variable Declaration Block. For example:

```
var
  TheFileName    : TFileName;
  AWindowCaption: TWindowCaption;
```

The first variable declaration above, `TheFileName`, reserves just enough memory to hold a character string of 12 characters maximum. It turns out that the actual amount of memory reserved for a string type is one more byte than the declared maximum string length. The size of the `TheFileName` variable is actually 13 bytes.

Each character of a string occupies one byte. The extra byte is needed to store the actual, dynamic length of the string, which may be anywhere from zero ("empty string") to the maximum declared number of characters, 12 in this case.

Figure 8.5 illustrates the memory layout for the `TheFileName` string. Notice the extra length byte at the very beginning of the array.

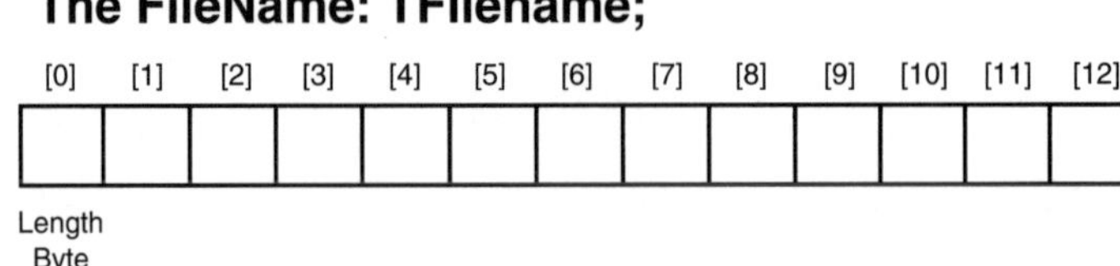

Figure 8.5.
The memory layout of `TheFileName` string variable declared in the text.

Strings are actually arrays of characters. With the exception of the first length byte, which is best interpreted as a number, all cells in a string can be occupied by character values. You can access the individual characters in a string the same way you access array elements: using an index expression within square brackets. For example, the expression

```
TheFileName[5]
```

gives you the fifth character in the string `TheFileName`. You can also assign individual characters anywhere within the actual, dynamic length of a string using the same syntax as for assigning values to character arrays. For example,

```
TheFileName[5] := 'B';
```

assigns the upper-case letter B as the fifth character in the string `TheFileName`.

As you might recall from Day 4, string variables are static in size: the *maximum allowable length* of a string is predetermined by its type declaration and cannot be changed at run-time. The maximum length determines the allocated string variable size. What is dynamic about a string is its *actual length*, up to the specified maximum. The actual length is the number of valid characters currently in the character array portion of a string variable.

When you are assigning individual characters to a string using the `StringName[Index]` syntax, you have to make sure that you are within the actual, "live," dynamic length of the string. There is not much point in assigning a value to a character cell that is beyond the current length of the string: the results will not be visible, at best. As far as strings are concerned, only the character cells within their current length are "active" and contain valid data.

To see an illustration of this concept, take a look at Listing 8.1.

Listing 8.1. Dynamic length versus static size of a string.

```
program Str2;

{
Illustrates the concept of a dynamic length of
a string and contrasts it with the static string
variable's size.
}

uses
  WinCrt;

type
  TFileName = String[12];

var
  FName    : TFileName;
  TheSize,
  TheLength: Byte;

```

continues

Listing 8.1. continued

```
begin
  FName := 'filename.txt';
  TheSize := SizeOf(FName);
  TheLength := Length(FName);
  WriteLn;
  WriteLn('FName         = ''',FName,'''');
  WriteLn('SizeOf(FName) = ',TheSize);
  WriteLn('Length(Fname) = ',TheLength);

  FName := 'a';
  TheSize := SizeOf(FName);
  TheLength := Length(FName);
  WriteLn;
  WriteLn('FName         = ''',FName,'''');
  WriteLn('SizeOf(FName) = ',TheSize);
  WriteLn('Length(Fname) = ',TheLength);

  FName := 'short.pas';
  TheSize := SizeOf(FName);
  TheLength := Length(FName);
  WriteLn;
  WriteLn('FName         = ''',FName,'''');
  WriteLn('SizeOf(FName) = ',TheSize);
  WriteLn('Length(Fname) = ',TheLength);

  FName := 'toolongafilename';
  TheSize := SizeOf(FName);
  TheLength := Length(FName);
  WriteLn;
  WriteLn('FName         = ''',FName,'''');
  WriteLn('SizeOf(FName) = ',TheSize);
  WriteLn('Length(Fname) = ',TheLength);
end.
```

The output from the program in Listing 8.1 should look similar to the following:

```
FName         = 'filename.txt'
SizeOf(FName) = 13
Length(FName) = 12

FName         = 'a'
SizeOf(FName) = 13
Length(FName) = 1

FName         = 'short.pas'
SizeOf(FName) = 13
Length(FName) = 9

FName         = 'toolongafile'
SizeOf(FName) = 13
Length(FName) = 12
```

The program declaration block in Listing 8.1 contains a uses-clause on lines 9 and 10 that imports the terminal style character I/O services of the `WinCrt` module.

The **`type`**-declaration block on lines 12 and 13 defines a string type of maximum 12 characters in length.

Lines 15 through 18 comprise a variable declaration block actually making use of the type declaration. The **`var`** block declares a `TFileName`-string variable `FName`. In addition, it declares two `Byte` variables, `TheSize` and `TheLength`, which will be used to store the calculated size of the string variable and its dynamic length, respectively.

The first assignment statement on line 21 within the executable **`begin-end`** block assigns the value of `'filename.txt'` to the string variable. Notice that the value happens to be exactly 12 characters in length, including the period. After the string assignment, the size of the string variable `FName` is calculated on line 22 by using the built-in function `SizeOf`, and assigned to the variable `TheSize`. `SizeOf(FName)` returns 13 as expected: the 12 bytes reserved for the string characters, and one byte for the string length.

Line 23 assigns the dynamic string length of `FName` to the variable `TheLength`. The dynamic length is obtained by calling the built-in function `Length`. `Length(FName)` returns 12 in this case, which gets assigned to `TheLength`.

The next four lines deal with outputting to the screen the values that were just calculated.

Line 24 inserts a blank line into the output.

Line 25 prints out the contents of the `FName` variable. The printout is prefixed with a label, that is, a constant string, so that it is easier to interpret for the user of the program. The actual value of the string is enclosed in quotes on the printout. Notice how putting a single quote into the label string constant was accomplished: by duplicating it within the enclosing string single-quotes.

The output generated from this first block of statements on lines 21 through 27 indeed verifies that although the declared maximum string length of `FName` is 12, the actual size of the variable is 13. The assigned string `'filename.txt'`, consisting of 12 characters, again takes up all the available character cells in the string.

Figure 8.6 illustrates the situation after the assignment on line 21 takes place.

The FileName: TFilename;

[0]	[1]	[2]	[3]	[4]	[5]	[6]	[7]	[8]	[9]	[10]	[11]	[12]
#12	f	i	l	e	n	a	m	e	.	t	x	t

Length Byte

Figure 8.6.
Memory layout after the assignment on line 21 of Listing 8.1.

The following group of statements, on lines 29 through 35, repeats similar actions. This time, however, a string of length 1 is assigned to FName. You can verify with the output that the size of the variable FName has not changed at all; it is still 13 because it is determined by the type declaration at compile-time, and not by the length of the string. The length has changed, of course, and is now 1.

Figure 8.7 illustrates the new situation created by the assignment on line 29.

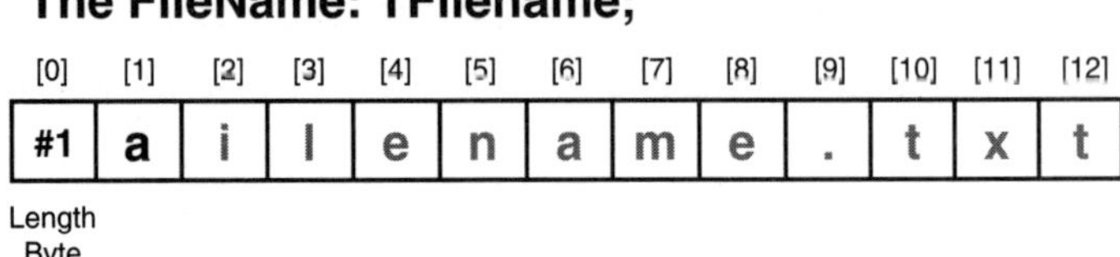

Figure 8.7.
Memory layout after the assignment on line 29 of Listing 8.1.

Notice what happened to the now-excessive characters of the previous 12-character string: They are still there, but not active or visible. Object Pascal knows how to handle strings and will not print out the garbage characters beyond the actual length of the string. But if you attempt to manipulate the string's characters by hand, using the array index expression, be careful not to go beyond the actual length, which is currently 1. Otherwise you will be picking up the garbage character leftovers. You can always check the current length of the string by using the `Length` standard function, in the same way it was done on line 31 previously.

History repeats itself again on lines 37 through 43. This time, a nine-character string `'short.pas'` is assigned to the variable FName.

The memory layout after the assignment on line 37 is illustrated in Figure 8.8.

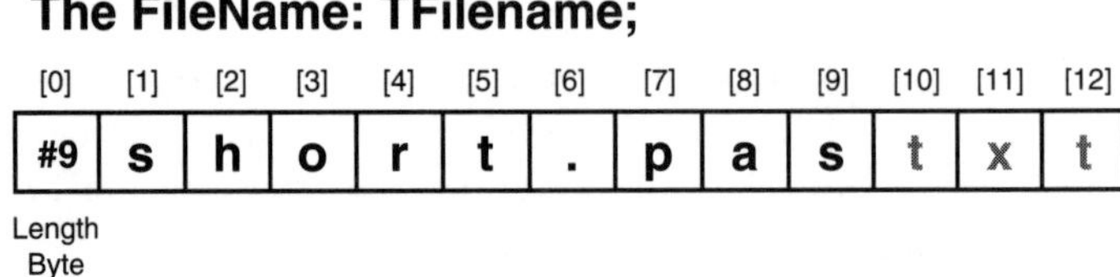

Figure 8.8.
Memory layout after the assignment on line 37 of Listing 8.1.

The last set of statements, on lines 45 through 51 of Listing 8.1, attempt something seemingly illegal. The assignment on line 45 attempts to assign a 16-character string `'toolongafilename'` to the variable FName. Observe what happened to the string: it did not "fit" within the declared size of the variable and was quietly truncated to the maximum allowable length, which was 12 characters. The resulting memory layout is illustrated in Figure 8.9.

Figure 8.9. *Memory layout after the assignment on line 45 of Listing 8.1.*

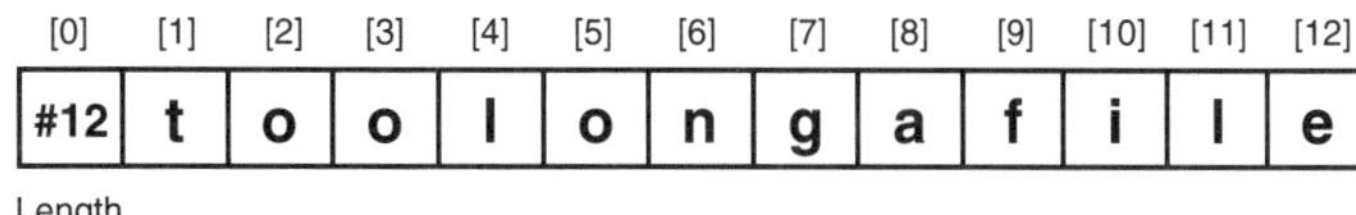

The important point to keep in mind is that Pascal string variables neither "grow" nor "shrink" as needed: their maximum length is fixed and declared at run-time. There are ways of accomplishing dynamic allocation of string variables in Object Pascal, but it requires more specialized knowledge of pointers and dynamic memory allocation; the power comes at a price.

String Manipulation

So far you have seen how to assign constant values to a string variable. Strings can be manipulated in a number of ways by using string expressions.

String Concatenation

The + (plus) sign is used to glue two strings together, or *concatenate* them. Bear in mind that the result of string concatenation cannot be longer than 255 characters, and additionally, that it is not very useful if it is longer than the declared size of the string variable to which you are trying to assign the value. In the former case, a run-time error is certain; in the latter, the string will simply be truncated.

Following are some examples of string concatenation using the + operator.

`'Object' + 'Pascal'` results in `'ObjectPascal'`

`'Object' + ' ' + 'Pascal'` results in `'Object Pascal'`

String Comparison

Very often you need to compare two strings to determine whether they contain the same values, and if not, which of the two values is "greater" or "smaller" than the other.

Although strings are not ordinal types, there is an associated ordering that can be applied to them. Every dictionary is an example of one such ordering.

The comparison of strings in Object Pascal proceeds from left to right, character by character. The ASCII values of the corresponding characters are compared, and the first mismatch determines which of the two strings will be considered "smaller." If the two strings being compared are of different length, but equal up to and including the last character of the shorter string, the longer string is considered "greater" and falls after the shorter in the resulting ordering.

Two strings are considered equal if and only if their lengths are the same and their contents match exactly, character by character.

Table 8.1 illustrates the relational operators that can be used to compare strings.

Table 8.1. String-comparison operators.

Operator	Meaning	Example
`=`	Equal	`'ABC' = 'ABC'`
`<`	Less-Than	`'ABC' < 'ABCD'`
`>`	Greater-Than	`'abc' > 'ABC'`
`<=`	Less-Than-Or-Equal	`'ABC ' <= 'ABCD'`
`>=`	Greater-Than-Or-Equal	`'a' >= 'ABCDEFGH'`
`<>`	Not-Equal	`'A ' <> ' A'`

Using the operators from Table 8.1, you can determine the ordering of any number of strings. For example, the following string-comparison expressions all resolve to the `Boolean` value `True`:

```
'Pascal' = 'Pascal'
'Pascal ' > 'Pascal'
'Object' > 'Pascal'
'1' < '2'
'1' < '1 '
'11' < '2'
'2'  > '1999999'
```

The following is an ASCII ordering of some strings according to the rules of string comparison in Object Pascal, from "smallest" to "largest":

```
DAY01
DAY02
DAY1
DAY1
DAY11
DAY12
DAY2
DAY21
DAY9
Day1
Day11
Day12
Day2
Day21
Day3
Day9
```

Note that the case of the string is significant, and that it disturbs what you would think to be the proper "dictionary" ordering of the strings.

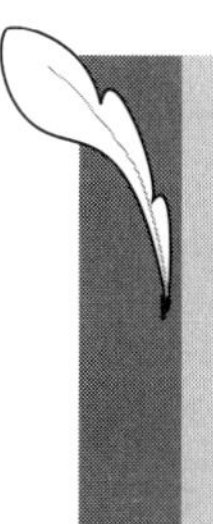

Note: The Pascal language is case-insensitive. This means that it does not matter whether you put an identifier's name in all-upper-, all-lower-, or mixed-case; the names are equivalent.

This does not mean, however, that when you compare string values in Pascal, the comparison would be case-insensitive: the value of a **`String`** constant or variable is taken verbatim and the ASCII values of the individual characters *do* matter in string comparisons.

String Subroutines

As a final take in this installment on strings, let's look at some of the common, built-in string-manipulation subroutines that you can use in your programs.

Built-In Subroutines

You have already encountered the `Length` standard function. Table 8.2 lists a number of additional built-in string subroutines available to you.

Table 8.2. Built-in string-manipulation subroutines. Square brackets [ ] indicate optional parameters.

Subroutine	Description	Examples
`function` `Concat(s1 [, s2,..., sn]: String): String;`	Concatenates (merges) several strings into one. If the result is longer than 255 characters, it is truncated.	`Concat('Object',' ',' Pascal','.')` returns `'Object Pascal.'`
`function` `Copy(S: String; Index, Count: Integer): String;`	Extracts a portion of length `Count` of the string `S`, starting at position `Index`. The parameter `S` is unaffected.	`Copy('Object Pascal',8,6)` returns `'Pascal'`.
`procedure` `Delete (`**`var`** `S: String; Index, Count:Integer);`	Deletes a portion of the string `S`, starting at position `Index`. The procedure modifies the actual parameter `S` passed to it.	Given `AString := 'Object Pascal'`; the expression `Delete(AString,7,7)` results in `AString` having the value of `'Object'`.

continues

Table 8.2. continued

Subroutine	Description	Examples
procedure Insert (Source: String; **var** S: String; Index: Integer);	Inserts a string Source into the target string S at position Index. The procedure modifies the actual parameter S but does not affect the Source.	Given AString := 'Pascal'; the statement Insert('Object ',1); results in AString assuming the value of 'Object Pascal'.
function Length (S: String): Integer;	Returns the actual length of the string S, as opposed to its declared maximum length.	Length('Pascal') returns 6.
function Pos(Substr: String; S: String): Byte;	Searches (case-sensitive) the string S for a substring specified as Substr and returns the position of the first character of the substring in S. If the substring is not found in S, 0 is returned.	Pos('Pas','Object Pascal') returns 7.
procedure Str(X [: Width [: Decimals]]; **var** S);	Converts the number X (integer or real) to its decimal string representation stored in S. With and Decimals are formatting parameters. Width specifies the minimum size of the string in which to right-justify the representation of the number. Decimals is applicable to real numbers only, and specifies the number of decimal digits (precision) to be output. See also Table 8.3 for the alternative IntToStr function.	Str(127,S) returns '127' in S.; Str(-12:5,S) returns ' -12' in S; Str(127.5789:10:2,S) returns ' 127.58' in S.

Subroutine	Description	Examples
procedure Val(S; **var** V; **var** Code: Integer);	Converts a string value S to its numeric representation returned in V. V can be an integer or real variable. A status code is returned in Code. If the string is invalid, the index of the first offending character is returned in Code; otherwise Code is zero. See also Table 8.3 for the alternative StrToInt.	Val('123',V,Code) returns 123 in V and 0 in Code; Val('12A',V,Code) returns 0 in V, and 3 in Code.

Additional Subroutines

In addition to the built-in subroutines listed in Table 8.2, there are a number of useful string-manipulation routines exported by the standard SysUtils unit. Unlike the built-in subroutines, which you can call right away without any special precautions, you must include SysUtils in the **uses** statement of the current module to use these additional routines.

Table 8.3 lists the string-manipulation routines exported by the SysUtils unit.

Table 8.3. String-manipulation routines from the SysUtils unit.

Subroutine	Description	Examples
function CompareStr(const S1, S2: string): Integer;	Compares two strings, S1 and S2, and returns 0 if they are equal, an integer less than zero if S1 < S2, an integer greater than zero if S1 > S2.	CompareStr('Cat', 'Dog') returns -1.
function CompareText(**const** S1, S2: String): Integer;	Makes a *case-insensitive* comparison between two strings, S1 and S2, returning 0 if the strings are equal, an integer less than zero if S1 < S2, an integer greater than zero if S1 > S2.	CompareText('Cat','CAT') returns 0.

continues

Table 8.3. continued

Subroutine	Description	Examples
`function Format const Format: String; const Args: array of const): String;`	Returns a string formatted according to the specification based on the `Format` parameter. The `Format` parameter works as a template for the output and allows the contents of numeric and character-based variables to be converted to string output. The `Args` parameter is an array of parameter variables to be formatted. The `Format` template string may contain special character codes called format specifiers, determining how the arguments passed into the function via `Args` array are to be formatted.	Format `('A=%5d',[123])` returns `'  123'`
`procedure FormatStr var Result: String; const Format: String; const Args: array of const);`	Formats a string in a similar way to `Format`, but instead of returning the formatted data as the function result, `FormatStr` fills the string `Result` passed in as a parameter. The meaning of the `Format` parameter is the same as in the case of the `Format` function.	Given a declaration `var Result: String;` after `FormatStr(Result, 'A=%5d',[123])` returns to the caller, the `Result` variable will have the value of `'  123'`.

Subroutine	Description	Examples
function `IntToHex Value: Longint; Digits: Integer): String;`	Converts the integer `Value` into a hexadecimal (base 16) string representation. If the hexadecimal representation contains less than the specified number of digits, the string is left-padded with zeros.	`IntToHex(1025,4)` returns '0401'.
function `IntToStr Value: Longint): String;`	Converts the integer `Value` into its decimal (base 10) string representation.	`IntToStr(245)` returns `'245'`.
function `LowerCase` **const** `S: String): String;`	Converts the string passed as `S` to all-lowercase.	`LowerCase('OBJECT')` returns `'object'`.
function `StrToInt` **const** `S: String): Longint;`	Converts a decimal (base 10) or hexadecimal (base 16) string representation of a number into an integer. If the string `S` does not represent a valid number, an exception is raised.	`StrToInt('123')` returns 123.
function `StrToIntDef(const S: String; Default: Longint): Longint;`	Converts a decimal (base 10) or hexadecimal (base 16) string representation of a number into an integer. If the string `S` does not represent a valid number, the `Default` value is returned.	`StrToInt('123',0)` returns 123; `StrToInt('XYZ',0)` returns 0.
function `UpperCase` **const** `S: String): String;`	Converts the string passed as `S` to all-uppercase.	`UpperCase('object')` returns `'OBJECT'`.

Sets

Sets are structured data types, each consisting of a collection of elements called *set members*. The elements in a set have no particular order. Another important characteristic of a set is that no element of a set is duplicated: every element is either represented (is a member of the particular set), or it is not (is missing from the set).

In other words, an element is either a member of a set, or it is not. Set manipulation is concerned with whether an element is in a set, rather than focusing on the order of the elements or the frequency of their occurrence.

Typical use for sets is to maintain a collection of independent "flags" describing different states that are *not* mutually exclusive. If they *are* mutually exclusive, an enumerated type is a better choice.

Set-Type Declarations

A set type is declared by specifying a pair of keywords, **set of**, after the equal sign in the type declaration.

Syntax

Declaration of Set Types

The syntax for declaring a set type is as follows:

```
type
  TypeName = set of ElementType;
```

Examples:

```
type
  Characters = set of Char;
  Numbers = set of Byte;
  MonthlyEntries = set of Month;
```

A specification of the type of set elements, called the *base* type of a set, follows in the **type**-declaration. All elements of a set must be of the same *ordinal* type. The element type cannot be a `Real`, nor an **array**, nor a **set**.

Note: An Object Pascal **set** can only hold up to 256 ordinal members. The set element type in the set definition (base type) must be narrow enough as to disallow any more than 256 values. Moreover, the ordinal value of the lowest-valued element of a set must not be less than zero. Likewise, the ordinal number of the highest-valued member of the set must not be more than 255.

Put all these requirements together, and you will see that they are all satisfied by enumerated types. You can thus use enumerated types as bases for your set declarations, both making the notation readable and ensuring that the above constraints are met.

Specifying Set Values

A particular set value is denoted by specifying a range of set elements enclosed in a pair of square brackets.

Depending on how the range of elements is specified, there are variations in the syntax of a set-value expression.

Syntax

Enumerated Set Notation

The syntax for specifying a value for a set by enumerating all of its elements is as follows:

```
[Element1, Element2, Element3, ..., ElementN]
```

Examples:

```
[1,2,3]
['A','B','C']
```

Syntax

Set Notation Using Ranges

The syntax for specifying a set value by listing subranges of base-type values is as follows:

```
[Range1, Range2, ..., RangeN]
```

Mixing explicit elements and ranges is also permitted.

Examples:

```
[-5..-1,1..5]
[1..5,9,23]
['A'..'F']
```

The *range* of all values of a particular set type is the collection of all possible subsets, including the empty set. What this really means is that you define a set type by specifying a range of possible values for the set elements.

For example, the definition

```
type
  CharSet = set of Char;
```

specifies a set, whose elements are all of type `Char`.

After the range of values of individual set elements is defined, that is, the set type is declared, you can define a variable of the set type. For instance:

```
var
  Chars: CharSet;
```

defines a variable of a set type `CharSet`, whose possible elements are all 255 characters. What are the possible values for the set variable now?

Each of the 255 possible characters can be in the set, or it might be missing. The total number of cases in which a particular selection of characters is represented in the set is clearly greater than 255.

To start with, there are 255 possible values where only one of the 255 characters is present. Each of the following elements:

```
['a']
['b']
['c']
['d']
 ...
```

is one of the distinct, possible values of the variable `Chars`. Now consider the possible values in which two of the 255 characters are present in the set. There are numerous combinations like these:

```
['a','b']
['a','c']
['a','d']
['a','e']
...
['b','c']
['b','d']
['b','e']
 ...
['c','d']
['c','e']
 ...
```

up until

```
['x','y']
['x','z']
['y','z']
```

Now consider the subsets consisting of exactly three elements, exactly four, and so on. You can see that the number of possible values is large, much larger than the number of elements of the base type itself.

Finally, there is the special value denoted by

```
[]
```

representing an *empty set*, that is, the set that has no elements.

To assign a particular value to a set variable, use the familiar assignment operator. A value for the set may be one of these combinations of the base type's values.

Listing 8.2 gives a few examples of assignment statements specific to the `CharSet` type.

Listing 8.2. Assigning values to set-typed variables.

```
 1: type
 2:   CharSet = set of Char;
 3:   NumberSet = set of Byte;
 4: var
 5:   Chars: CharSet;
 6:   Numbers: NumberSet;
 7: begin
 8:   Chars := [];
 9:   Chars := ['a','b','c'];
10:   Chars := ['a'..'f','x'..'z'];
11:   Chars := [#10, #13, 'A'..'Z'];
12:   Chars := ['9'];
13:   Numbers := [];
14:   Numbers := [9];
15:   Numbers := [1..100];
16:   Numbers := [1, 2, 3, 4, 5];
17:   Numbers := [0..255];
18: end
```

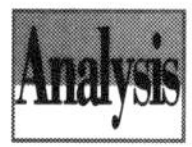

The **`type`**-declaration block on lines 1 to 3 of Listing 8.2 declares two set types: `CharSet`, which is a set of all characters in the range of `#0` to `#255`, and `NumberSet`, which is a set of `Byte`-sized numbers in the range of 0 through 255.

Lines 4, 5, and 6 form a variable declaration block defining two set variables: `Chars` and `Numbers`, of the `CharSet` and `NumberSet` types, respectively.

The executable **`begin-end`** block on lines 7 through 18 contains a number of assignment statements assigning sample values to the set variables.

Lines 8 and 13 both assign a value of an empty set, denoted by `[]`, to the variables `Chars` and `Numbers`, respectively. Note that the empty set is compatible with any set type; or in other words, the value of `[]` may be assigned to any set variable, regardless of its base type.

Line 9 assigns a particular set of three character values, `'a'`, `'b'`, and `'c'`, to the set variable `Chars`.

Line 10 illustrates the usage of subranges to specify members of a set. Instead of exhaustively listing the values as

```
['a','b','c','d','e','f','x','y','z']
```

a convenient shorthand subrange expression is used to specify the two contiguous ranges of set members.

The set being assigned to the set-variable `Chars` on line 11 uses a mixture of a subrange specification and element enumeration to specify its members. Notice the sharp-sign notation you learned previously to denote non-printable characters in the set.

Line 12 illustrates a set with just one member. It also highlights the fact that the notation `'9'` represents a character, not a number; hence there is no surprise in the fact that the set member `'9'` is a member of a set of *characters*. A corresponding set with a single *number* element is shown on line 14. It is being properly assigned to a number-set variable `Numbers`.

Line 15 illustrates a set defined as a range of numbers. After the assignment, the variable `Number` contains a set of 101 elements: each of the natural numbers 1 through 100, inclusive.

Line 16 shows a fully enumerated set of numbers.

Line 17 is interesting in that the set expression on the right-hand side of the assignment operator denotes a set consisting of all numbers in the base set type's range. A subrange expression is used to specify this set. One might justifiably say that the subrange defined is not a subrange, or at least not a *proper* subrange: it covers all the possible values in the entire range of the base type. This set is "full" in the sense that all possible elements are present.

Set Operations

One of the fundamental operations on a set is testing whether a particular value is a member of this set. The **`in`** set operator is used for that purpose.

Syntax

Testing Set Membership

The general syntax for a Boolean expression testing whether `AValue` is a member of a set `TheSet` is:

```
AValue in TheSet
```

The expression returns `True` if `AValue` is present in `TheSet`, `False` otherwise.

Examples:

```
if ('a' in CharSet) then
  DoSomething;

while not (ANumber in NumberSet) do
  PerformSomething;
```

The **`in`** operator for testing the set membership takes one element and tests it against one set. The result of applying the **`in`** operator to an element and a set is **`True`** if the element is a member of the set, **`False`** otherwise.

The mathematical set operations, such as set union, set difference, and set intersection, are supported by Object Pascal and give you the means to create new sets from existing ones. In particular:

8

- Set union is an operation that combines two sets into one. The elements of both original sets are grouped together in the resulting set and duplicate element values are discarded. Hence, the resulting set does not have any duplicate members and consists of the elements of both of the original sets. The order of operands for set union is not significant.

  The Pascal notation for the set union operation uses the symbol + (plus). For example:

```
[1,2,3] + [7,8,9]       = [1,2,3,7,8,9]
[7,8,9] + [1,2,3]       = [1,2,3,7,8,9]
[] + []                 = []
[1,2,3] + []            = [1,2,3]
[1,2,3] + [1,2,3]       = [1,2,3]
[1,2,3] + [1,2,3,4,5] = [1,2,3,4,5]
```

- Set difference is an operation performed on two sets whereby all elements that the first input set has in common with the second are removed. The result is the first input set, less the elements that it had in common with the second input set.

  Object Pascal set difference operator is a - (minus) sign. For example:

```
[1,2,3,4,5] - [1,2,3] = [4,5]
[1,2,3] - [7,8,9]       = [1,2,3]
[] - []                 = []
[] - [1,2,3,4]          = []
[1,2,3] - []            = [1,2,3]
[1,2,3] - [1,2,3]       = []
```

  Note that the order of operands in a set difference operation is significant. Consider the following two results that illustrate this:

```
[1,2,3,4] - [3,4,5,6] = [1,2]
[3,4,5,6] - [1,2,3,4] = [5,6]
```

- Set intersection describes the common elements of both input sets. The resulting set is constructed from all the elements that were present in both input sets.

  The set intersection is denoted by the symbol * (star, multiply) in Object Pascal. For example:

```
[1,2,3] * [7,8,9]       = []
[1,2,3] * [2,3,4]       = [2,3]
[] * []                       = []
[1,2,3] * [1,2,3]       = [1,2,3]
```

Object Pascal also supports a number of set-comparison operators that enable you to determine set relationships.

- Subset operator is denoted by <= (less-than symbol, immediately followed by the equal sign; looking identical to the arithmetic less-than-or-equal operator.) A set is a subset of another if all of its elements are also members of the other. For example the set `['a','b','c','d']` is a subset of the set `['a','b','c','d','e','f']`

  By definition, `A <= B` if, and only if, `A - B = []`.

  As an example, the following two expressions both return `True`:

  `['a','b','c','d'] <= ['a','b','c','d','e','f']`

  and

  `['a','b','c'] <= ['a','b','c']`

- Proper subset operator is denoted by < (less-than symbol). A set is a proper subset of another, when it is a subset and there is at least one element in the other, larger set that is *not* a member of the subset. In other words, the subset may not include all of the elements of the other set to be considered a proper subset.

  Again, by definition, `A < B` if, and only if, `A - B = []` and `B - A <> []`.

  For example, the set `['a','b','c']` is not a proper subset, but simply a subset, of `['a','b','c']`. On the other hand,`['a','b','c'] < ['a','b','c','d']`returns `True`: the first set is a proper subset of the second.

- Superset operator is denoted by the symbol >= (greater-than symbol, immediately followed by an equal sign; not to be confused with the arithmetic greater-than-or-equal operator.) A set is a superset of another if it contains all of the other set's elements, and possibly more.

  For example, the set `['a','b','c','d']` is a superset of `['a','b','c']` and the following expression yields `True`:

  `['a','b','c','d'] <= ['a','b','c']`

  The subset and superset relationships are closely related: if one set is a superset of another, the other is its subset, or formally, `A >= B` implies `B <= A`.

- Proper superset operator is denoted by the > (greater-than) sign. A set is a proper superset of another if it is a superset and contains at least one element that is not a member of the other.

  Again, a proper superset relationship corresponds to a proper subset relationship in the other direction.

  As an example, the set `['a','b','c','d']` is a proper superset of `['a','b','c']` but not the proper superset, although a superset, of `['a','b','c','d']`. Hence the following expression evaluates to `True`:

  `['a','b','c','d'] > ['a','b','c']`

- Set equality can be tested with the = (equal-sign) operator. Two sets are considered equal if they contain exactly the same elements.

  For example, the following expression is `True`:

  ```
  ['a','b','c'] = ['a','b','c']
  ```

  but the following one evaluates to `False`:

  ```
  ['a','b','c'] = ['a','b','c', 'd']
  ```

- Set inequality is expressed by the Pascal <> (not-equal) operator.

  For example, the following expression returns `True`:

  ```
  ['a','b','c'] <> ['a','b','c', 'd']
  ```

Records

Records are another kind of structure data types supported by the Object Pascal language.

NEW TERM A *record* is a collection of named data elements encapsulated and treated as a single entity. The individual data elements of a record are known as *fields*.

A record is essentially a collection of variables, called fields, glued together to form a single entity. The fields of a record are still individually accessible, but the record is treated as a whole for other purposes. This provides a simple and effective way to simplify programs: you can treat a number of variables that always appear together as a single entity for most purposes, while still retaining the flexibility of being able to access the individual elements.

Record-Type Declarations

A record type is declared by specifying the reserved word **`record`** after the equal sign in the type declaration.

Syntax

Record-Type Declaration

The general syntax for declaring record types is:

```
type
  TypeName = record
    Field1Name: Field1Type;
    Field2Name: Field2Type;
    Field3Name: Field3Type;
    ...
    FieldNName: FieldNType;
  end;
```

Example:

```
type
  PatientRecord = record
    FirstName: String[40];
    LastName : String[60];
    Age      : Integer;
    Sex      : Char;
    Insured  : Boolean;
  end;
```

The reserved word **record** is followed by an arbitrary number of field declarations. Each field declaration is terminated by a semicolon. The record declaration ends with the reserved word **end**.

The individual field definitions look remarkably similar to variable declarations. This is not surprising because fields are really variables that were cemented together to form a higher order structure. Each field declaration starts with a field name, which is a typical Pascal identifier, followed by a colon, and followed by a type declaration. Each field declaration is terminated with a semicolon.

The type declaration in a field definition can refer to any valid Pascal type.

A **record**-type declaration belongs inside a **type**-declaration block, within the declaration-part of a Pascal source code block.

Similar to how it was the case with variable declarations, consecutive record fields of the same type can be declared together, without repeating the type's name each time. For example, the following declaration

```
type
  TRectangle = record
    Left,
    Top,
    Right,
    Bottom: Integer;
  end;
```

declares a record type `TRectangle`. `TRectangle` is used extensively in Windows applications and provides a way of specifying the coordinates of a rectangular area of the screen, such as the dimensions of a window. This declaration defines four fields inside the type `TRectangle`, all of which are of the same type: `Integer`. The type name is specified only once, at the end of the declaration, whereas the individual field names are separated from each other by commas.

Using Records

Record types are one kind of a broad selection of Pascal types you can use to declare variables. Records are used very extensively to encapsulate chunks of related information of various types.

Record variables are declared in the same way you would declare other types of variables. In particular, you can declare a record variable whenever you could declare a simple variable of a built-in type.

To access an individual field of a record, you must specify the record variable together with the field's name.

Syntax

Accessing Record Fields

The general syntax for accessing record fields is:

```
RecordVariable.FieldName
```

Examples:

```
CustomerRecord.FirstName
InvoiceRecord.Number
```

The combination of a record variable, single period, and a field name acts in the same way as a variable of the type of the field.

NEW TERM The period, or dot, separating the variable-name part of a fully qualified field from the field-name part is an example of the *dot-notation*: a way of "qualifying" a symbol, or "navigating" your way to a particular data item of interest.

The dot-notation is used extensively and consistently in Object Pascal to allow you to resolve name conflicts among different symbols. It enables you to find your way and access a particular data item of interest, even if it is buried deeply inside a complex, nested structure.

As an example of accessing a record's fields, consider the code in Listing 8.3.

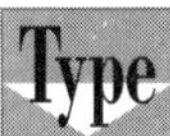

Listing 8.3. TCustomerRecord declaration and usage.

```
program Cust1;

uses
  SysUtils;

type
  TCustomerRecord = record
    FirstName      : String[20];
    LastName       : String[40];
    AmountOwed     : Real;
    DateLastOrdered: TDateTime;
    LastOrderAmount: Real;
  end;

var
  Customer1,
  Customer2: TCustomerType;

```

continues

Listing 8.3. continued

```
19: begin
20:   Customer1.FirstName := 'John';
21:   Customer1.LastName := 'Smith';
22:   Customer1.AmountOwed := 0;
23:   Customer1.DateLastOrdered := Date;
24:   Customer2 := Customer1;
25: end.
```

The declarations on lines 7 through 13 of Listing 8.3 define a `TCustomerRecord` type. The record consists of five fields: `FirstName`, `LastName`, `AmountOwed`, `DateLastOrdered`, and `LastOrderAmount`.

Lines 16 and 17 declare two variables, `Customer1` and `Customer2`, to be of the `TCustomerRecord` type. This is where the `TCustomerRecord` actually comes into existence.

The executable statements on lines 20 through 23 assign specific values to the individual fields of the `Customer1` variable. You can see that the fields are being qualified with the name of the record variable, using the dot-notation.

The assignment on line 23 is particularly interesting because it makes use of a standard function `Date`, returning a `TDateType` value equal to the current system date. This assignment is the reason for importing the services of the `SysUtils` unit on lines 3 and 4.

The assignment on line 24 shows a way of copying the contents of one record to another, provided the two are of the same type. Similar to what was the case with arrays, you can use the record variable as a single entity and assign its value to another record variable of the same type.

Note: The dot-notation and the concept of a record consisting of data fields is very closely related to, and in fact is a basis of, the object-oriented notions of an object and object fields. You will learn more about objects starting on Day 11. For now, keep in mind that objects look very much like records.

Anonymous Types

As with any other user-defined type, you can declare record variables directly, as part of the variable's definition. An example follows.

```
var
  ACustomer: record
    FirstName,
    LastName,
    Address: String;
  end;
```

The above declaration defines the variable `ACustomer` to be of an *anonymous* record type, the structure of which is explicitly spelled out in-line as part of the variable's declaration. The type is called "anonymous" because it does not have any explicit name. It is only used once, to define the single data entity `ACustomer`. There is no way to refer to the same type again—to declare another variable, for example. Even if you do declare another variable, say `AnotherCustomer`, in a similar way:

```
var
  AnotherCustomer: record
    FirstName,
    LastName,
    Address: String;
  end;
```

the two variables are considered to be of different types. If you attempt an assignment like the following

```
AnotherCustomer := ACustomer
```

the compiler will complain with a "Type mismatch" error.

The reason is that the second variable creates another anonymous type; there is no way to tell the compiler that your intention was to instantiate two variables of the same type. Your only recourse is to use an explicitly named type, in a **type**-declaration block, to declare both variables to be assignment-compatible:

```
type
  TCustomer: record
    FirstName,
    LastName,
    Address: String;
  end;

var
  ACustomer,
  AnotherCustomer: TCustomer;
```

Here, the type `TCustomer` is explicitly named, and both variables are declared to be of the same type.

The issue of anonymous types is not specific to record type. Any user-defined type can be declared anonymously; however, this practice should be avoided.

Records versus Arrays

Both records and arrays are structured Pascal types consisting of simpler elements. The important distinction between records and arrays is that the elements of an array must all be of the same type, whereas the fields of a record can each be of a different type.

Another important difference between the two types is in how the individual elements are accessed. The elements of an array are accessed by an index, typically an integer. The fields of a record are accessed by their name, using the dot-notation.

Summary

Today's long lesson introduced you to a number of Object Pascal data types. Here is what you have learned during today's lesson:

- Object Pascal enables you to define your own data types in addition to the rich collection of the built-in types it provides.
- A new type is defined in a Type-Declaration Block, or **type** block.
- Subrange types give you a way of creating restricted versions of existing ordinal types. Subranges are defined by specifying their first and their last value.
- Enumerated types provide means of creating entirely new types. Enumerated types are defined by listing all their values in order.
- Arrays are defined with the reserved word **array**. They are collections of elements of the same type.
- Individual elements of an array are accessible via their index. An index expression must be of ordinal type and is placed inside square brackets.
- Arrays can have one, two, or many dimensions, each indexed separately and independently.
- Pascal strings are special arrays of characters, the first element of which is a number specifying their actual length.
- The actual length of a string at run-time may range from zero to the maximum length defined in the type declaration.
- Sets represent unordered collections of up to 255 unique ordinal-type elements. You can test for set membership using the **in** operator.
- Records, unlike arrays, are collections of elements of possibly different types, called fields. Fields are individually accessible by their names, qualified with the name of the record variable.
- Anonymous types, declared within **var** blocks, although possible, should be avoided. Naming a type makes its use explicit.

Q&A

Q Can I define an array of records?

A Yes, an element of an array may be any defined Pascal type, including another array—or a record, for that matter. You can declare an array of records as follows:

```
type
  TRec = record
    Field1: Integer;
    Field2: String;
    Field3: Real;
  end;

  TArray = array[1..5] of TRec;
```

Q What is the largest record that can be defined in Object Pascal?

A The same restrictions apply for records as for arrays: the maximum size of any single data structure may not exceed 64KB.

Q Is there a way of handling strings longer than 255 characters in Object Pascal?

A The Pascal strings are limited to 255 characters. However, Object Pascal supports C-style null-terminated strings, which can theoretically be as big as 64KB. So, the answer is yes, there is a way, but not with Pascal strings. If you need to process text fragments longer than 255 characters, you must use null-terminated strings. These are considered advanced and were not covered in today's lesson nor in this book.

Q Can one use an enumerated type, say a list of weekdays, to loop through an array?

A Yes, an enumerated type is an example of an ordinal type, and can be used as a `for`-loop control variable, as well as an array index. Declare your loop variable (such as `Index`) to be of the enumerated type (such as `WeekDays`) and then run the loop as follows:

```
type
  WeekDays =
    (Monday, Tuesday, Wednesday, Thursday,
     Friday, Saturday, Sunday);
var
  Index: WeekDays;
  Week: array[Monday..Sunday] of ...;
begin
  ...
```

```
    for Index := Monday to Sunday do begin
      {Loop body goes here, e.g.}
      if Week[Index] ... then
        Week[Index] := ...;
      ...
    end;
  end;
```

Workshop

Quiz

1. True or False? The order of set members is determined by the ordinal number of each of the set elements.
2. True or False? The fields in a record may be accessed by their index, that is, their position in the record declaration.
3. True or False? A real number is a scalar type and hence can be used to index an array.
4. True or False? The `Ord` built-in function can be used to determine the ASCII value of a particular character in a string.
5. True or False? A subrange-type of real numbers must be contiguous and cannot exclude any elements "in the middle" of the range.
6. What is the result of the following set operations?

   a. `[100,102,104,105,106] + [100, 101, 102, 103, 104]`

   b. `[One, Two, Three, Four] - [Five, Four, Six]`

   c. `['a','b','c','D','E','F'] * ['A', 'B', 'c', 'd']`

Exercises

1. Define a subrange type to represent ages of people.
2. Define an enumerated type suitable for representing the gender of a person filling out a questionnaire. Make sure that you allow the representation of an unanswered question.
3. Define a record structure holding the following information: a book title, primary author, publisher, ISBN number, number of pages, price, and the current edition number. Build a simple `WinCrt`-based program that assigns sample values to the individual fields and then prints them out using WriteLn statements.

WEEK 2

9

Subroutines

Today's lesson is quite theoretical. It covers in a more formal way the topic of creating and using one of the most fundamental program building blocks: subroutines.

In today's lesson, you learn the following:

- What a subroutine is and what kinds of subroutines are available
- What a parameter is and how to pass data into and out of subroutines by means of parameters
- The structure of a subroutine declaration and implementation
- How to use procedures and functions
- The differences between procedures and functions
- Local declarations and how to use them
- Constant, built-in functions and how to use them in constant declarations and expressions

Pascal Subroutines

Most real-life programs are quite large, comprising tens to hundreds of thousands of statements. Although Object Pascal enables you to construct Windows programs in just a few lines of code, the reality is that you may still end up with a considerable body of code to learn, understand, and maintain.

To make the task of revising and maintaining Windows applications easier, Object Pascal defines ways to reduce the complexity of your program's code by enabling you to delegate tasks to subroutines. Partitioning into subroutines makes your programs more readable and easier to maintain.

NEW TERM A *subroutine*, often simply called a *routine*, is a named block of code consisting of a header, declarations, and a body of executable statements. Pascal offers essentially two kinds of subroutines: procedures and functions. Subroutines are one of the variety of Pascal building blocks from which you construct programs.

Subroutines support a programming technique called *information hiding*. You can encapsulate, or package, a portion of a program's functionality inside a subroutine, name it, and subsequently invoke it by calling it by name rather than repeating all the statements that would otherwise be required, whenever that functionality is needed. You are thereby "hiding" the details of how that functionality is achieved.

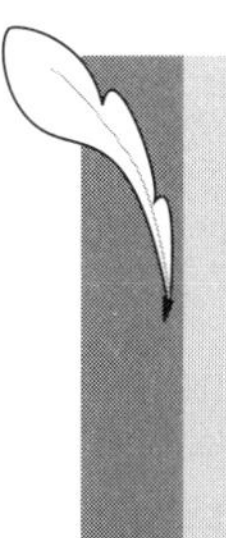

Note: Today's lesson is concerned with Pascal subroutines, that is, free-standing executable program elements. While you're reading about subroutines, keep in mind that almost everything you learn is directly applicable to object methods, which you learn about later. You can view methods as subroutines attached to objects. You have been using objects and methods already when building sample applications in Delphi. You learn more about object-oriented programming in another lesson. For now, bear in mind that a method is really a form of a subroutine: all the rules applicable to subroutines you learn today are, for the most part, also applicable to object methods.

Object Pascal provides a number of predeclared subroutines, collectively known as the Run-Time Library (RTL). The RTL comprises the pre-existing subroutines that you can use inside your programs. Examples include `Sin`, `Cos`, `Length`, `Log`, and so on. Whenever you use such a subroutine—for example, `Cos`, which calculates the cosine of an angle passed to it—you don't need to know exactly how to calculate the value of the cosine. The routine does it for you "automatically," and you don't have to concern yourself with the low-level details.

In addition to the predeclared standard routines, Object Pascal enables you to construct your own. This capability is one of the most powerful features of a high-level programming language. By using subroutines, you can structure your programs in meaningful ways, making them easier to read and maintain.

You should design subroutines in such a way that each serves a single, well-defined purpose. The purpose of the routine should be immediately visible or deducible from its name. Hence, the name should be clear, unambiguous, and meaningful. Equally important as it was in the case of constants and variables, the names you devise for your subroutines should be chosen carefully, with the reader of the program in mind.

You create subroutines to reduce a program's complexity. By using appropriately named subroutines, you can afford to deal with only a limited amount of code at a time, thereby reducing the local complexity with which you have to concern yourself at any given point. You can "hide" the complexity behind a simpler surface.

You can also localize a particular chunk of program logic, such as a complex or tricky calculation, to a single subroutine, thereby facilitating future changes. If a portion or all of the calculation changes, you need to fix it in only one place, rather than trying to find all places where this particular calculation is being performed.

Good structured-programming methodology encourages the notion that subroutines should be as independent and reusable as possible. This notion has not lost its appeal even in the age of object-oriented programming. A well-designed routine does not depend on anything outside itself, other than possibly the values passed into it through well-defined channels, called *parameters*.

NEW TERM A parameter to a subroutine provides a way of passing values to it from the outside. A subroutine arbitrarily can have many parameters, but you should avoid defining too many (five to seven are suggested as the maximum). Inside the subroutine, a parameter behaves simply as a variable. You can use it in evaluating expressions, or you can assign values to it.

Every aspect of a good subroutine should immediately be visible and easy to consider right on the spot, without your having to look up extensive references. A subroutine's well-defined purpose should be carried out cleanly and efficiently, possibly delegating any even lower-level tasks to lower-level subroutines. The "ideal" length for a subroutine has not been established, but the general consensus among software development practitioners is that the shorter, the better.

Another good reason to create subroutines is to avoid duplication of code and to promote code reuse. If you need to write nearly identical code in two or more places, always factor the common code out into its own subroutine, and then simply use the subroutine whenever its functionality is needed.

Anatomy of a Subroutine

An Object Pascal subroutine is a building block consisting of two parts:

- Optional subroutine declaration
- Subroutine implementation

Subroutine Declaration

The declaration part of a subroutine, if at all present, consists of a single element:

- A subroutine heading

You need a separate declaration of a subroutine only in two cases:

- If you are implementing the routine inside a unit, and you want the routine to be visible outside of this unit so that you can use it elsewhere, you must put its declaration in the unit's `interface` section. The implementation of a routine must always reside in the `implementation` section of a unit. It is not visible outside the unit unless you explicitly provide the declaration as part of the interface.

- If the routine is implemented in the same module in which it is used, you may still need to provide a separate declaration for it to be visible to other routines in the same module. If two subroutines are mutually dependent on each other, one of them must be declared so that the other can use it without the compiler having "seen" its implementation yet. The implementation of one of the routines typically follows further down in the module. You learn more about this mechanism called **`forward`** declarations on Day 15.

9

Subroutine Implementation

The implementation part of a subroutine potentially consists of up to three elements:

- A subroutine heading
- An optional local declaration block
- A statement block

Notice that if the subroutine declaration is present, the subroutine heading is repeated in both the declaration and in the implementation parts. As you soon see, the two copies of headings have a great deal in common but are not necessarily identical.

Figure 9.1 illustrates the block structure of a subroutine.

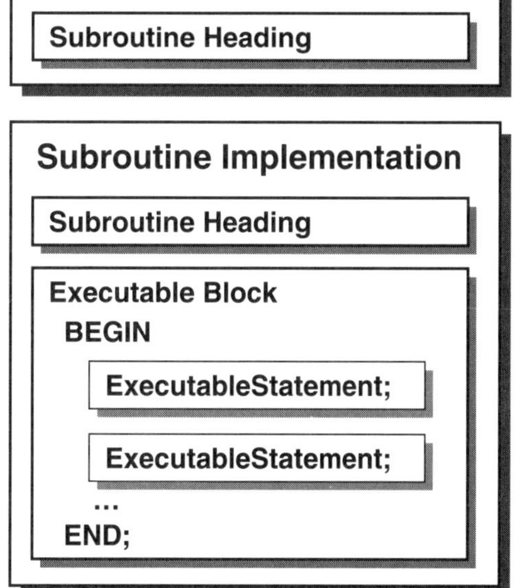

Figure 9.1.
Block structure of a Pascal subroutine.

Executable Statements Block

Every subroutine must have an executable statements block, which is a **begin-end** block containing zero or more executable statements.

Syntax

Executable Statement Block

The general syntax for a subroutine statement block is as follows:

```
begin
  Statement1;
  Statement2;
  ...
  StatementN;
end;
```

Example:

```
begin
  Initialize;
  Run;
  Terminate;
end;
```

A statement block enables you to write the actual instructions for the computer to perform. The pair of Pascal keywords **begin** and **end** encloses executable statements of a subroutine. You separate statements within the block from each other using semicolons. You place the semicolons immediately after almost every statement within a block.

The statements are performed top to bottom, in the order they are listed, unless the control of the execution is affected by a control statement, such as an **if-then-else** clause.

A statement block enclosed within the **begin-end** pair of keywords may contain individual statements; other executable blocks, such as **if-then-else** clauses, **case** statements, and so on; or nothing at all, in which case it is called an *empty block.*

Local Declaration Block

Subroutines can be regarded as little programs in their own right. They are often called *subprograms* for that reason. Each subroutine may have its own declarations, just like the main program. The declarations inside a subroutine are called *local* because they are visible and accessible only within that subroutine. They cannot be referenced from outside the subroutine's implementation block.

Just like you can declare constants, variables, typed constants, user-defined types, and subroutines inside your programs, units, and libraries, you can declare local constants, local variables, local typed constants, local types, and local subroutines inside subroutines.

Subroutines can be nested in this way to an arbitrary depth. In practice, you should probably avoid nesting more than one level deep because to do otherwise creates maintenance problems.

Local declarations appear inside the subroutine implementation blocks, between the subroutine's header and its body. The local declaration block of a subroutine may be, and often is, missing entirely.

Subroutine Headings

In Delphi, you can use two kinds of subroutines and, consequently, two kinds of subroutine headings. The two kinds of subroutines are

- Procedures

- Functions

In the following sections, you learn the rules for declaring the two varieties of headings. Notice that both have a lot in common.

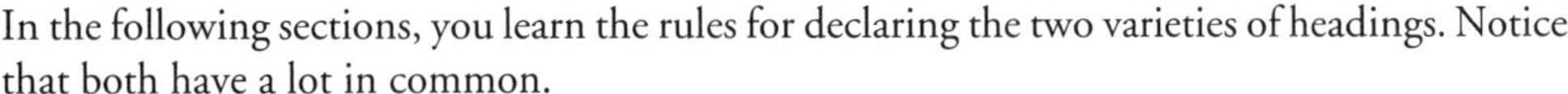

Procedure Headings

Procedures provide a convenient means of breaking executable statements of programs into smaller, more manageable chunks. Procedures are distinguished from one another by their headings, or signatures. A procedure heading includes its name and possibly a list of parameters. Consequently, there are two types of procedure headings: those with parameters and those without parameters.

Parameterless Procedure Headings

Syntax

The general syntax for a simple procedure heading without parameters is as follows:

```
procedure NameOfProcedure;
```

Examples:

```
procedure Paint;
procedure Run;
procedure InitializeRecalcEngine;
```

A heading for a procedure without parameters starts with the reserved word **procedure**, followed by the procedure's name. The name for a procedure is a Pascal identifier, and it obeys the same rules for identifiers as variable or constant names do. It must start with a letter or an underscore, which may be followed by any number of letters, digits, and underscore characters. Because the procedure has no parameters, a semicolon follows directly after the name and terminates the heading.

Figure 9.2 illustrates the block structure of a simple procedure heading.

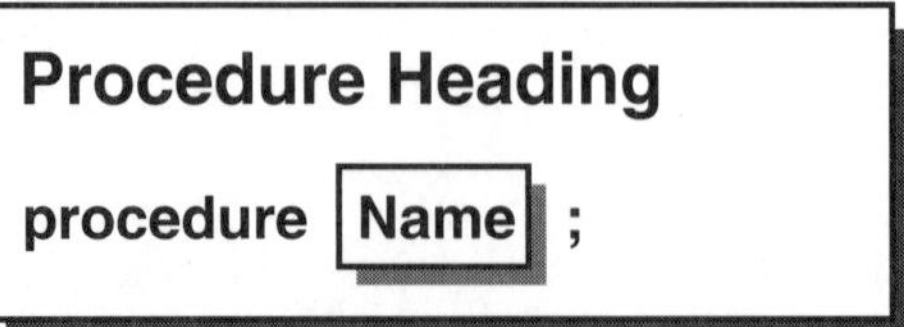

Figure 9.2.
The block structure of a procedure heading without parameters.

Syntax

Procedure Heading with Parameters

The general syntax for a procedure heading with parameters is as follows:

```
procedure Name
  (
...<Formal Parameter List>
  );
```

Examples:

```
procedure Rectangle(X, Y, Width, Height: Integer);
procedure Circle(X, Y, Radius: Integer);
procedure PrintReport(Name: String; PageCount: Integer);
```

A procedure with parameters has a heading that starts with the reserved word **procedure**, followed by the procedure name. After the name, a pair of parentheses enclosing a formal parameter list follows. Formal parameter lists are explained later in today's lesson. After the closing parenthesis of the formal parameter list follows a terminating semicolon.

Figure 9.3 illustrates the block structure of a procedure heading that declares parameters.

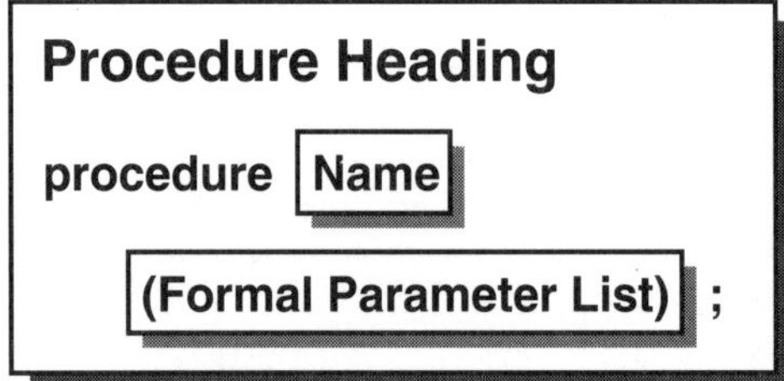

Figure 9.3.
The block structure of a procedure heading with parameters.

Function Headings

Functions not only provide a means of grouping executable statements and related declarations together, but also return intrinsic values. You can therefore use functions inside expressions and on the right-hand sides of assignment statements as if they were variables. The simplest expression involving a function consists of a single-function reference, leading to a single-function activation and evaluation.

After the function is done, a value computed by the function is returned and may be used inside the expression in which the function appeared.

In Delphi, you can use two types of function headings: those with parameters and those without them.

Syntax

Parameterless Function Headings

The general syntax for a simple function heading without parameters is as follows:

```
function Name: ResultType;
```

Examples:

```
function Count: Integer;
function Delimiter: Char;
function Name: String;
```

A function heading starts with the reserved word **function**, followed by the function's name. In functions that do not declare any parameters, the name is followed by a colon, a function return type, and a semicolon.

The function return type is the identifier of the type of the function result, and it can denote almost any Pascal type identifier, including user-defined, structured, nearly arbitrarily complex and sophisticated data types.

Figure 9.4 illustrates the block structure of a simple function heading.

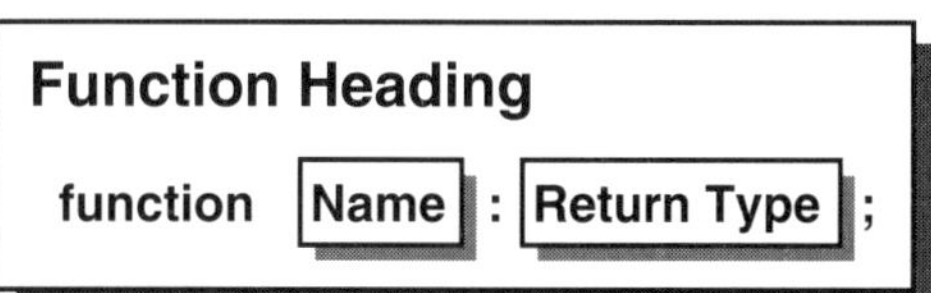

Figure 9.4.
The block structure of a function heading without parameters.

Syntax

Function Headings with Parameters

The general syntax for a function heading with parameters is as follows:

```
function Name
  (
...<Formal Parameter List>
  ): ReturnType;
```

Examples:

```
function UpCase(AChar: Char): Char;
function IsEven(ANumber: Integer): Boolean;
function Header(PageNumber, SectionNumber: Integer): String;
```

Function headings with parameters start with the reserved word **function**, followed by the function name, as before. A pair of parentheses encloses a formal parameter list (explained later in today's lesson) right after the function name and before the colon and the return type declaration.

Figure 9.5 illustrates the block structure of a function heading with parameters.

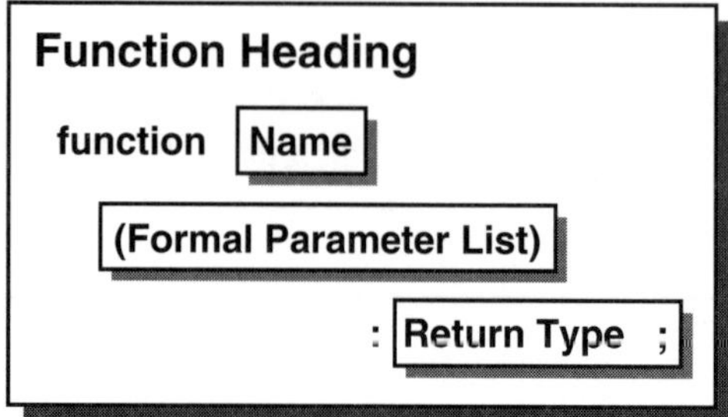

Figure 9.5.
The block structure of a function heading with parameters.

Local Variables and Constants

Consider the example of two subroutines with local declaration blocks given in Listing 9.1.

Listing 9.1. Unit SUB2 illustrating local declaration blocks.

```
unit Sub2;

interface

  function Average(var A: array of Integer): Real;
  procedure ReduceBias(var A: array of Integer);

implementation

function Average;
  {
  Returns the arithmetic average of the
  values in the array. The array A is an open array
  parameter.
  }
  var
    Sum  : Real;
    Count,
    Index: Integer;
  begin
    Sum := 0;
    for Index := Low(A) to High(A) do
      Sum := Sum + A[Index];
    Count := High(A) - Low(A);
    Result := Sum / Count;
  end;

procedure ReduceBias;
  {
  Decrements every element of the array A by the
  lowest value in the array.
  }
```

```
33:
34:   function Min(var Data: array of Integer): Integer;
35:     var
36:       Index: Integer;
37:     begin
38:       Result := Data[Low(Data)];
39:       for Index := Low(Data)+1 to High(Data) do
40:         if Data[Index] < Result then
41:           Result := Data[Index];
42:     end;
43:
44:   var
45:     Bias,
46:     Index: Integer;
47:   begin
48:     Bias := Min(A);
49:     for Index := Low(A) to High(A) do
50:       A[Index] := A[Index] - Bias;
51:   end;
52:
53: end.
```

The Pascal unit in Listing 9.1 defines and exports two subroutines: the function `Average` and the procedure `ReduceBias`. The `Average` function returns the arithmetic average of all elements in the array `A` passed to it. The array `A` is an open array parameter; that is, its size need not be defined in advance. The user of the function can pass integer arrays of different sizes as actual parameters.

Procedure `ReduceBias` also takes an open array `A` as its parameter. The purpose of the routine is to find the lowest number in the array `A`, called `Bias`, and then reduce all entries in the array by the value of the `Bias`. The entry or entries that originally had the lowest values are thereby reduced to zero.

On lines 5 and 6, both subroutines are defined and exported in the interface section of the unit. Here their signatures are defined, that is, the names, parameters and their types, as well as the return type for the function. By virtue of being declared in the interface section, both subroutines are made visible to any other module that uses the `Sub2` unit.

The implementation section of the unit in Listing 9.1 contains two subroutine implementation blocks. The `Average` function is implemented starting on line 10 and ending on line 26. The procedure `ReduceBias`'s implementation spans lines 28 through 51.

The `Average` function's header repeated on line 10 does not spell out the parameters and the return type explicitly, but it is understood that they are identical to the interface signature on line 5. Hence, the array `A`, an open array parameter passed into the function from outside, may be used inside the subroutine as if it were a locally declared variable. Notice that the array `A` is a **`var`** parameter (IN+OUT). Any changes made to the array are made to the actual parameter and will be visible outside after the routine terminates.

Several local parameters are declared inside the local declaration block on lines 16 through 19. The `Real` variable `Sum` declared on line 17 is used to compute the sum of values of all entries in the array. The calculation takes place on lines 21 through 23, where the variable is first initialized to zero, and then a **`for`** loop is run over all the entries in the array, accumulating the sum of their values as the loop progresses.

The variable `Count` calculates the number of entries in the array on line 24. The actual number of entries is not known until runtime. Depending on the size of the actual parameter used to call the function, the expression `High(A)` evaluates to the highest valid index of the actual array. The expression `Low(A)` currently always evaluates to zero.

The summation **`for`** loop on lines 22 and 23 uses the `Integer` variable `Index` as its counter. It also accesses the individual elements of the array `A` on line 23.

The executable block of the `Average` function, spanning lines 20 through 26, consists of the summation loop described previously on lines 21 to 23, the array size calculation on line 24, and the final calculation of the arithmetic average of all entries in the array on line 25. The result of the final calculation is assigned to the implicit variable `Result`, which is the function return value.

The `ReduceBias` procedure header on line 28 is an abbreviated version of the header declaration on line 6. The procedure receives a single, open-sized integer array parameter `A`.

Between the implementation header on line 28 and the executable block on lines 47 through 51 is a local declaration block spanning lines 34 through 46. The declaration block, in turn, contains a variable declaration block on lines 44 through 46 and a local subroutine declaration on lines 34 through 42.

Two local `Integer` variables are declared inside the procedure `ReduceBias`. `Bias` is used to store the value of the smallest element in the array. `Index` is a counter variable for a **`for`** loop running through all the elements in the array on lines 49 and 50, reducing their value by the value of `Bias`.

The locally declared and implemented function `Min` is visible only within the `ReduceBias` procedure's block. On line 48, `Min` obtains the minimum value in the array, which then initializes the local variable `Bias`.

`Min` also takes a single parameter, `Data`, which is an open array of integers. When `Min` is actually used on line 48, the array `A` is passed to it as the actual parameter. This way, the formal parameter `A` of the procedure `ReduceBias` becomes the actual parameter of the function `Min`, substituting for the formal parameter `Data`.

On lines 35 and 36, the function `Min` itself defines a local declaration block, where the local variable `Index` is declared. Notice that the `Index` variable declared locally to `Min` on line 36 is a distinct and separate entity from the local variable `Index` defined on line 46 inside `ReduceBias`. The former is not even visible inside the `Min` function because it is declared below the function's implementation. Neither is the `Index` variable of line 36 visible anywhere inside the `ReduceBias` subroutine, below line 42. It is strictly local to the function `Min`.

The purpose of the `Min` function is to find the smallest element in the array `Data` passed to it. It starts the process on line 38 by assigning the value of the first element of the `Data` array to the function result. Therefore, the minimum value in the array cannot be less than the value of the very first element in it.

The **`for`** loop spanning lines 39 through 41, whose body consists of a single **`if`** statement on lines 40 and 41, runs from the second element in the array, indexed by the expression `Low(data)+1`, to the last element with the index of `High(Data)`. In each case, a comparison is made to check whether the element in the array being looked at currently (`Data[Index]`) has an even smaller value than the smallest value seen so far (`Result`). If so, the value of the element becomes the "smallest value seen so far," by being assigned to the `Result` variable.

Once the loop is done, notice that the `Result` variable still holds the smallest value seen so far: it is also the smallest value in the entire array, and the `Result` variable is the result of the function.

Local variables are commonly used. Because they are created whenever the subroutine in which they are declared is invoked, and destroyed just before the subroutine returns control to the caller, their life span is relatively short. The memory allocated to them is freed when the subroutine returns. Thus, they are attractive for storing temporary values, intermediate results of calculations, or for temporary buffers.

Local variables exist only during the lifetime of a subroutine in which they are created; that is, they exist only when the subroutine is actively running. They do not exist in between calls to the subroutine.

The values of local variables are lost when the subroutine returns, that is, when the control returns to the calling program. All local variables must be reinitialized upon entry to the subroutine by explicit assignment statements.

Local typed constants, unlike regular variables, exist throughout the lifetime of the entire program. Hence, they preserve their values between calls to the subroutine that declares them. They behave like global variables, except that they are not visible and, consequently, not accessible from outside the subroutine that declares them.

Local constants don't "exist" in the sense that variables do. You may recall that no memory storage is allocated to constants at all. Local constants are names, or "labels," accessible from within the subroutine that declares them below their declaration. They are not accessible and cannot be referenced from outside the subroutine.

As you saw in Listing 9.1, local entities—whether they are constants, variables, typed constants, types, or subroutines—are distinct from local entities inside another subroutine, even though they may share the same names.

A local variable with a name that is the same as that of a global variable may be declared within a subroutine. The two variables are independent and distinct entities. The local declaration

"hides" the global one. Any unqualified references to the entity by name actually refer to the local copy.

As an example, suppose the implementation of the `ReduceBias` routine of Listing 9.1 were rearranged as shown in Listing 9.2.

Listing 9.2. Rearranged order of local declarations inside procedure `ReduceBias` from Listing 9.1.

```
1: procedure ReduceBias;
2:   {
3:   Decrements every element of the array A by the
4:   lowest value in the array.
5:   }
6:   var
7:     Bias,
8:     Index: Integer;
9:
10:   function Min(var Data: array of Integer): Integer;
11:     var
12:       Index: Integer;
13:     begin
14:       Result := Data[Low(Data)];
15:       for Index := Low(Data)+1 to High(Data) do
16:         if Data[Index] < Result then
17:           Result := Data[Index];
18:     end;
19:
20:   begin
21:     Bias := Min(A);
22:     for Index := Low(A) to High(A) do
23:       A[Index] := A[Index] - Bias;
24:   end;
```

The rearrangement of the local declarations shown in Listing 9.2 results in the local variable declaration block (lines 6 through 8) moving in front of the function `Min` (lines 10 through 18).

Even though the `Index` variable declared on line 8 of Listing 9.2 is now declared before, in the enclosing block, and is visible inside the function `Min`, the local declaration of `Index` on line 12 completely "hides" the variable from line 8 inside the `Min` function.

The reference to `Index` inside the executable block of `Min`, on line 15, refers to the closest local variable `Index`: the one defined on line 12.

On the other hand, the reference to `Index` on line 22 of Listing 9.2 is made to the `Index` variable declared inside the `ReduceBias` procedure on line 8. The declaration on line 12 is encapsulated inside the local function `Min` and not visible here.

Formal Parameter Lists

If a subroutine, such as a procedure or a function, has parameters, a formal parameter list appears inside parentheses in the subroutine's header declaration. A subroutine can have arbitrarily many formal parameters, although it is a good idea to keep their number to a minimum to decrease the complexity of the routine's interface.

NEW TERM A *formal parameter* to a subroutine is a placeholder that represents a variable defined inside the subroutine's header. Within the subroutine, a formal parameter can be used in the same way as a local variable.

NEW TERM An *actual parameter* to a subroutine, also called an *argument*, provides a particular value that gets passed to the subroutine at run-time in place of the corresponding formal parameter. The value must be of an appropriate type, as defined by the formal parameter declaration in the subroutine's heading. When calling a subroutine, you list the actual parameters in the same order as the order in which the subroutine's formal parameters are declared.

You declare the parameters to a subroutine in much the same way you declare variables within a variable declaration block; indeed, inside the routine, the formal parameters are used as ordinary variables.

Syntax

Formal Parameter List

The general syntax for declaring formal parameter lists is as follows:

```
<subroutine name>(
<modifier>
    Name11,
    Name12: Type1;
<modifier>
    Name21,
    Name22: Type2;
    ...
  <modifier>
    NameN1: TypeN
)
```

Example:

```
function MessageDlg(
  const Msg: String;
        AType: TMsgDlgType;
        AButtons: TMsgDlgButtons;
        HelpCtx: Longint
): Word;
```

A formal parameter list begins with a left parenthesis followed by an optional modifier. A modifier for a formal parameter declaration may be one of the reserved words: **var** or **const**. Later in today's lesson, you learn how a modifier changes the behavior of a formal parameter inside the subroutine.

Following the modifier, if any, is a formal parameter's declaration. An individual declaration consists of a name, followed by a colon, and then followed by a type name, much in the same way you declare variables. The name of a formal parameter obeys the same rules as the name of a variable. If you declare many formal parameters to be of the same type, you can list them one after another, separated by commas, along with a single colon and the type name—again, just like variables.

Figure 9.6 illustrates the block structure of the formal parameter list.

Figure 9.6.
The block structure of a formal parameter list.

Formal Parameter List

(
(Formal Parameter Declaration) ;
(Formal Parameter Declaration) ;
...
)

Syntax

Simple Formal Parameter List

In its simplest form without any modifiers, the syntax of the formal parameter list declaration is as follows:

```
<subroutine name>(
  Name11,
  Name12: Type1;
  Name21,
  Name22: Type2;
  ...
  NameN1: TypeN
)
```

Examples:

```
procedure DisplayStr(X, Y: Integer; Text: String)
procedure MoveArm(Angle: Real);
```

```
procedure EditStr(
  X, Y, EditX, EditY: Integer;
  Label, Edit, Default: String;
  MaxLen: Integer;
  Default: String
);
```

Each individual parameter declaration consists of a name, or a list of unique names separated with commas, followed by a colon, and then followed by a type name. Multiple parameter declarations are separated with semicolons within the formal parameter list.

The type declaration of a subroutine parameter plays the same role the type declaration of a variable does: it allows the compiler to reserve appropriate storage space for the values of the parameter, and it allows the compiler to check for any violations of type compatibility—for example, attempts to assign an incompatible value to the parameter, such as an attempt to assign a character string to an integer variable.

Syntax

Formal Parameter List with Modifiers

The general syntax of a formal parameter list is as follows:

```
<subroutine Name>(
  var
    Name11,
    ...
    Name1M: Type1;
  const
    Name21,
    ...
    Name2M: Type2;
  ...
    NameN1,
    ...
    NameNM: TypeN
)
```

The preceding syntax allows for **const** and **var** modifiers in any order.

Examples:

```
procedure QueryColumn(var ANumber: Integer)
procedure SetValue(const ANumber: Integer; const AString: String);
procedure Coordinates(var Number1, Number2: Real);
procedure Command(ANumber: Integer; var AResult: Boolean);
procedure CopyStr(const Src: String; var Dest: String);
```

Figure 9.7 illustrates the block structure of an individual formal parameter declaration, which can contain **var** or **const** modifiers.

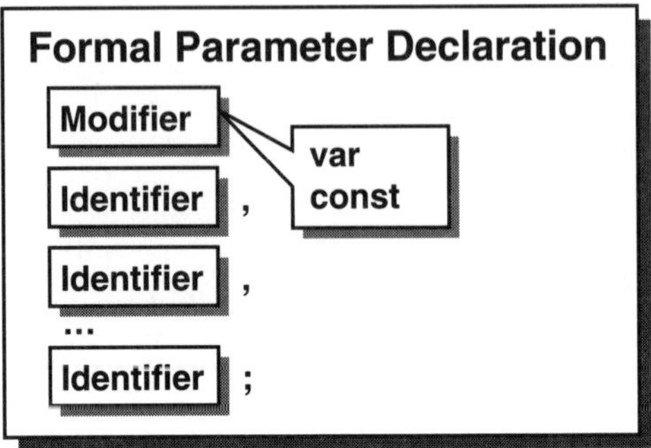

Figure 9.7.
The block structure of a formal parameter declaration.

The parameter modifiers change the assignment behavior of a formal parameter. Depending on whether a parameter is unqualified, or which of the two qualifiers appear in front of it, assigning a value to the parameter may be illegal, and the effect of doing so may only be localized to the subroutine, or it may actually propagate outside the subroutine.

The modifiers appearing inside the formal parameter lists change the meaning of the parameters that follow them, according to the rules summarized in Table 9.1.

The *Outside Effect* column of Table 9.1 designates two possible kinds of parameters: IN parameters, values of which are passed into the routine; and IN+OUT parameters, the passed values of which may be changed by the subroutine and reflected back on the outside. There are no OUT-only parameters in Pascal. You can think of function results as being OUT-only parameters.

The *Access* column in Table 9.1 specifies whether you can assign new values to the parameter inside the subroutine (Read-Write), or if you can only use the value in expressions (Read-Only).

Table 9.1. Formal parameter modifiers.

Modifier	Outside Effect	Access	Comments
<none>	IN	Read-Write	You can use the parameter as a variable inside the subroutine. The initial value of the variable is the value passed in as the actual parameter. Changes made to its value are not reflected outside the subroutine. The actual parameter may be any one of the following: an expression, a variable, a function, or a constant.

Modifier	Outside Effect	Access	Comments
`const`	IN	Read-Only	You can use the parameter as a constant inside the subroutine; that is, it may appear in expressions. The value of the constant is the value passed in as the actual parameter. The parameter cannot appear on the left-hand side of an assignment; hence, no changes can be made to its value. Neither can it be passed to another subroutine as a **`var`**-parameter. The actual parameter may be any one of the following: an expression, a variable, a function, or a constant.
`var`	IN+OUT	Read-Write	You can use the parameter as a variable inside the subroutine. The initial value of the variable is the value passed in as the actual parameter. Changes made to its value are reflected outside the subroutine. The actual parameter must be a variable to allow values to be assigned to it.

9

Following is the summary of the rules governing the declaration and usage of subroutine formal parameters:

- You declare parameters and their types inside parentheses in the function or procedure heading declaration.
- The parameters you declare inside a subroutine heading are called formal parameters and their declaration forms a formal parameter list.
- Within a subroutine, the formal parameters may be used in the same way as local variables. In particular, you can assign values to the formal parameters, just like you can to variables.
- Subroutines may have as many parameters as you need. You separate parameter declarations using semicolons. Each declaration within a single formal parameter list must introduce at least one, but possibly many, parameters of the same type.

- The declarations of parameter types in formal parameter lists must be type names, that is, identifiers that are either built-in or that have been declared prior to the subroutine declaration in question. In the process of declaring a parameter to a subroutine, you cannot declare new type specifications. The type for the parameter must have been named and defined first.

The use of modifiers in formal parameter declarations creates three distinct types of subroutine parameters. The three types of parameters are as follows:

- **Value parameters.** They are the unqualified formal parameters that permit communication into but not out of a subroutine. Actual parameters that are passed as value parameters are being passed "by value."
- **Variable parameters.** They are formal parameters qualified with a `var` modifier that allow the information to be passed back out of a subroutine. These parameters are passed "by reference."
- **Constant parameters.** They are formal parameters qualified with a `const` modifier. These parameters are protected in that you cannot assign values to them inside the subroutine. This restriction is useful whenever you need to protect the actual parameter from inadvertent assignments inside a subroutine. The **`const`** declaration explicitly assures the users of a subroutine that the parameters they pass to it will not be modified in any way.

Actual Parameters

Formal parameter lists declare the order and type of parameters for a subroutine. When the routine is being activated, however, a list of actual parameters, matching the formal ones in their type, order, and number, is passed to it by the caller or by the using code block.

Correspondence between actual and formal parameters is established based on the position of a parameter within a parameter list. An actual parameter is substituted for every formal parameter of a subroutine at the time of the activation, that is, at the time of a procedure call or function evaluation.

Consider the following procedure declaration:

```
procedure PerformAction(Row, Column: Integer; Command, Data: String; var Success:
Boolean);
```

Given the preceding declaration, you can use the procedure `PerformAction` as follows:

```
var
  Result: Boolean;
begin
  PerformAction(0,0,'Delete','',Result);
  PerformAction(10,12,'Add','Delphi',Result);
```

```
  PerformAction(-10,0,'Edit','Name',Result);
  PerformAction(1,1,'Copy','Attribute',Result);
end;
```

The formal parameters `Row` and `Column` get the values 0 and 0, respectively, in the first executable statement; 10 and 12, by the second; and so on. The formal string parameter `Command` corresponds to an actual string value each time the `PerformAction` procedure is called, that is, `'Delete'`, `'Add'`, `'Edit'`, and so on. The fourth parameter is also declared as `String` and gets its value from the literal strings in procedure invocation statements. The first invocation here, for example, passes an empty string in place of the formal parameter. Finally, the last parameter of `PerformAction`, `Result`, is a variable parameter, that is, an IN+OUT parameter. It is bound at runtime with the Boolean variable `Result` on each call. Presumably, the procedure indicates the success of its operation by setting the value of the `Success` formal parameter. When a procedure activation statement returns, the value of the actual parameter `Result` can be examined and used to determine the success or failure of the procedure's action.

Similarly, consider the following function declaration:

```
function AdjustedValue(Value, Modifier: Integer): Integer;
```

Given the preceding declaration for the function `AdjustedValue`, you can use it as follows:

```
var
  AValue: Integer;
begin
  AValue := AdjustedValue(100,1);
  AValue := AdjustedValue(AdjustedValue(17,1));
  AValue := (23 + AdjustedValue(10,2)) mod 3;
  AdjustedValue(100,33);
end;
```

In each of the preceding statements except the last one, the function `AdjustedValue` is part of an integer expression. The value of the expression is calculated by invoking the function. The function is invoked having its name listed, each time with a different set of actual parameters. Each function activation results in a value being computed and returned. The value returned from the `AdjustedValue` function participates in the expression evaluation. Once the value of the expression on the left-hand side of the assignment operator has been calculated, it is assigned to the variable `AValue` in each case.

The last example of `AdjustedValue`'s usage illustrates that you can discard the function result if it is not needed. The function in this case is called in the same way a procedure would be; that is, it is not a part of any expression. This technique is explained later in today's lesson.

Because each formal parameter must be declared to be of some type, the corresponding list of actual parameters passed into a subroutine at the time of the activation must not only match the number of formal parameters, but also the type of each actual parameter must be compatible with the type declared for the formal one. In other words, if a subroutine expects an `Integer` parameter, you can neither pass it a `String` value nor a `Real`-valued number.

Subroutine Declaration versus Implementation

Delphi offers two types of subroutine headings: the implementation heading, which appears together with the implementation of the subroutine; and a declaration heading, which may appear in the interface of a unit, for instance.

The first occurrence of a declaration of a subroutine heading must be complete; it must declare the name of the subroutine, all parameters and their types, as well as the return type, if the subroutine is a function.

The subsequent occurrence of a subroutine heading within a source module does not need to be complete. It is sufficient to provide the full name of the subroutine. You don't have to repeat the parameter declarations nor the return type for functions. It is assumed that they are the same as previously declared.

Consider the following procedure declaration, which may appear in the interface of a unit:

```
unit Unit1;

interface

  procedure SetLongFlag(var Aflag: LongInt; AMask: LongInt);

implementation

...
```

The preceding `SetLongFlag` procedure declaration defines the name of the procedure, its parameters—one of which is a `var` parameter—and their types.

The implementation of this procedure would reside in the implementation section of `Unit1`. The implementation may redeclare all parameters the same way they were specified in the interface:

```
...

implementation

  procedure SetLongFlag(var Aflag: LongInt; AMask: LongInt);
  begin
    {Executable Statements}
  end;

end.
```

Conversely, the implementation may specify only the name of the procedure, leaving out the parameter details:

```
...

implementation

  procedure SetLongFlag;
  begin
    {Executable Statements}
  end;

end.
```

If you decide to repeat the complete subroutine heading declaration at the implementation site, make sure that it is identical to the initial declaration given in the unit's interface. You must list the parameters in the same order and ensure that they have the same names, types, and modifiers as those in the interface declaration. Otherwise, the compiler complains that the subroutine's heading does not match its declaration.

Each of the two styles has advantages and disadvantages:

- Always repeating the declarations in the implementation headings makes them more readily available when you are constructing the code of the subroutine. You have them listed right there: no need to switch back and forth between the interface and the implementation. On the other hand, when you are changing the parameters of a routine or adding new ones during the development, you have to remember to change both the interface and the implementation. If the two don't match, the compiler flags an error.
- If you don't repeat the declarations in the implementation heading, you may need to switch back and forth between the interface and the implementation just to verify the spelling of a parameter's name so that you can use it inside the subroutine. But it is sufficient to change the heading in only one place.

Which of the two styles you use is something you have to decide for yourself.

Using Subroutines

Declaring and implementing a subroutine provides a script, or a detailed recipe, for the computer to perform some action at runtime. The script of a subroutine is actually performed whenever the routine is activated, or called.

A procedure is activated by a procedure call, or a procedure activation statement. A function is activated by a function call, or by reference to the function within an expression. A function is said to be evaluated when it is activated because it returns some value.

Implementing Procedures

To implement a procedure, you must provide a sequence of executable statements that make up its body. You must also provide the "packaging" in the form of

- An implementation procedure header
- Optionally, a local declaration block
- An executable **begin-end** block (the body)

Figure 9.8 illustrates the block structure of a complete procedure implementation.

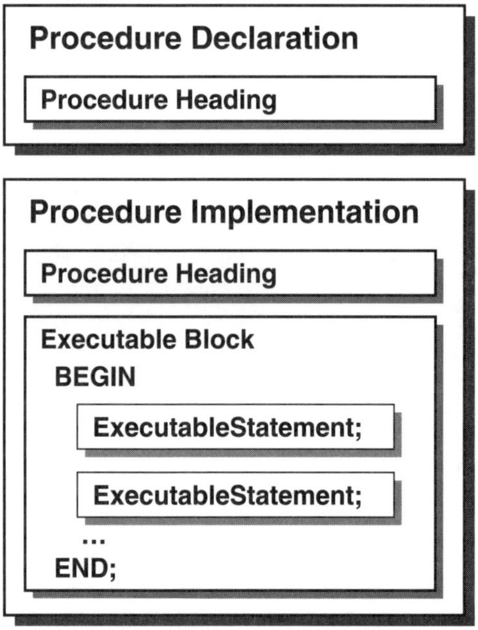

Figure 9.8.
The block structure of a procedure without local declarations.

Procedure Declaration
Procedure Heading

Procedure Implementation
Procedure Heading
Executable Block
BEGIN
ExecutableStatement;
ExecutableStatement;
...
END;

Figure 9.9 illustrates the block structure of a procedure containing a local declaration block. You may have any number of local declarations, including **type** blocks, **var** and **const** blocks, as well as subroutine blocks.

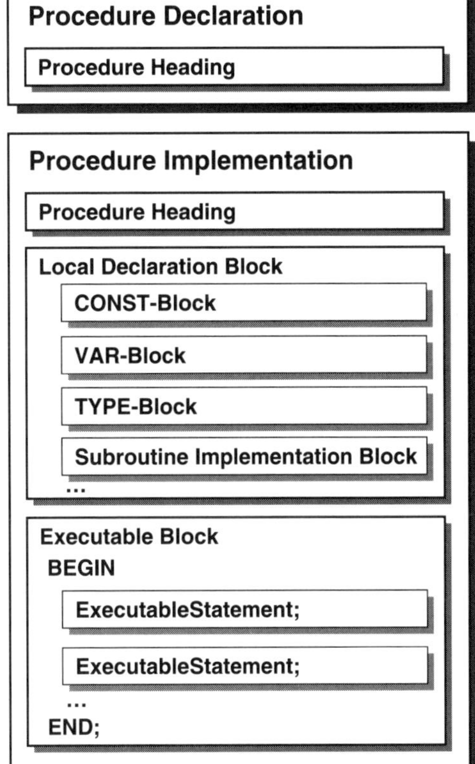

Figure 9.9.
Block structure of a procedure with local declarations.

Listing 9.3 provides an example of a procedure implemented inside a unit.

Listing 9.3. A procedure implemented inside a unit.

```
unit Proc1;

interface

  procedure AdjustNextEven(var ANumber: Integer;
    var Changed: Boolean);

implementation

  procedure AdjustNextEven;
    begin
```

continues

Listing 9.3. continued

```
12:        if (ANumber mod 0) <> 0 then
13:          begin
14:            ANumber := ANumber + 1;
15:            Changed := True;
16:          end
17:        else
18:          Changed := False;
19:      end;
20:
21: end.
```

The procedure AdjustNextEven in Listing 9.3 is implemented inside the unit Proc1. The procedure is first declared in the **interface** section of the unit, which is also where its parameters are defined, on lines 5 and 6.

Listing the procedure header in the interface of the unit makes it visible and usable outside this unit. To use it, the importing unit would also have to include Proc1 in its **uses** clause.

The implementation for the procedure Adjust begins on line 10, inside the *implementation* section of the unit. Note that in this particular implementation the procedure header does not repeat the parameters. The names and types of formal parameters are already defined in the interface declaration on lines 5 and 6.

The procedure AdjustNextEven first checks if the parameter ANumber is odd. The expression

```
(ANumber mod 0)
```

on line 12 results in zero for even numbers, and one for odd numbers. The results of the expression are tested against zero by the **if** statement's conditional clause on line 12.

If ANumber is odd, it is adjusted to the next highest even number on line 14. If ANumber is even, the **begin-end** block on lines 13 through 16 is skipped, and the **else** part on line 18 is executed.

Lines 15 and 18 set the value of an output-only variable Changed. Strictly speaking, it is not an output-only variable because it already contains some value upon entry to the subroutine, yet this value is ignored and explicitly set by either of the two branches of the **if-then-else** clause. The calling program may use this value to test whether an adjustment is needed, that is, whether ANumber was originally odd.

Notice that the procedure AdjustNextEven has two headers: one "signature," complete with formal parameter declarations on lines 5 and 6, and an abbreviated header again on line 10. You can replace the header on line 10 with an identical copy of the header from lines 5 and 6, if you want.

Also notice how ANumber is used as an ordinary variable inside the subroutine. Because it is a **var** parameter, any changes made to it are reflected on the outside when the routine terminates.

When the program is running, the executable statements take control one by one. When a procedure is called or a statement consisting of that procedure's name is encountered, the control

jumps from the caller to the **begin** statement of the executable block belonging to the called procedure. The statements inside the subroutine's **begin-end** block are executed in sequence. At the point where the program execution reaches the final **end** of the executable block of the called procedure, the control returns back to the caller. The next statement inside the caller, after the statement that led to the procedure call, is the next one executed.

Now consider this example:

```
begin
  Subroutine1;
  Subroutine2;
  Subroutine3;
end;
```

Assuming that `Subroutine1`, `Subroutine2`, and `Subroutine3` are names of procedures declared elsewhere in the program and visible here, executing the entire **begin-end** block here results in the following sequence of actions:

1. `Subroutine1` is called. The control jumps to the first statement inside `Subroutine1`.
2. Once `Subroutine1` has completed, the control returns to the first statement after the call, the one with `Subroutine2` on it.
3. `Subroutine2` is called. The control of execution is transferred to the executable statements inside the procedure `Subroutine2`.
4. Finally, upon return from `Subroutine2`, `Subroutine3` is called.
5. Upon completion of `Subroutine3`, the control arrives at the last statement in the block, the **end** keyword. At this point, the block has finished execution.

Using Procedures

Once you have built a procedure, you may want to *use* it. Using a procedure means calling it at runtime. You call a procedure simply by listing its name inside an executable block of statements, anywhere between the **begin-end** keyword pair. The statements inside the block are executed sequentially. Once the control of execution arrives at the subroutine call you specified, your subroutine is called in turn.

If the subroutine you want to call declares any *formal parameters*, at the time of the call you need to pass it the same number of *actual parameters* in an order corresponding to the order in which the formal ones were declared, match the formal parameters' types, and observe any modifiers that may have been specified.

Following are the simple rules to observe when passing parameters to subroutines:

- IN/Read-Write parameters (no modifier) and IN/Read-Only parameters (`const` modifier) can be passed as either an explicit value, an expression, including constant values and sub-expressions, or as variable references. If you specify a variable as an actual parameter, the variable's value is passed into the subroutine.

- You can specify entire expressions in place of individual formal, non-**var** parameters. The only restriction is that the type of the expression must match the type of the formal parameter.
- You can also pass function results to a subroutine by either calling the function itself in place of the actual non-**var** parameter or calling it as part of a more complex expression.
- You must pass IN+OUT/Read-Write parameters (**var** modifier) as variables. You cannot pass explicit values, function results, constants, or expressions as **var** parameters.

For example, given the following procedure declarations:

```
procedure DeleteElement(I: Integer);
procedure DrawRectangle(Left, Top, Width, Height: Integer);
procedure PrintReport(ATitle: String; NumPages: Integer);
```

you may make calls to these subroutines as follows:

```
const
  LeftOffset = 100;
  TopOffset = 60;
  HeaderPages = 3;

var
  ElementNo: Integer;

function GetPageCount: Integer;
  begin
    {Executable Statements}
  end;

begin
  DeleteElement(23);
  ElementNo := 100;
  DeleteElement(ElementNo+1);
  DrawRectangle(10,12,400,250);
  DrawRectangle(LeftOffset,TopOffset+23,240,100);
  PrintReport('Annual Report',10);
  PrintReport(IntToStr(1995)+
    ' Annual Report',HeaderPages+GetPageCount);
end;
```

Implementing Functions

To implement a function, you must provide a sequence of executable statements that make up its body, including an assignment to the function result. You must also provide the packaging in the form of

- A function header
- Optionally, a local declaration block
- An executable **begin-end** block (the body)

Figure 9.10 illustrates the block structure of a complete function implementation.

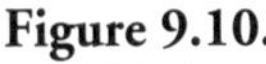

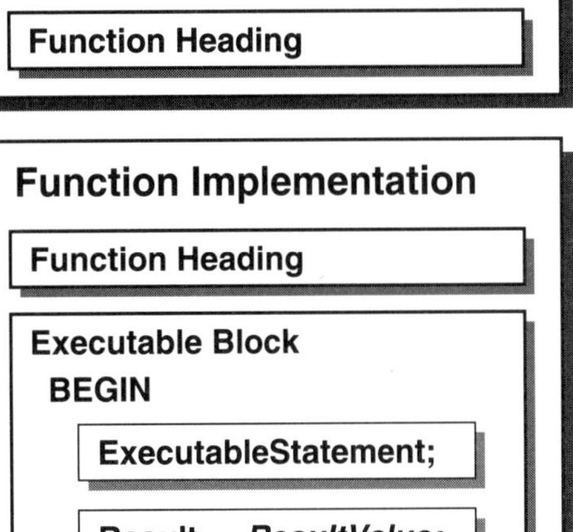

Figure 9.10.
The block structure of a function without local declarations.

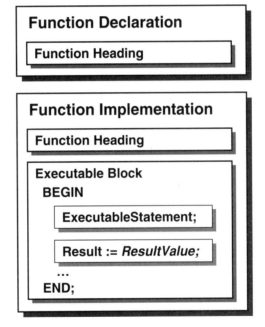

Figure 9.11 illustrates the block structure of a function containing a local declaration block. You may have any number of local declarations, including **type** blocks, **var** and **const** blocks, as well as subroutine blocks.

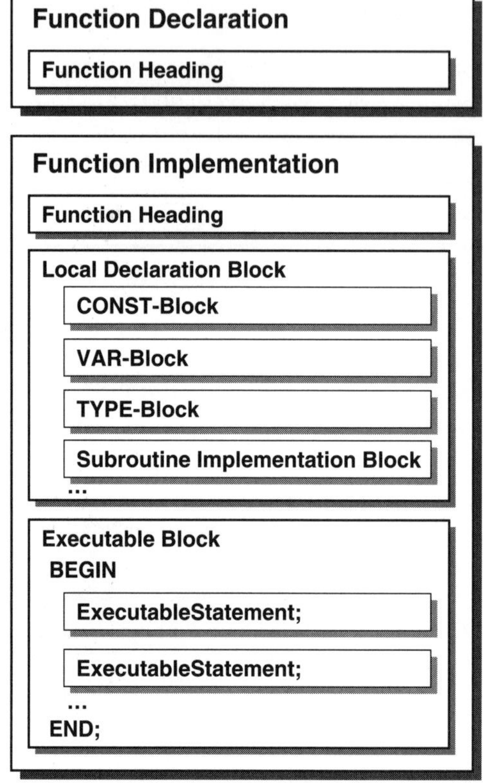

Figure 9.11.
The block structure of a function with local declarations.

The implementation of a function follows the same rules as the implementation of a procedure. Both have a list of executable statements enclosed in a `begin` and `end` pair. Like procedures, functions can have local declarations. The only difference in the implementation is that you must assign a value to a function at some point.

Note: If you don't explicitly assign a value to a function inside its executable statement block, the function result value is undefined. It is not zero or equivalent: it is undefined, or garbage.

So that you can assign a value to a function, at least one of the statements inside its executable block must be an assignment of a value to the name of the function, or to the special, implicit variable `Result`, of the same type as the function result.

Using Functions

Whenever a function's name appears within an expression, it is evaluated; that is, it is called and returns a value when it is done. In other words, a function is called whenever its name is used in a function call statement as part of an expression or assignment. A function call can, for the most part, only occur inside an executable block of statements, that is, within a **begin** and an **end**. In a few rare cases described later, you also find function calls inside constant declarations.

Calling a function means not only transferring the control of the program's execution to the function's executable block, but also obtaining the value the function was designed to compute upon its return.

Functions are used in expressions. Most often, functions are used either as a stand-alone or as part of a longer expression on the right-hand side of an assignment operator. For example, consider the following function:

```
function AddOne(ANumber: Integer): Integer;
  begin
    Result := ANumber + 1;
  end;
```

Given the preceding declaration, the statement

```
var
  Count: Integer;
begin
  Count := AddOne(3);
end;
```

causes the function `AddOne` to be executed, with the number 3 passed as the actual parameter. Upon return, the function's value—4, in this case—is assigned to the `Integer` variable `Count`.

Another typical usage for functions is computing the values of actual parameters passed to other subroutines on the fly. For example, given the declaration

```
procedure DrawRectangle(Left, Top, Width, Height: Integer);
begin
  {Draw the rectangle, as specified}
end;
```

the statement

```
DrawRectangle(AddOne(9),AddOne(9),100,100);
```

results in the following list of actual parameters to be passed to the procedure `DrawRectangle`: `(10,10,100,100)`. The `AddOne` function with an actual parameter of 9 is used here twice to compute the actual parameter for `Left` and for `Top` in the formal parameter list of the `DrawRectangle` procedure.

> **Note:** It is possible to use a function as an ordinary procedure; that is, discarding the function result upon its return. This capability is useful whenever you need to execute the function but are not interested in the actual result the function computes: you are interested in what the function does, not what its value is.
>
> User-defined functions may be called in exactly the same way procedures are called, provided that the extended syntax compiler option is enabled, either in the IDE (Project on the Options menu, Compiler page where the Extended Syntax check box should be checked) or through the compiler directive `{$X+}` in your code.
>
> You cannot use the standard (built-in) functions declared in the `System` unit in this way, however. They are always treated as functions.

You can "nest" function calls used to compute actual parameter values in the sense of the actual parameters of one function being supplied by calling another (or even the same) function. For example, a LISP-like expression:

```
Count := AddOne(AddOne(AddOne(AddOne(1))) + 2);
```

results in the `Count` variable getting the value of 7. Four calls to the `AddOne` function appear in the expression on the right-hand side, each incrementing the passed value 1 by one, and an explicit plus operator incrementing the actual parameter to the outermost `AddOne` function call by 2.

When this statement executes, first the innermost (last in this particular expression) `AddOne` function is called, with the actual parameter of 1 hard-coded. Upon its return, the resulting value of 2 is passed to the next `AddOne` function. The process of unwinding the actual parameters continues until the outermost (leftmost) `AddOne` function is evaluated, this time with the computed value of 4 returned from the last call to `AddOne` added to the hard-coded value of 2 to form the actual parameter. The outermost `AddOne` increments by one again, returning 7 as the result, which is then assigned to the `Count` variable.

In each case here, `AddOne` refers to the same function, that is, the same implementation. The `AddOne` function is called four times, starting with the rightmost reference to it, during the evaluation of the entire preceding expression.

Constant Functions

As a general rule, you can use function call statements only inside the executable blocks demarcated with a **`begin-end`** pair of keywords. They can be evaluated only at run-time by executing the code provided as their implementations. The functions listed in Table 9.2 also

known as intrinsic functions, are special in this regard, however. Their values can be computed at compile-time, and they do not change at run-time. They can therefore be used as constant expressions within, for example, constant declaration blocks.

Table 9.2. Built-in system functions evaluated at compile-time.

Function	Argument Type	Return Value	Return Value Meaning
`Abs`	Signed Integer-type, or Real	Same as argument	Absolute value of its real- or integer-typed actual argument. The return type is the same as that of the argument's.
`Chr`	Byte	Char	The character with the ordinal ASCII value corresponding to the value of the expression passed in as the argument.
`Hi`	Integer or Word	Byte	The high-order byte of the argument. The argument is always a two-byte entity.
`High`	Type identifier, or variable reference	Depends on the argument type	The highest value in the same range as the type denoted by the actual parameter. For ordinal types, this is the highest possible value; for array types, the highest allowable index; for string types, the declared size of the string; for open array parameters, the Word-typed value of the highest index.
`Length`	String	Byte	Length, or the number of characters of the string argument.
`Lo`	Integer or Word	Byte	The low-order byte of the argument. The argument is always a two-byte entity.

continues

Table 9.2. continued

Function	Argument Type	Return Value	Return Value Meaning
`Low`	Type identifier, or variable reference		Depends on the argument type. The lowest value in the same range as the type denoted by the actual parameter. For ordinal types, this is the lowest possible value; for array types, the lowest index; for string types and for open array parameters, zero, the lowest index.
`Odd`	Integer type	Boolean	True, if the argument is an odd number.
`Ord`	Ordinal type	LongInt	The ordinal number corresponding to the position of the argument within the set of values defined by the type.
`Pred`	Ordinal type	Same as argument	The ordinal predecessor of the argument. The return value is of the same type as the argument.
`Ptr`	Word, Word	Pointer	The pointer (memory address) constructed from a Word-sized segment and offset values.
`Round`	Real-type	LongInt	The integer value resulting from rounding of a Real value argument to the nearest whole number.
`SizeOf`	Type identifier or variable	Word reference	The number of bytes occupied by the variable argument, or by instances of the type, if the argument is a type identifier.

Function	Argument Type	Return Value	Return Value Meaning
`Succ`	Ordinal type	Same as argument	The ordinal successor of the argument. The return value is of the same type as the argument.
`Swap`	Integer or Word	Byte	Exchanges the low and high bytes of the two-byte argument.
`Trunc`	Real-type	LongInt	The integer value resulting from dropping the fractional part of the real-value argument.

9

As an example, you can declare constants using the following "constant" functions listed in Table 9.2:

```
const
  MachineWordSize = SizeOf(Integer);
  EndOfFileMark = Chr(26);
  ASCIIUpperCaseA = Ord('A');
```

The first declaration establishes `MachineWordSize` as a convenient label for the number of bytes required to store an `Integer` variable. The second declaration establishes a character constant whose value is the ASCII character 26 decimal, which denotes an end-of-file mark under DOS. Finally, the last statement labels the ASCII value of the uppercase character `'A'`, the value of 65, as `ASCIIUpperCaseA`.

Procedures versus Functions

The return type declared in the function heading is what makes a difference between a function and a procedure. A procedure is just a piece of executable code, encapsulated together with related declarations. A function, in addition to that, has a value that may be used in expressions and assignments.

The big difference between a procedure and a function is that functions return values. Whereas procedures give you means of writing statements, functions enable you to write expressions. A procedure call is always a statement. A function call is usually an expression but can also be a statement if needed.

A function can contain arbitrary executable code and is executed just like a procedure. In addition to performing some actions, however, a function's return value has to be computed and assigned as the value of the function upon return.

To assign a return value to a function, use either one of these two methods inside the function's **begin-end** block:

- Assign the return value to the function using the function's name on the left-hand side of an assignment statement. When the function's name appears on the left-hand side of an assignment operator, the compiler assumes that you mean the result value. For example,

  ```
  function AddOne(N: Integer): Integer;
  begin
    AddOne := N + 1;
  end;
  ```

  The preceding function adds one to the number passed in as parameter `N` and returns the incremented number as its result. The computed value `N + 1` is assigned to the function name, which means it becomes the result value of the function.

  You can assign return values to the function any number of times within that function. The ultimate result value is whatever was assigned to the function most recently, before the function returned to the caller.

  This approach is the traditional method of returning function values in Pascal. The drawback is that you cannot use the assigned function value inside the function itself. The second method eliminates this drawback.

- Assign the return value to an implicit variable called `Result`. You don't need to explicitly define `Result`: it is assumed and has the same type as the function result. For example,

  ```
  function AddOne(N: Integer): Integer;
  begin
    Result := N + 1;
  end;
  ```

  Again, the function adds one to the number passed in as parameter `N` and returns the incremented number as its result. The implicit `Result` variable is used to return the value. The `Result` variable is a true variable, which can be referenced inside the function on both sides of an assignment operator. You can use the `Result` variable as any other variable, except you don't need to declare it explicitly.

Note: Unlike the case with the return statement in C, assigning a value to the function result does not terminate the function. The execution of the function's code continues until the final **end** keyword is reached within the function's executable block. That's how it is possible to assign different result values in the course of execution of a single function. The ultimate value of the function depends on the last assignment made during the course of its execution.

A function may return only one result, determined by the declared function return type and computed during the function evaluation. Whenever you need to return more than one value from a subroutine, such as when you need to return the result of a computation as well as an error code or condition, use multiple **var** parameters (formal parameters with **var** modifiers) to pass the values from inside the procedure out. You can use a combination of a **var** parameter and the function result if you prefer to use a function.

DO / **DON'T**

DO use a function when you need a subroutine to return a single value.

DON'T use a function to return multiple values both through the function result and via **var** parameters. This use may be confusing to the reader of the program.

DO use a procedure with **var** parameters whenever you need a subroutine to return multiple values.

DON'T use a function whenever the action is emphasized and you merely want to return an error condition or code. Use an appropriately named (Verb+Object) procedure instead, with a **var** parameter to get the status value out.

Summary

Today's lesson introduced you to Object Pascal subroutines. You learned the following:

- Subroutines are free-standing program building blocks used to partition program modules into smaller, more manageable chunks. They support the concept of information hiding and allow for packaging of program elements together.
- Object Pascal offers two kinds of module-level subroutines: procedures and functions.

- Procedures are special kinds of subroutines. They perform actions but do not have any intrinsic value.
- Functions are subroutines that return a value and perform some action.
- An Object Pascal subroutine consists of an optional declaration and an implementation.
- A subroutine declaration is a header, or signature, defining its name, parameters, and the return type in case of a function.
- A subroutine's implementation provides the executable statements to be performed at run-time. It can also encapsulate local subroutine declarations consisting of any of the declaration building blocks: **`const`** blocks, **`var`** blocks, **`type`** blocks, local subroutines, and so on.
- Formal parameters of a subroutine are declared in its header as a formal parameter list enclosed in a pair of parentheses.
- A formal parameter list specifies the number of parameters, their order, and type.
- Modifiers in a formal parameter list specify the assignment properties of formal parameters. The two modifiers are **`const`** and **`var`**.
- Procedures are activated through procedure call statements; functions are evaluated inside expressions.
- Functions can also be used like procedures, provided the extended syntax compiler option is enabled.
- Some built-in functions, such as `SizeOf`, are treated as constants and are evaluated by the compiler at compile-time. You can use them within constant declarations.

Q&A

Q When should I use `var` parameters as opposed to non-qualified value parameters?

A You should use variable parameters whenever you need to affect a value of a variable passed to the subroutine, and you want the changes to be visible outside the subroutine when it terminates. Also consider another use of **`var`** parameters: You should use them whenever you are passing large structures, such as arrays or records, to and from subroutines. This way, you minimize the overhead of copying a possibly very large data structure. The caveat is that you have to be careful not to inadvertently modify the structure passed in as a **`var`** parameter. Remember, changes made to **`var`** parameters stick.

Q Because declaring a local variable "hides" any outside ones with the same name, the converse—not declaring a local variable with a particular name—should let me use the outside-declared one with that name, shouldn't it?

A Yes, you're right, but it is not recommended in general. This approach is called *up-level addressing* and has earned a reputation as a bad programming practice. If you have programmed in BASIC or other languages before, you may be used to numerous global variables accessible from anywhere. In Pascal, however, you are strongly encouraged to use the structured programming features of the language, such as using parameters to pass values into and out of subroutines. There are several reasons to do so. It is more difficult to use a subroutine that depends on a number of implicit values that are not passed explicitly through parameters. Unwanted side effects are possible; for example, changing a value of a global variable may cause unwanted effects outside the subroutine, and in many other subroutines that also use that value. These effects may be very hard to pinpoint. Trying to debug subroutines with unwanted side effects often changes into debugging the entire program at once: orders of magnitude more complex undertaking. The point is that you want to localize any effects a subroutine may have so that you can keep track of them more easily. Up-level addressing affects your program to the contrary.

Q How many parameters can a subroutine have?

A As many as you want. Keep in mind that defining too many parameters makes a routine harder to use. Having several parameters makes it harder to spot a problem in the order the parameters are passed or the values of the actual parameters that are being passed because you have so many of them. Keep parameters to a manageable number. If you really need to pass a lot of data at once, consider passing information encapsulated in records.

Workshop

Quiz

1. How many types of parameters does Object Pascal support? How are they declared?
2. Value parameters are like what type of variables? What modifier do you use when declaring value parameters?
3. True or False? A variable cannot be an actual parameter to a formal value parameter? To a formal constant parameter? To a parameter passed by reference?

Exercises

1. Build a unit of reusable string routines. At the minimum, it should define `LeftJustify`, `RightJustify`, and `Center` subroutines to left-justify, right-justify, and center, respectively, a string of text within a string field of a specified length. You should pad the unused portions of the target string with spaces.
2. Build a unit of reusable integer-array manipulation routines. At the minimum, the unit should include a routine for calculating averages (developed in today's lesson), a routine for calculating the sum of all elements, one to find the minimum, and one to find the maximum value in the array, as well as a routine to copy a specified contiguous portion of an integer array into another integer array. In all cases, use open array parameters to allow unrestricted use of the subroutines with arrays of varying sizes.

WEEK
2

Classes and Objects

Today's lesson introduces you to one of the hottest topics in programming today: object-oriented programming.

In today's lesson, you learn the following:

- The fundamental concepts of object-oriented programming: object, class, instance, object field, method, and so on
- How to convert and extend the capabilities of a structured, non-object-oriented solution to a common programming problem to take advantage of objects
- The major characteristics of object-oriented programming
- How to declare and deal with a class data type, including how to access the fields and other elements of an object at run-time
- What inheritance is and how to set up an inheritance hierarchy of classes

You also reexamine the code generated by Delphi for each form you create. You will discover that a form is really an object and that the components you place on a form using the Form Designer are objects, too.

Introduction to Object-Oriented Programming

Object-Oriented Programming (OOP) has become a natural method of choice for developing complex, graphical user interface-based software. Object-oriented techniques are powerful tools, enabling you to develop complex, sophisticated systems that are also robust and extendible. OOP is based on an object-oriented model that regards *objects* as fundamental entities of concern and that provides facilities for objects to interact with one another.

One of the myths of OOP is that it is easy to learn. It is not, especially if you haven't done it before. But it is well worth the effort, so don't feel intimidated by the unfamiliar terms or the general hype surrounding the object-oriented methodologies.

Another often-promulgated myth is that OOP is so powerful that it will literally turn your business around and provide magic, "silver bullet" solutions to age-old programming problems of insufficient documentation, inadequate analysis, lacking design, poor implementation, and the lack of resources. OOP is certainly not a panacea for all of today's programming problems. Learning it, however, will help you solve many of them. In the end, OOP could likely turn out to be the most powerful tool in your programming toolbox.

Object-oriented programming is best practiced with the support of a good *object-oriented programming language* (OOPL). It is not necessary to practice object orientation with an OOPL, but the convenience of object-oriented notation that an OOPL provides is one of the most important factors contributing to the power of object orientation. The same problem expressed

in object-oriented terms looks simpler, more natural than when it is expressed using some other method.

Object Pascal is an OOPL because, as you soon learn, it provides facilities for everything needed to support the object-oriented programming model.

Object Pascal is also often called a *hybrid* language, because not only does it support the object-oriented approach to programming, but it also enables you to write non-object-oriented programs in a traditional, structured fashion. The excitement and the action, however, are definitely with object orientation nowadays. The component-based architecture of Delphi would not be possible if it were not for objects. Delphi components are in a sense just specialized objects, and their operation depends on the object-oriented architecture of the *Visual Component Library* (VCL).

10

Many ways of providing support for OOP in a programming language are available, and Object Pascal offers one of the possible alternatives. Whether or not you have programmed with objects before, the Object Pascal model of OOP has specific characteristics that make it unique and perhaps different from any other OOP environment. You may need to take your time to familiarize yourself with the specifics of the Pascal object model. Although this book cannot be, and is not, a comprehensive study of object-oriented methodologies, the intention here is to get you started in the right direction on the way towards object-oriented programming using the Object Pascal language and Delphi.

Structured Programming

Before you can appreciate the power and convenience of an object-oriented view of the world, you may find it helpful to take a look at a typical programming problem as it is solved using the traditional, structured methods of program construction.

Customer Example

Consider a typical example of a data entity arising in many applications: a customer. Traditionally, a customer entity is represented as a data record, consisting of a number of fields describing a particular customer, as follows:

```
type
  RCustomer = record
    FirstName: String[25];
    LastName : String[40];
    Street   : String[80];
    City     : String[20];
    State    : String[2];
    Zip      : String[10];
    LastOrder: String[10];
  end;
```

The meaning of the preceding FirstName and LastName fields is obvious. Street refers to the street address; City, State, and ZipCode refer to the remaining portions of a full postal address. The LastOrder field should contain a date, in the form '1994-11-23', denoting the date on which a given customer placed his or her last order with your company.

The use of a **record** structure underscores the fact that you would like to treat a customer as a single entity, but with different internal attributes, such as the first and last name, address, and so on.

You can now declare variables of the type RCustomer as follows:

```
var
  Cust1,
  Cust2: RCustomer;
  ACust: array[1..100] of RCustomer;
```

Here, you have two *instances* of the RCustomer type, Cust1 and Cust2, defined individually, as well as 100 other instances combined in an array structure. You can use these instances of RCustomer to store information about your customers.

Initializing Customers

One of the first tasks you might want to perform on the instances of a customer is to initialize the fields so that the values represent and model your actual, real-life business clients. You already know that you can accomplish this task by writing straightforward code that sets the value of each field individually, as follows:

```
begin
  ...
  Cust1.FirstName := 'John';
  Cust1.LastName  := 'Smith';
  Cust1.Street    :=  '123 Anystreet';
  Cust1.City      := 'Anytown';
  Cust1.State     := 'CA';
  Cust1.Zip       := '99999-8888';
  Cust1.LastOrder := '';
  ...
end
```

You can write this code for all of your customers, but you will quickly recognize that you are repeating the same operations over and over, each time using a different RCustomer instance variable.

For example, statements to initialize the variable Cust2 look substantially similar:

```
begin
  ...
  Cust2.FirstName := 'Mary';
  Cust2.LastName  := 'Johnson';
  Cust2.Street    :=  '567 First Street';
  Cust2.City      := 'Citiville';
  Cust2.State     := 'NY';
```

```
  Cust2.Zip       := '11111-2222';
  Cust2.LastOrder := '';
  ...
end
```

The only significant difference with the preceding set of statements is that now `Cust2` is referred to and that different data values are assigned to the corresponding fields.

The typical way of dealing with repetitive statements like these is to turn them into a subroutine and to supply the particular variable instance to be operated upon and the values for its fields via the parameter list. You can initialize a customer instance in a single step by using the `Initialize` subroutine defined and implemented, for example, as follows:

```
procedure Initialize
  (
    var Cust: RCustomer;
    const FirstName,
      LastName,
      Street,
      City,
      State,
      Zip: String
  );
begin
  Cust.FirstName := FirstName;
  Cust.LastName  := LastName;
  Cust.Street    := Street;
  Cust.City      := City;
  Cust.State     := State;
  Cust.Zip       := Zip;
  Cust.LastOrder := '';
end;
```

Note that the preceding `Cust` parameter is a **`var`** parameter, so any changes to its value are reflected outside the routine in the value of any actual parameter passed during the call.

All fields of the generic `Cust` formal parameter are passed specific values as arguments to the subroutine. Only `LastOrder` is initialized to an empty string to indicate that no order has yet been received from the customer. By defining the subroutine, you achieve a greater encapsulation of the details of the initialization.

You can now reuse the `Initialize` procedure to initialize different variables of type `RCustomer`. Note how turning a set of individual program statements into a subroutine shifts the emphasis from dealing with minute details of initialization *every time* you want to initialize a variable of type `RCustomer` to a higher-level outlook on logically initializing it and disregarding the details.

A typical call to `Initialize` looks like the following:

```
begin
  ...
  Initialize(Cust1, 'John', 'Smith', '123 Anystreet',
    'Anytown', 'CA', '99999-8888');
  ...
end;
```

The variable representing the customer, Cust1, is passed to the procedure along with the values with which you initialize the customer instance. The subroutine call has hidden the details of how the initialization is taking place. You no longer have to attend to the detailed structure of the record when you need to initialize its value. All the low-level aspects of assigning the values to the appropriate fields are taken care of inside the subroutine, normally hidden from view.

The Initialize subroutine is specific to the RCustomer type: you cannot pass it a different type of variable and expect meaningful results. In fact, the Pascal strong typing mechanism would have prevented you from passing in anything other than an RCustomer-type variable. The connection between the RCustomer type and the Initialize procedure is not emphasized, however, in the definition of the type. It is therefore easy to overlook that you should use the Initialize procedure for all instances of RCustomer.

A related problem with the non-object-oriented approach is that the RCustomer-type variables, like all variables, can exist in an "undefined" state, when they have been declared in a **var** block but not yet initialized. Failure to initialize an RCustomer instance properly may result in bizarre program behavior later on. Yet there is nothing about the RCustomer definition that would ensure automatic initialization of the type's instances.

The preceding description provides just a few examples of the kinds of difficulties and concerns that object orientation easily solves.

Retrieving Customer Address

Another typical, repeated operation you are likely to want to perform on an instance of RCustomer is retrieving the values of its fields, such as the address. Again, you could manipulate each customer instance directly, retrieving the values of its fields individually, as follows:

```
var
  Address1,
  Address2,
  Address3: String;
begin
  ...
  Address1 := Cust1.FirstName + ' ' + Cust1.LastName;
  Address2 := Cust1.Street;
  Address3 := Cust1.City + ', ' + Cust1.State
    + ' ' + Cust1.Zip;
  ...
end
```

The preceding code retrieves the address of a customer, Cust1, in a form suitable for printing on an envelope, as three lines: Address1, Address2, and Address3.

As before, because the operation is likely to be repeated for many customers, it makes sense to put the code in a separate subroutine and pass a customer instance as a parameter to it so that you can use the same set of operations on many different customers. You can accomplish this goal using the following example procedure GetAddress:

```
procedure GetAddress
  (
    const Cust: RCustomer;
    var Address1,
      Address2,
      Address3: String
  );
  begin
    Address1 := Cust.FirstName + ' ' + Cust.LastName;
    Address2 := Cust.Street;
    Address3 := Cust.City + ', ' + Cust.State
      + ' ' + Cust.Zip;
  end;
```

As before, instead of hard-coding a particular customer variable, the procedure `GetAddress` refers to a generic variable `Cust` passed as a parameter. It is passed by reference as a **`const`** parameter, rather than by value, to avoid a potentially costly operation of copying the value of the actual argument into the local `Cust` parameter at the time of the call. The **`const`** modifier ensures that the variable is treated as a reference, not copied by value, and that it cannot be accidentally modified within the subroutine.

10

The parameters `Address1`, `Address2`, and `Address3` are out parameters through which the corresponding lines of a print-ready address are returned. They are therefore declared as **`var`** parameters so that changes to their values can be passed out of the subroutine.

Again, as before, you have a dedicated subroutine accessing the data and hiding the implementation details of the record being accessed. Nevertheless, this approach requires that the internals of the record declaration be exposed and does not make it clear that the routine and the `RCustomer` record type really belong together.

Binding Subroutines with Data

The customer record example shows a scenario typical for non-object-oriented programming. Here, data, the `RCustomer` record, is defined to a great extent independently of the subroutines that operate on that data: `Initialize` and `GetAddress`. Nothing in the way these entities were defined would particularly help you to make the logical connection between the code and the data. You either have to guess which subroutines go together with which data elements, or, even worse, you are tempted to circumvent the subroutines especially defined for a particular piece of data and access the record fields directly. In the latter case, you may be missing some actions that need to be performed and that have been defined within the subroutines.

Another part of the problem with the `RCustomer` record is that its definition is "open" and its details are exposed to all sorts of abuse. For example, nothing would prevent someone from assigning a value of `'John'` to the `LastOrder` field. Clearly, it is not a value this field was designed to hold. Nothing in the definition of the record would prevent a careless programmer from mixing the meaning of the fields, with some bizarre effects potentially showing up when the program is run.

Observe that the data in this non-object-oriented scenario is completely passive and cannot actively check for its own consistency and validity. The variables just wait to be passed into subroutines. A sharp separation exists between the data and the subroutine: the subroutine is active and performs operations on the data; the data itself is static and has no way of interfering with what is being done to it. The information about the close coupling between the specific type of data and the subroutine that operates only on this specific data type is lost in this scenario.

Because both `Initialize` and `GetAddress` routines are clearly meant to be used with `RCustomer`-type variables, from the perspective of implementation of these operations, it seems redundant to always have to explicitly indicate that only the instances of `RCustomer` data type are being operated upon by these two subroutines.

Also note that each time you do use a subroutine accessing a particular customer record, you have to explicitly pass it an `RCustomer` instance variable parameter. What you really need here is a way of automatically binding instances of customers with the valid operations that can be performed on them.

The object-oriented approach recognizes that the subroutines and the data they operate on are closely related. The object-oriented paradigm binds and encapsulates the data with the attached code that operates upon that data, thereby creating a single entity: an object.

Definition of Object-Oriented Programming

Object-oriented programming can be characterized by the following statements:

- OOP uses objects as its building blocks. An *object* is an active data entity.
- An object is a combination of both data elements and operations on those elements, packaged together for the convenience of reuse and for easier handling. The packaging of data and code is called *tight encapsulation*.
- Each object is an instance of some *class*. At run-time, objects interact with one another by invoking each others' methods, that is, subroutines specific to a particular class.
- *Classes* are related to each other by means of an *inheritance* relationship, with which objects can be extended and existing object definitions reused. Inheritance is one of the mechanisms by which a class of objects can tap into the services of another class of objects. It also provides a powerful modeling mechanism for representing real-world relationships.
- Class instances can be regarded as instances of their immediate class and, at the same time, instances of any one of their ancestor classes, thereby encouraging *polymorphism*. Polymorphism is a way of acting on a collection of objects of the same ancestry in a single pass, hiding the minute details of how each of the particular objects handles the

particular action. It is also the basis for extendibility of object-oriented code because it provides a way for old code to accept new data types that were not defined at the time the code was written.

No doubt, the most fundamental notion behind OOP is the notion of an *object*.

NEW TERM An *object* is a combination of data and code. In other words, an object, also known as an *instance* (of a class), is a chunk of data, the value or values of which define its current state, and a collection of subroutines operating on that data, known as *methods*, defining its *behavior*—that is, the way the object responds to outside stimuli.

A *class* is a unifying concept for a set of objects sharing common characteristics. A class also defines a common interface to the rest of the world, through which you can interact with the individual objects. All instances of a particular class are similar to each other because they present the same interface, that is, the same set of operations.

Objects

The concept of an *object* is the key to understanding object-oriented programming. *Object instances*, or simply *objects*, are regarded as active entities with certain responsibilities to perform. The responsibilities of an object comprise a "contract" with the outside world to provide specific *services*.

NEW TERM The terms *object* and *object instance* are used interchangeably here and denote a concrete instantiation, or embodiment, or specimen, constructed according to a class definition.

An object's behavior is described by its class definition: after all, an object is an instance of some class. Object instances are examples of both data entities and service providers:

- **Data entities.** As a data entity, an object looks like a Pascal record. It has fields, which can be assigned values, where each field may be of a different type. The combined values of all fields of an object amount to what is known as an object's *state*. Changing the value of a field logically changes the state of an object.
- **Service providers.** As a service provider, or a procedural entity, an object is a collection of methods, or subroutines, designed to operate on the object's fields. It looks like a subroutine library in that regard. Collectively, the methods define the object's *behavior*. Activating an object's method results in an action being performed by the object.

The combination of the two complementary views makes objects such powerful entities. They become a convenient tool for abstraction: the insides of an object can be treated as a "black box," accessed only through a well-defined interface of methods. Only the characteristics explicitly made visible become the *signature*, also known as the *protocol*, of an object.

Object-Oriented Terminology

Sometimes, the terminology can get in the way of understanding. OOP is laden with technical terms such as *object, class, instance, method,* and so on. To make matters worse, the usage of these terms, *object* and *instance* in particular, is somewhat fuzzy. It is therefore important to realize exactly what is meant when someone uses one of these terms. Table 10.1 helps you understand particular terms, depending on the context in which they are used.

Table 10.1. A vocabulary of object-oriented terminology.

Word	Synonym	Explanation
object	idea	A generic term denoting the abstract, logical notion of an object, as in "object-oriented," that is, a logical entity encapsulating both data and code.
	instance	A technical term denoting a particular unique object created at run-time based on a class definition. A variable referring to a particular run-time object entity.
	class	A technical term denoting a precise description of an object and its behavior, via Object Pascal code. A structured data type in Pascal.
class	description	A precise technical term denoting a Pascal structured data type defined with the keyword `class`. A passive description of the capabilities and memory layout of its run-time instances.
	instance factory	A term denoting an active run-time entity, capable of creating instances that conform to the class definition.
	method table	A term denoting an abstract, logical entity that dispatches the references to methods made through object instances. This entity corresponds roughly to the virtual method table the compiler creates in the final executable for each class you define.
instance	object	A particular run-time embodiment of an object. An instance looks like a record with all the fields defined for the class, plus a run-time reference to the class's method table to resolve method calls.
method	subroutine	This term denotes a subroutine; in other words, a procedure, a function, a constructor, or a destructor that has been defined within a particular class. A method always belongs to a class.

Word	Synonym	Explanation
property	data attribute	When used in this precise technical meaning, the term denotes an extension of the concept of a data field. A property is a member of a class definition and provides special protection to its related data, supporting automatic, custom processing upon a value lookup and upon a value change. In other words, a property is not merely data that is assigned and used; assigning and/or using the data may invoke special side effects.

As you can see from Table 10.1, the term *object* is used in at least three distinct meanings: in one context, *object* refers to the logical combination of data and subroutines, or an abstract model or architecture of an application; in another, it means a run-time *instance*, or a specific chunk of data that is an instance of a particular class and, through this class, has the capability of executing its methods; in yet another, it denotes the recipe for an instance, or the class definition. No wonder object-oriented programming is sometimes hard to grasp. Stay alert when you hear the term *object* being used; make sure you understand the context.

On another note, the term *property*, although appearing in Table 10.1 for completeness, may still be a bit fuzzy to you. You can expect this confusion. You learn more about the nature of object properties in future lessons.

Classes

A *class,* in one of the meanings of this term, is a structured data type in Object Pascal. The notion of a class enables you to capture a set of common characteristics a particular group of objects shares and to provide precise implementation details that allow all these objects, known as instances, to behave according to these characteristics.

A class is a description of how an instance looks and how it behaves. You can also consider a class as an entity responsible for creating new instances via facilities called *constructors*. After all, someone must create an instance before it can become active and start interacting with the world. You create instances by “asking” the prospective instance’s class to manufacture one for you and initialize it via a call to a particular constructor. You will soon see how this is accomplished.

A class is not responsible for destroying instances, however, because this capability is something that active instances can take care of themselves: object instances self-destroy when “asked” to do so via a method (subroutine) call.

A class declaration defines the structure of the instances of the class and the set of valid operations that can be performed on instances of that class.

Syntax

Class Declaration Block

You can declare a class inside a Pascal **type** block using the following syntax:

```
type
  ClassName = class(ParentClassName)
    <Class Definition>
  end;
```

Examples:

```
type
  TRectangle = class(TObject)
    ...
  end;

  TDate = class(TNumber)
    ...
  end;
```

A class declaration block begins like any other type declaration with a name, which is a Pascal identifier. The name is followed by an equal sign, which in turn is followed by the reserved word **class**. After the word **class** is possibly another identifier enclosed within a pair of parentheses. This identifier, if present, specifies the name of the parent class, which is explained later in this lesson. The entire class declaration block is terminated with the reserved word **end** and a semicolon.

Figure 10.1 provides a building-block diagram of a class declaration.

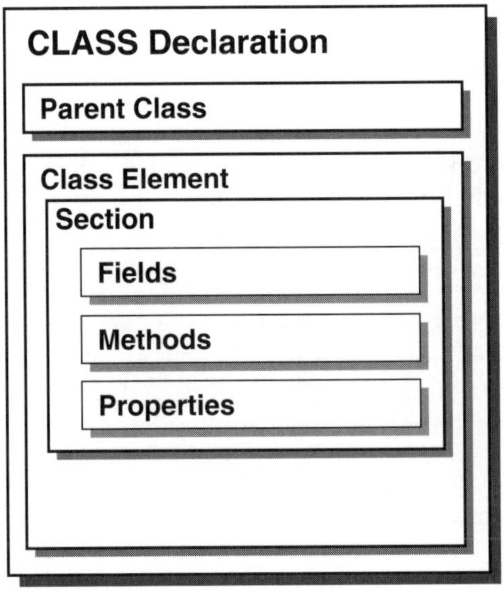

Figure 10.1.
The building-block structure of a class declaration.

An Empty Class

The following code example provides a skeleton unit containing the simplest possible class declaration:

```
unit Class1;

interface

type
  TClass = class
  end;

implementation

end.
```

The class `TClass` is not particularly useful as such, but it illustrates how to get started creating new class definitions in Object Pascal. The `Class1` unit is the simplest skeleton you can use to define your own object classes.

The contents of the class declaration block between the terminating **end** and after the **class** keyword are specific to each class and vary greatly. You learn exactly what kinds of elements or building blocks a class declaration contains during the remainder of today's and subsequent lessons.

Note: A class declaration is a declaration of *type*. It is primarily a static description of what an instance of the class will look like and how it will behave after it's created. You can view it as a recipe for a class instance, something that defines the characteristics and behavior of a live object. A class itself is not "live" but is a script or a screenplay for its instances.

To summarize, a class encapsulates the concept of data and that of action into a single, unified entity. Class declarations define three detailed characteristics of objects:

- **Object data.** The raw data attributes, also called fields, carried by each instance.
- **Object methods.** Also called operations, member functions, or actions in other programming languages.
- **Object properties.** Higher-order data attributes that are tightly coupled with dedicated data access methods.

A *class interface* is the collection of all elements of the class declaration, such as fields, methods, and properties. These elements are sometimes called the *features* of a class.

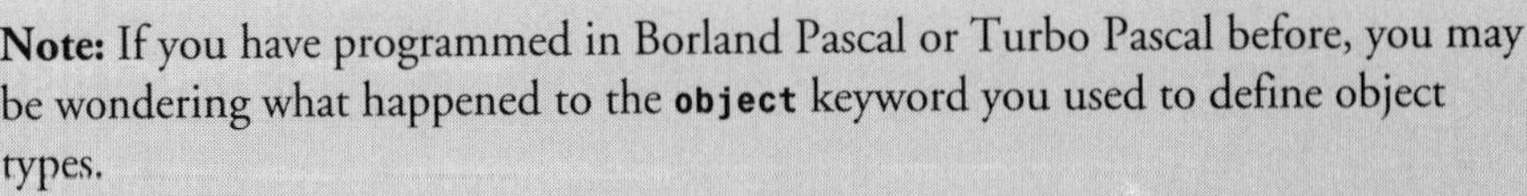

Note: If you have programmed in Borland Pascal or Turbo Pascal before, you may be wondering what happened to the **`object`** keyword you used to define object types.

The **`object`** keyword is still supported by Delphi to provide compatibility with old code. In any new code that you write, to take advantage of the tremendous improvements to the object model, however, you should use the **`class`** declarations exclusively.

The new **`class`**es are more powerful and flexible than **`object`**s. They are also the foundation of the Visual Component Library, the framework of predefined object classes provided along with Delphi.

Because the future of Pascal programming belongs to **`class`**-based objects, this book is concerned exclusively with **`class`**es, the new object entities. This note is the only reference to the old-style **`object`**s you will see during the entire 21 days of learning Delphi.

Inheritance

Classes can be related to one another in many ways. One of the fundamental concepts in object-oriented programming is the notion of class *inheritance* relating two classes in a parent-child relationship.

NEW TERM *Inheritance* is the capability of one class to reuse existing characteristics of another class. Inheritance captures the "kind of" relationship between two classes; for example, "a dog is a *kind of* mammal," "a mammal is a *kind of* animal," "an animal is a *kind of* living creature," and so on.

NEW TERM An *ancestor* is a class lending its capabilities and characteristics to another via the inheritance mechanism.

NEW TERM The class that reuses the characteristics of another class through inheritance is called its *descendant.*

NEW TERM The immediate ancestor of a class, the one from which the class directly descends, is called its *parent.*

This is not to be confused with the `parent` of a Windows control object as defined by some standard component classes such as the `TForm` class.

Object Pascal allows one class to be an immediate descendant (child) of another by specifying the parent of each class at the point of declaration in parentheses right after the **`class`** keyword.

Note: Object Pascal supports a model of inheritance known as *single inheritance*, which constrains the number of parents a particular class can have to a maximum of one. In other words, a user-defined class has exactly one parent.

The more powerful model of *multiple inheritance*, in which each class can potentially descend from an arbitrary number of parents, is not currently supported by Object Pascal/Delphi and Borland has indicated no plans to support it in the future.

A parent class designator is optional in a class declaration. If it is not given, the `TObject` class is assumed as the parent; if it is given, the specified class becomes the parent.

Syntax

Class Declaration Block with Parent

You can declare a class descending from a specific other class inside a Pascal **type** block by providing the parent-class designator in parentheses after the word **class** using the following syntax:

```
type
  ClassName = class(ParentClass)
    <Class Definition>
  end;
```

The syntax defines a class that is an immediate descendant of the specified class `ParentClass`.

Example:

```
type
  TPrinter = class(TOutputDevice)
    ...
  end;
```

Syntax

Class Declaration Block with No Parent

You can declare a class descending from the default object `TObject` inside a Pascal **type** block by omitting the parent-class designator altogether using the following syntax:

```
type
  ClassName = class
    <Class Definition>
  end;
```

The syntax defines a class that is an immediate descendant of `TObject`, the ultimate parent of all Object Pascal classes.

Example:

```
type
```

```
TRectangle = class
  ...
end;
```

You should choose the parent class, if given, in such a way that the essential "kind of" relationship is exemplified. For example, you cannot responsibly say, "A color printer is a kind of display monitor"; but you can say, "A color printer is a kind of output device." Descending a class representing the printer from a display-monitor class is not a good idea. After all, a printer is *not* a kind of monitor. Descending it from the hypothetical `OutputDevice` would be fine; a printer is an output device, and it likely shares many characteristics with other output devices.

Conceptually, every instance of the descendant class *is also an instance of its parent class*. If you can't say that with a straight face about some class in your inheritance hierarchy, you should consider a different inheritance scheme. For example, you might consider the two classes in question descending from a common ancestor you create just for the purpose of capturing and factoring out the common characteristics of both original classes.

Inheritance "adds up" capabilities in the sense that any descendant class has access to, or *inherits*, practically all resources (methods, fields, and properties) of the parent class and also of its ancestors all the way up to the top level of the hierarchy.

Establishing an inheritance relationship between two classes creates a close coupling between them. The descendant class is intimately tied with its ancestors. Keep in mind that every instance of a descendant is automatically an instance of any of its ancestor classes. The instances of a descendant class, for the most part, resemble those of its immediate ancestor. You soon see how descendants inherit data and code from their ancestors and how they can extend the definition to include new data fields and methods.

Object Fields

In at least one respect, an object (class type) is like a Pascal record: an object can be regarded as a collection of data *fields*, or *attributes*, grouped together under one name. The biggest difference between records and classes is that records cannot inherit from one another, nor can they have subroutines attached. Only classes can enter into inheritance schemes. Only classes define fields and associate subroutines (methods).

An attribute, or field, of an object instance is like a variable, except that it is tightly coupled together with the other attributes forming the particular instance.

Syntax

Object Field Declaration

The syntax to declare object fields is as follows:

```
type
  ClassName = class(ParentName)
    Field11,
    Field12,
```

```
    ...
    Field1N: Type1;
    Field21,
    Field22,
    ...
    Field2M: Type2;
  ...
    FieldX1,
    FieldX2,
    ...
    FieldXP: TypeX;
  end;
```

Example:

```
  type
    TColorRectangle = class
      Left,
      Top,
      Right,
      Bottom: Integer;
      Color : TColor;
    end;
```


You can define data fields inside a class declaration similarly to the way you define fields of a record. This process, in turn, is similar to the way you define variables. You can list one or more field names of the same type separated with commas and then provide a type name, which you separate from the list with a colon. You end the declaration with a semicolon after the type name.

All the field declarations together provide an instance layout, which is a memory map of an object instance specifying the relative size of the fields, in the order in which they were declared.

Figure 10.2 illustrates an instance layout for the `TColorRectangle` class declaration given as an example in the preceding syntax box.

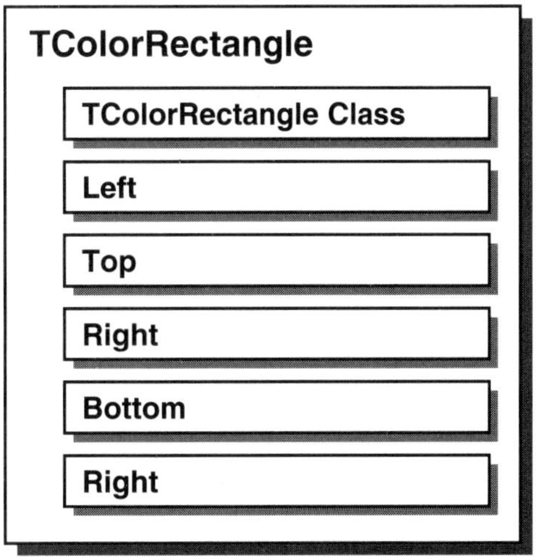

Figure 10.2.
The `TColorRectangle` instance layout.

Customer Example Continued

Now take another look at the Customer example you examined earlier in today's lesson. The `RCustomer` entity was originally defined as a record type, with several fields corresponding to the data attributes you would typically want stored about each customer.

You can now start converting the original, non-object-oriented approach to an object-oriented model. The first step is to define the data layout of an object representing a customer. Because all the data fields remain the same, the object-oriented definition of a customer looks almost exactly like the record definition from the earlier example.

Listing 10.1 shows the new object-oriented `TCustomer` entity with its data fields defined just as before.

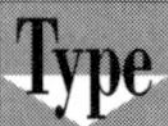

Listing 10.1. The data layout of `TCustomer`.

```
unit Cust1;

interface

type
  TCustomer = class
    FirstName: String[25];
    LastName : String[40];
    Street   : String[80];
    City     : String[20];
    State    : String[2];
    Zip      : String[10];
    LastOrder: String[10];
  end;

implementation
end.
```

Listing 10.1 shows the first step in creating a customer object: the definition of the data attributes and their layout within a customer instance. The data fields and their order are the same as in the earlier record-based example. At this point, the differences between the two techniques are minimal, so the superiority of the object-oriented approach is not yet apparent.

Right now the `TCustomer` class consists of exactly the same data elements as the `RCustomer` record. These class elements are currently as unprotected and open to misuse as the record elements were. It is not until you start building more complex entities that you see a substantial difference between the two approaches.

DO	DON'T

DO use class types as the default way of grouping related data attributes to represent real-life business and scientific entities.

DON'T use record types to merely group related attributes into meaningful entities; objects are more powerful.

Declaring Instance Variables

10

You should understand by now that merely declaring an object type is not sufficient for you to assign values to its fields or to otherwise use it. No memory is allocated for a **type** declaration, for example. Contrary to what is the case with classes, if you intend to use instances of a record type in your program, you simply need to declare a variable of that type to actually reserve the memory storage for the instance. (It is possible to dynamically allocate memory for traditional, non-object-oriented entities, but such techniques are beyond the scope of this book.)

Merely declaring a variable of a class type is still not sufficient to reserve appropriate storage for objects. Objects, in contrast to **var**-block-declared variables, are dynamic entities.

Just like any other variables in Pascal, class-instance variables must be initialized before they can be used. You can initialize a class-instance variable with a call to the class-instance constructor.

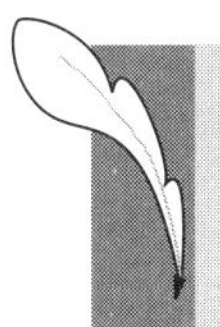

Note: A variable of a class type is not an instance of the class; it is merely a *reference* to an instance. It must therefore be initialized at run-time with a valid instance via a call to a constructor.

Recall that you can declare a record type as follows:

```
type
  TRecordType = record
    Field1: Type1;
    Field2: Type2;
    Field3: Type3;
  end;
```

To actually allocate memory for the record, you have to declare a variable of the preceding newly defined type, as follows:

```
var
  MyRecord: TRecordType;
```

The preceding declaration is sufficient to set aside a certain amount of memory to ensure that the variable exists and that its fields can be assigned values. The way the memory is set aside for the record instance is *static*; that is, it is done at compile-time.

Objects are different. Not only is declaring object class types not sufficient to obtain a valid instance, but neither is declaring a variable of the type. You must perform an extra step to initialize the variable. For example, the following declarations mimic the way you define a record variable:

```
 1: type
 2:   TColorRectangle = class
 3:     FLeft,
 4:     FTop,
 5:     FRight,
 6:     FBottom: Integer;
 7:     FColor : TColor;
 8:   end;
 9:
10: var
11:   ARect: TColorRect;
12:
13: begin
14:   ...
15: end;
```

On lines 2 through 8, the class declaration declares a class whose instances contain four `Integer` fields: `FLeft`, `FTop`, `FRight`, and `FBottom`. It also declares an `FColor` field of type `TColor`. `TColor` is a standard type provided by the `Classes` unit to denote a color as a single, `LongInt`-sized (32-bit) number.

The problem with the variable declaration on line 11 is that it still does not contain any instances of `TColorRect`. If you attempt to access a field of this object with a statement similar to what would work with an ordinary record—that is, if you write

```
ARect.Left := 10;
```

between the **`begin`** and the **`end`** on line 14—the attempt fails; a run-time error occurs, and your program terminates. The variable `ARect` is a reference variable but has not been initialized with a valid instance. You therefore cannot use it to refer to the fields or methods.

The variable is potentially capable of storing a reference to an instance of class `TColorRect`, but for the time being it does not actually hold a valid reference. It does not represent a valid instance until it is explicitly assigned one, typically via a call to an instance constructor.

The memory storage for the object instance is *dynamic,* allocated at run-time. Only a small amount of storage is allocated for the object *reference* statically when you declare a class-typed variable. The actual object instance is brought into life at run-time. Because a class-typed variable is merely a reference, it does not get any storage allocated for the values of the object's fields.

To summarize this section, just because a class variable may potentially refer to an object instance does not mean that it automatically does so merely by being declared. Something more must be done to it—namely, it must be dynamically *constructed* at run-time for you to use it.

Note: A class-typed variable must first be filled in with a valid object instance before it can be used. Declaring the variable by itself does not give you a valid instance; it leaves the variable in a state that all declared but uninitialized variables are in: undefined, or invalid. To obtain a valid instance, you must explicitly "ask" the class of the prospective object to supply you one dynamically at run-time and assign the reference to the instance thus obtained to the `class` variable.

10

The process of dynamically constructing a new instance, if successful, results in a valid object reference. The job of actually creating a valid instance is the responsibility of a special class subroutine called a *constructor*. Constructors are one of the possible kinds of object methods; you learn more about methods in tomorrow's lesson.

Accessing Object Elements

You can access an object's data fields and methods with the same "dot notation" you learned before to access the fields of a record. For example, given the following partial `TCircle` class declaration

```
type
  TCircle = class
    X,
    Y,
    Radius: Integer;
    ...
    constructor Create;
    procedure Move(NewX, NewY: Integer);
    procedure Scale(By: Integer);
  end;
```

and the corresponding instance variable `ACircle`, properly initialized with a call to a constructor,

```
var
  ACircle: TCircle;
begin
  ...
  ACircle := TCircle.Create;
  ...
end
```

you can access its fields as follows:

```
begin
  ...
  ACircle.X      := 10;
  ACircle.Y      := 25;
  ACircle.Radius := 17;
  ...
end;
```

You separate the field name from the variable name prefix using a single dot.

Not only can you access the fields of the given object type in this way, but all fields inherited from the ancestors can also be accessible. For example, consider the following class declaration derived from `TCircle`:

```
type
  TColorCircle = class(TCircle)
    BorderColor,
    InsideColor: TColor;
    constructor Create;
  end;
```

First, a valid instance of `TColorCircle` must be created with a call to its `Create` constructor as before. Once the variable `AColorCircle` is initialized with a valid instance, you can access its fields.

```
var
  AColorCircle: TColorCircle;
begin
  ...
  TColorCircle.Create;
  ...
  AColorCircle.BorderColor := clBlack;
  AColorCircle.InsideColor := clYellow;
  ...
  AColorCircle.X      := 10;
  AColorCircle.Y      := 25;
  AColorCircle.Radius := 17;
  ...
end;
```

In addition, as the last three statements illustrate, you can refer to the fields declared inside `TCircle` class because they are also part of a `TColorCircle` instance. These fields are inherited from `TCircle`, and you can specify them as if they were declared inside `TColorCircle`.

Eventually, you will learn to treat an instance as a single, indivisible, structured collection of *all* the inherited fields and methods together with the ones declared in the given class. This is what inheritance is all about: you don't have to specify the exact naming and layout of all the fields in the instance, just those that are new at a given level of inheritance.

DO	DON'T

DO study the entire inheritance chain up to the top-level class whenever confronted with a new or unfamiliar object. The object's structure and behavior are the sum of those of all of its ancestors, plus its own. After it successfully compiles, you can use the Object Browser to view the entire object hierarchy of your program.

DON'T forget to check the inheritance chain of a deceptively simple-looking class. Behind the apparent simplicity of a particular class may be hidden an enormous complexity of, and a wealth of potentially useful services provided by, its ancestors.

10

Accessing Fields: The *with* Statement

It is not unusual for you to want to refer to several fields of an object in short succession. For example, you typically initialize all the fields of an object within a constructor by assigning values to them one by one, or to access several fields of an object from outside its methods. So that you can do the latter, however, you have to prefix each reference to an object's fields with a name of an instance plus a period, for example, `Button1.Height`, `Form1.Caption`, and so on.

For example, consider the following long object class declaration:

```
type
  TSpecialButton = class
    FTop,
    FLeft,
    FHeight,
    FWidth: Integer;
    FCommand: Word;
    FText: String;
    FColorFace,
    FColorLightEdge,
    FColorDarkEdge: TColor;

    function GetTop: Integer;
    procedure SetTop(AValue: Integer);
    function GetLeft: Integer;
    procedure SetLeft(AValue: Integer);
    function GetWidth: Integer;
    procedure SetWidth(AValue: Integer);
    function GetHeight: Integer;
    procedure SetHeight(AValue: Integer);
    function GetCommand: Word;
    procedure SetCommand(NewCommand: Word);
    function GetText: String;
    procedure SetText(const NewText: String);
```

```
    function GetColorFace: TColor;
    procedure SetColorFace(NewColor: TColor);
    function GetColorLightEdge: TColor;
    procedure SetColorLightEdge(NewColor: TColor);
    function GetColordarkEdge: TColor;
    procedure SetColorDarkEdge(NewColor: TColor);
    constructor Create;
    destructor Destroy;
  end;
```

The `TSpecialButton` class mimics some of the properties of a Windows pushbutton. Among them are a set of fields determining the position and size—`FTop`, `FLeft`, `FHeight`, and `FWidth`—a set of fields determining the colors— `FColorFace`, `FColorLightEdge`, and `FColorDarkEdge`—a command value `FCommand`, and the visible label `FText`.

Note: By convention, you name object fields with a prefix of *F*, for *Field.* Examples include `FWidth` and `FTop`. This convention is not required but makes it easier to distinguish among similar-looking names of fields, variables, and methods.

Another naming convention has all the user-defined type names prefixed with a *T* for *Type.* Examples include `Tbutton` and `TRectangle`. Again, this convention is not required, but using it is convenient so that you can immediately recognize that a name like `TShape` refers to a type, not to a variable, for example.

Suppose that somewhere in your code you want to specifically control the position and size of a button instance. You would probably write code similar to the following:

```
var
  Button1: TSpecialButton;
begin
  ...
  Button1.Top := 10;
  Button1.Left := 120;
  Button1.Width := 42;
  Button1.Height := 24;
  ...
end;
```

Nothing is really wrong with this code, except that you have to repeat `Button1.` on every line, and somehow you still lose sight of the fact that these four statements are related. You are setting four fields of `Button1` to specific values to position the object on-screen. Each time you want to set a particular value, you have to repeat the `Button1.` prefix to denote that you are accessing a field of `Button1` as if it were a separate, independent action.

Object Pascal offers a shorthand notation—the **`with`** statement—that you use to avoid repetition of the instance prefix and to underscore the fact that you are accessing different fields of the same entity in what may be a single operation.

Syntax

The *with* Statement

The syntax of the **with** statement is as follows:

```
with Variable1, Variable2, ... do
  <Statement 1>;
```

or

```
with Variable1, Variable2, ... do begin
  <Statement 1>;
  <Statement 2>;
  ...
end;
```

Examples:

```
with Button1 do
  if Top > 10 then
    Top := 10;

with Button1 do begin
  Top := 10;
  Left := 120;
  Width := 42;
  Height := 24;
end;
```


The **with** statement belongs in the executable block, inside a **begin** and an **end** pair. The **with** keyword is followed by an arbitrary number of variable names, separated by commas. The variables are either object instance variables or records. The list is followed by the reserved word **do** and an executable statement. Typically, the executable statement is a **begin-end** block, a compound statement, in turn containing an arbitrary number of executable statements, each of which may refer to the object fields directly.

Note that inside the **with** statement the fields of the variable listed in the **with** part are accessible directly, without any prefixes. The **with** statement establishes a *context,* or *scope*, in which directly referring to the internals of the specific structured variable becomes possible.

Figure 10.3 illustrates the building-block structure of a **with** statement.

Note: You can use the **with** statement with **class** and **record** variables to establish a context suitable for accessing their fields directly.

The context established by a **with** statement relieves you from having to prefix each field name with the identifier denoting the variable of interest.

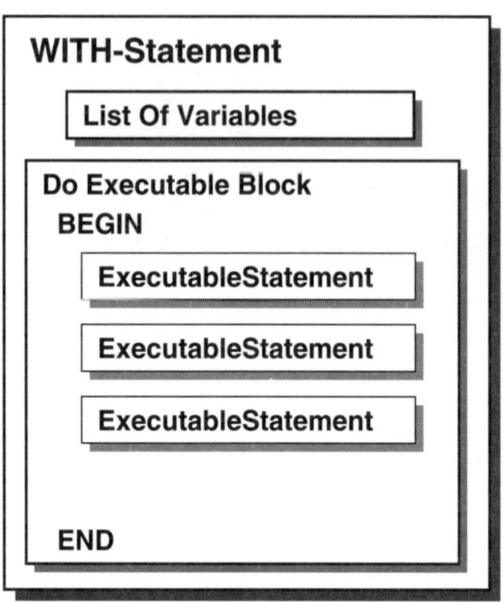

Figure 10.3.
The building-block structure of a `with` statement.

In case of any identifier conflicts—for example, a field name being identical to the name of a local variable or to the name of a formal parameter—you can still fully qualify the name of the field with the complete variable name so that it becomes clear which of the identically named entities is referenced.

Direct and Indirect Fields

You can define essentially two kinds of fields inside class instances: direct and indirect.

NEW TERM A *direct field* is a concrete piece of data directly embedded inside the instance. Examples are an integer number or a string. Direct attributes require the amount of storage in each instance to be equal to their declared size, so their values can be directly stored inside the instance.

NEW TERM An *indirect field* is a reference to another entity, typically another object instance. Indirect fields require only a comparatively small amount of storage to be embedded in the object instance for the value of the reference. The reference can give access to an arbitrary complex object instance in its own right.

Given the distinction between direct and indirect data attributes of an object, you can think of an object as "containing" other objects. An object can contain another in at least two ways:

- An object can *own* another object. The owning object is then responsible for both creating the owned instance when needed and destroying it when it is done with it. Typically, these two tasks are performed within a constructor and a destructor of the owning object, respectively. You will learn more about constructors and destructors in the next lesson.

- An object can be *associated with* other objects. An association, as opposed to ownership, allows an object to "know" other object instances, or to be able to refer to them, invoke their methods, and so on. But association does not imply the responsibility for creating and/or destroying those instances. Typically, the references to other instances are passed in through parameters to the object's constructor and stored inside the fields specifically designated for this purpose.

  When an associated object is being destroyed, it does not need to worry about destroying the associated instances; they were passed from outside, so presumably they are somebody else's responsibility. Hence, they are simply abandoned, rather than destroyed.

Forms as Classes

You are now ready to take a second look at Delphi forms, which are themselves instances of a form class. Each Delphi form you create becomes a separate class. When you create a blank form in a new project, for example, the Delphi IDE generates code that defines a new class by default called `TForm1`, which is a descendant of `TForm`. The generated class definition code looks like the following:

```
type
  TForm1 = class(TForm)
  private
    { Private declarations }
  public
    { Public declarations }
  end;
```

For now, ignore the contents of this declaration. You have not yet formally encountered the **`private`** and **`public`** keywords, which appear by default and which divide the class declaration into three sections: default public section, private, and an explicit public section. For your current purposes, however, it is sufficient simply to recognize the similarity between this declaration and the blank class declaration shown earlier in today's lesson. A simplified form class declaration can thus be represented as an empty shell descending from `TForm`:

```
type
  TForm1 = class(TForm)
    ...
  end;
```

Note that even though the class declaration looks simple, by inheriting from `TForm` you have already inherited a great deal of data and code.

A quick look inside the Object Inspector reveals a number of properties that even a blank form defines. These properties act programmatically like data fields so that you can, for example, access the current vertical position of the top-left corner of the form with a statement

```
Form1.Top := 16;
```

where `Form1` is an instance variable automatically defined by Delphi to correspond to the unique instance of the form that is automatically created at run-time, during the program initialization.

Creating the Example Form

Here's how to create the example form:

1. Create a new project with a blank main form. Save the form unit file under the name `CustLst` (CUSTLST.PAS, CUSTLST.FRM) and the project file under the name `NameList` (NAMELIST.PRJ).
2. Change the `Name` property of the form from `TForm1` to `CustList`.
3. Change the `Caption` property of the form to `'Customer List'`.
4. Place a `ListBox` component from the Standard page of the Component Palette on the form. Change its `Align` property to `Left`. The list box snaps to the window frame and fills the left-hand side of the form.
5. Place a `BitBtn` component from the Additional page on a free area on the form. After you change its `Kind` property to `bkCancel`, change its caption to `Close` (the `Kind` property reverts to `bkCustom`, but the Cancel button's *glyph*, or picture bitmap, remains in place).
6. Place an additional three Button components from the Standard page of the Component Palette onto the form. Name the buttons `ButtonAdd`, `ButtonDelete`, and `ButtonChange`, respectively. Then give them appropriate captions: `&Add`, `&Delete`, and `&Change`, respectively.
7. Place an edit box on the form, remove the contents of its `Text` property so that it appears blank, and name it `EditName`.

Your finished form should look similar to the one shown in Figure 10.4.

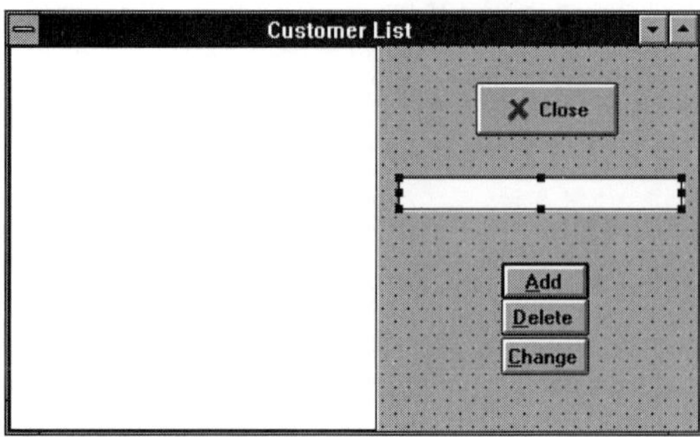

Figure 10.4.
The main form of the Customer List program as shown in the Form Designer.

Examining the Form Class

While you were creating the Customer List form, Delphi was quietly editing the source code of the `Custlst` unit in the background. Click the Code Editor window to make it fully visible, and take a look at the generated code for the `TCustList` class.

The generated code should look similar to what is shown in Listing 10.2.

Listing 10.2. `TCustList` class generated by Delphi.

```
unit Custlst;

interface

uses
  SysUtils, WinTypes, WinProcs, Messages, Classes,
  Graphics, Controls, Forms, Dialogs;

type
  TCustList = class(TForm)
    ListBox1: TListBox;
    EditName: TEdit;
    BitBtn1: TBitBtn;
    ButtonAdd: TButton;
    ButtonDelete: TButton;
    ButtonChange: TButton;
  private
    { Private declarations }
  public
    { Public declarations }
  end;

var
  CustList: TCustList;

implementation

{$R *.DFM}

end.
```

Analysis

As you can see in Listing 10.2, a form is an example of a class. A form is somewhat special in the sense that it corresponds to a visual interface element and that its definition is created interactively, by visually dropping components on the form inside the Form Designer. It is, however, a class like any other nevertheless: it has a parent (`TForm`) and defines a number of fields.

The blank skeleton for the `TCustList` class was created by Delphi when you requested a new form. Then the class declaration was filled with contents as you added components inside the Form Designer.

Note that all the components were added to the `TCustList` class definition in the section right after the **`class`** header on lines 11 through 16. You should never make changes to this first section of the form class definition by hand. This area is reserved for the Delphi automatic code generator. To add or remove a component from this section, go to the Form Designer and carry the action you want performed there. As you visually add components onto the form, appropriate fields are automatically added to the code. As you remove components, Delphi removes the fields that were added to the form definition.

The sections of the class definition marked **`private`** and **`public`** on lines 17 through 20 are left unchanged by Delphi and are available for you to define your own class elements.

On lines 11 through 16, the listing shows an example of a class with several fields. These fields represent the components you added to the form. Technically, all of these fields are object references; they act like reference variables through which you can access the component objects. `ListBox1`, `EditName`, `BitBtn1`, `ButtonAdd`, `ButtonDelete`, and `ButtonChange` are indirect fields referring to other object instances owned by the form at run-time.

Figure 10.5 illustrates the cluster of objects (*object ensemble*) instantiated at run-time, corresponding to the form design you have just created.

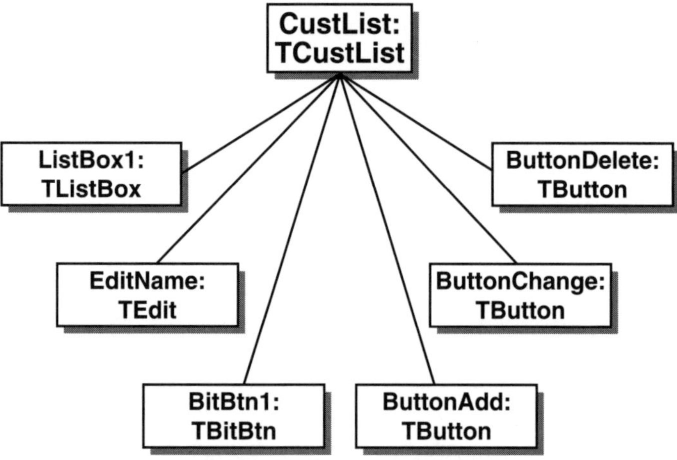

Figure 10.5.
The `TCustList` form's object ensemble.

Theoretically, because it is the responsibility of the form to both create and destroy the objects it owns, you should be handling the mechanics of creating the owned objects and of initializing the fields of the form with the proper references inside the `TCustList` class implementation somewhere. Fortunately, because Delphi creates the form class definition on-the-fly, it also takes the responsibility of managing the components at run-time. By making the `TCustList` class inherit from `TForm`, you have effectively ensured that all the proper initialization and destruction will take place automatically at the right time.

The **type** declaration block on lines 9 through 21 declares the internal structure of an instance. In addition to all the fields and properties the `TCustList` might have inherited from its ancestor, `TForm`, several new fields are added. The original class, `TForm`, has thus been extended and every instance of its descendant, `TCustList`, has a slightly larger memory footprint than it would have without your having placed the visual components on the form. Every instance of `TCustList` now carries the additional six variables, or fields, defined in the class declaration.

As you know now, merely declaring the `TCustList` form does not create an instance that could be used at run-time. Although Delphi automatically declared a variable on line 24 to reserve room for the instance reference, this variable is still unusable until something is done to initialize it. That something is the statement appearing in the main project source file, which creates a new instance of the form and assigns the reference to it to the instance variable `CustList`.

You can verify that the form is being created inside the main project file by selecting Project Source from the Delphi View menu. At the bottom of the source file that appears, you see code similar to the following:

```
begin
  Application.CreateForm(TCustList, CustList);
  Application.Run;
end.
```

The first statement after the initial **begin** is a call that eventually results in assigning the newly created instance of the `TCustList` class to the form variable `CustList`. The details of constructing the instance of the form are handled internally by the underlying application framework.

Because `CreateForm` is called as the first statement of the program, it is performed early, as part of the program initialization, thereby ensuring that the form instance is there and available as soon as you need to refer to it. You can use this instance reference to access the instance of the form after the program is running.

Observe that right now the program does not do anything. You have merely created the visual design for part of the program's user interface.

Summary

Today's lesson introduced you to the fundamental concepts of object-oriented programming. You have learned the following:

- Objects are conceptual entities that encapsulate data and code inside a single package.
- You define the structure and behavior of objects through class-type declarations.
- A class is technically a structured Object Pascal type declared with the reserved word **class**. Inside a class declaration, various elements can be defined, corresponding to the code and data that the class encapsulates. The elements of the class declaration form the class interface.

- The structure of an object that determines the size of memory it occupies and its memory layout depends on the definition of its fields, or data attributes of a class.
- The behavior of an object—that is, the protocol of operations that can be performed on it—is defined by implementing methods, or subroutines attached to a class declaration.
- Classes are related to each other via a mechanism called inheritance. Inheritance provides one way of reusing the capabilities of already defined objects.
- A class derived from a particular base class is called a descendant. The class lending itself to be extended through inheritance becomes an ancestor. A parent is an immediate ancestor.
- Object instances are related at run-time through association. One object can hold a reference to another, thereby typically gaining the ability to access the other and call its methods.
- You can conveniently access fields of an object or a record (and, in general, elements of a class) directly by setting up a context through a `with` statement.

Today's lesson was concentrated around the data elements of a class's fields. The study of objects continues in tomorrow's lesson with a detailed introduction to declaring, implementing, and using methods.

Q&A

Q How does object orientation help me model the real-life better than the traditional techniques?

A Object-oriented techniques of software development remove a "layer of indirection" when modeling the real world, in contrast to other techniques. The entities in the real world are more easily modeled in a straightforward, direct, and intuitive way with objects than with the traditional variables. It is easier to keep track of relationships among real-world entities by setting up their direct programmatic analogues inside the software.

Q What is the difference between a record and a class?

A Here are the fundamental differences:

- You cannot inherit a descendant entity from a record.
- You cannot declare methods, or subroutines, within a record.
- You cannot automatically ensure the initialization of a record's fields.
- You cannot hide the details of implementation of a record. All fields of a record are visible from the outside, or public.

Q Can I define a field in a descendant class with the same name as an already existing field in one of the ancestor classes?

A In general, no. If a field with a particular name already exists in an ancestor, you cannot define another with the same name in a descendant, provided that the ancestor's identifier is visible to a descendant. You learn about the visibility of class elements in tomorrow's lesson.

Workshop

The Workshop provides quiz questions to help you solidify your understanding of the material covered and exercises to provide you with experience in using what you've learned. Try to understand the quiz and exercise answers before continuing on to the next day's lesson. Answers are provided in the appendix at the end of this book.

Quiz

1. True or False? Variables of a class type are automatically initialized as soon as the program is run.
2. True or False? Polymorphism means the ability of an object to convert itself to another type of object.
3. True or False? The object state is determined by the collective values of all its fields, both direct and indirect. The object's state is therefore dependent on the states of potentially many other objects, which in turn depend on yet more distant objects...
4. True or False? You can set up a context for directly accessing more than one record variable in a single `with` statement.
5. True or False? You can mix and match any number of record and class variables in a single `with` statement, thereby setting up a context for directly accessing the fields of both kinds of multiple data entities.

Exercises

1. Define a data layout for a class `TDate` capable of holding a date value. Define interface methods that return the year, the month, and the day individually. Also define access methods that can affect any and all of the data elements of the class instances.
2. Define a data layout for a generic `TInvoice` object. Make sure you provide a facility for an invoice to refer to the related instance of the `TCustomer` class defined during today's lesson.

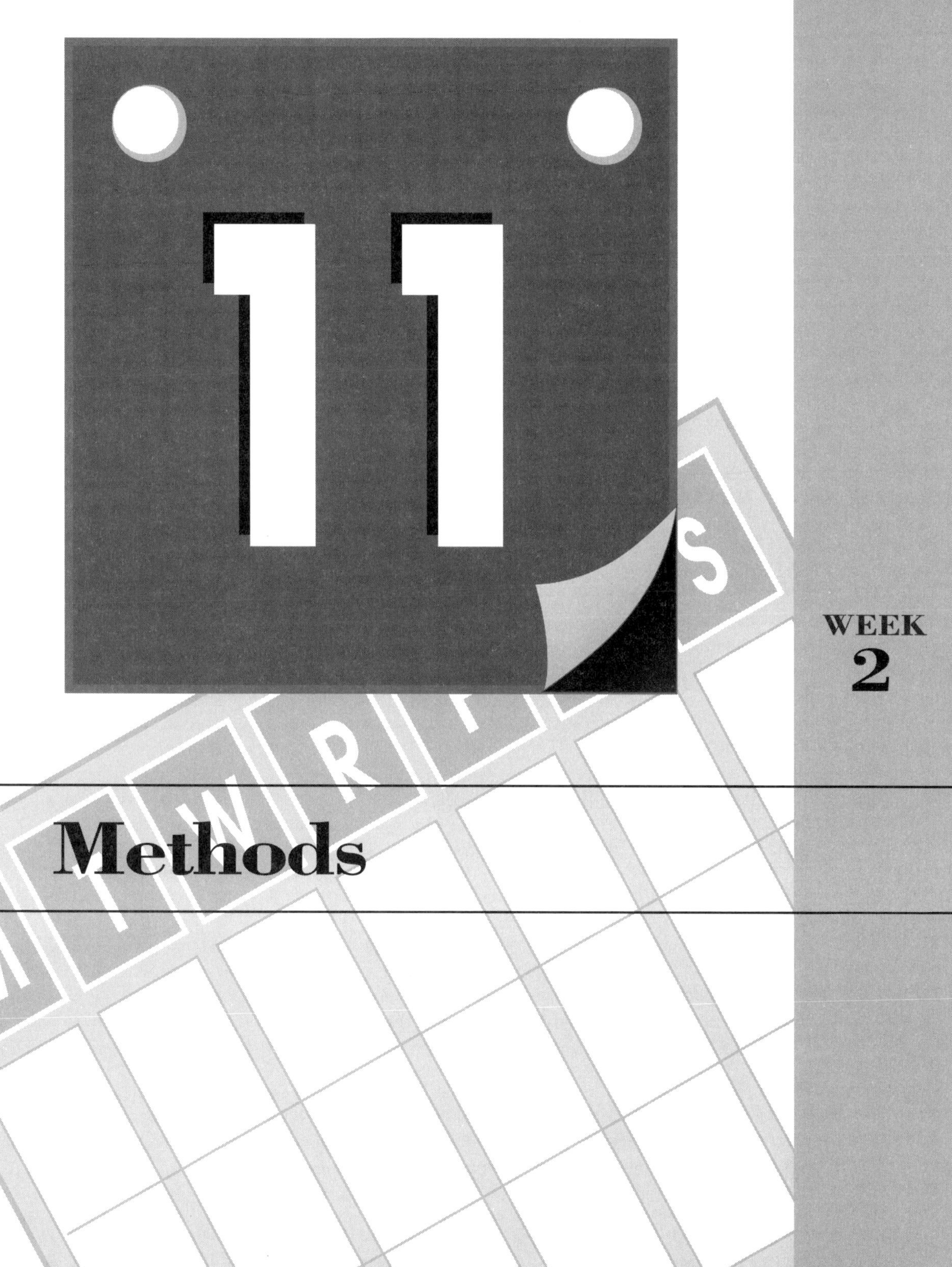

WEEK 2

11

Methods

In yesterday's lesson you were introduced to the fundamental concepts of Object-Oriented Programming (OOP).

Today, you will continue to explore the issues of OOP. You will learn the following:

- How to declare methods, including constructors and destructors
- How to implement methods
- How to use methods
- What class methods are
- How to hide and protect class elements

Introduction to Methods

You already know that objects encapsulate both data and code. The code, in the form of methods (that is, subroutines attached to an object), defines the behavior of an object. The set of all methods an object class defines determines the operations that can be performed on instances of the object.

The terms *operations* and *methods* both mean essentially the same thing: they refer to the concept of action, and to the process of execution of program instructions.

NEW TERM A *method* is a subroutine that is defined as part of, and encapsulated inside, a class.

It is the capability of objects to incorporate *both data and methods* that makes them so powerful and distinguishes them from simple records.

Recall from Day 9 that there are two types of stand-alone subroutines in Object Pascal: procedures and functions. These two correspond to the procedure and function methods, respectively. Objects define additional categories of methods. Overall, there are six different kinds of object methods, and they include:

- Procedure Methods

  Procedure methods correspond to the stand-alone procedures, except that they are "attached" to a particular class in which they are defined and can only be invoked through a valid instance of that class.

- Function Methods

  Function methods return values and behave like ordinary stand-alone functions, except that, like all methods, they are "attached" to a particular class in which they are defined and must be invoked through a valid instance of that class.

- Class Procedures

  Class procedures are conceptually even closer to ordinary, stand-alone procedures than are procedure methods. Class procedures do not require a valid object instance to be invoked. They are declared as part of the class and are invoked through a reference to the class itself, rather than to an instance. This will be explained later.

- Class Functions

  Similar to class procedures, *class functions* do not require a valid instance to be used. They are invoked through a reference to the class. Both kinds of class methods will be explained in more detail later.

- Constructors

  Constructors are special methods behaving like class functions, that is, being invoked through a reference to the class in which they are defined and returning a value. The returned value is a reference to a new instance of their class. This is how new object instances get created—you need to invoke a constructor to obtain a new instance of an object.

- Destructors

  Destructors are also special object methods, corresponding to and invoked essentially like procedures. Destructors have the responsibility of—you guessed it—destroying an instance of an object when you want to get rid of one. Destructors are instance methods; that is, like procedure and function methods, they require a valid instance to activate them.

We will now examine each kind of method in more detail.

Procedure and Function Methods

Procedure and function methods are declared just like ordinary procedures and functions, except that instead of being declared in the declaration section of a Pascal block, they are buried within a class declaration. The heading of a method looks very similar to a heading of a stand-alone subroutine.

Syntax

Procedure-Method Heading

The general syntax for declaring a procedure method is

```
type
  ClassName = class(ParentClassName)
    ...
    procedure Methodname(<Parameter List>);
    ...
  end;
```

Examples:

```
type
  TDataList = class(TPersistent)
    ...
    procedure EndUpdate;
```

```
    procedure LoadFromFile(const FileName: String);
    procedure SaveToFile(const FileName: String);
    ...
  end;
```

Syntax

Function-Method Heading

The general syntax for declaring a function method is

```
type
  ClassName = class(ParentClassName)
    ...
    function MethodName(<Parameter List>): ReturnType;
    ...
  end;
```

Examples:

```
type
  TClientWindow = class(TWindow)
    ...
    function Hide;
    function GetRect: TRect;
    function GetProperty(const AName: String): THandle;
    ...
  end;
```

There can be as many methods declared within a single class as needed. Procedure-method declarations can be interspersed among function methods and other types of methods. The declarations of class elements can be grouped in sections (you will learn about class declaration sections shortly). The only requirement is that within a single section of a class declaration all fields must appear before any methods.

Each procedure-method declaration inside a class definition starts with the reserved word **procedure**, followed by the method name. Each function-method declaration starts with the reserved word **function**, followed by the name.

An optional parameter list enclosed in parentheses may follow the method name. The syntax for the parameter list of a method is governed by the same syntax rules as those applicable to parameter lists of ordinary subroutines as described on Day 9.

In case of function-method declarations, a colon follows the closing parenthesis of the parameter list, or the function name if there are no parameters. The return type of the function appears after the colon.

In both cases, each method declaration must be terminated by a semicolon.

Following is an example of an almost-complete class declaration, with procedure and function methods, and fields. The purpose of the example is to show how to declare ordinary methods; hence the declaration is still missing a constructor and a destructor.

```
type
  TBook = class
    FAuthor: TAuthor;
    FTitle: String;
    function GetAuthor: TAuthor;
    procedure SetAuthor(const AnAuthor: TAuthor);
    function GetTitle: String;
    procedure SetTitle(ATitle: String);
  end;
```

The `TBook` class declaration introduces two data fields, `FAuthor` and `FTitle`, and a number of methods of both the procedure and function variety.

Constructors

Constructors are declared just like other methods, except that the reserved word **`constructor`** replaces the **`procedure`** or **`function`** keywords in the declaration.

NEW TERM A *constructor* is a special kind of a subroutine attached to a class. Its role is to create instances of a class. It behaves as a function returning a reference to the newly created object instance.

11

Syntax

Constructor Heading

The general syntax for declaring object constructors is as follows:

```
type
  ClassName = class(ParentClassName)
    ...
    constructor Name(<Parameter List>);
    ...
  end;
```

Examples:

```
type
  TClientWindow = class(TWindow)
    ...
    constructor Create(AnOwner: TWindow);
    constructor CreateOffDesktop;
    ...
  end;
```

A particular class may define many constructors. Typically, however, it would have just one constructor. The conventional name for the single constructor is `Create`.

A constructor declaration starts with the reserved word **`constructor`**, followed by the same pattern of elements—that is, a name, an optional parameter list, and a semicolon, as in the case of a procedure declaration.

Constructors are *used* more like functions than like procedures even though their declarations do not specify a return type and look generally like procedure declarations. A constructor is thus an implicit function: it returns a new instance of the class used to invoke it. There is no need to explicitly define the return type for a constructor because it is known at the time of the constructor invocation: it is the class type through which the constructor was called.

Destructors

Destructors are also declared similarly to procedures.

NEW TERM A *destructor* is a special kind of a subroutine attached to a class. Its role is to destroy instances of the class.

Syntax

Destructor Heading

The syntax for declaring object destructors is as follows:

```
type
  ClassName = class(ParentClassName)
    ...
    destructor Name(<Parameter List>);
    ...
  end;
```

Examples:

```
type
  TClientWindow = class(TWindow)
    ...
    destructor Destroy;
    destructor DestroyAndNotify(Receipient: TManager);
    ...
  end;
```

A single class may declare many destructors. Again, the most common situation is that it declares just a single, parameterless destructor called `Destroy`.

A destructor declaration starts with the reserved word **`destructor`**, followed by the same pattern of elements: a name, optional parameter list, and a semicolon, as in the case of a procedure declaration.

Declaring destructors with parameters is a very rare practice. Typically all a destructor needs to do is destroy the instance, for which all the information it needs is already accessible to it. The destructor syntax does, however, allow parameters for the infrequent occasions when they are needed.

As an example of declaring constructors and destructors, consider the following complete `TBook` class declaration, which is an extension of the one you saw earlier.

```
type
  TBook = class
    FAuthor: TAuthor;
    FTitle: String;
```

```
    constructor Create;
    destructor Destroy; override;
    function GetAuthor: TAuthor;
    procedure SetAuthor(const AnAuthor: TAuthor);
    function GetTitle: String;
    procedure SetTitle(ATitle: String);
  end;
```

Now the `TBook` object class defines a constructor `Create` and a destructor `Destroy`, which can be used to create and destroy `TBook` object instances, respectively. You will learn exactly how these methods are used later.

Observe the **`override`** keyword next to the declaration of the destructor `Destroy`. This keyword is needed whenever you declare a destructor called `Destroy`. The **`override`** essentially enables the default cleanup actions in case something goes wrong with the creation of the object instance. You learn more about this and other directives pertaining to method declarations in future lessons. For now, just observe the rule summarized in the following note.

Note: Destructor `Destroy` should always be declared without any parameters, and the declaration should always be followed with an **`override`** keyword.

```
destructor Destroy; override;
```

Class Procedures and Functions

In Object Pascal you can declare class methods. The most important difference between a regular method and a class method is that you don't need a valid instance of a class to be able to call a class method.

Class methods are declared in exactly the same way as ordinary methods, except that you put the reserved word **`class`** in front of the method declaration.

Syntax

Class-Procedure Declaration

The general syntax for declaring a class procedure is

```
type
  ClassName = class(ParentClassName)
    ...
    class procedure Methodname(<Parameter List>);
    ...
  end;
```

Examples:

```
type
  TDataList = class(TPersistent)
    ...
```

```
    class procedure FreeAll;
    class procedure SetDelimiter(ASymbol: Char);
    ...
  end;
```

Syntax

Class-Function Declaration

The general syntax for declaring a class function is

```
type
  ClassName = class(ParentClassName)
    ...
    class function MethodName(<Parameter List>): ReturnType;
    ...
  end;
```

Examples:

```
type
  TClientWindow = class(TWindow)
    ...
    class function NumInstances;
    class function DefaultCaption: String;
    class function DefaultWidth: Integer;
    ...
  end;
```

A class can arbitrarily declare many class methods, that is, both class functions and class procedures.

Each class-procedure declaration inside a class definition starts with the reserved word **`class`** followed by the reserved word **`procedure`**, followed by the method name. Each function-method declaration starts with the reserved word **`class`** followed by the reserved word **`function`**, followed by the name.

In both cases, the rest of the class method's declaration follows the same rules as for ordinary procedure or function methods, respectively.

Implementing Methods

After you have successfully declared a method in a class declaration, the next step is to *implement* it—that is, provide the description of the actions that the object is to perform when you call the method.

Fortunately, most of what you have learned about implementing stand-alone subroutines applies to methods, too.

Hidden Self

There is an important distinction between stand-alone subroutines and methods: access to instance data.

You may recall that data elements must be passed to subroutines, preferably in the form of parameters, for them to be able to act upon those data elements.

Stand-alone routines have access to any data declared globally in the unit or program in which they are implemented, and also to all global data from other units used via the **uses** clause.

Method implementations of ordinary methods (that is, methods other than class methods), on the other hand, not only have access to any data a subroutine in the same context would have access to, but they can implicitly access the fields of the class instance that made the call.

It is almost as if there were an extra parameter passed to every method representing the object instance through which the method was called, and as if there were an implicit **with** statement enclosing the entire body of a method. And there is!

Even though you don't see the extra parameter, called `Self`, in the method declaration, the parameter is there implicitly, accessible inside the method. The extra `Self` parameter is of the type of the class in which the method is defined.

There is an implicit **with** `Self` **do** statement enclosing the entire body of the method and giving the method access to the instance's (`Self`'s) fields, properties, and other methods.

The implicit **with** statement operates roughly as follows:

```
begin
  with Self do begin
    ...
    {Method's Code}
    ...
  end;
end;
```

The outer **begin-end** block represents the main block of a method. Inside it, the implicit **with** statement sets up a context for accessing the instance's fields.

Because the `Self` parameter is implicit inside a method, you don't even need to explicitly refer to it most of the time. The instance through which the method was called is implicitly available, the context for accessing it is prepared, and you can just refer to the instance's fields directly, without any prefixes.

Although you can prefix the names of object fields inside a method with `Self.`, this is not necessary. Inside a method, the `Self.` prefix is *assumed*, so you can simply refer to the fields of the object directly, as if they were local variables. You will see examples of this a little later.

There are rare circumstances, however, when you may need to refer to the `Self` parameter. In particular, you may need `Self` to resolve identifier conflicts inside a method.

Note: `Self` is a predefined identifier inside a method, so you can simply use it, even though it does not explicitly appear in the method declaration.

To resolve a name conflict using `Self`, for example, to refer to a local variable identifier with the exact same name as the object's field, prefix the object field name with `Self.` (that is, with `Self` followed by a period, such as `Self.FTitle`).

Class Methods are Simple Subroutines

The big difference between ordinary methods and class methods is that the latter do not have the implicit `Self` parameter.

Because class methods can be called *both* through a valid instance of a class *and* through a reference to the class itself (that is, without referring to a valid instance), it is not possible for a class method to access the fields of an instance. There is no implicit `Self` parameter inside the implementation of a class method, hence no way of referring to `Self`'s fields.

Since there is no hidden `Self`, class methods are in a sense no different than stand-alone subroutines. They are merely a convenient way of indicating that the method is somehow logically related to the class.

Implementing Procedure Methods

Ordinary procedure methods are implemented in a similar way to how standalone procedures are. You must provide the sequence of executable statements that make up the method's body.

Syntax

Procedure-Method Implementation

The general syntax for implementing procedure methods is

```
procedure ClassName.ProcName(<Parameters>);
  <Optional Declaration Block>
begin
  <Executable Statements>
end;
```

Example:

```
procedure TForm1.Button1OnClick(Sender: TObject);
  var
    Result: Boolean;
  begin
    Result := OpenDialog1.Execute;
    if Result then begin
      PerformAction;
    end;
  end;
```

Procedure-method implementation belongs in the implementation section of a unit, or inside a program or library, before the main **begin-end** block.

The implementation begins with the reserved word **procedure** and is followed by a fully qualified method name. *Fully qualified* means that the method name must be prefixed with the name of

the class the method belongs to and a period. The class-name prefix is an indication that what follows is not a standalone procedure implementation, but a method.

The remainder of the implementation follows the same rules as the implementation of a standalone procedure, which you learned on Day 9.

As mentioned, inside a method you have access not only to its local identifiers and any "visible" identifiers from outside, but also to the object-instance fields encapsulated within the class definition.

For example, the procedure method `SetTitle` of the `TBook` class, defined earlier, might look like the following:

```
procedure TBook.SetTitle(ATitle: String);
  begin
    FTitle := ATitle;
  end;
```

The procedure method `SetTitle` assigns a new value contained in `ATitle` passed as a parameter from outside, to the active instance's field `FTitle`. `ATitle` is a parameter to the method. `FTitle` is not explicitly defined as a local variable, but is equivalent to

```
Self.FTitle
```

that is, it is the field of the currently active instance of `TBook`.

Implementing Function Methods

Function methods are also implemented almost exactly like stand-alone functions. You must provide the sequence of executable statements that make up the method's body and, within those statements, explicitly assign a return value to the function.

Syntax

Function-Method Implementation

The general syntax for implementing function methods is

```
function ClassName.FuncName(<Parameters>): ReturnType;
  <Optional Declaration Block>
begin
  <Executable Statements>
  Result := ...
  <Executable Statements>
end;
```

Example:

```
function TForm1.CalculateScore(RawValue: Integer): Boolean;
  begin
    Result := CalcEngine.Score(RawValue);
  end;
```

Function-method implementation, like the implementation of a procedure method, belongs in the implementation section of a unit, or inside a program or library, before the main **begin-end** block.

The implementation begins with the reserved word **function** and is followed by a fully qualified method name. Again, "fully qualified" means that the method name must be prefixed with the name of the class the method belongs to and a period.

The remainder of the implementation follows the same rules as the implementation of a stand-alone function, which you learned on Day 9.

As before, throughout the method's implementation you have access to its local identifiers and any "visible" identifiers from outside, as well as to the object-instance fields encapsulated within the class definition.

For example, the function method `GetTitle`, belonging to the `TBook` class defined earlier, might be implemented as follows:

```
function TBook.GetTitle: String;
  begin
    Result := FTitle;
  end;
```

In this case, the function method `GetTitle` returns the value stored in the active instance's field `FTitle`.

Implementing Constructors

Constructors, as you already know, are special methods whose responsibility not only includes performing the executable statements placed inside their **begin-end** blocks, but first of all creating a brand-new instance. Fortunately, you don't have to worry about the details of creating the new instance in memory at run-time. By the time the program execution arrives at the first **begin** of the main **begin-end** block of a constructor, the instance has already been created automatically. The purpose of the code inside a constructor is to initialize the newly created instance.

Syntax

Constructor Implementation

The general syntax for implementing a constructor is

```
constructor ClassName.Name(<Parameters>);
  <Optional Declaration Block>
begin
  <Executable Statements>
  <Executable Statements>
end;
```

Example:

```
constructor TBook.Create(ATitle: String);
  begin
```

```
    inherited Create;
    FTitle := ATitle;
    FAuthor := Nil;
  end;
```

Constructor implementation, like all other method implementations, belongs in the implementation section of a unit, or inside a program or library, before the main **begin-end** block.

The implementation begins with the reserved word **constructor** and is followed by a fully qualified method name, complete with the class name and a period.

The remainder of the implementation follows the same rules as the implementation of a standalone *procedure* you learned on Day 9. Note, that even though a constructor is expected to return a value when you use it (that is, it is used as a function), it is being implemented more like a procedure. There is, for example, no explicit assignment of the return value within a constructor. This is possible because it is understood that the constructor *always* returns a reference to the newly created instance of the class in which the constructor was defined. There is no need to specifically assign any values.

Because inside a constructor, like inside almost any other method, you have access to all fields of the newly created instance, you are free and encouraged to initialize them to whatever values they need to be initialized to by default.

When the constructor exits, the instance it created is considered fully initialized and valid, unless the constructor terminates by calling a built-in `Fail` function, about which you will learn shortly.

DO	DON'T

DO make sure that there is an assignment statement, or that inside a constructor the value of every field a class declares changes from "undefined" to some known default value.

DON'T leave even a single field of an object uninitialized. The constructor should cover the initialization of all fields.

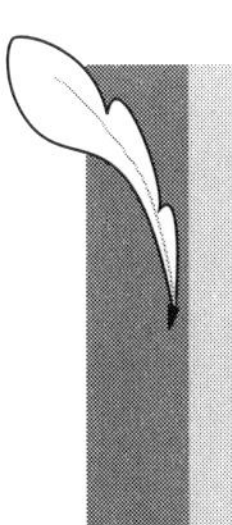

Note: The compiler does perform default initializations to fields of a class instance. This is the only exception to the rule in Pascal that all variables are uninitialized unless explicitly assigned a value. You can count on instance fields being automatically initialized to zero or the corresponding value for non-numeric types (**nil**, `False`). It is, however, a good idea to list all fields and explicitly assign default values to them inside the constructor. It makes the intent of your code clearer, showing that the initialization to zero was indeed deliberate rather than having happened by omission.

Inheriting Constructors

Consider a class-inheritance hierarchy consisting of three classes arranged as follows: the class `TBook` descends directly from the `TObject` base; `TTechnicalBook` is a particular specialization, or extension, of `TBook`. Figure 11.1 depicts the inheritance relationships among the three classes. Listing 11.1 shows one of the possible implementations of the book classes.

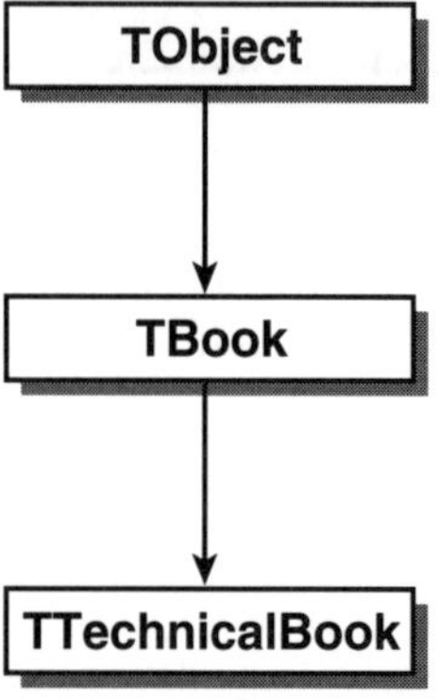

Figure 11.1.
Inheritance hierarchy of the book classes.

Listing 11.1. The implementation of the sample book classes.

```
unit Books1;

interface

uses
  Authors,
  Editors;

type
  TBook = class
    FAuthor: TAuthor;
    FTitle: String;
    constructor Create(AnAuthor: TAuthor; const ATitle: String);
    function GetAuthor: TAuthor;
    procedure SetAuthor(const AnAuthor: TAuthor);
    function GetTitle: String;
    procedure SetTitle(ATitle: String);
  end;

  TTechnicalBook = class(TBook)
    FTechEditor: TEditor;
    constructor Create(AnAuthor: TAuthor;
      const ATitle: String; AnEditor: TEditor);
    function GetTechEditor: TEditor;
    procedure SetTechEditor(AnEditor: TEditor);
  end;


```

```
implementation

{TBook}

  constructor TBook.Create;
    begin
      inherited Create;
      FAuthor := AnAuthor;
      FTitle := ATitle;
    end;


  function TBook.GetAuthor;
    begin
      Result := FAuthor;
    end;


  procedure TBook.SetAuthor;
    begin
      FAuthor := AnAuthor;
    end;


  function TBook.GetTitle;
    begin
      Result := FTitle;
    end;


  procedure TBook.SetTitle;
    begin
      FTitle := ATitle;
    end;


{TTechnicalBook}

  constructor TTechnicalBook.Create;
    begin
      inherited Create(AnAuthor,ATitle);
      FTechEditor := AnEditor;
    end;


  function TTechnicalBook.GetTechEditor;
    begin
      Result := FTechEditor;
    end;


  procedure TTechnicalBook.SetTechEditor;
    begin
      FTechEditor := AnEditor;
    end;

end.
```

Analysis

The Books1 unit in Listing 11.1 defines two specialized classes: TBook and TTechnicalBook.

The definition of the TBook class spans lines 10 through 18 of the unit. TBook inherits from the top-level TObject. An instance of TBook has two data fields: FAuthor and FTitle, naturally keeping track of the particular book's author and its title. The FTitle data attribute requires no special comments; it is a simple String variable.

The FAuthor, on the other hand, declared on line 11, is a reference to another object, representing the author of a given book. The type TAuthor denotes a type defined externally to this unit. It is assumed to be "imported" from the unit called Authors, which appears in the **uses** clause on line 6.

Even though the definition of TAuthor is not shown here, you can meaningfully perform certain operations on a TAuthor instance without knowing much about its implementation, as you will see shortly.

The TBook class defines a number of methods. The method that is of particular interest right now is the constructor Create, defined on line 13.

Create is implemented on lines 67 through 71. As a constructor, Create has the responsibility of initializing the newly created instance invisibly and implicitly passing to it as the Self. The two data attributes of TBook, FAuthor, and FTitle are being taken care of by the data passed in the two formal parameters defined for Create, AnAuthor, and ATitle. Lines 36 and 37 initialize the TBook fields.

Line 35 calls the inherited constructor to take care of any initialization the immediate parent of TBook, in this case TObject, may require.

Lines 14 through 17 define, and lines 41 through 62 implement, simple field-access methods to get and set the values of the TBook fields.

The second class defined within the unit in Listing 11.1, TTechnicalBook, extends the notion of a book by adding a reference to a technical editor to the inherited definition.

The extended class requires additional initialization that is not handled by the inherited constructor. This is the reason for declaring the local Create constructor on lines 22 and 23, and for implementing it on lines 67 through 71.

Again, TTechnicalBook.Create handles the initialization of the data field specific to the TTechnicalBook, that is, FTechEditor. It relies on the services of the constructor inherited from TBook, however, to handle the details of initializing the inherited fields.

Let's now take a closer look at the relationships among the three classes defined in Listing 11.1. TObject already has a default constructor called Create.

You may ask at this point: why does TBook need its own constructor, specific to TBook only, if one of the main reasons for setting up an inheritance hierarchy in the first place is to be able to reuse existing code? Why can't I re-use the already existing Create constructor of TObject for TBook as well?

The reason is simple: TBook introduces some TBook-specific data, which must therefore be initialized at TBook's level.

In other words, TObject's descendant, TBook, must define its own constructor to be able to initialize its own fields. The Create constructor inherited from TObject does not have any knowledge about TBook's fields—it only initializes whatever needs to be initialized at the TObject level.

A very similar situation exists between TBook and TTechnicalBook. Because TTechnicalBook introduces a new field, FTechEditor, the class needs a dedicated constructor to initialize this new field.

How should TTechnicalBook handle the initialization of the fields it inherited from its ancestor, TBook? Here is where object-oriented reuse and encapsulation show their capabilities. TTechnicalBook does not have to worry about the details of TBook's implementation. After all, TBook's Create constructor is already taking care of those details. Rather than attempting to *copy* the code already contained in TBook.Create, we opt to *reuse* it by calling the inherited constructor. The statement

```
inherited Create(AnAuthor,ATitle);
```

on line 69 of Listing 11.1 achieves just that. It delegates the responsibility of initializing the fields belonging to an ancestor object to the ancestor's constructor.

Note: You need to define a constructor for every class that introduces a new data field.

Syntax

Inheriting Constructors

A typical structure of a constructor is as follows:

```
constructor Class.MethodName(<Parameters>);
  <Local Declaration Block>
begin
  inherited MethodName(<Parameters>);
  <Initialization of Class-specific fields>
end;
```

Example:

```
constructor TBook.Create(AnAuthor: TAuthor; ATitle: String);
  begin
    inherited Create;
    FAuthor := AnAuthor;
    FTitle := ATitle;
  end;
```

To call an inherited constructor, use the **inherited** keyword, followed by the inherited constructor's name separated from the keyword by a blank space.

In general, you would call an appropriate **inherited** constructor as the first executable statement in the constructor's **begin-end** block.

Do I Need a Constructor?

Contrary to what you might think, constructors are not strictly necessary for every class you define. Remember that the role of a constructor is to initialize data fields specific to a given class.

What if the class does not introduce any new data fields, with respect to its ancestor? In that case, as you saw in the previous section, the ancestor would already have a constructor defined. There may be no need to define another one in the descendant if the descendant does not extend the original class.

As there are no new fields in the descendant class, even if you defined a `Create` constructor for it, its implementation would look as follows:

```
constructor TSomeClass.Create;
begin
  inherited Create;
end;
```

Because there is nothing to initialize other than what is already handled by the ancestor's constructor, the constructor in the descendant class is redundant in this case.

Failing Construction

There are cases when the construction of a new object cannot proceed, because—for any reason—the instance would be invalid if it did proceed. For example, if an object that is supposed to *contain* other objects at run-time cannot, for some reason, create one of its subordinates, exiting the constructor in the normal way would result in an invalid (incomplete) object being returned. After all, one of the owned objects that was supposed to be there, isn't.

In a case like this—that is, whenever an error is detected—there must be a way of aborting the construction process and returning control to the constructor's caller indicating the error condition.

The traditional way of aborting the construction process was by calling the predefined procedure `Fail`. If `Fail` has been called inside a constructor, the constructor immediately terminates and returns **nil** to the caller, thereby ensuring that no new instance will be created. The disadvantage of this approach is that the caller must explicitly check whether or not **nil** was returned.

A new way of failing construction is through the mechanism of *exceptions*. You will learn more about exceptions on Day 14. For today's lesson, just remember that the process of an object instance's construction *can* be aborted, if needed.

Note: The `Fail` procedure is available only inside object constructors. It is not available inside any other type of method, nor in stand-alone subroutines.

Borland recommends using the exception mechanism rather than the `Fail` procedure to terminate a constructor in mid-process.

The reference value returned by a `Fail`ed constructor is known as `Nil`.

NEW TERM The value of `Nil` indicates an invalid, or empty, reference. You can assign `Nil` to a class-typed reference variable explicitly as an initialization step, before a constructor is called, to ensure integrity of all references.

Assigning a value of `Nil` to a reference variable enables you to later test the variable again against `Nil` and to verify whether it refers to a valid object. When you see `Nil`, you know that the object has not yet been created. On the other hand, if you leave a reference variable uninitialized, you already know that you cannot rely on what is stored in it; its value is completely random and undefined.

Warning: Always assign a value to a reference variable as soon as practically possible after it has been declared. Either create an instance using the appropriate constructor, or explicitly assign `Nil`. Otherwise, you cannot rely on or use the value of the instance variable, nor can you test whether it actually refers to a valid instance.

Implementing Destructors

Destructors are another group of special methods. Their responsibility is essentially the opposite of that of constructors.

A destructor annihilates the object instance through which it was called, automatically releasing any dynamic memory storage previously allocated by the constructor. You call a destructor when you are done with a particular object.

Fortunately, you don't have to worry about the details of freeing the dynamic memory of the instance being destroyed: this is handled automatically by the destructor. You do, however, have the responsibility to call the destructors of any object that the object being destroyed owns.

In other words, if you have allocated a subordinate object inside a constructor, you are responsible to make sure that when the top-level object's destructor gets called, any objects that the top-level object owns also get destroyed. You will see examples of this in future lessons.

Syntax

Destructor Implementation

The general syntax for implementing a destructor is

```
destructor ClassName.Name(<Parameters>);
  <Optional Declaration Block>
begin
  <Executable Statements>
  <Executable Statements>
end;
```

Example:

```
destructor TBook.Destroy;
  begin
    FTitle := '';
    inherited Create;
  end;
```

Destructor implementation also belongs in the implementation section of a unit, or inside a program or library, before the main **begin-end** block.

The implementation begins with the reserved word **destructor** and is followed by a fully qualified method name, complete with the class name and a period.

The remainder of the implementation follows the same rules as the implementation of a stand-alone procedure you learned on Day 9.

One thing to remember about destructors, especially the "default" `Destroy` destructor, is that they can be called with only a partially initialized instance. The `Destroy` destructor can be called as a result of an exception occurring during the construction process. It must therefore be prepared to deal with only a partially initialized instance. If a constructor fails during the process of initializing an instance, the `Destroy` destructor will be dealing with some fields that have not yet been initialized beyond the default initialization to zero.

The contents of the **begin-end** block of the destructor must take care of any cleanup tasks. The cleanup must perform the destruction of any subordinate objects and the deallocation of any memory dynamically allocated during the lifetime of the object. It is not necessary, however, to explicitly reset the values of embedded (direct) fields to "zero".

Note: The difference between an *embedded* (direct) field and a *reference* (indirect) field is that an embedded field contains the actual value of the data attribute, whereas a reference field contains a reference to some other entity. The values of embedded fields are assigned directly. The values of reference fields must be assigned by accessing the referenced entity.

Inside a destructor you have access to all fields of the active instance as usual, so you can perform the cleanup job for each of the indirect fields as necessary.

After the destructor exits, the instance through which it was called no longer exists. Attempting to access this instance will result in a run-time error.

Undefined Instance Variables

There is a certain symmetry between the state of an instance variable before an object is constructed and the state of the variable after it has been destroyed.

Consider the example in Listing 11.2. Note that the program in the listing is incomplete and cannot be compiled. The ellipses (...) in the listing indicate arbitrary code that is not shown here.

Listing 11.2. Program fragment showing the lifetime of an object.

```
program Undef1;

{
This program illustrates the lifetime of an object
with emphasis on the two periods when an instance
variable is undefined/invalid: before construction, and after destruction.
}

type
  TCustomer = class
    ...
    constructor Create;
    destructor Destroy; override;
    ...
  end;

var
  ACustomer:

begin
  ...
  {ACustomer is undefined, i.e. invalid!}
  ...
  ACustomer := TCustomer.Create; {constructor}
  ...
  {The instance ACustomer is valid}
  ...
  ACustomer.Destroy; {destructor}
  ...
  {ACustomer is no longer valid!}
  ...
end.
```

The very simple (and incomplete) skeleton program in Listing 11.2 is meant to illustrate the lifetime of an object of type `TCustomer`.

The class definition of `TCustomer` on lines 9 through 15 shows a constructor and a destructor being defined.

Line 18 declares an instance variable of type `TCustomer`.

The executable code on lines 20 through 32 is effectively divided into three sections as follows:

At first, even though the `ACustomer` variable is visible and accessible on lines 21 through 23, it cannot be used because it has not been initialized. Its value is undefined at this point until it is explicitly assigned the result of a call to the `TCustomer.Create` constructor on line 24.

Lines 25 through 27 comprise the section of code in which the `ACustomer` variable represents a valid `TCustomer` instance. Here, `ACustomer` fields and methods can be accessed.

After the instance is destroyed on line 28, the `ACustomer` variable is no longer valid. You can no longer refer to its fields or methods on lines 29 through 31, just as it was not possible to do so on lines 21 through 23, before the instance was constructed. In both cases, the instance referred to by `ACustomer` does not exist.

Inheriting Destructors

Similar to what was the case with constructors, you would want to be able to reuse existing destructor code along the lines of the inheritance hierarchy.

Instead of each class taking care of all of the destruction details of the entire instance, the inheritance lattice conveniently partitions the task such that at any point you only need to be concerned about the elements that the current class *added* over and above those inherited. The current class then delegates the task of destructing any elements inherited from its ancestors to the inherited destructors.

Syntax

Inheriting Destructors

A typical structure of a destructor is as follows:

```
destructor Class.DestructorName(<Parameters>);
  <Local Declaration Block>
begin
  <Destruction of owned entities>
  inherited DestructorName(<Parameters>);
end;
```

Example:

```
destructor TBook.Destroy;
  begin
    FAuthor.Destroy;
    FTitle.Destroy;
    inherited Destroy;
  end;
```

To call an inherited destructor, use the **inherited** keyword, followed by the inherited destructor's name separated from the keyword by a blank space.

In general, you would typically call an appropriate **inherited** destructor as the *last* executable statement in the destructor's **begin-end** block.

Instead of using the **inherited** keyword, you are free to directly use the name of the ancestor class, followed by a period, followed by the ancestor destructor's name.

Note: It is very rare for a destructor to require any parameters. The job of a destructor is to clean up the instance immediately before that instance gets eliminated, performing any necessary shut-down operations for the object. Any other affirmative actions should have already been carried out inside other methods. A parameter passed to a destructor suggests that more than simply destroying the instance is being done and that some processing that uses the parameter occurs in addition to the destruction.

Do I Need a Destructor?

A simple rule of thumb is: If you created a constructor for a class, you will probably need a destructor too. In particular, if your constructor allocated something, or created other objects in the process, the destructor must typically free or destroy these. The notable exception to this rule is inside components, when you create other, owned, components and specify the current object as the owner. The subordinate component created in this way will automatically be destroyed when necessary.

The other exception to the rule of always providing a destructor when there is a constructor is when the class does not own any indirect data entities. There might be no need for a destructor if the instance of a class does not *own* nor *create* any subordinate instances or entities. In such a case, even though additional fields were added by the class declaration, the fields are not the responsibility of this class and can simply be abandoned.

Implementing Class Methods

The implementation of a class method is very simple. The same rules as for normal methods apply, except that the implementation header is preceded by the reserved word **class**.

The only thing that you should keep in mind is that you don't have access to any instance's fields inside a class method, even if the method was called through a valid instance of the class. Attempting to refer to an instance's field causes a compiler syntax error.

Other than that, simply treat the implementation as if you were writing a stand-alone subroutine.

Syntax

Class-Procedure Implementation

The general syntax for implementing a class procedure is

```
class procedure ClassName.ProcName(<Parameters>);
  <Optional Declaration Block>
begin
  <Executable Statements>
end;
```

Example:

```
class procedure TParser.SetDelimiter(const ASymbol: String);
  begin
    ParserDelimiter := ASymbol;
  end;
```

Class-procedure implementation belongs in the implementation section of a unit, or inside a program or library, before the main **begin-end** block, that is, in the same block of code where ordinary methods belong.

The implementation begins with the reserved word **class** followed by the reserved word **procedure**, followed by the fully qualified method name. Otherwise, the implementation looks the same as that of an ordinary method.

Syntax

Class-Function Implementation

The general syntax for implementing class functions is

```
class function ClassName.FuncName(<Parameters>): ReturnType;
  <Optional Declaration Block>
begin
  <Executable Statements>
  Result := ...
  <Executable Statements>
end;
```

Example:

```
class function TForm1.NumInstances: Integer;
  begin
    Result := GlobalInstanceCount;
    {GlobalInstanceCount is a unit-global variable}
  end;
```

Class-function implementation begins with the reserved word **class**, followed by the reserved word **function**, which in turn is followed by the fully qualified method name and the remainder of the heading declaration, as for ordinary methods.

Inside the implementation, you don't have access to any fields of instances belonging to the class in which the method is defined, but you can otherwise use any data to which a stand-alone subroutine would have access.

As always inside a function, there should be at least one statement assigning a return value to the function name, or to the pre-declared variable `Result`.

Invoking Methods

Because ordinary methods are attached to a particular class, they cannot be invoked by simply being called in the same way as subroutines. They can generally be activated only through an instance of the class in which they are defined.

Constructors and class methods, on the other hand, do not require a valid instance to operate. You have already seen examples of constructor calls. When you call a constructor, the call is made through a reference to a class, rather than through an instance. Similarly, with class methods you can call them by specifying the class. However, you can also call class methods via an instance, in the same way you call ordinary methods.

11

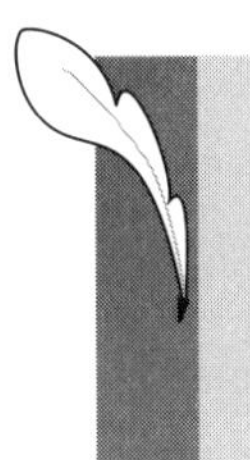

Note: The fundamental difference between a method and an ordinary subroutine is that a method is only accessible through the object of the class in which it was defined.

Furthermore, methods are considered to be embedded in the context of their class and therefore have access to the fields of the instance they are operating on at run-time.

You know now that ordinary methods are called as if there were an extra parameter at the end of the parameter list, one that links the method's code with a particular instance of the class at run-time. Any fields of the extra instance parameter `Self` are automatically accessible inside the method.

Invoking Constructors

The first method likely to be used with any kind of object is a constructor. To be able to use a constructor, you first need a valid class declaration and implementation. The class declaration must be accessible; that is, it must be visible from the point where you want to use it. The way you use a constructor, however, is somewhat different from the way you use most other methods.

If you haven't defined a constructor for a particular class, the specified constructor inherited from an ancestor class will be used. Ultimately, all objects have access to the `Create` constructor defined by `TObject`.

Syntax

Invoking a Constructor

The following is the syntax to invoke a constructor:

```
var
  AnInstance: ClassName;
begin
  ...
  AnInstance := ClassName.ConstructorName(<Parameters>);
  ...
end;
```

Example:

```
var
  FormInstance: TForm1;
begin
  FormInstance := TForm1.Create(Self);
end;
```

Note that unlike the case with most other methods, you invoke a constructor by referencing the class of the object. Because the instance does not yet exist, there is no way to refer to it. The *class* is thus being asked to construct an instance of itself.

Defining a class creates an active entity capable of creating instances of itself. Variables that you define to be of a **class** type are capable of storing references to the newly created class instances.

A **class** type in Object Pascal is therefore more than merely a static description of, or a recipe for, instances. A class is an active entity, existing in the program and capable of carrying out actions.

Invoking Instance Methods

After an instance of an object has been created, you can invoke any of the operations defined for this class of objects, that is, any of its methods.

Syntax

Method Activation

The syntax for calling, or activating, a method is

```
InstanceName.MethodName(<Parameters>);
```

The `InstanceName` denotes a valid instance reference variable, that is, an class instance variable previously initialized with a call to a constructor.

Examples:

```
Form1.Create;
Button1.Free;
```

The methods are accessed by specifying a valid instance and the corresponding method name, separated by a dot. The instance-name-plus-dot prefix creates what is called a *fully qualified* method name. You can, of course, use the **with** statement instead of fully qualified names to access methods of an object directly, just as it was possible to use the **with** statement to access fields.

Unlike in the case of records and record-access subroutines, however, you don't need to explicitly pass the active instance as a parameter to the method. The association is automatically made by Delphi. The compiler makes sure that inside the method you would be referring to the instance with which the method was called.

Invoking Destructors

Destructors are methods designed to clean up and destroy an instance of an object.

You invoke a destructor the same way you invoke most other methods of an object: through a valid object instance. The assumption here is that you must have first called the constructor of the class to obtain the instance in the first place, to then be able to destroy it by calling a destructor.

11

Syntax

Invoking a Destructor

The syntax to invoke a destructor is as follows:

```
InstanceName.DestructorName(<Parameters>);
```

Example:

```
Button1.Destroy;
```

Note that after calling a destructor, the instance variable is not valid. You cannot use it anymore to call any of the other methods. The only operation that can be performed on it would be to call its constructor to obtain another instance, if at all needed.

It is therefore advisable to explicitly assign the value of `Nil` to an instance variable that has already been destroyed. You can later detect an invalid instance and re-create it when needed.

Merely calling a destructor will not set the instance variable through which the call is being made to `Nil`. You must set the values of any variables that were referring to the destroyed instance explicitly.

Note: What if the instance variable through which you are attempting to call a destructor already is `Nil`? This virtually guarantees a General Protection Fault (GPF), or in other words, a program crash.

> In general, you should call the predefined `Free` method to get rid of an object's instance if you are using the default `Destroy` destructor. `Free` makes an additional check of whether the instance variable you are referring to is `nil`, preventing the GPF if it is.

Field-Access Methods

Even though a **`with`** statement can be used to access object fields directly, you might be surprised to hear that this practice is not recommended!

One of the big advantages of OOP is encapsulation and its support for information-hiding. If you are accessing, or just exposing, object fields directly, the result is that the implementation details of an object become known and can interact with the outside world, essentially voiding the benefits of encapsulation.

The users of the object in question would be affected should you decide to modify or optimize the implementation of the object. It pays to not provide direct access to the internal representation of an object and to shield its users from unnecessary details.

A much better approach would be to write methods to mediate the access to the object's fields, thereby providing true encapsulation and preventing direct modification of object data. Instead of accessing an object's fields, you call an appropriate method. The advantages to doing that are numerous. The following is a list of the major ones:

- Data Validation

  You can prevent a change in a data element by providing appropriate validation checks, thereby guaranteeing that the object is always in a consistent state.

- Referential Integrity

  You can ensure that, before a reference to an associated object is made, the reference field contains a correct value. Furthermore, if the value is incorrect (for example, the object being referred to no longer exists), you can initiate a corrective action, such as re-creating the associated object on demand.

- Desired Side Effects

  You can ensure that a specific action takes place whenever a particular field is referenced by the rest of the program. You can, for example, seamlessly track changes to a data value or to the number of times the data value was used by the program for accounting or billing purposes if the object is being provided on a pay-per-service basis.

- Information Hiding

  By accessing a piece of data owned by the object through methods only, you can hide the actual details of the implementation. If the implementation changes later, only the implementation of the access methods needs to be changed. The portions of the program that used the services of a particular class will not be affected.

Invoking Class Methods

Class methods can be invoked in two ways:

- Through instances, just like ordinary methods,
- Through the class type directly, without referring to any particular instance

Syntax

Class-Procedure Invocation

The syntax to invoke a class procedure is as follows:

```
begin
  ...
  InstanceName.ClassMethodName(<Parameters>);
  ...
end
```

or

```
begin
  ...
  ClassName.ClassMethodName(<Parameters>);
  ...
end
```

Example:

```
type
  TDatabase = class
    class procedure SetDateDelimiter(AChar: Char);
  end;

...

  class procedure TDatabase.SetDateDelimiter;
    begin
      ...
    end;

...

var
  TheDatabase: TDatabase;
begin
```

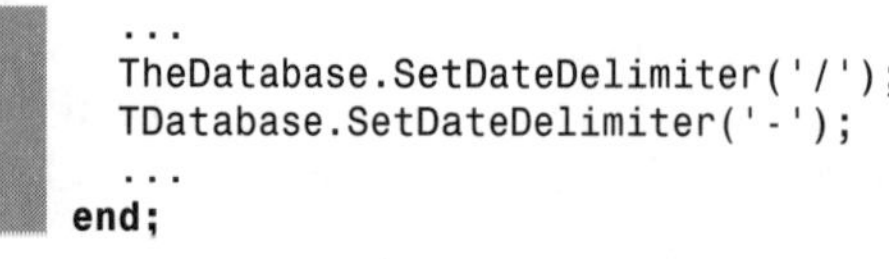

```
  ...
  TheDatabase.SetDateDelimiter('/');
  TDatabase.SetDateDelimiter('-');
  ...
end;
```

Syntax

Class-Function Invocation

The syntax of an assignment statement invoking a class function is as follows:

```
begin
  ...
  ReturnValue := InstanceName.ClassFunctionName(<Parameters>);
  ...
end
```

or

```
begin
  ...
  ReturnValue := ClassName.ClassMethodName(<Parameters>);
  ...
end
```

Just like the standalone functions, class functions can also be used inside expressions.

Example:

```
type
  TDatabase = class
    class function InsanceCount: Integer;
  end;

...

  class function TDatabase.InstanceCount;
    begin
      ...
      Result := ...
      ...
    end;

...

var
  TheDatabase: TDatabase;
  NumInstances: Integer;
begin
  ...
  NumInstances := TheDatabase.InstanceCount;
  NumInstances := TDatabase.InstanceCount;
  ...
end;
```

As already explained, the only difference between calling class methods and invoking the ordinary methods is that class methods can also be called through a class type, not just through an instance.

Visibility of Object Elements

Before we can proceed with the discussion of how to use methods that have successfully been declared and implemented, let's discuss a few more cosmetic issues of class declaration.

So far, we have assumed that all fields and methods of a particular object are equally visible and accessible, provided a valid instance reference is available and used to access them. Whereas it is certainly true with respect to variables of type **record**, the assumption about visibility does not necessarily apply to objects.

The abstraction power of a programming construct can be greatly enhanced by hiding the internal details of its representation. The information-hiding techniques are fundamental to object-oriented programming. They allow you to take a step back and treat a programming construct, such as an object, as a "black box" with well-defined input and output, but inaccessible internals. By removing the drudgery of the internal details from consideration, this technique enables you to concentrate on building the architecture of your system at an appropriate abstraction level.

Object Pascal defines several standard keywords, known as *directives*, that modify the visibility of elements declared within a class interface.

A class declaration may be divided into an arbitrary number of sections, each of which starts with one of the keywords known as *standard directives*: **private**, **protected**, **public**, and **published**.

Syntax

Class-Interface Visibility Directives

The following is the syntax for dividing a class declaration into visibility sections:

```
type
  ClassName = class(Parent)
      <field or method declaration>
      ...
      <field or method declaration>
    <directive>
      <field or method declaration>
      ...
      <field or method declaration>
    ...
    <directive>
      <field or method declaration>
      ...
      <field or method declaration>
  end;
```

Example:

```
type
  TColorRectangle = class(TObject)
```

```
private
  Left,
  Top,
  Right,
  Bottom: Integer;
  Color : TColor;
protected
  function GetLeft: Integer;
  function GetTop: Integer;
  function GetRight: Integer;
  function GetBottom: Integer;
  function GetColor: TColor;
public
  constructor Create;
  destructor Destroy;
end;
```

There are four standard directive keywords related to visibility of class-interface elements:

- **private**

  Used to denote the highest level of restriction on visibility of a class-declaration element. The class-interface elements declared as **private** are only visible within the module (that is, the unit) in which the particular class is defined. Outside of this module, **private** class-interface elements are not visible nor accessible. If several classes are defined within a module, they can "see" each other's **private** interface sections as if they were **public**.

- **protected**

  Denotes a partially restricted visibility of a class-declaration element. A **protected** element is only visible within descendants of the class that declares them as **protected**. It is not possible to get at a **protected** element from the code outside of the code belonging to the "protecting" class; that is, outside of the methods of the class defining the protected element, the protected element is not visible. A descendant can be declared and implemented separately, however, and the **protected** elements are still visible inside its methods.

- **public**

  Denotes full visibility. Class elements declared as **public** are visible at any point when a class instance itself is visible. In other words, once you have a valid object instance that is visible as a whole, its **public** elements are also visible to you (that is, you can always refer to its **public** interface elements, whether from the methods of that class or from the outside).

- **published**

  You will have to wait for a true explanation of the meaning of the **published** directive until we get around to discussing object properties. For now, consider **published** class-interface elements as effectively the same as **public**. You will see later that they are in fact more than just **public**, because they provide an extended level of accessibility.

Note: By default, if no directive is given, a class-declaration element is considered to be **`published`** (that is, it is accessible and visible to all, even beyond the **`public`** accessibility).

The first section of any class declaration, before any visibility directive is given, is **`published`** by default.

Using Methods

A method, as you understand by now, is a piece of code, essentially a procedure or a function, attached to a particular class type.

The fact that a method is part of a class declaration suggests that methods should be accessible using the same dot- or **`with`** notation that is used to access object fields.

Indeed, similar to accessing object fields, most object methods must be accessed by your referring to an instance, the class of which defines a particular method. This is a way of asking an object to *do* something. An object, regarded as an active entity, can be "told" what to do by your invoking one of its methods.

To call a method of an object, you must have access to an instance of that object. You can then invoke methods of that particular instance by prefixing the method name with the instance-variable name and a period (for example, `Form1.Close` or `ListBox1.Clear`).

Descendants' Methods

You can—and often will—call other methods of a particular class, whether inherited or defined at the same level, from within a method.

A particular class does not "know" anything about any of its potential descendants. There can be many descendants of a particular class, in fact almost infinitely many, and each of them might define its own specific methods and fields. The base class of all of these descendants might have been developed and compiled long before the descendants were defined.

Searching for Methods

Let us now take a quick look at how the compiler determines which particular method implementation to call when you specify a method call in your code.

When you attempt to use a method of a particular object, the compiler looks in the object's class definition to find the implementation of the method defined for that class. If the class defines a method with the name you specified, all is well—that particular method will be called at run-time.

If the given class does not define a method of the name you specify, the compiler will look up within the immediate ancestor type for an implementation of that method. If the method is found, the compiler will make it the target of your call. If it is not found, the process of searching for the given method continues to the next ancestor type.

If the compiler ends up going all the way up to the top-level class without finding a method definition of the name you specified, you will get a compile-time error: "Unknown identifier."

This message is rather cryptic, but in this context it means that the compiler could not find a method declaration with the name you specified, after it has searched the entire inheritance chain, all the way up to the top-level class (`TObject`).

Summary

Today's lesson explored the topic of object methods. You have learned, among other things, the following:

- Methods are subroutines attached to objects. They provide the behavior for instances of a class and define the protocol through which that behavior can be activated.
- Methods are called through object instances in which they are defined. The connection between a particular method and the instance that called it is made at run-time through a hidden parameter called `Self`.
- Constructors and class methods are called through the object type, that is, by referring to the class rather than an instance.
- Class methods, unlike constructors, do not have access to an instance's fields.
- Ordinary methods, constructors, and destructors have direct access to the fields of the instance with which they were called. In the case of constructors, it is the newly created instance to which their `Self` parameter refers.
- Methods are implemented like ordinary subroutines except that ordinary methods can take advantage of the direct access to the active instance's fields.
- Class declarations can be partitioned into sections, each with a different "visibility." There are **`private`**, **`protected`**, **`public`**, and **`published`** sections in which class elements, such as methods and fields, can be defined.

Q&A

Q What happens if I define in a descendant a method with the same name as one already existing in one of the ancestor classes?

A You are said to have overridden the method in question of the ancestor class. Whenever the descendant class refers to a method with a name as the one in question, the

new, overriding method will be used instead of the one provided by the ancestor. You will learn more about overriding methods in tomorrow's lesson.

Q Can I define a constructor for a built-in data type, so that variables of that type are automatically pre-initialized when they are created?

A No. Built-in data types are not objects and cannot have constructors defined for them. You have to manually initialize the value of every variable of a predefined type using an assignment statement.

Q Can I create multiple constructors with the same name but different parameter lists?

A No, not inside a single class. What you are asking for is called function-name overloading and is not supported by Delphi/Object Pascal.

Q What are class methods good for anyway? Why can't I simply use stand-alone subroutines to accomplish whatever the class method accomplishes?

A In general, you *can* use stand-alone subroutines for whatever purpose the corresponding class method is used. In addition, the idea of class methods is related to the issue of object-oriented design. In design, you would like to preserve the subtle relationships among different classes and their attached methods. Sometimes the stand-alone subroutine is not so much stand-alone, because it in fact is closely related to the class as a whole.

A typical example of that would be a function returning the number of currently available instances of a given class. It is entirely possible to create it as a stand-alone function at the `unit` level in which the class itself is defined, but because that function is so intimately tied to the class itself, it is more elegant to make it part of the class definition. Turning it into a class function makes the close, logical proximity of the function to the class obvious even to the casual reader of your code, and highlights that the function is related to the class by design.

Q Can I define class fields, analogously to defining class methods? That is, can I define a field which would be only applicable to the class as a whole, not to each instance of the class?

A Unfortunately, no. All fields defined within a class declaration are instance fields, that is, they are repeated in every instance of a class. Once you learn more about defining properties, you will see how you can create an implicit class property.

Workshop

The Workshop provides quiz questions to help you solidify your understanding of the material covered and exercises to provide you with experience in using what you've learned. Try to understand the quiz and exercise answers before continuing on to the next day's lesson. Answers are provided in the appendix at the end of this book.

Quiz

1. True or False? Constructors can be used as functions returning results inside expressions.
2. True or False? Class methods work exactly like stand-alone subroutines.
3. Which of the following statements is false?
   a. Function methods must be invoked through a valid instance of a class.
   b. Class functions can be invoked via a valid instance of a class.
   c. Constructors are essentially class functions.
   d. Constructors must be invoked through a valid instance of a class.
   e. Class procedures, class functions, and instance constructors are all invoked through reference to a class in which they are defined.
4. An object class inherits and can make direct use of all elements of its ancestors **except**:
   a. Public fields
   b. Private fields
   c. Protected and private fields
   d. Protected fields and methods
   e. Private fields and methods

Exercises

1. Complete the `TDate` class you defined as part of the exercises on Day 10 and provide the implementations of all the methods, including any constructors and destructors, that you declared as part of the class interface.
2. Provide a complete implementation in a separate unit called `Customer` of the `TCustomer` class you encountered on Day 10. Make sure that the unit compiles with Delphi.
3. Complete the definition by giving an implementation of the `TInvoice` class you encountered as part of the exercises on Day 10.

12

WEEK 2

Inheritance and Polymorphism

by Namir Shammas

The popularity of object-oriented programming (OOP) stems from the use of classes, inheritance, and polymorphism. The previous chapters have introduced you to classes that encapsulate fields and the methods that manipulate these fields. Inheritance empowers software developers to extend classes by declaring descendant classes that receive the fields and methods of parent classes. Polymorphism empowers classes to support the appropriate response of their instances. In this chapter you will learn about the following topics:

- Inheritance
- Constructors and destructors
- Virtual methods
- Dynamic methods
- Overriding methods
- Polymorphism
- Class hierarchies

Inheritance

The concept of inheritance is important to object-oriented programming. Inheritance enables you to spin off a new *descendant* class from an existing one. You can repeat the creation of descendant classes to generate a hierarchy of classes. The first ancestor class is called the *base class.* The classes from which a descendant class is derived are called *ancestor classes.* The immediate ancestor class is called the *parent class.* The significance of inheritance comes from the fact that the descendant class needs not reinvent the wheel by redeclaring all of the data field and methods. Instead, only the new data fields need declaration. As for the methods, the descendant class declares the new methods and also those that override the inherited ones. Overriding inherited methods is often needed to provide an adjusted operation suitable to the descendant class.

Note: Inheritance is often viewed as a *specialization* of type. Because inheritance is equivalent to an "is-a" or "kind-of" relationship, a descendant of a class is said to be a specialization of that class since the descendant may appear anywhere the ancestor can, but not necessarily the other way around.

Reuse Through Inheritance

Inheritance empowers a descendant to refine its parent class by adding more specialization. The descendant class inherits all of the fields and methods of its ancestor classes. The declaration of

descendant class shows the new methods, the overriding methods, and the new fields. It is worth pointing out that while a descendant class can override an inherited method, it cannot uninherit any field. Let's look at an example:

```
TStrArray = class
  public
    constructor Create(theMaxSize : Integer);
    destructor Destroy; override;
    function store(aVal: String;
                   index : Integer) : Boolean;
    function recall(var aVal: String;
                   index : Integer) : Boolean;
  protected
    data : ^string;
    maxSize : Integer;
    workSize : Integer;
  private
    function checkIndex(index : Integer) : Boolean;
end;

TSortedStrArray = class (TStrArray)
  public
    constructor Create(theMaxSize : Integer);
    destructor Destroy; override;
    procedure sort;
    function search(key : String) : Integer;

  protected
    function linearSearch(key : String) : Integer;
    function binarySearch(key : String) : Integer;

    isSorted: Boolean;

  private
    procedure fastSwap(index1, index2 : Integer);
end;
```

12

The above code declares the class `TStrArray`. This class declares the following identifiers:

- The public constructor `Create`.
- The public destructor `Destroy`.
- The public function `store`.
- The public function `recall`.
- The protected field `data`.
- The protected field `maxSize`.
- The protected field `workSize`.
- The private function `checkIndex`.

The above code also declares the class `TSortedStrArray` as a descendant of class `TStrArray`. The descendant class inherits all of the fields and methods of class `TStrArray`, but can access only the public and protected fields and methods of the parent class. The descendant class declares the following identifiers:

- The public constructor `Create`.
- The public destructor `Destroy`.
- The public procedure `sort`.
- The public function `search`.
- The protected function `linearSearch`.
- The protected function `binarySearch`.
- The protected field `isSorted`.
- The private procedure `fastSwap`.

The field `isSorted` supports the new sorting feature of the descendant class. The methods `sort`, `search`, `linearSearch`, and `binarySearch` support sorting the array and searching in its elements. These methods assist the descendant class in its specialized operations: namely, sorting and searching array elements.

DO | **DON'T**

DO delegate different levels of operations to classes in a hierarchy, where each descendant class refines the operations of its parent class. This approach empowers you, and other hierarchy users, to further extend the classes in an efficient and easy manner.

DON'T forget that the divide-and-conquer concept works well in the design of class hierarchies.

Declaring Base and Descendant Classes

You declare a base class as independent of any other class. Note that Delphi Pascal allows you to use either the `class` or `object` keywords. The keyword `class` is new to Delphi's Pascal, allowing it to better work with the visual component. The keyword `object` appears in Turbo Pascal 5.5, which was the first version of Borland's Pascal with object-oriented programming language extensions. The keyword `object` first appeared in Apple Computer's Object Pascal (the first Pascal implementation with object-oriented extensions), a few years before Turbo Pascal 5.5 was developed. Since Borland wanted to build on the Object Pascal syntax, the company used the keyword `object` (and not `class`) to signify a class. Moreover, the Borland manuals used the term "object" to mean "class" because of the keyword `object`. This is somewhat unfortunate, because the rest of the commercial Pascal implementations and other OOP languages call a class

a class. The keyword `class` comes with Delphi, which needed to create a slightly different kind of class to support visual components.

You should use `class` to declare your own object types in Delphi programs. The `object` keyword is considered obsolete and will be phased out in subsequent releases of Delphi.

The general syntax of a base class:

Syntax

```
Type
  TClassName = class
        public
               <public fields>
               <public methods>
        protected
               <protected fields>
               <protected methods>
        private
               <private fields>
               <private methods>
        published
               <published fields>
               <published methods>
  end;
```

The class type has four possible sections that control the accessibility of its fields and methods. The public section declares fields and methods to have no access restrictions—the class instances and descendant classes can have access to these fields and methods. The protected section declares fields and methods to have some access restrictions—the descendant classes can have access to these fields and methods. The private section declares fields and methods to have severe access restrictions—they cannot be accessed by class instances or descendant classes. The published section is like the public section, but offers special information to the Object Inspector.

Example:

```
Type
        TTimeClass = class
               public
                      constructor Initialize;
                      procedure SetHour(dHour : Integer);
                      procedure SetMinute(dMinute : Integer);
                      procedure SetSecond(dSecond : Integer);
                      function GetHour : Integer;
                      function GetMinute : Integer;
                      function GetSecond : Integer;
```

```
                        function GetSeconds : Integer;
                protected
                        Hour : Integer;
                        Minute : Integer;
                        Second : Integer;
        end;
```

The `TTimeClass` declares three protected fields: `Hour`, `Minute`, and `Second`. The class declares methods to initialize, set, and query the protected fields, as well as return the number of seconds since midnight.

You declare a descendant class by specifying the parent class, which is enclosed in parentheses after the keyword `class`.

Syntax

The General Syntax of a Descendant Class

```
Type
  TClassName = class(ParentClassName)
        public
               <public fields>
               <public methods>
        protected
               <protected fields>
               <protected methods>
        private
               <private fields>
               <private methods>
        published
               <published fields>
               <published methods>
  end;
```

This syntax resembles the one for a non-descendant class (also called the *base class*). Notice that the keyword `class` is followed by the name of the parent class enclosed in parentheses.

Example:

```
Type
        TTimeClass = class
               public
```

```
                Hour : Integer;
                Minute : Integer;
                Second : Integer;
                constructor Initialize;
                function GetSeconds : Integer;
end;

TDateTime = class(TTimeClass)
      public
                Year : Integer;
                Month : Integer;
                Day : Integer;
                constructor Initialize;
                function GetDayNumber : Integer;
end;
```

The class `TDateTime` is a descendant of class `TTimeClass` and inherits the fields `Hour`, `Minute`, and `Seconds`. The descendant class also inherits the method `GetSeconds`. The class `TDateTime` overrides the inherited method `Initialize` and declares the method `GetDayNumber`.

Constructors and Destructors

Many classes need to initialize and destroy their instances. The initialization of class instances ensures that these instances start up with the correct field value to work properly. Likewise, the destruction of class instances ensures that valuable resources are recuperated and made available to future class instances. This section discusses the use of constructors and destructors to initialize and destroy class instances, respectively.

Constructors

Constructors are special procedures that initialize the class instance data. This initialization includes assigning values to all or some of the fields, allocating dynamic memory, opening files, and so on. Invoking the constructor also sets up a Virtual Method Table (VMT) for the class. Delphi Pascal allows you to declare several constructors. The typical name of the constructor is `Create`.

When you call a class constructor, memory for the instance data block is allocated from the heap, that memory block is filled with zeros, and then the code of the constructor is executed. The instance data of Delphi classes is guaranteed to be initialized to zero before the constructor is executed. (This was not guaranteed in previous Borland Pascal products.)

Syntax

The General Syntax for the Constructor

```
Type
  TClassName = class(TParentClassName
        public
               <public fields>
               constructor Create(<parameters>);
               <public methods>
        protected
               <protected fields>
               <protected methods>
        private
               <private fields>
               <private methods>
        published
               <published fields>
               <published methods>
  end;
```

The above syntax declares the class constructor with the keyword `constructor` followed by the constructor name and an optional parameter list.

```
Type
        TTimeClass = class
               public:
                       Hour : Integer;
                       Minute : Integer;
                       Second : Integer;
                       constructor Init(vHour, vMinute, vSecond : Integer);
                       constructor defInit;
                       function GetSeconds : Integer;
        end;
```

The class `TTimeClass` declares two constructors, `Init` and `defInit`. The constructor `Init` initializes the fields `Hour`, `Minute`, and `Second` with the arguments of parameters `vHour`, `vMinute`, and `vSecond`, respectively. The constructor `defInit` performs a default value initialization to fields `Hour`, `Minute`, and `Second`.

DO	DON'T
DO declare at least one constructor if the class has a virtual method.	
DON'T forget to invoke the constructor with the class instance before invoking any other method.	

Destructors

Destructors are special procedures that destroy the class instances. This destruction includes deallocating dynamic memory, closing files, and so on. After the destructor's code is executed, the instance data block is released and returned to the heap.

If your class needs to add behaviors to its destructor (usually to clean up something its constructor allocated), be sure to declare the destructor to *override* the default `Destroy` destructor your class inherits from `TObject`. You can declare a new destructor for your own purposes, but when you're creating a Delphi component class it's important to make sure the component's standard `Destroy` destructor releases the resources the component uses. Any custom destructors you declare will not be used by VCL when it destroys your components for you.

Syntax

The General Syntax for the Destructor

```
Type
  TClassName = class(TParentClassName)
        public
               <public fields>
               constructor Create(<parameters>);
               destructor Destroy; overide;
              <public methods>
        protected
               <protected fields>
               <protected methods>
        private
               <private fields>
               <private methods>
        published
               <published fields>
               <published methods>
  end;
```

This syntax declares the class destructor with the keyword `destructor` followed by the destructor name.

```
Type
        TStrArray = class
               public
                       constructor Create(theSize : word);
                       destructor Destroy; override;
                       function store(aStr : string;
                                            index : Integer) : Boolean;
                       function recall(var aStr : string;
                                            index : Integer) : Boolean;
               protected
                       data : ^string;
                       MaxSize : word;
                       workSize : word;
        end;
```

The class `TStrArray` declares the constructor `Create` and the destructor `Destroy`. The constructor `Create` initializes the class instances by allocating dynamic space for the array of strings. The destructor `Done` deallocates the dynamic space.

When do you declare a destructor in a class? The answer is, when you need to recuperate resources that were allocated by the class, such as dynamic memory or file buffers.

12

DO	DON'T

DO call the destructors of class instances when these instances are no longer needed.

DO *override* the default `Destroy` destructor to release any resources allocated by your class. In the situations where VCL will free components for you, VCL only calls `Destroy`.

DO call the inherited method from the body of your constructors and destructors. If you don't, the instance data will not be initialized correctly, or resources will not be freed correctly.

DON'T create custom destructors except as a convenience for code you write, because only code you write will use them.

DON'T call destructors directly. Call the `Free` method inherited from `TObject`. `Free` checks to make sure the instance pointer is not nil before calling `Destroy`. `Free` is a little sanity check that you should get into the habit of using.

Creating Instances

Creating a class instance involves the following steps:

1. Declare a variable of the class type.
2. Invoke a constructor with the class-type identifier and assign the new instance into the class instance variable.

Syntax

The Creation of a Class Instance

```
var
  classVar : TClassName;

begin
  ...
  classVar := TClassName.ConstructorName(<parameters>);
  ...
end;
```

The above syntax declares a class-type variable, constructs an instance, and then assigns that instance into the variable.

```
var
  stateNames : TStrArray;

begin
  ...
  stateNames := TStrArray.Create(50);
  ...
end;
```

The above example declares the `TStrArray`-type instance variable `stateNames`. The code also initializes the instance using the constructor `Create`.

Destroying Instances

Destroying a class instance involves the simple invocation of the destructor with that instance.

Syntax

The Destruction of a Class Instance

```
var
  classVar : TClassName;

begin
  ...
  classVar := TClassname.ConstructorName(<parameters>);
  ...
  classVar.destructorName;
  ...
end;
```

The above syntax declares a class-type variable, constructs an instance, and then calls the destructor to destroy the instance.

```
var
        stateNames : TStrArray;

begin
     ...
        stateNames := Create(51);
        ...
        stateNames.Destroy;
end;
```

The above example declares the `TStrArray`-type instance `stateNames`. The code also initializes the instance using the constructor `Create`. The code then destroys the class instance by using the destructor `Destroy`.

12

Virtual Methods

Delphi's Object Pascal supports four kinds of methods: static, virtual, dynamic, and message methods. Each kind of method uses a different technique to resolve method calls—that is, to figure out what machine code should be called based on the source code you typed in.

The methods of a class are static by default. The compiler resolves calls to static methods at compile-time. This approach is basically the traditional way of resolving subroutine calls in Pascal. When the program starts executing, the call addresses are already figured out, so there is no run-time decision process to slow things down. Executing the program is a matter of systematically following the sequence of routine calls.

Virtual methods offer a more sophisticated way for resolving method calls. A virtual method call allows you to implement different behaviors for the same-named method in different classes—the very definition of *polymorphism* (literally, "many shapes"). The choice of which implementation to execute is made at run-time based on the class instance data used to make the call, instead of at compile-time. The next subsections discuss the syntax and usage of virtual methods.

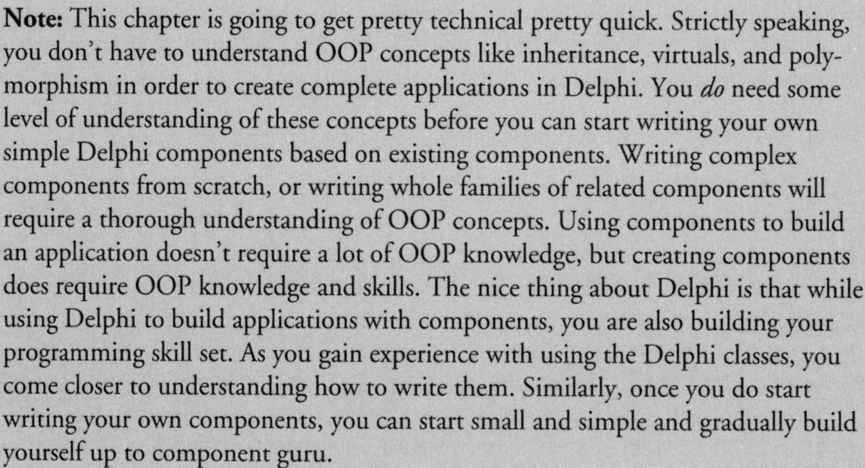

Note: This chapter is going to get pretty technical pretty quick. Strictly speaking, you don't have to understand OOP concepts like inheritance, virtuals, and polymorphism in order to create complete applications in Delphi. You *do* need some level of understanding of these concepts before you can start writing your own simple Delphi components based on existing components. Writing complex components from scratch, or writing whole families of related components will require a thorough understanding of OOP concepts. Using components to build an application doesn't require a lot of OOP knowledge, but creating components does require OOP knowledge and skills. The nice thing about Delphi is that while using Delphi to build applications with components, you are also building your programming skill set. As you gain experience with using the Delphi classes, you come closer to understanding how to write them. Similarly, once you do start writing your own components, you can start small and simple and gradually build yourself up to component guru.

If this is your first stab at learning about the mechanics of OOP, don't be discouraged if it doesn't "click" the first time through. Sometimes it takes a second or third reading before the high-level concepts and low-level mechanics mesh with your Delphi programming experience. (You'd better be sitting down when the "click" does hit you, because revelations that change your view of the world (like OOP) are often classified as "mind-altering experiences!")

If you want or need to get into writing Delphi components immediately, understanding the concepts in this chapter is critical.

Declaring Virtual Methods

Declaring the methods to be virtual causes the run-time system to carry out an additional step in resolving method calls in a smarter way. The basic idea behind this call-resolution scheme is as follows. The compiler needs to keep track of the virtual methods of the various object types. A special table, called the Virtual Method Table (VMT), is established for this purpose. Delphi's Object Pascal has the following rules concerning virtual methods:

1. The `virtual` keyword declares methods as virtual. This keyword appears in a separate statement after the routine heading inside the object type declaration. The `virtual` keyword **must not** appear in the definition of the method body.
2. `Virtual` always introduces a new virtual method that is completely unrelated to any other methods by that name the class may inherit. `Override` allows a descendent to replace or extend an existing virtual method inherited from an ancestor class. (BP7 programmers, wake up! This is one of the biggest language differences you'll notice between Delphi and Borland Pascal 7. In the old-style "object" type, `virtual` plays many roles. In the Delphi "class" type, `virtual` has exactly one role: to introduce a new virtual method.

   Each descendent class has its own name scope that preempts the name scope of all methods it inherits. Consequently, it is possible to "obscure" an inherited method by declaring a same-named static or virtual method in a descendent class. There is no relationship between the two same-named methods unless the descendent method is declared to override a virtual method inherited from the ancestor.

   You should never intentionally create new virtual methods in a descendent class with the same names as virtual methods in an ancestor class. The reason this name scoping exists is to make classes less sensitive to changes in their ancestors. For example, say you write a class `TMyClass` that descends from `TBaseClass`, and you declare a new virtual method `Draw` in your descendent. If you later get a new version 2 of `TBaseClass` that adds a new `Draw` method of its own, you could have a problem. In previous versions of Borland Pascal, you would have to change your `TMyClass.Draw` declaration to something else before you could compile your class using the new version 2 of the ancestor. With Delphi's class types, though, the compiler can deal with that situation, and the two same-named but unrelated virtual methods could coexist without breaking any code.

   This situation is not ambiguous to the compiler, but it could be very confusing to someone reading the source code, so you should never intentionally create same-named virtual methods. For your own sanity, always use override when you want to override, and use a unique name when you declare new virtual methods.
3. Although the parameter lists of same-named static methods in descendant class types can be different, the parameter list of a virtual method cannot be changed when

12

overridden. There is no relationship between same-named static methods and same-named new virtual methods in descendent classes. There is a very strong relationship between a virtual method and all its overriden variations: they must all have the same parameter list, because calling the virtual method could result in any one of the descendent implementations being called at run-time.

Syntax

The General Syntax for Declaring a Virtual Method

```
procedure methodName(<parameters>); virtual;

function methodName(<parameters>) : returnType; virtual;

constructor methodName(<parameters>); virtual;

destructor methodName(<parameters>); virtual;
```

Example:

```
Type
        TStrArray = class
              public
                     constructor Create(theSize : word);
                     destructor Destroy; override;
                     function store(aStr : string;
                                          index : Integer)
                                          : Boolean; virtual;
                     function recall(var aStr : string;
                                          index : Integer)
                                          : Boolean; virtual;
              protected
                     data : ^string;
                     MaxSize : word;
                     workSize : word;
        end;
```

The class `TStrArray` declares the methods `store` and `recall` as virtual.

Dynamic Methods

Dynamic methods are another form of virtual method, functionally equivalent but differing in implementation. The primary difference between virtual and dynamic methods is how the code address pointers are stored in the compiler-generated method tables. Dynamic Method Tables (DMTs) are much more space efficient than VMTs.

The Virtual Method Table of a particular class type contains pointers for every virtual method declared in that class type, as well as for all virtual methods that class inherits from its ancestors. If a base class has 10 virtual methods and 10 classes descend from that base class, you will have 11 VMTs containing 10 method pointers each — even if those 10 descendants don't declare anything of their own. That's 110 pointers, or 440 bytes of memory occupied by VMTs that contain nearly identical information. You should see that this propagation of ancestral virtual methods entries in every descendant's VMT can add up quickly.

A Dynamic Method Table contains only method pointers for the dynamic methods that are explicitly declared (or overriden) in a particular class type. The class's DMT contains a pointer to its parent's DMT, and so on up the inheritance chain. Dynamic methods that the class inherits are not recorded in that class's DMT, but are located at run-time by searching back through the DMTs of its ancestors until a method pointer is found whose compiler-generated index matches the compiler-generated index of the desired method. Thus, DMTs are many times more compact than VMTs.

Nothing comes without a price, of course. The price for the DMT's space efficiency is performance. A VMT method lookup is a simple table offset, a one-instruction operation. A DMT method lookup often involves an active search, which could take hundreds of instruction cycles.

DMTs provide the smallest possible storage of code pointers. VMTs provide the fastest possible storage of code pointers (or very nearly so, anyway).

Dynamic method declarations are often used for methods that are called infrequently, where the performance cost is not a factor. Methods that are called thousands of times per second would probably feel the performance cost of DMTs and should be declared as virtual instead. Except for that extreme case, the performance difference between dynamic methods and virtual methods is usually imperceptible.

12

Because there is no functional difference between methods declared `virtual` and methods declared `dynamic`, the examples and text of the rest of this chapter will use only `virtual` methods, in the interest of clarity and simplicity. Just keep in mind that wherever you see `virtual`, it's equally valid to put `dynamic`.

Syntax

The General Syntax for Declaring a Dynamic Method

The declaration of a dynamic method uses the directive `dynamic`. Like `virtual`, `dynamic` always introduces a new method name unrelated to any inherited method by the same name.

```
procedure methodName(<parameters>); dynamic;
```

or

```
function methodName(<parameters>) : returnType; dynamic;
```

Example:

```
Type
        TStrArray = class
              public
                     constructor Create(theSize : word);
                     destructor Destroy; overrid;
                     function store(aStr : string;
                                         index : Integer)
                                         : Boolean; dynamic;
                     function recall(var aStr : string;
                                         index : Integer)
                                         : Boolean; dynamic;
              protected
                     data : ^string;
                     MaxSize : word;
                     workSize : word;
        end;
```

The class `TStrArray` declares the methods `store` and `recall` as dynamic.

Overriding Virtual Methods

The whole point of having a virtual method is to enable descendent classes to modify the behavior of a method introduced in an ancestor class. The `override` directive is how you tell the compiler that's what you want to do — modify (extend or replace) the implementation of an inherited virtual method.

Note: The differences between methods declared `virtual`, `dynamic`, or `override` are significant primarily in the class declaration. In terms of how you call or use these methods in code, they are equivalent and are lumped together under the general term `virtual` methods. `Virtual` method refers exclusively to a method declared with the `virtual` directive. `Virtual` method is a general term referring to any kind of `virtual`, `dynamic`, or `override` method.

The virtual and dynamic directives always introduce a new method name, while override always indicates a new implementation of an existing inherited method.

An override method declaration must match the declaration of the ancestor's original virtual or dynamic method exactly in method name, parameter count, parameter names, parameter types, and (for functions) function result type. If the method name does not exist somewhere in the class's line of ancestry, or the inherited method is not virtual, dynamic, or override, or the method declarations do not match, the compiler will report an error.

Syntax

The General Syntax for Declaring a Virtual Method Override

```
procedure methodName(<parameters>); override;

function methodName(<parameters>) : returnType; override;

constructor methodName(<parameters>); override;

destructor methodName(<parameters>); override;
```

Example:

```
Type
       TStrArray = class
              public
                     constructor Create(theSize : word);
                     destructor Destroy; override;
                     function store(aStr : string;
                                          index : Integer)
                                          : Boolean; virtual;
                     function recall(var aStr : string;
                                          index : Integer)
                                          : Boolean; virtual;
              protected
                     data : ^string;
                     MaxSize : word;
                     workSize : word;
       end;
```

The class TStrArray declares the destructor Destroy to override the Destroy destructor it inherits from TObject.

Virtual Methods: See How They Run

Listing 12.1. VCLASS.PAS—A unit of classes for exploring the operation of virtual methods.

```
unit Vclass;

interface

type
  TBaseClass = class
  protected
    Indent: Integer;
  public
    procedure First; virtual;
    procedure Second; virtual;
    procedure Report(const Msg: String);
  end;

  TChild1 = class(TBaseClass)
    procedure First; override;
  end;

  TChild2 = class(TBaseClass)
    procedure First; override;
  end;

  TGrandChild1 = class(TChild1)
    procedure First; override;
    procedure Second; override;
  end;

  TGrandChild2 = class(TChild2)
    procedure Second; override;
  end;

implementation

uses SysUtils, WinCRT;

procedure TBaseClass.First;
begin
  Report('TBaseClass.First');
end;

procedure TBaseClass.Second;
begin
  Report('TBaseClass.Second');
end;

procedure TBaseClass.Report(const Msg: String);
begin
  writeln('':Indent,Msg);
end;
```

```
procedure TChild1.First;
begin
  Report('TChild1.First calling inherited ');
  Inc(Indent,2);
  inherited First;
  Dec(Indent,2);
  Report('TChild1.First');
end;

procedure TChild2.First;
begin
  Report('TChild2.First');
end;

procedure TGrandChild1.First;
begin
  Report('TGrandChild1.First calling inherited ');
  Inc(Indent,2);
  inherited First;
  Dec(Indent,2);
  Report('TGrandChild1.First');
end;

procedure TGrandChild1.Second;
begin
  Report('TGrandChild1.Second calling inherited ');
  Inc(Indent,2);
  inherited Second;
  Dec(Indent,2);
  Report('TGrandChild1.Second');
end;

procedure TGrandChild2.Second;
begin
  Report('TGrandChild2.Second');
end;

end.
```

The VCLASS.PAS unit shown in Listing 12.1 defines a small hierarchy of simple classes designed to illustrate how virtual methods work and where execution goes when you call a virtual method.

TBaseClass defines two virtual methods, First and Second, which simply write a message to the WinCRT window when called. The Report method is a utility routine to help indent the output to indicate nested calls to these methods. TBaseClass has a protected Indent field that tells the Report routine how many spaces to insert before the output text. That "writeln('':Indent)" statement writes an empty string in an area *Indent* spaces wide—a cheap way to generate whitespace.

12

Two classes descend from `TBaseClass` (`TChild1` and `TChild2`) and each of those has a descendent class (`TGrandChild1` and `TGrandChild2`). Each of these four descendants override one or both of the virtual methods they inherit from their ancestors. When called, all the methods report their name and what they are doing. This will let us see the path of execution through the methods (in a manner that can be displayed and followed in print!). `TChild1.First` and `TGrandChild1.First` call their inherited method as part of their execution — they *extend* or add to the behavior they inherit from their ancestors. `TChild2.First` and `TGrandChild2.Second` do not call their inherited method—they *replace* or block the behavior they inherit.

Whether you should write an overridden virtual method to extend or replace its inherited behaviors depends upon the situation and the design intent of the ancestor class. Most of the time, descendants extend the behaviors they inherit, following the OOP adage: "A descendant class is everything its ancestor is, and more." The only time you should replace inherited behavior by not calling the inherited method is when the author or documentation of the ancestor class tells you to do so.

The `VClass` unit gives us an interesting test-bed in which to explore what happens when you call a `virtual` method, which is what the next code sample will actually do.

Listing 12.2. VIRTUALS.DPR illustrates virtual method calls in action.

```
program Virtuals;

uses SysUtils, Wincrt, Vclass;

var
  BC : TBaseClass;
  C1 : TChild1;
  C2 : TChild2;
  GC1: TGrandchild1;
         GC2: TGrandchild2;

begin
  writeln('TBaseClass instance: ');
  BC := TBaseClass.Create;
  BC.First;
  BC.Second;
  BC.Free;

  writeln;
  writeln('TChild1 instance: ');
  C1 := TChild1.Create;
  C1.First;
  C1.Second;
  C1.Free;

  writeln;
  writeln('TChild2 instance: ');
```

```
28:  C2 := TChild2.Create;
29:  C2.First;
30:  C2.Second;
31:  C2.Free;
32:
33:  writeln;
34:  writeln('TGrandChild1 instance: ');
35:  GC1 := TGrandChild1.Create;
36:  GC1.First;
37:  GC1.Second;
38:  GC1.Free;
39:
40:  writeln;
41:  writeln('TGrandChild2 instance: ');
42:  GC2 := TGrandChild2.Create;
43:  GC2.First;
44:  GC2.Second;
45:  GC2.Free;
46:end.
```

The VIRTUALS.DPR program shown in Listing 12.2 creates an instance of each of the five class types defined in the `VClass` unit, calls the `First` and `Second` methods, and then destroys the instance. Notice how similar each block of code is to the others — we'll come back to that shortly.

The source code of VIRTUALS.DPR isn't as interesting as the output of the program, shown in Listing 12.3. You could follow the execution path of the program by keeping one finger in Listing 12.2 and another in Listing 12.3, but to experience the full effect of this example you really should step through the program line by line in the Delphi integrated debugger.

To step through the sample code in the Delphi debugger, load the VIRTUALS.DPR project into the Delphi IDE, then make sure that the Integrated Debugging option is enabled (checked) in the Options: Environment dialog, on the Preferences page. From the Delphi main menu, select Trace Into to compile, run, and step to the first executable line in the program, line 13 in Listing 12.3. F7 is the Trace Into hotkey if you're using the default or classic IDE key mappings. Trace Into is also on the IDE speedbar, the button with, as Neil Rubenking describes it, "the flea jumping into the blue box."

Continue stepping through the program one line at a time. When you reach line 15 (`BC.First;`), notice that Trace Into takes you *into* the procedure or function call. In this case, it takes us to `TBaseClass.First`. When you step out of `TBaseClass.First`, the debugger takes you back to the main program, ready for the next call.

Continue stepping to line 22 (`C1.First;`). When you trace into this method call, you wind up in `TChild1.First`, which should seem pretty reasonable. `TChild1.First` reports that it is about to call its inherited method, then it calls the inherited method. Tracing into the inherited call takes you to `TBaseClass.First`.

Continue stepping until you get back to line 23 (`C1.Second`). `TChild1` does not do anything to alter the `Second` method it inherits from `TBaseClass`. Sure enough, when you trace into the call to `C1.Second`, you wind up in `TBaseClass.Second`.

Similar behavior can be seen in the call `GC1.Second`, when the `TGrandChild1.Second` method's call to inherited `Second` winds up in `TBaseClass.Second`.

Finally, notice the difference in execution between `C1.First` and `C2.First`. `TChild1.First` extends the behavior of `TBaseClass.First` by calling the inherited method and doing additional work. `TChild2.First` replaces the inherited behavior, since it does not call the inherited method. The same is true in the difference in output between `GC1.First` and `GC2.Second`.

If you want to run the program again to watch a particular aspect of this virtual call sample program, select Run: Run to return control to the sample program, Alt+F4 to terminate the sample program, then select Run|Trace Into to start the program again.

Listing 12.3. The output of the VIRTUALS.DPR sample program.

```
TBaseClass instance:
TBaseClass.First
TBaseClass.Second

TChild1 instance:
TChild1.First calling inherited
  TBaseClass.First
TChild1.First
TBaseClass.Second

TChild2 instance:
TChild2.First
TBaseClass.Second

TGrandChild1 instance:
TGrandChild1.First calling inherited
  TChild1.First calling inherited
    TBaseClass.First
  TChild1.First
TGrandChild1.First
TGrandChild1.Second calling inherited
  TBaseClass.Second
TGrandChild1.Second

TGrandChild2 instance:
TChild2.First
TGrandChild2.Second
```

Polymorphism

Polymorphism is the third and most powerful facet of object-oriented programming (the first two are encapsulation and inheritance). Polymorphism can be described as *behavioral abstraction,* the ability to invoke an action or behavior by name on a particular object instance without knowing exactly which implementation will be invoked, or even what type the actual object instance is. The class type of the instance and the method implementation that will be invoked cannot be completely determined at compile-time, but will be completely determined at run-time. What's more, these determinations are made dynamically—the same machine code may invoke `method1` of `descendantclass1` in one pass, but invoke `method1` of `descendantclass2` in the next pass, if each pass uses a different object instance.

Polymorphism is only possible when you have:

- An ancestor class that defines one or more virtual methods
- One or more descendant classes which may override those virtual methods
- An instance variable whose declared type is the ancestor class, but which actually contains an instance of one of the descendant classes

For example, you can develop a class hierarchy of simple graphical shape classes (dots, lines, rectangles, ellipses, circles, and so on) all descended from a `TShape` base class that defines the methods common to all the shape descendants. One such method might be a virtual `Draw` method. Each specific shape descendant would override this `Draw` method to implement the particular drawing required by that class. If you wanted to store a list of such shapes, you could create an array variable declared as an array of `TShape`, then assign instances of `TCircle`, `TSquare`, `TLine`, etc. into slots in the array variable.

12

Here's where things get interesting: you can write a simple loop to call the `Draw` methods of all the instances in the array, without having to check to see which kind of shape is stored in each array slot. Like this:

```
var ShapeArray: array [1..10] of TShape;
begin
...
for x := 1 to ShapeCount do
  ShapeArray[x].Draw;
```

That's polymorphism: The loop code only has to know about the ancestor type, which defines the virtual methods overriden by the descendant classes. At run-time, the right method will be called depending upon the object instance stored in the generic instance variable (in this case, an array of `TShape`).

VMTs Make Your Head Spin

How is this magic possible? Recall that virtual methods are managed and accessed through a compiler-generated structure called the Virtual Method Table (VMT). This table is actually an array of pointers to the code of each of the virtual methods declared in a class. Every class type has its own unique VMT. Every object instance data block contains a hidden pointer to the VMT of the class type for that object instance. When the compiler generates code for a call to a virtual method, it generates code to get the VMT pointer from the object instance data, get the code address of the desired virtual method from its precalculated slot in the VMT, and call that address. The actual machine instructions involve only two steps, so the size and performance costs of this run-time polymorphism magic is quite small.

The key for virtual methods is the code pointers in the VMT; the key for polymorphism is that the VMT appropriate to an object instance's type is obtained from the object instance data at run-time.

Example of Polymorphic Behavior

Remember back in the VIRTUALS.DPR example that we noted how similar each of the statement groups were to each other? Let's now reduce all that repetitive *almost* identical code down to a simple subroutine, using polymorphism. We'll use the same VCLASS.PAS unit as before, but change the main program to POLYMRPH.DPR, shown in Listing 12.4.

Listing 12.4. The source code for POLYMRPH.DPR, which simplifies the earlier example by taking advantage of polymorphism.

```
program Polymrph;

uses SysUtils, Wincrt, Vclass;

procedure RunTest(AnInstance: TBaseClass);
begin
  writeln;
  writeln(AnInstance.ClassName,' instance: ');
  AnInstance.First;
  AnInstance.Second;
  AnInstance.Free;
end;

var
  X : TBaseClass;

begin
  X := TBaseClass.Create;
  RunTest(X);

  X := TChild1.Create;
```

```
    RunTest(X);

    RunTest( TChild2.Create );    { Assigning to a variable really isn't necessary }
    RunTest( TGrandChild1.Create );
    RunTest( TGrandChild2.Create );
end.
```

The new `RunTest` procedure takes a parameter of the generic `TBaseClass` type, writes out the class name of the received instance (using the `ClassName` method inherited from `TObject`) and makes the same calls to `First` and `Second` that were made separately for each class type in the VIRTUALS.DPR program. To call the virtual method `First`, the compiler generates code to get the VMT pointer from the instance data, get the address pointer from the `First` method's slot in the VMT, and then call that address. That's how the call winds up going to the correct method for the type of instance this `RunTest` subroutine is given, without requiring `RunTest` to know anything about the descendant classes of `TBaseClass`. You could even add more classes to the `VCLASS.PAS` unit; the machine code generated for `RunTest` would not change one bit (or byte), but it would support the new classes just as well.

Since `RunTest` frees the object instance that was passed to it, there is no real need for the main program block to use a variable to keep track of the object instance—the object instance can be created and immediately passed to the `RunTest` procedure, which will use the instance and then destroy it. The first two calls use an `X` variable just to make it easier to see the correspondence between the new code and the old. The last three calls are more like what one would find in a real program.

Though the implementation of the main program has been reduced a great deal, the output of POLYMRPH.DPR is identical to VIRTUALS.DPR (output is Listing 12.3). Take this new program for a spin in the internal debugger, and trace into the calls to `First` and `Second` to verify that your understanding of what is going on matches what the code really does.

RTTI versus Polymorphism

Run-time type information (RTTI) is compiler-generated descriptions of classes and other types used in the program, which the compiler stores in the exe. Normally, type information like the name of a class type or the name and type of a property in a class is thrown away after the compiler has gleaned what it needs from the source code declarations. RTTI allows a program to use this information at run-time for such diverse tasks as deciding whether two object instances are type compatible or for reading data into component properties. RTTI makes Delphi's visual form designer and object inspector possible, and is responsible for many of the no-effort-required aspects of Delphi programming. On Day 14 you will learn more about run-time type information as related to the class operators `as` and `is`.

RTTI and polymorphism are at opposite ends of the abstraction spectrum. Polymorphism requires and promotes abstraction — the use of generic processes to control related specific behaviors. In this sense, polymorphism is a kind of *leveraging*, enabling a small amount of code to control a larger set of behaviors.

RTTI is most easily used to defeat abstraction, to find out specific details of the object instance at hand, such as its class or properties. To get maximum benefit from the leveraging power of polymorphism, you should use RTTI sparingly.

Class Hierarchies

Class libraries are made up of one or more interrelated class hierarchies. Each class hierarchy begins with general and simple classes and ends up with descendant classes that support very specialized operations. Delphi Pascal supports only linear inheritance. That is, each descendant class has only one parent class. Some languages, like C++, support multiple inheritance, where a descendant class can have two or more parent classes. Multiple inheritance has sparked heated debate between OOP software engineers and purists. The OOP purists state that every class hierarchy design that uses multiple inheritance can be replaced with a better design that uses linear inheritance. Since Delphi Pascal does not support multiple inheritance, we should all feel fortunate that we are forced to use the *better* inheritance scheme!

The *TObject* Class

The `System` unit defines an abstract class `TObject`, which is the default base class of all newly declared objects. This very basic common ancestry supports polymorphic behavior for all classes you define. In fact, Delphi's Object Pascal automatically assumes that your newly defined classes are descendants of class `TObject` if you do not specify a parent class. The class `TObject` contains the rudimentary constructor `Create` and destructor `Destroy`.

The Standard Class Library

The `Classes` unit exports the declarations for many of the base classes that are used in Delphi applications. When you generate a new form, Delphi automatically adds the `Classes` unit to the uses clause. Here are some of the classes declared in the `Classes` unit:

- The class `TComponent` is the abstract base class for all the component classes and provides these classes with some basic common behavior. Each component that you draw on the form is represented by a class that is a descendant of `TComponent`.
- The class `TFiler` is the abstract base class for the reader and writer classes used by Delphi to recall and save forms and components in form files.

- The class `THandleStream` is a stream class that reads and writes data through a file handle. File handles are most often associated with disk files (see below), but can also be associated with virtual files in memory, such as the resource file data stored in a program's `exe` or `dll` disk file. `THandleStream` doesn't care what the handle is associated with, it just uses the handle for reading and writing data.
- The class `TFileStream` is a stream class that stores its data in a disk file. `TFileStream` descends from `THandleStream`, which already does all the work of reading and writing data to a file handle. `TFileStream` merely opens a disk file by name to obtain a handle, then lets the methods it inherits from `THandleStream` do the rest.
- The class `TList` maintains and manages a list of items and objects.
- The class `TMemoryStream` is a stream class that stores its data in dynamic memory.
- The class `TPersistent` is the abstract base class for all objects stored and loaded on Delphi stream classes.
- The class `TReader` is a specialized filer class that reads data from its associated stream.
- The class `TStream` is an abstract class representing a medium that can store binary data. Delphi offers various useful descendants of class `TStream` that store their data in memory or in disk files.
- The class `TStringList` maintains a list of strings. This class empowers a component to manage and maintain a list of strings.
- The class `TStrings` assists components in manipulating and managing strings.
- The class `TWriter` is a specialized filer class that writes data to its associated stream.

The *TComponent* Class

The last subsection mentions the class `TComponent` as the abstract base class for all component classes. Typically you need not work with class `TComponent` unless you are developing new components. In this case you need to learn about the internal details of class `TComponent`. Here is a list of some of the components in the Visual Component Library (VCL):

TApplication	TDDEClientItem	TOutline
TBatchMove	TDDEServerConv	TPaintBox
TBCDField	TDDEServerItem	TPanel
TBevel	TDirectoryListBox	TPopupMenu
TBitBtn	TDrawGrid	TPrintDialog
TBlobField	TDriveComboBox	TPrinterSetupDialog
TBooleanField	TEdit	TQuery
TButton	TField	TRadioButton

TBytesField
TCheckBox
TColorDialog
TComboBox
TCurrencyField
TDatabase
TDataSource
TDateField
TDateTimeField
TDBCheckBox
TDBComboBox
TDBEdit
TDBGrid
TDBImage
TDBListBox
TDBLookupCombo
TDBLookupList
TDBMemo
TDBNavigator
TDBRadioGroup
TDBText
TDDEClientConv
TFileListBox
TFilterComboBox
TFindDialog
TFloatField
TFontDialog
TForm
TGraphicField
TGroupBox
THeader
TImage
TIntegerField
TLabel
TListBox
TMainMenu
TMaskEdit
TMediaPlayer
TMemo
TMemoField
TMenuItem
TNotebook
TOLEContainer
TOpenDialog
TRadioGroup
TReplaceDialog
TReport
TSaveDialog
TScreen
TScrollBar
TScrollBox
TSession
TShape
TSmallIntField
TSpeedButton
TStoredProc
TStringField
TStringGrid
TTabbedNotebook
TTable
TTabSet
TTimeField
TTimer
TVarBytesField
TWordField

TApplication
TBCDField
TBlobField
TBooleanField
TBytesField
TCurrencyField
TDateField
TDateTimeField
TField
TFloatField
TGraphicField
TIntegerField
TMemoField
TMenuItem
TScreen
TSession
TSmallIntField
TStringField
TTimeField
TVarBytesField
TWordField

Summary

This chapter discussed topics related to inheritance and polymorphism. You learned about the following topics:

- Inheritance empowers you to create descendant classes that inherit fields and methods from their ancestor classes. The new descendant classes can declare new fields, new methods, and override existing virtual method implementations to support the specialized class operations. Inheritance supports code reuse in class hierarchies.
- Constructors and destructors are special methods that initialize and destroy class instances, respectively. Delphi's Object Pascal uses the keywords `constructor` and `destructor` to declare a constructor and a destructor, respectively.
- Virtual methods support run-time resolution of method calls. Using virtual methods, you can provide the appropriate response to indirect calls to these methods. Virtual methods support polymorphic behavior.
- Methods declared `virtual` are stored for fastest execution. Methods declared `dynamic` are stored for the most efficient use of memory, at a small performance cost.
- `Virtual` and `dynamic` always introduce a new method name, unrelated to any inherited method with the same name. `Override` always associates the method with an existing, inherited `virtual` or `dynamic` with the same name and parameter list.
- Polymorphism supports and enhances abstraction to allow the same high-level code to operate on many specific types of related objects instances.
- Class libraries are made up of hierarchies of classes that support different levels of the same operations and support new operations. Delphi's Object Pascal supports the visual components using a sophisticated class hierarchy.

Q&A

Q Can I mix classes declared using the `class` and `object` keywords?

A No, you will get a compiler error.

Q How do I refer to the class itself in any one of its methods?

A Use the identifier `Self` for self-reference.

Q How do I override a virtual method in a descendant class and change the parameter list of the overriding method?

A You can't. An overriden virtual method must be able to take the place of the ancestor's virtual method, so the parameter lists must be identical. You can "change" the parameter lists of same-named static methods, but these do not participate in polymorphism.

Q Can I use a class as an extendible record?

A Yes, by declaring public fields in the class. Using this approach, you can create a hierarchy of classes that simply add new fields.

Q What is an abstract class?

A An abstract class is a class that supports operations that are common to its descendants, but is not useful by itself.

Q Does Delphi Pascal offer a special syntax for abstract classes?

A No, it does not.

Q Do abstract classes always reside at the root of class hierarchies?

A Not necessarily. Abstract classes can appear anywhere in a class hierarchy.

Q Can I override the declaration of an inherited field?

A No, you cannot.

Workshop

The Workshop provides quiz questions to help you solidify your understanding of the material covered and exercises to provide you with experience in using what you've learned. Try to understand the quiz and exercise answers before going to the next day's lesson.

Quiz

1. What is wrong with the following code?

```
TStrArray = class
  public
    constructor Create(theMaxSize : Integer);
    destructor Destroy; override;
    function store(aVal: String;
                   index : Integer) : Boolean;
    function recall(var aVal: String;
                   index : Integer) : Boolean;
  protected
    data : ^string;
    maxSize : Integer;
    workSize : Integer;
  private
    function checkIndex(index : Integer) : Boolean;
end;
TSortedStrArray = class (TStrArray)
  public
    constructor Create(theMaxSize : Integer);
    destructor Destroy; override;
```

```
    procedure sort;
    function search(key : String) : Integer;
  protected
    function linearSearch(key : String) : Integer;
    function binarySearch(key : String) : Integer;
    workSize: Word;
    isSorted: Boolean;
  private
    procedure fastSwap(index1, index2 : Integer);
end;
```

2. What is wrong with the following code?

```
TStrArray = class
  public
    procedure Create(theMaxSize : Integer);
    procedure Destroy; override;
    function store(aVal: String;
                   index : Integer) : Boolean; virtual;
    function recall(var aVal: String;
                   index : Integer) : Boolean; virtual;
  protected
    data : ^string;
    maxSize : Integer;
    workSize : Integer;
  private
    function checkIndex(index : Integer) : Boolean;
end;
```

3. What is wrong with the following code?

```
     TStrArray = class
   public
     constructor Create(theMaxSize : Integer);
     destructor Destroy; override;
     function store(aVal: String;
                   index : Integer) : Boolean;
     function recall(var aVal: String;
                   index : Integer) : Boolean;
   protected
     data : ^string;
     maxSize : Integer;
```

12

continues

```
    workSize : Integer;
  private
    function checkIndex(index : Integer) : Boolean;
end;
TSortedStrArray = object (TStrArray)
  public
    constructor Create(theMaxSize : Integer);
    destructor Destroy; override;
    procedure sort;
    function search(key : String) : Integer;
  protected
    function linearSearch(key : String) : Integer;
    function binarySearch(key : String) : Integer;
    workSize: Word;
    isSorted: Boolean;
  private
    procedure fastSwap(index1, index2 : Integer);
end;
```

4. What is wrong with the following code?

```
    TStrArray = class
  public
    constructor Create(theMaxSize : Integer);
    destructor Destroy(removeAll : Boolean); override;
    function store(aVal: String;
                   index : Integer) : Boolean;
    function recall(var aVal: String;
                   index : Integer) : Boolean;
  protected
    data : ^string;
    maxSize : Integer;
    workSize : Integer;
  private
    function checkIndex(index : Integer) : Boolean;
end;
```

Exercises

Extend the VCLASS.PAS class declarations to include new dynamic and static methods.

1. Start by adding to TBaseClass a function named Third returning an integer and make it dynamic. Add a procedure named Fourth and leave it as a static method (no virtual, dynamic, or override directive). In the body of the Fourth method, call the other methods in TBaseClass (First, Second, and Third). In the POLYMRPH.DPR programs RunTest routine, add a call to Fourth. Step through this code in the debugger and observe the results for all five classes. Explain what you find.
2. Try adding new methods to the descendant classes. Override the new Third method in TGrandChild1, for example. Step through your code in the debugger to verify it works.
3. How does adding a new static method named Fourth to the TGrandChild2 class affect the execution of the program?
4. How does adding a new virtual method (virtual, not override) named Second to TChild2 affect the execution of the program? Which part of this chapter discusses this phenomenon?

12

WEEK
2

Properties and Windows Messages

by Namir Shammas

This chapter introduces you to class properties, Windows API functions, and Windows messages. The properties support the visual and functional attributes of a form and its components. The Windows messages animate Windows applications and call API functions. You will learn about the following topics:

- Declaring properties in a class
- The general overview of Windows API functions
- The general categories of Windows messages
- Declaring event-handlers that trap specific Windows messages

Properties

A *property* is an attribute of a form or a component that influences either the visual behavior or the operations of the form or component. For example, the `Visible` property determines whether a component is visible. Likewise, the `Enabled` property decides whether the control is enabled or disabled. Regarding behavior-related properties, you can consider the `BorderStyle` property as an example. The setting of this property in a form determines how the form appears as well as whether or not you can resize it.

The following subsections discuss various aspects of declaring properties.

Declaring Properties

Delphi supports a special syntax that allows a class declaration to contain the declaration or properties.

Syntax

The General Syntax for Declaring a Property

```
Property propertyName : type
  [read {propertyField ¦ readMethod} ]
  [write {propertyField ¦ writeMethod}]
  [default defaultValue];
```

The `propertyName` parameter specifies the property name. The `type` component indicates the type of the property. Delphi allows you to declare properties that are of simple types, enumerated types, sets, objects, and arrays. The optional `read` clause specifies how to read the property setting. The optional `write` clause indicates how to write a new value for the property. The optional `default` clause specifies the default value for the property.

Example:

```
property Count : Integer
  read FCount
  write SetCount
```

```
  default 0;
End.
```

This code shows the property `Count` with the `read`, `write`, and `default` clauses. The next sections discuss what the content of each clause means.

Note: The declaration of a property does not parallel the declaration of a field or a variable—a property declaration never creates a memory location to store the property values.

The *Read* Clause

The `read` clause in the property declaration specifies how to access the value for the property. Typically, the class stores the value of the property in one of the fields. If the `read` clause is omitted, the property is write-only (useful for a password property, perhaps). Delphi allows two ways to read the property value:

- Direct Access. This route involves using a class field that stores the value of the property. The field must have the same type as the property. The suggested convention for naming such a field is starting the name with an uppercase F. Thus, the field that stores the value for a property called `Count` should be named `FCount`.
- Indirect Access. This route involves using a method that accesses the value of the property. For simple properties, the read method must be a function with no parameters that returns the property value. For indexed properties, the read method must be a function with a single integer parameter that returns the property value. For array properties, the read method must be a function that takes the same number and type of parameters as the index(es) in the property's array declaration, and the function must return the property value. The method must be declared in the class declaration prior to any property declaration that references it.

  The method must return a value that has the same type as the property. The suggested convention for naming such a method is starting the name with the word `Get`. Thus the method that reads the value for a property called `Count` should be named `GetCount`. Here is an example of declaring an implementing a class with the property `Count` and the method `GetCount`:

```
Type
   TMyCtrl = class(TComponent)
      private
         FCount : Integer;
      protected
```

13

```
            function GetCount() : Integer;
    published
            property Count : Integer
               read GetCount;
End;

function TMyCtrl.GetCount() : Integer;
Begin
   GetCount := Fcount;
End;
```

Listing 3.1 shows the declaration of class `TButton`. Consider the declaration of property `Cancel` in line 26. This property has the predefined type `Boolean` and uses the field `FCancel` to read the property's value. Line 4 declares the field `FCancel`, which also has the same type as the property `Cancel`.

Listing 3.1. The declaration of class `TButton`.

```
 1: TButton = class(TButtonControl)
 2:  private
 3:   FDefault: Boolean;
 4:   FCancel: Boolean;
 5:   FActive: Boolean;
 6:   FReserved: Byte;
 7:   FModalResult: TModalResult;
 8:   procedure SetDefault(Value: Boolean);
 9:   procedure CMDialogKey(var Message: TCMDialogKey);
10:     message CM_DIALOGKEY;
11:   procedure CMDialogChar(var Message: TCMDialogChar);
12:     message CM_DIALOGCHAR;
13:   procedure CMFocusChanged(var Message: TCMFocusChanged);
14:     message CM_FOCUSCHANGED;
15:   procedure CNCommand(var Message: TWMCommand);
16:     message CN_COMMAND;
17:  protected
18:   procedure CreateParams(var Params: TCreateParams);
19:     override;
20:   procedure CreateWnd; override;
21:   procedure SetButtonStyle(ADefault: Boolean); virtual;
22:  public
23:   constructor Create(AOwner: TComponent); override;
24:   procedure Click; override;
25:  published
26:   property Cancel: Boolean
27:     read FCancel
28:     write FCancel
29:     default False;
30:   property Caption;
31:   property Default: Boolean
32:     read FDefault
33:     write SetDefault
34:     default False;
```

```
    property DragCursor;
    property DragMode;
    property Enabled;
    property Font;
    property ModalResult: TModalResult
      read FModalResult
      write FModalResult
      default 0;
    property ParentFont;
    property ParentShowHint;
    property PopupMenu;
    property ShowHint;
    property TabOrder;
    property TabStop default True;
    property Visible;
    property OnClick;
    property OnDragDrop;
    property OnDragOver;
    property OnEndDrag;
    property OnEnter;
    property OnExit;
    property OnKeyDown;
    property OnKeyPress;
    property OnKeyUp;
    property OnMouseDown;
    property OnMouseMove;
    property OnMouseUp;
  end;
```

The *Write* Clause

The `write` clause in the property declaration specifies how to write a new value for the property. If the `write` clause is omitted, the property is read-only, a handy way to protect data fields from being modified. Delphi allows two ways to write the property value:

- Direct Access. This route involves using a class field that stores the value of the property. The field must have the same type as the property. If the `read` and `write` clauses of a property refer to a field, they must refer to the same field.
- Indirect Access. This route involves using a method that writes the new value of the property. In all cases, the method used to write the property must be a procedure with a parameter whose type matches the property type. For a simple property, that is the only parameter of the write method. For an indexed property, the first parameter of the write method must be an integer index, and the second parameter the property data. For an array property, the write method must have the same number and type of parameters as the array property's index(es), and the last parameter must be the property data. The property data parameter in all cases must be a pass-by-value or `const` parameter: `var` parameters are not allowed. The method must be declared in the class declaration prior to any property declaration that references it.

The suggested convention for naming such a method is to start the name with the word Set. Thus the method that reads the value for a property called `Count` should be named `SetCount`. Here is an example of declaring an implementing a class with the property `Count` and the method `SetCount`:

```
Type
    TMyCtrl = class(TComponent)
        private
            FCount : Integer;
        protected
            function GetCount() : Integer;
            procedure SetCount(Value : Integer);
        published
            property Count : Integer
                read GetCount;
                write SetCount;
    End;

    procedure TMyCtrl.SetCount(Value : Integer);
    Begin
        FCount := Value;
    End;

    function TMyComponent.GetCount() : Integer;
    Begin
        GetCount := Fcount;
    End;
```

Refer back to Listing 3.1 and examine the declaration of property `Default` in line 31. This property has the predefined type `Boolean` and uses the field `FDefault` to read the property's value. The property uses the method `SetDefault` to write the property value. Line 8 declares the method `SetDefault`. This method has the parameter `Value`, which is of the `Boolean` type.

DO	DON'T

DO use the suggested naming convention to make it easier for you and for others to read your code.

DON'T forget to use the same field if both `read` and `write` clauses specify fields for direct access.

The *Default* Clause

A `default` value clause allows you to indicate what value the property will be initialized to by the class constructor. Examples of the `default` clause appear in lines 29 and 34 in Listing 3.1. Line 29 specifies the default value of `False` for the `Cancel` property. Line 34 specifies the default value of `False` for the `Default` property.

Here is an example of declaring an implementing a class with the property `Count` and the `default` clause:

```
Type
    TMyCtrl = class(TComponent)
        private
            FCount : Integer;
        protected
            function GetCount() : Integer;
            procedure SetCount(Value : Integer);
        public
            constructor Create(AOwner : TComponent);
                override;
        published
            property Count : Integer
                read GetCount;
                write SetCount;
                default 1;
    End;

    constructor TMyCtrl.Create(AOwner : TComponent);
    Begin
        inherited Create(AOwner);
        FCount := 1;
    End;

    procedure TMyCtrl.SetCount(Value : Integer);
    Begin
        FCount := Value;
    End;

    function TMyCtrl.GetCount() : Integer;
    Begin
        GetCount := FCount;
    End;
```

Notice that the constructor code assigns the default value of 1 to the field `FCount`, which stores the property value.

If no default clause is specified, a default value of zero is assumed.

Only simple types can be specified in a `default` value clause: integers, enumerated types, character, and set types. Properties whose type is string, floating point, array, or record types cannot have a `default` value clause.

13

`Default` can also be used on array properties, but for a different purpose, as you will see in the next section.

Note: The `default` value clause does *not* set the value of the property—you are responsible for writing the code to actually assign the default value into the property in the class's constructor. The `default` value clause informs the compiler of what you will be initializing the property to. This information allows the automatic property streaming system (for loading and storing forms and components in files) to know whether a property value needs to be written to the file. If the property value is the same as that declared in the `default` value clause, it doesn't need to be written, and that saves file space.

Declaring Array Properties

You can declare a property to provide access to an array of values. This kind of property requires one or more indices to access an individual value of the array property.

Syntax

The General Syntax for Declaring an Array Property

```
Property propertyName[Index1 : Index1Type {; Index2: Index2Type...}] : type
  [read {propertyField ¦ readMethod} ]
  [write {propertyField ¦ writeMethod}]
  [default];
```

The *propertyName* parameter specifies the property name. The *type* component indicates the type of the property. One or more index parameters enclosed in square brackets make this an array property declaration. The optional `read` clause specifies how to read the property setting. The optional `write` clause indicates how to write a new value for the property. The optional `default` clause makes this array property the default array property for the class.

Example:

```
type
  TArrayPropSample = class
  protected
    function GetDays(Index: Integer): String;
    procedure SetDays(Index: Integer; const Value: String);
    function GetDaySum(Index: String): Real;
    procedure SetDaySum(Index: String; Value: Real);
  public
    property Days[Index : Integer] : String
      read GetDays
      write SetDays;
```

```
    property DaySum[Index : String] : Real
      read GetDaySum
      write SetDaySum;
  end;
```

The property `Days` represents an array of strings accessed by an integer index. The property uses the methods `GetDays` and `SetDays` to access the individual elements of the `Days` array property.

The second property, `DaySum`, represents an array of floating-point values accessed by a string index. The property uses the methods `GetDaySum` and `SetDaySum` to access the individual elements of the array.

A default array property is the one array property in a class that can be used in a shorthand notation that omits the name of the property. Normally, the `Items` property would be accessed with an instance variable like this:

```
S := Listbox1.Items[10];
```

If `Items` were declared with a `default` clause (which it is, in TListbox), you could use the shorthand version to reference that property, like this:

```
S := Listbox1[10];
```

Only one array property can be the default array property of a class. Once the array default property is set, it can be inherited in descendent classes but it cannot be changed by descendants. Declaring a second default array property will produce a compiler error.

The Windows API Functions

If you are familiar with the Windows API functions, you can skip this section. If not, read on. This section is for the reader who is new to programming Windows applications. Windows 3.1 has just over 1000 API Windows functions. Under Windows 3.1 are the following three groups of API functions:

- *Windows manager interface functions* manage message processing, create system output, and create, move, and alter windows. Table 3.1 shows the types of Windows manager interface functions.

Table 3.1. The types of Windows manager interface functions.

API Functions Type	Purpose
Message	Read and process Windows messages in an application's queue.
Window-creation	Create, destroy, alter, and retrieve information about windows.

continues

Table 3.1. continued

API Functions Type	Purpose
Display & movement	Show, hide, move, and return information regarding the number and positions of windows on the screen.
Input	Take control of the system devices, disable input from system devices, specify the special action to be carried out by Windows when an application receives input from the system devices.
Hardware	Alter and query the state of input devices (Windows employs the mouse and the keyboard as input devices).
Painting	Ready a window for painting and offer practical general graphics functions.
Dialog box	Create, change, test, and remove dialog boxes and the controls inside the boxes.
Scrolling	Control the scrolling of a window and of the window's scroll bars.
Menu	Create, alter, and remove menus.
Information	Retrieve information about the number and location of windows on a screen.
System	Return information about the system metrics, color, and time.
Clipboard	Perform the exchange of data between Windows applications and the Clipboard.
Error	Display system errors and request a response from the user to handle the error.
Caret	Create, remove, display, hide, and change the blink time of the caret.
Cursor	Set, move, show, hide, and restrict the cursor movements.
Hook	Manage system hooks.
Property	Create and retrieve the window's property list.
Rectangle	Set and query the information about rectangles in a window's client area.

- *Graphics Device Interface (GDI) functions* perform device-independent graphics operations for Windows applications. These operations include drawing a wide assortment of lines, text, and bitmapped images on several output devices. Table 3.2 shows the types of GDI functions.

Table 3.2. The types of Graphics Device Interface (GDI) functions.

API Functions Type	Purpose
Device-context	Create, delete, and restore device contexts that link a Windows application, a device driver, and an output device.
Drawing-tool	Create and remove the drawing tools that GDI utilizes when it generates output on a device.
Color-palette	Provide a device-independent method for accessing colors of a display device.
Drawing-attribute	Influence the output image of a Windows application (which can appear as a brush, line, bitmap, or text).
Mapping	Set and query the GDI mapping mode information.
Coordinate	Convert between custom and screen coordinates, and determine the location of an individual point.
Region	Create, modify, and obtain information about regions. A region is an elliptic or polygonal area within a window that can be supplied with a graphical output.
Clipping	Create, change, and test clipping regions.
Line-output	Create both simple and complex line output using a selected pen drawing tool.
Ellipse & Polygon	Draw ellipses and polygons.
Bitmap	Display bitmaps.
Text	Write text on a device of display surface, obtain text information, change text alignment, and modify text justification.
Fonts	Select, create, delete, and obtain information about fonts.
Metafile	Create, copy, close, remove, retrieve, play, and obtain information about metafiles.
Device-control	Obtains the information about a device and alters its initialization.
Printer-control	Obtain the printer's capabilities, and alter its initialization state.
Printer-escape	Permit an application to access the facilities of a specific device that is not directly available through GDI.
Environment	Set and query the information related to the environment of the output device.

- System services interface functions access code and data in modules, allocate local and global memory, manage tasks, load program resources, manipulate strings, change the Windows initialization files, offer debugging aid, perform port communication and file I/O, and create sound. Table 3.3 shows the types of system services interface functions.

Table 3.3. The types of system services interface functions.

API Functions Type	Purpose
Module-management	Set and query information regarding Windows modules.
Memory-management	Manage global and local system memory.
Segment	Allocate, deallocate, lock, and unlock memory segments.
OS interrupt	Permit assembly-language programs to carry out certain DOS and NETBIOS interrupts without directly coding the interrupts.
Task	Change the execution status of a task (that is, a single Windows application call), retrieve the information related to a task, and obtain the information about the environment within which a task is executing.
Resource-management	Locate and load application resources (such as cursors, icons, bitmaps, strings, and fonts) from a Windows executable file.
String-manipulation	Offer frequently used string-manipulation functions, such as string copy, comparison, case conversion, and character test.
Atom-management	Create and manage atoms (an *atom* is a unique integer-index to a string).
Initialization-file	Set and query information from the WIN.INI Windows initialization file, or any other private initialization file (usually with an .INI extension).
Communications	Performs serial and parallel communications via the system's ports.
Sound	Create sound and music for the system's sound generator.
File I/O	Create, open, close, read from, and write to files.
Debugging	Assist in catching errors in Windows applications and modules.
Application-exec	Allow one Windows application to execute another Windows or DOS program.

Windows Messages

Windows applications contain various types of objects that interact with each other, via messages, in response to events. The Windows metaphor resembles the working office that is made up of employees, managers, departments, and material resources (computers, typewriters, photocopying machines, phones, faxes, and so on). Each employee (who, for the sake of the discussion, corresponds to a Windows object) has a role to play as defined by his or her job description (which corresponds to a class declaration). The activities of an office are stimulated by events from the outside world, events directed to the outside world, and internal events. To respond to these events, the various employees and departments need to communicate with each other via messages. In a similar manner, the Windows environment and its applications interact with each other and with the outside world (that is, the input and output devices) using messages. These messages can be generated from the following sources:

- User-generated events, such as typing on the keyboard, moving the mouse, and clicking on the mouse button. These events result in user-generated messages.
- A Windows application can call Windows functions and result in Windows sending messages back to the application.
- A Windows application can send internal messages aimed at specific program components.
- The Windows environment can send messages to a Windows application.
- Two Windows applications can send dynamic data exchange (DDE) messages in order to share data.

Windows 3.1 has the following types of message categories:

- *Windows-management messages* are sent by Windows to an application when the state of a window is altered. Table 3.4 shows a selection of Windows-management messages.

Table 3.4. A selection of Windows-management messages.

Message	Meaning
WM_ACTIVATE	Sent when a window becomes active or inactive.
WM_CLOSE	Sent when a window is closed.
WM_MOVE	Sent when a window is moved.
WM_PAINT	Sent when either Windows or an application requests to repaint part of an application's window.
WM_QUIT	Signifies a request to end an application.
WM_SIZE	Sent after a window is resized.

- *Initialization messages* are sent by Windows when an application constructs a menu or a dialog box. Table 3.5 shows the initialization messages.

Table 3.5. The initialization messages.

Message	Meaning
WM_INITDIALOG	Sent right before a dialog box is displayed.
WM_INITMENU	Request to initialize a menu.
WM_INITMENUPOPUP	Sent right before a pop-up menu is displayed.

Note: Delphi apps do not generate or receive wm_InitDialog messages, because Delphi does not use the Windows dialog manager. Delphi 'dialogs' are modal forms which to Windows are just plain windows, not special dialog windows.

- *Input messages* are emitted by Windows in response to an input through the mouse, keyboard, scroll bars, or system timer. Table 3.6 shows a selection of input messages.

Table 3.6. A selection of input messages.

Message	Meaning
WM_COMMAND	Sent when you select a menu item or click on a button.
WM_HSCROLL	Sent when you click the horizontal scroll bar with the mouse.
WM_KEYDOWN	Sent when a non-system key is pressed.
WM_KEYUP	Sent when a non-system key is released.
WM_LBUTTTONDBLCLK	Sent when you double-click on the left mouse button.
WM_LBUTTONDOWN	Sent when you press the left mouse button.
WM_LBUTTONUP	Sent when you release the left mouse button.
WM_MOUSEMOVE	Sent when you move the mouse.
WM_RBUTTONDBLCLK	Sent when you double-click the right mouse button.
WM_RBUTTONDOWN	Sent when you press the right mouse button.
WM_RBUTTONUP	Sent when you release the right mouse button.

Message	Meaning
WM_TIMER	Sent when the timer limit set for a specific timer has elapsed.
WM_VSCROLL	Sent when you click the vertical scroll bar with the mouse.

- *System messages* are sent by Windows to an application when the user accesses the application's control menu, scroll bars, or size box. Most of the Windows applications do not respond to these messages directly but instead pass them to the `DefWindowProc` function for default processing.
- *Clipboard messages* are sent by Windows to your application when other applications attempt to access the data you've placed on the clipboard.
- *System-information messages* are sent by Windows when a system-level change is made that affects other Windows applications. Among such changes are those that affect the fonts, color palette, system color, time, and the contents of the WIN.INI file.
- *Control-manipulation messages* are sent by Windows applications to a child control, such as a push-button, list box, combo box, and edit control. The control messages result in performing a specific task, and also return a value that indicates the outcome.
- *Control-notification messages* notify the parent window of a control about the actions that have occurred within that control.
- *Scroll-bar notification messages* include the WM_HSCROLL and WM_VSCROLL messages. The scroll bars send these messages to their parent windows when you click the bars.
- *Nonclient-area messages* are sent by Windows to create and update the non-client area (that is, the area outside the working or client area of a window). You will seldom be required to override the default responses to these messages in your Delphi applications.
- *Multiple Document Interface (MDI) messages* are sent by an MDI frame window to a child client window. These messages result in operations such as activating, deactivating, creating, removing, arranging, and restoring client windows.

Sending Messages

Windows allows your application to send messages to itself, other applications, or to Windows itself. The Windows API functions `SendMessage`, `PostMessage`, and `SendDlgItemMessage` provide important tools for sending messages. The `SendMessage` function sends a message to a window and requires that window to handle the emitted message. The `SendMessage` function is declared as follows:

```
function SendMessage(Wnd: HWnd;
                Msg, wParam: Word;
                lParam: LongInt): LongInt;
```

The parameter Wnd is the handle of the window receiving the message. The parameter Msg specifies the message sent. The parameters wParam and lParam designate additional optional information. You can use the SendMessage function to communicate with other windows and controls.

The PostMessage is similar to SendMessage except that it lacks the sense of urgency—the message is posted in the window's message queue. The message is handled later by the targeted window when it is convenient for that window. The declaration of the Boolean PostMessage function is as follows:

```
function PostMessage(Wnd: HWnd;
        Msg, wParam: Word;
        lParam: LongInt): Bool;
```

The parameter Wnd is the handle of the window receiving the message. The parameter Msg specifies the message sent. The parameters wParam and lParam designate additional optional information.

The SendDlgItemMessage function sends a message to a particular item in a dialog box. Since you already have direct access to all the components in your Delphi forms, this function is useless in a Delphi app, but it might be useful when using windows and dialogs implemented in external DLLs.

The declaration of the SendDlgItemMessage function is

```
function SendDlgItemMessage(Dlg: HWnd;
          IDDlgItem: Integer;
          Msg, wParam: Word;
          lParam: LongInt): LongInt;
```

The parameter Dlg is the handle of the dialog box that contains the targeted control. The parameter IDDlgItem indicates the integer identifier of the dialog box item that receives the message. The parameter Msg specifies the message sent. The parameters wParam and lParam designate additional optional information.

User-Defined Messages

Windows allows you to define the names of new messages. The constant WM_USER (see Table 3.7) is associated with the number of the first message. You need to declare constants that represent the offset values for your custom messages. For example, you can use the const clause to define the names of new messages:

```
const
   WM_USER1  = WM_USER + 0;
   WM_USER2  = WM_USER + 1;
   WM_USER3  = WM_USER + 2;
```

Table 3.7 shows the range of Windows messages for Windows 3.1.

Table 3.7. The range of Windows messages.

Constant	Value	Message Range	Meaning
		0x0000-0x03FF	Windows messages
WM_USER	0x0400	0x0400-0x7FFF	Programmer-defined window messages
		0x8000-0xBFFF	Reserved for use by Windows
		0xC000-0xFFFF	String messages for use by applications

Declaring Windows Message Handlers

Delphi enables you to declare methods as Windows message handlers.

Syntax

The General Syntax for Declaring a Message Method

```
procedure methodName(var Message : MsgRecordType);
    message WM_XXXX;
```

The *methodName* specifies the name of the method in a class. The identifier *Message* is the name of the message-passing parameter. *MsgRecordType* can be any record type, usually specific to the particular message this method is designed to handle. The keyword `message` indicates that the method is a message handler. The identifier *WM_XXXX* is an integer constant or expression that defines the Windows message number that the method will handle. Message methods must be procedures.

Message methods have the special property that any type can be used for the message parameter, as long as the parameter is a `var` parameter. The name of the method is not important to its message handling; only the message number is used to match a received message with a message method.

Example:

```
TMyCtrl = class (TComponent)
    { other declarations }
    procedure MyOwnBtnClick(var Message : TWMRBUTTONDBLCLK);
        message WM_RBUTTONDBLCLK;
    { other declarations }
End;
```

The preceding script declares method `MyOwnBtnClick` as the handler of the Windows message `WM_RBUTTONDBLCLK`.

TMessage is a generic message type, but you'll see in a moment that you should endeavor to use message-specific record types whenever possible. TMessage has the following declaration:

```
TMessage = record
  Msg: Word;
  case Integer of
    0: (
      WParam: Word;
      LParam: Longint;
      Result: Longint);
    1: (
      WParamLo: Byte;
      WParamHi: Byte;
      LParamLo: Word;
      LParamHi: Word;
      ResultLo: Word;
      ResultHi: Word);
end;
```

Delphi has record types pre-declared for all the standard Windows messages and Delphi internal messages. This takes all the pain out of extracting the message data packed into cryptic WParam and LParam data fields.

This use of record types to decode the packed message data will also play an important role in making your Delphi apps portable to the Win32 environment. In the move to 32 bits, some of the Windows messages shifted their data packings around a bit. Any programs that are written to directly decode the message data will require source code modifications before they can be compiled and run as 32-bit Windows applications. Delphi's use of record types shields your program from the specifics of the message data packing. The record types for some messages will be slightly rearranged in the move from 16 to 32 bits, but the data field names your program code uses will not change, so your code is insulated from this porting headache.

Whenever possible, use record types to access data packed in messages instead of the generic TMessage record.

Message methods operate as static methods if called directly in code. Like static methods, there is no name or parameter list relationship between message methods declared in an ancestor and in a descendent, so it is perfectly valid to have declarations like the following:

```
type
  TBaseClass = class
    procedure WMFoo(var M: TMyRec); message 407;
  end;

  TChildClass = class
    procedure WMBar(var X: TYourRec); message 407;
  end;
```

The only link between these two message methods is the message index number 407.

Dispatching Messages

If you want to call a message method directly, you have to know the exact method name and parameter type of the target message method in the particular class, just as with static method calls. Direct calls to message methods never exhibit any sort of polymorphism.

To send a message to an object instance polymorphically, use the `Dispatch` method found in `TObject`. `Dispatch` takes a single `var` parameter of any type. It treats the first word of the parameter data as a message number, and starts a search for a matching message handler method in the object instance's message methods. The search proceeds up the inheritance chain until a matching method is found or you run out of ancestors. If this sounds familiar, it should: message methods are indexed and searched for using the same internal structures and code as DMT methods, described in Chapter 12.

If a matching message method is found, it is executed with the `var` parameter given to Dispatch.

If no matching message method is found, the instance's `DefaultHandler` method is called and the processing of the message is terminated.

Calling Inherited Message Methods and Default Handlers

In the body of a message method, you will often want to allow your ancestor to see the message before or after you have done your work with it. However, since message methods are basically static in nature, you have no idea what the name of the ancestor's corresponding message handler might be, so you can't just call `inherited` *<methodname>*, as you would with virtual methods.

Instead, you just write `inherited;` all by itself. In the context of a message method, the compiler knows that this means you want to dispatch the current message with the current message parameter to any qualifying inherited message methods.

13

As each message method calls its inherited method on up the inheritance tree, you will eventually run out of inherited message methods, at which point the instance's `DefaultHandler` method is called. `DefaultHandler` is a virtual method defined by `TObject` and overriden by some component classes to pass unhandled Windows messages on to Windows default handlers such as `DefWindowProc`, `DefMDIProc`, or `DefMDIChildProc`.

This means that when you call `inherited;` you don't have to worry about whether your class is the last in the inheritance chain to handle this message number. This is a big improvement over Borland Pascal's OWL library, where the last method in the inheritance chain was responsible for calling a default handler instead of any (possibly non-existent) inherited handler. ("The last person out should lock the door.") If your ancestor class was later changed to process that same message, your OWL code would need to change in many descendent classes to get things working again. ("The next-to-last person locks the door through force of habit, inadvertently locking the last person inside.")

In Delphi, message handling methods almost always call `inherited;` and therefore never have to think about calling a default handler. When `inherited;` runs out of rope, it will call the default handler automatically. ("The door locks itself when the room is empty.")

Message Processing Opportunities

A Delphi component has three opportunities to process messages: before any message method has seen the message, in message methods, and after every qualified message method has seen the message. Pre-processing can be done by overriding `TControl.WndProc`. Post-processing can be done by overriding `TObject.DefaultHandler`. The distribution of messages is a diamond-shaped graph: All messages go through `WndProc`, then they are split up and dispatched to their specific message methods, then they all converge on `DefaultHandler`.

There is a fourth opportunity for you to process messages in your application: the `Application.OnMessage` event. You can assign a method of your form to this event property in the form's `OnCreate` event. The `Application.OnMessage` event gets to see all messages that pass through the application's message loop, for all the windows in the application. Be careful not to do anything time-consuming in this event, or you'll slow down the whole application.

If you look at the declaration of class `TButton` in Listing 3.1, you see a number of Windows message handlers in lines 9 to 17. Notice that these handlers use different message types for the `Message` parameter. Each message handler uses a type that is particular to the Windows message handled. For example, line 15 contains the declaration of the method `CNCommand`. This message responds to the CN_COMMAND Windows message. The parameter `Message` for this method has the type `TWMCommand`.

Summary

Today's lesson discussed properties, Windows API functions, and Windows messages. You learned about the following topics:

- Declaring properties in a class. The chapter discussed how to declare a property and set the `read`, `write`, and `default` clauses. The `read` and `write` clauses access the value of the property.
- The general overview of Windows API functions. These functions provide the underlying support for Windows. You learned about the various groups of Windows API functions.

- The general categories of Windows messages. These messages animate the various kinds of windows. The chapter briefly discussed the various groups of Windows messages.
- Declaring message handlers that respond to specific Windows messages. Delphi supports a special syntax that allows a method to become the handler of a Windows message. The syntax involves placing the keyword `message` after the declaration of the method, followed by the name of the associated Windows message.

Q&A

Q How does Windows support object-oriented features?

A Windows is not a true object-oriented environment because it relies on API functions (which are mostly coded in C and assembly).

Q Should the read and write methods of a property be non-public?

A Yes, it is best to make them protected.

Q How do I send a Windows message while handling another message?

A `PostMessage` and `SendMessage` can both be used to send the new message. `PostMessage` is generally safer, since it avoids the infinite recursion issues possible with `SendMessage`, but `SendMessage`'s synchronous call model is usually easier than `PostMessage`'s asynchronous nature.

Workshop

The Workshop provides quiz questions to help you solidify your understanding of the material covered and exercises to provide you with experience in using what you've learned. Try to understand the quiz and exercise answers before continuing on to the next day's lesson.

Quiz

1. True or False? The declaration of a property never allocates memory space for the property value.
2. True or False? You can use different fields when directly accessing the property value.
3. How many parameters are there in the method listed as a `read` clause of a property?
4. How many parameters are there in the method listed as a `write` clause of a property?
5. What group of Windows API functions perform device-independent graphics operations for Windows applications?
6. What group of Windows API functions handles sound?
7. What group of Windows messages includes the WM_CLOSE message?

Exercise

1. Use a file viewer to browse (but not edit!) the file STDCTRLS.INT in the DELPHI\DOC directory. Examine the classes declared in that file and study the properties and Windows message handlers.

14

WEEK 2

Exceptions Handling and RTTI

by Namir Shammas

Almost every program experiences run-time errors. These errors occur when the program's code is unable to deal with conditions that arise due to a particular user action, hardware state (such as a drive with its door open, a printer that is not ready, and so on), computational values, or other reasons. In this chapter you will look at handling run-time errors and using run-time type information services. Today you will learn about the following topics:

- What are exceptions?
- Exception syntax
- Exception classes
- Run-time type information (RTTI)

What Are Exceptions?

Exceptions are a means to communicate run-time error conditions or other "exceptional" situations from the site where the situation is first discovered to a handler that is prepared to deal with that situation. Exceptions can arise from various conditions such as mathematical errors, using an out-of-range array index, stack overflow, memory-allocation errors, invalid data, and not-ready hardware status, to mention just a few.

NEW TERM An *exception* is a notification of a run-time error or other situation that requires abandoning the normal flow of program execution.

The traditional approach to dealing with run-time errors is often called *defensive programming*, which means checking that input data is reasonable before attempting an operation on it. This can only go so far in preventing problems, so you usually have to put in checks after a statement to verify that the statement did not actually encounter or produce an error. An example of defensive programming is making sure a filename exists before attempting to open it for input. After opening the file, you have to check that the operation was successful. After each read from or write to the file, you are supposed to check that the operation was successful. As you can imagine, this continuous checking for errors can take up a lot of code—more than the code that actually does the work! Consequently, it is very rare that a programmer writes code to cover every possible error condition and respond or report it to the user in an orderly fashion.

Advanced programming languages, such as C++, Ada, and Delphi's Object Pascal, offer constructs that formalize the process of communicating errors to the code that needs to know about them in a reliable and orderly fashion. The next section discusses the exception-handling constructs in Delphi. Before we jump into the syntax, though, let's explore the fundamental operation of exceptions and exception handling.

Exception handling differs from traditional error handling in that it allows you to separate the code that detects an error condition from the code that reacts to the error condition, and provides an automatic and unobtrusive communication channel between the two. The code that detects

an error *raises* an exception to signal the error condition. The code that responds to that signal is an *exception handler*. When an exception is raised, a search begins for a suitable exception handler. When a handler is found, execution jumps to that handler, never to return to the code that raised the exception. The code in the handler is executed, and then program execution resumes at the next statement following the handler, or resumes the search for another handler, depending on the kind of exception handler it is.

This search walks back through the call stack of the program, looking for markers that point to exception-handler information generated by the compiler. Recall that when procedure A calls procedure B, A's state is stored on the stack. In a sense, the state of procedure A is waiting for the completion of procedure B. If procedure B then calls another routine, C, B's state is stored on the stack and it waits while C executes.

If procedure A contains an exception handler, and C raises an exception, execution will jump from C directly to A. All of the state information on the stack for C, B, and A will be thrown away. If you imagine the call stack as something like A->B->C, then when C raises an exception, the exception-handler search will look on the stack for an exception-handler marker in C (and find none), then work its way back up the stack through procedure B (and find none), and then back up the stack still further to procedure A, where it finds a marker for an exception handler.

Exception handling is also different from traditional error handling in that it can dramatically change the execution path of a program. That can take some getting used to, but it is a key strength of exception handling. It means that code that is going to use the results of a calculation, or that is waiting for a subroutine call to return a value, will not be executed if an exception is raised in that calculation or subroutine because the exception will zoom past them in its search for an exception handler.

The result of all this is that exceptions can allow you to write code to assume that if you can obtain the results of a subroutine call or calculation, those results must be valid. The justification is that if the subroutine encountered an error that would prevent it from returning valid results, the subroutine is expected to raise an exception. That exception protects the calling routine from having to deal with invalid data, and that means the caller does not have to dedicate as much code or run-time performance to check every operation and subroutine call for errors.

Used responsibly, exceptions can help you write most of your middle-level code in a straightforward, get-the-job-done manner, without all the distractions or overhead of checking for error flags in every other statement. Data checking doesn't go away—your low-level routines that synthesize or obtain data will still need to perform data checks as before, but now those routines can raise an exception to signal invalid data instead of reserving data values (like 0 or -1) to indicate error states. Exceptions can streamline your code by removing the error-communication mechanism from the midst of your everyday program logic and replacing it with an automatic and reliable built-in error communication system that kicks in only when rare, *exceptional* situations arise.

If you find yourself writing an exception handler for nearly every individual statement in your program, you've missed the point. If you often find yourself reading code and thinking, "If execution made it this far, everything prior to this must have gone well," you've got the right idea.

Now that you have an idea of how exceptions work in general, let's look at Delphi's Object Pascal language features that support raising and handling exceptions.

The *try-finally* Construct

The first form of exception handling deals with protecting resources, such as dynamic memory, files, Windows resources, and objects. The `try-finally` statement ensures that the program executes statements that release resources whether or not an exception is raised. If entered by an exception, a `try-finally` block does not kill the exception—after the `finally` code is executed, the exception goes on to the next eligible exception handler.

Syntax

The General Syntax for the *try-finally* Block

```
resource allocating statements

try

 other statements

finally

 resource releasing statements

end;
```

The `try` clause contains the statements that might raise an exception. The `finally` clause contains the statements that release the resources. When an exception is raised in a statement in the `try` block, execution jumps to the `finally` clause, the code in the `finally` clause is executed, and then the search for an exception handler is resumed. If no exceptions occur in the `try` block, the `finally` clause is executed anyway, and program execution continues with the statement following the `try-finally` block. No matter what happens (short of a power failure), the code in the `finally` clause will always be executed as program execution exits the `try` block.

Example:

```
procedure TForm1.TestBtnClick(Sender: TObject);

const MAX = 100;

var i, j: Integer;
  d: ^Integer;

begin
```

```
 GetMem(d, MAX * SizeOf(Integer));
 try
  j := 0;
  For i := 0 to MAX - 1 do
   d^ := 1000 div j;
  ListArray;
  inc(j);
  For i := 0 to MAX - 1 do
   d^ := 1000 div j;
  ListArray;
 finally
  FreeMem(d, MAX * SizeOf(Integer));
 end;
end;
```

This code example dynamically allocates an array of 100 integers in the `try` block. When the division statement raises an exception, the code execution jumps to the `finally` clause to deallocate the dynamic array, then jumps to the next-outward exception handler found on the call stack. If the code in the `try` block could complete without an exception (impossible in this example), the `finally` block would be executed to deallocate the dynamic array as part of normal operations.

DO	DON'T

DO allocate the various resources before the `try` block (if possible). This approach ensures that the `finally` block can handle proper resource deallocation.

DON'T shy away from including non-resource-related statements in the `finally` clause, if these statements must be executed whether or not an exception occurs.

The *try-except* Construct

The second kind of exception handler is the `try-except` statement. Code in the `except` block is executed only when an exception occurs, not during normal program execution. What's more, the `except` block can contain multiple exception handlers, each designed for a particular type of exception. When the code of an `except` block has been executed, the exception is killed—the search process ends and execution resumes at the statement following the `try-except` statement.

Syntax

The General Syntax for the *try-except* Block

```
try

 statements

except

 cleanup statements
```

```
end;
```

The try block contains the statements that may raise an exception. The except block contains the statements that perform a cleanup operation. When an error occurs in a statement in the try block, the program jumps to the except clause. If no error occurs, the program skips the except block statements.

Example:

```
procedure TForm1.TestBtnClick(Sender: TObject);

var z, y, x : Integer;

begin
 x := 100;
 y := 0;
 try
  z := x div y;
 except
  z := -1;
 end;
 MessageDlg('z = ' + IntToStr(z),
       mtInformation, [mbOK], 0);
end;
```

The above example divides two integers. When the division statement raises an exception, the code execution jumps to the except clause to assign -1 to the variable z. The code then displays the value of variable z in a message dialog box.

The *on-do* Clause

The except keyword is usually followed by a list of exception handlers made up of various on-do statements.

Syntax

The General Syntax for *on-do* Statements

```
try

 statements

except

 on exceptionclass1 do begin
   cleanup statements #1;
 end;
 on exceptionclass2 do begin
   cleanup statements #2;
 end;
 on exceptionclass3 do begin
   cleanup statements #3;
 end;
```

```
 other on-do statements
 else
  default cleanup statements;
end;
```

When an exception occurs in the `try` block, program execution jumps to the `except` clause, where the class type of each `on-do` statement is tested for type compatibility with the current exception instance. An `on-do` statement's type is compatible with the exception instance if it is equal to or an ancestor of the type of the exception object instance. (More on that in the next section.) If there is no compatible handler in the `except` clause, the `else` clause is executed, if present. If there is no matching exception handler and no `else` clause, the search for an exception handler continues with the next outward `try` block on the call stack.

Example:

```
procedure TForm1.TestBtnClick(Sender: TObject);

var z, y, x : Integer;

begin
 x := 100;
 y := 0;
 try
  z := x div y;
 except
  on EDivByZero do z := -1;
 end;
 MessageDlg('z = ' + IntToStr(z),
       mtInformation, [mbOK], 0);
end;
```

The above example divides two integers. When the division statement raises an exception, the code execution jumps to the `except` clause. This clause has the `on EDivByZero do` statement, which matches the division-by-zero error (see Table 14.1). The statement associated with this `on-do` clause assigns `-1` to the variable `z`. The code then displays the value of variable `z` in a message dialog box.

DO	DON'T

DO use the `on-do` statement to offer a specific response to particular exceptions.

DON'T systematically use the `else` clause because its statements end up handling unanticipated errors. In other words, use the `else` clause only when you *really* know what your code is doing!

Table 14.1 shows the *run-time library* (RTL) exceptions that are exported by the `SysUtils` unit.

Table 14.1. The run-time library (RTL) exceptions.

Value	Meaning
`EInOutError`	Input/output error, such as file not found or read past end of file.
`EOutOfMemory`	Insufficient space on the heap to complete the requested operation.
`EInvalidPointer`	Attempt to dispose of a pointer that points outside the heap. Usually, this means the pointer was already disposed of.
`EDivByZero`	Attempt to divide by zero (integer division).
`ERangeError`	Number or expression out of range.
`EIntOverflow`	Integer operation overflowed.
`EInvalidOp`	Processor encountered an invalid floating-point operation.
`EZeroDivide`	Attempt to divide by zero (floating-point math).
`EOverflow`	Floating-point operation overflowed.
`EUnderflow`	Floating-point operation underflowed.
`EInvalidCast`	Invalid typecast.
`EConvertError`	Numeric-to-string and string-to-number conversion error.
`EFault`	Base exception object from which all fault objects descend.
`EGPFault`	General protection fault, usually caused by an uninitialized pointer or object.
`EStackFault`	Illegal access to the processor's stack segment.
`EPageFault`	The Windows memory manager was unable to correctly use the swap file.
`EInvalidOpCode`	Processor encountered an undefined instruction. This usually means the processor was trying to execute data or uninitialized memory.
`EBreakpoint`	The application generated a breakpoint interrupt.
`ESingleStep`	The application generated a single-step interrupt.

Nested Exception Handlers

Delphi allows you to nest the `try-finally` and `try-except` handlers. *Nested* handlers enable you to implement a sophisticated scheme to handle an exception.

Syntax

The General Syntax for Nested *try* Blocks

```
try
 statements
 try
   statements
 {except ¦ finally}
   cleanup code
 end;
{except¦finally}
 cleanup code
end;
```

The above syntax shows you that you can nest `try-finally` blocks, `try-except` blocks, and the combination of these `try` blocks. You can nest exception blocks in any combination and to any depth.

Reraising an Exception

When you want a piece of code to execute only in the event of an error, that code should go in an `except` block exception handler. However, you often don't want your cleanup code to be responsible for the full handling of the exception, including reporting the error to the user—you just want some code to execute in an error condition, and then permit the exception to proceed in its quest for the next exception handler.

Delphi provides the keyword `raise` to support reraising the current exception. The following example shows one use of nested `try` blocks and re-raising an exception:

```
type
 PXRef = ^TXRef;
 TXRef = record
  Name: String[10];
  Link1: Integer;
  Link2: Integer;
 end;

function LoadXRefTable(const Filename: String): TList;
var
 F: Text;
 X, Count: Integer;
 Node: PXRef;
begin
 Assign(F, Filename);
```

```
Reset(F);
try
 Readln(F, Count);
 Result := TList.Create;
 try
  for X := 1 to Count do
  begin
   New(Node);
   Result.Add(Node);
   Readln(F, Node^.Name);
   Readln(F, Node^.Link1);
   if (Node^.Link1 > MaxLinks) or (Node^.Link1 < 0) then
    raise Exception.CreateFmt('Invalid Link1 (%d) in node "%s".',
                [Node^.Link1, Node^.Name]);
   Readln(F, Node^.Link2);
   if (Node^.Link2 > MaxLinks) or (Node^.Link2 < 0) then
    raise Exception.CreateFmt('Invalid Link2 (%d) in node "%s".',
                [Node^.Link2, Node^.Name]);
  end;
 except
  for X := 0 to Result.Count-1 do
   Dispose(PXRef(Result[X]));
  Result.Free;
  raise;
 end;
finally
 Close(F);
end;
end;
```

This example has a `try-except` statement nested inside a `try-finally` statement. The outer `try-finally` statement ensures that the file handle will be closed in the course of normal execution and in the event of an exception. The inner `except` block will be executed only if an exception (any exception) occurs during the reading of the file and creation of nodes in the list. That `except` block ensures that memory allocated to the incomplete list is destroyed before allowing the exception to proceed to the next outward exception handler. There is no need to assign an error-indicating data value to `Result` (like `nil`) because all error conditions in this routine will exit the routine via an exception. Therefore, in the event of an error, the caller will never get the opportunity to use the function result. `Raise` by itself reraises the currently active exception.

The Exception Class

The current trend in OOP languages that support exception-handling statements such as the `try` block is to manage exceptions using classes and their instances. This section looks at how Delphi applies the programming trend of using classes to manage exceptions.

The *Exception* Class

Delphi provides the class `Exception` as the root of its exception classes. Any class can be used to raise an exception, but the convention is to use descendants of `Exception` to raise exceptions. The `SysUtils` unit defines exception classes (see Table 14.1) as descendants of class `Exception`. Some of the classes in Table 14.1 are not direct descendants of the class `Exception`. Instead, they are descendants of other classes that are in turn the direct descendants of `Exception`. For example, the `SysUtils` unit declares the class `EProcessException` as a descendant of class `Exception` and the parent or ancestor of classes `EFault`, `EGPFault`, `EStackFault`, `EPageFault`, `EInvalidOpCode`, `EBreakpoint`, and `ESingleStep`.

Declaring New Exception Classes

You can easily declare your own exception class as a descendant of class `Exception`.

Syntax

The General Syntax for Declaring an Exception Class

```
Type
  exceptionClassName = class (Exception);
  exceptionClassName = class (Exception)
   fields
  end;
```

This syntax shows two forms of exception classes. The first form merely declares the custom exception class name. The second form includes fields that can store information that describes the state of the custom exception class.

Example:

```
Type
   ECalcOpError = class(Exception);
   ECalcOprErr = class(Exception)
   public
   ErrCode: integer;
   ErrMsg: string;
  end;
```

The above example declares the class `ECalcOpError` as a descendant of class `Exception`. This declaration includes no fields. By contrast, the class `ECalcOprErr` includes the fields `ErrCode` and `ErrMsg`, which allows the exception to carry more information about the error condition from the site of the error to the exception handler.

DO	DON'T

DO declare fields in exception classes to support multiple states for the custom exception.

DON'T declare non-public fields in custom exception classes unless you also declare methods to access these fields.

Handling New Exceptions

To define new exception classes, just create a class type like any other. By convention, exception classes are usually descendants of the `Exception` base class, but this is not a language requirement.

To raise your new exception, use the same syntax shown earlier: `raise` followed by an instance of your exception class. This instance is usually created on-the-fly by calling the class's constructor.

You don't have to do anything to destroy an exception instance that is raised. The exception instance will be destroyed as soon as the exception is handled.

Using Exception Instances

One reason for using object instances in exception handling is so that information about the error condition can be carried from the site of the error to the handler of the error. But how does the exception handler access the data in the exception object instance? By declaring an exception instance identifier in the `on` clause, as in the following:

Syntax

The General Syntax for Using Exception Instances

```
try
 { statements which raise an exception }
except
on AnIdentifier : exceptionClassName do
 begin
 { statements which use AnIdentifier to access the fields
  of the exception instance of type exceptionClassName }
 end;
end;
```

Example:

```
procedure TForm1.CalcBtnClick(Sender: TObject);

var x, y, z : Integer;
```

```
begin
 y := 0;
 x := 1;
 try
  z := x div y;
 except
  on ErrorInstance : EDivByZero do
    MessageDlg(ErrorInstance.Message,
          mtInformation, [mbOK], 0);
 end;
end;
```

The preceding code example declares the identifier `ErrorInstance` in the `on` clause and uses that instance identifier to access the `Message` field of the exception instance.

Note: The `on E: ExceptionClassName do` syntax does *not* declare a new variable `E` (with its own memory address), but merely declares a new identifier that maps onto the already existing exception object instance in memory. You do not initialize `E`, nor do you destroy `E`. The exception instance identifier simply gives you access to an object instance in memory that is created elsewhere and will be destroyed elsewhere.

Let's look at an example that uses exception handlers. The next program project, CALC1, represents a command-oriented calculator shown in Figure 14.1. The form has the following controls:

- The edit box with the associated label Operand 1. You type in the first operand in this edit box.
- The edit box with the associated label Operator. You type in the operator in this edit box. The program supports the operators `+`, `[nd]`, `/`, and `*`.
- The edit box with the associated label Operand 2. You type in the second operand in this edit box.
- The edit box with the associated label Result. This edit box displays the result of the operation you request.
- The Execute button, which performs the operation you specify in the Operator edit box.
- The Close button, which closes the application.

The program handles the following errors:

- Typing in numbers with bad formats, which causes subroutines like `StrToInt` to raise the predefined exception `EConvertError`.

- Typing in an invalid operator, which causes the program code to raise a custom exception.
- Performing operations that cause an overflow, underflow, or division-by-zero errors.

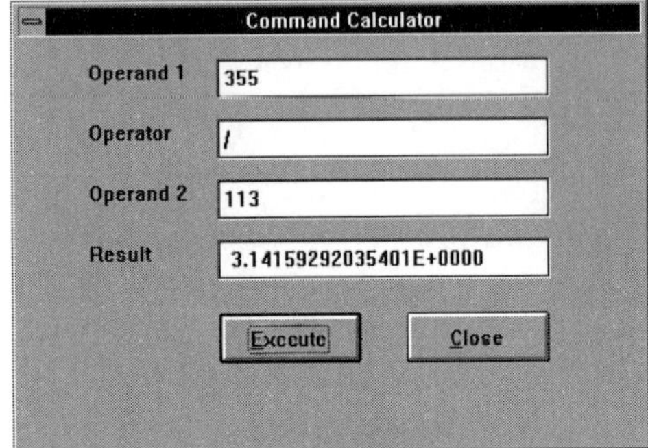

Figure 14.1.
The Command Calculator screen.

Table 14.2 shows the table of components and customized properties. Listing 14.1 shows the source code for the CALC1 program. The bold lines show the code you need to insert to customize the program. The program has two event-handling methods, namely, `CloseBtnClick` and `ExecuteBtnClick`.

Table 14.2. The customized properties of the form and components of the CALC1 program project.

Component	Property	New Value
`Form1`	Caption	Command Calculator
`Edit1`	Text	(empty string)
	Name	Operand1Box
`Edit2`	Text	(empty string)
	Name	OperatorBox
`Edit3`	Text	(empty string)
	Name	Operand2Box
`Edit4`	Text	(empty string)
	Name	ResultBox
`Label1`	Caption	Operand 1
	Name	Operand1Lbl
`Label2`	Caption	Operator
	Name	OperatorLbl
`Label3`	Caption	Operand 2
	Name	Operand2Lbl

Component	Property	New Value
Label4	Caption	Result
	Name	ResultLbl
Button1	Caption	&Execute
	Name	ExecuteBtn
Button2	Caption	&Close
	Name	CloseBtn
	ModalResult	

Listing 14.1. The source code for the CALC1 program.

```
unit Ucalc1;

interface

uses
 SysUtils, WinTypes, WinProcs, Messages, Classes,
 Graphics, Controls, Forms, Dialogs, StdCtrls;

type
         TForm1 = class(TForm)
          Operand1Box: TEdit;
          Operand1Lbl: TLabel;
          OperatorLbl: TLabel;
          OperatorBox: TEdit;
          Operand2Lbl: TLabel;
          Operand2Box: TEdit;
          ResultBox: TEdit;
          ExecuteBtn: TButton;
          CloseBtn: TButton;
          ResultLbl: TLabel;
          procedure CloseBtnClick(Sender: TObject);
          procedure ExecuteBtnClick(Sender: TObject);
         private
          { Private declarations }
         public
          { Public declarations }
         end;

         EOperatorErr = class(Exception);

        var
         Form1: TForm1;

        implementation

        {$R *.DFM}

        procedure TForm1.CloseBtnClick(Sender: TObject);
```

continues

Listing 14.1. continued

```
39:        begin
40:         Close;
41:        end;
42:
43:        procedure TForm1.ExecuteBtnClick(Sender: TObject);
44:
45:        var
46:         x, y, z : real;
47:
48:        begin
49:          { clear result box }
50:          ResultBox.Text := '';
51:          { obtain the first operand }
52:          x := StrToFloat(OperandBox1.Text);
53:          { obtain the second operand }
54:          y := StrToFloat(OperandBox2.Text);
55:          { execute the operation }
56:          case OperatorBox.Text[1] of
57:           '+': z := x + y;
58:           '-': z := x - y;
59:           '*': z := x * y;
60:           '/': z := x / y;
61:          else
62:           raise EOperatorError.CreateFmt(
63:               'Invalid operator: "%s"',[OperatorBox.Text[1]]);
64:          end;
65:          { display the result }
66:          ResultBox.Text := FloatToStr(z)
67:
68:        end;
69:
70:        end.
```

Listing 14.1 shows the customized code in bold lines. Line 29 declares the custom exception class `EOperatorErr` as a descendant of class `Exception`.

Lines 43 to 68 implement the method `ExecuteBtnClick`. Line 46 declares local variables used in the calculation.

Line 52 obtains the string from the Operand 1 edit box, converts the string to a number, and then stores that number in the local variable `x`. The `SysUtils` function `StrToFloat` performs the conversion and checks for errors. If the string cannot be converted into a number, `StrToFloat` will raise an `EConvertError` exception.

Line 54 obtains the second operand from the Operand 2 edit box, just as was done for the first operand.

Line 56 extracts the operator character from the Operator edit box and uses a `case` statement to execute the requested operation and store the result in the local variable `z`. If the operator character doesn't match any of the `case` selections, the `else` clause is executed, which raises an `EOpErr` exception.

Line 66 converts the value of variable `z` into a string and copies that string to the Result edit box.

Notice that this code does not perform any explicit exception handling. That's because the default VCL exception handler will display the exception message in a message box. All you have to do to ensure that the user is informed of his error is to raise exceptions as needed and use subroutines that raise exceptions.

Notice that there is no special code to avoid copying `z` into the `ResultBox` edit box in the event of an error. This might be necessary with traditional error-checking code, but because calculation overflows or data conversion problems will raise exceptions in this program, you can safely assume that if execution reaches line 66, everything prior to that went well, and therefore `z` contains valid data that should be displayed.

Finally, notice that there is no special code to pre-check the operands for special values, like zero in a division operation. If you were to check for that situation explicitly, all you would do would be to display an error message to the user—which the division by zero exception will do automatically with no work on your part.

It's no small irony that the pinnacle example of the chapter on exception handling doesn't contain an exception handler. That's the way most of your code will be written, and that's the whole point of exception handling—let the system take care of processing and reporting the errors that come up.

Run-Time Type Information

Run-time type information (RTTI) involves the management and query of data types at run-time. The next sections discuss topics common to RTTI.

Value Typecasting

Value typecasting is the operation of changing the type of an expression to another type. The expression type and the specified type must both be either an ordinal type or a pointer type. In the case of ordinal types, the resulting value is obtained by modifying the expression, which may include truncation or extension of the original value if the size of the specified type is different from that of the expression. In cases where the value is extended, the conversion process maintains the sign of the value.

14

Variable Typecasting

Delphi offers the operator `as` to allow you to perform a safe typecasting of a variable or a class instance. The operator `as` tests the types of variables at run-time and then carries out safe typecasting. The `as` operator performs safe typecasts by combining the test performed by the operator `is` with a typecast.

Syntax

The General Syntax for the *as* Operator

```
AnObject as TObjectType
```

This syntax is equivalent to

```
if AnObject is TObjectType then

 TObjectType(AnObject)

else

 raise EInvalidCast.Create;
```

Using the operator as raises an `EInvalidCast` exception if `AnObject` is not of a compatible type.

Example:

```
type

 EDivByZeroErr = class(Exception);

var
 Err: Exception;
 XErr: EDivByZeroErr;

begin
    try
       Err := XErr as Exception;
    except
       on EInvalidCast do
           MessageDlg('Invalid conversion',
                 mtInformation, [mbOK], 0);
    end;

end;
```

This example uses the operator as to typecast the variable `XErr` (an instance of class `EDivByZeroErr`) into an `Exception` type.

Object Type Checking

Delphi offers the Boolean operator `is` to test whether one class is type-compatible with another—that is, whether the type of the left operand is equal to or a descendant of the type of the second operand.

Syntax

The General Syntax for the *is* Operator

```
AnObject is TObjectType
```

This statement returns `TRUE` if the instance `AnObject` is of type `TObjectType`, or a descendant of `TObjectType`.

Example:

```
begin
if EditBox is TEdit then
TextMmo.Lines.String[0] := TEdit(EditBox).Text
end;
```

The above example tests if the variable `EditBox` is an instance of class `TEdit` before executing the statement in the `then` clause.

Class References

Delphi supports the creation of *class references*, which are special pointers to classes. Class reference variables don't carry object instance information, but instead carry type information. With a class reference variable, you can achieve a kind of polymorphism in constructing object instances: You can write code that doesn't know exactly what type it is constructing until that line of code gets executed at run-time.

The Delphi IDE uses this polymorphism of instance creation all the time, in the Component Palette. Imagine that the Component Palette contains an array `CompList` of class references. You could fill that array with the types of the many components: `CompList[1] := TMenu; CompList[2] := TButton;` and so on.

Now, when you click on an item in the Component Palette, you're selecting an index into that array. When you click on the form, all the IDE has to do to create an instance of the kind of component you clicked on is this: `CompList[n].Create(Form1);`

Syntax

Declaring Class References

```
Type
classRef = class of classType;
Var
classRefVar: classRef;
```

The `classRef` represents the class reference to class `classType`. The `classRefVar` is a class reference variable.

Example:

```
type

 TClassRef = class of TChildClass1;
 TChildClass1 = class(TObject)
  public
   field1: Integer;
 end;
 TChildClass2 = class(TChildClass1)
  public
   field2: Integer;
 end;

var
 ClassRef: TClassRef;
 AChild1, AChild2: TChildClass1;
begin
 ClassRef := TChildClass1;
 AChild1 := ClassRef.Create;
 ClassRef := TChildClass2;
 AChild2 := ClassRef.Create;
 writeln(AChild1.ClassName); { displays TChildClass1 }
 writeln(AChild2.ClassName); { displays TChildClass2 }
end;
```

The preceding code example shows you that the instance of reference class `TClassRef` can access the method `Create` of the instances of classes `TChildClass1` and `TChildClass2`. The statements to create `AChild1` and `AChild2` look the same, but because the type stored in the class reference variable was different for each statement, the type of instance created is different. The `writeln` statements prove that the types of the object instances created are different.

Summary

Today's lesson discussed handling run-time errors and run-time data type information. You learned about the following topics:

- An *exception* is a notification of a run-time error or other situation that requires abandoning the normal flow of program execution.
- Delphi provides the `try-finally` and `try-except` statements to support resource protection and exception handling, respectively. You also learned that you can use the `on-do` statements in the `except` clause to handle specific exceptions.
- Delphi uses object instances to carry information about the error condition signaled by raising an exception. (Table 14.1 lists the RTL exception classes.) You also learned that you can define and raise your own exceptions.
- Run-time type information (RTTI), which includes using the operators `as` and `is`, and using class reference variables. The Boolean operator `is` determines if an instance

is of a specific class. The operator as performs a safe typecasting operation. The text showed you that class reference variables can be used to create object instances polymorphically.

Q&A

Q Can I place a `try-except` statement inside an `except` block?

A Yes, you can. Here is a trivial example of placing a `try-except` statement inside an `except` block:

```
procedure TForm1.Button1Click(Sender: Tobject);

var x, y, z, w : integer;

begin
 try
  x := 1;
  y := 0;
  z := x div y;
 except
  on EDivByZero do begin
   z := -1;
   try
    w := x div y;
   except
   on EDivByZero do
    w := -1;
   end
  end;
 end

end;
```

Q What would placing a `try-except` statement inside an `except` block achieve?

A This scheme empowers you to deal with secondary exceptions that arise from dealing with the main exceptions.

Q How do I implement a silent exception handler?

A Use the `Abort` statement, which prevents the display of the exception message dialog box in the VCL default exception handler.

Q Does the `is` operator work with class references in the context of class references (that is, can I write the statement like `AnObject is a class TObject`)?

A No, the operator `is` does not work in a broad sense.

Workshop

The Workshop provides quiz questions to help you solidify your understanding of the material covered and exercises to provide you with experience in using what you've learned. Try to understand the quiz and exercise answers before continuing on to the next day's lesson.

Quiz

1. What is wrong with the following code?

```
procedure TForm1.TestBtnClick(Sender: Tobject);

const MAX = 100;

var i, j: Integer;
 d: ^Integer;

begin
 try
  GetMem(d, MAX * SizeOf(Integer));
  j := 0;
  For i := 0 to MAX - 1 do
   d^ := 1000 div j;
  ListArray;
  inc(j);
  For i := 0 to MAX - 1 do
   d^ := 1000 div j;
  ListArray;
 except
  FreeMem(d, MAX * SizeOf(Integer));
 end;
end;
```

2. True or False? The order of the `on-do` statement in an `except` block is relevant.

3. True or False? The following expression that uses the `is` operator yields `TRUE`.

```
Type
 ClassA = class
  public
   field1: integer;
 end;
 ClassB = class(ClassA)
  public
   field2: integer;
 end;

Var B: ClassB;
 Ok: Boolean;

Begin
 ...
 Ok := B is ClassA;
 ...
End;
```

4. How can you implement the operator `as` if you only have the operator `is`?

Exercise

1. Create program CALC2 from program CALC1 by adding support to the ^ power operator. Implement this operation using the statement `z := exp(y * ln(x));`.

14

WEEK 2 IN REVIEW

8 9 10 11 12 13 14

Congratulations! You have reached the end of the second week of your Delphi training. One of the most important issues discussed during this week was the notion of object-oriented programming. You have also completed the tutorial on Object Pascal.

- You learned how to define your own data types, including structured and enumerated data-types that greatly extend the capabilities of Object Pascal.
- You became acquainted with various Pascal data-types, including arrays, records, sets, enumerated types, subranges of ordinal types, and character strings.
- You now understand how subroutines are built and that there are two kinds of subroutines in Pascal: procedures and functions.
- You've gained an understanding of the fundamental concepts of object-oriented programming, the concepts of encapsulation, inheritance, and polymorphism, and how they can be used to your advantage.

- You understand the meaning of directives such as `virtual`, `dynamic`, and `message`, and how methods declared with one of these directives are different from static methods.
- You've learned the mechanisms of exception handling and how exceptions can help you make your code cleaner and more streamlined.

The third week of Delphi training will take you to some of the more advanced concepts of programming with Delphi.

WEEK 3

AT A GLANCE

15

16

17

18

19

20

21

This last week of study starts off by showing you how programs are constructed from numerous building blocks, how these blocks interconnect, and how they depend on one another.

Later in the week you'll be introduced to a number of techniques and areas of concern in Windows programming, including drawing, painting, and printing, creating your own custom Delphi components and dynamic link libraries.

One of this week's lessons, Day 19, is entirely devoted to the issue of database programming with Delphi. You'll learn how to access data tables and how easy it is to set up and manage a one-to-many relationship using standard Delphi data-aware components.

WEEK
3

Program Architecture Blocks

by Namir Shammas

This chapter discusses the Pascal program blocks as another kind of program component. It looks at how to manage variables in these blocks and also covers the topic of open arrays. Open array parameters play a pivotal role in creating general-purpose routines that process arrays of different sizes. In this chapter you will learn about the following topics:

- Scope of identifiers
- Visibility of identifiers
- Types of variables
- Open array parameters
- Open string parameters
- On-the-fly open arrays
- Type-safe open arrays

Scope of Identifiers

The scope of an identifier is its life span in a sequence of declarations and statements. Therefore, the scope of an identifier determines its accessibility. The next subsections discuss how different program components affect the scope of identifiers.

Note: The scope of an identifier begins where it is declared and ends at the end of the code block enclosing the declaration. For example, the scope of a constant, variable, type, or other symbol declared in a procedure ends with that procedure's `end` statement.

Scope in the Units

A unit is made up of an interface section and an implementation section. The identifiers declared in the interface section are accessible to all other units and programs that use the unit. In addition, the identifiers (especially constants, data types, variables, classes, and objects) are accessible to the implementation section. In contrast, the identifiers declared in the implementation sections are strictly local to that section. Once you declare a constant, data type, variable, class, or an object in the implementation section, it is accessible to subsequent constants, data types, variables, classes, objects, and all the routine implementations.

Here is an example of a simple unit:

```
unit MyArray;

interface
```

```
const MYARRAY_SIZE = 100;

type ArrayType = array [1..MYARRAY_SIZE] of String;

procedure Init(var arr : ArrayType;
               initVal : real);
procedure sort(var arr : ArrayType;
               numElems : Integer);
function binarySearch(var arr : ArrayType;
                      key : String;
                      numElems : Integer) : Integer;
function linearSearch(var arr : ArrayType;
                      key : String
                      numElems : Integer) : Integer;

implementation

function checkIndex(index : Integer) : Boolean;
begin
  { statements to validate index }
end;

procedure swap(var arr : ArrayType;
               index1, index2 : Integer);
begin
  { swap elements at indices index1 and index2 }
end;

procedure Init(var arr : ArrayType;
               initVal : real);
begin
  { statements to initialize array elements }
end;

procedure sort(var arr : ArrayType;
               numElems : Integer);
begin
  { statements to sort array elements }
end;

function binarySearch(var arr : ArrayType;
                      key : String;
                      numElems : Integer) : Integer;
begin
  { statements to search in ordered array elements }
end;

function linearSearch(var arr : ArrayType;
                      key : String
                      numElems : Integer) : Integer;
begin
  { statements to search in unordered array elements }
end;

end.
```

This unit declares the following identifiers in the interface section:

- The constant MYARRAY_SIZE.
- The array type ArrayType.
- The procedure Init.
- The procedure sort.
- The function binarySearch.
- The function linearSearch.

These identifiers are accessible to all unit clients (or users, if you prefer). The constant and data type are also accessible in the implementation section. The implementation section declares the following identifiers:

- The function checkIndex.
- The procedure swap.

These identifiers are accessible only to the implementations of the routines declared in the interface section. No client unit or client program can use the routines checkIndex and swap.

Scope in the Main Program

The source code for the main program unit may declare constants, data types, classes, variables, objects, functions, and procedures. The procedures and functions have access to the constants, data types, classes, variables, and objects that are already declared in the main program (or imported from units). Here is an example of a main program:

```
program myProgram;

const MYARRAY_SIZE = 100;

type ArrayType = array [1..MYARRAY_SIZE] of String;

var i, j, k : Integer
    elem : real;

function checkIndex(index : Integer) : Boolean;
begin
  { statements to validate index }
end;

procedure swap(var arr : ArrayType;
               index1, index2 : Integer);
begin
  { swap elements at indices index1 and index2 }
end;

procedure Init(var arr : ArrayType;
               initVal : real);
begin
```

```
  { statements to initialize array elements }
end;

procedure sort(var arr : ArrayType;
               numElems : Integer);
begin
  { statements to sort array elements }
end;

function binarySearch(var arr : ArrayType;
                      key : String;
                      numElems : Integer) : Integer;
begin
  { statements to search in ordered array elements }
end;

function linearSearch(var arr : ArrayType;
                      key : String
                      numElems : Integer) : Integer;
begin
  { statements to search in unordered array elements }
end;

procedure getArray(var arr : ArrayType;
                   numElems : Integer);
begin
  { statements to obtain array }
end;

var myArray : ArrayType;

begin
  { statements to manipulate the array }
end.
```

This program declares the following identifiers:

- ☐ The constant `MYARRAY_SIZE`.
- ☐ The array type `ArrayType`.
- ☐ The variable `elem`.
- ☐ The variables `i`, `j`, and `k`.
- ☐ The procedure `Init`.
- ☐ The procedure `sort`.
- ☐ The function `binarySearch`.
- ☐ The function `linearSearch`.
- ☐ The function `checkIndex`.
- ☐ The procedure `swap`.
- ☐ The procedure `getArray`.
- ☐ The variable `myArray`.

The constant MYARRAY_SIZE, data type ArrayType, and variables elem, i, j, and k are accessible to the routines declared in the main program. In contrast, the variable myArray is not, because it is declared after the program's routine. The scope of the variable myArray is the main begin-end block. The other variables are accessible in the begin-end blocks of the program's routines as well as the main begin-end block.

Scope in Routines

Procedures and functions declare parameters and local identifiers (constants, data types, variables, and nested routines). The scope of the parameters and local identifiers is limited to the host routine and any nested routines. No program component *outside* the routine may access the routine's parameters and local identifiers. The parameters and local identifiers of a routine have the same block level, which is one level deeper than the host program component.

Here is a new version of myProgram that shows detailed implementation of the function linearSearch. Also notice that the program no longer declares variables elem, i, j, and k.

```
program myProgram;

const MYARRAY_SIZE = 100;

type ArrayType = array [1..MYARRAY_SIZE] of String;


function checkIndex(index : Integer) : Boolean;
begin
  { statements to validate index }
end;

procedure swap(var arr : ArrayType;
               index1, index2 : Integer);
begin
  { swap elements at indices index1 and index2 }
end;

procedure Init(var arr : ArrayType;
               initVal : real);
begin
  { statements to initialize array elements }
end;

procedure sort(var arr : ArrayType;
               numElems : Integer);
begin
  { statements to sort array elements }
end;

function binarySearch(var arr : ArrayType;
                      key : String;
                      numElems : Integer) : Integer;

begin
```

```
  { statements to search in ordered array elements }
end;

function linearSearch(var arr : ArrayType;
                      key : String
                      numElems : Integer) : Integer;

var notFound : Boolean;
    i : Integer;

begin
  i := 1;
  notFound := True;
  while (i <= numElems) and notFound do begin
    if arr[i] <> key then
      inc(i)
    else
      notFound := False;
  end;
  if notFound then
    Result := -1
  else
    Result := i;
end;

procedure getArray(var arr : ArrayType;
                   numElems : Integer);
begin
  { statements to obtain array }
end;

var myArray : ArrayType;

begin
  { statements to manipulate the array }
end.
```

The function declares the parameters `arr`, `key`, and `numElems`. The scope of these identifiers is limited to the function's body. The function also declares the local variables `notFound` and `i`. The scope of these identifiers is also limited to the function's body. No other external routine or program component can access the parameters or local variables.

Scope in Nested Routines

Nested routines can access the identifiers declared in the host unit or program component and in the parent routine. The parameters and local identifiers of nested routines are accessible only to these routines and their own nested routines. The parameters and local identifiers of a nested routine have a block level that is lower than the host routine. Here is an example that uses an implementation of the function `sort` with a nested routine `fastSwap`.

```
procedure sort(var arr : ArrayType;
               numElems : Integer);
```

```
  var inOrder : Boolean;

  procedure fastSwap(i1, i2 : Integer);

  var temp : real;

  begin
    temp := arr[i1];
    arr[i1] := arr[i2]
    arr[i2] := temp;
    inOrder := False;
  end;

  var offset, i, j : Integer;

begin
  offset := numElems;
  repeat
    offset := (8 * offset) div 11;
    if offset = 0 then offset := 1;
    inOrder := True;
    for i := 1 to numElems - offset do begin
      j := i + offset;
      if arr[i] > arr[j] then
        fastSwap(i, j);
    end;
  until (offset = 1) and inOrder;
end;

end;
```

The nested function `fastSwap` declares the parameters `i1` and `i2` and also declares the local variable `temp`. The nested function accesses the parameter `arr` and the variable `inOrder`, which is already declared in procedure `sort`. In contrast, the procedure `sort` cannot access the parameters and local variable of the nested routine `fastSwap`.

Scope in the Classes

Classes impose their own special rules for scoping. The public, protected, and private sections of a class define the scope of class components with regard to class instances and descendant classes. Table 15.1 summarizes the scope of class components.

Table 15.1. The scope of class components.

Fields/Methods	Class Methods	Access to Class Instances	Descendant Classes
Public	Yes	Yes	Yes
Protected	Yes	No	Yes
Private	Yes	No	No

Here is a simple example:

```
TStrArray = class
  public
    constructor Create(theMaxSize : Integer);
    destructor Destroy; override;
    function store(aVal: String;
                   index : Integer) : Boolean;
    function recall(var aVal: String;
                   index : Integer) : Boolean;
  protected
    data : ^string;
    maxSize : Integer;
    workSize : Integer;
  private
    function checkIndex(index : Integer) : Boolean;
end;

TSortedStrArray = class (TStrArray)
  public
    constructor Create(theMaxSize : Integer);
    destructor Destroy; override;
    procedure sort;
    function search(key : String) : Integer;

  protected
    isSorted: Boolean;
    function linearSearch(key : String) : Integer;
    function binarySearch(key : String) : Integer;

private
    procedure fastSwap(index1, index2 : Integer);
end;
```

This code declares the class `TStrArray`. This class declares the following public identifiers:

- The constructor `Create`.
- The destructor `Destroy`.
- The function `store`.
- The function `recall`.

These public identifiers can be accessed by all class methods, class instances, and descendant classes. The class declares the following protected identifiers:

- The field `data`.
- The field `maxSize`.
- The field `workSize`.

These protected identifiers can be accessed by all class methods and descendant classes. The class also declares the private function `checkIndex`. This method cannot be accessed by class instances or descendant classes.

The preceding code declares the descendant class `TSortedStrArray` as a descendant of class `TStrArray`. The descendant class can access all the public and protected identifiers of the parent class. The descendant class declares public, protected, and private identifiers that follow the same rules of accessibility as the parent class.

Visibility of Identifiers

The scope of an identifier deals with the existence of that identifier. Accessing that identifier is possible only if it is not overshadowed by another identifier with the same name that resides in a nested block. Here is an example:

```
program myProgram;

const MYARRAY_SIZE = 100;

type ArrayType = array [1..MYARRAY_SIZE] of String;

var arr : ArrayType;

function linearSearch(var arr : ArrayType;
                      key : String
                      numElems : Integer) : Integer;

var notFound : Boolean;
    i : Integer;

begin
  i := 1;
  notFound := True;
  while (i <= numElems) and notFound do begin
    if arr[i] <> key then
      inc(i)
    else
      notFound := False;
  end;
  if notFound then
    Result := -1
  else
    Result := i;
end;

procedure getArray(var arr : ArrayType;
                   numElems : Integer);
begin
  { statements to obtain array }
end;

begin
  { statements to manipulate the array }
end.
```

The program declares the variable `arr` before declaring the routines `linearSearch` and `getArray`.

These routines declare the array-parameter `arr`, which has the same name as the global array `arr`. Within each routine, the identifier `arr` refers to the parameter and not the global variable. In other words, the global variable `arr` is not visible inside the routines, even though its scope extends almost throughout the program. The global array `arr` is visible in the main `begin-end` block.

The Types of Variables

Delphi's Object Pascal supports three types of variables that differ in the way they are created and the way they maintain data. The next subsections discuss the different kinds of data types.

Automatic Variables

Most of the variables you employ in a program are automatic. That is, the run-time system creates them, initializes them, and then removes them. When the compiler comes across a `var` section, it creates run-time instructions to create that variable (by allocating a memory location for it). When the program execution reaches the end of that variable's scope, the run-time system removes that variable from memory. The advantages of using automatic variables are that they are easy to manage and the compiler determines their memory location and space requirements before you start running the program. The disadvantage of using automatic memory is that the variables lose their data once they are out of scope. This is especially true for variables declared inside routines.

Note: Automatic variables are not initialized to any particular value when they are allocated. Always assign a value into an automatic variable before using it in an expression or as a parameter.

The Static Variables

Static variables are those that reside inside routines and can maintain their values between calls to the routines. Delphi's Object Pascal supports static variables using typed constants. A typed constant is associated with an explicit data type and has an initial value.

Let's look at an example. The next program, STATVAR, has two buttons and a static label on a form. Table 15.2 shows the new settings for some of the properties of the components for the STATVAR program. Table 15.3 shows the list of events handled by the various components of program STATVAR. When you click on the Test Static Var button, you display the new value of the static variable using the static label component. The static variable resides in the method

`TestBtnClick`. Listing 15.1 shows the source code for the STATVAR1.PAS file. Figure 15.1 shows a sample session with program STATVAR.

Table 15.2. The new settings for some of the properties of the components for the STATVAR program.

Component	Property	New Value
Button1	Name	TestBtn
	Caption	&Test Static Var
Button2	Name	CloseBtn
	Caption	&Close
Label1	Name	StaticLbl
	Caption	Number is
Form1	Caption	Static Variable Demo

Table 15.3. The events handled by the various components of program STATVAR.

Component	Event	Event-Handler
CloseBtn	OnClick	CloseBtnClick
TestBtn	OnClick	TestBtnClick

Listing 15.1. The source code for the STATVAR1.PAS file.

```
unit Statvar1;

interface

uses
  SysUtils, WinTypes, WinProcs, Messages,
  Classes, Graphics, Controls,
  Forms, Dialogs, StdCtrls;

type
  TForm1 = class(TForm)
    StaticLbl: TLabel;
    TestBtn: TButton;
    CloseBtn: TButton;
    procedure CloseBtnClick(Sender: TObject);
    procedure TestBtnClick(Sender: TObject);
  private
    { Private declarations }
```

```
19:     public
20:       { Public declarations }
21:     end;
22:
23:   var
24:     Form1: TForm1;
25:
26:   implementation
27:
28:   {$R *.DFM}
29:
30:   procedure TForm1.CloseBtnClick(Sender: TObject);
31:   begin
32:     Close;
33:   end;
34:
35:   procedure TForm1.TestBtnClick(Sender: TObject);
36:
37:   const number : Integer = 1;
38:
39:   begin
40:     StaticLbl.Caption := 'Number is ' + IntToStr(number);
41:     inc(number);
42:   end;
43:
44:   end.
```

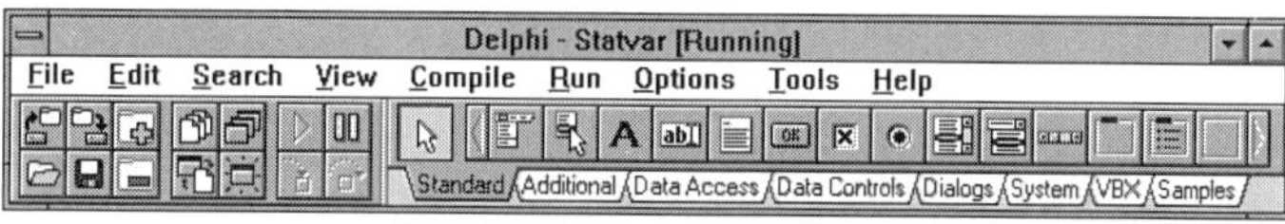

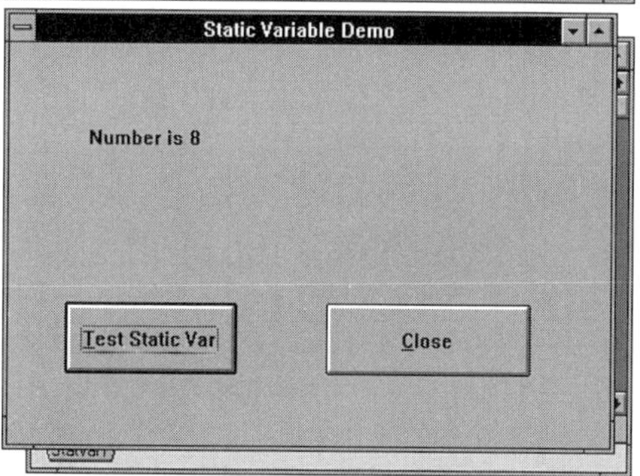

Figure 15.1.
A sample session with the program STATVAR.

Line 37 in Listing 15.1 declares the typed constant `number`. This identifier acts as a static variable. The source code initializes the static variable `number` with `1`. Every time you click the Test Static Var button, the method `TestBtnClick` displays the current value of variable `number` and then increments it. The variable number retains its current value between calls to method `TestBtnClick`.

The Dynamic Variables

Dynamic variables are created and removed at run-time. Such variables reside in the heap part of the memory. Dynamic variables are versatile because they can deal with different combinations of data at run-time. For example, you can use a dynamic variable to create an array with a size dictated by conditions determined during program execution. You create a dynamic array using the `GetMem` and `FreeMem` statements.

DO	DON'T

DO use dynamic variables to support dynamic structures (arrays, stacks, queues, trees, and so on) whose size depends on run-time conditions.

DON'T forget to remove a dynamic variable when it is no longer needed.

DON'T forget that dynamic variables are themselves nameless and are accessed using pointers.

Let's look at an example. The next program, DYNVAR, has two buttons and a static label on a form. Table 15.4 shows the new settings for some of the properties of the components for the DYNVAR program. Table 15.5 shows the list of events handled by the various components of the program DYNVAR. When you click on the Test Dynamic Var button, you display the new value of the dynamic variable using the static label component. Listing 15.2 shows the source code for the DYNVAR1.PAS file. Figure 15.2 shows a sample session with the program DYNVAR.

Table 15.4. The new settings for some of the properties of the components for the DYNVAR program.

Component	Property	New Value
Button1	Name	TestBtn
	Caption	&Test Dynamic Var
Button2	Name	CloseBtn
	Caption	&Close
Label1	Name	DynamicLbl
	Caption	Number is
Form1	Caption	Dynamic Variable Demo

Table 15.5. The events handled by the various components of program DYNVAR.

Component	Event	Event-Handler
CloseBtn	OnClick	CloseBtnClick
TestBtn	OnClick	TestBtnClick
Form1	OnCreate	FormCreate
	OnDestroy	FormDestroy

Listing 15.2. The source code for the DYNVAR1.PAS file.

```
unit Dynvar1;

interface

uses
  SysUtils, WinTypes, WinProcs, Messages,
  Classes, Graphics, Controls,
  Forms, Dialogs, StdCtrls;

type
  TForm1 = class(TForm)
    StaticLbl: TLabel;
    TestBtn: TButton;
    CloseBtn: TButton;
    procedure CloseBtnClick(Sender: TObject);
    procedure TestBtnClick(Sender: TObject);
    procedure FormCreate(Sender: TObject);
    procedure FormDestroy(Sender: TObject);
  private
    { Private declarations }
  public
    { Public declarations }
  end;

var
  Form1: TForm1;

implementation

{$R *.DFM}

var pNumber : ^Integer;

procedure TForm1.CloseBtnClick(Sender: TObject);
begin
  Close;
end;

```

continues

Listing 15.2. continued

```
39:  procedure TForm1.TestBtnClick(Sender: TObject);
40:  begin
41:    StaticLbl.Caption := 'Number is ' + IntToStr(pNumber^);
42:    inc(pNumber^);
43:  end;
44:
45:  procedure TForm1.FormCreate(Sender: TObject);
46:  begin
47:    new(pNumber);
48:    pNumber^ := 1;
49:  end;
50:
51:  procedure TForm1.FormDestroy(Sender: TObject);
52:  begin
53:    dispose(pNumber)
54:  end;
55:
56:  end.
```

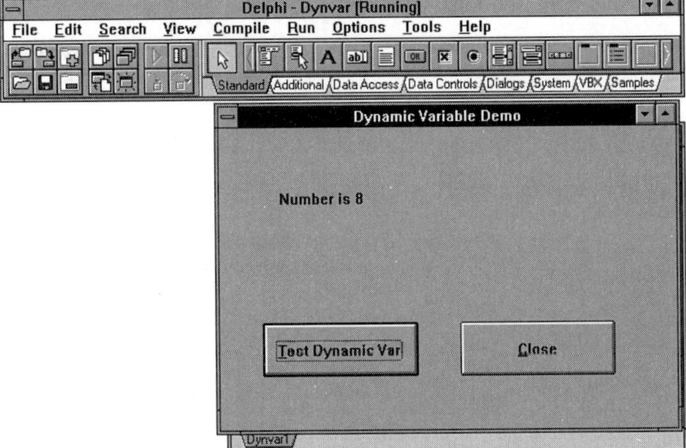

Figure 15.2.
A sample session with the program DYNVAR.

The implementation section of Listing 15.2 declares the pointer `pNumber` in line 32. This identifier is a pointer to an `Integer` type. The method `FormCreate` (lines 45 to 49) uses the `new` statement to allocate the space for the dynamic variable. The pointer `pNumber` accesses the dynamic variable. The method then assigns 1 to the dynamic variable. The method `TestBtnClick` (lines 39 to 43) displays the value of the dynamic variable and then increments its value. The method `FormDestroy` (lines 51 to 54) deallocates the dynamic variable using the `dispose` statement.

Open Parameters

One of the main keys to developing general-purpose routines is the ability to handle arrays of varying sizes. Pascal allows you to specify parameters that are array types having a specific number of elements. Such parameters require that their arguments be of the same data type. This requirement limits the usefulness of such routines. The other option is to use open arrays, which allow you to specify the basic array type but not the size. The argument for an open array parameter must have the same element type.

Syntax

The General Open Array Syntax

openArray : array of *elemType*

The parameter `openArray` has the basic data type `elemType` but has no fixed array size. The parameter `openArray` is mapped onto the index range `0` to `N-1`, where `N` is the number of elements in the argument of parameter `openArray`.

Example:

```
function sumArray(var arr : array of real) : real;
procedure linearRegression(var X, Y : array of real;
                           var slope, intercept, R2 : real);
```

The function `sumArray` has the parameter `arr`, which is an open array of `real`. The procedure `linearRegression` has two open array parameters, namely `X` and `Y`.

DO	DON'T

DO use open array parameters to develop general-purpose routines that manipulate arrays of data.

DON'T forget that the lowest index of an open array is *always* 0, not 1.

The Low and High Functions

The predefined functions `Low` and `High` return the lower and upper indices of an array, including an open array parameter. Use these functions (or at least function `High`) to process the entire array. Here is an example of implementing the function `sumArray` using the function `High`:

```
function sumArray(var arr : array of real) : real;
var i : word;
begin
  Result := 0.;
```

```
    { access all of the array elements }
    for i := 0 to High(arr) do
       Result := Result + arr[i];
  end;
```

This example uses the `for` loop to iterate over the range `0` to `High(arr)` to access the elements of the open array parameter `arr`.

DO	DON'T

DO use function `High` to accurately access the highest index of an open array parameter.

DON'T overload the stack by passing large array elements. To avoid overloading the stack, use the `var` or `const` in the declaration of open array parameters.

Strings as Open Arrays

The Pascal String type is limited to 255 characters. You can use `array of char` type to develop routines that process strings that can exceed the 255-character limit. The rule to watch is that such strings terminate with the null character (that is, ASCII 0, or #0). Such strings are called *ASCIIZ strings*. Here is an example of a procedure that converts an ASCIIZ string into uppercase:

```
procedure toUpcaseStr(var aStr : array of char);

var i : Integer;

begin
  i := 0;
  while (aStr[i] <> #0) and
        (i <= High(aStr)) do begin
    aStr[i] := UpCase(aStr[i]);
    inc(i);
  end;
end;
```

The arguments for parameter `aStr` are arrays of characters.

On-the-Fly Open Arrays

Delphi allows you to create an on-the-fly array and immediately use it as an argument to an open array parameter. This kind of array contains comma-delimited values contained in square brackets. Here is an example:

```
function sumArray(arr : array of real) : real;
var i : word;
```

```
begin
  Result := 0.;
  { access all of the array elements }
  for i := 0 to High(arr) do
     Result := Result + arr[i];
end;

sum := sumArray([1.2, 3.4, 6.5, 7.6, 3.8]);
```

This example uses the on-the-fly array `[1.2, 3.4, 6.5, 7.6, 3.8]`.

DO | **DON'T**

DO use on-the-fly arrays to pass relatively small arrays.

DON'T pass on-the-fly arrays as arguments to `var` open array parameters.

Type-Safe Open Arrays

Delphi supports a special kind of open array of `const`, which permits an open array of items of more than one data type to be safely passed to a procedure or to a function. One example of where this feature is used by Delphi is the `Format` string formatting routine that accepts varying numbers of items of diverse types. The following function declaration shows you how to use an `array of const` in the declaration of a string formatting function. The parameter `arguments` is an open array that holds any number of variables, each having any data type:

```
function Format(const formatStr : string;
                const arguments : array of const) : string;
```

The compiler regards the `array of const` as identical to the array of `TVarRec`. The `TVarRec` type is declared as follows:

```
const
  vtInteger  = 0;
  vtBoolean  = 1;
  vtChar     = 2;
  vtExtended = 3;
  vtString   = 4;
  vtPointer  = 5;
  vtPChar    = 6;
  vtObject   = 7;
  vtClass    = 8;

type
  TVarRec = record
    case Integer of
      vtInteger:  (VInteger: Longint; VType: Byte);
      vtBoolean:  (VBoolean: Boolean);
      vtChar:     (VChar: Char);
```

```
    vtExtended: (VExtended: PExtended);
    vtString:   (VString: PString);
    vtPointer:  (VPointer: Pointer);

    vtPChar:    (VPChar: PChar);
    vtObject:   (VObject: TObject);
    vtClass:    (VClass: TClass);
end;
```

The `VType` tag field allows the subroutine to know the simple type of each parameter passed in the open array. The `vt` integer constants are the values that may appear in the VType tag of the `TVarRec` structure.

Summary

This chapter discussed how to manage identifiers using different kinds and levels of blocks. You learned about the following topics:

- The scope of identifiers in units, the main program, routines, and nested routines. The text discussed how units show and hide identifiers, and how the main program shares identifiers with its routines. The chapter also discussed identifiers that are local to routines and nested routines.
- The visibility of identifiers in routines and nested routines. The text discussed how identifiers can mask other identifiers with the same name and type.
- The automatic, static, and dynamic variables. The chapter discussed how the run-time system creates and later removes automatic variables. Automatic variables are not initialized to any particular value. The text also discussed how to implement static local variables using typed constants. Such variables retain their values between routine calls. The text also discussed the creation and removal of dynamic variables, which are accessed by pointers.
- The support of the open array parameter syntax, which empowers you to write general-purpose routines. These routines are able to handle one-dimensional arrays with varying numbers of elements.
- The use of `array of char` parameters to manage null-terminated (also called ASCIIZ) strings. These strings exceed the 255-character limitation of the Borland Pascal String type.
- The extended syntax of Delphi Pascal, which supports on-the-fly open arrays. These arrays are arguments to open arrays that create a comma-delimited list of values and simultaneously use it as an argument to an open array parameter.

- The type-safe open array, `array of const`, is a general-purpose parameter structure that allows you to pass a variable number of parameters of various types to a routine, and allows the routine to know the number of parameters passed and the type of each.

Q&A

Q How do I resolve accessing two identifiers that have the same name and which are exported by two separate units?

A Use the unit name to qualify the access. Consider the following example. Your program uses units `unitA` and `unitB`, and both units export the identifier `WriteString`. To access each identifier, you use `unitA.WriteString` and `unitB.WriteString`.

Q What is the golden rule in placing variables at different block levels?

A Follow the "need to know" rule in placing variables. Do not give access to a variable unless it is needed.

Q Do the scoping rules in a program component, routines, and nested routines apply some kind of an inheritance scheme?

A Yes indeed. For example, the constants, types, and variables in a main program are accessible to the subsequently declared routines. The parameters, local constants, local types, and local variables in each routine are accessible to the subsequently declared nested routines, and so on. Each program component inherits the identifier declared in the host (or parent, if you prefer) program component.

Q Do open array parameters support two-dimensional arrays?

A Not directly. Open array parameters can support two-dimensional arrays by managing arrays of pointers. Each pointer handles a column or row in the two-dimensional array.

Q Why not use pointers to emulate open array parameters?

A You certainly can use pointers to emulate open array parameters. The advantage of open array parameters is the ability to use the function `High` to reliably get the highest array index. In addition, the implementation code for the open array parameter has the same syntax as normal arrays.

Workshop

The Workshop provides quiz questions to help you solidify your understanding of the material covered and exercises to provide you with experience in using what you've learned. Try to understand the quiz and exercise answers before continuing on to the next day's lesson.

Quiz

1. Where is the error in the following code?

```
unit FileIO;

interface

   procedure WriteReal(x : real);

implementation

   procedure WriteReal(x : real);
   begin
   { implementation statements }
   end;

end.

unit ScreenIO;

interface

   procedure WriteReal(x : real);

implementation

   procedure WriteReal(x : real);
   begin
   { implementation statements }
   end;

end.

program IO;

uses FileIO, ScreenIO;

procedure getReal(var x : real);
begin
  { implementation statements }
```

15

```
end;

var x : real;

begin
  getReal(x);
  WriteReal(x);
end.
```

2. Where is the error in the following code?

```
program myProgram;

const MYARRAY_SIZE = 100;

var i, j, k : Integer
    elem : real;

function checkIndex(index : Integer) : Boolean;
begin
  { statements to validate index }
end;

procedure swap(var arr : ArrayType;
               index1, index2 : Integer);
begin
  { swap elements at indices index1 and index2 }
end;

procedure Init(var arr : ArrayType;
               initVal : real);
begin
  { statements to initialize array elements }
end;

procedure sort(var arr : ArrayType;
               numElems : Integer);
begin
  { statements to sort array elements }
end;

function binarySearch(var arr : ArrayType;
```

```
                        key : String;
                        numElems : Integer) : Integer;
begin
  { statements to search in ordered array elements }
end;

function linearSearch(var arr : ArrayType;
                        key : String
                        numElems : Integer) : Integer;
begin
  { statements to search in unordered array elements }
end;

procedure getArray(var arr : ArrayType;
                     numElems : Integer);
begin
  { statements to obtain array }
end;

type ArrayType = array [1..MYARRAY_SIZE] of String;

var myArray : ArrayType;

begin
  { statements to manipulate the array }
end.
```

3. True or false? The parameters and local variables of a procedure or function have the same block level.

4. What is the value in the global variable `i` at the end of the program?

```
program myProgram;

var i, j : Integer;

procedure Double;
begin
  i := 2 * i;
end;

procedure Triple(var i : Integer);
begin
```

```
    i := 3 * i;
  end;

  procedure Halve(var i : Integer);
  begin
    i := i div 2;
  end;

  begin
    i := 1;
    j := 2;
    Double;
    Triple(j);
    Halve(j);
    Halve(i);
    Write(i);
    Write(j);
  end.
```

5. Where is the error in the following code?

```
function sumArray(var arr : array of real) : real;
var i : word;
begin
  Result := 0.0;
  { access all of the array elements }
  for i := 0 to High(arr) do
     Result := Result + arr[i];
end;

sum := sumArray([1.2, 3.4, 6.5, 7.6, 3.8]);
```

6. How is the following code vulnerable to run-time errors?

```
function sumArray(var arr : array of real;
                  numElems : word) : real;
var i : word;
begin
  Result := 0.;
  { access all of the array elements }
  for i := 0 to numElems - 1 do
     Result := Result + arr[i];
end;
```

Exercise

1. Write the procedure `toLoCaseStr`, which converts an ASCIIZ string into lowercase using an `array of char` parameter.
2. Write the procedure `MinMax`, which returns the smallest and largest value in an array of reals. Use an open array parameter to make the procedure work with arrays of different sizes.

WEEK
3

Drawing, Painting, and Printing

Windows is called a Graphical User Interface, and not without a reason. The crucial distinguishing characteristic of generating visible output in Windows is that all output, whether it's text or pictures, is graphical in nature.

During today's lesson you will, among other things, learn the following:

- The basics of generating graphical output in Delphi
- The fundamentals of using the `Canvas` object and its properties and methods
- How to draw on a form
- How to use the Delphi facilities for printing

Windows Graphics

As mentioned, all output generated by Windows programs is graphical in nature. In addition to text, geometric shapes, such as lines, rectangles, circles, ellipses, and so on, can be drawn.

Even text itself is a graphical object, the properties of which are encapsulated in the `Font` class.

There are several types of output devices you will have to deal with when generating any kind of graphical output in Delphi. The two most commonly used are the display and the printer.

When you need to display any information on the display screen, Windows—the operating system—provides you with window-oriented graphics. This means that, for example, each Delphi form is treated like a separate drawing surface. Anything you draw on it is clipped to the form's boundaries.

When you draw inside a form's window, the default drawing coordinates are set up so that the origin (the point with the coordinates (0,0)) is, by default, in the upper-left-hand corner of the window's drawing area, known as the client area of the window.

NEW TERM The *client area* of a window is the area inside the window's frame in which an application can display text and graphics.

Objects being drawn inside a window are automatically clipped to the boundary of the window. When your program draws inside a window, only the parts of the drawings being created that fit within the window are displayed. This approach ensures that one application's drawing does not gobble up the client area of another application. This kind of "protection" of designated display areas is the basis for the "windowing" effect, that is, the appearance of overlapping windows partially obscuring one another as if they were flat surfaces stacked on top of one another.

Similarly, each visual Delphi component that you place on the form is a separate, independent drawing surface. Each such component is responsible for drawing itself, that is, displaying text and graphics in its client area.

There are a number of standard built-in Windows user interface elements, such as text and edit boxes, list boxes, combo boxes, scrollbars, pushbuttons, and so on, the support for which is provided by Windows itself. You typically don't have to draw these interface elements. Windows takes care of drawing them whenever appropriate. You are typically only responsible for supplying the data values for drawing and for defining the characteristics of user interaction with the control, such as choosing between a single-selection versus a multiple-selection list box, or between a word-wrapping and non-wrapping edit box.

16

Delphi encapsulates the standard Windows interface elements inside the components on the Standard page of the Component Palette.

An important fact to remember is that the visual appearance of the client area of any form, and the appearance of any custom visual control that you develop, is your responsibility. You have to explicitly provide code that draws the appropriate shapes on the screen when needed.

The *Canvas*

To generate graphical output from a Delphi program, you need to interact with a Delphi object known as `Canvas`. A `Canvas` is an object with a number of properties and methods that allow you to control the output to the graphical devices such as the display screen, printers, and plotters.

`Canvas` encapsulates the interaction with the graphical engine inside Windows known as *Graphic Device Interface* (GDI). GDI is a collection of graphic-output subroutines and related data structures that enable applications to display information visually. GDI is the most fundamental facility for creating graphical displays under Windows. GDI handles all graphic output destined for the display screen and for the various kinds of printers and plotters. Windows itself uses GDI internally to display graphics.

Unfortunately, direct interaction with GDI is tedious, error-prone, and just plain difficult. The concept of `Canvas`, and its implementation as the standard `TCanvas` class, encapsulates the complexity of GDI and presents a relatively simple, uniform interface that's much easier to deal with for the programmer.

A very important advantage of using `Canvas` is that you can use exactly the same abstraction to access the drawing surface of both the display and the printer. You simply use the `Printer` object's `Canvas` to print, and a visual object's `Canvas` to display shapes and text. There is no need to approach the two kinds of devices differently, which makes it a lot easier on you, the programmer, who have to support both types of output. GDI does not provide that kind of uniformity across different types of devices and requires that you take somewhat different steps when preparing a printer device for access from when you are accessing the display.

`Canvas` itself is also a property of other visual Delphi objects. In general, whenever an object has a `Canvas` property, it is possible to draw on its "surface" to achieve various graphical effects.

Following are the important characteristics of the `Canvas` property of visual Delphi objects:

- The `Canvas` property is never a published property. It is only available to you at run-time, so you can only manipulate it programmatically, by writing Object Pascal code.
- `Canvas`, if present, is always a read-only property. This means that you cannot programmatically assign a different `Canvas` to an object and that it is the responsibility of each visual object to manage its own `Canvas`.

You can think of `Canvas` as a virtual sheet of paper on which you can draw. It encapsulates all the low-level details of drawing and writing text on Windows devices.

Note: If you have been programming in Windows using other, more traditional, development environments, you may be interested in the relationship between a `Canvas` and the Windows device context. The `Canvas`, while actually encapsulating the Windows device context, does give you direct access to it through the `Handle` property.

The analogy of the `Canvas` as a sheet of paper breaks down, however, upon closer scrutiny. This is because the surface of `Canvas`, when you look at it very, very closely, is not smooth, but consists of discrete points, called pixels. At a very low level, you can draw on the `Canvas` surface by lighting up appropriate pixels in a desired color.

NEW TERM A *pixel* is the fundamental unit of graphical output. It represents a single point, or in fact, the smallest rectangular area, that can be explicitly addressed on a device's drawing surface, and be made to appear in any of the colors available on that device.

Canvas' Properties

The most important properties of the `TCanvas` object class are:

- `Pen`, for drawing lines.
- `Brush`, for filling the insides of shapes with colors and patterns.
- `Font`, for drawing text.
- `Handle`, for directly accessing the Windows device context through the low-level GDI calls.

The `TCanvas` class is defined in the standard `Graphics` unit.

In addition to the aforementioned properties, `Canvas` provides a way for you to access the individual pixels of the image you are composing for the ultimate in control. If you really wish

to deal with your drawings in terms of individual pixels, you can use the public `Pixels` property, which lets you treat the drawing surface of the Canvas as a two-dimensional array of pixels.

Typically, however, you would use the built-in drawing capabilities of the `Canvas` object as much as possible, rather than relying on controlling the colors of the individual pixels in the image. It is important to realize that a `Canvas` is not a smooth surface, but one consisting of pixels, and that the number and the relative size of the pixels available depends on the particular device.

16

You can view the various drawing methods of `TCanvas`, about which you will learn shortly, as simply convenient ways of manipulating a whole lot of pixels at once. A subroutine that draws a line, for example, is a shortcut for calculating the positions and changing the color of the appropriate pixels that happen to be aligned to visually form a straight line.

Similarly, drawing rectangles or ellipses is just a convenient way to turn the color of a whole bunch of pixels to the current value of the `Canvas.Pen`'s color, and turning others to the color of the `Canvas.Brush`.

Canvas' Methods

Of course, if all you could do in order to be able to draw were to highlight individual pixels, the process would be very tedious indeed. To make it simpler to draw graphic objects, `Canvas` provides a number of shortcuts for drawing common geometric shapes, such as lines, rectangles, and ellipses.

Following is an overview of the most commonly used methods of the `TCanvas` class that let you draw a variety of shapes and lines:

- `Rectangle`, to draw rectangles and squares.
- `Ellipse`, to draw ellipses and circles.
- `MoveTo` and `LineTo`, to draw straight lines.
- `Polygon` and `Polyline`, to draw closed and open shapes, respectively, consisting of multiple line segments.
- `TextOut`, to draw text.

Rectangle

The `TCanvas.Rectangle` method is defined as follows:

```
TCanvas = class(TPersistent)
  ...
```

```
public
  ...
  procedure Rectangle(X1, Y1, X2, Y2: Integer);
  ...
end;
```

The rectangle to be drawn is defined in terms of the opposing corners. The method takes four parameters describing the coordinates of the rectangle to be drawn. `X1` and `Y1` parameters describe the horizontal (`X1`) and the vertical (`Y1`) coordinates of one corner of the rectangle, respectively. The two other parameters, `X2` and `Y2`, describe the corresponding coordinates of the opposite corner.

In fact, to be absolutely precise, the `X2,Y2` pair does not specify the opposite corner as much as it specifies a point adjacent to the opposite corner of the rectangle, that is, a point just one pixel away from the corner. The actual corner of the rectangle is at `(X1-1, X2-1)`.

Even more precisely, you can view the coordinates used in drawing as not representing the pixels, but the points between pixels. Figure 16.1 illustrates this idea.

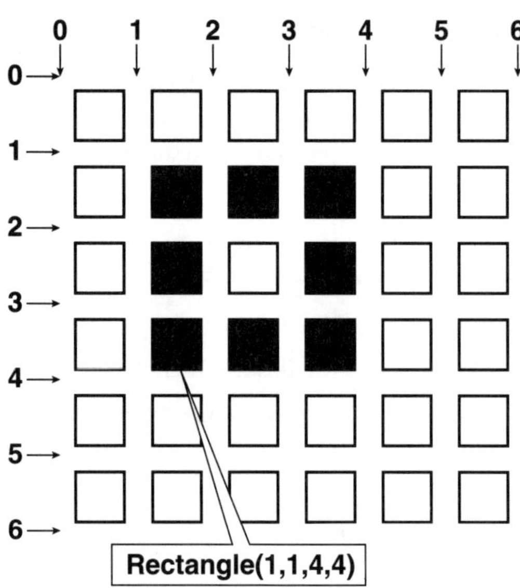

Figure 16.1.
Windows device coordinates.

When you use the `Rectangle` method, supplying the required coordinates to it, a rectangle is drawn using the current properties of the canvas `Pen` for the borders, and the current properties of the canvas `Brush` for the inside area of the rectangle.

For example, the following statement

```
TForm1.Canvas.Rectangle(10,10,210,110);
```

draws a rectangle with an upper-left-hand corner at `10,10` and the lower-right-hand corner at `210,110` using the current `Pen` for the border and filling the interior of the rectangle with the current `Brush` of the `Form1.Canvas`.

The smallest rectangle you can draw using the `Rectangle` method is a square two pixels across, consisting of just the border, for example

```
Canvas.Rectangle(1,1,3,3);
```

16

You cannot turn an individual pixel to the current `Pen`'s color by coding

```
Canvas.Rectangle(1,1,2,2);
```

Nothing appears because the GDI seems to assume that such a rectangle is actually empty and does not attempt to draw it. The above statement would have to be replaced by the following to turn the pixel at (1,1) to the current `Pen`'s color:

```
Canvas.Pixels[1,1] := Canvas.Pen.Color;
```

Note: There is no `Square` method explicitly defined by the `TCanvas` class. A square is simply a rectangle with all sides equal.

Ellipse

The `TCanvas.Ellipse` procedure method is declared in a similar way to the `Rectangle` method:

```
TCanvas = class(TPersistent)
  ...
public
  ...
  procedure Ellipse(X1, Y1, X2, Y2: Integer);
  ...
end;
```

The parameters to the `Ellipse` method have exactly the same meaning as the parameters to the `Rectangle` method: they define a rectangular region. In the case of an ellipse, however, the rectangle defined by the set of coordinates `X1,Y1` and `X2,Y2` is the bounding rectangle within which the ellipse is to be drawn.

In other words, the ellipse is defined in terms of its bounding rectangle. The bounding rectangle is the smallest rectangle enclosing the desired ellipse, oriented along the major axes, that is, not rotated in any way. It is important to realize that the bounding rectangle is hidden. Windows uses the concept of the bounding rectangle to draw the shape, but the rectangle itself does not become visible.

You can use the Ellipse method as follows; for example

```
TForm1.Canvas.Ellipse(10,10,210,110);
```

draws an ellipse, the major axis of which extends from 10 to 210 pixels, and the minor axis from 10 to 110 pixels.

You will notice that TCanvas does not define a Circle method. Just as a square is a rectangle with both dimensions equal, a circle is simply an ellipse with both axes equal. It would not be very difficult to define a supplemental Circle subroutine based on the Rectangle method.

As was the case with the Rectangle method, Ellipse draws the circumference of the ellipse with the Canvas's Pen and fills its interior with the current Brush.

MoveTo and *LineTo*

To draw simple lines, a pair of methods—MoveTo and LineTo—can be used. For line-drawing purposes, the Canvas maintains a property called the current pen-drawing position, or PenPos. You can either set PenPos directly, by assigning a TPoint-typed value to the property, or you can affect the current position by issuing a call to the MoveTo method.

In either case, the imaginary pen touches the Canvas's drawing surface at the specified position. You can then use a series of calls to the LineTo method to actually draw line segments. LineTo affects the current pen position as well, so that if you are drawing several lines radiating from the same position, you have to call MoveTo to reset your pen position to the origin of the drawing.

The two line-drawing routines are defined as follows:

```
TCanvas = class(TPersistent)
  ...
public
  ...
  procedure LineTo(X, Y: Integer);
  procedure MoveTo(X, Y: Integer);
  ...
end;
```

In both cases, two parameters, X and Y, specify the coordinates of a point on the two-dimensional X-Y plane representing the Canvas's drawing surface, X being the horizontal coordinate and Y being the vertical one.

Remember that in the default situation, the (0,0) origin of the coordinate system for drawing is in the upper-left-hand corner of the drawing surface, with the X-coordinate growing to the right and the Y-coordinate growing downward.

A call to MoveTo does not result in anything being drawn, but merely repositions the current Pen. LineTo actually draws the line, starting at the current pen position and ending at the coordinates specified as the actual parameters to the LineTo method.

For example, the following series of calls results in an outline of a rectangle being drawn at the same coordinates as were the example rectangle and ellipse from the previous sections:

```
Form1.Canvas.MoveTo(10,10);
Form1.Canvas.LineTo(210,10);
Form1.Canvas.LineTo(210,110);
Form1.Canvas.LineTo(10,110);
Form1.Canvas.LineTo(10,10);
```

16

The first of the above statements, `MoveTo`, positions the pen (without actually drawing anything) at one of the corners of the rectangular outline to be drawn, at position (10,10).

The remaining four calls to the `Canvas.LineTo` method actually draw the four sides of the desired rectangle. Note that the interior of the rectangle is not filled in this case, as the four `LineTo` statements result only in an outline of the rectangle being drawn. Each of these statements advances the pen position to the specified point, drawing the line with the current pen along the way.

Polygon and *Polyline*

The example you just saw of drawing several lines in succession illustrates a common need. The support for successive drawing of multiple line segments has therefore been distilled into a pair of separate methods that allow you to conveniently (and quickly!) draw *polylines* (multiple connecting line segments) and *polygons* (closed figures consisting of multiple connecting line segments). Unlike the case of a rectangle, with its four sides, a polygon can have an arbitrary number of sides.

The two poly-segment drawing methods, `Polyline` and `Polygon`, are defined as follows:

```
TCanvas = class(TPersistent)
  ...
public
  ...
  procedure Polygon(Points: array of TPoint);
  procedure Polyline(Points: array of TPoint);
  ...
end;
```

Both methods take a single argument: an open array of `TPoints`. The concept of an open array is a very convenient technique of enabling you to pass a variable number of arguments to a Pascal subroutine. The exact number of `TPoint`-typed arguments in the array is determined automatically by the compiler. You can therefore use the same method to pass arrays of points of varying sizes, thereby defining polylines with varying numbers of segments, or polygons with varying numbers of sides.

The `Polyline` drawing routine can be used as follows:

```
TForm1.Canvas.Polyline([Point(10,10),Point(210,10),
  Point(210,110),Point(10,110),Point(10,10)]);
```

Note how the open array of points is being constructed on-the-fly, without being defined anywhere. Each of the points is constructed by your calling the standard `Point` function, which returns a `TPoint` structure.

The single call to `Polyline` above is exactly equivalent to the series of `LineTo` method calls, preceded by a call to the `MoveTo` method given in the previous section. The resulting figure, although closed, is treated as a polyline; that is, the figure is just an outline and is not filled.

To achieve the same result as the `Rectangle` method achieves, you can use the `Polygon` method as follows:

```
TForm1.Canvas.Polygon([Point(10,10),Point(210,10),
  Point(210,110),Point(10,110)]);
```

In this case, you don't even need to specify the end-point for the last line segment, because it is understood that the created figure will be closed. The interior of a polygon is filled with the current brush.

Of course, you are not limited to four line segments when using the `Polyline` and `Polygon` methods. You can use as many points describing the figure being drawn as necessary.

You can construct the arrays of points describing the figures being drawn either dynamically or on-the-fly as shown previously, or you can pass ready-made arrays to these methods. The open nature of the array parameters of the `Polyline` and `Polygon` methods will in each case ensure that an appropriate number of line segments gets drawn, as defined in the actual arguments.

TextOut

The nice feature of a graphical interface like Windows is that you can combine graphics and text in a uniform way and seamlessly output both on a single page or in a single display window. This is possible because text is being treated as a graphical element too, and is literally being *drawn* on the drawing surface of a `Canvas`.

You can use the `TextOut` method defined by the `TCanvas` class to display text.

The `TextOut` method is declared as follows:

```
TCanvas = class(TPersistent)
  ...
public
  ...
  procedure TextOut(X, Y: Integer; const Text: String);
  ...
end;
```

The first two parameters of `TextOut` define the coordinates at which the text is to appear. Again, the concept of a bounding rectangle is helpful here. The `X` and `Y` coordinates you need to pass to the `TextOut` method define the upper-left-hand corner of the rectangle bounding the text string to be displayed. The text itself is passed as the third, `Text` parameter to the method.

Since the text is "drawn" using the `Font` property of the `Canvas`, you can achieve any desired visual effect by simply varying the values of the various properties of the `Font`. The possibilities are truly endless. You can control the size, color, and font-family characteristics, along with style attributes such as bolding or underlining. Note that the text background's color is controlled via the `Canvas.Brush.Color` and the `Canvas.Brush.Style` properties. An example of that is shown later.

After you set the desired combination of properties for the `Canvas.Font`, the text will faithfully appear at the specified coordinates—provided, of course, that you have the corresponding font installed on your system. Otherwise, the text will appear in a font with characteristics that Windows determines as "closely matching" the desired ones.

As an example of the usage of the `TextOut` method, consider how the following statement results in the message `'Hello world!'` being displayed in the current font, at position 10,10 of the `Form1` surface:

```
Form1.Canvas.TextOut(10,10,'Hello world!');
```

Note that `TextOut` takes a `String` argument in the third position. If you need to display a numeric value, such as an `Integer`, you must convert it to a string before you can pass it to the `TextOut` method. You can achieve the conversion by calling the standard `IntToStr` function, for example:

```
Form1.Canvas.TextOut(10,10,'The answer is '+IntToStr(42));
```

The statement above displays the number 42 at the specified position (10,10).

`TextOut`, similar to the line-drawing methods, affects the current drawing position. The value of the `PenPos` property of a `Canvas`, after a call to `TextOut`, will be referring to the point just past the text string displayed.

The `TCanvas` methods you have learned so far enable you to build some actual example programs.

Random Lines Example Program

As the first exercise in using the `Canvas` for drawing, you will create a program that continuously displays random lines.

The lines will be drawn directly over the main form's background.

- ☐ Create a new project called `Rand1` and save it in a newly created, empty directory as `rand1.dpr`, with the corresponding form unit saved as `rand1f.pas`.
- ☐ Select the `OnActivate` event from the Object Inspector's Events page. Double-click the value column on the right of the event's name to create an event-handler's shell method: `TForm1.FormActivate`.

Delphi responds to the double-clicking on the event's value by creating an empty event-handler method of the main form. This event handler is where the action of drawing the lines will actually take place. You will now proceed by filling the internals of the form's `OnActivate` event handler.

The `TForm1.FormActivate` event handler will consist of a loop, continuously drawing new lines, in different colors, at random locations on the screen. The code for the method is given in Listing 16.1.

Listing 16.1. Random line-drawing example.

```
 1: procedure TForm1.FormActivate(Sender: TObject);
 2: begin
 3:   if Running then
 4:     Exit;
 5:   Running := True;
 6:   Done := False;
 7:   repeat
 8:     Canvas.Pen.Color := RGB(Random(255),Random(255),Random(255));
 9:     Canvas.MoveTo(Random(ClientWidth),Random(ClientHeight));
10:     Canvas.LineTo(Random(ClientWidth),Random(ClientHeight));
11:     Application.ProcessMessages;
12:   until Done;
13:   Running := False;
14: end;
```

The main drawing loop spans lines 7 through 12 of Listing 16.1. A **`repeat-until`** loop is used for this purpose. Inside the loop, the pen color is chosen by being assigned randomly generated numbers. The color value is constructed from its three base components, red, green, and blue, by means of the standard RGB function. Each of the components is independently, randomly generated by a call to the standard function `Random`. The resulting composite `TColor` value is assigned to the `Color` property of the `Canvas.Pen` and is used to draw the next line. The color will change at every new iteration through the loop, because new random numbers will be generated for the base color components.

Lines 9 and 10 of Listing 16.1 define the position and direction of the line being drawn at every iteration. Again, the standard library function `Random` is used to generate the coordinate values for the end-points of the line segments. New, random values will be generated each time through the loop.

The statement on line 11 ensures that, as the drawing **`repeat`** loop is running, the rest of Windows will not come to a halt. The call to `Application.ProcessMessages` ensures that other applications get a chance to run and process their messages, even as the `FormActivate` method busily draws the random lines. This act of good will on behalf of the example application is necessary due to the cooperative nature of Windows multitasking. Each application has the responsibility to ensure that other applications are allowed to run also.

There is an interesting anomaly that results from calling `Application.ProcessMessages` at this point. Each time the user of the program switches away from and then back to this application, the `FormActivate` event handler is re-entered in response to the window activation. To prevent multiple instances of the **`repeat-until`** loop starting each time, a Boolean flag `Running` is maintained as an instance variable of the form. Initially `False`, on line 5 this flag is turned to `True` just before the loop starts running. Then, on any subsequent entry to the routine, the value of the flag is being checked. If the test performed on line 3 returns `True`, it means that the loop is already running and that there is no need to set up another. In this case, the method exits immediately to the caller as a result of the `Exit` statement on line 4.

16

The loop on lines 7 through 12 uses a Boolean variable `Done` to control when to terminate. Similar to the `Running` flag, this variable will be defined as an instance variable of the form, because you need to ensure that at least one other method will have access to it. You will need to be able to have the `FormClose` method, the event handler for the main form's `OnClose` event, to change the value of the `Done` variable and ultimately to ensure loop termination.

☐ Enter the code as shown in Listing 16.1 inside the empty `FormActivate` event-handler method.

As noted in the previous Analysis section, to ensure that your application does not draw the lines forever, you must provide a way for it to exit the **`repeat-until`** loop implemented inside the `OnActivate` event handler.

☐ Create an empty event-handler method for the `OnClose` event of the main form. As before, double-click the value column next to the event name inside the Object Inspector to generate the skeleton code for the handler.

As before, Delphi generates the event handler and positions the cursor inside the executable **`begin-end`** block.

The code you need to enter to ensure the termination of the program is very simple:

```
procedure TForm1.FormClose(Sender: TObject; var Action: TCloseAction);
begin
  Done := True;
end;
```

The single line of code inside the event handler that you need to enter changes the value of the form variable `Done` to `True`, thereby causing the **`repeat`** loop inside the `FormActivate` event handler to terminate.

This change will only occur upon the `OnClose` event, that is, after the user of the program requests that the main form of the applet be closed.

☐ Enter the

```
Done := True;
```

statement inside the newly generated `FormClose` event.

In summary, Listing 16.2 provides the code for the `Rand1F` form unit in its entirety.

Listing 16.2. The main form unit of the `Rand1` example program.

```
unit Rand1F;

interface

uses
  SysUtils, WinTypes, WinProcs, Messages, Classes, Graphics, Controls,
  Forms, Dialogs;

type
  TForm1 = class(TForm)
    procedure FormActivate(Sender: TObject);
    procedure FormClose(Sender: TObject; var Action: TCloseAction);
  private
    Running,
    Done: Boolean;
  public
    { Public declarations }
  end;

var
  Form1: TForm1;

implementation

{$R *.DFM}

procedure TForm1.FormActivate(Sender: TObject);
begin
  if Running then
    Exit;
  Running := True;
  Done := False;
  repeat
    Canvas.Pen.Color := RGB(Random(255),Random(255),Random(255));
    Canvas.MoveTo(Random(ClientWidth),Random(ClientHeight));
    Canvas.LineTo(Random(ClientWidth),Random(ClientHeight));
    Application.ProcessMessages;
  until Done;
  Running := False;
end;

procedure TForm1.FormClose(Sender: TObject; var Action: TCloseAction);
begin
  Done := True;
end;

end.
```

The code in Listing 16.2 has already been discussed. Most of the listing's contents have been generated by Delphi automatically.

You just needed to add the declaration of the `Running` flag on line 14 and the `Done` field on line 15, and the code for the two methods: `FormActivate` and `FormClose`.

The `FormActivate` method, the code for which you entered and which is listed on lines 29 through 39, performs the actual drawing of the random lines.

The single line of code, line 44, inside the `FormClose` method ensures proper termination of the program and makes sure, by setting the variable `Done` to `True`, that the loop inside `FormActivate` terminates as soon as the user indicates a desire to close the main form of the application.

Figure 16.2 illustrates the visual appearance of the random line-drawing applet.

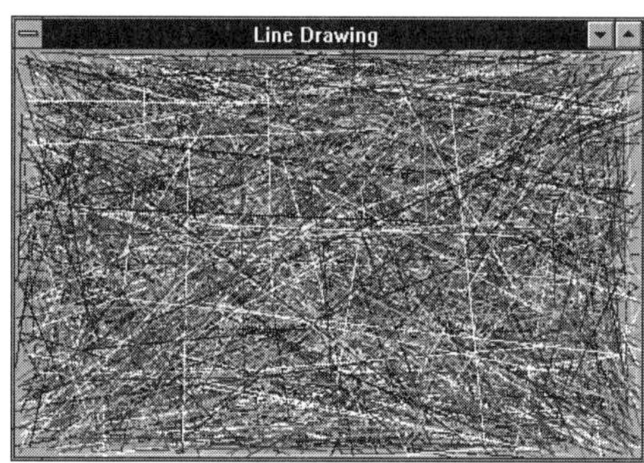

Figure 16.2.
Random line-drawing application `Rand1`.

☐ Run the application now.

Notice the line-drawing subroutines in action as the `Rand1` application is running. Also note that even though the lines are being drawn continuously in a tight loop, you have ensured just enough "breathing space" for Windows so that other applications can also run alongside `Rand1`.

Enhancing the *Rand1* Program

As a minor variation on the theme of drawing random lines, and more importantly as an illustration of how you can programmatically affect the characteristics of the lines being drawn, consider the following example code, shown in Listing 16.3.

Listing 16.3. A variation on random line-drawing.

```
 1: procedure TForm1.FormActivate(Sender: TObject);
 2: begin
 3:   Done := False;
 4:   repeat
 5:     Canvas.Pen.Color := RGB(Random(255),Random(255),Random(255));
 6:     Canvas.Pen.Width := Random(30);
 7:     Canvas.MoveTo(Random(ClientWidth),Random(ClientHeight));
 8:     Canvas.LineTo(Random(ClientWidth),Random(ClientHeight));
 9:     Application.ProcessMessages;
10:   until Done;
11: end;
```

The code in Listing 16.3 is identical to the `FormActivate` method's code from Listing 16.2, with the exception of one additional statement, on line 6 here.

The statement on line 6 changes the `Width` of the pen used to draw the random lines to yet another random number, this time in the range of 0 through 30 (the limit of 30 is entirely arbitrary here).

You can see the visual difference changing the width of the line the pen makes by running the modified `Rand1` program, which incorporates the additional statement as shown in Listing 16.3.

Drawing versus Painting

You will often encounter the terms "drawing" and "painting" when dealing with the creation of graphical output in Delphi. The two terms are related and often used interchangeably, but for greater clarity it is convenient to distinguish them. Let us first start with the term "drawing":

NEW TERM *Drawing* is the process of creating individual, simple graphical elements and shapes, such as circles, rectangles, polygons, and so on by means of calling appropriate output subroutines.

You would call various `Canvas` methods, such as `Rectangle`, `Ellipse`, and `MoveTo`/`LineTo`, to accomplish drawing graphics on its surface.

"Painting," on the other hand, is the term reserved for a special occasion.

NEW TERM *Painting* is the act of responding to a request from Windows to redraw the appearance of, typically, the entire surface of a Windows element, such as a window or control.

The term "painting" is thus reserved for the process of potentially (re-)creating the *entire* appearance of a visible object. At certain times Windows determines that an object needs to be repainted and sends it a message to cause it to repaint itself. As you can tell, painting involves drawing on the `Canvas`, but occurs only upon a specific request from Windows.

Now that you understand the distinction between drawing and painting, you are ready to build another graphical example. This time, the output you create will be generated upon request from Windows, in response to the `OnPaint` event.

The Drawing Shapes Example

You are about to create a new example program that will illustrate the process of painting on a form. Follow the steps outlined below:

- ☐ Create a new project called `Draw1` and save it in a newly created, empty directory as `draw1.dpr`, with the corresponding form unit saved as `draw1f.pas`.
- ☐ Select the `OnPaint` event from the Object Inspector's Events page. Double-click the value column on the right of the event's name to create an event-handler method's skeleton: `TForm1.FormPaint`.

Listing 16.4 gives you the code you need to enter inside the newly created `OnPaint` handler.

Listing 16.4. Canvas drawing example program `Draw1`.

```
unit Draw1F;

interface

uses
  SysUtils, WinTypes, WinProcs, Messages, Classes, Graphics, Controls,
  Forms, Dialogs;

type
  TForm1 = class(TForm)
    procedure FormPaint(Sender: TObject);
    procedure FormResize(Sender: TObject);
  end;

var
  Form1: TForm1;

implementation

{$R *.DFM}

procedure TForm1.FormPaint(Sender: TObject);
var
  Count,
  Current,
  Step: Integer;
  R   : TRect;
begin
  R := ClientRect;
  InflateRect(R,-10,-10);
```

continues

Listing 16.4. continued

```
  {Draw Frame and Background}
  Canvas.Brush.Color := clYellow;
  Canvas.Pen.Color := clBlack;
  Canvas.Rectangle(R.Left,R.Top,R.Right,R.Bottom);

  {Draw horizontal grid}
  Step := 15;
  Current := Succ(Step);
  Canvas.Pen.Color := clLime;
  while Current < R.Bottom do begin
    Canvas.MoveTo(Succ(R.Left),Current);
    Canvas.LineTo(Pred(R.Right),Current);
    Inc(Current,Step);
  end;

  {Draw Vertical Lines}
  Step := 3;
  Current := 85;
  Canvas.Pen.Color := clRed;
  for Count := 1 to 2 do begin
    Canvas.MoveTo(Current,Succ(R.Top));
    Canvas.LineTo(Current,Pred(R.Bottom));
    Inc(Current,Step);
  end;

  {Draw some shapes and their labels}
  {Ellipses}
  with Canvas do begin
    Pen.Color := clBlack;
    Brush.Color := clFuchsia;
    Ellipse(230,40,360,60);
    Brush.Color := clAqua;
    Ellipse(200,40,260,90);
    Brush.Color := clPurple;
    Ellipse(220,20,300,80);
  end;

  {Rectangles}
  with Canvas do begin
    Pen.Color := clBlack;
    Brush.Color := clRed;
    Rectangle(130,120,230,160);
    Brush.Color := clWhite;
    Rectangle(100,110,160,140);
    Brush.Color := clBlue;
    Rectangle(120,100,200,130);
  end;


  {Polylines}
  with Canvas do begin
    Pen.Width := 3;
    Pen.Color := clBlack;
    PolyLine([Point(230,240),Point(250,200),Point(210,220),
```

```
 86:       Point(300,160),Point(280,240),Point(230,240)]);
 87:     Pen.Color := clFuchsia;
 88:     PolyLine([Point(360,230),Point(230,210),Point(260,250),
 89:       Point(190,210),Point(240,190),Point(360,230)]);
 90:   end;
 91:
 92:
 93:   {Text Labels}
 94:   with Canvas do begin
 95:     Brush.Style := bsClear;
 96:     TextOut(120,50,'Ellipses');
 97:     TextOut(250,130,'Rectangles');
 98:     TextOut(120,210,'Polylines');
 99:     Brush.Style := bsSolid;
100:   end;
101: end;
102:
103:
104: procedure TForm1.FormResize(Sender: TObject);
105: begin
106:   Invalidate;
107: end;
108:
109: end.
```

Listing 16.4 shows the entire form unit of the `Draw1` project you are currently developing. The skeleton code for this unit, including the class declaration on lines 9 through 13, has been generated by Delphi, as usual.

The code inside the `TForm1.FormPaint` event-handler method on lines 22 through 101 is what you need to enter manually. This is the code that exercises some of the `Canvas` drawing methods and results in the graphical output being generated.

The `FormPaint` event handler should be installed as a handler for the form's `OnPaint` event. This means that the code inside the `FormPaint` method will be executed every time Windows makes a request to the `Draw1` application to repaint its main window. In response to the paint request, you will be drawing some shapes and labeling them with text.

At first, on lines 29 and 30, a rectangular area inside the form is being defined. This rectangular area will become the basis for the drawing, and will be filled with a background color.

The `ClientRect` property retrieved on line 29 refers to the bounding coordinates of the rectangular area inside the window frame, known as the client area.

The subsequent call to the standard Windows API subroutine `InflateRect` on line 30 shrinks the retrieved rectangle by 10 pixels on each side. This is done to leave a margin of the window background color around the drawing.

After the bounding rectangle for the drawing inside the window has been established, you can proceed with erasing the rectangle with an appropriate background color.

The code in Listing 16.4 makes a heavy use of the `Canvas` methods you learned a little earlier during today's lesson to actually draw the required shapes, lines, and so on.

In particular, lines 32 through 35 paint the background rectangle yellow, with a black frame, by first assigning the `clYellow` color constant to the form's `Canvas.Brush` on line 33. Similarly, the `clBlack` constant is assigned to the `Color` property of the `Canvas.Pen` on line 34. After both the `Brush` and the `Pen` are set up as desired, calling the `Rectangle` method of the `Canvas` uses both to actually perform the drawing and color-filling of the specified rectangle.

Next, on lines 37 through 45, a horizontal grid is being drawn in green (`clLime` constant) to simulate the visual appearance of a standard office notepad. The effect is achieved by running a **`while`** loop on lines 41 through 45 that draws the horizontal grid lines, one-by-one, utilizing the `MoveTo`/`LineTo` sequence of method calls.

The loop is initialized on lines 38 through 40 to draw the lines 15 pixels apart. There is no magic to the number 15 here; it is completely arbitrary, and you can in fact experiment with your own settings to see what kind of visual effect you can achieve.

The only important consideration is that no matter what `Step` value you choose, the loop should eventually terminate by incrementing the `Current` vertical coordinate value beyond the boundary of the rectangle.

Lines 47 through 55 achieve the simulated left-margin marker for the notepad by drawing two vertical, parallel, red lines across the simulated page.

A **`for`** loop is used for this purpose, on lines 51 through 55. Note how the current pen color is changed on line 50, before the loop starts.

Up to this point, your code was dealing with simulating the appearance of a yellow notepad. It is about time you actually drew some shapes on the notepad.

Start with drawing a few sample ellipses on lines 58 through 67. The `Canvas.Ellipse` method is used for the occasion. Each time, before the ellipse is being drawn, the `Brush` property of the form's `Canvas` is set to a new color. Hence, the ellipses are each filled with a different color.

The **`with-do`** block on lines 59 through 67 makes it possible to refer to the `Ellipse` method without any qualification on lines 62, 64, and 66, and to the `Pen` and `Brush` on lines 60, 61, 63, and 65. Otherwise, you would have to prefix each of these statements with the `Canvas` qualifier.

Similar to the ellipses, some rectangles are drawn on lines 69 through 78. Again, as before, the inside color of these rectangles is explicitly controlled by an assignment statement to the `Canvas.Brush.Color` property, just before the `Rectangle` method is invoked. The rectangles are displayed at arbitrary locations, again, just to illustrate how you could use the `Rectangle` method. Feel free to experiment with changing the coordinates and the order of execution of the statements inside the **`with`** block on lines 70 through 78 to achieve the visual effect of changing the apparent order in which the rectangles are stacked on top of one another.

The section on lines 81 through 90 is more interesting, because it makes use of the `Polyline` method of the `Canvas`.

Two polygonal outlines are constructed on-the-fly on lines 85 through 89 using Delphi's dynamic array feature. Since drawing polylines involves using a `Pen`, you can control the appearance of these polygonal shapes by setting the `Pen` properties.

Finally, text labels are drawn next to the respective groups of shapes by executing the statements on lines 94 through 100.

To actually display the text, the `TextOut` method of the `Canvas` is used.

Worth noting is the statement on line 95 and then again on line 99. You can control whether the text is being drawn against an opaque background, or whether the background is being erased in the current `Brush` color, or whether the background becomes transparent, allowing the objects underneath to show through.

Setting the `Brush.Style` property to `bsClear` has the effect of making the text background transparent such that drawing the text allows the existing background pattern to show through. By default, however, the `Brush.Style` property is set to `bsSolid`, which results in the background of the text's bounding rectangle to be erased with the current `Canvas.Brush` color as the text is being drawn.

It seems like a lot of code for a simple paint method! Keep in mind that this code will get called many times during the course of the execution of the application. Windows will likely ask you to repaint the client area of the window often, whenever it becomes invalid, that is, whenever it is being uncovered from under another window.

One remaining piece of business is to ensure that the size of the drawing follows the changes in the dimensions of the window itself. To achieve a relative size independence, that is, to make the drawing of the form accommodate changes in the form's size, it is desirable to respond to the `OnResize` event of the form.

In this case, because the `FormPaint` method already handles the task of retrieving the paint area dimensions each time it is invoked, the only outstanding consideration is to make sure that the window gets repainted as soon as it changes in size. To achieve that, the `Invalidate` method is called inside the `OnResize` event-handler method of the form: `FormResize`, on lines 104 to 107. `Invalidate` will ultimately cause Windows to send a paint request to your application and will force the window to be repainted.

The `Draw1` example you have developed illustrates the use of the various drawing methods of the form's `Canvas` object, used to paint on the form's surface.

- ☐ Run the example program and see how the shapes are being drawn.

The visual appearance of `Draw1` at run-time is illustrated in Figure 16.3.

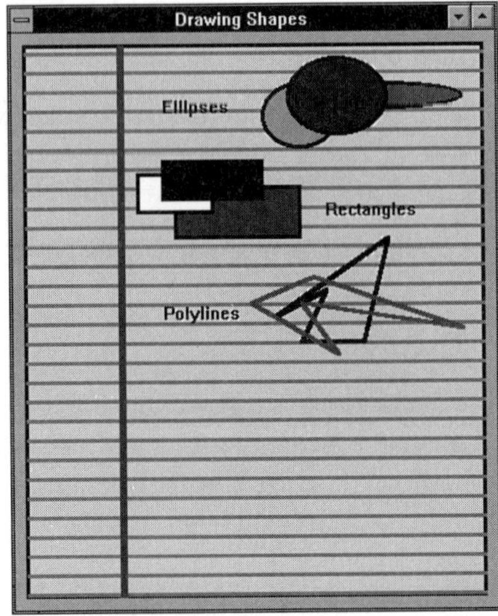

Figure 16.3.
The Drawing Shapes example program `Draw1` *running.*

The techniques you used to draw on a form's `Canvas` can be used to draw on other canvases. In particular, the same drawing methods you used to display shapes on-screen can be used to print them.

Printed Output with Delphi

The task of printing under Windows has traditionally been regarded as an arcane art, best left to the narrow circle of the initiated. Despite the fact that Windows supports a great degree of device independence, the support for generating printed output has traditionally been insufficient.

One of the main reasons for the difficulty in printing under Windows is that Windows does not encapsulate the details of the application's interaction with the printer device drivers as completely as it encapsulates the details of the interaction with the display device drivers. Printing has always required additional preparation and the knowledge of more advanced programming techniques.

Another reason for printing being inherently more complicated than displaying is that you don't have to deal with multiple paper sizes or orientations when drawing on a video screen, nor do they have to deal with multiple video display cards simultaneously!

Fortunately, Delphi removes most of the difficulty of printing by providing a truly uniform interface that works across different devices, even across devices as disparate as the printer and the display screen.

16

Standard Output

Probably the simplest way to produce printed output from a Delphi application is by using the built-in support for `Write` and `WriteLn` procedures.

You can use `Write` and `WriteLn` in a print mode in much the same way you used them during the earlier lessons to generate the output to the `WinCRT` screen. The only difference is that you need to do some preparation to connect the `Write` family of procedures to the printer.

In order for the output of `Write` and `WriteLn` to go to the printer, you must first include `Printers` in the **`uses`** clause of your unit or program. `Printers` is the standard Delphi unit where the support for seamless printing is defined.

Before you can use `Write` or `WriteLn`, you must assign a `Text` file variable to the printer. You can do that by executing a pair of statements:

```
var
  AFile: System.Text;
begin
  ...
  AssignPrn(AFile);
  Rewrite(AFile);
  ...
end;
```

where `AFile` is a `Text`-file variable defined in the **`var`**-declaration just above the executable block.

The `AssignPrn` statement associates the `Text`-file variable `AText` with the printer. The `Rewrite` opens the file for output. After executing these statements, you can use the standard `Write` and `WriteLn` procedures to generate printed textual output.

Before you undertake developing your own application that uses the printing capabilities of `Write` and `WriteLn` procedures, take a look at the following checklist of limitations of this method of printing:

- ☐ You can only print text. No graphics can be printed using the `Write` and `WriteLn` procedures.
- ☐ You have only a very rudimentary control over the appearance of the printout. In particular, you can only control the attributes of the font used globally for the printout. There is no easy way of printing individual snippets of text with different attributes on the same page and within the same paragraph.

  For example, you cannot individually highlight a section of a paragraph, or a single word with boldface, nor can you underline an individual word, and so on.
- ☐ You cannot stop or abort printing in progress. There is no typical Printing dialog box with the Cancel button to give the user of your program more control over the process of printing.

These complaints result simply from the fact that, although `Write` and `WriteLn` give you a convenient way to generate some quick-and-dirty printer output under Delphi, they are nevertheless no substitute for the "real thing," that is, directing the printer output through the `Printer.Canvas`.

`Write` and `WriteLn` automate some of the tasks you need to perform when printing text, such as advancing to the next line and performing the equivalent of a carriage return upon `WriteLn`, but they take away a lot in terms of what you can do. The good news is that `Write` and `WriteLn` both use the `Canvas` of the pre-defined `Printer` object. Because you already know how to deal with `Canvas`, you can simply generate the printed output of both text and graphics by using the now-familiar `Canvas` drawing methods.

Instead of spending the time investigating the `Write/WriteLn` technique any further, let us move on to building an example program using the `Printer.Canvas` directly.

Printer Canvas

As you realize by now, using the `Printer`'s `Canvas` directly gives you total control over the appearance of the printed page. You can print text in any and all available fonts, graphics such as bitmaps, and line graphics utilizing the `Canvas` drawing methods, all on a single output page. You are in control.

The object encapsulating the `Printer`'s `Canvas` is given to you in the form of `Printer`, a pre-defined instance of the class `TPrinter`, instantiated for you by the `Printers` unit in its initialization code.

Because you really only need one instance of the `TPrinter` class to attend to all of your printing needs, all you need to do to actually use the `Printer` object is to declare `Printers` in your **`uses`** clause. The object will be automatically created and made available to you via the `Printer` variable.

Specifically, you don't have to deal with the explicit creation of an instance of the `TPrinter` object, nor with the destruction of it when it's no longer needed. All of these details are already taken care of for you.

You can access the `Canvas` property of the `Printer` as usual, that is, as

```
Printer.Canvas
```

and all methods available to you when drawing on a display `Canvas` are also available here.

You are now going to develop a sample application that uses the `Printer` object to print some text.

The Note Printer Application

The application you are going to design and create now, called Note Printer, or `NotePrnt` for short, is essentially a very simple text editor that can print the contents of a text file that the user manually creates or loads from disk. The application prints by using the `Printer.Canvas` drawing methods you have learned today.

16

Creating the *NotePrnt* Application

- ☐ Create a new, blank Delphi project. Name the form unit of the main form of the application `Note1` (note1.pas). Name the project itself `NotePrnt` (noteprnt.dpr).
- ☐ Place the following components on the form:
  - ☐ A `Memo` and a `MainMenu`, both from the Standard page.
  - ☐ An `OpenDialog` from the Dialogs page of the Component Palette.

The components you just placed become `Memo1`, `MainMenu1`, and `OpenDialog1`, respectively.

- ☐ Change the `Align` property of the `Memo1` component to `alClient`.

The edit box will fill the entire client area of the main form.

- ☐ Clear the `Lines` property of `Memo1` so that the edit box is blank.
- ☐ Double-click the `MainMenu1` component inside the Form Designer window to open the Menu Designer.
- ☐ Inside the Menu Designer, create a single item of the main menu, "File."
- ☐ Underneath the File main-menu selection, create the following popup-menu entries:

```
&New
&Open
<divider>
&Print
<divider>
E&xit
```

The menu you have just created consists of six entries, two of which are merely dividers, with the rest being commands that will actually effect some actions inside your application.

You have to enter a dash "-" as the `Caption` property of the menu item to make it a divider.

The ampersand symbol (`&`), when you make it part of a menu item's `Caption`, will cause the letter following it in the `Caption` to be underlined when the menu is displayed. The underlined letter will then act as the menu shortcut key.

- ☐ After you have entered the details of the main menu, close the Menu Designer window, for instance by double-clicking its system-menu button.
- ☐ Select the `OpenDialog1` component and change its `Filter` property to provide an easy access to the most common filename extensions.

There are several ways of entering the value of the `Filter` property, as you will learn on Day 18. Right now, simply double-click the value of the `Filter` property to bring up the custom property editor: the Filter Editor shown in Figure 16.4.

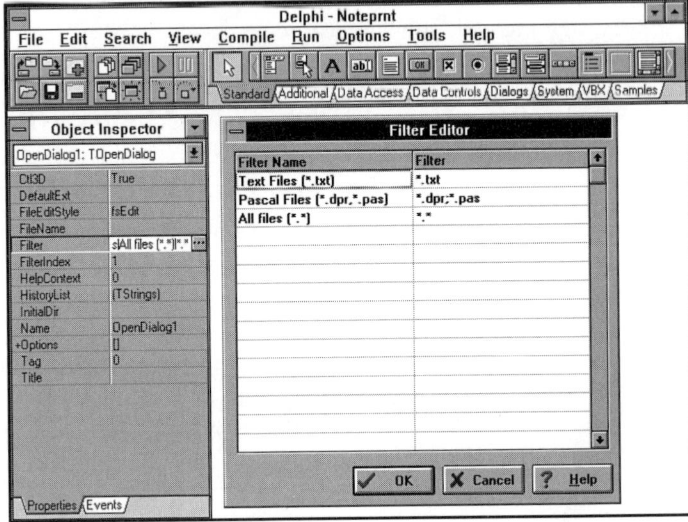

Figure 16.4.
`OpenDialog`'s `Filter` custom property editor.

- ☐ Inside the Filter Editor's window, enter the filename extensions of the filter entries as shown in Figure 16.4. You will learn about the details of entering various filters on Day 18. Right now, just follow the example as given.

The Print Command

The actual purpose of the `NotePrnt` example program is to print the contents of a text file the user loaded. To accomplish that goal, you need to provide the code that implements the File|Print command.

- ☐ Create the default event handler for the Print command on the File menu by simply clicking the Print option on the File menu prop inside the Form Designer.
- ☐ Inside the newly created `TForm1.Print1Click` handler, enter the following line of code:

```
PrintCurrentFile;
```

You are going to create a new method dedicated to printing but separate from the User Interface event handlers. Actually separating the code that does the work from the user interface code makes your applications more easily portable, should the user interface change in the future.

Printing the Hard Copy

You are now going to create the method that actually does the printing. First, you must declare the procedure `PrintCurrentFile` as a custom method of the form class you are building: `TForm1`.

- Enter the following line inside the public section of the `TForm1` class declaration:

```
procedure PrintCurrentFile;
```

You have thereby declared a new method of the `TForm1` class. Note that you placed the declaration in the public section near the end of the class declaration, replacing the comment that Delphi puts there by default. It is worth remembering that you are free to declare your own methods, fields, and properties as part of a form-class declaration.

A form class, which is any descendant of `TForm`, is just like any other ordinary class. The only part of its declaration that you should not touch in code, but rather deal with through the combination of the Object Inspector and the Form Designer, is the first section of the class declaration, right after the keyword **`class`**. The subsequent sections, the first of which is introduced by the reserved word **`private`**, are there for you to use.

You can extend the form to let it support any other methods and data fields that you may need by declaring them in these sections.

By default, Delphi creates two such sections: a **`private`** and a **`public`** section, placing comment lines instead of method or field declarations inside them.

Note: You are free to introduce new sections to a form's class declaration, as well as to declare new methods and fields inside the existing sections, except the first, which is being managed by Delphi's code-generation facilities.

To enforce changes to the first, implicitly **`published`** section of the form's class declaration, use the combination of the Object Inspector and the Form Designer.

You have reached the point when there are no more excuses: you have to actually implement the printing code. How hard could that be?

Let's see. Listing 16.5 reveals it all: the implementation of the `PrintCurrentFile` method in addition to the methods already discussed.

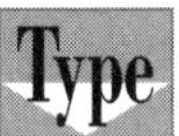

Listing 16.5. The main form unit of the `NotePrnt` example.

```
unit Note1;

interface

```

continues

Listing 16.5. continued

```
uses
  SysUtils, WinTypes, WinProcs, Messages, Classes, Graphics, Controls,
  Forms, Dialogs, Menus, StdCtrls, Printers;

type
  TForm1 = class(TForm)
    Memo1: TMemo;
    MainMenu1: TMainMenu;
    OpenDialog1: TOpenDialog;
    File1: TMenuItem;
    Open1: TMenuItem;
    New1: TMenuItem;
    N1: TMenuItem;
    Exit1: TMenuItem;
    Print1: TMenuItem;
    N2: TMenuItem;
    procedure Open1Click(Sender: TObject);
    procedure Print1Click(Sender: TObject);
    procedure Exit1Click(Sender: TObject);
    procedure New1Click(Sender: TObject);
  private
    { Private declarations }
  public
    procedure PrintCurrentFile;
  end;

var
  Form1: TForm1;

implementation


procedure TForm1.PrintCurrentFile;
  var
    LeftMargin,
    LineCoord,
    LineOnPage,
    CurrentLine,
    TextHeight,
    LinesPerPage: Integer;

  procedure StartDoc;
    begin
      LeftMargin := Printer.Canvas.PixelsPerInch;
      Printer.Canvas.Font := Memo1.Font;
      {Must TextOut or else TextHeight gets miscalculated!!!}
      Printer.Canvas.TextOut(0,0,'');
      TextHeight := Abs(Printer.Canvas.Font.Height);
      LinesPerPage :=
        Printer.PageHeight div TextHeight;
      CurrentLine := 0;
    end;

  function MorePages: Boolean;
    begin
```

```
      Result := (CurrentLine < Memo1.Lines.Count)
        and not Printer.Aborted;
    end;

  procedure StartPage;
    begin
      LineOnPage := 0;
      LineCoord := 0;
    end;

  procedure NextPage;
    begin
      if MorePages then
        Printer.NewPage;
    end;

  function MoreLines: Boolean;
    begin
      Result := (LineOnPage < LinesPerPage)
        and not Printer.Aborted;
    end;

  procedure NextLine;
    begin
      Inc(LineOnPage);
      Inc(LineCoord,TextHeight);
      Inc(CurrentLine);
    end;

  procedure PrintLine;
    begin with Printer.Canvas do begin
      TextOut(LeftMargin,LineCoord,Memo1.Lines[CurrentLine]);
    end end;

  begin
    if Memo1.Lines.Count = 0 then
      Exit;
    Printer.Title := Caption;
    Printer.BeginDoc;
    StartDoc;
    while MorePages do begin
      StartPage;
      while MoreLines do begin
        PrintLine;
        NextLine;
        Application.ProcessMessages;
      end;
      NextPage;
    end;
    Printer.EndDoc;
  end;

{$R *.DFM}

procedure TForm1.Open1Click(Sender: TObject);
begin
```

continues

Listing 16.5. continued

```
116:   if not OpenDialog1.Execute then
117:     Exit;
118:   Memo1.Lines.LoadFromFile(OpenDialog1.FileName);
119:   Memo1.SelStart := 0;
120:   Memo1.Modified := False;
121:   Caption := ExtractFileName(OpenDialog1.FileName);
122: end;
123:
124: procedure TForm1.Print1Click(Sender: TObject);
125: begin
126:   PrintCurrentFile;
127: end;
128:
129: procedure TForm1.Exit1Click(Sender: TObject);
130: begin
131:   Close;
132: end;
133:
134: procedure TForm1.New1Click(Sender: TObject);
135: begin
136:   Memo1.Lines.Clear;
137:   Caption := 'Note Printer';
138: end;
139:
140: end.
```

Listing 16.5 illustrates all the code necessary to drive the main form of the `NotePrnt` application. In addition to the methods already discussed in the text, that is `Open1Click`, `Print1Click`, `Exit1Click`, and `New1Click` on lines 114 through 138, respectively, you will notice the rather long implementation of the `PrintCurrentFile` procedure method starting on line 37 and continuing through to line 110.

Note however, that despite its length, the procedure is neatly organized in a series of local subroutines.

The main executable body of the `PrintCurrentFile` method invokes these local subroutines on lines 95 through 109.

At first, on lines 95 and 96, a check is made to see if it is worth executing the body of the subroutine at all. If the form's memo component, `Memo1`, contains no text, there is not much to print, so the subroutine immediately terminates via the standard `Exit` clause on line 96.

Assuming that there is text in the `Memo1` component, line 97 defines the title of the print job. This is what is going to appear as the job's title inside the Print Manager's list. The code as shown simply designates the file name as the title, but you are free to enhance the print job title to make it even more descriptive to the user, for example, prefixing it with the application's name.

Line 98 is where you actually start printing. The statement

```
Printer.BeginDoc
```

"opens" the printer currently associated with the `Printer` component and makes it possible for you to send output to that printer.

Line 99 calls upon the `StartDoc` local subroutine to initialize the various variables controlling the printing of your document. You will examine the `StartDoc` subroutine shortly.

Lines 100 through 108 designate a **`while`** loop running through all of the pages of the document and printing them one-by-one. The **`while`** loop is used because it is not readily known in advance how many pages there are to print.

Note that inside the main **`while`** loop running page-by-page, right after the `StartPage` local subroutine call initializing the current page on line 99, there is another **`while`** loop, on lines 102 through 106.

This second, embedded **`while`** loop takes care of printing the text line-by-line, on the current page.

In particular, inside the line-oriented loop there is a call to the local `PrintLine` on line 103, which outputs exactly one line of text, followed by another local call to `NextLine` on line 104, whose purpose is to advance the printing to the next logical text line.

Line 105, with the `Application.ProcessMessages` statement, is especially worth noting. The `ProcessMessages` method does not have anything to do with printing *per se*. The purpose of including the call here is, as before, to let Windows "breathe" while you are printing your document. Without that call, all activity within Windows would come to a halt until you completely finished printing.

With the `ProcessMessages` call in place, the user can still interact with other applications, and the system is still responding to input events, even as the text of the note inside the `Memo1` component is being printed.

As soon as all the lines on the current page have been printed, the local call to the `NextPage` subroutine on line 107 advances the page count and lets the whole history repeat itself with the text of the next page.

After you are done printing all pages of the currently loaded document, the statement with the call to the `Printer`'s `EndDoc` method on line 109 ensures that the printing properly terminates, that the printed page is actually ejected from the printer, and that any resources devoted to printing that have been allocated in the background are released.

Note that up until now you have handled mostly the top-level logic involved with breaking the text stream inside the `Memo1` component into pages and lines. You have not actually printed anything just yet!

Before you rush to discover how the details of printing are being handled, take a look at the variable-declaration block on lines 38 through 44. All the variables declared in the block are accessible by the local subroutines below the **var** block. The block declares a number of control variables enabling you to keep track of the current line number being printed, your position relative to the total number of lines on the page and overall, and so on.

The `CurrentLine` variable declared on line 42 keeps track of the number of lines printed so far within the file.

The related `LineOnPage` variable declared on line 41 keeps track of the lines being printed on the current page. Both of these variables are incremented each time a new line is printed. The `NextLine` procedure defined on lines 82 to 87 is responsible for incrementing these line numbers. The same `NextLine` procedure is also responsible for incrementing the current pixel-based coordinate value of the `LineCoord` variable declared on line 40. `LineCoord` is calculated independently of the logical line number and describes the vertical position on the printed page at which each successive line is being printed. The position is expressed in terms of device pixels rather than logical line numbers. You need the pixel-based position to actually draw anything on the page.

The `LinesPerPage` variable declared on line 44 lets the printing algorithm decide when it is time to quit printing one page and start printing another. The `LinesPerPage` variable gets its initial value inside the `StartDoc` procedure, as you will shortly see, and that value never changes during the course of printing a document.

Similarly, the `TextHeight` variable, also initialized inside the `StartDoc` procedure, is calculated only once, at the beginning of a print job, to determine the actual height of a text line, expressed in device pixels. This value lets you advance the drawing of each successive line of text by an appropriate number of pixels so that the text lines do not appear crammed on top of one another, nor do they appear too widely spaced.

The remaining variable, `LeftMargin`, declared on line 39, is purely for esthetic reasons. It allows you to adjust the left margin so that the text does not appear too close to the left edge of the sheet of paper. The left margin is arbitrarily set to one inch on line 48, inside the `StartDoc` procedure. The value of `LeftMargin` is never recalculated again and remains valid throughout the entire process of printing a document.

Let's now begin a closer scrutiny of the local subroutines defined inside the `PrintCurrentFile` method, on lines 46 through 92.

`StartDoc` on lines 46 through 56, as mentioned before, initializes the various measurements to make the printing possible.

The trick to make the measurements accurate is to first assign the desired font to the `Printer`'s `Canvas`. It is the `Font`'s characteristics, in particular its vertical or point size, that determine the

number of lines on a page, and ultimately the number of pages it takes to print the entire document.

Line 51 shows an example of a quick solution that has experimentally been proven to work to enable making the text-size measurements. Attempting to output a blank character on the page actually initializes the printing mechanism and makes it possible to take accurate font-size measurements off the `Printer.Canvas`. Without the `TextOut` statement on line 51, the result returned by the subsequent statement on line 52 reflects the height of the font in terms of display pixels rather than in printer pixels.

Line 52 actually measures the height of a character in the currently selected font. Taking the `Abs` (the absolute value) of the `Font.Height` property is necessary because the result is typically negative, reflecting a design convention adopted by Windows GDI. The resulting value expressed in the device pixels is stored for the convenience of controlling the printing in the local variable `TextHeight`.

After you know the actual, device-dependent text height, you can calculate the number of lines that will fit on a page.

This is done through the statement on lines 53 and 54. The `Printer.PageHeight` property is used to obtain the actual vertical dimension of the printed page, again expressed in device pixels.

Line 55 initializes the overall line counter to zero, and the printing can begin.

The `MorePages` function defined on lines 58 through 62 is responsible for ensuring that the printing will actually terminate. The Boolean function returns `True` when there are more text lines to print, as indicated by the current printing position in the `CurrentLine` variable. Once the `CurrentLine` counter reaches the total number of text lines inside the memo component on the form, it is time to terminate printing.

The `MorePages` subroutine also checks whether the `Printer.Abort` method has been called. You may wish to provide a Printing... dialog box in your programs giving the user an opportunity to terminate a print job before it finishes. Typically, such a dialog box would have a Cancel button. If the Cancel button has been pressed, you call `Printer.Abort`, and then `Printer.Aborted` returns `True`. To obey the user's command, `MorePages` returns `False` in this case. The example program as is does not show the Printing... dialog box.

The procedure `StartPage`, defined on lines 64 through 68, is invoked every time a new page is about to be printed. It ensures that the counter variables local to, and meaningful only within the context of, a single page, `LineOnPage` and `LineCoord`, are always initialized afresh before a new page begins printing.

The procedure `NextPage`, defined on lines 70 through 74, is called after each page is being printed. It causes the page that has just finished printing to be ejected from the printer. The call to Printer.NewPage is only executed, however, if there are more pages pending. Otherwise the terminating call to Printer.EndDoc, already discussed, causes the ejection of the last page.

The Boolean function MoreLines, defined on lines 76 through 80, is expected to decide whether or not the current page being printed has been completed. A page is completed, naturally, when the LineOnPage counter reaches the LinePerPage limit.

Another reason to terminate the printing of a page might be the user pressing the Cancel button inside the Printing... dialog box. As before, checking Printer.Aborted will reveal the user's intent, and will force the printing to terminate if indeed the printing process was aborted.

Every time a new line has been printed, the NextLine procedure, defined on lines 82 through 87, ensures that the two counter variables, LineOnPage and CurrentLine, are properly updated. The procedure also ensures, on line 85 of the listing, that the next line of text to be drawn on the printed page does not overlap with the current line. It increments the value of the LineCoord variable with the value previously calculated and stored as the TextHeight.

Finally, something you have been waiting for all along! The PrintLine procedure on lines 89 through 92 implements the code that actually draws something on the Printer's Canvas. The TextOut statement on line 91 is where the text line is actually retrieved from the memo component via the Memo1.Lines[CurrentLine] property-access attempt.

If it seems like a lot of code to merely dump the contents of a text file to the printer, note that most of the code deals with the generic task of breaking the text into pages and lines.

Also note that after you have written down the basic outline of the printing algorithm, it becomes almost trivial to enhance the printing routine to also display graphical shapes and pictures, for example.

DO	DON'T

DO remember to include a call to Application.ProcessMessages inside any kind of a potentially lengthy processing loop, to let Windows run other applications too.

DON'T mix the display-based measurements with printer-based measurements. The actual height, in device pixels, of a character in 10-point Arial font is significantly different on a 96-pixel-per-inch display than it is on a 600-pixel-per-inch laser printer!

You can use the example program to quickly print out the contents of text files under Windows. Figure 16.5 shows the appearance of its main form, which is in a sense similar to the standard Windows Notepad.

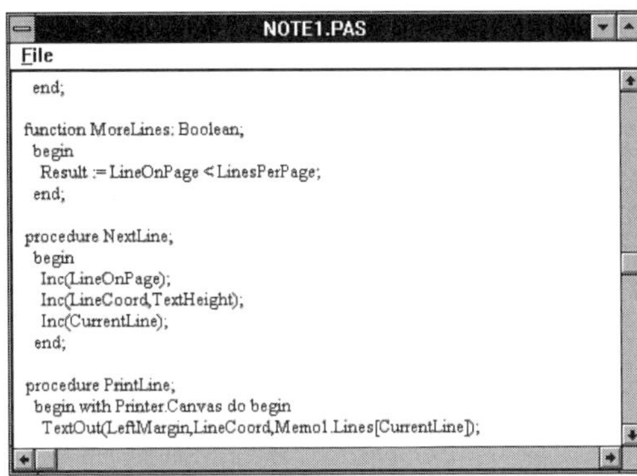

Figure 16.5.
NOTEPRNT, the Note Printer Application.

The above example of printing a text file concludes our limited (of necessity) discussion of drawing and painting with Delphi. The most important message to remember after today's lesson is that you display graphics and text using the methods of a `Canvas`.

Summary

Today's lesson revolved around the issues of displaying graphical output under Delphi. In particular, you learned the following:

- To generate output to either a display or a printer, you need to interact with a Delphi object known as `Canvas`.
- `Canvas` is a read-only, run-time-only property of all visual Delphi controls. In some cases it may not have been made visible by the owning class, however.
- The `Canvas` object has a number of properties defining how text and graphics are being drawn.
- `Pen` is a `Canvas` tool used to draw lines. `Brush` is another `Canvas` tool that is used to fill the inside areas of closed shapes, the most common example of which is a rectangle. `Font` describes the characteristics of the text being displayed. The combination of these three `Canvas` properties gives you full control over the appearance of the graphics you draw.
- The `Canvas` object also defines a number of methods that allow you to draw anything from a simple line (`MoveTo`/`LineTo` methods), to a `Rectangle`, to an `Ellipse`, to an arbitrarily complex `Polyline` (an open shape) or `Polygon` (a closed one), among others.

- You can also use the `TextOut` method, together with the properties of the `Font` and—to some extent also—`Brush`, to control the placement and the appearance of the text you draw.
- Delphi makes it relatively easy to generate printed, graphical output by fully encapsulating the low-level details of interacting with the printer device drivers and hiding them behind the familiar paradigm of a `Canvas`.
- To print, simply include the `Printers` unit in your **uses** clause and use the `Printer`'s methods to control the paper handling, and the `Printer.Canvas` to draw.

Q&A

Q How can I determine the physical size of the surface I am drawing on? Aren't the logical dimensions of the drawing surface dependent on the type and resolution of the output device?

A Yes, both the actual physical dimensions of the output device's display area and the resolution of the device, that is, the number of pixels per inch of the device's display, affect the number of pixels you have ultimately available to draw on. You also have to accommodate the fact that even the same device can be accessed in different resolution modes. If your drawing is dependent on physical coordinates, such as measurements in inches or millimeters, your best bet may be to change the default mapping mode of the device you are drawing on to one expressed in the units that will agree with your measurements. You can change the mapping mode of an output device by directly interacting with the so-called *device context* via Windows API (see the next question).

Q I am used to drawing in Windows using the built-in GDI subroutines, which I learned from the examples in many books available on the subject. The concept of `Canvas` seems to prevent me from doing some of the low-level detailed output rendering I was able to accomplish by using a handle to a Windows device context. Can I still use the traditional Windows subroutines for drawing?

A Yes. The `TCanvas` class encapsulates a lot of the GDI's functionality, providing the most useful methods, but it does not provide them all. You can still access the standard Windows GDI routines, however. Just make sure that you have included `WinProcs`, and usually `WinTypes`, in the **uses** clause of your unit. All GDI drawing subroutines expect you to supply a handle to the *device context*, which identifies the drawing surface of a particular device. The `Canvas.Handle` property *is* the device context, and it is accessible at run-time so that you can use it directly in calls to the Windows GDI. Not surprisingly, the `Canvas` itself uses calls to the GDI subroutines to produce any actual output.

Q How do I draw a bitmap?

A You can draw a bitmap on a `Canvas` by creating and preparing the bitmap, such as loading the actual image from a .bmp file on disk, and then using the `Canvas.Draw` method to display the bitmap.

The `Draw` method is defined as

```
procedure Draw(X, Y: Integer; Graphic: Tgraphic);
```

where the `X` and `Y` parameters are the coordinates of where the upper-left-hand corner of the bitmap should be placed, and the `Graphic` represents a graphical object to be displayed—a `Bitmap` in this case. The `TBitmap` class is a direct descendant of `TGraphic` and can be substituted polymorphically whenever a `TGraphic` is expected.

Workshop

The Workshop provides quiz questions to help you solidify your understanding of the material covered and exercises to provide you with experience in using what you've learned. Try to understand the quiz and exercise answers before continuing on to the next day's lesson.

Quiz

1. True or False? You cannot change the visual appearance of the standard Windows controls; they are drawn by Windows and there is no way to customize their look.
2. True or False? You can simultaneously use multiple pens to draw lines with different characteristics, for example, to draw several lines each in a different color.
3. True or False? You can accomplish every visual effect that is possible to accomplish with any and all of the `Canvas` methods by simply lighting appropriate pixels in designated colors.
4. True or False? In response to a paint request from Windows, you are required to redraw the entire surface of the visual control.
5. True or False? The set of graphics-drawing services encapsulated inside the VCL introduces considerable overhead and makes graphics operations slower by essentially inserting an additional layer of indirection between the application and the GDI.

Exercises

1. Create a simple program capable of loading and printing a bitmap from disk. Hint: Use a `Picture` component from the Additional page.

2. Modify the example `NotePrnt` program developed during the course of today's lesson for it to display a Printing dialog box that would enable the user to cancel a lengthy printing operation in progress.

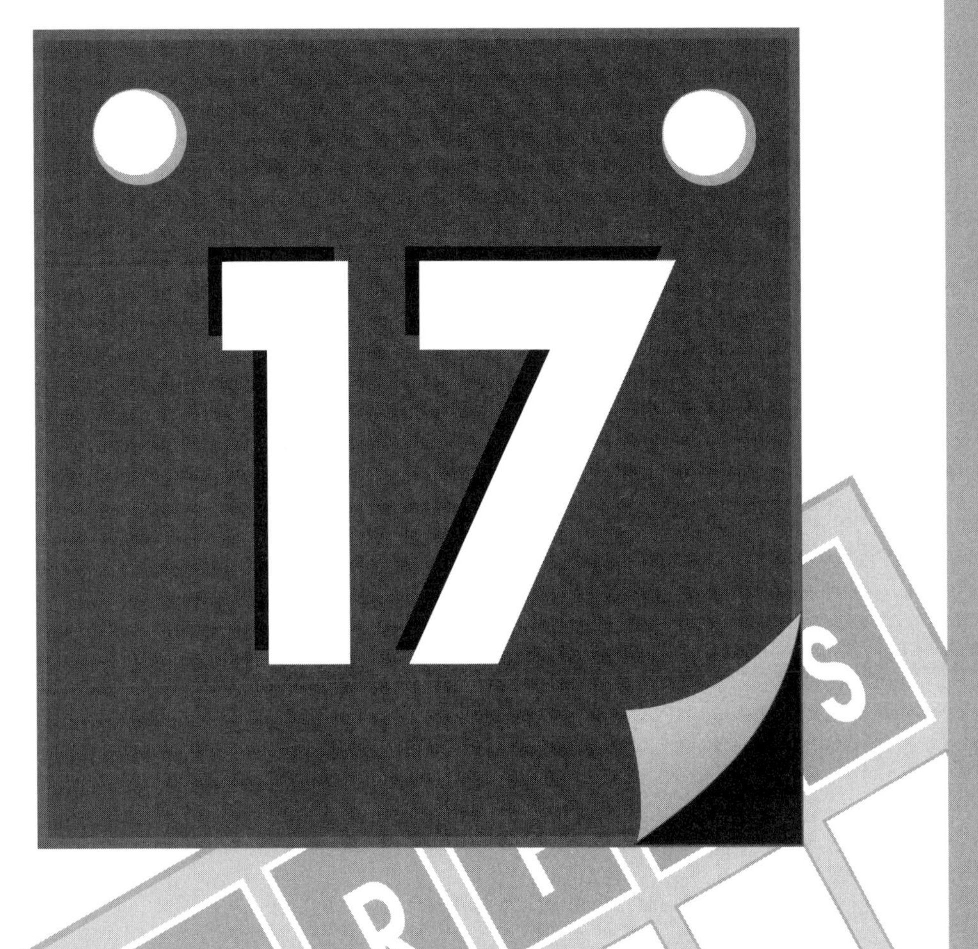

WEEK 3

Standard Windows Components

Today's lesson gives you more in-depth coverage of the standard, built-in Windows controls encapsulated by the Delphi components on the Standard page of the Component Palette.

You will learn about the following Delphi components:

- The menus—`MainMenu` and `PopupMenu`—used to invoke commands
- Labels
- Single-line `Edit` and multiline `Memo` text boxes
- Push-buttons, including the standard `Button` and the enhanced `BitBtn` components
- List boxes, including their single-selection and multiple-selection variants
- Combo boxes in their three variants of simple, drop-down, and drop-down lists
- Scroll bars
- Group boxes, including the custom `RadioGroup` component
- Panels

Menus

Menus are one of the key characteristics of Windows programs. Almost all Windows programs have a menu through which the user can interact with the application. Menus provide the user of a program with the means of invoking commands and requesting actions from the application.

Menus used to be the primary means of invoking program actions in most, if not all, Windows applications. If for no other reason, this was because menus were the simplest of all possible techniques the application designers could use to make their programs respond to user commands. Creating menus was, and still probably is, the simplest way of providing a means for invoking program commands.

Today, in the age of floating toolbars, speedbars, and fancy custom controls, menus often serve as a secondary means of controlling a program's actions. Do not underestimate the importance of menus, however. Menus still are an important element of the overall user interface.

Consider the following:

- Laptop and mobile users do not always appreciate having to use a mouse or another kind of pointing device to invoke common program actions.
- Data-entry operators do not like having to switch their mode of operation between entering data via the keyboard and invoking commands with the mouse. It is important for them to be able to control every aspect of the program directly from the keyboard.

- Menus serve as a "table of contents" for your application. Just by opening and looking at the available menu choices, new and inexperienced users can start learning about what your program has to offer in terms of functionality. For that reason, the main menu of an application should contain all the major commands that your program is capable of performing, even if there are other means of activating the same functionality, such as a button on a toolbar.

Using Menus

A menu must be associated with a window. In Delphi parlance, a visible window corresponds to a form so that you can associate menus with forms.

You can associate two kinds of menus with your Delphi forms:

- A main menu, which is displayed at the top of a window just below the title bar.
- A pop-up menu, which can be displayed by pressing the right mouse button anywhere within the window's frame.

17

Using the *MainMenu* Component

A main menu of a form is represented at run-time by a menu bar that appears inside the form's window just below the caption bar. The main menu consists of one or more choices, such as File, Edit, and Help, which are the entry points for the corresponding drop-down menus.

To display a drop-down menu, the user can click one of the choices displayed in the window menu bar, or press the Alt key followed by one of the underlined mnemonic characters displayed in the main menu bar.

The `MainMenu` component, which can be found on the Standard page of the Component Palette, encapsulates the functionality of a main application menu. You can select the `MainMenu` component and drop it on your form to give it the capability to automatically display a menu.

After you install a `MainMenu` component on your form, the menu becomes visible and operational even inside the Form Designer.

Although selecting a main menu choice at run-time invokes the program's action, selecting the choice from the Form Designer's prop menu at design-time enables you to easily associate an action with that menu choice.

A Menu Example Program

Although you have created example programs with menus before, you now will examine the process of creating and maintaining program menus in more detail and in a more systematic way.

Today, you will create a simple, blank, temporary project so that you can explore the ins and outs of menus. You will create a new project based on a blank form in a directory that you can dedicate to it and easily remove afterward.

Creating a Main Menu

To associate a main menu with a form, select a `MainMenu` component from the Standard page of the Component Palette and drop it on the form.

A small icon representing the menu component appears on the form, but the form window does not display any menus yet. The menu component you dropped on the form is empty initially; there are no items defined for it.

To define items for the menu, you need to open the Menu Editor, which is a custom Property Editor for menus. Double-click the `MainMenu1` icon on the form inside the Form Designer.

The Menu Designer's window opens. Initially, the main menu bar inside the Menu Designer is empty, as shown in Figure 17.1.

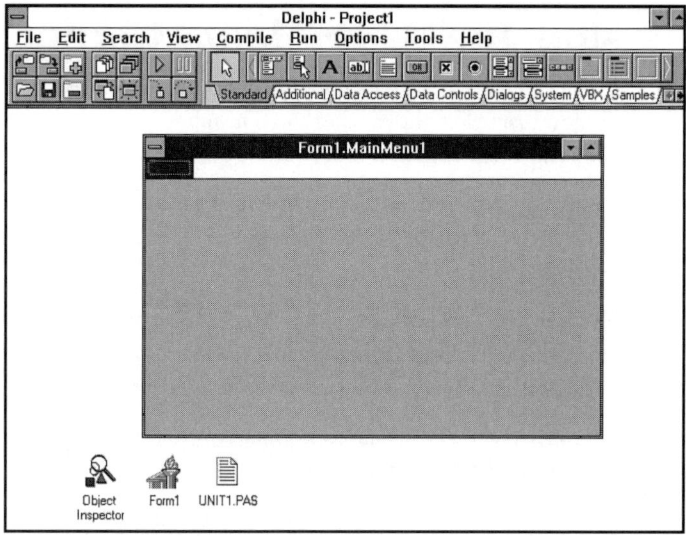

Figure 17.1.
An empty Menu Designer window.

The Menu Designer is effectively a custom Property Editor for the `Items` property of a `MainMenu` component. You examine the remaining properties of a `MainMenu` shortly.

With the Menu Designer window open, begin typing. Type `&File`, for example, and press Enter.

The text you entered ends up inside the `Caption` property of a newly created `MenuItem`.

After you press Enter, a new component is added to the form's class definition. There is a component inside your form's class for every menu item you create on the menu. You can access these menu item components at run-time inside the methods of your form and manipulate menu items and their properties dynamically.

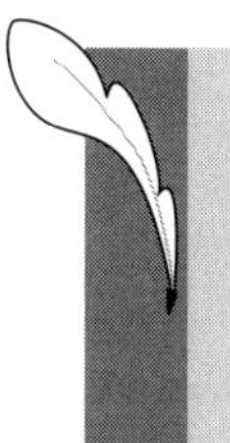

Note: If you do not want to access the methods and properties of the individual menu items programmatically at run-time, which is by far the most common situation, you can remove safely all but one reference to `TMenuItem` from the form's class definition to conserve space. More important, removing these references simplifies the form's class and makes it easier to understand.

You must leave one `TMenuItem` in the class definition of the form to enable the VCL to automatically register the class with the form loader. It does not matter which menu item you leave inside the class definition, as long as you leave at least one item.

17

A `MenuItem` (of `TMenuItem` class) is a Delphi component representing a single choice on a menu. It can represent a title for a drop-down menu or a cascading submenu, or a particular menu choice invoking a program's command.

Because you were typing while the highlight bar of the Menu Designer was positioned inside the main menu bar, you have created an item for the main menu bar. Now you have two choices:

- After you pressed Enter, the highlight bar of the Menu Designer was placed below the File item. If you continue there and enter more items, you will be building the File drop-down menu.
- You can place the Menu Designer's highlight bar in the main menu bar, after the File item you entered, and continue entering the main menu titles.

You thus can grow your menu in essentially two directions: by extending its main bar, or by appending or inserting items for the drop-down menus.

To append an item to a menu, position the Menu Designer's highlight bar in the blank spot at the end of the menu and start typing the menu item's caption.

To insert a new item in the middle of existing items, press Ins and start typing the new item's caption.

Now you can finish entering the items for the File drop-down menu. Within the Menu Designer, place the highlight bar on the first item position, just below the File title, and enter `New`.

Complete the File drop-down menu with the following items:

```
"&Open..."
"&Save"
"Save &As..."
"-"
"&Print..."
"P&rint Setup..."
"-"
"E&xit"
```

You immediately will recognize that this is a standard File menu—one identical to the menu you developed for the `NotePrnt` example program on Day 16.

You now add a new menu title in the main menu bar. Position the Menu Designer's highlight bar just after the File title on the main menu bar and type `&Edit`. Below the &Edit title, enter the following list of menu items:

```
"&Undo"
"-"
"Cu&t"
"&Copy"
"&Paste"
```

You have created a standard Edit menu.

After you enter some menu items, you can rearrange their order and position by dragging them with the mouse. To move an item to another location, select it with the mouse and then drag it to its new position while still holding the left mouse button. Then release the mouse button.

You can drag a menu item outside of its native menu—for example, from one pop-up menu to the main menu bar, or to another pop-up menu. You have complete freedom in how you want to arrange the menu items.

Here are some more hints on menu editing:

- To delete a menu item or an entire submenu, select the item you want to delete inside the Menu Designer and press the Delete key.
- To select a contiguous block of more than one menu item for a subsequent operation (such as to drag several items to a new location, or to delete several items in one step), highlight the first item of the block. Then, while pressing Shift, highlight the last item of the block. All items between the first item and the last item that you indicated are selected.
- To select a noncontiguous collection of multiple menu items in preparation for a subsequent operation, select successive items while pressing Ctrl. All items that you click while pressing Ctrl are selected. You can toggle the selection state of individual items on a menu by clicking them with the mouse while pressing Ctrl.

- To enter a separator line in place of a menu item (for example, to separate two groups of menu items), enter a single dash (-) character (ASCII #45, decimal) as the `Caption` of the `MenuItem` component. You can create separators in drop-down menus and cascaded pop-up menus, but not on the main menu bar. In the main menu, the dash appears verbatim as a separate choice.
- To create a cascading submenu attached to the right-hand side of a menu item in a drop-down menu, press the right-arrow key while you press Ctrl. Menu items that lead to cascading submenus are marked with a right-pointing triangle at run-time, indicating that the menu item opens another submenu instead of executing a command.

17

Although there are no limits to the depth of nesting of cascading menus, the use of deeply nested cascading menus (and, in fact, of cascading menus in general) is not recommended. Multilevel cascading menus are very difficult for the user to manipulate, because every time an item is chosen from the bottom-level menu, the entire cascade disappears. The user must navigate explicitly all the way down through the cascade to restore his or her context in the menu. It also is very easy to issue a wrong, unintended command when in a cascading menu.

Note: When defining a horizontal main menu bar, avoid using multiword phrases or titles containing blank spaces. Spaces make it confusing for the user to discern a single, multiword, drop-down menu title from several single-word titles.

Menu choices can be accessed by the users of your programs in a number of ways; they can make a choice by selecting it with a mouse, by pressing Alt or F10 and navigating to the desired item with the arrow keys, and so on.

Choices also can be accessed by their mnemonic access characters, which are underlined in menu titles and menu item captions.

Note: Each menu item's caption should contain an underlined mnemonic access character that gives your users direct access to the menu items through the keyboard. Remember that not everyone can use a pointing device, such as a mouse, to invoke menu commands.

To make a particular character in a menu title or caption a mnemonic (to make it appear underlined), prefix it with an ampersand character (&)—ASCII #38, decimal. This is precisely what you were asked to do when creating the example File and Edit menus earlier.

You should avoid using the same mnemonic character for two items in the same menu. The Menu Designer will not catch this condition, and the result will be that only one of these menu items will be accessible via the keyboard.

Another way of accessing the functionality of most frequently used menu items is by direct keyboard shortcuts known as *accelerators*. A menu accelerator gives the user the capability to invoke a particular command by using the keyboard in a single step. The shortcut key combinations usually are displayed to the right of the corresponding menu item's caption.

Delphi makes it very easy to create menu shortcuts. Every menu item component you create inside the Menu Designer has a `ShortCut` property. You can assign the `ShortCut` property of a menu item to the name of a keyboard key.

By default, the `ShortCut` property defines no accelerator keys. You can change that by using the drop-down list of some of the available keyboard shortcuts that can be associated with the `ShortCut` property inside the Object Inspector. You can also type the key names directly: for example, `Home`.

When you change the value of the `ShortCut` property of a menu item, the shortcut you define is displayed automatically in the menu to the right of the item caption, as required.

Try to associate some shortcuts with the menu you have been creating so far. Associate the following shortcuts with the Edit menu items:

Ctrl+Z	Undo
Ctrl+X	Cut
Ctrl+C	Copy
Ctrl+V	Paste

These shortcuts are considered standard in Windows version 3.1 and higher.

Captions of menu items associated with actions that require some more information from the user before the action can be initiated should be followed by an ellipsis (...)—three periods (each being the ASCII character #46 decimal).

The "Open..." item in the File menu you created earlier contains such an ellipsis, because typically the user would be prompted for a filename before the open action could be completed.

Make sure that you always omit the ellipsis, however, if there is a possibility of a menu item invoking an immediate action. When users see an ellipsis in a menu item, they are expecting a dialog box to pop up so that they can enter the additional required information or cancel the action.

Creating a Pop-Up Menu

A pop-up menu is the second kind of a menu supported by Delphi. The `PopupMenu` component (`TPopupMenu` class) is different from the `MainMenu`, because it can be associated with many visible Delphi controls.

Pop-up menus are menus that appear upon user request. They appear to be floating over the background and are not visually attached to the application's menu bar.

Often, a context-sensitive pop-up menu appears after the user clicks the right mouse button. The items that appear on the menu and, consequently, the commands available from the menu, change depending on where the user's cursor was when the button was pressed. Each visible object on the display can have its own pop-up menu with commands that pertain only to this object.

17

Try right-clicking on the Delphi Code Editor window to see an example of a pop-up menu.

Notice that the Code Editor's pop-up menu has no fixed position. Unlike the main menu, which always has a menu bar with the submenu titles, a pop-up menu appears wherever the user happened to right-click the mouse.

Pop-up menus offer an attractive alternative to invoking commands via the main menu bar or a toolbar. Unlike the main menu, pop-up menus appear "in-place," at the location of the mouse cursor, eliminating the need for the user to move the mouse pointer to the menu bar. Pop-up menus appear only on demand, and do not take up any of the screen's precious real estate. On the other hand, they give no indication to the user that such a functionality even exists and how to activate it.

Follow these steps:

1. To create a pop-up menu for the main form of your application, drop a `PopupMenu` component from the Standard page of the Component Palette on the form.
2. Double-click the newly dropped `PopupMenu1` component icon to open the custom Property Editor for the menu `Items`: the Menu Designer.

   You now can enter the menu item captions as before, defining the contents of the pop-up menu. Because you are building a pop-up menu that will be associated with the form, you can choose a subset of the main menu commands to appear on the pop-up menu, for the convenience of the user.
3. Enter the following items inside the newly created pop-up menu, `PopupMenu1`:

```
"&New"
"&Open..."
"&Save"
"-"
"&Copy"
"&Paste"
"-"
"E&xit"
```

4. Close the Menu Designer window.
5. Click the form to select the form itself, `Form1`, as the current component in the Object Inspector and click the form's `PopupMenu` property. Open the drop-down list of the pop-up menus available and associate `PopupMenu1` with this property.
6. Compile and run the application.

   Notice that, in addition to the main menu you created earlier, after you click the right mouse button on the form, a pop-up menu appears from which you can select commands.

   Of course, as is, neither the main menu nor the pop-up menu causes the program to do anything, so the next step is to associate events with the menu commands.
7. Close the application to return to design mode.

Associating Menu Events

When the user of your program selects a menu item at run-time, an `OnClick` event is generated for that menu item. You can trap that event by writing your own handler, which invokes the corresponding action in response to the user selection.

There are many ways to associate `OnClick` events with menu items. The simplest way in the case of a `MainMenu` component is by selecting the menu item on the menu prop created for you by Delphi inside the Form Designer. In other words, you interact with the form's menu just as the user would, pulling down the submenus you want and selecting a particular command.

At design-time, the action that occurs after you select a menu item is different from the action at run-time. When you click a form's main menu item inside the Form Designer, Delphi responds by creating an empty skeleton event handler in the Code Editor. You then can enter the code that you want to be executed for that menu item at run-time.

You will now associate some actions with the menu items you created in previous steps:

1. Select the Exit item from the File drop-down menu on your sample form.

   Delphi responds by creating an empty event handler like the following:

   ```
   procedure TForm1.Exit1Click(Sender: TObject);
   begin

   end;
   ```

   You now can enter the code you want to be executed after the user chooses Exit from the File menu. The code for this event is very simple and consists of a single line only.
2. Enter the following statement inside the `Exit1Click` handler:

   ```
   Close;
   ```

The action you just defined closes the main form of the application, terminating the program.

Checking and Unchecking Menu Items

Typically, a menu item invokes an action—a process. Sometimes, it is convenient to provide menu items that change some program settings.

As an example, take a look at the View menu inside Delphi. At the bottom of the Delphi View menu, there is a group of two items—Speedbar and Component Palette—separated from the rest of the items by a horizontal divider.

Speedbar toggles the visibility of the Delphi toolbar, and Component Palette toggles the visibility of the Component Palette. Both items have checkmarks next to the respective item's caption.

You can use such checkmarked menu items to let the user set the values of data properties inside your own programs. Every menu item has a `Checked` property that is of type `Boolean`. The value of this property can be set at design-time, and dynamically at run-time, to properly reflect the value of the setting to which it corresponds.

17

Typically, you would set the initial or default value of the `Checked` property at design-time, and let your application toggle the checkmark in response to the user actions at run-time.

The following code, for example, ensures that the checkmark is visible in front of the menu item designated as the `Underline1` component:

```
Underline1.Checked := True;
```

Changing Menus

Although only one main menu can be active on a form at any given time, there is nothing that prevents you from dropping more than one `MainMenu` component on a single form. You can define several menus for any given form and switch among them at run-time. This method gives you the capability to equip your programs with context-sensitive menus that change their appearance and composition depending on the current state of the application.

It also is possible to remove an individual drop-down menu title from a window at run-time. According to the official user-interface guidelines published by Microsoft, you can remove a drop-down menu title from the main menu bar in an application that supports different document types or different views and displays a different menu depending on which document type currently has the focus. If no views are open inside an application like that, there may be no way to decide which menu bar to display.

You can remove the drop-down titles that no longer are applicable and leave only those that are valid, even if there are no open documents. A typical example of this technique is eliminating the text-formatting commands from the menu of a word processing program when there is no text loaded. If the commands no longer are applicable, or are temporarily not applicable, the simplest way to remove them from the menu is by dynamically, at run-time, selecting a different menu—one that does not contain the redundant commands—to be the main menu of an application's window.

Note that Microsoft guidelines suggest graying out, rather than removing, menu options in programs that support only one document type. This has the effect of educating the user of possible choices the program offers. Otherwise, the user may not even be aware that a particular action *can* be performed.

Labels

Labels (class `TLabel`) are one of the most commonly utilized components in any Delphi project. You place a label on the form whenever you need to annotate another component, such as an edit box, or whenever you simply need to display some text inside a form. A label describes the meaning or function of the control it annotates, and also provides a way to access directly the annotated control with the keyboard, by using a mnemonic shortcut.

A `Label` component has a number of properties that enable you to control the appearance of the text the label displays—for example, the font with which the label is being drawn, the positioning and sizing of the label, and other attributes.

You also can associate event handlers with a number of mouse-related events that the `TLabel` component defines, such as `OnClick`, `OnDblClick`, `OnMouseDown`, `OnMouseMove`, and so on.

Note: Delphi labels should not be confused with the standard Windows static text controls.

Although very similar in functionality, Delphi `Labels` serve a more narrowly defined purpose of simply displaying text. The standard static text controls actually are capable of displaying themselves as rectangles of various colors, in addition to being displayed as text.

The implementation of Delphi `Labels` is not based on the standard static text control, but is native to Delphi. Unlike the standard static controls, Delphi labels are not true windows but merely visual adornments painted by the application. Delphi labels are much less wasteful of Windows resources than are the standard static controls.

Labels typically display read-only, static text. The text is static in the sense that the user cannot change it by typing over it. The text may be altered by the application by assigning a new value to the `Caption` property during the course of the application's execution to reflect the current state of processing.

The most important property of a label is undoubtedly its `String`-typed `Caption` property. You can change the text the label component displays by assigning a value to the caption. You also can read the value of the caption to determine what is being displayed.

To change the contents of the label by assigning a string value to the `Caption` property, use a statement such as the following:

```
Label1.Text := 'This is a label';
```

Although you can control the appearance of a label's text by assigning appropriate values to its `Font` property, you are limited to using a single font per label. The entire label is displayed in a particular typeface, size, and color. You cannot highlight or modify the visible properties of just a portion of the label.

17

Edit Boxes

The `Edit` component encapsulates the idea of a text-entry box in which you can type information. A blinking current-position or insertion-point indicator, also known as the *caret*, is a characteristic feature of edit boxes. This blinking caret appears when the edit box has the focus.

An *edit box* is a standard Windows control used by many, if not all, Windows applications. The `TEdit` Delphi class encapsulates this standard edit control in its capacity as a single-line edit box. It may be possible to enter more text into the box than fits within the visible boundaries of the control, for example, but line breaks are not permitted. The overflow text will scroll horizontally, "sliding" underneath the edit box.

You can insert text inside the edit box by assigning a string value to its `Text` property. Of course, you can read the value of the `Text` property back to programmatically find out about the contents of the edit box.

As was the case with the label component, you can control the appearance of the text inside an edit box by assigning appropriate values to its `Font` property. You can control the selection of the typeface, size, color, and other attributes of the font. Just as before, the font settings affect all text in the control at once. You cannot control the appearance of the individual characters or individual words within the standard edit box.

You can control separately the color of the control's background by assigning the desired value to its `Color` property.

An edit box can be designated as auto-sizing by its `AutoSize` property being set to `True`. In this case, the edit box dynamically changes its height depending on the currently selected `Font`. The larger the font used for the edit box, the greater the height of the control. This property is `True` by default. If you change it to `False`, the edit box retains its height regardless of the changes in the size of the font associated with it. On the other hand, setting `AutoSize` to `False` may make your edit box clip its text when run on systems configured with large fonts—not a pretty sight.

You can limit the maximum number of characters that can be entered into an edit box by assigning an appropriate numeric value to its `MaxLength` property. Due to Windows limitations, the absolute theoretical maximum amount of text that an edit box control can handle is 64KB, but for many practical reasons, you will never be able to achieve that maximum. In particular, if you assign text to an edit box via the `Caption` property, the maximum length of a Pascal string, 255 characters, is your limiting factor. This value may be sufficient for many applications, but if you ever need more, just keep in mind that it is possible. Unfortunately, the explanation of how to manage more text in an edit box is beyond the scope of this book (look up the `GetTextBuf`/`SetTextBuf` methods of the `TEdit` class in the on-line help, if you are curious).

You can force the characters the user types inside an edit box to all uppercase or to all lowercase, depending on the value of the `CharCase` property. By default, `CharCase` is `ecNormal`, allowing mixed-case text entry. You can change it to `ecUpperCase` or `ecLowerCase` to force all uppercase or all lowercase.

An interesting effect that you can achieve with an edit box involves the `PasswordChar` property. By default, this `Char`-type property has the value of #0. If you change it to some other character value (for example, an asterisk), each character the user types into the edit box appears as the designated `PasswordChar` (in this case, *), instead of showing the actual character typed. This capability is useful for data entry in which confidentiality is required, such as with login password dialog boxes.

Finally, the `ReadOnly` property of an edit box can be used to designate it as a read-only control. Its appearance does not change after you set the `ReadOnly` property to `True`, but its functionality does: the user is prevented from changing the text displayed in the control.

Memo Boxes

A `Memo` (`TMemo` class) is another type of an edit box: one that allows multiline text entry. In a `Memo`, lines can extend beyond the right boundary of the control, just like in the case of the simple edit boxes. Alternatively, lines may wrap to the next line, forming a paragraph spanning multiple visible lines. To control whether the excess text is being wrapped, you can assign a Boolean value to the `WordWrap` property of a `Memo` component.

A `Memo` may present scroll bars for navigation through the text that extends outside the control's boundaries. The `ScrollBar` property controls whether the horizontal and vertical scroll bars are visible. You can assign one of four values to the `ScrollBar` property: `ssNone`, `ssVertical`, `ssHorizontal`, or `ssBoth`.

`Memo` supports many of the same properties as the edit box. The `Memo` component is built around the same edit box standard Windows control as the one that forms the basis for the edit box. This time, the Windows edit box is used in its capacity as a multiline editor.

Some properties, however, apply only to multiline memos. A `Memo` does not have a `Text` property, for example. Instead, its `Lines` property enables you to control the contents of the memo. You can use the `TStrings` methods and properties to manipulate the text lines inside a memo.

At design-time, inside the Object Inspector, you can open the `Lines` property and simply enter the text in the provided custom Property Editor. At run-time, you may use the programmatic interface of the `Lines` property of a memo to rearrange and modify the text lines. In particular, you can append or insert new text lines, delete or replace existing lines, and so on.

17

You see an illustration of how a `TStrings`-typed property is used in the context of a list box control later in today's lesson. Note, however, that the descendants of the `TStrings` component serving as the `Lines` property of a memo can be manipulated in the same way as the `Items` property of a list box, so that everything that applies to manipulating list box items also is applicable to manipulating individual text lines in a memo.

Buttons

A `Button` component, also known as a push-button standard Windows control, is a control displayed as a labeled, gray push-button that the user can press by clicking it with the mouse to initiate an action.

The user also can select most buttons by pressing a key on the keyboard that corresponds to the mnemonic shortcut. The shortcut appears as an underlined letter on the button's face.

A push-button initiates commands; it provides another way for the user to invoke an application's action, and is an alternative to menus.

`Buttons` are labeled with text. As was the case with the `Label` component, the textual label of the button is controlled by assigning string values to the `Caption` property.

You can control the details of the appearance of a button's label by defining the properties of its font. In particular, you can change the typeface, size, and color of the text label.

The action associated with a particular button takes place when the user releases the mouse while the cursor is over the push-button.

You can assign the action to a `Button` component by creating an `OnClick` event handler for it. Inside the Form Designer, double-click the particular `Button` component for which you want to create an `OnClick` handler. Alternatively, with the `Button` component selected, double-click the value column of the `OnClick` event on the `Events` page of the Object Inspector to create an appropriate skeleton handler:

```
procedure TForm1.Button1Click(Sender: TObject);
begin

end;
```

The code you put inside this event handler is executed after the user chooses that button.

A Button component defines a number of unique properties related to its function as a command initiator.

Cancel Property

The Cancel property of a button, if set to True, binds the button's action to the Esc key on the keyboard. Whenever the user of the program presses Esc, the first button in the tab order whose Cancel property is set to True executes its OnClick event handler as if it were selected by the user directly.

Typically, Esc is used to close a modal dialog box; it is associated with a push-button labeled Cancel or Close.

Default Property

The Default property of a push-button determines the behavior of the form when the user presses Enter.

After the user of the program presses Enter, the first button in the tab order in which the Default property is set to True executes its OnClick method. However, if another button was selected explicitly by the user and has the focus at the time, its OnClick handler executes instead. This, as well as the Cancel button behavior described earlier, is part of the standard Windows behavior that you will observe in just about all modal dialog boxes.

ModalResult Property

The ModalResult property of a Button component is meaningful only when the form on which the button resides is displayed in a modal state, as a dialog box. If the form is displayed using the ShowModal method, it stays up until the user dismisses it by choosing an appropriate action. Typically, the user is expected to choose the OK button to accept the data on the form, or the Cancel button to reject the data. As mentioned earlier, the user can press Enter or Esc to achieve the same results.

To let the block of code in which the modal form was displayed know which of the possible actions took place (whether the user accepted or canceled the form, for example), the ShowModal method of the form returns a numeric value—a *modal result.*

A `Form` component has a `ModalResult` property, which is zero by default. Whenever the value of this property becomes nonzero, the form closes and the value of its `ModalResult` is returned as the `ShowModal` function's result.

A `Button` component defines a `ModalResult` to make it possible for you to define different results for different buttons and, consequently, to determine which button was pressed to close a modal form.

If you provide a nonzero value for the `ModalResult` property of a button, you don't have to write a dedicated `OnClick` event handler just to close the form. By assigning this nonzero value to the `ModalResult` property of the form, which is done automatically, you can close the form and return this value to the caller.

17

BitBtn

The `BitBtn` component is a natural and attractive extension of the standard push-button concept. It can be found on the "Additional" page of the Delphi Component Palette.

A `BitBtn`, whose class `TBitBtn` is a direct descendant of the `TButton`, provides support for displaying text labels and icons inside the button.

For a quick tour of built-in possibilities, try changing the `Kind` property of a `BitBtn` component.

If you have not yet done so, place a copy of a `BitBtn` component on the current form to allow yourself to see its properties in the Object Inspector.

Changing the kind of a `BitBtn` from the default `bkCustom` to one of the predefined kinds enables you to see some of the built-in *glyphs*—bitmaps or pictures associated with different standard functions.

Changing the kind of a `BitBtn` to `bkOk`, for example, reveals a green checkmark, while `bkCancel` shows a red X sign.

Use the `Kind` property to quickly tune a `BitBtn` to perform one of several standard functions and associate an appropriate standard picture with it.

On the other hand, when you want more control over the appearance of the button, or simply want to introduce your own picture not included in the standard set of glyphs, you can use the `Glyph` property to associate any Windows bitmap with the button.

Other than by its appearance, the `BitBtn` does not differ from its standard counterpart and is equivalent functionally to that of a standard push-button.

Check Boxes

Check box controls enable the user to select an On or Off state for an individual choice or setting. When the choice is turned on, the check box is *checked*—it appears with an X inside it. When the choice is turned off, the check box is blank.

The `State` property of a check box determines the visual state of the control. The `State` property allows one of *three* possible values: `cbChecked`, `cbUnchecked`, and `cbGrayed`. The `cbGrayed` state is considered to represent an indeterminate state—neither checked, nor unchecked, also meaning "not applicable."

As a matter of principle, check box controls are used to display one of two binary states: On or Off, True or False, Included or Excluded, and so on. The third, indeterminate state (`cbGrayed`) is used when other settings make it impossible to determine the current check value for the check box.

Radio Buttons

A *radio button control*, also known as an *option button*, displays a single choice in a set of mutually exclusive options. In any group of radio buttons, the user can select one button, and only one button, at any given time. That is, when several radio buttons are placed in a single container, such as a group box, they become mutually exclusive.

A selected radio button is displayed as a circle filled in the middle. An unselected radio button is an empty circle. Assign the value of `True` or `False` to the `Checked` property of a radio button to change its visual state.

You can use groups of radio buttons to allow the user to select one from a limited set of choices—usually no more than four or five. If the number of choices exceeds four, you may want to consider alternatives that are less demanding as far as the screen area is concerned, such as list boxes or combo boxes.

See also the discussion of the `RadioGroup` component later in today's lesson.

List Boxes

List boxes are amazingly versatile controls that allow the user to select one or more choices from a list of possible options. The choices available may be represented by text captions, graphics, or a combination of the two.

The common theme among the different kinds of list boxes is the actual lists of items they maintain. The most common type of a list box item is a text string. You will find text-string-oriented list boxes in almost any application. The user can scroll through the contents of the list

box and choose from among many more options than otherwise would physically fit on the display.

You might want to consider using a list box under the following circumstances:

- When the user must select from many choices, making it impractical to use radio buttons.
- If the list of choices is not static, but changes dynamically at run-time. For example, new choices are added, some are removed, and so on.

A `ListBox` component defines the `Items` property, which is simply a list of `String`-typed items. The `Items` property is defined in the following:

```
property Items: TStrings read FItems write SetItems;
```

The `Items` property is assigned a concrete `TStrings` descendant, such as an instance of a `TStringList`, which you can manipulate directly to add or delete strings from the list box.

To add a string to the list box `ListBox1` at run-time, for example, you simply can use its `Items.Add` method, as in the following example:

```
ListBox1.Items.Add('Sample string');
```

Similarly, to insert a new string at a specified position into the list box, you can use the `Insert` method:

```
ListBox1.Items.Insert(0,'This becomes the first string');
```

This line inserts the sample literal string as the first item in the list box, at position zero.

Note: List box items are numbered using a zero-based scheme. The first item is item number 0, the second is the item number 1, the third is item number 2, and so on.

Similarly, to delete a string at a specified position, use the Delete method, as in the following example:

```
ListBox1.Items.Delete(2);
```

This statement deletes the *third* item in the list box (remember that list box item indexes are zero-based).

As you can see, it is fairly easy to manipulate the items in a list box at run-time, thereby affecting the choices the user sees inside the box.

Single-Selection List Boxes

By default, a `ListBox` component becomes a single-selection list box (when you drop a new instance of it from the Component Palette on the form, for example).

Only one item in such a list can be selected at any given time. This selected item is highlighted and the highlight can be moved by the user via the up- and down-arrow keys.

You can retrieve the current selection index by querying the value of the `ItemIndex` property. The `ItemIndex` is an `Integer`-typed property available only at run-time, which enables you to determine which of the list box items has the selection in a single-selection list box.

Usually, double-clicking an item in a single-selection list box invokes some default action on that item. On modal dialog forms, for example, double-clicking an item in a list box often selects that item and closes the dialog box.

Single-Selection List Box Example

To investigate the behavior of single-selection list boxes, create a very simple example application by following these steps:

1. Create a new project and drop an instance of a list box from the Standard page of the Component Palette on the form.
2. Size the newly dropped `ListBox` component (by default, named `ListBox1`) so that it takes up most of the form's area. You also can change its `Align` property to `alClient` to make it fully cover the form's client area and to adjust automatically to the current size of the form.
3. Double-click in the right-hand column (the value) of the `Items` property. Alternatively, choose the ellipsis (...) button that appears after you select the `Items` property in the Object Inspector to open the String List Editor window.

   The String List Editor is a custom Property Editor for the `TStrings`-typed properties and any `TStrings`-descendant-typed properties.

   The Editor enables you to enter free-form text, arranged in lines, at design-time, thereby providing the initial contents for the list box.
4. Enter the following lines of text inside the String List Editor:

```
One
Two
Three
Four
Five
Six
Seven
```

```
Eight
Nine
Ten
```

5. Choose OK.

The lines you entered fill the list box at design-time and run-time.

You now can run your application to test the behavior of a single-selection list box.

Note how the highlighting selection bar moves whenever you click an item in the list box, or whenever you press the up- or down-arrow key.

The key point is that only one selection is visible at any given time, and you can query that selection by examining the value of the `ItemIndex` property at run-time.

You can use an assignment statement similar to the one that follows to obtain the current list box selection index:

```
var
  AnIndex: Integer;
begin
  ...
  AnIndex := ListBox1.ItemIndex;
  ...
end;
```

Multi-Item Selection List Boxes

Occasionally, you will need a list box in which the user has the capability to select more than one item at a time.

You can toggle the value of the `MultiSelect` property of a list box to `True` to turn it into a multiple-selection list box.

The multi-item selection list boxes fall into two categories:

- Extended-selection
- Multiple-selection

The difference in the behavior of multiple-selection versus extended-selection depends on the value of the `ExtendedSelect` property of a list box.

Extended-Selection List Boxes

Extended-selection list boxes enable the user to select multiple items from the list. A list box has an extended-select behavior when both the `MultiSelect` and `ExtendedSelect` properties are set to `True`.

Extended-selection lists support the selection of both contiguous and disjoint blocks of items with the mouse or the keyboard.

Consider the following examples:

- Clicking an item and dragging the mouse extends the current selection, forming a contiguous block of selected items. This behavior is characteristic for an extended-selection list box.
- Clicking the mouse on an item, in addition to moving the focus to that item, toggles its selection state. It also deselects all other items that already may have been selected. This behavior is virtually identical to that of a single-selection list box.
- Similarly, pressing the spacebar toggles the selection state of the currently focused item, deselecting all other items.
- Clicking an item other than the currently focused item while Shift is pressed extends the selection to form a contiguous block of selected items.
- Clicking an item while pressing Ctrl toggles the selection state of that single item without affecting any other items. This is characteristic of multi-selection list boxes.

Keep in mind that this is not meant as an exhaustive list of features of extended-selection list boxes under Windows. Instead, it should leave you with the impression that an extended-selection list box behaves just like a single-selection list box if no special keys are pressed. Clicking an item with the mouse while the Shift or Ctrl is pressed enables the user to control exactly which items in a multiple-selection list box actually are selected.

In particular, extended-selection list boxes enable the user to easily select contiguous blocks of items by selecting the first (or last) item, and extending the selection from there.

Note that setting `ExtendedSelect` to `True` has no effect when the `MultiSelect` property is `False` (when the list box is not a multiple-selection list box, that is).

An Extended-Selection List Box Example

Modify the single-selection list box example you created earlier in this chapter to investigate the behavior of extended-selection list boxes. Follow these steps:

1. At design-time, inside the Object Inspector, toggle the `MultiSelect` property of `ListBox1` to `True`.
2. Make sure that the `ExtendedSelect` property is still `True`, as it is by default.
3. Run the application and experiment with selecting and deselecting individual items in noncontiguous and contiguous groups, by pressing Shift or Ctrl while clicking the items, as appropriate.

Multiple-Selection List Boxes

Multiple-selection list boxes are useful whenever the user must select several entries from a list, but these entries are not grouped in any meaningful way. In other words, there is no reason to provide the extended-selection capability to select contiguous blocks of items, because the user is likely to toggle the selection state of individual items on a one-by-one basis.

Simply toggle the `ExtendedSelect` property of a multi-selection list box to `False` to achieve an ordinary multiple-selection list box optimized for disjoint selections.

A Multiple-Selection List Box Example

Change the extended-selection example program you created earlier in this chapter to now appreciate the behavior of a nonextended, multiselect list box. Follow these steps:

17

1. At design-time, inside the Object Inspector, toggle the `ExtendedSelect` property of `ListBox1` to `False`.
2. Make sure that the `MultiSelect` property is still `True`.
3. Run the program now and observe that you no longer can extend the selections by dragging the mouse or clicking the list box items while Shift is pressed. Each item now must be selected or deselected individually and independently of others.

Note: Delphi uses the traditional technique of marking the selected items in a multiple-selection list box with a highlighting bar, displaying the selected items in reverse video. This is a built-in Windows behavior and requires no additional programming on your part beyond making sure that the `MultiSelect` property of the list box is set to `True`. The official Windows interface guidelines, however, recommend that a check box be used to precede each item in the list box to indicate whether the item is in a selected or an unselected state.

The multiple-selection list box with check marks is not a predefined Windows control, and supporting this recommendation requires you to create an owner-drawn list box. In fact, few applications currently support this style.

Owner-Drawn List Boxes

The need for owner-drawn list boxes arises whenever the standard, textual, list-item captions are not sufficient to represent an item.

A common application of owner-drawn list boxes arises, for example, when you need to display a graphic in addition to the standard text caption for each item inside the list box.

Also, because the standard automatic drawing of list box items is done in a single color using a single font (the attributes of the `Font` property of the list box, for example), you have to resort to an owner-drawn list box whenever you need to display several types of items, with each item type possibly using a different font.

To create an owner-drawn list box, change the value of the `Style` property from `lbStandard` to `lbOwnerDrawFixed` or `lbOwnerDrawVariable`.

The `lbOwnerDrawFixed` style assumes that all list box items are of the same, fixed height. An `OnMeasureItem` event is generated once during the lifetime of the control's window. This event can be trapped by the owner form to redefine the standard height of the list box items to a custom value. The default item measurement depends on the value of the `ItemHeight` property, whose default, in turn, depends on the font being used in the list box. Of course, you don't have to provide the `OnMeasureItem` event handler if you do not want to change the default item height.

The `lbOwnerDrawVariable` style enables the owner form to determine the height of each item individually by providing an event handler for the `OnMeasureItem` event. You should provide the `OnMeasureItem` handler because the list box cannot make any assumptions about the height of any individual item.

Note: The Windows implementation of the `lbOwnerDrawVariable` list box has a bug that prevents it from correctly handling the Page Down key. You must provide a workaround for this bug by creating a custom control based on `Listbox`, and handling the `WM_VSCROLL` Windows message yourself if you intend to use the `lbOwnerDrawVariable` style.

In both cases, designating a list box as `lbOwnerDrawXXXX` in the first place puts the additional burden of providing the mechanism for drawing the items on the "owner" of the list box—typically, the form on which the control appears.

Owner-drawing means additional work on your part, but gives you an opportunity to greatly enhance the display of list items. In addition to the string stored by the list box, you can refer to data outside the list box, such as to object references you may maintain separately, to provide the enhanced and more detailed look for the items.

To perform owner drawing, you must provide an event handler for the `OnDrawItem` event. These events are generated only for owner-drawn list boxes, so make sure that the `Style` property is not `lbStandard` if you intend to use the handler at run-time; otherwise, the handler never will be called!

Inside the `OnDrawItem` handler you provide, the code to actually draw the item can be as simple or as complex as you want.

Fill the `OnDrawItem` event handler shell that Delphi generates with the code to actually display an individual item. You are given enough context information and access to the control's canvas, so that drawing a single item at a time becomes possible.

The standard empty shell for an `OnDrawItem` handler follows, as it is generated by Delphi:

```
procedure TForm2.ListBox1DrawItem(Control: TWinControl; Index: Integer;
  Rect: TRect; State: TOwnerDrawState);
begin

end;
```

17

The `Index` parameter tells you which item is to be drawn. The `Rect` parameter defines the boundaries of the individual item. The `State` parameter is a set in which its members are defined inside the standard `StdCtrls` unit as the following code:

```
TOwnerDrawState = set of
  (
    odSelected,
    odGrayed,
    odDisabled,
    odChecked,
    odFocused
  );
```

You can test the value of the `State` parameter for a particular flag to tell you whether the item currently is selected; whether to display the item grayed out, disabled, or checked; and whether the item currently has the focus.

For example, the statement

```
if (odSelected in State) then
  begin
  end
else
  begin
  end;
```

executes its **`then`** part if the item being drawn happens to be selected at the time. You should draw the item in the highlight colors, or reverse video, instead of the normal list box colors to indicate to the user that the item is selected.

The `Control` parameter is perhaps not as useful as you would have expected, because it only gives you access to the `TWinControl` interface, which does not include the `Canvas`.

Fortunately, because you know the control from which this event is arriving, you can use the Object Pascal's safe typecasting mechanism to gain access to the canvas of the list box, or simply ignore the `Control` parameter altogether and use the list box component reference defined inside your form.

For example, you can say

```
(Control as TListBox).Canvas.Font.Color := clRed;
```

or

```
ListBox1.Canvas.Font.Color := clRed;
```

In both cases, you will have gained access to the list box `Canvas` to change the color with which you draw the item's text.

To actually display the item, use the `Canvas` drawing tools you learned about on Day 16. You can issue a call to the `TextOut` method to display the textual caption of the item, for example, but you also can draw lines, shapes, pictures, and so on as part of the individual item's appearance.

Note that if you do nothing (choose not to draw anything inside your `OnDrawItem` handler, for example) the list *appears* empty. If there actually were items inside the list box, scrolling would work as expected, for example. The user would not be able to see the results of the scrolling actions, however, because in an owner-drawn list box, Windows performs no default drawing actions beyond merely erasing the background. Drawing the items is your responsibility in this case.

In an owner-drawn setting, it is also your responsibility to provide the distinctive appearance for the selected items, as well as to draw the focus rectangle, if desired.

You can draw the focus rectangle simply by calling the `Canvas.DrawFocusRect` method, passing it the `Rect` record structure you received as one of the parameters to your `OnDrawItem` handler.

Combo Boxes

A *combo box* derives its name from the fact that it is a combination of an edit box and a list box. There are three types of combo boxes:

- Standard
- Drop-down
- Drop-down list

The `Style` property of the `ComboBox` component determines the type of combo box to be displayed.

True to its name, a combo box operates a little like a list box, and a little like an edit box.

A combo box has both the `Text` property like an `Edit` component, and the `Items` and `ItemIndex` properties like a `ListBox`. The details of exactly how the two subcomponents are interconnected depend on the combo box's style.

Drop-Down Combo Boxes

When you drop a new instance of a `ComboBox` component from the Standard page of the Component Palette on a form, it appears by default as a drop-down combo box. Its `Style` property has the value of `csDropDown` (combo style, drop-down).

Drop-down combo boxes include both a text box and a drop-down list. The drop-down list normally is closed. To the left of the edit box, there is a drop-down button that a user can choose to display the drop-down portion of the list. There is a characteristic gap between the edit box and the drop-down button, which distinguishes a drop-down combo from its drop-down list variation.

The idea behind a drop-down combo box is that it enables the user to easily find and pick an existing element from a list, but also enables free-form entry of text inside the edit box. Furthermore, the drop-down aspect of this combo box style saves space on-screen, enabling more controls to fit in the same area of the screen.

When the drop-down list is closed, a drop-down combo takes little more room than what an equivalent edit box would take.

Standard Combo Boxes

Standard combo boxes comprise a list box and an edit box, both simultaneously visible and arranged in such a way that the edit box is placed directly above the list. The left border of the list box is characteristically indented to the right from the edit box.

You can create a standard combo box on your form by changing the `Style` property of the `ComboBox` component from the default `csDropDown` to `csSimple`. When you do that at design-time, observe that the list box portion of the combo box does not become immediately visible. You must explicitly resize the component on the form, by dragging its bottom edge down, to show the list box.

The function of a standard combo box is the same as that of a drop-down combo box, except that it can be used when space is not at a premium. It saves the user from having to click an extra time to open the list; the list is open and available at all times.

Drop-Down Lists

A drop-down list is another variation of a `ComboBox` component's `Style`: `csDropDownList`. Contrary to the other variations of the combo box family, it does not give the user the freedom to enter a value free-form, but only enables the selection to be made from the drop-down list, just like a regular list box does. The point is, there is no way to select a value different from what already is on the list.

Unlike with the regular list box, when the drop-down portion is closed, the user can see only a single item at a time. To see more of the list and to be able to scroll through its contents, the user must open the drop-down portion of the combo box by clicking the drop-down button next to it.

You also can provide owner-drawn capabilities for a drop-down list, just as was possible with regular list boxes. This is the purpose of the remaining two combo box `Style` values, `csOwnerDrawFixed` and `csOwnerDrawVariable`. Both of these styles imply a drop-down list combo box.

Scroll Bars

A `ScrollBar` component can be used to adjust a value of a numeric parameter through a continuum. The value being adjusted may be the relative position of a picture inside a window, for example, or it may be an abstract numeric value being controlled (temperature or pressure, for example).

A scroll bar does not exist all on its own. Every scroll bar has to be ultimately tied to another control or widget so that the changes in the position on the scroll bar perform some action, such as scrolling an image or updating some data.

Note: What may look like a scroll bar component on the outside may, in fact, not be one. Forms and, in general, windows can define scroll bars as part of their frame decoration. These scroll bars are intimately tied to the window that displays them, rather than being separate, stand-alone scroll bar components. They are limited to appearing at the right-hand and/or bottom edges of the window to which they belong. Stand-alone scroll bar components can appear anywhere within a form's window.

You will need a stand-alone scroll bar if it is to be displayed in a custom location inside the form. There are two kinds of scroll bars:

- Vertical (`sbVertical`)
- Horizontal (`sbHorizontal`)

The `Kind` property of the `ScrollBar` component toggles between these two states.

- You can set the minimum and the maximum values for the scrolling range. The `Min` and `Max` properties accept `Integer` values in the range –32768...+32767.

- To determine and control the current position of the scroll bar, access the `Position` property. When you set the value of the position, the scroll bar's thumb indicator moves accordingly.

Finally, you can adjust two other properties that relate to the way a scroll bar operates:

- Set the `SmallChange` property to a value by which you want the position to change after the user presses the scroll-arrow buttons at the ends of the scroll bar. This value determines the line-by-line, item-by-item, or pixel-by-pixel scrolling rate.
- Set the `LargeChange` property to a value by which you want the position to change after the user clicks the gray area inside the scroll bar, between the thumb in the middle and the arrow button at each end. This value determines the page-by-page, fast-forward scrolling rate.

Group Boxes

A `GroupBox` component, also found on the Standard page of the Component Palette, provides for a visual grouping of related controls and gives them a more organized look that includes a group caption.

A group box influences the keyboard interface because all components belonging to a particular group can be treated as a single tab-order entity. Tabbing into a group box should move the focus to the first component in the group. Tabbing out of any control inside the group should move the focus to the next component *outside* the group. To move focus *within* a group of check boxes, for example, the user would press the arrow keys instead of the Tab key.

A `GroupBox` component (`TGroupBox` class), as their parent, manages the controls it encloses. Deleting a group box from the form at design-time also deletes all the components belonging to that group.

A typical usage of a group box is for visually and functionally grouping check boxes or radio buttons. In fact, the latter use is so common that it prompted Borland to provide a ready-made `RadioGroup` component, described next.

Radio Groups

A `RadioGroup` component is simply a group of several radio buttons arranged inside a group box. The individual radio buttons are mutually exclusive choices—only one can be selected at any given time.

A *radio group* provides the `Items` property for the design-time convenience of entering just the captions for the radio buttons, and letting the component automatically figure out the placement and proper alignment of the subordinate radio button controls.

Because the radio buttons inside a group are meant to be treated as mutually exclusive options, the `ItemIndex` property of a radio group enables you to treat the entire group as a whole. It works very much like a single-selection list box, by enabling you to just designate with a simple `Integer` property which of the enclosed radio buttons is supposed to be selected at any time.

Panels

Last in today's lesson, but certainly not least, comes the `Panel` component, with its underlying `TPanel` class. Panels are very simple, but extremely versatile visual components.

At the very least, a *panel* can be used to achieve the goal of visually grouping related controls together on a form. You can provide a panel with a raised or lowered look by changing its two bevel properties: `BevelOuter` and `BevelInner`. By varying the values of these two properties independently, choosing `bvNone`, `bvLowered`, or `bvRaised` for each, you can achieve different visual 3-D effects.

You also can set the numeric value of the `BevelWidth` property for additional visual effect.

The usefulness of the panel component does not end with merely providing visual appearance. Another application of `TPanel` is to place other controls on it, and use the `Align` property of the panel to automatically ensure proper positioning of all the controls in the group relative to the enclosing window (form). You can designate a panel as `alTop`-aligned and never worry about the proper positioning of the panel even as the form is being resized at run-time, for example.

This leads to another discovery: a panel is an ideal candidate for providing the now ubiquitous functionality of a toolbar (also known as a speedbar, a button bar, or any number of other more or less proprietary names).

A top-aligned (or bottom-, right-, or left-aligned) panel can serve as a backdrop for `SpeedButtons` to be placed on it, creating very visual and spectacular toolbars.

Similarly, you can use a single panel, or a panel with other panels anchored in it, to build various status bars and similar information areas where the current status of the application can be displayed.

Note, however, that if all you want from a panel is the appearance of a lowered or raised bevel, there is a much simpler and less resource-intensive `Bevel` component on the Additional page of the Component Palette that you can use instead of a panel.

Summary

Today you studied the properties and behavior of the standard Windows controls encapsulated by Delphi components.

You learned the following:

- A `MainMenu` component should be used to create a menu bar for the top-level application's window or windows.
- A pop-up menu can be made to appear after the user right-clicks a visible component with the mouse. Pop-up menus are detached from the main menu bar and appear on demand. The `PopupMenu` property of many visual controls enables you to automatically pop up a menu after the user right-clicks the control with the mouse.
- `Label` components annotate edit boxes and other components.
- Edit boxes enable the user to enter a single line of text. `Memo` components provide support for entering multiple lines of text.
- `Button` components, and their more visually appealing `BitBtn` equivalents, can be used to invoke program actions, especially in a modal dialog box scenario.
- A check box offers a way to toggle the state of a setting or parameter with two possible values. Check boxes often are grouped inside a `GroupBox` component.
- Groups of `RadioButton` components can be used to select one of several possible choices. Radio buttons, like check boxes, often are grouped inside a group box. A `RadioGroup` standard component encapsulates the functionality of a group box with several radio button combinations.
- Single-selection list boxes (a `ListBox` component with the `MultipleSelect` property set to `False`), enable the user to choose one from possibly many options and are functionally equivalent to a group of radio buttons.
- Multiple-selection list boxes (`ListBox` components with the `MultipleSelect` property set to `True`) are to some extent equivalent to a group of check boxes and enable the user to select more than one from a list of choices.
- Owner-drawn list boxes give you the ultimate control over the appearance of the list box items, making it possible to mix graphics and different types of text within the same list box.
- `TStrings` is a generic component that can be used to maintain multiple text-string items, whether representing the items in a list box or lines of text in a memo, as well as in many other settings and with other components not described here.
- A `ComboBox` component is a combination of an edit box and a list box. Combo boxes come in three distinct flavors: a simple combo, a drop-down combo, and a drop-down list, depending on the value of their `Style` property.
- Scroll bars can be defined as part of the "decoration" of a particular form or other type of a window. The stand-alone `ScrollBar` component is used to place scroll bars at arbitrary locations within a form.

- The `Panel` component is a versatile and powerful building block that enables you to provide modern toolbars and status bars in your applications.

Q&A

Q Can I somehow save the items defined within a menu component so that I can reuse the same basic menu structure in other applications I will be building?

A Yes. You can save the entire menu as a template and later load it into another application. After you finish defining the structure of the menu, right-click inside the Menu Designer to display its pop-up menu. Then choose Save as Template. A Save Template dialog box appears, enabling you to name the menu template for later retrieval.

To retrieve an existing template menu in a new project, right-click inside the Menu Designer to display the pop-up menu again. Then choose Insert from Template. Inside the Insert Template dialog box that appears next, select the template you are interested in and choose OK. The menu stored in a template is inserted into the current position inside the Menu Designer.

A number of menu templates are supplied with Delphi, such as the standard File and Edit menus, so you never need to create these from scratch.

Q How can I automatically sort the contents of a standard list box control in alphabetical order?

A Set the `Sorted` property of the `ListBox` to `True`. The list box automatically sorts the items as they are inserted.

Q What is the purpose of the `IntegralHeight` property of a list box?

A This property determines whether the list box displays partial lines at the bottom. This property is important if the size of the box is not an exact multiple of an individual item's height. If `IntegralHeight` is set to `True`, the list box may shrink somewhat at run-time and will show only full lines of text, with no partial lines at the bottom.

Q What happens if I designate two panel components as being top-aligned, both on the same form?

A Try it! Both panels are aligned at the top, both visible at the same time. VCL correctly handles the situation by making the two panels appear one underneath the other, rather than literally aligning both to the top of the form, thus rendering one of them invisible. You easily can create two or more toolbars in this way.

Workshop

The Workshop provides quiz questions to help you solidify your understanding of the material covered, and exercises to provide you with experience in using what you have learned. Try to understand the quiz and exercise answers before continuing on to the next day's lesson. Answers are provided in Appendix E at the end of this book.

Quiz

1. True or False? You cannot use the standard `Edit` component to allow the user to enter a single line of right-justified text, such as for numeric-only data entry. You must use the memo for this purpose, even though only a single line of text is desired.
2. True or False? A `Label` component, because it is not a true window but rather a static piece of text, cannot have its own cursor, and it cannot respond to mouse clicks.
3. True or False? The standard `ComboBox` component, when used in its simple or drop-down variation, does not provide any support for owner-drawing of items.
4. True or False? You can create your own combo boxes by combining any two visual controls in a single component.

Exercises

1. Create an equivalent of a simple combo box on a form by using separate edit box and list box components.
2. Create a mini Program Manager application in which the user can maintain a single list of the most frequently used programs, including their command-line parameters, and invoke them by double-clicking a program's name on the list.

18

WEEK
3

Standard Dialogs and File Components

by Namir Shammas

Windows supports a number of standard dialog boxes that allow you to open a file, save a file, select a font, choose a color, print, and set up the printer. Delphi supports these standard dialog boxes and also offers you components that allow you to select files, directories, drives, and file filters. This chapter covers the following topics:

- The `OpenDialog` component
- The `SaveDialog` component
- The `FontDialog` component
- The `ColorDialog` component
- The `PrintDialog` component
- The `PrinterSetupDialog` component
- The `FindDialog` component
- The `ReplaceDialog` component
- The `FileListBox` component
- The `DirectoryListBox` component
- The `DriveComboBox` component
- The `FilterComboBox` component

The *OpenDialog* Component

Windows supports a standard dialog box used to open files. Figure 18.1 shows a sample Open dialog box. The dialog box contains controls that allow you to select groups of files by wildcard, navigate through directories, and select different drives.

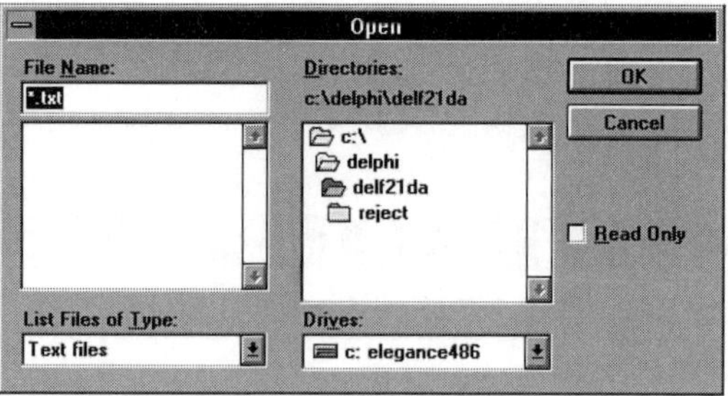

Figure 18.1.
The Open dialog box.

The next subsections discuss the relevant properties of the `OpenDialog` component and of the `Execute` method, which invokes the Open dialog box.

DO	DON'T

DO use the standard dialog boxes to implement applications that have an interface with which the user is familiar.

DON'T forget that the standard dialog boxes do not perform any task beyond exchanging information with the user.

The *Ctl3D* Property

The Boolean `Ctl3D` property determines whether the controls of the Open dialog box appear with the 3-D look. When the value for this property is `True`, the controls have a 3-D look that gives the appearance of depth. By contrast, when the value of this property is `False`, the controls appear with a 2-D look.

18

The *DefaultExt* Property

The `DefaultExt` property is a three-character string that specifies the extension that is added to the filename the user types in the File Name edit box (if the user doesn't include a filename extension in the filename). When the user includes an extension for the filename, the value of the `DefaultExt` property is ignored. If the value of the `DefaultExt` property stays blank, the dialog box adds no extension to the input filename.

Examples of setting the `DefaultExt` are as follows:

```
OpenDialog1.DefaultExt := 'bat';
If OpenDialog1.Execute then
    LoadFile(OpenDialog1.FileName);

OpenDialog1.DefaultExt := 'EXE';
If OpenDialog1.Execute then
    Print(OpenDialog1.FileName);

OpenDialog1.DefaultExt := 'INI';
If OpenDialog1.Execute then
    CopyFile(OpenDialog1.FileName, 'MYINI.INI');
```

Do not include the period character, which delimits the filename and its extension.

DO	DON'T

DO use the `DefaultExt` property to help the user skip typing in the default file extension.

DON'T forget to exclude a dot from the string assigned to the `DefaultExt` property.

The *FileName* Property

The `FileName` property specifies the filename that appears in the File Name edit box when a form opens the dialog box. The user may choose the displayed filename or specify any other filename. When the user selects a filename and then clicks the OK button, the value of the `FileName` property changes to the name of the most recently selected file. You can include a path in the value of the `FileName` property. Here are examples of using the `FileName` property:

```
OpenDialog1.FileName := 'WIN.INI';
If OpenDialog1.Execute then
    MyPrint(OpenDialog1.FileName);

OpenDialog1.FileName := 'C:\WINDOWS\SYSTEM.INI';
If OpenDialog1.Execute then
    MyPrint(OpenDialog1.FileName);
```

The first example sets just the filename. By contrast, the second example includes a drive and path.

The *Files* Property

The `Files` property is a run-time and read-only property. The value of the `Files` property holds a list of all the filenames chosen in the Open dialog box. The list includes the path names. To support the selection of multiple filenames in the dialog box, include the value `ofAllowMultiSelect` in the `Options` property set.

Here is an example of using the `Files` property:

```
OpenDialog1.Options := [ofAllowMultiSelect];
If OpenDialog1.Execute then
    For i := 0 to OpenDialog1.Files.Count - 1 Do
        MyPrint(OpenDialog1.Files.Strings[i]);
```

The above example sets the `ofAllowMultiSelect` in the `Options` property set and then invokes the Open dialog box. The code then prints the selected files, one at a time.

DO	DON'T

DO support multiple file selection to make it convenient to process these files in one swoop.

DON'T forget to include the value in the `ofAllowMultiSelect` in the `Options` property to support the selection of multiple files.

The *Filter* Property

The `Filter` property is a string that determines the file masks accessible to the user for use in deciding which files appear in the list box of the dialog box. The *file mask* is made up of one or more file filters. Each file filter has two substrings. The bar character delimits each substring and the file filters. The first substring in each file filter is some meaningful text that indicates the type of file. The second substring in each file filter is the *file wildcard*. You can string multiple wildcard file filters together using the semicolon character as the delimiter. The value of the `Filter` property is a string that can hold up to 255 characters. Here are examples of using the `Filter` property:

18

```
OpenDialog1.Filter := 'Text files *.txt¦*.txt';
if OpenDialog1.Execute then
    MyPrint(OpenDialog1.FileName);

OpenDialog1.Filter := 'Text files¦*.TXT' +
                      'Document files¦*.DOC¦' +
                      'BMP files¦*.BMP¦' +
                      'INI files¦*.INI¦';
if OpenDialog1.Execute then
    MyPrint(OpenDialog1.FileName);

OpenDialog1.Filter := 'Text files¦*.TXT, *.DOC';
if OpenDialog1.Execute then
    MyPrint(OpenDialog1.FileName);
```

The first example shows a single file filter, the *.txt files. The second example shows multiple file filters (*.TXT, *.DOC, *.BMP, and *.INI wildcards). The third example shows a single file filter with two file wildcards, *.TXT and *.DOC. Here are examples of using the `Filter` property:

```
OpenDialog1.Filter := 'Text files *.txt¦*.txt';
if OpenDialog1.Execute then
    MyPrint(OpenDialog1.FileName);

OpenDialog1.Filter := 'Text files¦*.TXT' +
                      'Document files¦*.DOC¦' +
                      'BMP files¦*.BMP¦' +
                      'INI files¦*.INI¦';
```

```
if OpenDialog1.Execute then
    MyPrint(OpenDialog1.FileName);
```

These examples show file filters with single and multiple filters.

The *FilterIndex* Property

The `FilterIndex` property is an integer index that specifies which file filter specified in the `Filter` property appears as the default file filter in the List Files of Type drop-down list box. For example, if you assign 3 to the `FilterIndex` property, the third file filter listed in the `Filter` property becomes the default filter when the dialog box appears. The default value for the `FilterIndex` property is 1. If you specify a value that exceeds the number of file filters in the `Filter` property, the dialog box selects the first filter (so much for trying to outsmart that little dialog box!). Here is an example of using the `FilterIndex` property:

```
OpenDialog1.Filter := 'Text files¦*.TXT' +
                      'Document files¦*.DOC¦' +
                      'BMP files¦*.BMP¦' +
                      'INI files¦*.INI¦';
OpenDialog1.FilterIndex := 2;
if OpenDialog1.Execute then
    MyPrint(OpenDialog1.FileName);
```

This example selects the second file filter (*.DOC) to appear as the default file filter in the List Files of Type drop-down list box.

The *InitialDir* Property

The `InitialDir` property selects the current directory when the dialog box first comes into view. Moreover, the value of the `InitialDir` property appears as the current directory in the directory tree. The File Name list box of the Open dialog box shows only the files in the current directory. State the full path name when specifying the initial directory. If you do not pick an initial directory, or if you select a nonexistent directory, the current directory remains as such. Here is an example of using the `InitialDir` property:

```
OpenDialog1.Filter := 'Text files¦*.TXT' +
                      'Document files¦*.DOC¦' +
                      'BMP files¦*.BMP¦' +
                      'INI files¦*.INI¦';
OpenDialog1.InitialDir := 'C:\WINDOWS';
if OpenDialog1.Execute then
    MyPrint(OpenDialog1.FileName);
```

This example shows that the directory C:\WINDOWS is the initial directory for the Open dialog box.

The *Options* Property

The `Options` property fine-tunes the appearance and operations of the Open dialog box. The `Options` property is a set of values. Table 18.1 shows these values.

Table 18.1. The values for the `Options` property set.

Value	Meaning
`ofAllowMultiSelect`	When `True`, this option allows users to select multiple files in the File Name list box.
`ofCreatePrompt`	When `True`, this option shows a message dialog box with a warning if the user enters a nonexistent filename in the File Name edit box and then clicks OK. The warning informs the user that the file doesn't exist and asks if the user wishes to create a new file with that name.
`ofExtensionDifferent`	This option is set when the filename returned from the dialog box has an extension that differs from the default file extension (that is, the value in the `DefaultExt` property). The program may utilize this information. Setting an `ofExtensionDifferent` value with the Object Inspector has no meaning.
`ofFileMustExist`	If `True`, this option shows a message dialog box with a warning if the user enters a nonexistent file in the File Name edit box and then clicks OK. The warning tells the user the file can't be found and requests the user to enter the correct path and filename.
`ofHideReadOnly`	If `True`, this option hides the Read Only check box in the dialog box.
`ofNoChangeDir`	If `True`, this option sets the current directory to whatever the current directory was when the dialog box first appeared and ignores any directory changes the user made while using the dialog box.
`ofNoReadOnlyReturn`	If `True`, the dialog will not allow the user to select a read-only file. Use this option when you are planning to write to the file the user selects.

continues

18

Table 18.1. continued

Value	Meaning
`ofNoTestFileCreate`	This option applies only when the user wishes to save a file on a create-no-modify network share point, which can't be opened again once it has been opened. If property `ofNoTestFileCreate` is `True`, your program will not verify for write protection, a full disk, an open drive door, or network protection when saving the file because this verification generates a test file. Your application will then have to handle file operations carefully so that a file isn't closed until you really want it to be.
`ofNoValidate`	If `True`, this option doesn't stop the user from keying in invalid characters in a filename. If `ofNoValidate` is `False` and the user types in invalid characters for a filename in the File Name edit box, a message dialog box appears telling the user that the filename contains invalid characters.
`ofOverwritePrompt`	If `True`, this option displays a message dialog box if the user tries to save a file that already exists. The message tells the user that the file already exists and lets the user elect whether or not to overwrite the existing file.
`ofReadOnly`	If `True`, the Read Only check box is checked when the dialog box is displayed.
`ofPathMustExist`	If this option is `True`, the user may enter only existing path names as part of the filename in the File Name edit box. If the user enters a nonexistent path name, a message box appears telling the user that the path name is invalid.
`ofShareAware`	If `True`, the dialog box ignores all sharing errors and returns the name of the selected file even though a sharing violation occurred. If `ofShareAware` is `False`, a sharing violation results in a message box informing the user of the problem.
`ofShowHelp`	If `True`, this option displays a Help button in the dialog box.

Here is an example of using the `Options` property:

```
OpenDialog1.Filter := 'Text files¦*.TXT' +
                    'Document files¦*.DOC¦' +
                    'BMP files¦*.BMP¦' +
                    'INI files¦*.INI¦';
```

```
OpenDialog1.Options := [ofReadOnly, ofShowHelp];
if OpenDialog1.Execute then
    MyPrint(OpenDialog1.FileName);
```

This example shows the Open dialog box with the Read Only check box checked and also shows the Help button.

The *Title* Property

The `Title` property determines the text that appears in the title bar of the dialog box. Here is an example of using the `Title` property:

```
OpenDialog1.Filter := 'Text files¦*.TXT' +
                      'Document files¦*.DOC¦';
OpenDialog1.Title := 'Open Document File';
if OpenDialog1.Execute then
    MyPrint(OpenDialog1.FileName);
```

This example shows the Open dialog box with the title "Open Document File."

18

The *Execute* Method

The `Execute` method invokes the dialog box in the application and yields `True` when the user clicks the OK button. Typically, the code of an application has statements that execute if the method `Execute` yields `True`. Occasionally you may want the code to execute statements to handle the outcome of clicking either the OK or Cancel button.

Note: The `Execute` method applies for all the other dialog box components. The exception is the `PrintSetupDialog` component, in which the `Execute` method is a procedure and not a function.

The *SaveDialog* Component

Windows supports a standard dialog box used to save files. Figure 18.2 shows a sample Save dialog box. The dialog box contains controls that allow you to select groups of files by wildcard, navigate through directories, and select different drives.

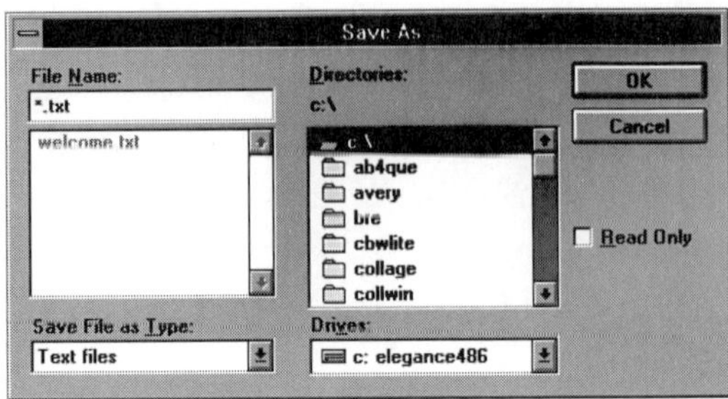

Figure 18.2.
The Save As dialog box.

The SaveDialog component has the same properties as the OpenDialog component. Moreover, the Execute method invokes the SaveDialog component just like the OpenDialog component.

The *FontDialog* Component

Windows supports a standard dialog box to select fonts. Figure 18.3 shows a sample Font dialog box. The dialog box contains controls that enable you to select the type, size, style, and color of a font.

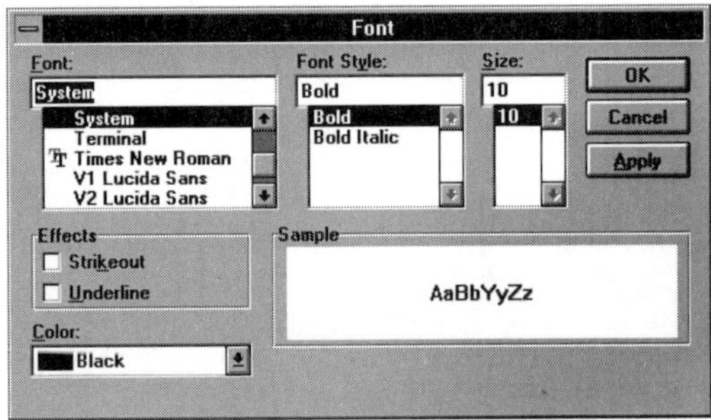

Figure 18.3.
The Font dialog box.

The next subsections discuss the relevant properties of the FontDialog component.

The *Device* Property

The Device property allows you to control which fonts are shown in the font dialog. Table 18.2 shows the values for the Device property.

Table 18.2. The values for the `Device` property.

Value	Meaning
`fdScreen`	List only screen fonts
`fdPrinter`	List only printer fonts
`fdBoth`	List both screen and printer fonts

Here is an example for using the `Device` property:

```
FontDialog1.Device := fdBoth;
if FontDialog1.Execute then
    dFont := FontDialog1.Font;
```

Note: If you set the `Device` property to `fdPrinter` or `fdBoth`, the Font dialog box will show fonts that are compatible with the printer that is currently selected in the Delphi Printer component. Different printers support different fonts, so if you have multiple printers at your disposal, you should configure the Printer component to refer to the appropriate printer device before executing the `FontDialog`.

18

The *Font* Property

The `Font` property specifies the initial font of the dialog box and also the font returned by the user. The `Font` property has nested properties, such as `Name`, `Color`, `Style`, and `Size`, which provide detailed information on the font. Here is an example for using the `Font` property:

```
var dFont : TFont;

begin
    ...
    if FontDialog1.Execute then begin
        dFont := FontDialog1.Font;
        { check font style }
        if dFont.Name = 'Courier' then begin
            { check font size }
            if dFont.Size > 12 then
                dFont.Size := 12;
            MyPrint('AUTOEXEC.BAT', dFont);
        end;
    end;
    ...
end;
```

This example copies the selected font to the variable `dFont` and then examines the font properties `Size` and `Name`.

The *MaxFontSize* Property

The `MaxFontSize` property uses integer values to specify the biggest font size available in the Font dialog box. This property enables you to limit the font sizes available to the user. To make the value of the `MaxFontSize` effective, include the value `fdLimitSize` in the `Options` property set (of the Font dialog box). Otherwise, the value of the property `MaxFontSize` has no effect. Here is an example for using the `MaxFontSize` property:

```
FontDialog1.MaxFontSize := 24;
FontDialog1.Options := [fdLimitSize];
if FontDialog1.Execute then begin
    ...
end;
```

This code example sets the maximum font size to 24.

The *MinFontSize* Property

The `MinFontSize` property uses integer values to specify the smallest font size available in the Font dialog box. This property enables you to limit the font sizes available to the user. To make the value of the `MinFontSize` effective, include the value `fdLimitSize` in the `Options` property set (of the Font dialog box). Otherwise, the value of the property `MinFontSize` has no effect. Here is an example for using the `MinFontSize` property:

```
FontDialog1.MinFontSize := 4;
FontDialog1.Options := [fdLimitSize];
if FontDialog1.Execute then begin
    ...
end;
```

This example sets the minimum font size to 4.

DO | **DON'T**

DO support font size limits to prevent size selection from ending up with unreasonable values.

DON'T forget to include the `fdLimitSize` value in the `Options` property to enforce font size limits.

The *Options* Property

The `Options` property enables you to fine-tune the operations of the Font dialog box. Table 18.3 shows the values for the `Options` property.

Table 18.3. The values for the `Options` property of the Font dialog box.

Value	Meaning
`fdAnsiOnly`	If `True`, the user can chose fonts that only utilize the Windows character set. When `False`, the OEM character set is available.
`fdEffects`	If `True`, the Effects check boxes and the Color list box appear in the Font dialog box. The user employs the Effects check boxes to select strikeout or underlined text and the Color list box to choose a color for the selected font. If `fdEffects` is `False`, the Effects check boxes and Color list box remain hidden.
`fdFixedPitchOnly`	If `True`, only monospaced fonts appear in the Font combo box.
`fdForceFontExist`	If `True` and the user enters a font name in the Font combo box and then clicks OK, a message dialog box appears informing the user the font name is invalid.
`fdNoFaceSel`	If `True`, when the dialog box appears, there is no font name selected in the Font combo box.
`fdNoOEMFonts`	If `True`, only fonts that aren't vector fonts appear in the Font combo box.
`fdNoSimulations`	If `True`, only fonts that aren't GDI font simulations (that is, fonts that are directly supported by the given device) appear in the Font combo box.
`fdNoSizeSel`	If `True`, when the dialog box appears, there is no selected size in the Size combo box.
`fdNoStyleSel`	If `True`, when the dialog box appears, there is no selected style in the Style combo box.
`fdNoVectorFonts`	Same as `fdNoOEMFonts`.
`fdShowHelp`	If `True`, a Help button appears in the dialog box.
`fdTrueTypeOnly`	If `True`, only TrueType fonts appear in the Font list box.
`fdWysiwyg`	If `True`, only fonts that are accessible to both the printer and the screen appear in the Font combo box.

Here is an example for using the Options property:

```
FontDialog1.MinFontSize := 4;
FontDialog1.Options := [fdLimitSize, fdWysiwyg];
if FontDialog1.Execute then begin
   ...
end;
```

This code example sets the minimum font size to 4 and shows fonts that are accessible to both the printer and the screen.

The *ColorDialog* Component

Windows supports a standard dialog box to select colors. Figure 18.4 shows a sample Color dialog box. The dialog box contains controls that enable you to select a color.

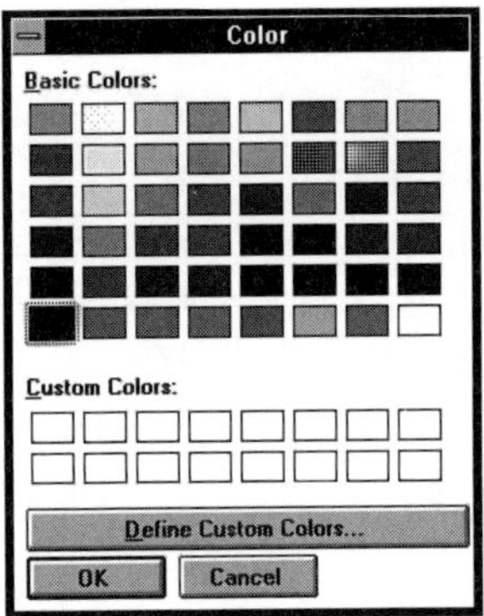

Figure 18.4.
The Color dialog box.

The next subsections discuss the relevant properties of the ColorDialog component.

The *Color* Property

The Color property allows you to set the initially selected color when the Color dialog box appears. The Color property also reports the color selected by the user if the method Execute returns True. Here is an example for using the Color property:

```
ColorDialog1.Color := clRed;
if ColorDialog1.Execute then begin
    Color := ColorDialog1.Color;
end;
```

This example makes red the initially selected color of the Color dialog box. If the Execute method yields True, the code assigns the selected color to the form's Color property.

The *Options* Property

The `Options` property fine-tunes the operations and appearance of the Color dialog box. Table 18.4 shows the values for the `Options` property.

Table 18.4. The values for the `Options` property of the Color dialog box.

Value	Meaning
`cdFullOpen`	Displays the custom coloring options when the Color dialog box opens.
`cdPreventFullOpen`	Disables the Create Custom Colors button in the Color dialog box to prevent the user from creating his own custom colors.
`cdShowHelp`	Adds a Help button to the Color dialog box.

Here is an example for using the `Options` property:

```
ColorDialog1.Color := clRed;
ColorDialog1.Color := [cdFullOpen, cdShowHelp];
if ColorDialog1.Execute then begin
    Color := ColorDialog1.Color;
end;
```

This script shows the custom coloring options when the Color dialog box opens. Moreover, the Color dialog box includes the Help button.

The *PrintDialog* Component

Windows supports a standard dialog box to start printing the contents of a file. Figure 18.5 shows a sample Print dialog box. The dialog box contains controls that enable you to select a printer, the printed page range, printer setup, and so on.

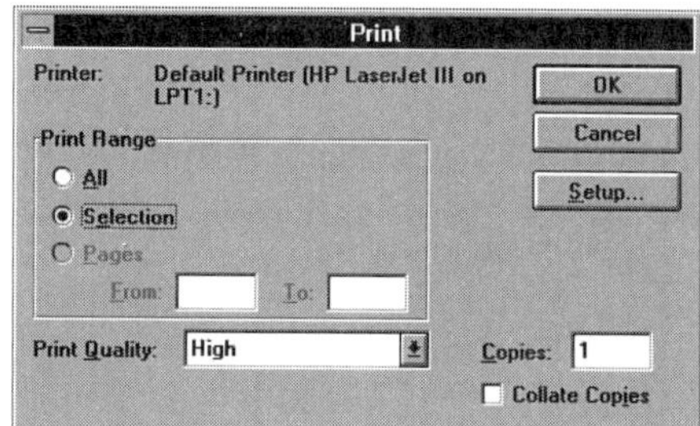

Figure 18.5.
The Print dialog box.

The next subsections discuss the relevant properties of the PrintDialog component.

The *ChangeDefault* Property

The ChangeDefault property is a Boolean flag that indicates whether the user selected a new printer setup using the Printer Setup dialog box.

Here is an example for using the ChangeDefault property:

```
if PrintDialog1.Execute then begin
    if PrintDialog1.ChangeDefault then
     MessageDlg('You changed the printer setup',
                mtInformation, [mbOK], 0);
end;
```

This code example displays a message dialog box if the user changed the printer setup.

The *Collate* Property

The Collate property is a Boolean flag that determines whether or not to check the Collate check box and also to select collating. The property also reports the state of the Collate check box after closing the Print dialog box. The default value of the Collate property is False.

Here is an example for using the Collate property:

```
if PrintDialog1.Execute then begin
      if PrintDialog1.Collate then
      MessageDlg('You selected to collate pages',
                 mtInformation, [mbOK], 0);
end;
```

This script displays a message dialog box if the user checked the Collate check box.

The *Copies* Property

The Copies property represents the number of copies of the print job to print. You may set the value of the Copies property at design-time. This value becomes the default value in the edit box control when the Print dialog box appears.

Here is an example for using the Copies property:

```
PrintDialog1.Copies := 10;
if PrintDialog1.Execute then begin
    For i := 1 to PrintDialog1.Copies do
        MyPrint(theFilename);
end;
```

This example sets the default number of copies to 10 before invoking the Print dialog box. The example also uses the value of the Copies property to print the specified number of copies.

DO / DON'T

DO use the `Copies` property to prevent run-away printing of a large number of copies.

DON'T forget that the application code is responsible for producing the number of copies.

The *FromPage* Property

The `FromPage` property is the integer value that specifies the starting page number for a print job.

Here is an example for using the `FromPage` property:

```
if PrintDialog1.Execute then begin
    i1 := PrintDialog1.FromPage;
    i2 := PrintDialog1.ToPage;
    For pageNum := i1 to i2 do
        MyPagePrint(theTextFile, pageNum);
end;
```

This script uses the `FromPage` property to determine the starting page for printing a file.

18

The *ToPage* Property

The property `ToPage` is the integer value that specifies the ending page number for a print job.

Here is an example for using the `ToPage` property:

```
if PrintDialog1.Execute then begin
    i1 := PrintDialog1.FromPage;
    i2 := PrintDialog1.ToPage;
    For pageNum := i1 to i2 do
        MyPagePrint(theTextFile, pageNum);
end;
```

This example uses the `FromPage` and `ToPage` properties to determine the starting and ending page for printing a file, respectively.

The *MaxPage* Property

The `MaxPage` property specifies the highest page number the user can select when choosing a range of pages to print. When the selected page number exceeds the value in the `MaxPage` property, the dialog box displays a warning message box. This dialog box requests that the user either enter a valid number or close the dialog box. To permit the user to print specific page numbers, include the value `poPageNums` in the `Options` property.

Here is an example for using the MaxPage property:

```
PrintDialog1.MinPage := 1;
PrintDialog1.MaxPage := 50;
if PrintDialog1.Execute then begin
    i1 := PrintDialog1.FromPage;
    i2 := PrintDialog1.ToPage;
    For pageNum := i1 to i2 do
        MyPagePrint(theTextFile, pageNum);
end;
```

This code example uses the MaxPage property to prevent the user from printing more than 50 pages.

The *MinPage* Property

The MinPage property specifies the lowest page number the user can select when choosing a range of pages to print. When the selected page number is below the value in the MinPage property, the dialog box displays a warning message box. This dialog box requests that the user either enter a valid number or close the dialog box. To permit the user to print specific page numbers, include the value poPageNums in the Options property.

Here is an example for using the MinPage property:

```
PrintDialog1.MinPage := 10;
PrintDialog1.MaxPage := 50;
if PrintDialog1.Execute then begin
    i1 := PrintDialog1.FromPage;
    i2 := PrintDialog1.ToPage;
    For pageNum := i1 to i2 do
        MyPagePrint(theTextFile, pageNum);
end;
```

This example uses the MinPage property to specify that the user cannot print the first 10 pages.

DO	DON'T

DO use the MinPage and MaxPage properties to limit the range of printed pages. Such a limitation helps to focus on only the altered document pages.

DON'T forget to include the value poPageNums in the Options property to support page numbers.

The *Options* Property

The `Options` property allows you to fine-tune the appearance and operations of the Print dialog box. Table 18.5 shows the values for the `Options` property.

Table 18.5. The values for the `Options` property of the Print dialog box.

Value	Meaning
`poHelp`	If `True`, the dialog box includes a Help button.
`poPageNums`	If `True`, the Pages radio button is enabled and the user can select a range of pages to print.
`poPrintToFile`	If `True`, a Print to File check box appears in the dialog box, enabling the user to print to a file instead of to a printer.
`poSelection`	If `True`, the Selection radio button is enabled and the user may elect to print selected text.
`poWarning`	If `True` and if no printer is installed, a warning message appears when the user clicks OK.

18

Here is an example for using the `Options` property:

```
PrintDialog1.MinPage := 10;
PrintDialog1.MaxPage := 50;
PrintDialog1.Options := [poHelp, poPageNums,
                        poSelection];
if PrintDialog1.Execute then begin
    i1 := PrintDialog1.FromPage;
    i2 := PrintDialog1.ToPage;
    For pageNum := i1 to i2 do
        MyPagePrint(theTextFile, pageNum);
end;
```

This code example uses the `Options` property to specify that the Print dialog box includes a Help button, supports page numbering, and supports printing the selected text.

The *PrintRange* Property

The `PrintRange` property is a set of values that determines the type of print range the application uses to print a file. Table 18.6 shows the values for the `PrintRange` property.

Table 18.6. The values for the `PrintRange` property of the Print dialog box.

Value	Meaning
`prAllPages`	If set at run-time, the user elected to print all pages of the print job. When you set the Print Range to `prAllPages` at design-time, the All Pages radio button is selected when the Print dialog box first appears.
`prSelection`	If set at run-time, the user elected to print only the selected text. When you set the Print Range to `prSelection` at design-time, the Selection radio button is selected when the Print dialog box first appears.
`prPageNums`	If set at run-time, the user elected to designate a range of pages to print. When you set Print Range to `prPageNums` at design-time, the Pages radio button is selected when the Print dialog box initially appears, and the user can designate a print range by page numbers. The page numbers are defined by the `MinPage` and `MaxPage` properties.

Here is an example for using the `PrintRange` property:

```
PrintDialog1.MinPage := 1;
PrintDialog1.MaxPage := 50;
PrintDialog1.Options := [poHelp, poPageNums,
                        poSelection];
if PrintDialog1.Execute then begin
if prAllPages in PrintDialog1.PrintRange then
    MyFilePrint(theTextFile)
else begin
    i1 := PrintDialog1.FromPage;
    i2 := PrintDialog1.ToPage;
    For pageNum := i1 to i2 do
        MyPagePrint(theTextFile, pageNum);
end;
```

This example uses the `PrintRange` property to determine whether the user wants to print all of the pages or just a range of pages.

The *PrintToFile* Property

The `PrintToFile` property is a Boolean flag that determines whether the user wishes to send the print job to a file instead of a printer. When the value of this property is `True`, the user has checked the Print to File check box. By contrast, when the Property is `False`, the user has not checked the Print to File check box. When you set the `PrintToFile` property to `True` at design-time, the Print to File check box is checked when the Print dialog box appears. It's worth mentioning that the Print to File check box appears in the Print dialog box only if the `Options` property is set to `poPrintToFile`. Otherwise, printing to a file is not an available option.

Here is an example for using the `PrintToFile` property:

```
PrintDialog1.MinPage := 1;
PrintDialog1.MaxPage := 50;
PrintDialog1.Options := [poHelp, poPageNums,
                        poSelection, poPrintToFile];
if PrintDialog1.Execute then
    if PrintDialog1.PrintToFile then
        MyPrintToFile(theTextFile)
    else
        MyPrint(theTextFile);
```

This script uses the `PrintToFile` property to determine whether the user wants to print to a file to a printer.

The *PrinterSetupDialog* Component

Windows supports a standard dialog box to set up the printer. Figure 18.6 shows a sample Print Setup dialog box. The dialog box contains controls that allow you to select a printer, the paper orientation, paper size, and other options.

18

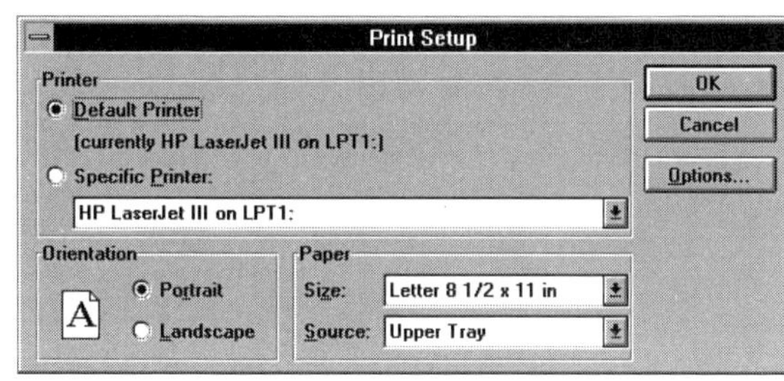

Figure 18.6.
The Print Setup dialog box.

The most relevant property for the `PrinterSetupDialog` is the `ChangeDefault` property. This property works like the one in the `PrintDialog` component.

Note: You can invoke the Print Setup dialog box from within the Print dialog box. Consequently, you should place the `PrinterSetupDialog` component in a form only if you want to directly invoke the Print Setup dialog box.

The *FindDialog* Component

Windows supports a standard dialog box to find text. Figure 18.7 shows a sample Find dialog box. The dialog box contains controls that enable you to specify the search text, search direction, case sensitivity, and whole-word matching mode. It is important to point out that the Find dialog box is modeless. This means that the dialog box remains in view during and after search operations.

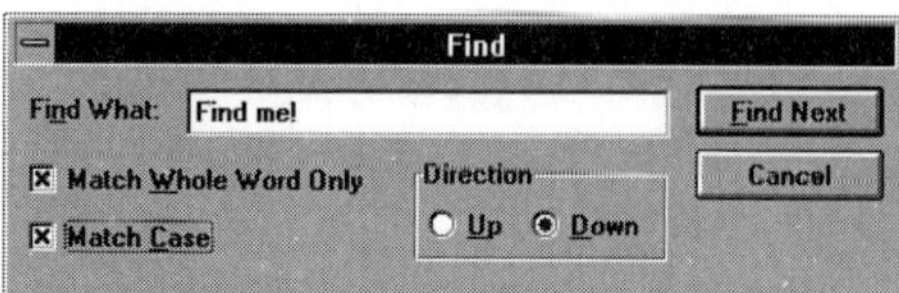

Figure 18.7.
The Find dialog box.

The next subsections discuss the relevant properties, the `CloseDialog` method, and the `OnChange` event of the `FindDialog` component.

The *FindText* Property

The `FindText` property stores the search string. You can set the value of this property before invoking the Find dialog box to specify the initial search string in the Find What edit box. The program's user has the option of either accepting the initial search string or entering a different string. After the user clicks the OK button, the `FindText` property contains the most recent string that appeared in the Find What edit box before closing the dialog box.

Here is an example for using the `FindText` property:

```
FindDialog1.FindText := '[Sound]';
filename := 'WIN.INI';
if FindDialog1.Execute then
    SearchInFile(filename, FindDialog1.FindText);
```

This example uses the `FindText` property to set the initial search string to `[Sound]`. The code also uses the same property in searching for the text after the user closes the Find dialog box.

The *Options* Property

The `Options` property empowers you to fine-tune the appearance and operations of the Find dialog box. Table 18.7 shows the values for the `Options` property.

Table 18.7. The values for the `Options` property of the Find dialog box.

Value	Meaning
`frDisableMatchCase`	When `True`, the Match Case check box appears grayed and is disabled. When it is `False`, the Match Case check box can be checked.

Value	Meaning
frDisableUpDown	When True, the Direction Up and Down buttons are grayed and disabled. When it is False, the user can choose either the Direction Up or Down button.
frDisableWholeWord	When True, the Match Whole Word check box is grayed and disabled. When it is False, the user can check the check box.
frDown	When True, the Down button is selected in the dialog box and the downward search direction is set. When frDown is False, the Up button is selected, and the upward search direction is set.
frFindNext	When True, the user has clicked the Find Next button. Consequently, the program should start searching for the text in the FindText property.
frHideMatchCase	When True, the Match Case check box is hidden. When the property is False, the Match Case check box is visible.
frHideWholeWord	When True, the Match Whole Word check box is invisible. When it is False, the Match Whole Word check box is visible.
frHideUpDown	When True, the Direction Up and Down buttons are invisible. When the property is False, the Direction Up and Down buttons are visible.
frMatchCase	When True, the Match Case check box is checked. When the property is False, the Match Case check box is unchecked. You can set frMatchCase at design-time, or users can change the value at run-time.
frReplace	A flag set by the system to induce the program to replace the current occurrence of the FindText string with the ReplaceText string. frReplace applies only to the Replace dialog box.
frReplaceAll	A flag set by the system that indicates your application should replace all occurrences of the FindText string with the ReplaceText string. frReplaceAll applies only to the Replace dialog box.
frShowHelp	When True, a Help button appears in the dialog box when the dialog box displays. When frShowHelp is False, no Help button is present.
frWholeWord	When True, the Match Whole Word check box is checked in the dialog box.

Here is an example for using the `Options` property:

```
FindDialog1.FindText := '[Sound]';
FindDialog1.Options := [frDown, frMatchCase,
                        frWholeWord];
filename := 'WIN.INI';
if FindDialog1.Execute then
    SearchInFile(filename,
            FindDialog1.FindText,
            FindDialog1.Options);
```

This example uses the `Options` property to select the Down button, Match Case check box, and Match Whole Word check box when the Find dialog box first appears. The sample code also passes the `Options` property to the search procedure to enable that routine to determine how to search for the text in the targeted file.

The *CloseDialog* Method

The `CloseDialog` method closes the modeless Find dialog box. The declaration of the `CloseDialog` method is

```
procedure CloseDialog;
```

The *OnFind* Event

Because the Find dialog box is modeless, you can trigger a text search while the dialog box remains opened. To support this feature, implement an event handler for the `OnFind` event. This event occurs when you click the Find Next button in the Find dialog box. The general syntax for the `OnFind` event handler is

```
procedure TForm1.FindDialog1Find(Sender: TObject);
begin
    { statements to search for text }
end;
```

The *ReplaceDialog* Component

Windows supports a standard dialog box to replace text. Figure 18.8 shows a sample Replace dialog box. The dialog box contains controls that allow you to specify the search text, replacement text, search direction, case sensitivity, and whole-word matching mode. It is important to point out that the Replace dialog box is modeless, just like the Find dialog box.

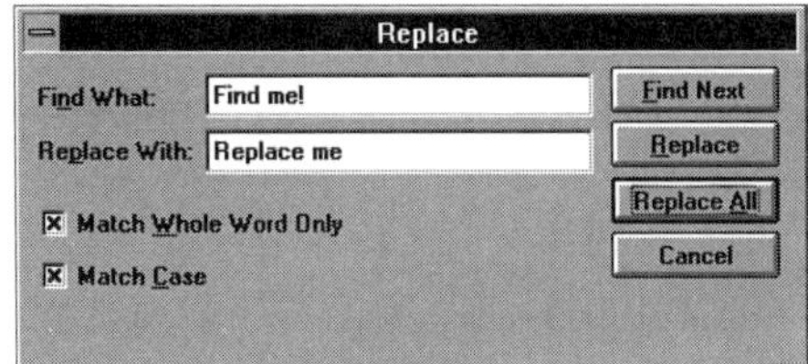

Figure 18.8.
The Replace dialog box.

You can think of the Replace dialog box as the Big Brother of the Find dialog box. Both dialog boxes share many properties, methods, and events. The `ReplaceDialog` component has the same `FindText` property, `Options` property, `CloseDialog` method, and `OnFind` event. The next subsections present the `ReplaceText` property and `OnReplace` event.

The *ReplaceText* Property

The `ReplaceText` property stores the replacement string. You may set the value of this property before invoking the Replace dialog box to specify the initial search string in the Replace With edit box. The program's user has the option of either accepting the initial replacement string or entering a different string. After the user clicks the OK button, the `ReplaceText` property contains the most recent string that appeared in the Replace With edit box before closing the dialog box.

18

Here is an example for using the `ReplaceText` property:

```
ReplaceDialog1.FindText := '[sounds];
ReplaceDialog1.ReplaceText := '[Sound]';
filename := 'WIN.INI';
if ReplaceDialog1.Execute then
    SearchInFile(filename,
        ReplaceDialog1.FindText
         ReplaceDialog1.ReplaceText);
```

This example uses the `ReplaceText` property to set the initial search and replacement strings to `[sounds]` and `[Sound]`, respectively. The code also uses the same property in replacing the text after the user closes the Replace dialog box.

The *OnReplace* Event

Because the Replace dialog box is modeless, you can trigger a text replacement while the dialog box remains opened. To support this feature, implement an event-handler for the `OnReplace` event. This event occurs when you click the Replace or Replace All button in the Replace dialog box. The general syntax for the `OnReplace` event handler is

```
procedure TForm1.ReplaceDialog1Replace(Sender: TObject);
begin
    { statements to replace text }
end;
```

The *EDT1* Example

Let's look at a program that implements a simple text editor that invokes the Open, Save, Print, Find, Replace, Color, and Font dialog boxes. Figure 18.9 shows the form for the EDT1 program project at design-time.

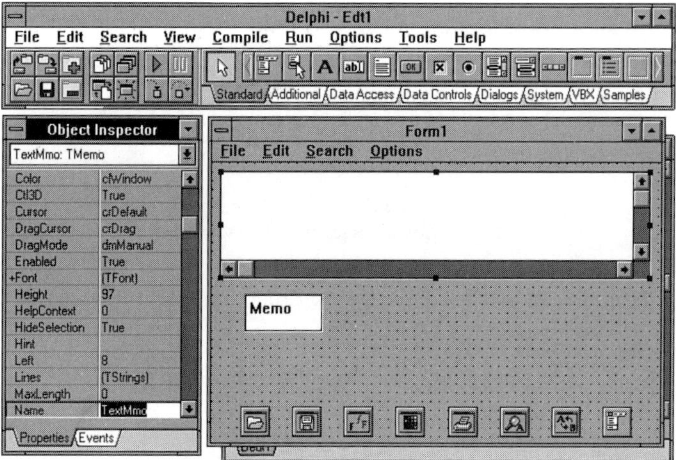

Figure 18.9.
The form for the EDT1 program project at design-time.

The Menu System

The EDT1 program has a menu bar with the options File, Edit, Search, and Options. Table 18.8 shows the menu system and lists the menu options and selections. The table also shows the shortcut keys and click events associated with menu selections. Use the information in Table 18.8 to build and customize the menu system.

Table 18.8. The menu system for the EDT1 program.

Option/Selection	Name	Shortcut	Event Handler
&File	`FileOpt`		
&New	`NewSel`		`NewSelClick`
&Open...	`OpenSel`	Ctrl+O	`OpenSelClick`
&Save	`SaveSel`	Ctrl+S	`SaveSelClick`
&Save As...	`SaveAsSel`		`SaveAsSelClick`

Option/Selection	Name	Shortcut	Event Handler
(separator)	N1		
&Print...	PrintSel	Ctrl+P	PrintSelClick
(separator)	N2		
&Exit	ExitSel	Ctrl+E	ExitSelClick
&Edit	EditOpt		
C&ut	CutSel	Ctrl+X	CutSelClick
Cop&y	CopySel	Ctrl+C	CopySelClick
&Paste	PasteSel	Ctrl+V	PasteSelClick
&Delete	DeleteSel	Del	DeleteSelClick
Select &All	SelectAllSel		SelAllSelClick
&Search	SearchOpt		
&Find	FindSel	Ctrl+F	FindSelClick
&Replace	ReplaceSel	Ctrl+F	ReplaceSelClick
&Options	OptionsOpt		
&Color...	ColorSel		ColorSelClick
&Font...	FontSel		FontSelClick

18

The Customized Settings of Components

The program's form contains the following components:

- Two memo components
- An `OpenDialog` component
- A `SaveDialog` component
- A `ColorDialog` component
- A `FontDialog` component
- A `FindDialog` component
- A `ReplaceDialog` component

Table 18.9 shows the new settings for some of the properties of the components for the EDT1 program. Use the information in this table to draw and customize the form and its components. After you draw the components, you need to specify the event handlers for the menu selections and for the components. Table 18.10 lists the events handled by the various non-menu components of program EDT1.

Compile and run the EDT1 program (see the bold lines in Listing 18.1, which show the code you need to insert in unit Uedt1). Use the text-editing features to load, edit, print, and save text, as well as change text font and background color. The program uses the following menu selections to invoke the different standard dialog boxes:

- The File|Open selection invokes the Open dialog box.
- The File|Save As selection invokes the Save dialog box. The File|Save selection invokes the same dialog box if you are saving new text to a file.
- The File|Print selection invokes the Print dialog box. This dialog box supports printing the entire text or just the selected text.
- The Options|Color selection invokes the Color dialog box, which allows you to select the background color.
- The Options|Font selection invokes the Font dialog box, which enables you to choose a new font style, font size, font effects, and font color.
- The Search|Find selection brings up the Find dialog box. The current program version only supports forward, case-sensitive searches of text. When the Find dialog box appears, it displays the selected text in the Find What edit box. Clicking on the Find Next button searches for the sought text and selects the next matching text in the memo control. If there is no matching text (at least in the remaining part of the memo component), the program displays a message dialog box and resets the search parameters.
- The Search|Replace selection brings up the Replace dialog box. The current program version only supports replacing all of the text in the memo component. The text replacement is case-sensitive. The Find Next button works just like it does in the Find dialog box. When the Replace dialog box appears, it displays the selected text in the Find What edit box. If you click the Replace button, you get a message dialog box telling you that the single text-replacement feature is not supported. When you click the Replace All button, the program replaces all of the text in the Find What edit box with the text in the Replace With edit box.

Table 18.9. The new settings for some of the properties of the components for the EDT1 program.

Component	Property	New Value
MainMenu1	Name	MainMnu
Memo1	Name	TextMmo
	ScrollBars	ssBoth
	Name	Memo
OpenDialog1	Name	OpenDlg

Component	Property	New Value
SaveDialog1	Name	SaveDlg
PrintDialog1	Name	PrintDlg
FindDialog1	Name	FindDlg
ReplaceDialog1	Name	ReplaceDlg
ColorDialog1	Name	ColorDlg
FontDialog1	Name	FontDlg

Table 18.10. The list of events handled by the various non-menu components of program EDT1.

Component	Event	Event Handler
Form1	OnCreate	FormCreate
	OnResize	FormResize
TextMmo	OnChange	TextMnuChange
FontDlg	OnApply	FontDlgApply
FindDlg	OnFind	FindDlgFind
ReplaceDlg	OnFind	ReplaceDlgFind
	OnReplace	ReplaceDlgReplace

Listing 18.1 shows the source code for the Uedt1 unit. The bold lines indicate the code that you need to insert. This code includes declarations and statements for the various event handlers; declarations of auxiliary fields; and the declaration and implementation of protected auxiliary methods. The listing shows the implementation of the various methods in alphabetical order. Such an order makes it easy to locate the implementation of a method in a relatively long listing.

Listing 18.1. The source code for the Uedt1 unit.

```
unit Uedt1;

interface

uses
  SysUtils, WinTypes, WinProcs, Messages, Classes,
  Graphics, Controls, Forms, Dialogs, Menus, StdCtrls,
  { insert next unit }
  Printers;

type
```

continues

Listing 18.1. continued

```
  TForm1 = class(TForm)
    MainMnu: TMainMenu;
    TextMmo: TMemo;
    FileOpt: TMenuItem;
    SearchOpt: TMenuItem;
    NewSel: TMenuItem;
    OpenSel: TMenuItem;
    SaveSel: TMenuItem;
    SaveAsSel: TMenuItem;
    N1: TMenuItem;
    PrintSel: TMenuItem;
    N2: TMenuItem;
    ExitSel: TMenuItem;
    OptionsOpt: TMenuItem;
    ColorSel: TMenuItem;
    FontSel: TMenuItem;
    FindSel: TMenuItem;
    ReplaceSel: TMenuItem;
    OpenDlg: TOpenDialog;
    SaveDlg: TSaveDialog;
    FontDlg: TFontDialog;
    ColorDlg: TColorDialog;
    PrintDlg: TPrintDialog;
    FindDlg: TFindDialog;
    ReplaceDlg: TReplaceDialog;
    EditOpt: TMenuItem;
    CutSel: TMenuItem;
    CopySel: TMenuItem;
    PasteSel: TMenuItem;
    DeleteSel: TMenuItem;
    SelectAll1: TMenuItem;
    Memo: TMemo;
    procedure FormCreate(Sender: TObject);
    procedure FormResize(Sender: TObject);
    procedure ExitSelClick(Sender: TObject);
    procedure ColorSelClick(Sender: TObject);
    procedure FontSelClick(Sender: TObject);
    procedure FontDlgApply(Sender: TObject; Wnd: Word);
    procedure NewSelClick(Sender: TObject);
    procedure TextMmoChange(Sender: TObject);
    procedure OpenSelClick(Sender: TObject);
    procedure SaveSelClick(Sender: TObject);
    procedure SaveAsSelClick(Sender: TObject);
    procedure FindSelClick(Sender: TObject);
    procedure FindDlgFind(Sender: TObject);
    procedure PrintSelClick(Sender: TObject);
    procedure CutSelClick(Sender: TObject);
    procedure CopySelClick(Sender: TObject);
    procedure PasteSelClick(Sender: TObject);
    procedure DeleteSelClick(Sender: TObject);
    procedure SelectAll1Click(Sender: TObject);
    procedure ReplaceDlgFind(Sender: TObject);
    procedure ReplaceDlgReplace(Sender: TObject);
    procedure ReplaceSelClick(Sender: TObject);
```

```
  private
    { Private declarations }
    fNewFile: Boolean;
    fFilename: string;
    fFindStr: string;
    fCharIdx: Byte;
    fByteSum: Integer;
    fLineIdx: Integer;

    procedure ClearMemoText;
    function QuerySave : Word;
    procedure FindString(const findStr: string);
    procedure ReplaceAllStrings(const findStr,
                                     replStr: string);
    procedure SaveFile(const filename: string);
    procedure LoadFile(const filename: string);
    function XPos(const findStr, mainStr: string;
                  const start: byte) : byte;
    procedure MyMessage(Msg: string);
  public
    { Public declarations }
  end;

var
  Form1: TForm1;

implementation

{$R *.DFM}

const
   NEW_TITLE = 'UNTITLED.TXT';

procedure TForm1.ClearMemoText;

begin
  TextMmo.Lines.Clear;
  Caption := NEW_TITLE;
  TextMmo.Modified := False;
  fNewFile := True;
end;

procedure TForm1.ColorSelClick(Sender: TObject);
begin
  if ColorDlg.Execute then
    TextMmo.Color := ColorDlg.Color;
end;

procedure TForm1.CopySelClick(Sender: TObject);
begin
  TextMmo.CopyToClipboard;
end;

procedure TForm1.CutSelClick(Sender: TObject);
begin
```


continues

Listing 18.1. continued

```
  TextMmo.CutToClipboard;
end;

procedure TForm1.DeleteSelClick(Sender: TObject);
begin
  TextMmo.ClearSelection;
end;

procedure TForm1.ExitSelClick(Sender: TObject);

var msgRes: Word;

begin
  { select response for the case when
    file is already saved }
  msgRes := mrNo;
  { ask user to Save text if not already saved }
  if TextMmo.Modified then
     msgRes := QuerySave;
  { act on save-file outcome }
  if msgRes = mrCancel then
    Exit
  else
    Close;
end;

procedure TForm1.FindDlgFind(Sender: TObject);

var findStr: string;

begin
  if fFindStr <> FindDlg.FindText then begin
    fFindStr := FindDlg.FindText;
    { reset the character and line
      indices for the text search }
    fCharIdx := 0;
    fByteSum := 0;
    fLineIdx := 0;
  end;
  FindString(FindDlg.FindText);
end;

procedure TForm1.FindSelClick(Sender: TObject);

var findStr: string;

begin
  if TextMmo.Lines.Count > 0 then begin
    fFindStr := TextMmo.SelText;
    FindDlg.FindText := fFindStr;
    { reset the character and line
      indices for the text search }
    fCharIdx := 0;
    fByteSum := 0;
```

```
    fLineIdx := 0;
    FindDlg.Execute;
  end
  else
    MyMessage('No text to search');
end;

procedure TForm1.FindString(const findStr: string);

var
   notFound: Boolean;
   i, n : Integer;
   aStr: string;

begin
  notFound := True;
  n := Length(findStr);
  { search for text }
  while notFound and (fLineIdx < TextMmo.Lines.Count) do begin
    { get line at index fLineIdx }
    aStr := TextMmo.Lines.Strings[fLineIdx];
    i := XPos(findStr, aStr, fCharIdx + 1);
    if i > 0 then begin
      notFound := False;
      { update character index }
      fCharIdx := i;
      { select matching text }
      TextMmo.SelStart := fByteSum + i - 1;
      TextMmo.SelLength := n;
      TextMmo.SetFocus;
    end
    else begin
      fCharIdx := 0;
      inc(fLineIdx);
      inc(fByteSum, Length(aStr) + 2);
    end;
  end;
  if notFound then begin
    MyMessage('String "' + findStr + '" was not found');
    { reset the character and line
      indices for the text search }
    fCharIdx := 0;
    fByteSum := 0;
    fLineIdx := 0;
  end;
end;

procedure TForm1.FontDlgApply(Sender: TObject; Wnd: Word);
begin
  TextMmo.Font := FontDlg.Font;
end;

procedure TForm1.FontSelClick(Sender: TObject);
begin
  if FontDlg.Execute then
```

continues

Listing 18.1. continued

```
    TextMmo.Font := FontDlg.Font;
end;

procedure TForm1.FormCreate(Sender: TObject);
begin
  TextMmo.Top := 0;
  TextMmo.Left := 0;
  TextMmo.Height := ClientHeight;
  TextMmo.Width := ClientWidth;
  TextMmo.Modified := False;
  Memo.Visible := False; { hide secondary memo }
  fNewFile := True;
  Caption := NEW_TITLE;
end;

procedure TForm1.FormResize(Sender: TObject);
begin
  TextMmo.Height := ClientHeight;
  TextMmo.Width := ClientWidth;
  Memo.Height := ClientHeight;
  Memo.Width := ClientWidth;
end;

procedure TForm1.LoadFile(const filename: string);
begin
  TextMmo.Lines.LoadFromFile(filename);
  TextMmo.Modified := False;
  fNewFile := False;
end;

procedure TForm1.MyMessage(Msg: string);
begin
  MessageDlg(Msg, mtInformation, [mbOK], 0);
end;

procedure TForm1.NewSelClick(Sender: TObject);

var msgRes : Word;

begin
  if TextMmo.Modified then begin
     msgRes := QuerySave;
    { act on save-file outcome }
    if msgRes = mrCancel then
      Exit;
  end;
  { clear memo text }
  ClearMemoText;
end;

procedure TForm1.OpenSelClick(Sender: TObject);

var msgRes: Word;

```

```
begin
  if TextMmo.Modified then begin
     msgRes := QuerySave;
    { act on save-file outcome }
    if msgRes = mrCancel then
      Exit;
  end;

  { set the file filters }
  OpenDlg.Filter := 'All files|*.*|' +
                    'Text files|*.txt|' +
                    'INI files|*.ini|' +
                    'Batch files|*.bat|';
  OpenDlg.FilterIndex := 2;
  if OpenDlg.Execute then begin
    fFilename := OpenDlg.FileName;
    Caption := fFilename; { update form caption }
    LoadFile(fFilename);
  end;
end;

procedure TForm1.PasteSelClick(Sender: TObject);
begin
  TextMmo.PasteFromClipboard;
end;

procedure TForm1.PrintSelClick(Sender: TObject);

var
  i: Integer;
  PrtText: System.Text;

begin
  PrintDlg.Options := [poWarning, poSelection];
  If PrintDlg.Execute then begin
    If poSelection in PrintDlg.Options then begin
      { print selected text }
      { exit if there are no selected text }
      If TextMmo.SelLength = 0 Then
        Exit;
      { copy the selected text from TextMmo to Memo
        using the clipboard }
      TextMmo.CopyToClipboard;
      Memo.PasteFromClipboard;
      AssignPrn(PrtText);
      Rewrite(PrtText);
      { use the TextMmo's font }
      Printer.Canvas.Font := TextMmo.Font;
      For i := 0 to Memo.Lines.Count - 1 do
        Writeln(PrtText, Memo.Lines[i]);
      CloseFile(PrtText);
    end
    else begin
      { print entire memo text }
      AssignPrn(PrtText);
      Rewrite(PrtText);
```


continues

Listing 18.1. continued

```
      Printer.Canvas.Font := TextMmo.Font;
      For i := 0 to TextMmo.Lines.Count - 1 do
        Writeln(PrtText, TextMmo.Lines[i]);
      CloseFile(PrtText);
    end;
  end;
end;


procedure TForm1.ReplaceAllStrings(const findStr,
                                         replStr: string);

var
  i, j, findLen, replLen : Integer;
  StrLine: string;

begin
  findLen := Length(findStr);
  replLen := Length(replStr);
  for i := 0 to TextMmo.Lines.Count - 1 do begin
    StrLine := TextMmo.Lines.Strings[i];
    j := Pos(findStr, StrLine);
    while j > 0 do begin
      Delete(StrLine, j, findLen);
      Insert(replStr, StrLine, j);
      j := j - findLen + replLen;
      j := Pos(findStr, StrLine);
    end;
    TextMmo.Lines.Strings[i] := StrLine;
  end;
  TextMmo.Refresh;
  TextMmo.SetFocus;
end;

procedure TForm1.ReplaceDlgFind(Sender: TObject);
begin
  if fFindStr <> ReplaceDlg.FindText then begin
    fFindStr := ReplaceDlg.FindText;
    { reset the character and line
      indices for the text search }
    fCharIdx := 0;
    fByteSum := 0;
    fLineIdx := 0;
  end;
  FindString(ReplaceDlg.FindText);
end;

procedure TForm1.ReplaceDlgReplace(Sender: TObject);
begin
  if frReplaceAll in ReplaceDlg.Options then begin
    fFindStr := ReplaceDlg.FindText;
    ReplaceAllStrings(fFindStr, ReplaceDlg.ReplaceText);
    { reset the character and line
    indices for the text search }
```

```
    fCharIdx := 0;
    fByteSum := 0;
    fLineIdx := 0;
  end
  else
    MyMessage('Feature is currently not supported');
end;

procedure TForm1.ReplaceSelClick(Sender: TObject);
begin
  if TextMmo.Lines.Count > 0 then begin
    fFindStr := TextMmo.SelText;
    ReplaceDlg.FindText := fFindStr;
    { reset the character and line
      indices for the text search }
    fCharIdx := 0;
    fByteSum := 0;
    fLineIdx := 0;
    ReplaceDlg.Execute;
  end
  else
    MyMessage('No text to search/replace');
end;

procedure TForm1.SaveFile(const filename: string);
begin
  TextMmo.Lines.SaveToFile(filename);
  TextMmo.Modified := False;
  fNewFile := False;
end;

procedure TForm1.SaveAsSelClick(Sender: TObject);

var msgRes: Word;

begin
  { set the file filters }
  SaveDlg.Filter := 'All files¦*.*¦' +
                    'Text files¦*.txt¦' +
                    'INI files¦*.ini¦' +
                    'Batch files¦*.bat¦';
  SaveDlg.FilterIndex := 2;
  if SaveDlg.Execute then begin
    fFilename := SaveDlg.FileName;
    Caption := fFilename; { update form caption }
    SaveFile(fFilename);
  end;
end;

procedure TForm1.SaveSelClick(Sender: TObject);
begin
  if fNewFile then
    SaveAsSelClick(Sender)
  else
    SaveFile(fFilename);
end;
```

continues

Listing 18.1. continued

```
procedure TForm1.SelectAll1Click(Sender: TObject);
begin
  TextMmo.SelectAll;
end;

procedure TForm1.TextMmoChange(Sender: TObject);
begin
  { reset character and line indices for text search }
  fCharIdx := 0;
  fByteSum := 0;
  fLineIdx := 0;
end;

function TForm1.QuerySave : Word;
begin
  Result := MessageDlg('Save text?', mtConfirmation,
                       mbYesNoCancel, 0);
  { save the file }
  if Result = mrYes Then
    SaveFile(fFilename);
end;

function TForm1.XPos(const findStr, mainStr: string;
                     const start: byte) : byte;

var
  i: Integer;
  copyStr: string;

begin
  copyStr := Copy(mainStr, start, 255);
  i := Pos(findStr, copyStr);
  if i > 0 then
    Result := i + start - 1
  else
    Result := 0;
end;

end.
```

The next subsections discuss the various relevant parts of the program.

Note: When the following discussion mentions the memo component, it refers to the visible memo. The program uses a second memo component, which is kept invisible, to support printing selected text.

The Auxiliary Fields

Lines 68 to 73 declare a group of auxiliary fields that support the various dialog boxes in the EDT1 program. These fields are as follows:

- The field `fNewFile` is a flag that tells the program whether or not the memo component contains new text.
- The field `fFilename` stores the name of the file associated with the contents of the memo component.
- The field `fFindStr` stores the most recent search string. The program uses this field mainly to detect changes in the search string while the Find and Replace dialog boxes are still in view.
- The field `fCharIdx` stores the character index of the matching string in the memo line specified by field `fLineIdx`.
- The field `fByteSum` stores the sum of bytes of the first `fLineIdx - 1` lines.
- The field `fLineIdx` stores the index of the currently searched memo line.

18

Lines 75 to 84 declare a group of auxiliary methods that support the various dialog boxes in the EDT1 program. These methods are:

- `ClearMemoText`, which clears the text in the memo component, resets the form caption, and resets other fields.
- `QuerySave`, which asks the user to save the modified contents of the memo component. If you click the OK button of the message dialog box, the method saves the text to a file and then returns the numeric code of the button you clicked.
- `FindString`, which conducts the text search in the memo component.
- `ReplaceAllStrings`, which replaces text in the memo component.
- `SaveFile`, which saves the text of the memo component in a file.
- `LoadFile`, which loads the text of the memo component from a file.
- `XPos`, a version of the predefined procedure `Pos`, which searches for a string starting at a specified character.
- `MyMessage`, which implements a short version of the method `MessageDlg`.

The *OpenDialog* Component Code

The method `OpenSelClick` (implemented in lines 280 to 303) uses the `OpenDialog` component `OpenDlg`. The method first determines if the current text in the memo component needs to be saved. Lines 285 to 290 handle saving the text if needed. The `if` statement in line 285 examines the memo's Boolean property `Modified` to determine if the text in the memo needs saving. If the property is `True`, the code invokes the method `QuerySave` in line 286.

Lines 293 to 296 assign the file filters to the `Filter` property of the `OpenDlg` component. These filters specify the wildcards `*.*`, `*.txt`, `*.ini`, and `*.bat`. Line 297 assigns 2 to the `FilterIndex` property of the `OpenDlg` component. This assignment selects the wildcard `*.txt` as the initial file type. The statement in line 298 invokes the Open dialog box by sending the OOP message `Execute` to the object `OpenDlg`. This OOP message appears as the condition of an `if` statement. If the message returns `True`, the program executes the statements in lines 299 to 301. The statement in line 299 copies the value of the property `FileName` to the field `fFilename`. Line 300 updates the caption of the form using the selected filename. Line 301 loads the contents of the selected file in the memo component by invoking the auxiliary method `LoadFile`.

The *SaveDialog* Component Code

The method `SaveAsSelClick` (implemented in lines 425 to 441) uses the `SaveDialog` component `SaveDlg`. Lines 431 to 434 assign the file filters to the `Filter` property of the `SaveDlg` component. These filters specify the wildcards `*.*`, `*.txt`, `*.ini`, and `*.bat`. Line 435 assigns 2 to the `FilterIndex` property of the `SaveDlg` component. This assignment selects the wildcard `*.txt` as the initial file type. The statement in line 436 invokes the Save dialog box by sending the OOP message `Execute` to the object `SaveDlg`. This OOP message appears as the condition of an `if` statement. If the message returns `True`, the program executes the statements in lines 437 to 439. The statement in line 437 copies the value of the property `FileName` to the field `fFilename`. Line 438 updates the caption of the form using the selected filename. Line 439 saves the contents of the memo component in the selected file by invoking the auxiliary method `SaveFile`.

The *PrintDialog* Component Code

The method `PrintSelClick` (implemented in lines 310 to 347) uses the `PrintDialog` component `PrintDlg`. Line 317 sets the printer options `poWarning` and `poSelection` in the `Options` property of the `PrintDlg` object. The statement in line 318 invokes the Print dialog box by sending the OOP message `Execute` to the object `PrintDlg`. This OOP message appears as the condition of an `if` statement. If the message returns `True`, the program executes the statements in lines 319 to 345. The `if` statement in line 319 determines if the user elected to print the selected text. The `if` statement in line 322 determines if there is no selected text. If there is no selected text, the method merely exits. Otherwise, the program executes the statements in line 326 and beyond. The statement in line 326 copies the selected text to the Clipboard by sending the OOP message `CopyToClipboard` to the memo `TextMmo`. Line 327 pastes the Clipboard's contents to the invisible memo component (the method `FormCreate` hides this component, which is used strictly to print selected text) by sending the OOP message `PasteFromClipboard` to the invisible memo `Memo`. Lines 328 and 329 set up the printer. Line 331 selects the printer's font to match that of the memo object `TextMmo`. The `for` loop in lines 332 and 333 prints the lines of the invisible memo. Line 334 closes the printer's buffer.

Lines 337 to 345 handle printing the entire text of the memo object `TextMmo`. Lines 338 and 339 set up the printer. Line 340 selects the printer's font to match that of the memo object `TextMmo`. The `for` loop in lines 341 and 342 prints the lines of the invisible memo. Line 343 closes the printer's buffer.

The *ColorDialog* Component Code

The method `ColorSelClick` (implemented in lines 108 to 112) uses the `ColorDialog` component `ColorDlg`. The statement in line 110 invokes the Color dialog box by sending the OOP message `Execute` to the object `ColorDlg`. This OOP message appears as the condition of an `if` statement. If the message returns `True`, the program executes the statements in line 111. This statement assigns the `Color` property of the object `ColorDlg` to the `Color` property of the memo object `TextMmo`.

The *FontDialog* Component Code

The method `FontSelClick` (implemented in lines 227 to 231) uses the `FontDialog` component `FontDlg`. The statement in line 229 invokes the Font dialog box by sending the OOP message `Execute` to the object `FontDlg`. This OOP message appears as the condition of an `if` statement. If the message returns `True`, the program executes the statements in line 230. This statement assigns the `Font` property of the object `FontDlg` to the `Font` property of the memo object `TextMmo`.

The `FontDlg` object uses the method `FontDlgApply` to respond to the user clicking the Apply button in the Font dialog box. The method `FontDlgApply` is implemented in lines 222 to 225 and contains a single statement in line 224. This statement assigns the `Font` property of the object `FontDlg` to the `Font` property of the memo object `TextMmo`.

The *FindDialog* Component Code

The Find dialog box employs several methods to support its operations. These methods are `FindSelClick`, `FindDlgFind`, and `FindString`. The next subsections discuss these various methods.

The Method *FindSelClick*

The method `FindSelClick` (implemented in lines 163 to 180) uses the `FindDialog` component `FindDlg`. The `if` statement in line 168 determines if there are any text lines. If there are, the method executes the statements in lines 169 to 176. The statement in line 169 copies the selected text into the field `fFindStr`. The statements in lines 173 to 175 reset the search parameters, which are stored in fields `fCharIdx`, `fByteSum`, and `fLineIdx`. Line 176 invokes the Find dialog box by sending the OOP message `Execute` to the object `FindDlg`.

The Method *FindDlgFind*

The method `FindDlgFind` (implemented in lines 147 to 161) responds to the user clicking the Find Next button in the Find dialog box. The `if` statement in line 152 compares the string in field `fFindStr` with the string in property `FindDlg.FindText`. If these two strings do not match, the method executes the statements in lines 153 to 158. These statements reset the search parameters, which are stored in fields `fCharIdx`, `fByteSum`, and `fLineIdx`. Line 160 triggers the text search by invoking the auxiliary method `FindString`. The argument for this method is the property `FindDlg.FindText`.

The Method *FindString*

The method `FindString` (implemented in lines 182 to 220) searches for the targeted string in the memo component. The method examines the lines of the memo starting with line `fLineIdx` and with character `fCharIdx`. The method uses a `while` loop to search for the text and updates the value of field `fByteSum` if it finds no match in the current line. The lines 202 to 204 select the matching string and set the focus to the memo component in order to display the matching string as selected text. If the method finds no match for the search string, it displays a message dialog box (line 213) and resets the search parameter (lines 216 to 218). Therefore, when you attempt to search beyond the last occurrence of a string, you get the message dialog box. The next time you search for the same string you will obtain the first occurrence of that string. Cool!

The *ReplaceDialog* Component Code

The Replace dialog box employs several methods to support its operations. These methods are `ReplaceSelClick`, `ReplaceDlgReplace`, `ReplaceDlgFind`, `ReplaceAllStrings`, and `FindString`. The next subsections discuss these various methods (except `FindString`, which was discussed above).

The Method *ReplaceSelClick*

The method `ReplaceSelClick` (implemented in lines 402 to 416) uses the `ReplaceDialog` component `ReplaceDlg`. The `if` statement in line 404 determines if there are any text lines. If there are, the method executes the statements in lines 405 to 412. The statement in line 405 copies the selected text into the field `fFindStr`. The statements in lines 409 to 411 reset the search parameters, which are stored in fields `fCharIdx`, `fByteSum`, and `fLineIdx`. Line 412 invokes the Replace dialog box by sending the OOP message `Execute` to the object `ReplaceDlg`.

The Method *ReplaceDlgReplace*

The method `ReplaceDlgReplace` (implemented in lines 387 to 400) responds to the user clicking the Replace Next button in the Replace dialog box. The `if` statement in line 389 determines

whether the user clicked the Replace or Replace All button. If the tested condition is true, the method executes the statements in lines 390 to 396. The statement in line 390 copies the string of property `FindText` to the field `fFindStr`. Line 391 replaces the strings in the memo component by invoking the auxiliary method `ReplaceAllStrings`. The arguments for this method are field `fFindStr` and property `ReplaceDlg.ReplaceText`. The statements in lines 394 to 396 reset the search parameters, which are stored in fields `fCharIdx`, `fByteSum`, and `fLineIdx`. The `else` clause in line 398 displays a message dialog box (line 399) to tell the user that single text replacement (requested by clicking the Replace button) is not supported.

The Method *ReplaceDlgFind*

The method `ReplaceDlgFind` (implemented in lines 347 to 385) responds to the user clicking the Find Next button in the Replace dialog box. The `if` statement in line 376 compares the string in field `fFindStr` with the string in property `ReplaceDlg.FindText`. If these two strings do not match, the method executes the statements in lines 377 to 382. These statements copy the search text into field `fFindStr` and reset the search parameters, which are stored in fields `fCharIdx`, `fByteSum`, and `fLineIdx`. Line 384 triggers the text search by invoking the auxiliary method `FindString`. The argument for this method is the property `ReplaceDlg.FindText`.

18

The Method *ReplaceAllStrings*

The method `ReplaceAllStrings` (implemented in lines 349 to 372) replaces the string of parameter `findStr` with the string of parameter `replStr`. The method performs a line-by-line replacement for all the occurrences of the string in parameter `findStr`. The method uses the property `TextMmo.Lines.Strings` to read and write the lines in the memo component.

The *FileListBox* Component

The `FileListBox` component is a list box dedicated to list all the files in the current directory. The next subsections discuss the relevant properties of this component. The file list component can handle events generated by mouse clicks, mouse buttons, gain of focus, loss of focus, and pressing keys. The most relevant event is `OnChange`. Handling this event enables a program to respond to changes in the file list box.

The *Directory* Property

The `Directory` property is a string that specifies the current directory for the file list box component. The file list box shows the files in the directory specified in the `Directory` property.

Here is an example of using the `Directory` property:

```
FileListBox1.Directory := '\';
```

This example sets the `Directory` property to the root directory of the current drive.

The *Drive* Property

The `Drive` property stores the character designation for the current drive. This property is only available at run-time. When you change the value of the `Drive` property you select another drive. This change affects the list of files displayed in the file list box.

Here is an example of using the `Drive` property:

```
FileListBox1.Directory := '\';
FileListBox1.Drive := 'C';
```

The above example selects the root directory of drive C: by assigning `'\'` and `'C'` to the `Directory` and `Drive` properties, respectively.

The *FileEdit* Property

The `FileEdit` property enables you to echo the name of the currently selected file in a separate edit box. When there is no selected file, the associated edit box shows the file mask used to display the list of files.

Here is an example of using the `FileEdit` property:

```
FileListBox1.FileEdit := Edit1;
```

This example associates the edit box `Edit1` with the file list box `FileListBox1`, using the `FileEdit` property.

The *FileName* Property

The `FileName` property specifies which file name is selected in the file list box.

Here is an example of using the `FileName` property:

```
Memo1.Lines.LoadFromFile(FileListBox1.FileName);
```

This code example loads text into a memo component from the currently selected file in the list box `FileListBox1`.

The *FileType* Property

The `FileType` property selects which files appear in the file list box depending on the attributes of the files. The value of this property is a set of values, shown in Table 18.11.

Table 18.11. The values for the FileType property.

Value	Meaning
`ftReadOnly`	When `True`, the list box displays any files with the read-only attribute.
`ftHidden`	When `True`, the list box displays any files with the hidden attribute.
`ftSystem`	When `True`, the list box displays any files with the system attribute.
`ftVolumeID`	When `True`, the list box displays the volume name.
`ftDirectory`	When `True`, the list box displays directories.
`ftArchive`	When `True`, the list box displays files with the archive attribute.
`ftNormal`	When `True`, the list box displays files with no attributes.

Here is an example of using the `FileType` property:

```
FileListBox1.FileType := [frReadOnly, ftArchive,
                         ftNormal, ftHidden, ftSystem];
```

This example displays the files with the attributes read-only, archive, normal, and hidden in the list box `FileListBox1`.

18

The *Mask* Property

The `Mask` property specifies the files that appear in the file list box. A file mask is made up of one or more filename wildcards, delimited by the semicolon character.

Here is an example of using the `FileMask` property:

```
FileListBox1.FileMask := '*.txt; *.doc';
```

The above example displays the files with the extensions .TXT and .DOC in the list box `FileListBox1`.

The *MultiSelect* Property

The `MultiSelect` property is a Boolean flag that specifies whether the file list box supports selecting multiple files.

Here is an example of using the `MultiSelect` property:

```
If ManyFilesCheckBox.State = cbChecked then
    FileListBox1.MultiSelect := True;
else
    FileListBox1.MultiSelect := False;
```

This example sets or clears the `MultiSelect` property depending on the checked state of a check box.

The *Selected* Property

The `Selected` property verifies whether a particular item is selected in the file list box. The declaration of the `Selected` property is

```
property Selected[Index: Integer]: Boolean;
```

The parameter `Index` is the positional index of the tested list member. The index of the first item is 0. The value of the `Selected` property reports the selected state of the targeted item. This property works in conjunction with the `MultiSelect` property.

Here is an example of using the `Selected` property:

```
For i := 0 to FileListBox1.Count - 1 do begin
    if FileListBox1.Selected[i] then
        MyPrint(FileListBox1.Items.Strings[i])
end;
```

This code example prints the selected files by using the `Selected` property.

The *ShowGlyphs* Property

The `ShowGlyphs` property is a Boolean flag that determines whether *glyphs* (bitmaps) appear to the left of the filenames in the file list box. The default value for this property is `False`, causing the bitmaps to be hidden.

Here is an example of using the `ShowGlyphs` property:

```
FileListBox1.ShowGlyphs := True;
FileListBox1.Mask := '*.txt; *.doc; *.exe';
FileListBox1.EditFile := Edit1;
```

The above example shows the bitmaps in the list of .TXT, .DOC, and .EXE files.

The *TopIndex* Property

The `TopIndex` property is the numeric index of the item appearing as the first displayed item in the file list box. Setting a value to the `TopIndex` property empowers you to select which filename appears at the top of the file list box.

Here is an example of using the `TopIndex` property:

```
FileListBox1.ShowGlyphs := True;
FileListBox1.Mask := '*.txt; *.doc; *.exe';
FileListBox1.TopIndex := 3;
```

This example shows the a list of .TXT, .DOC, and .EXE files and selects the third list item to be at the top of the list box.

The *DirectoryListBox* Component

The `DirectoryListBox` component is a list box dedicated to displaying the directory structure of the current drive. When the application runs, the user can use the directory list box to change directories, which changes the value of the `Directory` property. The next subsections discuss the relevant properties of the directory list box. The directory list component can handle events generated by mouse clicks, mouse-button management, gain of focus, loss of focus, and pressing keys. The most relevant event is `OnChange`. Handling this event allows a program to respond to changes in the directory list box.

The *Directory* Property

The `Directory` property is a string that specifies the current directory for the directory list box component.

Here is an example of using the `Directory` property:

```
procedure TForm1.DirectoryListBox1Change(Sender: TObject);
begin
  FileListBox1.Directory := DirectoryListBox1.Directory;
end;
```

This example shows how to synchronize the changes between the directories of a file list box and a directory list box.

The *DirLabel* Property

The `DirLabel` property enables you to associate a label component with a directory list box. This association causes the label component to display the current directory. When the current directory changes in the directory list box, the label automatically reflects the change.

Here is an example of using the `DirLabel` property:

```
DirectoryListBox1.DirLabel := CurDirLbl;
```

This code example associates the label `CurDirLbl` with the directory list box `DirectoryListBox1`, using the `DirLabel` property.

The *Drive* Property

The `Drive` property stores the character designation for the current drive. This property is only available at run-time. When you change the value of the `Drive` property, you select another drive. This change also affects the directory list box and the file list box, because these components display the current directory and files of the newly selected drive.

Here is an example of using the `Drive` property:

```
procedure TForm1.DriveComboBox1Change(Sender: TObject);
begin
  DirectoryListBox1.Drive := DriveComboBox1.Drive;
  FileListBox1.Directory := DirectoryListBox1.Directory;
end;
```

This example synchronizes the change in drive between a drive, directory, and file list boxes. This process involves the `Drive` and `Directory` properties.

The *FileList* Property

The `FileList` property associates a directory list box with a file list box. This association allows the file list box to automatically update its contents when the directory list box has a new current directory.

Here is an example of using the `FileList` property:

```
DirectoryListBox1.FileList := FileListBox1;
```

This example associates the file list box `FileListBox1` with the directory list box `DirectoryListBox1`, using the `FileList` property.

The *DriveComboBox* Component

The `DriveComboBox` component is a combo box dedicated to displaying all the drives available at run-time. The next subsections discuss the relevant properties of the drive combo box. The drive combo component can handle events generated by mouse clicks, mouse buttons, gain of focus, loss of focus, and pressing keys. The most relevant event is `OnChange`. Handling this event enables a program to respond to changes in the drive combo box.

The *DirList* Property

The `DirList` property associates a drive combo box with a directory list box. This association enables the directory list box to display the current directory of a new drive selected in the drive combo box.

Here is an example of using the `DirList` property:

```
DriveComboBox1.DirList := DirectoryListBox1;
```

This example associates the directory list box `DirectoryListBox1` with the drive combo box `DriveComboBox1`, using the `DirList` property.

The *Drive* Property

The `Drive` property, which is available only at run-time, specifies which drive is displayed in the edit control of the combo box. This property maintains the current drive and is updated automatically when the user selects another drive using the drive combo box.

Here is an example of using the `Drive` property:

```
DriveComboBox1.Drive := 'C';
```

This example selects drive C: by assigning the character C to the `Drive` property of the drive list box.

The *Text* Property

The `Text` property is a read-only property that is available only at run-time. This property represents the first item that appears in the combo box. The setting of the `Drive` property sets the value of the `Text` property in a drive combo box.

Here is an example of using the `Text` property:

```
filename := DriveComboBox1.Text + '\MYDATA.DAT'
```

This code example appends the value of the `Text` property to a filename.

The *TextCase* Property

The `TextCase` property specifies whether the volume name in the `Text` property appears in uppercase or lowercase. The values of this property are presented in Table 18.12.

Table 18.12. The values for the `TextCase` property.

Value	Meaning
`tcLowerCase`	The volume name set in the `Text` property appears in lowercase letters.
`tcUpperCase`	The volume name set in the `Text` property appears in uppercase letters.

Here is an example of using the `TextCase` property:

```
if DriveComboBox1.TextCase = tcLowerCase then
    filename := DriveComboBox1.Text + 'MYDATA.DAT'
else
    filename := DriveComboBox1.Text + 'mydata.dat';
```

This example uses the `TextCase` property to determine whether to create the filename in uppercase or lowercase characters.

The *FilterComboBox* Component

The `FilterComboBox` component is a combo box that is dedicated to presenting the user with a selection of file filters. The next subsections discuss the relevant properties of the filter combo box. The filter combo component can handle events generated by mouse clicks, mouse buttons, gain of focus, loss of focus, and pressing keys. The most relevant event is `OnChange`. Handling this event enables a program to respond to changes in the filter combo box.

The *FileList* Property

The `FileList` property associates a filter combo box and a file list box. This association allows the file list box to be automatically updated when you select a different filter in the filter combo box.

Here is an example of using the `FileList` property:

```
FilterComboBox1.FileList := FileListBox1;
```

This code example connects the file list box `FileListBox1` with the filter combo box `FilterComboBox1`, using the `FileList` property.

The *Filter* Property

The `Filter` property is the file filter string. This property uses the same file filter format as in the Open and Save dialog boxes.

Here is an example of using the `Filter` property:

```
FilterComboBox1.Filter = 'Text files¦*.txt¦' +
                    'Document files¦*.doc¦' +
                    'Programs¦*.exe¦';
```

This example sets the file filters to select .TXT, .DOC, and .EXE files.

The *Mask* Property

The `Mask` property is a read-only property that is available only at run-time. This property is the string selected as the filter in the filter combo box.

Here is an example of using the `Mask` property:

```
procedure TForm1.FilterComboBox1Change(Sender: TObject);
begin
   Label1.Caption := 'Mask: ' + FilterComboBox1.Mask;
end;
```

This example displays the new mask in a label component.

The *Text* Property

The `Text` property is a read-only property that is available only at run-time. This property represents the first item that appears in the combo box. The value of the `Filter` property specifies the value of the `Text` property in a filter combo box. When the `Filter` property lists multiple filters, the first filter in the `Filter` string appears first in the filter combo box.

The VIEW1 Program

Let's look at a program that uses the file list box, directory list box, drive combo box, and filter combo box components. The next program project, VIEW1, uses these components in a dialog box form. The program has two forms: the main form and the bottom-buttons dialog box form. Figure 18.10 shows the dialog box form for the VIEW1 program project at design-time.

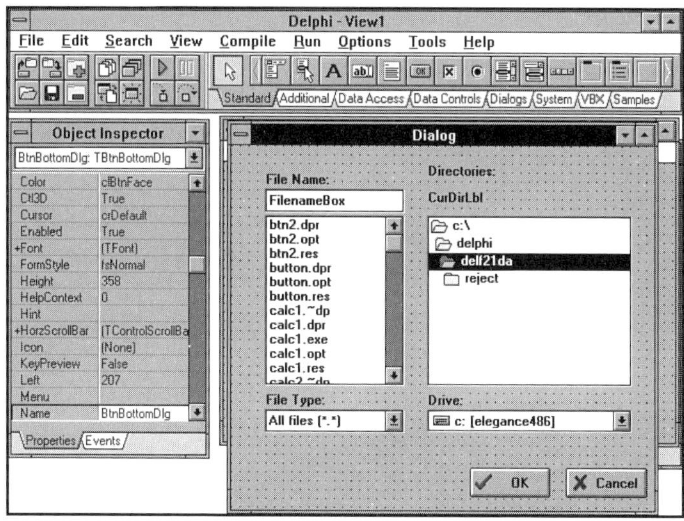

Figure 18.10.
The dialog box form for the VIEW1 program project at design-time.

The main form has a main menu component and a memo component. Table 18.12 shows the menu system for the main form in the VIEW1 program. Use the table's information to create the menu option and selection. Set the `Name` property of the memo component to `TextMmo`. The form-creation method handles further customization of the memo's properties. Table 18.13 lists the events handled by the form of program VIEW1.

Table 18.12. The menu system for the main form in the VIEW1 program.

Option/Selection	Name	Shortcut	Event Handler
&File	`FileOpt`		
&Open...	`OpenSel`	Ctrl+O	`OpenSelClick`
&Exit	`ExitSel`	Ctrl+E	`ExitSelClick`

Table 18.13. The list of events handled by the form of program VIEW1.

Component	Event	Event Handler
`Form1`	`OnCreate`	`FormCreate`
	`OnResize`	`FormResize`

The dialog box form contains the following components:

- The current directory label
- The filename edit box
- The file list box
- The file filter combo box
- The directory list box
- The drive combo box
- The OK button
- The Cancel button
- The labels for the filename edit box, file filter combo box, drive combo box, and directory list box.

Remember to delete the Help button and the bevel component that Delphi automatically includes in the dialog box form. Table 18.14 shows the new settings for some of the properties of the components in the dialog box form of the VIEW1 program. Table 18.15 lists the events handled by the dialog box form of program VIEW1. Use the information in these tables to customize the components in the dialog box form and set up the event handlers.

Table 18.14. The new settings for some of the properties of the components in the dialog box form of the VIEW1 program.

Component	Property	New Value
Label1	Name	CurDirLbl
	Caption	CurDirLbl
Label2	Name	FilenameLbl
	Caption	File Name:
Label3	Name	FileTypeLbl
	Caption	File Type:
Label4	Name	DirsLbl
	Caption	Directories:
Label5	Name	DriveLbl
	Caption	Drive:
Edit1	Name	FilenameBox
FileListBox1	Name	FileLst
DirectoryListBox1	Name	DirLst
FilterComboBox1	Name	FilterCmb
DriveComboBox1	Name	DriveCmb

Table 18.15. The list of events handled by the dialog box form of program VIEW1.

Component	Event	Event Handler
BtnBottomDlg	OnCreate	FormCreate
OKBtn	OnClick	OKBtnClick
CancelBtn	OnClick	CancelBtnClick
FileLst	OnDblClick	FileLstDblClick

Listing 18.2 shows the source code for the Uview11 unit. Listing 18.3 shows the source code for the Uview12 unit. The bold lines in these listings show the manually inserted code.

Listing 18.2. The source code for the Uview11 unit.

```
unit Uview11;

interface

uses
  SysUtils, WinTypes, WinProcs, Messages, Classes,
  Graphics, Controls, Forms, Dialogs,
  Menus, StdCtrls,
  { insert next unit name }
  Uview12;

type
  TForm1 = class(TForm)
    TextMmo: TMemo;
    MainMenu1: TMainMenu;
    FileOpt: TMenuItem;
    OpenSel: TMenuItem;
    ExitSel: TMenuItem;
    procedure FormCreate(Sender: TObject);
    procedure FormResize(Sender: TObject);
    procedure ExitSelClick(Sender: TObject);
    procedure OpenSelClick(Sender: TObject);
  private
    { Private declarations }
  public
    { Public declarations }
  end;

var
  Form1: TForm1;

implementation

{$R *.DFM}

procedure TForm1.FormCreate(Sender: TObject);
begin
  TextMmo.Top := 0;
  TextMmo.Left := 0;
  TextMmo.ScrollBars := ssBoth;
  TextMmo.Color := clAqua;
  TextMmo.Font.Name := 'Courier';
  TextMmo.Font.Size := 10;
  TextMmo.Lines.Clear;
  TextMmo.ReadOnly := True;
  Caption := 'File Viewer';
end;

procedure TForm1.FormResize(Sender: TObject);
begin
  TextMmo.Width := ClientWidth;
  TextMmo.Height := ClientHeight;
end;

```

```
procedure TForm1.ExitSelClick(Sender: TObject);
begin
  Close;
end;

procedure TForm1.OpenSelClick(Sender: TObject);

var filename : string;

begin
  if BtnBottomDlg.ShowModal = IDOK then begin
    filename := BtnBottomDlg.selFilename;
    if FileExists(filename) then begin
      TextMmo.Lines.LoadFromFile(filename);
      Caption := 'File Viewer ' + filename;
    end
    else
      MessageDlg('Error in opening file ' + filename,
                  mtWarning, [mbOK], 0);

  end;
end;

end.
```

Listing 18.3. The source code for the Uview12 unit.

```
unit Uview12;

interface

uses WinTypes, WinProcs, Classes, Graphics, Forms,
  Controls, Buttons, StdCtrls, FileCtrl;

type
  TBtnBottomDlg = class(TForm)
    OKBtn: TBitBtn;
    CancelBtn: TBitBtn;
    FileLst: TFileListBox;
    FileNameLbl: TLabel;
    FilenameBox: TEdit;
    FilterCmb: TFilterComboBox;
    FileTypeLbl: TLabel;
    DirLbl: TLabel;
    CurDirLbl: TLabel;
    DirLst: TDirectoryListBox;
    DriveLbl: TLabel;
    DriveCmb: TDriveComboBox;
    procedure FormCreate(Sender: TObject);
    procedure OKBtnClick(Sender: TObject);
    procedure CancelBtnClick(Sender: TObject);
    procedure FileLstDblClick(Sender: TObject);
  private
```

continues

Listing 18.3. continued

```
    { Private declarations }
  public
    { Public declarations }
    selFilename: string; { selected filename }
  end;

var
  BtnBottomDlg: TBtnBottomDlg;

implementation

{$R *.DFM}

procedure TBtnBottomDlg.FormCreate(Sender: TObject);
begin
  { connect components }
  FileLst.FileEdit := FilenameBox;
  DirLst.FileList := FileLst;
  DirLst.DirLabel := CurDirLbl;
  DriveCmb.DirList := DirLst;
  FilterCmb.FileList := FileLst;

  FilterCmb.Filter := 'All files|*.*|' +
                      'Text files|*.txt;*.doc|' +
                      'Batch files|*.bat|' +
                      'Pascal files|*.pas|' +
                      'Delphi projects|*.dpr|';
end;

procedure TBtnBottomDlg.OKBtnClick(Sender: TObject);
begin
  selFilename := FilenameBox.Text;
  ModalResult := mrOK;
end;

procedure TBtnBottomDlg.CancelBtnClick(Sender: TObject);
begin
  ModalResult := mrCancel;
end;

procedure TBtnBottomDlg.FileLstDblClick(Sender: TObject);
begin
  OKBtnClick(Sender);
end;

end.
```

The code in Listing 18.3 is relevant to the file-related components. Listing 18.2 merely provides the custom code to make the program work. Therefore, this discussion will focus on the code of Listing 18.3.

Line 30 declares the public field `selFilename`, which reports the name of the selected filename to the main form.

Lines 40 to 54 implement the method `FormCreate`. The statements in lines 43 to 47 connect the various components to support automatic updates between them. Line 43 connects the Filename edit box with the file list box, using the property `FileEdit`. Line 44 connects the file list box `FileLst` with the directory list box `DirLst`, using the `FileList` property. Line 45 connects the label `CurDirLbl` with the directory list box `DirLst`, using the property `DirLabel`. Line 46 connects the directory list box `DirLst` with the drive combo box `DriveCmb`, using the property `DirList`. Line 47 connects the file list box `FileLst` with the filter combo box `FilterCmb`, using the `FileList` property. The statement in lines 49 to 53 assigns the file filter string to the `Filter` property of the filter combo box.

Lines 56 to 60 implement the method `OKBtnClick`. This method assigns the value of property `FilenameBox.Text` to the field `selfFilename`. The method then assigns the predefined constant `mrOK` to the property `ModalResult`. This assignment closes the dialog box form and returns `IDOK`.

Lines 62 to 65 implement the method `CancelBtnClick`. This method assigns the predefined constant `mrCancel` to the property `ModalResult`. This assignment closes the dialog box form and returns `IDCancel`.

18

Lines 67 to 70 implement the method `FileLstDblClick`. This method merely invokes the method `OKBtnClick`. Consequently, when you double-click on an item in the file list box, you select that item and close the dialog box.

Summary

This chapter presented the components that support the standard Windows dialog boxes as well as file-related components. You learned about the following topics:

- The `OpenDialog` component is a modal standard dialog box that enables you to select a file to open. The dialog box contains controls that allow you to select a drive, directory, and file type in order to find the file you want to open.
- The `SaveDialog` component is a modal standard dialog box that enables you to select a file to use for saving data. The dialog box contains controls that allow you to select a drive, directory, and file type in order to specify the file to which you want to save.
- The `FontDialog` component is a modal standard dialog box that enables you to select a font. The dialog box contains controls that enable you to select the font type, style, size, effects, and color.
- The `ColorDialog` component is a modal standard dialog box that enables you to select a color. The dialog holds controls that enable you to select a predefined color or customize a color.

- The `PrintDialog` component is a modal standard dialog box that enables you to specify how to print a document. The dialog box possesses controls that enable you to select a printer, what part of the document to print, if you want to collate the output, the number of copies to print, and whether to print to file.
- The `PrinterSetupDialog` component is a modal standard dialog box that enables you to set up the printer. The dialog box maintains controls that enable you to select a printer and specify output orientation, paper size, and paper source.
- The `FindDialog` component is a modeless standard dialog box that enables you to search for text. The dialog box contains controls that enable you to specify the search text, search direction, whole-word search mode, and the case sensitivity of the search.
- The `ReplaceDialog` component is a modeless standard dialog box that enables you to search and replace text. The dialog box contains controls that enable you to specify the search text, the replacement text, whole-word search mode, and the case sensitivity of the search/replacement.
- The `FileListBox` component is a list box dedicated to displaying files in the current directory.
- The `DirectoryListBox` component is a directory list box dedicated to displaying directories in the current drive.
- The `DriveComboBox` component is a combo box dedicated to displaying the drive currently available in a machine.
- The `FilterComboBox` component is a combo box dedicated to displaying file filters.

Q&A

Q Can I use the Color dialog box to select the color of the font?

A Yes. There is no reason for font color selection to be monopolized by the Font dialog box.

Q Why are the standard Find and Replace dialog boxes modeless?

A These dialog boxes are modeless to allow them to remain in view after you click on the search/replace buttons.

Q What is the advantage of shifting the focus to the edit box or memo component affected by a Find or Replace dialog box?

A Shifting the focus to the edit box or memo component enables you, for example, to display selected text in that component.

Q How can I tell whether a user clicked the Replace or Replace All button in a Replace dialog box?

A Test if the value `frReplaceAll` is in the `Options` property in the method that handles the event `OnReplace`.

Q Is connecting the file component more convenient than using similar properties to synchronize updating these components?

A Indeed! Delphi offers two routes to connect file components. The first route requires that you copy the values of similar properties (ones that have the same name) for the different file components. The second route uses the component-associating properties that establish the automatic link. The program VIEW1 uses the second route and therefore shows you how short the code is for keeping these components synchronized.

Workshop

The Workshop provides quiz questions to help you solidify your understanding of the material covered and exercises to provide you with experience in using what you've learned. Try to understand the quiz and exercise answers before continuing on to the next day's lesson.

Quiz

1. Where is the error in the following code?

```
OpenDialog1.DefaultExt := '.bat';
If OpenDialog1.Execute then
    LoadFile(OpenDialog1.FileName);
```

2. True or False? You can include a full path in the `FileName` property of an `OpenDialog` component.
3. Where is the error in the following code?

```
OpenDialog1.Options := [];
If OpenDialog1.Execute then
    For i := 0 to OpenDialog1.Files.Count - 1 Do
        MyPrint(OpenDialog1.Files.Strings[i]);
```

4. What is the size limit for the file filter string?
5. How do you create a file filter with multiple wildcards?

6. What file filter appears in the Open dialog box for the following code?

```
OpenDialog1.Filter := 'Text files¦*.TXT' +
                      'Document files¦*.DOC¦' +
                      'BMP files¦*.BMP¦' +
                      'INI files¦*.INI¦';
OpenDialog1.FilterIndex := 10;
```

7. What Font dialog box properties control the minimum and maximum font size the user can select?
8. What Print dialog box property controls the number of copies?
9. How do you control the range of printed pages in a Print dialog box?

Exercise

1. Modify the program EDT1 to make the Find and Replace dialog boxes fully operational.

WEEK
3

Database Programming

One of the big advantages of Delphi over some more traditional Windows programming tools and environments is its built-in support for accessing and manipulating databases.

Today's lesson introduces you to the concepts and techniques related to database development. In particular, you learn the following:

- The database terminology and some basic notions related to databases
- The properties and usage of the most commonly used database components
- How to connect database components together to form a cohesive, cooperating team responsible for managing database data under the user control
- The most commonly occurring patterns in the database application design

Databases

Although this book is not a formal introduction to database theory, you need to understand some of the database terminology to be able to make proper use of the database tools available in Delphi. In this section, you learn the most important database concepts.

NEW TERM *Data* denotes information stored inside the database.

Databases can be structured in many ways. Delphi supports the relational database model, a well-known and widely used database paradigm. Relational databases consist of data tables, each with a fixed structure of columns.

NEW TERM A *database* is a collection of data tables.

Databases can be local; that is, they may simply be a collection of dBASE or Paradox tables in one subdirectory on your local hard drive or on the local area network file-server volume. Or they can be remote, in which case the database is maintained by a database server, such as Sybase, Oracle, Informix, or Interbase.

NEW TERM A *table* conceptually consists of a grid of rows and columns in which data values are stored.

NEW TERM A *record* corresponds to a single row in a database table. Each record in a table has the same structure; it is divided into the same fields laid out in the same order.

NEW TERM A *column* in a database table is a named collection of all values of a particular field across the entire table, together with information describing the type of data and the structure of the individual field.

NEW TERM A *field* in a data record is the simplest element meaningful from the perspective of the database theory. A field is the individual element in the grid of data rows and columns; it is the intersection of a single column with a single row. Fields contain data values.

The database structure is "fixed" in the sense that all records in an entire table have the same format; in other words, each record consists of the same fields throughout the table. Each individual field within a record in turn contributes to the creation of columns of data values of the same type.

Figure 19.1 illustrates the fundamental database concepts.

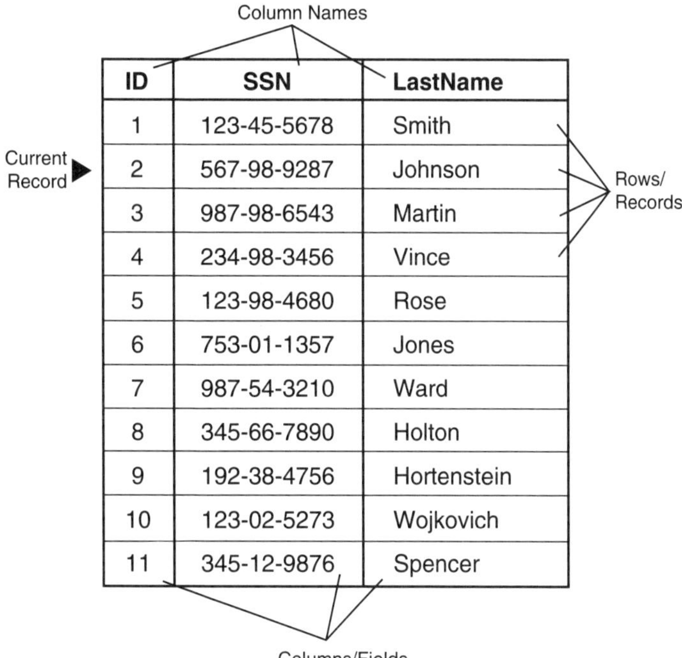

ID	SSN	LastName
1	123-45-5678	Smith
2	567-98-9287	Johnson
3	987-98-6543	Martin
4	234-98-3456	Vince
5	123-98-4680	Rose
6	753-01-1357	Jones
7	987-54-3210	Ward
8	345-66-7890	Holton
9	192-38-4756	Hortenstein
10	123-02-5273	Wojkovich
11	345-12-9876	Spencer

Figure 19.1.
Fundamental database concepts.

In addition to the concepts already described, there is a notion of a current position, or current record, within a data table. The facility responsible for setting and maintaining the current position within a data table is called a cursor.

NEW TERM A *cursor* is the database facility responsible for maintaining the current position within a data table and distinguishing the data record that is the current focal point, or that is receiving the attention at any given time from all other records in the table.

Note: Don't confuse the term *cursor* as used in the context of traversing database tables with the term *cursor* as used in connection with pointing devices, such as the mouse cursor. The two types of cursors are completely unrelated. The only characteristic that they have in common, other than the name, is that both have to do with somehow indicating a position within their respective domains.

Analogous to the concept of the current record, it also is sometimes desirable to distinguish a particular field within the current record. This leads to the concept of a current field. The current field is a specific field that is of particular interest in the current record. The concept is typically used in Delphi applications that display data fields and make them editable. Only a single record is considered current at any given time, and only a single field within the current record is current, or is currently focused on. Any editing actions affect only the current field.

Databases are identified by logical names called aliases. An alias is a logical name for the entire database. The user can assign aliases to denote and identify a particular database via a meaningful symbol rather than a system-dependent designator. For example, for local databases, instead of designating a database by using its full drive and path location, you can set up an alias such as WORKDATA or ACCOUNTS and refer to the database using that alias.

Another benefit of aliases is that they give you the flexibility to move the data tables some place else on your hard-drive or within the network, and the only reference you need to change is the alias information. Your programs using the alias will be completely unaffected.

Relational databases can often be manipulated by the SQL (Structured Query Language) queries.

NEW TERM *SQL* (Structured Query Language) is a dedicated language for defining and manipulating relational databases.

Although SQL is recognized as an international standard, many flavors or dialects of SQL exist, implementing various vendor-specific extensions. You have to be aware of any limitations of and/or extensions to SQL supported on the particular database platform for which you are writing.

One last database-oriented buzzword you need to know is the often misused term *client/server*.

NEW TERM The term *client/server*, for the purposes of this book, means a database architecture where data is stored in a central location—the *server*—and is being made available to any number of *clients*, that is, applications using and manipulating the contents of the server database.

This approach allows for centralized and controlled storage of large volumes of data, while making it possible to optimize access to the data, manage multiple simultaneous requests for the same data, and distributing the cost of a high-performance machine required to manage the data over many clients.

Typically, the clients and the server are running on different machines connected with one another through a network.

Examples of database servers include Oracle, Sybase, Informix, or Interbase database servers. Delphi, on the other hand, provides you with all the facilities and tools required for developing and maintaining client applications that access data managed by a server.

This book makes no claim to the ultimate definition of client/server. For the purposes of this book, you have a client/server application whenever you use a database server to access the data.

Architecture of Delphi Database Applications

Delphi provides a set of tools and facilities so that you can develop database applications easily. All Delphi database applications share certain common characteristics.

Figure 19.2 illustrates the typical high-level architecture of a Delphi database program. The general architecture consists of three layers.

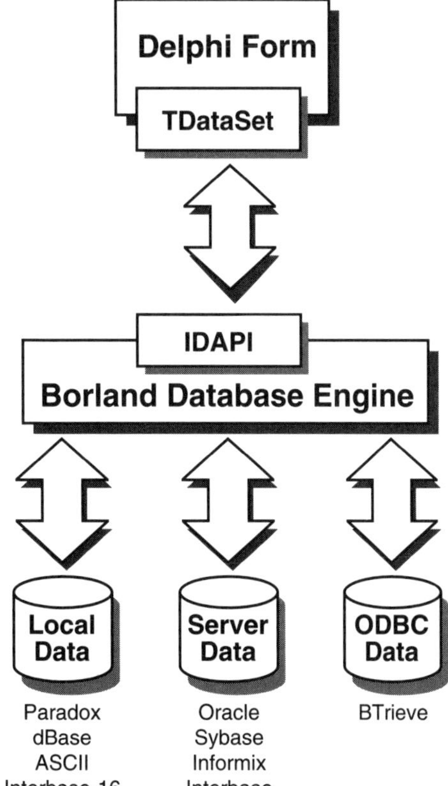

Figure 19.2.
The architecture of a Delphi database program.

- At the top is the Delphi application in need of managing data. The easiest way for the application to gain the capability of accessing and manipulating databases is by making use of the standard database components provided with Delphi.
- The application's database components in turn make use of the Borland Database Engine (BDE), which is shown as the intermediate layer in Figure 19.2. The components interface with the BDE via a collection of subroutines and services made available by the BDE Application Programming Interface (API, previously known as IDAPI).
- The lowest layer in Figure 19.2 provides access to the actual physical data stored in database tables and is composed of the actual database management systems, both local, such as Paradox or dBASE tables, and remote, such as data residing in a database managed by an Oracle, Sybase, Informix, or Interbase server.

The whole idea of this layered architecture is to insulate you, the Delphi programmer, from the complexities and details of supporting all the different data-table formats and all the different interface conventions available. It also provides you with the ability to access all the different databases in a heterogeneous environment, where some portions of the data may reside in a local table, whereas others may be accessed remotely.

All that you need to concern yourself with has been encapsulated in the form of the Delphi database components. All that the components themselves deal with is a relatively uniform and consistent realm of the low-level interface to the BDE.

Database Components

The key to unleashing Delphi's database potential is using the database components. The standard Delphi class library provides two major groups of database components:

- *Data-access* components directly manipulate data tables, in general known as data sets. You use the data-access components to obtain and change values of fields within records, and to obtain and manipulate meta-data (data about data) in a database, such as table definitions, lists of tables defined within a database, and so on. Examples of data-access components include `Database`, `Table`, `Query`, and so on, from the Data Access page of Delphi's Component Palette. The data-access components encapsulate the low-level interface to the Borland Database Engine, so that you don't need to worry about the non-object-oriented details of how BDE expects the applications to use it.
- *Data-aware* controls are visual controls such as list boxes, edit fields, drop-down combo boxes, and so on, that not only represent windows control elements, but are also wired to and capable of displaying data fields of a table. Examples of data-aware controls include `DbGrid`, `DbLabel`, `DbEdit`, `DbListBox`, and so on, from the Data

Controls page of Delphi's Component Palette. The data-aware controls are just like the standard Windows user-interface components, except that their visual contents are "automatically" obtained from the appropriate database tables and you don't need to worry about setting their values explicitly. All you need to do is to hook them together with a table component via an intermediary called a `DataSource`.

In addition to the preceding two groups are a number of additional standard components that perform a variety of functions, such as connecting the data-access components with corresponding data-aware controls to make the data visible (`DataSource` component), or encapsulating the higher-order concept of a database as opposed to a single table (`Database` component).

Data-Access Components

The data-access components are capable of establishing connections with the physical databases via BDE, but they do not provide any facilities for actually displaying the data on a form.

All data-access components descend from the `TDataSet` abstract class encapsulating the interface to the Borland Database Engine. The specific descendants of `TDataSet`, such as `TTable` and `TQuery`, can be instantiated inside your application and used to manipulate databases.

TTable

19

The `Table` component (`TTable` class) encapsulates the concept of a database table. You can use a single or multiple instances of `TTable` whenever you need to access a specific table or a set of database tables. The `Table` component enables you to access or delete existing records in a given table and insert new ones.

Figure 19.3 shows the `Table` component icon from Delphi's Component Palette.

Figure 19.3.
The `Table` component's icon.

To activate a `Table` component, you must first put it on the form. Then you can adjust the values of some of its properties.

1. To access a local database (a set of dBASE or paradox tables in a directory) using the Object Inspector, enter the directory where the database resides as the `DatabaseName` property.
2. Change the `TableName` property to reflect the name of the table you want to access. If the database you are accessing contains more than one table, you can select one from a drop-down list inside the Object Inspector's property editor for `TableName`.

The `Table` component gives you access to all columns and all rows of a data table. At any given time, a `Table` component refers or points to a particular row of the associated data table (the current record).

To obtain access to a particular field of the current record by its ordinal integer number, you can use the `Fields` array property as follows:

```
AField := Table1.Fields[1];
```

The preceding code line retrieves a reference to field number one. The disadvantage of accessing fields by ordinal number is that your program is dependent on a particular ordering of fields within the table. A better, more flexible approach would be to refer to a field by its logical name. You can accomplish this by using `TTable`'s `FieldByName` method as follows:

```
AField := Table1.FieldByName('NAME');
```

The reference retrieved by the preceding call to `FieldByName` is always guaranteed to be to the `NAME` field, even if you've restructured the database. The `NAME` field must, of course, exist; otherwise, the reference is not found. Once you have obtained a reference to the field, which is an object of type `TField`, you can use any of the `TField`'s facilities to, for example, get and set data values explicitly.

To make the data visible, you can associate a visual component, such as a `DBGrid` from the Data Controls page of the Component Palette, with the table component via a `DataSource`, which is explained later in this chapter.

A `Table` component gives you access to all columns of a particular table. An implicit order is associated with the database columns. You can change the selection of columns and the order in which they are displayed inside data-aware controls, such as `TDbGrid`, by using the Data Set Designer.

TTable Properties

The `TTable` component defines a number of properties giving you access to some of the `TTable`'s functionality. The following sections describe these properties.

DatabaseName

You need to set the `DatabaseName` property in order to determine which database—of the possibly many available—the table you want to access belongs to. In case of a local database, such as a collection of Paradox or dBASE tables, you can specify a directory name on the disk where the data resides in place of the database name. You can also use an alias, a surrogate name that the Borland Database Engine knows and uses to identify a local or remote database.

When you enter the value of this property at design-time, you can use the drop-down list of alias names to pick a particular database.

TableName

Using the `TableName` property, you can specify which of the possibly many tables belonging to a particular database you want the `TTable` component to be connected to. Using the Object Inspector at design-time, after you select the database name, you can use the drop-down list of the `TableName` property to choose from an inventory of available tables.

ReadOnly

Setting the `ReadOnly` property of a `Table` to `True` prevents any attempts to change the data in the table. You can use this property to ensure that a particular table is viewed only in a lookup mode so that the user cannot enter new data or change any existing fields.

Exclusive

Setting the `Exclusive` property of a `TTable` to `True` prevents any other user, including any other process on your own machine, to open that table until you release it by setting `Exclusive` to `False`. Note that you cannot change the value of the `Exclusive` property if the table is already open, that is, its `Active` property is already `True`. Also note that this property only applies to local tables, not to server-based SQL-manipulated tables.

IndexName

You can optionally set the `IndexName` property of a `TTable` to a name of a secondary index, if the table has any secondary indices. A secondary index allows the database components to traverse through the records in a database in an order other than the default record order. For example, you may use an index defined to traverse the COUNTRY sample table in the alphabetic order of the capitals, rather than the default order of countries.

If the table specified in the `TableName` property does not define any secondary indices, or you simply want to use the default (primary) ordering of records to traverse the table, leave the `IndexName` property blank.

MasterSource

You can use the `MasterSource` property to link two tables in a master-detail relationship. On the detail-table, you can set the `MasterSource` property to the name of the primary table. The designated `MasterSource` will thus become the "master" for the relationship and will determine the selection of records that the "detail" table displays.

Each time you move the current position inside the master table, the corresponding records from the detail table are retrieved for manipulation and display. To fully specify the relationship, you must also set the `MasterFields` property to determine the common fields that define the link between the master and the detail tables.

MasterFields

If you want to link two tables in a master-detail relationship, set the value of `MasterFields` to a string consisting of one or more names of fields that are meant to define the link between the tables. Note that the fields you specify must exist in both tables. You can link the two tables on more than one field name by separating each pair of field names inside this property with a semicolon. Each time the current record in the master table changes, the new values in the specified fields are used to select corresponding records from the secondary table for display and manipulation.

A better approach to defining a master-detail relationship would be to use the custom property editor for the `MasterFields` property. If you double-click in the value column of `MasterFields` inside the Object Inspector, Field Link Editor is activated. You see an example of a master-detail relationship involving the use of the Field Link Editor later in today's lesson.

Active

Set the `Active` property of a `Table` to `True` to actually "open" the table, that is, to establish a connection to a database table and to make its data available for retrieval, display, and manipulation. Interestingly enough, you can open the table at design-time, in which case you can see live data inside the data-aware controls on the form!

Note that once you set the `Active` property to `True`, you cannot change many of the other table properties: the table is opened in a particular mode, and to change that mode you must first close the table by setting `Active` to `False`.

TTable Methods

The `TTable` class defines a number of methods accessible to you at run-time. Using these methods, you can control the behavior of a `Table` component.

As usual, you can obtain the list of all the available methods from the on-line help. Just click on the `TTable` component inside the Form Designer; then press F1 to get to the `TTable` page in the on-line help system. In the following sections, you concentrate on only a few of the most important methods.

Open and *Close* Methods

You have an alternative to setting the value of the `Active` property for a table to either `True` or `False`, depending on whether you want to "open" or "close" the table, respectively. You can use the `Open` and `Close` methods explicitly, thus programmatically affecting the value of the `Active` property.

Calling `Open` is exactly equivalent to setting the `Active` property to `True`. `Open` itself does that internally. `Close` sets the `Active` property to `False`.

FieldByName Method

The `FieldByName` function method gives you access to the field-definition structure of a particular field at run-time. The function returns a `TField` object, which you learn about later in today's lesson. Note, however, that `FieldByName` takes a `String` parameter denoting the name of the field, and that it involves searching through a list of strings designating all the fields in the associated table. A search operation of that sort may be costly and may affect the performance, especially if the technique is used frequently.

The capability that makes this method interesting and useful is that it effectively translates a logical name of a field, a string of characters, into a run-time object you can use to manipulate the data of a particular field. This translation is important because it enables you to use logical field names, as defined within the data table, as opposed to the physical sequential number of the field within the database structure.

There is an alternate approach to obtaining direct access to the `TField` objects that you should be aware of. You can use the Fields Editor to define `TField`-typed instance variables of the form. Just double click a `TTable` component inside the Form Designer, and the Fields Editor will appear. You can then add the fields you use most directly to the definition of the form's class. As you know by now, this makes them available to every method of the form's class without any need to perform string searches.

Navigational Methods

The `TTable` class defines a number of methods whose purpose is to move the data cursor to another position within the table. This group of "navigational" methods includes `First`, `Last`, `Prior`, and `Next`, which move the position within the table to the first record, last record, previous record, and next record, respectively.

The latter two methods move the position by one record in the specified direction, relative to the current record position. You can thus step through the table by initially calling `First`, and then repetitively calling `Next` until you get to the end of the table.

You can determine whether you have reached the end of a table by checking the value of its `EOF` (end-of-file) property. This value becomes `True` whenever you attempt to move the data cursor beyond the last record of the table.

Following is the skeleton code enabling you to traverse a database table in the forward direction:

```
begin
  ...
  Table1.First;
  while not Table1.EOF do begin
    ...
    Table1.Next;
  end;
  ...
end
```

Conversely, you can call the `Last` method and then repetitively call `Prior` to step through the table starting at the end and progressing backward. The value of the table's `BOF` (beginning-of-file) property enables you to determine when you have reached the first record.

The skeleton code for traversing a database table in the reverse direction is as follows:

```
begin
  ...
  Table1.Last;
  while not Table1.BOF do begin
    ...
    Table1.Prior;
  end;
  ...
end
```

In addition to the preceding, you can gain greater control over how many records are skipped in either direction when you are traversing a database by using the `MoveBy` method. `MoveBy` is defined as follows:

```
procedure MoveBy(Distance: Integer);
```

This method enables you to specify the number of records to skip in its `Distance` parameter. If you pass a negative parameter to the `MoveBy` routine, the data cursor is moved by the number of records specified back from the current position. A positive parameter skips the number of records indicated forward, toward the end of the table.

Of course, in all cases, when it becomes logically impossible to move the data cursor any further, these routines do nothing. For example, when you call `Next` while the data cursor is already beyond the end of file, that is, when the `EOF` property is `True`, the routine does not have any effect. Similarly, if you call `Prior` when the cursor is already at the beginning of the file, the routine does not have any effect.

Extending Data Tables

Two of the `TTable` methods deal with the creation of new table rows. The `Insert` method creates the new row before the current data cursor position. The `Append` method creates the new row at the end of the table. In both cases, calling the method moves the current position to the newly created record and puts the table in the edit-mode, thus making it available for editing.

Disabling Associated Controls

`TTable` inherits two very useful methods dealing with the issue of updating the associated data-aware controls that display the table's data. These methods are: `DisableControls` and `EnableControls`.

The `DisableControls` method allows you to temporarily suspend the coupling between the table and the associated data-aware controls such that the controls do not get updated whenever the

table's cursor moves to a new position. This facility allows you to, for example, iterate through and process all the records in a table without distracting the user with the data flashing by on the display whenever the current position changes. Disconnecting the visual updates also considerably improves the performance.

The `EnableControls` method reverses the action of `DisableControls` by re-establishing the connection between the cursor position and the data displayed by the associated data-aware controls.

TTable Events

The `TTable` class defines several events triggered by the actions taking place within the table. The following sections describe these events in more detail.

OnNewRecord

One example of an event you may want to trap inside your code is the creation of a new record. Whenever a new data row is created, the `OnNewRecord` event is triggered, enabling you to initialize the fields of the new record with default values, for example.

An `OnNewRecord` event handler you may want to install must have the following skeleton structure:

```
procedure TForm1.Table1NewRecord(DataSet: TDataSet);
begin
  ...
end;
```

The `DataSet` parameter of the `OnNewRecord` handler allows the handler to know which of the possibly many `TTables`, which are `TDataSet` descendants, triggered the event.

Open and *Close* Events

`TTable` defines several event pairs related to a particular action. The `Open` action, for example, is enclosed in a pair of events `BeforeOpen` and `AfterOpen`. Using these events, you can install handler methods, typically belonging to the form in which the `TTable` control resides and to enhance or customize the table opening action either right before it takes place or just after.

The `BeforeOpen` event is triggered just before the table is about to be opened. You may want to perform some additional user validation or display a `Connecting...` message to the user at this point by installing a handler for the `BeforeOpen` event.

A `BeforeOpen` event handler has the following structure:

```
procedure TForm1.Table1BeforeOpen(DataSet: TDataSet);
begin
  ...
end;
```

The AfterOpen event is triggered immediately after the table is opened. Typically, you may want to position the data cursor to a specific starting point within the table or to perform some additional initialization in response to this event.

The AfterOpen event handler has the following structure:

```
procedure TForm1.Table1AfterOpen(DataSet: TDataSet);
begin
  ...
end;
```

The BeforeClose event of the TTable class occurs just as the table is about to be closed. The purpose of the event is to give you a chance to perform some last-minute update to the contents of the table, after all the user-initiated changes have been completed.

A BeforeClose event handler that you may want to install has a structure exactly like the other notification events you have encountered so far:

```
procedure TForm1.Table1BeforeClose(DataSet: TDataSet);
begin
  ...
end;
```

The AfterClose event associated with the TTable class is triggered whenever you successfully close the table in question. At this point, you can perform any cleanup and termination tasks that you may need in response to this event.

The AfterClose event handler again has the same structure as the corresponding BeforeClose one:

```
procedure TForm1.Table1AfterClose(DataSet: TDataSet);
begin
  ...
end;
```

So far, you have seen event pairs and skeleton event handlers for two actions that can be performed on a TTable: Open and Close. Here is a list of other actions for which Before*XXXX* and After*XXXX* notification events exist:

- Delete (BeforeDelete, AfterDelete)
- Edit (BeforeEdit, AfterEdit)
- Insert (BeforeInsert, AfterInsert)
- Post (BeforePost, AfterPost)

In all these cases, the event handler's structure is identical to the ones you have already seen.

In summary, keep in mind that the purpose of the Table component (TTable class) is to encapsulate the notion of a relational database table with rows and columns of data, and some common actions, such as moving the position of the data cursor, adding new rows, deleting or updating existing rows, and so on.

TQuery

The `Query` component (`TQuery` class) provides a way for you to access a database using SQL statements. With the `Query` component, you can build SQL queries and execute SQL statements against both local dBASE and Paradox tables, and against databases on remote SQL servers.

Figure 19.4 shows the `Query` component's icon on Delphi's Component Palette.

Figure 19.4.
The `Query` component's icon.

To use a `Query` component, place it on the form and change its properties as follows:

1. Using the Object Inspector, change the `DatabaseName` property of the `Query` component to reflect the name (a path or alias) of the database you want to access.
2. Use the Object Inspector to enter an SQL statement inside the SQL property of the `TQuery`. The statement is used to manipulate the database. Probably the easiest way to enter this statement is to select the SQL property in Object Inspector and then click on the ellipsis (...) button next to the property value. An editor is then activated, enabling you to enter long and complex SQL queries easily.

Note that the `TQuery` component, unlike `TTable`, does not provide a way of specifying the table name as a property in the Object Inspector. Instead, the table name must always be a part of the SQL statement comprising the actual query.

19

Similar to what was the case with `TTable`, you can invoke the Data Set Designer to control the selection and order of fields to which a query has access. To activate the Data Set Designer, however, you have to right-click on the `TQuery` component inside the Form Designer and select Data Set Designer from the menu that shows up.

Data-Aware Controls

The data-aware controls know how to display the data sent to them from the database but know nothing about the structure and the current state of the table from which they receive and to which they send the data. Most data-aware components are enhanced versions of standard Windows controls, such as edit boxes, list boxes, radio buttons, and check boxes. The only difference between them and the standard Windows controls is their data-awareness, making it simple to connect them to various data sources.

You can connect a data-aware component to a data source at design-time, using the Object Inspector, and programmatically at run-time. The common property among all data-aware controls is the `DataSource` property, which specifies from where the control gets its data.

TDbEdit

The data-aware version of a standard `Edit` component, `DbEdit`, found on the Data Controls page of the Component Palette, defines the `DataSource` and `DataField` properties. Thus, it is possible to connect the control to a source of database data. The `DataField` property specifies which of the columns of the underlying table to use as the source of data for the control.

The `DbEdit` component does not define any specific methods or events other than those defined by the standard edit control. Everything that you can do with a standard `Edit` component you can also do with `DbEdit`.

TDbGrid

You can find the `DbGrid` component (`TDbGrid` class) on the Data Controls page of the Component Palette. It is an example of a powerful data-aware control that is not simply an enhancement of a standard Windows control, but a brand-new custom control specifically designed to display database data. The `DbGrid` component enables you to display the entire contents of a data table in a tabular format, with rows representing records and fields arranged into columns.

By default, when you link a `DbGrid` to a `DataSource`, in turn linked to an active data `Table`, all columns of the table are displayed. If you want to limit the number of columns displayed, you can use the Data Set Designer tool to specify explicitly which of the columns you want to see and in what order. As you will learn, you also can use the Data Set Designer to define new calculated or virtual columns that are not part of the physical database but are calculated dynamically at run-time.

`DbGrid` allows the user to rearrange its columns at run-time. Using the mouse, you can grab the title of a column by clicking and holding down the left mouse button. You can drag the column across the horizontal dimension of the grid. After you release the mouse button, the column snaps into its new position, which is indicated by a thick, vertical line while you are dragging it.

You can also change the order of the columns displayed by the grid at run-time. In this case, the change is not permanent and affects only the currently running instance of the program.

You can also resize the columns of the grid dynamically at run-time by dragging the vertical bars dividing the column headers across the horizontal dimension of the grid. To permanently redefine the widths of the columns displayed by the grid, you must use the Data Set Designer and make the fields explicit components of the form. Once the fields are accessible through Object Inspector, you can set their properties, including the `DisplayWidth`. The Data Set Designer is described later in today's lesson.

Miscellaneous Database Components

In addition to the two main groups of database-related components, Delphi provides the ubiquitous `DataSource` component, which is present on any form displaying database data.

The *DataSource* Component

Because the data-aware controls can only display information provided to them, and the data-access components can only connect to databases and provide the information but cannot display it, you need an intermediate link in the chain of database-related components that connects and manages these two disparate groups of components. The "missing link" is the `DataSource` component (`TDataSource` class).

Every form using any of the data-aware controls must contain at least one `DataSource` component. A `DataSource` acts as an intermediary between one of the data-access components, such as `Table` or `Query` on one hand, and one or more of the visual data-aware controls, such as `DbEdit` or `DbGrid`, on the other.

When you place a `DataSource` component on a form in one of your projects, one of the first things you need to do with it is set its `DataSet` property. A `DataSource` is connected to exactly one `DataSet`, such as a `Table` or `Query`. Multiple `DataSource` components can be connected to the same `DataSet`, although a more common setup involves exactly one `DataSource` for each `DataSet`.

Each `DataSource` is referenced by the `DataSource` property of one or more data-aware controls on the form. You can use the `Enabled` property to control whether the communication channel between a `DataSet` and the visual data-aware controls is active. You can assign a Boolean value to the property as follows:

```
DataSet1.Enabled := False;
```

Typically, you set the `Enabled` property to `False` whenever you want to process a significant number of records in a single pass, that is, whenever you need to move the data cursor through a large number of records. Disabling the `DataSource` in this way prevents the visual controls from being updated every time the data cursor moves to another record. As a result, you see a dramatic improvement in performance, and the user is not annoyed with the data flashing on the screen.

Note that when you disable a `DataSet`, all of its connected data-aware controls become blank! The data disappears. If this behavior is not what you desire, take a look at the `DisableControls`/`EnableControls` pair of methods belonging to a `TDataSet` and therefore available in all `TDataSet` descendants, such as `TTable` and `TQuery`. These methods were described in one of the preceding sections of today's lesson.

You can use the `AutoEdit` property of the `DataSource` component to prevent the database's data from being unintentionally changed. This gives the user some extra protection from inadvertent changes to the data, when he or she intended merely to look through the data. You can set the `AutoEdit` property to a Boolean value as follows:

```
DataSource1.AutoEdit := False;
```

Once the property value has been set to `False`, the user cannot change any data within the data-aware controls associated with the `DataSource`. The controls behave as if placed in a Read-Only mode. To permit modifications to the data while the `AutoEdit` property is set to `False`, you can call the `Edit` method.

You can achieve roughly the same effect by explicitly setting the `ReadOnly` property of any data-aware controls, such as `DbEdits`, to `True`. Doing so prevents the user from modifying the data being displayed. This approach, however, is awkward because it requires setting the `ReadOnly` property of all the controls connected to a particular `DataSource`. The `AutoEdit` mechanism provides a more elegant and centralized way of disabling data modifications.

Both the `AutoEdit` and the `Enabled` property are also accessible through the Object Inspector so that their values can be set at design-time in addition to being determined programmatically.

`DataSource` defines an `OnDataChange` event, which you can use to centrally monitor any changes to the contents of the data-aware controls attached to the particular instance of `TDataSource`. Install an `OnDataChange` event handler to intercept notifications about the changes inside the data-aware controls. The handler is of the following form:

```
procedure TForm1.DataSource1DataChange(Sender: TObject; Field: TField);
begin
  ...
end;
```

The `Sender` parameter identifies the object sending the notification, that is, one of the data-aware controls. The `Field` parameter tells you which of the table's fields has been affected by the change.

Another useful event you may want to intercept is the `OnUpdateData` event, occurring whenever an actual change to the data table has been made. The handler that you may want to install for this event looks like the following:

```
procedure TForm1.DataSource1UpdateData(Sender: TObject);
begin
  ...
end;
```

In this case, the `Sender` parameter is the table in which the change occurred.

The *TField* Component

A `Field` is one of the most fundamental database components, yet you cannot find it on the Component Palette directly. All other standard database components rely on the `Field`

component, which encapsulates the concept of a table's column. A `Field` component incorporates properties describing a column's structure (data type), current value, display and edit formats, and so on.

Typically, you do not need to worry about creating the instances of `TField` at run-time because the database components that use the fields take care of that for you. For example, when you set the `Active` property of a table to `True`, the field components corresponding to the fields defined in the table are created for you automatically.

The field objects are normally dynamically re-created based on the actual physical structure of the database every time you set the `Active` property of a data-access component to `True`.

Note: Be careful about keeping variables referring to field objects around. These variables become obsolete as soon as you close their corresponding data-set. Even if the data set is subsequently re-opened, the values of these references are invalid and must be explicitly updated through an assignment.

The Data Set Designer accessible at design-time from both `TTable` and a `TQuery` components enables you to interfere with the default process of field component creation and to define field objects accessible throughout the active life of the associated `Table` or `Query` component. The Data Set Designer is described in more detail later in this chapter.

When you decide to make a particular field static, a field component is added to the form. The reference to the field is accessible from any method of the form at any time.

19

The *Database* Component

The `Database` component (`TDatabase` class) provides the ability to further define the details of a connection to a database in addition to those provided by a `DataSet` descendant (`TTable`, `TQuery`). Using instances of the `TDatabase` class, you can maintain persistent database connections, provide password security for your database, and take advantage of the transaction control features of the Borland Database Engine.

You can place a `Database` component on a form on which you are using `Table` or `Query` components. When you set the `DatabaseName` property of the `Database` component to the same value as the corresponding property in one or more of the `TDataSet` descendants, you are effectively controlling the access to the database through the `Database` component.

`TDatabase` defines a number of properties giving you further control over the details of a database connection.

You need to set the DatabaseName property to determine to which of the possibly many databases available you want to connect. In case of a local database, such as a collection of Paradox or dBASE tables, you can specify a directory name on the disk where the data resides. You can also use an alias (a surrogate name that the Borland Database Engine uses to identify a local or remote database) as the value of the DatabaseName property. When you enter the value of this property at design-time, you can use the drop-down list of database names to select an available database.

The Connected property determines whether the Database component is actually connected to the physical database. Set this property to True to establish a connection to the database specified in the DatabaseName property.

Architecting Database Applications

After this necessarily superficial introduction to some of the Delphi database components, you are ready to delve into hands-on experimentation. The examples in the remainder of today's lesson are intended to give you a better understanding of how the various database components fit together and how they interact with each other.

Database Application Structure

It should be clear to you by now that you build Delphi applications by means of selecting appropriate components and assembling them together to form an integrated, interacting whole. Building *database* applications in Delphi is no different in this regard. The database components described in the preceding sections encapsulate the functionality you need to access and manipulate database data.

Some common patterns of component interactions are likely to occur more often than others in your applications. First, take a look at a generic model for creating database programs with Delphi. Figure 19.5 illustrates the typical architectural arrangement of components in a database application built using Delphi.

At a high-level of architectural abstraction, a Delphi database-aware form interacts with the actual database via the BDE facilities. In more detail, the Delphi form typically contains some visual data-aware controls whose responsibility is to display the data from the database. These controls are hooked up with instances of the non-visual DataSource component. The role of the DataSource component is to mediate the interaction between a single table on one hand and a set of data-aware controls that are displaying the data from the table on the other.

Each instance of the DataSource component on the form interfaces with exactly one data-access component, such as a Table or Query. A Table component is responsible for abstracting and encapsulating the functionality of a database table. It does that by either interfacing with the BDE directly or by making the data available to the DataSources that may require it.

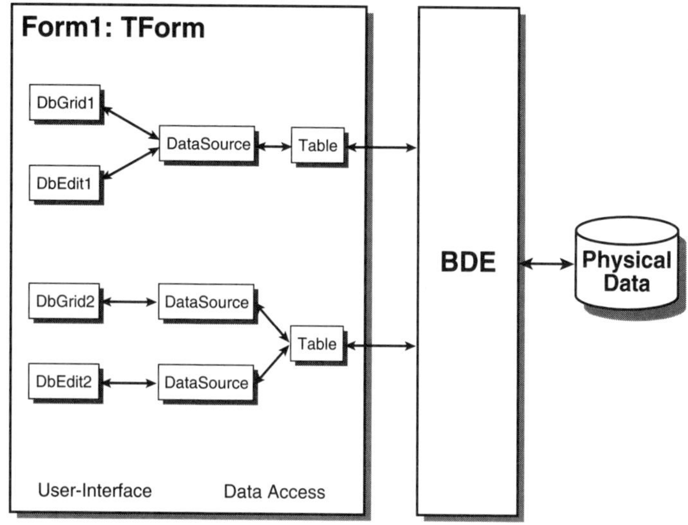

Figure 19.5.
A Delphi database application's architectural details.

Component-Based Database Development Patterns

Some arrangements of components are more likely to occur than others inside Delphi database applications. The following sections give you some idea of the most common uses for the database components.

Table Browser

One of the most common database tasks involves visually browsing through the records of a database. This common task leads to an architectural pattern involving a triad of components: `TTable`, `TDataSource`, and `TDbGrid`, hooked together to form a typical Table Browser.

Table Browser Example

Now you're ready to begin building a Table Browser. It is probably the simplest of all possible database applications you can build using Delphi. The functionality a Table Browser provides—viewing a data table in its entirety—is commonly needed.

1. Before you begin building the example browser program, create a new directory called DBROWSER on your disk.
2. Create a new project (select New Project from the File menu) and save it as DBROWSER.DPR in the DBROWSER directory.

3. Select a `Table` component from the Data Access page of the Component Palette, and place it on the form. Delphi names it `Table1` by default and places a `Table1` field declaration of type `TTable` inside the main form's class definition.
4. Select a `DataSource` component from the Data Access page of the Component Palette, and place it next to the `Table` on the form. Delphi names the new component `DataSource1`.
5. Select a `DbGrid` component from the Data Controls page of the Component Palette, and place it on the form. The default name for the grid is `DbGrid1`.
6. Change `DbGrid1`'s `Align` property to `alClient`. Delphi responds by making the grid component occupy the entire form.

So far, you have completed the design of the visual appearance of the form. The form should look like the one shown in Figure 19.6.

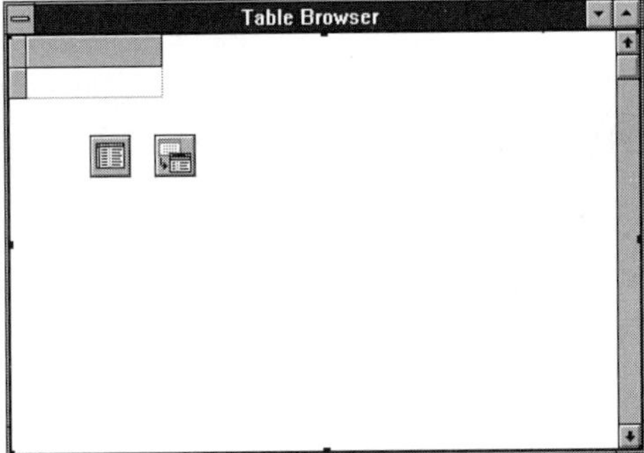

Figure 19.6.
The Table Browser example program, as shown in the Form Designer.

7. Select `Table1` component in the Form Designer, and use Object Inspector to change its `DatabaseName` property to `D:\DELPHI\DEMOS\DATABASE`, where `D:` is the drive and `\DELPHI` is the directory in which you installed Delphi.

This action connects the `Table1` component with the demo database provided with Delphi.

8. Click on the `TableName` property of `Table1` inside Object Inspector. Use the drop-down list to select COUNTRY.DB.

The `Table1` component is now connected to the demo database and hooked up with the COUNTRY table inside this database. Later, you learn how to make the Database Browser program more generic and allow it to browse any of the available tables.

9. Select the `DataSource1` component inside the Form Designer's window. Using Object Inspector, change its `DataSet` property to `Table1`.

Here you connected the `DataSet1` component with `Table1`. The `DataSet1` can now supply data to any of the data-aware controls that might be present on the form. In this case, `DbGrid1` is the component you hook up with the `DataSource1`.

10. Select the `DbGrid1` component by clicking on it inside the Form Designer. Using Object Inspector again, change its `DataSource` property to `DataSource1`.

You have finished defining the connections among the database-related components on the form. All you have to do now is make the connection to the database active. Then you can see live data from the COUNTRY table inside the grid right in the design mode.

11. Select the `Table1` component again. Change its `Active` property from `False` to `True`.

You can now see live data appearing almost instantaneously inside the grid. The grid itself adjusts to reflect the structure of the table, and shows the columns `Name`, `Capital`, `Continent`, and so on, of the COUNTRY table. You may not see some of the columns because they fall beyond the right edge of the form. At run-time, you can scroll horizontally to see all these columns.

Figure 19.7 shows the appearance of the Data Browser example form after you set the `Active` property of the `Table1` component to `True`.

Table Browser

Name	Population	Area	Average Area
Argentina	32300003	2777815	
Bolivia	7300000	1098575	
Brazil	[illegible]0400000	85111968	
Canada	26500000	9976147	
Chile	13200000	756943	
Colombia	33000000	1138907	
Cuba	10600000	114524	
Ecuador	10600000	455502	
El Salvador	5300000	20865	
Guyana	800000	214969	
Jamaica	2500000	11424	
Mexico	88600000	1967180	

Figure 19.7.
The Data Browser's main form after setting *`Table1.Active to True.`*

12. Save the project and run it now.

When you run the project, notice the highlighting bar that appears inside the grid. The position of the highlight indicates the particular field of interest, or the current field, the value of which you can change at will.

To convince yourself that you are indeed dealing with live data here, try to edit the `Capital` field of Canada. Move the highlighting bar to the appropriate grid element, at the intersection of the `Capital` column and the row with `Canada` as the value of the `Name` field, either by using the arrow keys or by clicking inside the cell. You can either press Enter to activate the edit mode of the grid or simply start typing. Type **`Vancouver`** inside the cell and press Enter. (No, this city is not geographically correct. You revert back to the correct value shortly.)

Now close the active form to return to the design mode; then run the program again. Upon second invocation, the value of the capital of Canada is still Vancouver; it has been permanently preserved in the database.

You can see now how easy it is to access and modify database tables using Delphi. It is just about as easy to insert new records into the database. Press the Insert key while the highlight bar is still in the row with Canada. A new, blank row is inserted just above the highlight and made the current row. You can now enter data for the fields in the newly created row. Again, you can easily verify that the data you input is indeed permanently added to the table.

At this point, it is probably easy to guess how you delete records from the table, using the functionality of the grid component. Just press the Delete key to get rid of the currently selected row of data.

Notice that the changes you make to the database at run-time are not reflected in the design-time grid shown inside the Form Designer because the Form Designer fetches the data once—when you set the `Table1`'s `Active` property to `True`. To see the new or changed data inside the Form Designer, temporarily change the `Active` property of `Table1` to `False` and then back to `True`. You can see the current state of the database again.

Enhancing the Table Browser

Now you learn how to customize the default behavior of the data-grid control to suit your needs better at run-time. As usual, the keys to quick customization of a component's behavior are the events, for which you can write individual handlers.

Suppose you want double-clicking on the data grid to also activate the edit mode inside the cell that has been double-clicked. By default, double-clicking inside the grid control does nothing. Follow these steps to change the default behavior:

1. Make sure you are in design mode and that the example Table Browser is not running.
2. Select the `DbGrid1` component. Then, inside Object Inspector, activate the Events page.
3. Double-click the `OnDoubleClick` event. Delphi responds by activating the code editor and creating a skeleton for the `TForm1.DBGrid1DblClick` procedure inside it. This procedure becomes the event handler for the `OnDblClick` event of the `DbGrid1` component.
4. Enter the following single line of code inside the newly created `TForm1.DBGrid1DblClick` procedure:

   ```
   DbGrid1.EditorMode := True;
   ```

   The preceding code activates the edit mode of `DbGrid1` whenever you double-click inside a cell. This is accomplished by simply setting the `EditorMode` property of `DbGrid` to `True`.
5. Run the program.

You can now try to revert the value of the capital of Canada from Vancouver back to Ottawa, this time activating the edit mode by double-clicking on the `Capital` cell of the Canadian record.

Using the Data Set Designer

The example Table Browser program from the previous section used the physical structure of the COUNTRY data table to determine what to display in the visual grid control. The layout of the data displayed within the grid's columns—that is, the order and the selection of the columns—corresponded directly to the layout defined in the database table. The grid showed all columns, and the columns were ordered the same as in the table.

You did have control, however, over how the columns were ordered at run-time. You could grab the column title with the mouse and drag it across the grid to move the column elsewhere, relative to the other columns. The feature of the data-grid control enabling you to rearrange the columns at run-time had some disadvantages, however. One disadvantage was the fact that any changes you made to the order of the columns being displayed were not preserved from session to session. The next time you ran the Table Browser, the columns reverted back to their original order. Another disadvantage was that you had no way of specifying that only some columns be displayed and no way of suppressing the display of the remaining ones.

These disadvantages disappear when you use the Data Set Designer, a custom property editor for the `Table` component. The purpose of the Data Set Designer is to give you better control over the selection and order of the fields of a table that are used for display. Using the Designer, you can select only the fields of interest. Proceed as follows:

1. To use the Data Set Designer, double-click on the `TTable` component inside the Form Designer. Or you can right-click on the `Table` (or `Query`) component and select Data Set Designer from the pop-up menu.

The Data Set Designer window appears, as shown in Figure 19.8.

Figure 19.8.
The Data Set Designer.

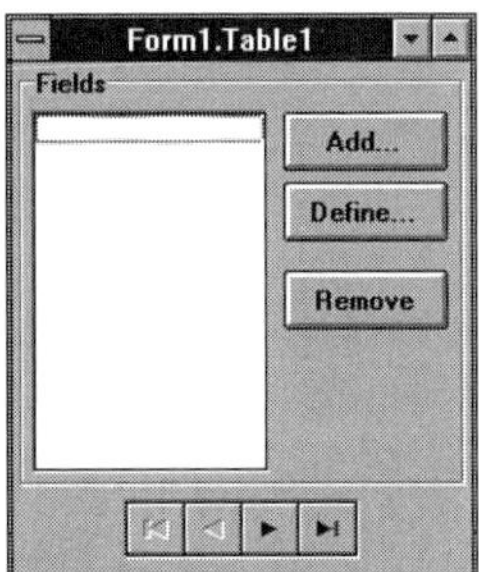

You can use the Data Set Designer to force a particular selection of data columns to be made available by a `Table` component (`TTable` class) to its associated `DataSources`.

2. Click on the Add button inside the Data Set Designer to see the list of available data columns. The list of available columns has multi-selection capabilities.
3. Select the `Name`, `Area`, and `Population` columns. Then click on the OK button.

The columns you selected appear inside the main Data Set Designer's list. Note that—as you make the selections—only the specified columns appear inside the `DataGrid` on the form being designed.

4. Practice rearranging the selected columns by dragging their titles inside the Data Set Designer's main list box.

The changes to the order of the columns you make inside the Data Set Designer are permanent for the program. Every time the application starts, only the specified columns appear in the data grid in the exact order you defined. Note that as you rearrange the columns inside the Data Set Designer, the appearance of the Form Designer's grid changes as well, responding to your actions immediately.

Creating Calculated Fields

After you are satisfied with the order of the specified columns, you can close the Data Set Designer's window. The design-time changes are then saved. Don't close the window just yet because you can take this opportunity to create a calculated field to be displayed in the grid.

NEW TERM A *calculated field* displays values that are not permanently stored in a database table, but instead are calculated on-the-fly by the program as it displays successive records.

You are going to create a calculated field called `AvgeDensity` to display the average density of population—that is, the number of people per square mile—for each country from the COUNTRY table. The `AvgeDensity` field is not stored in the database. Its values are calculated dynamically, as needed. Proceed as follows:

1. To create a calculated field, click on the Define button inside the Data Set Designer. A Define Field dialog box appears.
2. Inside the Field name edit box, enter **`AvgeDensity`** as the name of the new calculated field to be created. In general, you can also select an existing name from the drop-down list.

   The name of the component corresponding to the field, through which you can programmatically access the field at run-time, is automatically displayed in the Component name edit box as you type. Of course, you can change the default component name to your liking.
3. From the Field type list box, select the type of the field to be created. In this case, select `FloatField`.
4. Make sure the Calculated check box is checked; the check mark must appear. If you do not check this box, the table will most likely fail to open.

5. Click on the OK button. The newly created field is added to the list of fields defined within the main window of the Data Set Designer. It also appears inside the Form Designer grid, thus giving you the opportunity to preview the visual effect of adding the field.

   The fields defined inside the Data Set Designer are components, just like the other components you visually placed on the form. You can access the properties and events of a `TField` component by selecting it inside the Data Set Designer. Its corresponding properties and events are accessible via the Object Inspector as usual.

6. Select the newly created `AvgeDensity` field inside the Data Set Designer window.
7. Inside the Object Inspector window, change the `ReadOnly` property of the `AvgeDensity` field to True.
8. Change the `DisplayLabel` property of the field to `Average Density`. In other words, spell out the logical purpose of the field in plain English rather than as a cryptic abbreviation.

   Notice that the name of the field, `AvgeDensity`, remains unchanged, but the title of the column displayed in the Form Designer changes to the value of the `DisplayLabel` property.

After you define a calculated field, you must provide code to calculate its value for every record of the table. Proceed as follows:

1. Select the `Table1` component by picking it from the drop-down list at the top of the Object Inspector window.
2. From the Events page of the Object Inspector, select the `OnCalcFields` event and double-click on its value to create the event handler for it.
3. Inside the newly created `TForm1.Table1CalcFields` event handler in the Code Editor window, enter the following code:

   ```
   Table1AvgeDensity.Value := Table1Population.Value / Table1Area.Value;
   ```

   The preceding code calculates the value of the `AvgeDensity` field by taking the value of the `Population` field, the number of inhabitants of a given country, and dividing it by the value of the `Area` field, the area of the country. The result is the average density of population, or the number of people per square mile. The result is then assigned to the value of the `AvgeDensity` field of `Table1`.

   The executable statement inside the `TForm1.Table1CalcFields` event handler is automatically called whenever there is a need to recalculate the value of the `AvgeDensity` field for a particular record.

4. Run the program and observe the values displayed inside the column entitled `Average Density`. Note that Brazil and Canada have very low densities of population, whereas El Salvador and Jamaica have by far the highest of all American nations.

The problem with the display of the calculated data is that the result of the calculation is shown with too high a precision. Notice the number of digits after the decimal point. Typically, you would want to format this data so that only one or two decimal places are shown. Time to go back to the design mode.

1. Open the Data Set Designer for the `Table1` component by double-clicking on the component inside the Form Designer window.
2. Inside the list of fields shown, select the `AvgeDensity` field. The `AvgeDensity` field's properties become available in the Object Inspector window.

Note: You can select a particular field component in one step by selecting it from the drop-down list at the top of the Object Inspector window.

3. Change the `DisplayFormat` property of the `Table1AvgeDensity` field to `###.##`. This is a *mask* that will be used to format the field for the display.
4. Run the program and notice how the display of the calculated `Average Density` field changes and how it is now more readable and manageable.

As you can see, you have a great degree of control over how the data inside the grid is displayed. Even though the default formatting may be sufficient for most purposes, you may find that occasionally you need to override it with custom formats. The preceding example shows you how to access the `DisplayFormat` property of a data field to provide a formatting mask.

Form Browser

The previous example of a Table Browser illustrated a grid-oriented, or table-oriented, solution to the problem of browsing database records. A form-oriented, or entry-screen-oriented, model of a database browser is also fairly common in real-world applications.

Form Browser Example

Now you are going to build a simple form-oriented browser for the COUNTRY table. The initial steps required to create the example Form Browser are nearly identical to the steps you followed before.

1. Create a new directory called FBROWSER on your disk.
2. Create a new project (File | New Project) and save it as FBROWSER.DPR in the FBROWSER directory.
3. Select a `Table` component from the Data Access page of the Component Palette, and place it on the form. Delphi names it `Table1` by default and places a `Table1` field declaration of type `TTable` inside the main form's class definition.

4. Select a `DataSource` component from the Data Access page of the Component Palette, and place it next to the `Table` on the form. Delphi names the new component `DataSource1`.
5. Select the `Table1` component in the Form Designer, and use Object Inspector to change its `DatabaseName` property to `D:\DELPHI\DEMOS\DATABASE`, where `D:` is the drive and `\DELPHI` is the directory in which you installed Delphi.
6. Click on the `TableName` property of `Table1` inside the Object Inspector. Use the drop-down list to select COUNTRY.DB.
7. Select the `DataSource1` component inside the Form Designer's window. Using the Object Inspector, change its `DataSet` property to `Table1`.

You have connected the data-access components to the table of interest. Now you provide the visual controls so that the data can be displayed. Proceed as follows:

1. Add four `DBEdit` components from the Data Controls page of the Component Palette to the form.

   Delphi names the `DbEdit` instances you just added `DbEdit1` through `DbEdit4`.
2. On the form, align `DbEdit1` through `DbEdit4` boxes vertically in a column, one below another as shown in Figure 19.9.

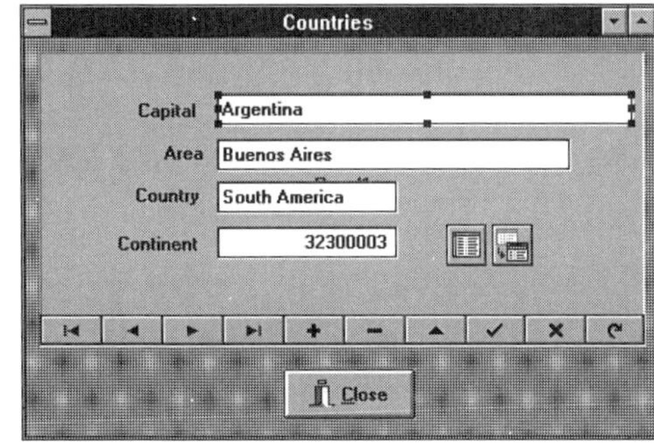

Figure 19.9.
Form Browser program's main form.

3. Add four `Label` components from the Standard page of the Component Palette. Arrange them each in front of a `DbEdit` box. Change their captions to `Country`, `Capital`, `Continent`, and `Population`, respectively.
4. Change the `DataSource` property of `DbEdit1` to `DataSource1` and its `DataField` property to `Name`.
5. Change the `DataSource` property of `DbEdit2` to `DataSource1` and its `DataField` property to `Capital`.
6. Change the `DataSource` property of the remaining two `DbEdit` boxes to `DataSource1`, and their `DataField` properties to `Continent` and `Population`, respectively.

7. From the Data Controls page of the Component Palette, select a `DBNavigator` control and place it on the form.
8. Change the `DataSource` property of the newly added `DbNavigator1` to `DataSource1`.
9. Place a `BitBtn` control from the Additional page of the Component Palette at the bottom of the form.
10. Change the `Kind` property of the newly added `BitBtn1` to `bkClose`.
11. As the final step in the process of building the form, change the `Active` property of `Table1` to `True`.
12. Run the program now. Step through the records of the COUNTRY table by clicking on the buttons of the `DbNavigator` control.

The program you have built is an example of a simple, flat File Browser. With it, you can browse a specific table with a predefined set of fields.

Using the `DbNavigator`'s buttons, you can easily add new records to the table and delete existing ones. Try to expand the scope of the table by including some other countries.

Master-Detail Browser

A more complex example of a database application design pattern that frequently occurs in real-life applications is one involving a master-detail relationship. In this scenario, multiple detail records are retrieved and manipulated for every currently selected master record.

Whenever you move the data cursor position in the master table, the detail data set is updated to reflect the details corresponding to the selected master.

A typical example illustrating the need for a master-detail relationship involves providing support for browsing invoices. An invoice typically consists of some header data describing the customer and a collection of details corresponding to the items sold or services being invoiced.

Whenever you select a different invoice from a list of all invoices, the master table, the details of the selected invoice must also change to reflect the actual master. This common task of linking a detail table to its master has been made very simple by Delphi. You now have a chance to build an example program linking a master customer record with the details of the customers orders.

Master-Detail Example

You are about to create a Delphi database application, MASTER, which uses a master-detail paradigm to show the details of a customer order. The ORDERS table is used as the master table for the master-detail relationship you are currently building. For each order, you display its details showing items sold and their price. The order detail data is retrieved from the ITEMS table.

1. Before you begin creating the example master-detail program, create a new directory called MASTER on your disk.
2. Create a new project (File | New Project) and save it as MASTER.DPR in the MASTER directory.
3. Select a `Table` component from the Data Access page of the Component Palette, and place it on the form. Delphi names the newly added component `Table1`.
4. Change the `DatabaseName` property of `Table1` to `D:\DELPHI\DEMOS\DATABASE`, where `D:` is the drive and `\DELPHI` is the directory in which you have installed Delphi. Setting this property connects the `Table1` component with the demo database provided with Delphi.
5. Change the `TableName` property of `Table1` to `ORDERS.DB`. This action indicates that the `Table1` component on the form is connected to the ORDERS table, which is a demo Paradox table provided with Delphi and containing a fictitious list of orders.
6. Select a `DataSource` component from the Data Access page of the Component Palette, and place it next to `Table1` on the form. Delphi gives the new component the name `DataSource1`.
7. Connect the `DataSource1` component to the table by setting the `DataSet` property of `DataSource1` to `Table1`.
8. Change the `Active` property of `Table1` to `True`. Once you have done that, the `Table1` component is fully connected to the database and may be used to access the master ORDERS table.

You now have to provide facilities to connect to the detail table called ITEMS. Proceed as follows:

1. From the Data Access page of the Delphi Component Palette, select a `Table` component again, and place it on the form. The table component assumes the name `Table2`.
2. Change the `DatabaseName` property of `Table2` to `D:\DELPHI\DEMOS\DATABASE`, where `D:` is the drive and `\DELPHI` is the directory in which you have installed Delphi, just as before, to connect the `Table2` component with the demo database.
3. Change the `TableName` property of `Table2` to `ITEMS.DB`. Now the `Table2` component on the form is connected to the ITEMS table, which is used as the details table in the relationship.
4. Select another `DataSource` component from the Data Access page of the Component Palette, and place it on the form. Change the `DataSet` property of this `DataSource2` component to `Table2`.
5. Change the `Active` property of `Table2` to `True`. Once you have done that, the `Table2` component is fully connected to the database and can be used to access the detail ITEMS table.

So far, you have opened two tables, ORDERS and ITEMS, by activating the corresponding `TTable` components on the form: `Table1` and `Table2`. You have also connected these tables with two `DataSource` components, `DataSource1` and `DataSource2`, respectively. In doing all this, you have used non-visual components only. Now it's time to give visibility to the data you are retrieving from the database.

1. Place a `DBGrid` component from the Data Controls page of the Component Palette on the form.
2. Change the `Align` property of the newly placed `DbGrid1` component to `alBottom`. The data grid then snaps to the bottom of the form.
3. Adjust the size of the `DBGrid1` data grid by dragging its top edge using the mouse so that the grid takes up about two-thirds of the form's total height.
4. Change the `DataSource` property of `DBGrid1` to `DataSource2`.

You have hereby achieved a live connection between the grid and the data table `Table2`. You should now be able to see the data inside the grid.

Inside the grid, you see the contents of the ITEMS table in its entirety. If you compile and run the program, you can see that the grid contains multiple entries with the same order number, but it also shows all the items for all the orders together.

The situation now is effectively equivalent to the simple Data Browser example you built before. You have a single table connected with a single data grid via a `DataSource` component. You have not established the master-detail relationship yet. What you are after is the ability to step through the master ORDERS table, a record at a time, and to see the details of the currently selected order only.

You are now going to add some indication of where you currently are in the master ORDERS table as well as the ability to navigate through the master table.

1. Select the `DBEdit` component from the Data Controls page of the Component Palette, and place it on the form in the area left above the data grid. The edit control assumes the name `DbEdit1`.
2. Change the `DataSource` property of the newly added `DbEdit1` component to `DataSource1`.
3. Change the `DataField` property of `DbEdit1` component to `OrderNo`.

   The `DBEdit1` component is now connected to the ORDERS table via `DataSource1`. Its contents now reflect the value of the first order number in the ORDERS table—for example, `'1003'`.
4. Place a `DbNavigator` component from the Data Controls page of the Component Palette on the form, next to `DbEdit1`. The `DbNavigator` instance becomes `DbNavigator1` once placed on the form.

The `DbNavigator` control consists of a set of buttons for navigating databases and for inserting and deleting records, posting transactions, and so on. Now you are interested only in the navigational capabilities of this control, so you need to make the unnecessary buttons disappear.

5. Inside Object Inspector, with `DbNavigator1` still selected, double-click on the `VisibleButtons` property name. Make sure you double-click on the property name—on the left-hand side of the list of properties where the little plus sign is next to the property name—and not on the property value—not on the right-hand column of the property list.

The `VisibleButtons` property expands into subordinate properties, including `nbFirst`, `nbPrior`, `nbNext`, `nbLast`, `nbInsert`, `nbDelete`, `nbEdit`, `nbPost`, `nbCancel`, and `nbRefresh`. Each of these visibility subproperties is True by default; the corresponding button shows in the Form Designer.

6. Turn all the `VisibleButton` subproperties to `False`, except for `nbFirst`, `nbPrior`, `nbNext`, and `nbLast`.

The corresponding four buttons of `DbNavigator1` still appear in the Form Designer, but the remaining buttons are now hidden. Figure 19.10 illustrates the appearance of the grid as shown in the Form Designer at this point.

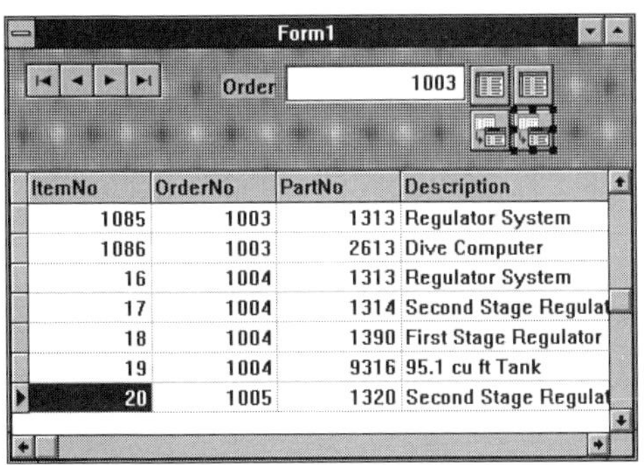

ItemNo	OrderNo	PartNo	Description
1085	1003	1313	Regulator System
1086	1003	2613	Dive Computer
16	1004	1313	Regulator System
17	1004	1314	Second Stage Regulat
18	1004	1390	First Stage Regulator
19	1004	9316	95.1 cu ft Tank
20	1005	1320	Second Stage Regulat

Figure 19.10.
The main form of the example Master Program as shown in the Form Designer.

7. Connect `DbNavigator1` to the ORDERS table so that you can navigate through all orders in the table. To do that, change the `DataSource` property of `DbNavigator1` to `DataSource1`.

8. Try to run the MASTER program at this point and see what happens.

As you can see, there is still no connection established between the ORDERS master table with its currently selected order and the details of that order from the ITEMS table. You can now step through the ORDERS table by clicking on the `DBNavigator`'s buttons, and your changing position within that table is reflected by the changing order number in the DbEdit1's window. The data grid at the bottom of the form, however, remains unaffected.

Now you're going to establish the master-detail relationship between the two tables and their corresponding visual display controls.

1. Temporarily change the `Active` property of `Table2` from `True` back to `False`, thereby closing the table. The data then disappears from the grid.

   You need to take this step because you cannot establish master-detail links while the detail table is open.

2. Select the `Table2` component on the form, and change its `MasterSource` property from blank to `DataSource1`.

The effect of this change is that `Table2` is now aware of the master ORDERS table. To accomplish the master-detail connection, you now must tell `Table2` which of the common field(s) to use for the join.

Using Field Link Designer

To use the Field Link Designer, proceed as follows:

1. With `Table2` still selected, double-click on the `MasterFields` property inside the Object Inspector to open the Field Link Designer property editor.

A custom property editor called Field Links Designer appears, as shown in Figure 19.11. You use the Field Links Designer to define the details of a the master-detail relationship between two tables.

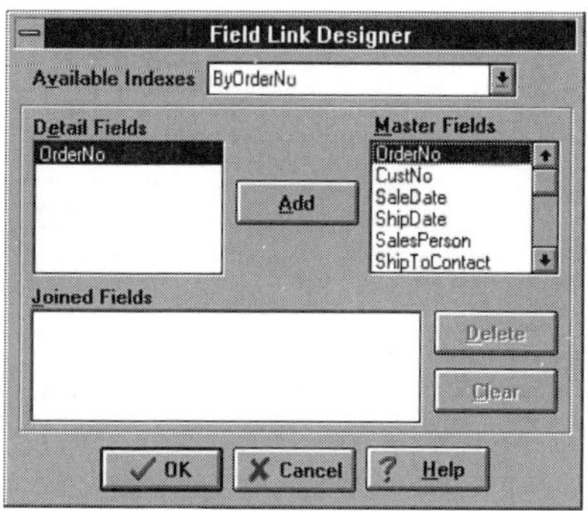

Figure 19.11.
The Field Links Designer custom property editor for the `MasterFields` property of `Table` components.

Note that the Detail Fields list box on the left shows only `ItemNo` as the field available to link the master table with. This field is of no use to you now, because the master table does not have an `ItemNo` field. You are interested in linking on the `OrderNumber` field, present in both the master and the detail table.

2. Because you can link detail tables via an indexed field only, change the currently selected index of the ITEMS table, `Table2`, from `Primary` to `ByOrderNo`. Observe that the field name available inside the Detail Fields list box changes to `OrderNo`.
3. Select the `OrderNo` field in both the `Detail` and the `Master` list. As you are making this change, the Add button becomes active.
4. Click on the Add button to define the criteria for the table join.

   An entry

   ```
   OrderNo -> OrderNo
   ```

   is then added to the Joined Fields list box at the bottom of the Field Link Designer, reflecting the fact that you have selected the `OrderNo` field both from the master table (ORDERS) and the detail table (ITEMS). Hence, the tables are joined on the `OrderNo` field.
5. Accept the join by clicking on the OK button. The Field Link Designer disappears.

   Notice that upon your return to the Object Inspector, `Table2`'s properties have changed somewhat. The `MasterFields` property appears as `OrderNo` now. The `IndexName` property, which was previously blank (assuming the primary record ordering by default), appears as `ByOrderNo` now.
6. Change the `Active` property of `Table2` back to `True`.

Congratulations! You have created a master-detail relationship based on the `OrderNo` field between the ORDERS and ITEMS tables, respectively.

You can easily tell even in the Form Designer that the details displayed in the grid now are filtered out and show only the ones pertaining to the currently selected master record. The order numbers shown next to each item detail correspond to the number shown inside `DbEdit1` control. Instead of all items, the grid shows only the items with the selected `OrderNo`.

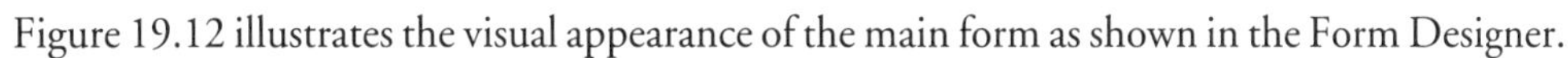

Figure 19.12 illustrates the visual appearance of the main form as shown in the Form Designer.

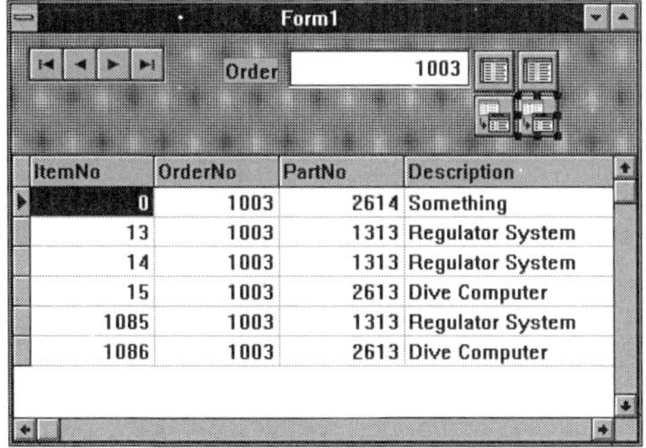

Figure 19.12.
The main form of the MASTER program after the master-detail relationship has been established.

Running the Master-Detail Example

Now you're ready to run the master-detail example. Proceed as follows:

1. Compile and run the program.
2. Click on the buttons of the `DbNavigator` to scroll through the master ORDERS table.

As the master order number inside the edit box changes at the top of the form, the contents of the data grid also change, reflecting the details for the selected master only. This is precisely what you were after.

Enhancing the Master-Detail Example

The example master-detail program is now in its raw state as far as its user-friendliness is concerned. The master-detail link works correctly, but the display of data still leaves a lot to be desired. You are now going to enhance the program to be more user-friendly.

1. Add a second `DbEdit` control, `DbEdit2`, to the form beneath `DbEdit1`. Change its `DataSource` property to `DataSource1` and its `DataField` property to `CustNo`.
2. Place two standard labels from the Standard page of the Component Palette in front of the edit boxes, and change their `Caption` properties to `Order No.` and `Customer No.`, respectively.

By running the program, you can now verify that the master data is updated as you move through the ORDERS table; both Order No. and Customer No. edit boxes change to reflect the data in the current record. Both `DbEdit1` and `DbEdit2` are connected to the same data source: `DataSource1`.

Now you can introduce a second visual enhancement to the program. Note that the main form is resizeable at run-time. You can resize it like almost any other program window, yet the size of the data grid at the bottom remains unchanged. You gain nothing by making the window longer: the maximum number of grid elements displayed remains the same. To rectify the problem, install a custom event handler for the form's `OnResize` event as follows:

1. Click on the blank area of the form inside the Form Designer to select the form itself.
2. Make the Events page of the Object Inspector visible by clicking on the appropriate tab.
3. Double-click on the value side of the `OnResize` event.

   Delphi responds by creating a skeleton `TForm1.FormResize` event handler.
4. Enter the following code inside the event handler:

   ```
   DbGrid1.Height := ClientHeight - (DbEdit2.Top + DbEdit2.Height + 10);
   ```

   The preceding code resizes the data grid as the user resizes the form at run-time. The grid's `Height` property is set to the height of the client area (the inside) of the form, minus some room for the controls at the top.

To calculate how much room to leave for the edit controls and the navigator, the height of the control closest to the grid, `DbEdit2.Height` in this case, is added to the actual vertical position of this control, `DbEdit2.Top`. The result is the vertical coordinate of the bottom edge of `DbEdit2`. To that result an arbitrary number, 10, is added to make more room and the overall effect more pleasing. The final result, after being subtracted from the total height of the form, becomes the new height of the grid control.

Setting the height of the grid is all that is required here. The grid automatically positions itself at the bottom edge of the form, stretching through its entire width, because its `Align` property is set to `alBottom`.

5. Run the program to verify that the grid resizes in conjunction with your resizing the form. Long detail listings are now easier to view because you can make more of them visible at once.

The current appearance of the master-detail example program is shown in Figure 19.13.

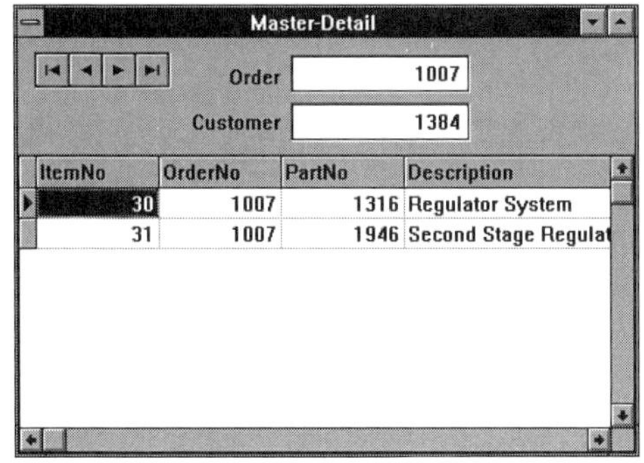

Figure 19.13.
The master-detail program with an automatically resizeable detail data grid.

Summary

Today's lesson introduced you to the notions of database programming and to the common Delphi database components. You learned the following:

- Databases are collections of tables, each of which consists of columns and rows of data.
- A database table, encapsulated by the `TTable` component, as well as a query, a `TQuery` component, support the concept of a current record. The abstract entity you use to traverse the records of a table or query is called a cursor.
- You use the `TQuery` component to access databases via Structured Query Language (SQL) statements, or queries. `TTable` and `TQuery` are examples of a generic `TDataSet` component that encapsulates a great deal of the functionality common to both queries and tables.

- You can make a TField component explicitly accessible within your forms by adding the fields of interest using the Data Set Designer, a custom property editor of TTable and TQuery. A TField encapsulates the notion of a data field, giving you programmatic access to the field definition and its data.
- You can use the Data Set Designer to create calculated fields whose values are programmatically computed on-the-fly.
- TDataSource is a component acting as a connector between a database-access component, such as TTable, and one or more data-aware controls, such as DbGrid.
- A triad of components—TTable, TDataSource, and TDbGrid—is all that you need to create useful table-oriented data browsers.
- Replacing TDbGrid with a set of TDbEdit components in the preceding triad enables you to create form-oriented browsers, in which the user can view and edit one record at a time. You typically need an instance of TDbNavigator on the form as well to allow the user to move from one record to another.
- You can create a powerful master-detail browser by using the support for this type of relationship built into the TTable component. The MasterSource and MasterFields properties of the TTable class enable you to seamlessly create a relational link between a master and a detail table on one or more fields.
- You can use the custom property editor of the MasterFields property of TTable, the Field Link Designer, to make defining the master-detail relationship even easier. Using the Designer, you can specify the details of the relationship visually.

Q&A

Q How can I dynamically determine the structure of any given table at run-time? In other words, how can I get a list of all fields of a given table?

A You can use a FieldDefs property of a data-set component, such as a TTable or TQuery, to gain access to the field definitions. FieldDefs is a list of all fields the table defines. You can enumerate the fields by setting up a loop like this:

```
var
  AFieldDef: TFieldDef;
  AField: TField;
begin
  ...
  for FieldNo := 1 to Table1.FieldCount do
  begin
    ...
    AFieldDef := Table1.FieldDefs.Items[FieldNo];
    AField := AFieldDef.Field;
    ...
```

```
  end;
  ...
end
```

Q All I want is to simply access an individual dBASE table and read some values from it. Do I have to go through the hoops of adding a `Table` and `DataSource` components to my form?

A Yes, if you are going to use any of the data-aware controls. The data set derivatives, such as `Table` or `Query`, encapsulate the low-level details of accessing the Borland Database Engine. They shield you from the drudgery of reading database files, parsing their formats, and so on.

Nothing in the Delphi environment or language prevents you from using third-party data-access Pascal libraries, or libraries you have developed that access dBASE data tables directly, completely bypassing BDE. Keep in mind, however, that by using what effectively is a "manual" process, you end up having to take care of many details that normally are taken care of for you within the BDE+VCL framework, such as the support for multiple users on a network, updating of visual controls, representing data cursors, and so on.

Another important factor is that your application will not necessarily be easily scaleable to a client/server or 32-bit format. Bypassing the BDE and going at the dBASE data directly is like insisting on assembling your car from scratch every time you want to take a ride: its not very effective, but it is time consuming and error prone.

Workshop

The Workshop provides quiz questions to help you solidify your understanding of the material covered and exercises to provide you with experience in using what you've learned. Try to understand the quiz and exercise answers before continuing on to the next day's lesson.

Quiz

1. True or False? A single table is not a database.
2. True or False? The `Database` component is not strictly needed to access databases. It is only useful whenever you need additional security or more control over the connection with the physical database.
3. True or False? You cannot have more than one `DataSource` connected to the same `Query` component.

4. True or False? You need instances of at least three database components present on the form to have a working database application: a data-access component, a data-source, and a data-aware control.
5. True or False? The calculated fields defined via the Data Set Designer must be numeric fields. Only numeric values can be calculated in response to the `OnCalcFields` event.

Exercises

1. Extend the Table Browser program to make it possible for the user to choose a particular table to view at run-time.
2. Extend the enhanced Table Browser from Exercise 1 to enable the user to specify both a database and a table at run-time, making it a generic Data Browser.
3. Create a master-detail-detail—also known as a one-to-many-to-many, or 1-M-M relationship—application enabling you to step through all CUSTOMER records and view ORDERS placed by the selected customer and, for each order, the details of the order from the ITEMS table.

WEEK
3

Creating Custom Components

So far, you have learned how to use existing components to build Delphi applications. You have mastered the techniques involved in creating your own applications by assembling them from preexisting components and customizing these components at the application-level to suit the specific needs of each application. Today, you learn how to create your own components within the Delphi environment.

In particular, you learn the following:

- How to create a new component by descending a new component class from an existing specialized class
- How to create a new visual component from scratch by descending its class from an existing base, non-specialized component class
- How to create a new custom control: a point diagram enabling you to display data points on its surface

Delphi Components

Delphi is a powerful programming environment because it provides support for both sides of the component-based development equation. It supports building applications from preexisting components, and it supports the creation of new components, all within the same environment.

The main advantages of having the capability of extending Delphi via your own components are that you are not constrained with the limitations of the environment, you are not limited to the repertoire of choices available out-of-the-box, and you can confidently embark on a project of any size knowing that, as a worst-case scenario, you may have to develop a custom component or two from scratch. But you know that you will not hit any walls, that you will not encounter any severe limitations of the development environment itself that would prohibit you from accomplishing something you need to accomplish.

The transition from your being a component consumer to a component producer becomes less of a paradigm shift and more of a daily routine when you can build applications and components from which the applications are made using the same familiar concepts, conventions, and tools.

If you have the ability to create your own components smoothly and seamlessly and integrate them so that they blend with the development environment just as if they were built-in, new possibilities for code reuse present themselves, and increased productivity reigns. The rarely told truth of the software development industry is that software reuse has not happened, despite promises and pronouncements to the contrary. The proverbial wheel is being reinvented everywhere all the time. It is not true that you need to build in reuse right from the start. This kind of approach rarely pays off because you end up spending a great deal of time creating reusable components no one reuses. The fact is that reusability evolves. A reusable component is discovered through a painstaking process of creating numerous applications and abstracting the patterns common to all or most of them.

Delphi has the capability to change the process of creating reusable software building blocks. With it, you start developing applications using existing components. When you discover a need that no existing component addresses, you don't typically jump to develop your own component immediately. At first, you try to address the need by writing custom code around the existing components.

You may also try to customize a component specifically for the purposes of a single application that needs the functionality. A new class is thus created, inheriting from one of the existing ones, modifying the behavior or properties of the existing one in some way.

Finally, when you discover that you need the functionality repeatedly, you can rearrange the code so that a component is born.

What is important here is that the process of evolving the component is a gradual, stepwise refinement rather than a radical or revolutionary change. You do not lose the snippets of code you created in the initial phase of addressing the specific needs of your application. You do not need to "port" or translate the code. Everything blends right in, within the same environment. You simply rearrange the interfaces so that the resulting building block becomes increasingly autonomous and increasingly reusable. A new component is thus born.

On the dark side, however, writing components is no longer an exercise in visual programming. There is no jazzy development environment, no tools to support the component developer in his or her endeavors. It's back to the old style of programming: rigorously and painstakingly developing lines of code. The rewards are potentially tremendous, which makes it all worthwhile, but you have to realize that Delphi does not necessarily make it too easy for you to develop your own custom components.

The Definition of a Component

For the purposes of this book, a *component* is simply whatever Delphi chooses to call a component. If it can be placed on the Component Palette, if it can be dropped onto a form and its properties can be examined with the Object Inspector, it is a component.

From the perspective of an application programmer, someone who uses components to create applications, a component is something you can choose from the Component Palette, make part of the application being developed, and customize with event-handling code.

For a component developer, a Delphi component is an Object Pascal class descending either directly or indirectly from `TComponent`.

The great news for all developers is that you may be wearing both the application developer's and a component developer's hat because the transition between the two roles is relatively smooth and painless, thanks to the integrated nature of Delphi. Writing components need not be any more difficult than writing applications, although admittedly, it introduces a new level of complexity such as possibly having to deal with the Windows Application Programming Interface (API) directly.

The complexity of custom components and the corresponding difficulty of writing them form a spectrum from the simplest modifications of existing components to the arbitrarily complex, custom-designed subsystems. Writing components typically requires more knowledge of object-oriented programming and more thoughtful design.

Only the sky is the limit for the component developer, and the good news is that you can reach the sky step by step. You don't need a sudden elevation to the new heights of component-writing sophistication, and the associated fear of flying and dizziness, to be able to reach new levels of skill and understanding. It is all gradual and quantitative rather than radical and qualitative in Delphi, which makes it much easier to develop custom components than in other existing programming environments for Windows.

Developing Custom Components

The key to developing and integrating custom components successfully with Delphi is in being able to comply with various requirements and conventions of interface and behavior that the Delphi environment expects of components.

The fact that a custom component is an Object Pascal class that descends from `TComponent` makes it essentially compliant with most of the basic requirements. It gives, for example, the new component the capability to appear on the Component Palette and the capability to interact with the Form Designer and the Object Inspector. Beyond these basic capabilities, however, a component may define arbitrarily complex behavior and may exhibit an arbitrarily rich set of attributes to the component user, who is the application programmer. These additions to the standard, minimal behavior of a component are the responsibility of the component writer.

The most important thing to keep in mind about customizing components is that you can customize them in different ways. Almost every ready-made component allows some degree of customization at design-time and run-time through its properties and events. A good component provides many entry points, such as properties that you can change and events that you can handle, to give you the ability to modify the component's appearance or behavior to suit the needs of your application. This is called *design-time* or *run-time customization*, depending on whether you are setting the properties at design-time or whether you are accessing them programmatically at run-time.

Inevitably, you will hit a limitation with or a deficiency in just about every component. Eventually, you will need a particular behavior that the component writer has not foreseen that extends the component into a new direction. Or you will need to make the component do something fundamentally different, something that it was not designed to do in the first place. Once you are in this situation, it is reassuring to know that in most cases your alternatives are

not reduced to the dreaded "start from scratch and build your own" predicament that plagued developers before Delphi.

Typically, you already have a component that does nearly everything you want, and you need to change it only slightly to suit your needs. Whenever you face such a situation, first ask yourself whether you have properly understood the event hooks and properties provided by the component designer in the first place. Maybe the component can already do what you want, but you just don't know how. If you are reasonably sure that the component cannot do what you want, then you must roll up your sleeves and get your hands dirty with component customization.

Customizing an Existing Component

The easiest way of creating new components in Delphi is through the process of subclassing, or deriving from, the existing ones. You can use any of the standard components that come with Delphi as the basis to derive your own.

You may, for example, want to change a default value associated with a particular property of a standard component so that this new default value takes effect automatically whenever you place the component on the form. If you often find yourself entering the same sequence of method calls to set up a component at run-time, or you discover that you tend to change the value of a property as soon as you place the component on the form, chances are that you may benefit from creating a new component that does all that by default and therefore requires no special initialization beyond merely being placed on the form.

Another reason for you to want to customize an existing visual control is that, in cases of some of the standard Windows controls, such as edit boxes, list boxes, and combo boxes, you may want to use one of their more exotic flavors, which require you to set special, optional flags at creation time to inform Windows of your preferences. To be able to tell Windows, at the time of control creation, that you need one of these other flavors of the basic control, you need to create a custom control that overrides the creation attributes Windows uses to give the visual appearance to the control.

Following are the main steps you need to follow to create a new component based on an existing one:

1. Create a new unit.
2. Declare a new component class, descending from an existing class.
3. Define the extensions to the base class that make the derived component class different from the base component.
4. Ensure that the component becomes properly registered with Delphi.
5. Install the component using the Delphi IDE.

Creating a New Unit

Typically, when deriving a new component, you create a new Object Pascal unit to contain the component's declaration and implementation. In this case, you select "New Unit" from the "File" menu to create a new Pascal unit.

Sometimes you may prefer to add the new component to an already existing unit, for example, when several components form a closely, logically interrelated group. In this case, you select Open File from the File menu to gain access to the source code for an existing unit.

Note: Beware of third-party components that are distributed exclusively as precompiled .DCU files. The binary format of precompiled units is likely to change in new versions of Delphi. If you don't have the complete source code to be able to rebuild the component's .DCU file, you have to rely on the component's vendor to provide you with an updated version of the component whenever the .DCU format changes.

The newly created unit consists of nothing but a bare minimum skeleton, as shown in Listing 20.1. Your job is to provide the contents of this unit.

Type

Listing 20.1. A minimum skeleton for an Object Pascal unit created by Delphi.

```
1: unit Unit1;
2:
3: interface
4:
5: implementation
6:
7: end.
```

The unit in Listing 20.1 is a minimal compilable Object Pascal unit. This skeleton for a unit is created by Delphi whenever you select New Unit from the File menu.

The section between the **`interface`** and the **`implementation`** keywords (line 4), called the *interface section*, is the place where you place global public declarations.

The section after the **`implementation`** keyword and before the final **`end.`** (line 7) is called the *implementation section* and may contain declarations and implementation of the entities declared throughout the unit.

Anything appearing after the final **`end.`** is ignored by the compiler.

Declaring a New Component Class

You define a new component by creating a class declaration in the interface section of the component's Object Pascal unit. As you may recall from previous lessons, you must place a new class declaration as part of a **type** declaration block because it defines a new Pascal type.

Every Delphi component descends either directly or indirectly from the `TComponent` class. In the case of modifying an existing component, you descend your new component from the base, existing Delphi component, such as `TListBox` or `TMemo`, as follows:

```
type
  TMyComponent = class(TListBox)
  end;
```

You should not be surprised to hear that the component you declared in the preceding three lines of code is a fully functional `ListBox` component. You do not have to do anything special beyond deriving it from `TListBox` to inherit all the functionality of the `ListBox`.

You could proceed to the next step of registering the component with Delphi and place this newly created component on the Component Palette. Of course, there is no advantage in doing so because `TMyComponent` defines no new or modified behavior, nor does it extend the existing component in any way. The behavior and properties of `TMyComponent` are identical to those of a regular `TListBox`. Typically, you extend or customize the newly derived component so that it differs from its parent.

Once you declare even a bare minimum component class, you can register and install it on Delphi's Component Palette.

Registering a Component with Delphi

After you declare the new component class, you can make it available to the Delphi IDE so that it becomes possible to install this new class as a component on the Delphi palette. To make it available as an installable component, you must provide facilities for registering the new class using Delphi.

In the simplest case, all you need to do is to declare a procedure named `Register` in the interface section of the component's unit as follows:

```
unit Unit1;

interface

type
  TMyComponent = class(TComponent)
    ...
  end;

procedure Register;
```

```
11:
12: implementation
13:    ...
14: end.
```

The declaration on line 10 makes it possible for Delphi to install the components declared within the unit, `TMyComponent` in this case, on the Component Palette.

Note: If you add a component to a unit that already defines other components, chances are that the `Register` procedure is already declared there, and you don't need to do anything about the declaration.

Now you need to provide the implementation of the Register procedure you declared in the interface section of the component's unit.

A typical implementation of the Register procedure looks like the following:

```
procedure Register;
begin
  RegisterComponents('Special',[TMyComponent]);
end;
```

The `Register` procedure calls the standard `RegisterComponents` procedure with two parameters:

- The name of the Component Palette page on which to place the new component or components
- A set of component class names (type identifiers)

The name of the Component Palette page does not need to refer to an existing page. If the name specifies a page that does not yet exist, it is created by Delphi when you actually install the component with the IDE. The set of components to register, that is, the second argument to the `RegisterComponents` subroutine, lists the class names of all the components you want to be placed on the specified page.

The following example shows you a more elaborate registration procedure, in which multiple components are placed on multiple pages:

```
procedure Register;
begin
  RegisterComponents('Custom',[TTabbedListBox,TNonWrapMemo]);
  RegisterComponents('Special',[TMyComponent]);
  RegisterComponents('Additional',[TWidget, TGadget, TSplitter]);
end;
```

As you can see, the `Register` procedure enables you to install new pages of components (for example, `'Custom'`, `'Special'`) and extend existing pages (for example, `'Additional'`) with one or more component classes at a time.

Once you have provided the registration facilities for the new component or components, you are ready to install them using Delphi.

Installing a New Component

A newly created component becomes available to your applications once it is installed within the active Component Library.

NEW TERM A *Component Library* is an executable Windows module, typically with the filename extension .DCL, containing the executable code of all the components installed within Delphi and available to the Form Designer and the Object Inspector at design-time. The Component Library provides the behavior to the components manipulated at design-time. The executable code for components created at run-time is linked directly with the application program from the individual precompiled unit files (.DCU).

The default Component Library, COMPLIB.DCL, resides in the same directory in which the main Delphi executable, DELPHI.EXE, is installed, that is, D:\DELPHI\BIN, where D: is the Delphi drive you selected at installation, assuming that you used the default directory structure when installing Delphi.

You can initiate the process of installing a new component from within Delphi by selecting Install Components from the Options menu. The Install Components dialog box appears, as shown in Figure 20.1. From within the Install Components dialog box, you can both add and remove components.

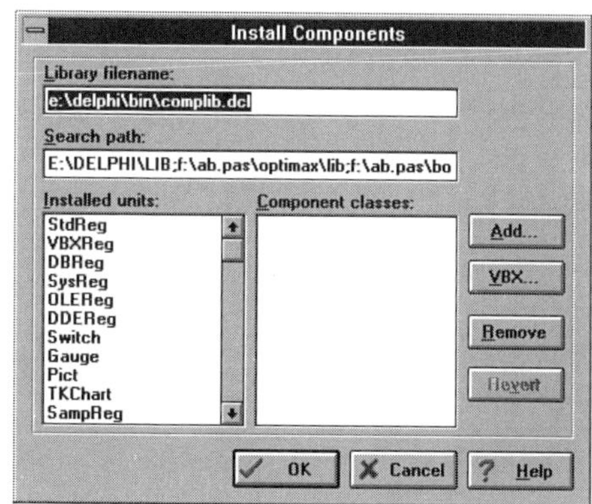

Figure 20.1.
The Install Components dialog box.

Note: It is always a good idea to create a new, custom component library when you are installing additional components beyond those provided by Delphi. You always have the original working set of base components to revert to in case something goes wrong with the library build process. Select Open Library from the Options menu to either switch to a different existing library or to specify a new library name.

To add a set of components defined within an Object Pascal component unit to the currently selected Component Library, click on the Add button. Then click on the Browse button inside the Add Module dialog box. Use the standard Windows file selection dialog box to locate either the Object Pascal source file or the compiled .DCU file containing the new component or components. Click on the OK button inside the Add Module dialog box, and the unit you selected is then added to the Installed units list of the Install Components dialog box.

You can add several component units in succession by repeating the steps just described. After you are done and are ready to re-create the Component Library, click on the OK button in the Install Components dialog box. Delphi first closes any open projects that you may have; then it starts rebuilding the Component Library. After the few seconds it takes to rebuild the library, you notice the new component pages, if any, and the new components appearing in the Component Palette, which is the visible manifestation of the contents of the Component Library.

Extending the Component Class

The bulk of the work related to creating new components is naturally relegated to the code you write that provides the implementation of the component. The amount of code that you need to write varies tremendously, depending on the type of component and on how much the contemplated derived component's behavior differs from that of its parent. In the case of components derived from existing, fully functional ones, the amount of implementation code may be minimal indeed.

Example Listbox-with-Tabs Component

To give you an idea of how easy it is to derive new components based on the existing ones, consider `ListBoxTabs`, or a "list box with tabs," component that enables you to use the tab alignment facility of the standard Windows list box. The goal is to provide an easy way of aligning a few columns of text within a standard list box in a grid-like fashion.

The naive approach to solving the problem as stated would be to try to visually align the columns of the list box by filling the strings with an appropriate number of blanks, that is, the space character (ASCII 32, decimal). Although this approach works when the list box contents are displayed in a fixed-pitch font (such as Courier New), in general the alignment breaks down in a situation in which a proportional font is used (such as Times New Roman or Arial). The non-blank portions of the string, the ones containing actual text, end up having different display lengths, depending on the exact composition of characters.

Windows provides a simple solution to this problem by allowing its standard list box control to handle tab stops. A list box with tab stops enabled accepts strings with embedded tab characters (ASCII 9, decimal) and attempts to expand the tabs and display the text after each tab character at the predefined tab stop position. This gives the impression of a columnar layout inside the list box.

Figure 20.2 illustrates the concept of a list box with tabs. Each of the lines shown within the list box consists of a string of the form

```
'This'#9'is'#9'line'#9'number N'
```

Each line contains three tab characters.

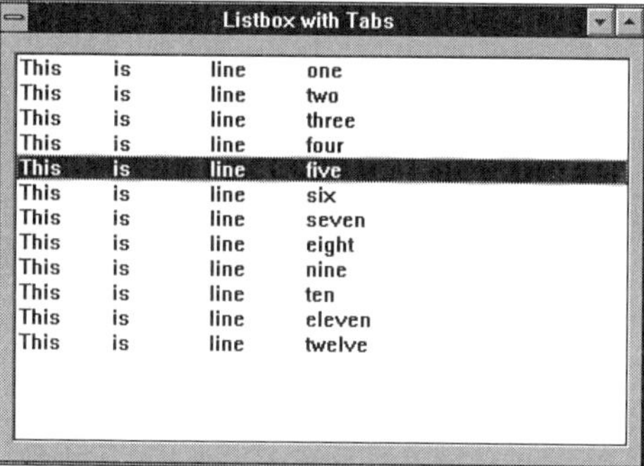

Figure 20.2.
A ListBox with Tabs control.

The standard Delphi component, `ListBox`, does not encapsulate the tab stop functionality although it is based on the standard Windows control. You need to roll out your own list box-based component to support tab stops. Fortunately, it is a simple task.

1. Define a new unit by selecting New Unit from the File menu. Save the newly created skeleton unit under the name `LbTabs` (LBTABS.PAS.)
2. Define a new class called `TListBoxTabs` inside the interface section of the unit.
3. Provide the implementation of the `TListBoxTabs` class according to the code in Listing 20.2.

Listing 20.2. List box control with tabs—Delphi component implementation.

```
 1: unit LbTabs;
 2:
 3: interface
 4:
 5: uses
 6:   Controls,
 7:   StdCtrls;
 8:
 9: type
10:   TListBoxTabs = class(TListBox)
11:   public
12:     procedure CreateParams (var Params: TCreateParams); override;
13:     procedure SetTabStops (Val: array of Word);
14:   end;
15:
16: procedure Register;
17:
18: implementation
19:
20: uses
21:   WinTypes, WinProcs, Classes, Messages;
22:
23: procedure TListBoxTabs.CreateParams;
24: begin
25:   inherited CreateParams( Params );
26:   with Params do
27:     Style := Style or lbs_UseTabStops;
28: end;
29:
30: procedure TListBoxTabs.SetTabStops;
31: begin
32:   SendMessage(Handle, LB SETTABSTOPS,
33:     High (Val) - Low (Val) + 1, LongInt (@Val));
34: end;
35:
36: procedure Register;
37: begin
38:   RegisterComponents('Special', [TListBoxTabs]);
39: end;
40:
41: end.
```

Analysis Listing 20.2 implements a useful list box component with tabs. The component's class is declared on lines 9–14 of the unit's interface section. The most important method declared as part of the class protocol is the `CreateParams` procedure on line 12. The implementation of `CreateParams` on lines 23 to 28 ensures that the visible Windows control corresponding to the list box component at run-time is created with a flag enabling it to recognize and expand tabs automatically inside the strings it displays. The assignment statement on line 27 makes sure that the Windows `lbs_UseTabStops` flag is set before the component is created.

This example also points out the fact that there is more to component creation than knowing the Delphi/VCL environment well. The `lbs_UseTabStops` flag is part of the generic Windows Application Programming Interface (API). When you're creating new components, you may be forced to program directly with the Windows API; therefore, your knowledge of it helps you design and implement your own custom components. (The discussion of the Windows API is, for the most part, beyond the scope of this book. You need to use other resources, such as other specialized books, at your disposal to gain more knowledge in this area.)

The `SetTabStops` routine declared on line 13 of Listing 20.2 and implemented on lines 30 to 34 complements the class interface with a way of actually setting the tab stops inside the list box. The `SetTabStops` method takes an open array of `Words` specifying the positions of tab stops and utilizes a call to another standard Windows API subroutine, `SendMessage`, to actually define the tab stops. A standard Windows message identified with the `LB_SETTABSTOPS` mnemonic is sent to the list box window to establish the tabs inside the list box control.

Finally, the `Register` procedure declared on line 16 and implemented on lines 36–39 makes it possible to install the control on Delphi's Component Palette. A new component page, Special, is created as part of the installation process, if necessary, and the component's icon is placed there.

The implementation of the `TListBoxTabs` component in Listing 20.2 is sufficient for the purposes of illustrating the principles of creating derived components. In reality, to create a production quality component, you would probably enhance it with additional ways of setting the values of tab stops and with a way of retrieving their values. In particular, you would probably consider providing a run-time array property `Tabs`, containing all the tab stop values. You may also consider making the `Tabs` property a design-time feature, with a custom property editor to allow the application designer to enter the values for the tab stops statically.

Even as it stands, however, the component is ready to be installed in the library.

4. Install the `LbTabs` unit and the `TListBoxTabs` component it contains by selecting Install Components from the Options menu.

   The component then appears on the newly created Special page inside the Component Palette.

Using Listbox-with-Tabs

You can use the `TListBoxTabs` component you just created in the same way you can use a standard list box. The only difference is that now you can use the `SetTabStops` method to establish the positions of the tab stops inside a list box-with-tabs at run-time. You can also add strings containing tabs to the list box. The tabs are automatically expanded, and the portions of the string delimited with tabs are aligned at tab stops inside the control.

For example, the following code establishes tab stops at positions 30, 60, and 120, respectively, inside list box control ListBox1:

```
const
  Tabs: array[0..2] of Word = (30, 60, 120);
begin
  ...
  ListBox1.SetTabStops(Tabs);
  ...
end
```

Note that the tab stops you indicate are given in so-called dialog units that do not directly correspond to pixels. It may take a bit of experimentation to get the column widths right. Now you can insert strings like the following to the list box:

```
begin
  ...
  ListBox1.Add('ID'#9'Name'#9'Surname'#9'SSN');
  ListBox1.Add('1'#9'Andrew'#9'Wozniewicz'#9'888-88-8888');
  ListBox1.Add('2'#9'John'#9'Doe'#9'999-99-9999');
...
end
```

The strings you Add are displayed properly aligned in four columns inside the control.

Creating New Visual Components

You have learned how to customize existing, specialized components by deriving new class types from one of the Delphi VCL classes. Next in your series of adventures with component creation is to derive a brand new component from one of the non-specialized component classes.

Note that creating a "brand new" visual component still entails deriving a new class from one of the existing VCL classes. The only difference between merely extending an existing specialized component and creating a new one is that, in the latter case, you would be deriving from one of the less-specialized classes, such as TWinControl or TGraphicControl, rather than from a specialized control, such as a TLabel, TMemo, or TCheckBox.

The fact that you are deriving from a less specialized class, however, does put more responsibilities into your hands, as the component creator. You have to take care of the details of the interaction of the component with the program's user and the details of the design-time interface.

One of the biggest distinctions between component users and component writers is the fact that the users are concerned with the creation and the manipulation of object instances, whereas the writers create and manipulate object types. Even in the simplest case of creating new derived components from the specialized, existing ones, as you learned in the preceding sections, you need to deal with deriving new Delphi classes.

As the introduction to today's lesson indicated, the transition you have to make from being a component user to becoming a component creator is one of degree. The customization of a component that is being accomplished through delegation, as is the case of a component user, is easily converted into customization accomplished through inheritance, as practiced by a component writer. The degree of how much of the built-in support for various component-like behaviors is inherited depends on how far from the bottom of the inheritance hierarchy you decide to descend your new object.

Protected Interfaces

When you are creating new components, you have access to the protected interface of an object, the interface the user of a component does not see. Recall that Object Pascal defines four levels of protection, or access control, over class elements: private, protected, public, and published. By specifying levels of protection, you can control the context in which the class elements can be accessed and who can access them from which blocks of code.

The user of a component has access to the public and published elements of an instance. The writer of a component, at the minimum, has access to published, public, and protected elements. In addition, if the derived class is defined in the same compilation unit as the base class, the private elements are also accessible.

The purpose of declaring class elements as private is to hide the details of their implementation from any client code accessing the instances of the class outside the unit in which it was defined. Making class elements private de-couples the interface of the class—that is, the published, public, and to some extent, protected elements—from its implementation. You can change the implementation later without affecting the client code. The class users are free to access the publicly available elements and need not concern themselves with the details of implementation.

The situation of component writers, however, is somewhat of a dilemma. On one hand, they may need to access the details of class implementation to modify or enhance the behavior provided by the parent class. On the other hand, a component writer deriving a new class from an existing component is also a user of the component in the sense that he or she delegates as much as possible to the base class and does not want to be concerned with the details of implementation of the base class.

The solution to this dilemma in Object Pascal is provided in the form of a protected interface. Protected level of access control gives just enough access for a descendant component writer to make extending or modifying the component by way of inheritance possible. The class encapsulation to the outside world, or to the component users, is still preserved intact so that the benefits of class encapsulation are not lost.

The important consideration when you are deriving new component classes is the decision as to which class to make the parent of the new class being defined. You need to study the existing class hierarchy to determine which aspects of the protected component interface you need to inherit and which aspects you do not need.

Remember that once a particular class element has been made public, it cannot be made private or protected again. Similarly, once a class element has been published, it stays published and visible in the Object Inspector window in all descendants of that class.

Point Diagram Example

You are now going to build a complete example of a Delphi custom control. The component you are about to construct is a simple data point diagram in which individual points are plotted on a two-dimensional Cartesian plane.

The example control is purposefully unsophisticated as far as its plotting capabilities are concerned. The purpose here is to illustrate the process of its creation rather than give you a complete implementation of the component. Hopefully, knowing the process of component writing will enable you to extend and modify the sample component in any number of ways to make it more sophisticated and production-like.

Creating the Unit

Here's how to create the unit:

1. Create a new project (select "New project" from the "File" menu). Then save it as project name `DiagRun` in a new directory DIAGRAMS. Also save the main form of the project as `FormDiag`.

   The Delphi project you have just created will serve as a test bed for your new component. You return to it later.

   As the first step in the process of creating the sample `PointDiagram` component, you create the component's unit and registration mechanism.

2. Select New Unit from the File menu. A new Object Pascal source code unit `Unit2` is created.
3. Save the new unit under the name `Diagms` using File | Save File As.

Installing the Component

Delphi creates a minimal, skeleton unit with no real code in it, so the next step is for you to provide the minimum support required for hosting a component inside the unit. Enter the necessary code, as shown in Listing 20.3, to provide sufficient support for installing it as a Delphi component unit.

Listing 20.3. A minimal Delphi visual component unit.

```
 1: unit Diagms;
 2:
 3: interface
 4:
 5: uses
 6:   WinProcs,
 7:   WinTypes,
 8:   Classes,
 9:   Graphics,
10:   Controls;
11:
12: type
13:   TPointDiagram   = class(TGraphicControl)
14:
15:   end;
16:
17: procedure Register;
18:
19: implementation
20:
21: procedure Register;
22: begin
23:   RegisterComponents('Custom',[TPointDiagram]);
24: end;
25:
26: end.
```

The code in Listing 20.3 shows a minimal Object Pascal unit necessary for supporting components. The interface of the unit, lines 3–18, declares a component class on lines 12–15 and a **uses** clause on lines 5–10 to make all the supporting units visible to this module.

The declaration of the `TPointDiagram` class is minimal at this point because the only relationship it establishes is the inheritance from `TGraphicControl` as its parent class. `TGraphicControl` was chosen as the parent class, as opposed to—for example—`TCustomControl`, because the custom component you are creating does not require its own window handle. Descending from `TGraphicControl` means that the control does not have its own window handle and that it draws itself on its parent's `Canvas`, thereby conserving scarce Windows resources.

Descending from `TGraphicControl` is sufficient to establish the new class as a legitimate component, however. All that is required for Delphi to accept the newly created component into its Component Library and onto the Component Palette is the registration mechanism.

The required procedure, `Register`, is declared on line 17 and implemented inside the implementation section of the unit on lines 21–24. The procedure registers the new component with Delphi by calling the `RegisterComponents` standard subroutine.

When you attempt to install the unit with Delphi, a new page called `Custom` is created on the Component Palette, and a default icon representing the component is placed on that page.

Once you have entered the supporting code inside the `Diagms` unit as shown in Listing 20.3, install the component as follows:

1. Select Install Components from the main Delphi Options menu.
2. Click on the Add... button inside the Install Components dialog box that appears.
3. Click on the Browse... button inside the Add Module dialog box.
4. Navigate your way to the newly created component unit, DIAGMS.PAS, select the file, and click on the OK button.
5. Click on the OK button inside the Add Module dialog box.
6. Click on the OK button inside the Install Components dialog box to rebuild the Component Library incorporating your new component unit in it.

After Delphi rebuilds the library, you see a new Custom page on the Component Palette, containing a single icon. When you select the Custom page by clicking on its tab and place the mouse cursor over the new component's icon, you see the name of the new component, `PointDiagram`, appearing as the user hint.

The component is ready to be placed on the form now. You know that it is not doing anything special right now, but you can verify that you can place it on the project's main form, and that it shows up in the Object Inspector.

1. Place the `PointDiagram` component on the project's main form. Verify that the component appears in the Object Inspector.
2. Delete the instance of the `PointDiagram` component from the form.

You return to designing the form later in this chapter.

Defining the Properties

Now you can provide the implementation of the `PointDiagram` component so that it becomes functional and useful. Here is a list of the required features the `PointDiagram` component is to support:

- The component allows for visual display of up to 12 data points on a two-dimensional grid.
- The user can select the background color and other brush properties of the grid as well as the color and other properties of the pen used to draw the grid.
- The user can select the color of the dots representing data points on the grid.
- The data point coordinates are to be supplied at run-time only.

- The density of the diagram's grid, that is, the distance between consecutive lines of the grid, is to be under the component user's control at design-time and run-time. The distance between horizontal lines is to be independently controlled from the distance between vertical lines.
- Any change in the visual properties of the diagram must be immediately reflected on the screen so that the user can interactively design the appearance of the diagram.

You must first decide what properties the diagram component needs to support the preceding requirements. Here is a list of properties that seem to be necessary:

- `UnitHorizontal`: An integer specifying the distance between consecutive grid lines in the horizontal direction, that is, determining the distance between consecutive vertical lines.
- `UnitVertical`: An integer specifying the distance between consecutive grid lines in the vertical direction, that is, controlling how far apart the horizontal lines are drawn.
- `BackgroundBrush`: A `TBrush` object supporting the design-time interface to setting the visual properties of the diagram's background, such as its background color.
- `BackgroundPen`: A `TPen` object used to draw the grid lines. You can control the appearance of the grid lines by setting the appropriate properties of `BackgroundPen`.
- `DataBrush`: Another `TBrush` object to control the appearance of the inside area of the data points. The data points are drawn as small circles, and in addition to filling their insides with an appropriate color, their borders are independently controlled too.
- `DataPen`: A second `TPen` object to control the appearance of the borders around the tiny circles representing the data points.
- `Points`: An array of `TPoint` structures representing the data point coordinates so that the component user can set and retrieve their values. This will be a run-time only property.

Some of the preceding properties require a specialized subroutine (method) for setting their values, some require an access function to retrieve a value, and some need both.

Listing 20.4 shows an expanded `TPointDiagram` class declaration that results from considering supporting the required properties.

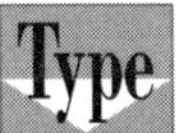

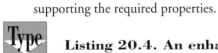

Listing 20.4. An enhanced `TPointDiagram` class declaration.

```
type
  TPointDiagram  = class(TGraphicControl)
  private
    FBkgndPen,
    FDataPen    : TPen;
    FBkgndBrush,
```

continues

Listing 20.4. continued

```
 7:     FDataBrush  : TBrush;
 8:     FPoints     : array[0..MaxTPoints-1] of TPoint;
 9:     FHorzUnit,
10:     FVertUnit   : Integer;
11:   protected
12:     function GetPoint(Index: Integer): TPoint; virtual;
13:     procedure SetPoint(Index: Integer;
14:       APoint: TPoint); virtual;
15:     procedure SetHorzUnit(AValue: Integer); virtual;
16:     procedure SetVertUnit(AValue: Integer); virtual;
17:   public
18:     constructor Create(AnOwner: TComponent); override;
19:     destructor Destroy; override;
20:     property Points[Index: Integer]: TPoint
21:       read GetPoint write SetPoint;
22:   published
23:     property DataBrush: TBrush read FDataBrush;
24:     property DataPen: TPen read FDataPen;
25:     property BackgroundBrush: TBrush read FBkgndBrush;
26:     property BackgroundPen: TPen read FBkgndPen;
27:     property UnitHorizontal: Integer
28:       read FHorzUnit write SetHorzUnit;
29:     property UnitVertical: Integer
30:       read FVertUnit write SetVertUnit;
31:   end;
```

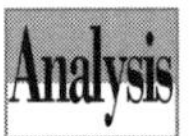

The **`published`** section of the class declaration on lines 20–31 of Listing 20.4 declares most of the properties mentioned. The corresponding **`private`** section on lines 3–10 declares the fields, also known as instance variables, that provide the data storage needed to support these properties. The **`protected`** section from line 11 to 16 declares the data-access methods for these properties. Finally, the **`public`** section declares additional methods on lines 18 and 19 and a run-time only property `Points` on lines 20 and 21.

The four drawing-related properties—`DataBrush`, `BackgroundBrush`, `DataPen`, and `BackgroundPen`—require no **`read`** functions. In each case, the instance variable can be accessed directly to retrieve the corresponding object. The four properties are read-only because **`write`** access is not needed in their case: the corresponding objects are completely managed by the enclosing `TPointDiagram` instance. This means that the user of the component cannot replace them with extraneous instances created outside the component's control. The user can of course still modify the properties of these pens and brushes.

The values of the `UnitHorizontal` and `UnitVertical` properties, controlling the density of the background grid, may be accessed directly from their respective instance variables. But changing the horizontal or vertical grid unit at design-time or run-time should affect the display so that the updated look is visible to the user. Consequently, specialized **`write`** methods `SetHorzUnit` and `SetVertUnit` are defined on lines 15 and 16, and referenced by the property declaration on

lines 28 and 30, respectively. These specialized methods make sure that, in addition to setting the corresponding values, the display is updated.

The only remaining property, `Points`, is declared in the **`public`** section on line 20 is an array property. It encapsulates the access to the data point coordinates. The implementation of the `Points` property is straightforward. An array of `TPoint` structures is declared as `FPoints` field on line 8. The array is indexed from 0 to `(MaxTPoints-1)`, where `MaxTPoints` is the maximum number of points allowed.

The preceding requirements stated that up to 12 points must be supported. Making the "magic number" 12 into a constant enables you to change the class implementation easily, should the requirements ever change. Remember to avoid polluting your code with embedded "magic numbers" like the 12 here. Always turn them into named constants. The listing assumes that the constant has been declared in the scope prior to the **`type`**-block declaration on line 1.

The implementation of the `Points` property as a static array of `TPoints` poses some practical problems. First of all, you cannot support an arbitrary number of points with it because you know that the absolute maximum for the size of any structure is 64K. A `TPoint` structure is defined in a `WinTypes` unit as follows:

```
type
  TPoint = record
    X: Integer;
    Y: Integer;
  end;
```

Consequently, each `TPoint` record consisting of two `Integer` fields, takes up `2*sizeof(Integer)`, or 8 bytes on a 16-bit system. Dividing 64K by 8 gives you a rough estimate of over 8,000 points per diagram. This number sounds reasonably large. The problem of statically declaring an array of points that large as part of the `TPointDiagram` class, however, is that every instance of `TPointDiagram` has to carry the storage necessary to accommodate all 8,000-plus points, regardless of whether it actually needs to display them all. This sounds like a big waste of memory space, and there are far better ways of coping with this problem than a naive array implementation.

The implementation here opts for simplicity, however. Because the maximum number of points a diagram must support is relatively small, you can get away with declaring an array of 12 points for every instance of `TPointDiagram` you create, even if all it displays is a single data point.

Another problem with the implementation of the `Points` property as an array of `TPoints` is that the component's client, which may be yourself in your capacity as the application programmer, may inadvertently attempt to access a point beyond the allowable range. Even with the 12 data point limit imposed by the requirements, nothing prevents you from accessing point number 12 or 13 (remember that the `FPoints` array index is zero-based) with potentially disastrous consequences.

To guard against mistakes like this, the array implementation of the `Points` property is never accessed directly, but instead two access methods are declared as part of the `TPointDiagram` class: `GetPoint` on line 12 and `SetPoint` on line 13. This way, you can build range checks right into the property access protocol.

As the final issue regarding the `TPointDiagram`'s class declaration, you know that the instances of the class, when created, each have to own two brush and two pen objects. These objects are dynamic class instances owned by the diagram instance and must be explicitly created when the diagram object itself is created and destroyed when the diagram is destroyed. As a result, you need to declare a dedicated constructor and a destructor to take care of these allocations and deallocations. The constructor `Create` is therefore declared on line 18, and the destructor `Destroy` is declared on line 19. Note that you cannot change the signatures (the subroutine headers) of the `Create` and `Destroy` methods.

The `Create` constructor is declared as follows:

```
constructor Create(AnOwner: TComponent); override;
```

You are *not* free to change the declaration so that it introduces additional parameters, for example, because it is meant to **`override`** a declaration in an ancestor class. It must therefore be identical to the ancestral declaration in all respects or else the compiler complains about the **`override`** directive.

You *cannot* introduce another constructor, for instance, with a different name and a different set of parameters, either. In general, you know that it is possible for a class to declare more than one constructor. In the case of components, however, the VCL mechanism for automatically instantiating forms from their binary definitions (.DFM files linked into your application) relies on the fact that there is a `Create` constructor whose declaration looks exactly like the preceding one. If you do not define it, the fields of your component are left essentially uninitialized when the object is created from a form file or inside the Form Designer.

If you need to pass some data to a component being created, use properties or methods defined for that purpose. The role of a component's constructor is to create a "default" instance of the component, one with its attributes initialized to some default values known in advance. Any customization beyond construction must be done after the component has already been created with a call to `Create`.

Remember that it is not you who calls the `Create` constructor for your component, but that it is called automatically in the process of the creation of the form on which it was placed.

The declaration of the `TPointDiagram` class is fairly complete as it stands. You eventually add a few methods that are needed to support the painting of the component.

Implementing the Methods

You are now ready to provide the implementation of the methods you introduced to the class declaration of `TPointDiagram`.

Setting the Grid Units

First, you provide the implementation for the `SetHorz` method of the `TPointDiagram` object. The `SetHorz` method is responsible for setting the value of the `UnitHorizontal` property and updating the display to reflect the change to the grid unit immediately.

Here is a possible implementation:

```
procedure TPointDiagram.SetHorzUnit(AValue: Integer);
begin
  FHorzUnit := AValue;
  Invalidate;
end;
```

The call to the inherited `Invalidate` method tells Windows to update the area of the display where the control is shown at the earliest convenience. This has the effect of updating the visual appearance of the control almost instantaneously but without disrupting the flow of Windows messages.

The implementation of the corresponding `SetVertUnit` method is almost identical:

```
procedure TPointDiagram.SetVertUnit(AValue: Integer);
begin
  FVertUnit := AValue;
  Invalidate;
end;
```

Enter the implementation of the `SetHorzUnit` and `SetVertUnit` methods inside the implementation section of the `Diagms` Object Pascal unit.

20

Defining the Data Points

Another task requiring specialized methods is to set and retrieve the values of the data points. Remember that you need to build some range-checking code into these methods to avoid raising exceptions at runtime.

Here is a suggested implementation for the `SetPoint` property access method:

```
procedure TPointDiagram.SetPoint;
begin
  if (Index >= 0) and (Index < MaxTPoints) then
    FPoints[Index] := APoint;
  Invalidate;
end;
```

The underlying property value stored in the `FPoints` array is accessed only if the value of the `Index` supplied by the user is within the valid range.

The call to `Invalidate` at this point warrants some explanation. The implementation of the `TPointDiagram` that you are building uses a marker value to determine which of the `TPoint` cells in the `Points` array are valid, or used for actual points, and which of them are "empty," or unused.

You can use a `TPoint` value of `(X:-1; Y:-1)` to indicate an unused cell. This value is not likely to create any conflicts with any actual data values because the diagram is capable of displaying points with non-negative coordinates only.

Initially, all elements of the `FPoints` array are set to the marker value `(-1,-1)` to indicate that they are unused. During the course of the program's execution, the user may assign specific values to some of the points in the array. Once the value changes from `(-1,-1)` to a coordinate pair supplied by the user, the specific point may become visible on the diagram. The call to `Invalidate` ensures that all points that should be visible are indeed visible at all times. Whenever a particular point's coordinates change from the "unused" marker to some valid data values, the diagram is redrawn.

To retrieve the values of a particular data point's coordinates, you use the `GetPoint` function. Here is the suggested implementation:

```
function TPointDiagram.GetPoint;
begin
  if (Index >= 0) and (Index < MaxTPoints) then
    Result := FPoints[Index]
  else
    Result := Point(-1,-1);
end;
```

As before, the first line after the **begin** checks to see whether the `Index` argument passed by the user is within the allowable range. If it is not, the marker value is returned. Note how a marker `TPoint` structure is constructed on-the-fly. The call to the standard `Point` function returns a `TPoint` filled with the specified coordinate values. This shorthand is convenient for assigning a value to each of the `TPoint`'s fields without having to access them separately.

If the `Index` value passed to the `GetPoint` function is within the allowable range, the corresponding point from the `FPoints` array is returned by the expression

```
Result := FPoints[Index]
```

Painting the Control

The `TPointDiagram` is a visual component. All the properties and methods implemented so far would not be of much use if there were no way to display the diagram control.

So that you can paint a custom control you develop, the control's class needs to override the ancestor's `Paint` method. The `Paint` method is called by the VCL framework at appropriate times in response to requests from Windows to repaint all or part of the control, for example, after the user uncovers it from under another window.

The implementation of the `Paint` method you provide determines exactly how the control appears to the user.

Here are the steps you need to undertake inside the `Paint` method of your `TPointDiagram` class to provide the desired appearance to the control:

1. Erase the background with the `BackgroundBrush` to ensure that the control appears in the user-selected color and texture.
2. Display the horizontal and vertical lines forming the background grid.
3. Plot the data points supplied earlier by the user and stored inside the `Points` array against the grid background.

The preceding steps suggest the implementation for the `TPointDiagram.Paint` method shown in Listing 20.5.

Listing 20.5. The `TPointDiagram's Paint` method implementation.

```
procedure TPointDiagram.Paint;
var
  I,
  X,
  Y: Integer;
begin
  with Canvas do begin
    {Paint background}
    Brush := FBkgndBrush;
    Pen := FBkgndPen;
    Rectangle(0,0,Width,Height);

    {Draw Vertical Gridlines}
    I := UnitHorizontal;
    while I < Width do begin
      MoveTo(I,0);
      LineTo(I,Height);
      Inc(I,UnitHorizontal);
    end;
    {Draw Horizontal Gridlines}
    I := Height;
    while I > 0 do begin
      MoveTo(0,I);
      LineTo(Width,I);
      Dec(I,UnitVertical);
    end;

    {Plot Data Points}
    Brush := FDataBrush;
    Pen := FDataPen;
    for I := 0 to MaxTPoints do begin
      X := Points[I].X;
```


continues

Listing 20.5. continued

```
33:         if (X <> -1) then begin
34:           Y := Points[I].Y;
35:           Ellipse(X-3,Height-(Y-3),X+3,Height-(Y+3));
36:         end;
37:       end;
38:     end;
39: end;
```

To be able to paint anything on the control's surface, you need to access the component's `Canvas` property inherited from an ancestor. `Canvas` encapsulates the drawing and painting functionality for Delphi Windows applications. To seamlessly access the public properties and methods of the control's `Canvas`, the entire executable **`begin-end`** block of the `Paint` method in Listing 20.5 is enclosed within a

```
with Canvas do begin
end
```

statement. The opening **`with`** part of the statement appears on line 7 of the listing, and the closing **`end`** appears on line 38.

Inside the **`with`** statement, the three main steps of the painting algorithm outlined previously are carried out. Lines 8–11 deal with painting the background. Before painting, `Canvas`'s `Brush` and `Pen` properties are initialized with the respective objects native to the `TPointDiagram` control to ensure that the diagram is painted with the visual preferences as defined by the user of the component.

The call to the `Rectangle` method of the `Canvas` on line 11 actually erases the background.

The next step of painting, or drawing the grid lines, is divided into two phases. At first, lines 13–19 deal with the drawing of the vertical grid lines. A **`while`** loop controls the repetitive task of drawing the next vertical grid line, `UnitHorizontal` pixels to the right of the previous one, until the entire visible surface of the control is covered. Each time through the loop, the temporary variable `I`, holding the current horizontal position, is incremented by the number equal to the value of `UnitHorizontal` property on line 18.

Lines 21–26 deal with drawing the horizontal grid lines. The horizontal lines are drawn bottom-up; each line is drawn `UnitVertical` pixels above the previous one. The repetitive nature of this task is also under the control of a **`while`** loop and terminates once the entire visible surface is covered. Each time through the loop, the temporary variable `I`, holding the current vertical position, is decremented by the value of the `UnitVertical` property on line 25.

Drawing the horizontal grid lines in the bottom-up direction highlights the fact that a translation occurs between the screen vertical coordinates, starting at zero at the top of the screen and growing downward, to the grid coordinates, starting at the bottom edge of the grid and growing upward. The translation between the screen-based and grid-based direction of the

vertical (Y) coordinate reflects the fact that the grid-based approach is more appropriate for a data-plotting control because it corresponds to the normal orientation of standard Cartesian coordinates on a plane traditionally used in mathematics and sciences.

In both cases of drawing the grid lines, a sequence of calls

```
MoveTo(X,Y)
LineTo(X,Y)
```

first positions the `Canvas`'s imaginary "drawing position" cursor at an appropriate starting position with the call to the `MoveTo` method and then draws the line to the specified end position with the `LineTo` method.

The final step of drawing the diagram on lines 29–37 displays the data points.

A **`for`** loop is run through the entire array `FPoints` of the data points, skipping the marker values and displaying only the valid data points.

The **`if`** test on line 33 determines whether to skip a point by testing the X-coordinate of the current cell in the `FPoints` array against the marker value `-1`.

If the particular point is to be plotted, a call to the `Ellipse` method of the `Canvas` accomplishes the task. By default, the points are drawn as small circles, six pixels in diameter, in the color defined by the `DataBrush` property of the diagram. Because the data point circles are so small, it is not necessary to perform any calculations to ensure that they show up as circles instead of ellipses. The distortion, if any, from the perfect circular shape resulting from different display resolutions along the vertical and the horizontal axes is negligible in this case.

Once the data points are plotted, the `Paint` method is done.

Creating the Component

The only remaining concern with respect to the custom `TPointDiagram` component is the implementation of its constructor and destructor. You know already that the constructor must be called `Create` and must be declared to override the inherited constructor `Create` so that the VCL mechanism can properly instantiate your component along with the rest of the components on a form.

The job of the overriding constructor is to initialize the fields of a new instance of your component. In particular, the `TPointDiagram` class defines two `Brush` and two `Pen` objects, which it maintains. The constructor's job is to create the `DataBrush`, `BackgroundBrush`, `DataPen`, and `BackgroundPen` objects. This is done with a series of statements, like the following:

```
{Create pens and brushes}
FDataPen := TPen.Create;
FDataBrush := TBrush.Create;
FBkgndPen := TPen.Create;
FBkgndBrush := TBrush.Create;
```

The constructor should also initialize the data fields and any inherited properties of the object. In particular, the `Width` and `Height` property inherited from an ancestor should be set to an appropriate value so that the component appears conveniently sized when it is dropped onto a form in the design mode. The grid units need also be initialized:

```
Width := 144;
Height := 144;
FHorzUnit := 24;
FVertUnit := 24;
```

Finally, the constructor has to take care of initializing the data points to the marker value signifying an "unused" cell in the data points array:

```
{Initialize data points}
for I := 0 to MaxTPoints do begin
  Points[I] := Point(-1,-1);
end;
```

The finished constructor is shown in Listing 20.6.

Listing 20.6. The `Create` constructor for the `TPointDiagram` class.

```
 1: constructor TPointDiagram.Create;
 2: var
 3:   I : Integer;
 4: begin
 5:   inherited Create(AnOwner);
 6:
 7:   {Initialize data fields}
 8:   Width := 144;
 9:   Height := 144;
10:   FHorzUnit := 24;
11:   FVertUnit := 24;
12:
13:   {Create pens and brushes}
14:   FDataPen := TPen.Create;
15:   FDataBrush := TBrush.Create;
16:   FDataPen.OnChange := CtrlStyleChanged;
17:   FDataBrush.OnChange := CtrlStyleChanged;
18:   FBkgndPen := TPen.Create;
19:   FBkgndBrush := TBrush.Create;
20:   FBkgndPen.OnChange := CtrlStyleChanged;
21:   FBkgndBrush.OnChange := CtrlStyleChanged;
22:
23:   {Initialize data points}
24:   for I := 0 to MaxTPoints do begin
25:     Points[I] := Point(-1,-1);
26:   end;
27: end;
```

The code in Listing 20.6 has already been explained in the text. The only additions worth noting are the series of statements on lines 16, 17, 20, and 21. These statements assign the `OnChange` property of the `Brush` and `Pen` components to a `TPointDiagram` method

CtrlStyleChanged to let the control capture notifications of any changes to the state of its brushes and pens used in drawing. You need to do that to be able to force a redraw of the visible control every time some characteristic of a pen or a brush changes so that the visual appearance reflects the settings of the component's properties at all times.

Also note that inside the Create constructor, the inherited constructor is called first. The call to the inherited constructor ensures that the instance is properly created and that the portions of it inherited from parent objects are properly initialized before you attempt to interact with them inside the constructor.

The remaining lines inside the constructor in Listing 20.6 have already been discussed. In particular,

- The data fields and inherited attributes are initialized on lines 7–11.
- The required pens and brushes are created and initialized on lines 13–21.
- The data points are initialized to the default marker value by a **for** loop on lines 23–26. This **for** loop is also the reason for declaring a counter variable I on lines 2 and 3.

Note: As a general rule of the component creation, remember to call the inherited Create constructor first.

The constructor described here makes use of an OnChange event handler, CtrlStyleChanged, that is supposed to be supplied by the TPointDiagram class in order to capture changes to the pens and the brushes of the diagram object at runtime. The implementation of this event handler is simple because the only task it has to carry out is making sure that the component is redrawn in response to a change in one of the associated objects. This is accomplished by calling the inherited Invalidate method as follows:


```
procedure TPointDiagram.CtrlStyleChanged;
begin
  Invalidate;
end;
```

Destroying the Instance

Destroying an instance of a TPointDiagram is simpler than creating it. Here are the only considerations that you have to keep in mind:

- All the associated objects owned by the component, the pens and brushes in this case, must be properly destroyed.
- The inherited destructor must be called to make sure that the inherited parts are properly deallocated and destroyed.

You implement the resulting destructor as follows:

```
destructor TPointDiagram.Destroy;
begin
  FDataPen.Free;
  FDataBrush.Free;
  FBkgndPen.Free;
  FBkgndBrush.Free;
  inherited Destroy;
end;
```

The Complete Implementation

Listing 20.7 summarizes everything that has been said about the `TPointDiagram` component's implementation.

Listing 20.7. The complete implementation of the `TPointDiagram` component.

```
unit Diagms;

{
Point Diagram:
A simple, custom Delphi visual-control component
featuring a 2-D diagram against which data points
can be plotted.
}

interface

uses
  WinProcs,
  WinTypes,
  Classes,
  Graphics,
  Controls;


const
  MaxTPoints = 12;
    {Maximum number of points per diagram}

type
  TPointDiagram  = class(TGraphicControl)
  private
    FBkgndPen,
    FDataPen    : TPen;
    FBkgndBrush,
    FDataBrush  : TBrush;
    FPoints     : array[0..MaxTPoints-1] of TPoint;
    FHorzUnit,
    FVertUnit   : Integer;
  protected
    function GetPoint(Index: Integer): TPoint; virtual;
```

```
    procedure SetPoint(Index: Integer;
      APoint: TPoint); virtual;
    procedure SetHorzUnit(AValue: Integer); virtual;
    procedure SetVertUnit(AValue: Integer); virtual;
    procedure Paint; override;
  public
    constructor Create(AnOwner: TComponent); override;
    destructor Destroy; override;
    procedure CtrlStyleChanged(Sender: TObject);
    property Points[Index: Integer]: TPoint
      read GetPoint write SetPoint;
  published
    property DataBrush: TBrush read FDataBrush;
    property DataPen: TPen read FDataPen;
    property BackgroundBrush: TBrush read FBkgndBrush;
    property BackgroundPen: TPen read FBkgndPen;
    property UnitHorizontal: Integer
      read FHorzUnit write SetHorzUnit;
    property UnitVertical: Integer
      read FVertUnit write SetVertUnit;
  end;


procedure Register;


implementation


constructor TPointDiagram.Create;
var
  I : Integer;
begin
  inherited Create(AnOwner);

  {Initialize data fields}
  Width := 144;
  Height := 144;
  FHorzUnit := 24;
  FVertUnit := 24;

  {Create pens and brushes}
  FDataPen := TPen.Create;
  FDataBrush := TBrush.Create;
  FDataPen.OnChange := CtrlStyleChanged;
  FDataBrush.OnChange := CtrlStyleChanged;
  FBkgndPen := TPen.Create;
  FBkgndBrush := TBrush.Create;
  FBkgndPen.OnChange := CtrlStyleChanged;
  FBkgndBrush.OnChange := CtrlStyleChanged;

  {Initialize data points}
  for I := 0 to MaxTPoints do begin
    Points[I] := Point(-1,-1);
  end;
```


continues

Listing 20.7. continued

```
end;
destructor TPointDiagram.Destroy;
begin
  FDataPen.Free;
  FDataBrush.Free;
  FBkgndPen.Free;
  FBkgndBrush.Free;
  inherited Destroy;
end;
procedure TPointDiagram.CtrlStyleChanged;
begin
  Invalidate;
end;
function TPointDiagram.GetPoint;
begin
  if (Index >= 0) and (Index < MaxTPoints) then
    Result := FPoints[Index]
  else
    Result := Point(-1,-1);
end;
procedure TPointDiagram.SetPoint;
begin
  if (Index >= 0) and (Index < MaxTPoints) then
    FPoints[Index] := APoint;
  Invalidate;
end;
procedure TPointDiagram.SetHorzUnit;
begin
  FHorzUnit := AValue;
  Invalidate;
end;
procedure TPointDiagram.SetVertUnit;
begin
  FVertUnit := AValue;
  Invalidate;
end;
procedure TPointDiagram.Paint;
var
  I,
  X,
```

```
145:    Y: Integer;
146: begin
147:   with Canvas do begin
148:     {Paint background}
149:     Brush := FBkgndBrush;
150:     Pen := FBkgndPen;
151:     Rectangle(0,0,Width,Height);
152:
153:     {Draw Vertical Gridlines}
154:     I := UnitHorizontal;
155:     while I < Width do begin
156:       MoveTo(I,0);
157:       LineTo(I,Height);
158:       Inc(I,UnitHorizontal);
159:     end;
160:     {Draw Horizontal Gridlines}
161:     I := Height;
162:     while I > 0 do begin
163:       MoveTo(0,I);
164:       LineTo(Width,I);
165:       Dec(I,UnitVertical);
166:     end;
167:
168:     {Plot Data Points}
169:     Brush := FDataBrush;
170:     Pen := FDataPen;
171:     for I := 0 to MaxTPoints do begin
172:       X := Points[I].X;
173:       if (X <> -1) then begin
174:         Y := Points[I].Y;
175:         Ellipse(X-3,Height-(Y-3),X+3,Height-(Y+3));
176:       end;
177:     end;
178:   end;
179: end;
180:
181:
182: procedure Register;
183: begin
184:   RegisterComponents('Custom',[TPointDiagram]);
185: end;
186:
187: end.
```

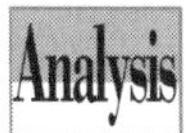

Because various bits and pieces of the code in Listing 20.7 have already been discussed, the commentary here is limited to giving you a general outline and referring to the previous sections whenever applicable.

The interface section of the `Diagms` unit declares the `TPointDiagram` class on lines 24–56. The details of the declaration were discussed in the "Defining the Properties" section.

The constant declaration on lines 20–22 ensures that the implementation is easy to change when the number of required data points changes, within a reasonable range.

The declaration of the `Register` procedure on line 59 ensures that you can install the component using Delphi and that it shows up on the Component Palette. Lines 182–185 implement the `Register` procedure as discussed in the "Registering the Component with Delphi" section.

The implementation section of the unit on lines 62–187 implements all the methods discussed in the previous sections, including

- The constructor `Create` (see "Creating the Component") on lines 65–91
- The destructor `Destroy` (see "Destroying the Instance") on lines 94–101
- The various property access methods (see "Setting the Grid Units" and "Defining the Data Points") on lines 110–116, 119–124, 127–131, and 134–138
- The `Paint` method responsible for displaying the control (see "Painting the Control") on lines 141–179
- The `CtrlStyleChanged` event handler (see "Creating the Component") on lines 104–107

The Test Application

To test the appearance and behavior of the diagram control you have implemented in today's lesson, you are now going to complete the `DiagRun` project you created in the beginning.

Make sure you have rebuilt the Component Library with the final version of the `Diagms` unit before you continue with the example program. Select Rebuild Library from the Delphi Options menu to recompile the library.

The test program displays a `PointDiagram` component and lets the user interact with it by setting the values of the data points at runtime.

Listing 20.8 shows the textual representation of the main form of the `DiagRun` project in its final shape.

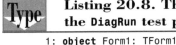

Listing 20.8. The textual representation of the main form of the `DiagRun` test project.

```
object Form1: TForm1
  Left = 200
  Top = 98
  Width = 435
  Height = 300
  ActiveControl = BitBtn1
  Caption = 'Point Diagram'
  Font.Color = clBlack
  Font.Height = -11
  Font.Name = 'MS Sans Serif'
  Font.Style = [fsBold]
  PixelsPerInch = 96
  OnActivate = FormActivate
```

```
object PointDiagram1: TPointDiagram
  Left = 16
  Top = 29
  Width = 288
  Height = 216
  DataBrush.Color = clRed
  DataPen.Color = clRed
  DataPen.Width = 1
  BackgroundBrush.Color = clWindow
  BackgroundPen.Width = 1
  UnitHorizontal = 72
  UnitVertical = 72
end
object Label1: TLabel
  Left = 332
  Top = 148
  Width = 9
  Height = 13
  Caption = 'X'
end
object Label2: TLabel
  Left = 332
  Top = 174
  Width = 9
  Height = 13
  Caption = 'Y'
end
object BitBtn1: TBitBtn
  Left = 324
  Top = 48
  Width = 89
  Height = 33
  TabOrder = 0
  Kind = bkClose
  NumGlyphs = 2
end
object ComboBox1: TComboBox
  Left = 326
  Top = 106
  Width = 85
  Height = 20
  TabOrder = 1
  TabStop = True
  Items.Strings = (
    '1'
    '2'
    '3'
    '4'
    '5'
    '6'
    '7'
    '8'
    '9'
    '10'
    '11'
```


continues

Listing 20.8. continued

```
      '12')
    ItemHeight = 13
    OnChange = ComboBox1Change
  end
  object EditXCoord: TEdit
    Left = 354
    Top = 144
    Width = 57
    Height = 20
    TabOrder = 2
  end
  object EditYCoord: TEdit
    Left = 354
    Top = 170
    Width = 57
    Height = 20
    TabOrder = 3
  end
  object Button1: TButton
    Left = 326
    Top = 206
    Width = 87
    Height = 23
    TabOrder = 4
    Caption = '&Save'
    OnClick = EditCoordChange
  end
end
```

The declarative pseudo-code in Listing 20.8 gives you a way of quickly and unambiguously re-creating the form exactly as it was meant to appear. You can enter the text of the listing exactly inside the Code Editor and save it as a form file (*.DFM). Delphi will convert the text into the binary .DFM format.

Figure 20.3 shows the final appearance of the form inside the Form Designer window.

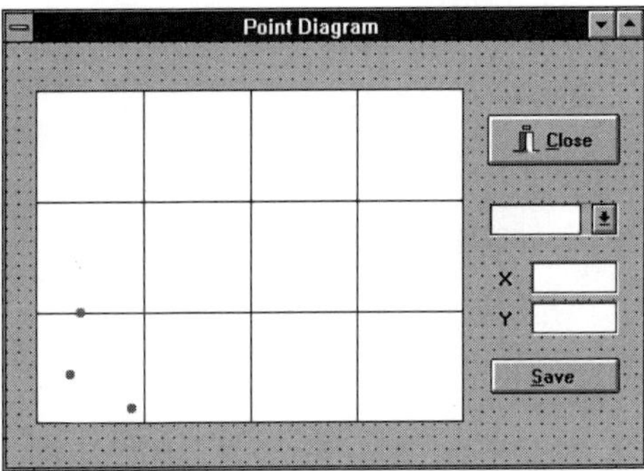

Figure 20.3.
The final appearance of the `DiagRun` *form.*

To create the equivalent form visually, follow these steps:

1. Place the `PointDiagram` component on the form. Resize it as shown in Figure 20.3. Then change its `DataBrush.Color` and `DataPen.Color` subproperties to `clRed`, and its `UnitVertical` and `UnitHorizontal` properties to `72`.
2. Place a `ComboBox`, two `Edit` components, and a `Button` on the form, as shown in Figure 20.3.
3. Rename the `Edit` components to `EditXCoord` and `EditYCoord`, respectively. Add appropriate `Labels` next to each.
4. Rename the button `Button1` to `ButtonSave`. Change its caption to `&Save`.
5. Enter the values for the `Items` property of the combo box. The values are lines of text; each contains a whole number, consecutively in the range of 1 to 12, indicating the 12 possible data points on the diagram.
6. Select the `ComboBox1` component on the form, and click the Events tab of the Object Inspector. Double-click the `OnChange` event to create an empty `ComboBox1Change` handler for it.
7. Inside the `ComboBox1Change` handler enter the following code:

   ```
   procedure Form1.ComboBox1Change(Sender: TObject);
   var
     P: TPoint;
   begin
     P := PointDiagram1.Points[ComboBox1.ItemIndex];
     EditXCoord.Text := IntToStr(P.X);
     EditYCoord.Text := IntToStr(P.Y);
   end;
   ```

   The preceding code fires every time you select a different number from the combo box. It retrieves the value of the diagram's data point at index `ComboBox1.ItemIndex` and places its coordinates inside `EditXCoord` and `EditYCoord` edit boxes, respectively, converting them to displayable strings in the process.

   The user can change the values displayed by the edit boxes and save them back to be stored in the diagram's `Points` array by clicking on the Save button—after you provide the button's `OnClick` event handler in the next step.
8. Create an `OnClick` handler for the Save button (`ButtonSave` component), rename the handler to `EditCoordChange`, and enter the following code in it:

   ```
   procedure TForm1.EditCoordChange(Sender: TObject);
   var
     P: TPoint;
   begin
     P := Point(StrToInt(EditXCoord.Text),StrToInt(EditYCoord.Text));
     PointDiagram1.Points[ComboBox1.ItemIndex] := P;
   end;
   ```

The preceding code updates the diagram's `Points` value indexed by the currently selected item inside the `ComboBox1` component with the coordinates specified inside the respective edit boxes. The code is called whenever the user clicks on the Save button, presumably after changing the contents of the coordinate edit boxes. You can thereby change the coordinates of the points displayed in the diagram dynamically at run-time.

9. Create an empty event handler for the form's `OnCreate` event. Insert the following code inside the handler's main **`begin-end`** block:

```
procedure TForm1.FormCreate(Sender: TObject);
begin
  PointDiagram1.Points[0] := Point(32,45);
  PointDiagram1.Points[1] := Point(64,72);
  PointDiagram1.Points[2] := Point(23,172);
  PointDiagram1.Points[3] := Point(124,34);
end;
```

   The form's `OnCreate` handler defines a few sample data points to be plotted in the diagram.

The complete code of the resulting form unit `FormDiag` is shown in Listing 20.9.

Listing 20.9. The complete code inside the `DiagRun` project's main form unit.

```
unit FormDiag;

interface

uses
  SysUtils, WinTypes, WinProcs, Messages, Classes, Graphics, Controls,
  Forms, Dialogs, Diagms, StdCtrls, Buttons;

type
  TForm1 = class(TForm)
    PointDiagram1: TPointDiagram;
    BitBtn1: TBitBtn;
    ComboBox1: TComboBox;
    EditXCoord: TEdit;
    EditYCoord: TEdit;
    Label1: TLabel;
    Label2: TLabel;
    Button1: TButton;
    procedure FormCreate(Sender: TObject);
    procedure ComboBox1Change(Sender: TObject);
    procedure EditCoordChange(Sender: TObject);
  private
    { Private declarations }
  public
    { Public declarations }
  end;

var
```

```
29:   Form1: TForm1;
30:
31: implementation
32:
33: {$R *.DFM}
34:
35: procedure TForm1.FormCreate(Sender: TObject);
36: begin
37:   PointDiagram1.Points[0] := Point(32,45);
38:   PointDiagram1.Points[1] := Point(64,72);
39:   PointDiagram1.Points[2] := Point(23,172);
40:   PointDiagram1.Points[3] := Point(124,34);
41: end;
42:
43: procedure TForm1.ComboBox1Change(Sender: TObject);
44: var
45:   P: TPoint;
46: begin
47:   P := PointDiagram1.Points[ComboBox1.ItemIndex];
48:   EditXCoord.Text := IntToStr(P.X);
49:   EditYCoord.Text := IntToStr(P.Y);
50: end;
51:
52: procedure TForm1.EditCoordChange(Sender: TObject);
53: var
54:   P: TPoint;
55: begin
56:   P := Point(StrToInt(EditXCoord.Text),StrToInt(EditYCoord.Text));
57:   PointDiagram1.Points[ComboBox1.ItemIndex] := P;
58: end;
59:
60: end.
```

Analysis The code of Listing 20.9 has already been discussed in the preceding text. The `Form1` form component declared on lines 10–26 defines the main form of the example program. The form class declares its own components as well as the three event handlers it needs to support the user interaction with the controls: `FormCreate`, `ComboBox1Change`, and `EditCoordChange`.

The implementation section defines these event handlers as described previously.

Running the Example Program

When you run the example program, you can change the coordinates of the individual points displayed on the diagram by selecting the data point number from the combo box's drop-down list, entering new coordinates inside the edit boxes, and clicking on the Save button.

Figure 20.4 illustrates the running example program, with all its 12 points actively displayed.

The example program and the current state of the custom point diagram component show you some of the possibilities for creating your own components. You can extend the diagram custom control in many ways to support events, multiple layers of data points, and many other features.

Look into the Exercises section at the end of today's lesson for more ideas on how to extend and enhance the diagram component.

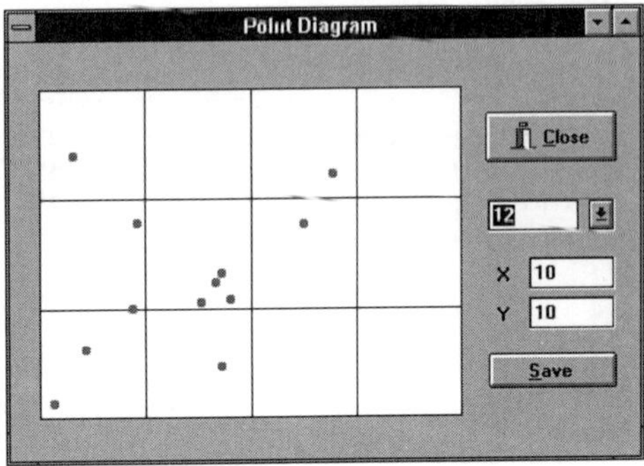

Figure 20.4.
The example `DiagRun` *program displaying 12 data points.*

Summary

Today's lesson walked you through the process of designing and implementing custom components using Delphi. Specifically, you have learned the following:

- Delphi enables you to create custom components within the same environment and with the same programming language you can use to create applications.
- Creating a new component involves defining a new Object Pascal class.
- All custom components created with Delphi must descend directly or indirectly from `TComponent`.
- You can create new components by customizing an existing specialized component, such as `Edit`, `Memo`, `ListBox`, and so on.
- You also can create new components from scratch, by subclassing one of the non-specialized component classes, such as `TComponent`, `TControl`, `TGraphicControl`, or `TWinControl`.
- Creating a new component frequently involves creating a new unit, declaring and implementing a new object class, and providing the `Register` procedure for registering the new component's class with Delphi.
- The component creator has to deal with additional levels of complexity in addition to what a component user encounters. In particular, a component writer must deal with the protected interfaces only available to the descendants of a component class but unavailable to the component's clients. A component writer must exhibit a greater understanding of OOP issues like inheritance, polymorphism, and so on.

- You are free to define new properties to extend the functionality of an existing component, whether specialized or not.
- The properties declared in the **published** section of a component class declaration are visible to the Object Inspector at design time.
- The class elements declared in the **protected** section of a component's class are visible only to the component that declares them and its descendants.
- If a constructor is needed to initialize the data values of a component's fields, it must be declared to override the virtual `Create` constructor of the generic `TComponent` class.
- If a destructor is defined for a component, it must override the virtual `Destroy` destructor of the `TComponent` class.
- You must remember to call the inherited constructor as the first statement inside your component's `Create` constructor, and to call the inherited destructor as the last statement inside your component's `Destroy` destructor.
- To enable a custom, visual component to display itself at runtime, you must override the virtual `Paint` method inherited from either `TGraphicControl` or `TCustomControl`, inside which you can draw on the component's visible surface using the `Canvas` property also inherited from an ancestor.

Q&A

Q Do I have to descend every object inside my application from `TComponent`?

A No, of course not. You can derive many useful classes directly from `TObject`. For example, many "business objects," or objects encapsulating abstract business entities such as an `Invoice` or a `BankAccount`, may successfully be implemented as `TObject` descendants. You must derive from `TComponent` or one of its descendants if you want to create a "component," that is, an entity that can be installed in the Component Library and on the Component Palette, and manipulated via the Form Designer or the Object Inspector.

Q Is it possible to hide inherited properties?

A No, unfortunately Delphi does not let you hide a property that has been made public, nor does it allow you to unpublish a property inherited from an ancestor class. Once published, always published is the rule. Hopefully, Borland will consider changing that rule in future revisions of Delphi and let you unpublish an unneeded property, although there is no indication that this will ever happen. All you can do at this point is to "override" a property by providing another one of the same name and defining its access methods to be blank, or to display a warning message, and so on.

Q How can I direct Delphi to automatically use a constructor other than the default `Create` to construct my component at runtime? I absolutely must pass some additional data to the component at creation time.

A In short, you can't. The VCL framework uses the `Create` constructor to instantiate components, and there is no straightforward way of instructing it otherwise. Remember that you can always pass the information you need to pass to your component via appropriately declared properties, or through method parameters. The purpose of the `Create` constructor is to instantiate a component with the default values of its instance variables.

Q I have declared a `Create` constructor for my component with a proper signature, that is, as a virtual method with a single parameter of type `TComponent`, but the data fields of my object are not being initialized. In fact, when I put a breakpoint inside the `Create` constructor, the program never stops; the breakpoint is never reached. What have I done wrong?

A Make sure that you declare your constructor with the **`override`** directive rather than with **`virtual`**. When you use a **`virtual`** directive, you are effectively introducing another virtual method with the same name as a method of an ancestor's. The **`override`** directive, on the other hand, ensures that your intent of overriding the ancestor's method is observed by the compiler.

Workshop

The Workshop provides quiz questions to help you solidify your understanding of the material covered and exercises to provide you with experience in using what you've learned. Try to understand the quiz and exercise answers before continuing on to the next day's lesson. Answers are provided in Appendix B at the end of this book.

Quiz

1. True or False? You can redeclare **`public`** properties of a component to make them **`published`** and accessible through the Object Inspector.
2. True or False? You can change the initial value of a property by assigning the desired value inside the component's constructor.
3. True or False? You can change the initial, default value of a component's property by specifying a **`default`** directive after the property declaration.
4. True or False? Constructors and destructors must always be declared **`public`**.
5. True or False? Side effects are dangerous phenomena that make programs hard to read and maintain, and they should therefore be avoided. Property access methods that use side effects are dangerous.

6. True or False? Non-visual components are always descended from the `TComponent` class.

Exercises

1. Extend the `TPointDiagram` component you have developed during the course of this lesson to allow each data point to be labeled with an individual text label.
2. Extend the `TPointDiagram` component you have developed during the course of this lesson to allow multiple (up to three) layers of data points, displayed and managed independently on the same diagram.
3. Extend the `TPointDiagram` component you have developed during the course of today's lesson to allow some basic events, such as mouse clicks, drag-and-drop events, and so on, to be captured.

WEEK
3

Dynamically Linked Libraries (DLLs)

Programs running in Windows can share subroutines located in executable files called *dynamic link libraries* (DLLs). Typically, DLLs are used in the context of a large system or application, where many common routines are shared among many programs.

During today's lesson, you will learn the basics of creating and using DLLs. In particular, you will learn the following:

- How to create your own DLLs in Delphi.
- How to declare import units to automatically make the subroutines in a DLL available to Delphi programs.
- How to use subroutines implemented in DLLs.
- How to take control over loading the DLLs and over resolving the subroutine addresses at run-time.

In the process of learning about DLLs, you are going to create your own DLL containing useful string-manipulation subroutines.

Understanding DLLs

DLLs are one of the most important elements of Windows. DLLs exist primarily to provide services to application programs. Windows itself uses DLLs to make Windows subroutines and resources available to Windows applications. It probably is fair to say that DLLs are the most fundamental concept of Windows architecture.

Windows itself consists largely of three DLLs called KERNEL, USER, and GDI. These libraries contain the code and data for the Windows Application Programming Interface (API).

NEW TERM A *dynamic link library* (*DLL*) is an executable module containing subroutines that Windows programs can call in order to perform common, useful tasks.

A Delphi application program is an executable file that consists of one or more forms or windows. A program interacts with the user at run-time; it retrieves messages and events from a message queue maintained on its behalf by Windows.

In contrast, DLLs are separate libraries of subroutines, containing procedures and functions that can be called by other programs. DLLs are not themselves directly executable, however, and come into play only when another Windows module calls one of the subroutines in the library. Specifically, DLLs do not have their own message queues and rely on the flow of messages and events in the using application.

A user can run several copies, called *instances*, of a program simultaneously. All these instances share the same code in memory. If, however, you run several programs containing the same subroutine library, the same executable code will be cloned in memory. The same routines will be residing in memory in multiple copies.

In other words, if you link the common routines shared among many programs statically to each individual program, as units, you end up with identical code linked into many executable modules. If you consider that each of the various individual programs can be running simultaneously on the same system, you see that virtually identical code may be loaded unnecessarily into memory in multiple copies.

The fact that multiple copies of the same routine may exist in memory results in space being wasted instead of being used for application programs' needs. The solution to this problem is in the form of DLLs and in the process of dynamic linking that eliminates the duplication of common code.

NEW TERM *Dynamic linking* is the process that Windows uses to link a subroutine call in one executable module to the actual function in a dynamic library module at run-time.

NEW TERM *Static linking* refers to the process of resolving subroutine calls by the Delphi integrated compiler/linker at link-time, which occurs right after compilation and is totally transparent to the user. In Delphi, the compile and link steps are integrated so that they both appear to be part of the compilation process.

Furthermore, if you change any of the subroutines in the common, static subroutine library, you must rebuild all the programs that use the library.

If, however, you extract the common subroutines and put them into a separate dynamic library, then only the library contains the routines required by all programs.

There is only one copy of a dynamic library loaded in memory at run-time, no matter how many programs happen to use the services of the library. Additionally, if you change a subroutine in the common library, you need only recompile the library module. The programs that use the library remain intact, unless you have changed the interfaces to the library.

DLLs are similar in concept to Object Pascal units. They represent an additional step in the quest for the separation of concerns among different subsystems, or modules comprising a program, however—another step in the process of modularization of a program.

Object Pascal units are only separate until compile/link-time, at which point they are melted together to form a single executable file. DLLs remain separate even at the time of deployment of an application. DLLs therefore are more autonomous than units and utilize the operating system's (Windows') facilities rather than the language/compiler facilities to achieve modularization and integration of separate modules. The integration occurs at run-time—late in the development cycle, which is desirable from the perspective of reusability and flexibility.

In addition to letting applications share executable code, you can use DLLs to share other resources, such as data and hardware. Windows fonts, for example, actually are shared text-drawing data, and Windows device drivers actually are special DLLs that enable applications to share hardware resources.

Although a dynamic link library can have any valid file name extension, the standard extension is DLL. Only libraries with the default extension of DLL can be loaded automatically by Windows. If the library file has a different extension, it must be loaded explicitly by the program that wants to use it. An application can invoke the standard API `LoadLibrary` function to explicitly load a DLL. You see an example of that later during today's lesson.

Dynamic Linking

When a Windows program is loaded into memory, the calls to the Windows API are resolved to point to the entry of the subroutines in the appropriate DLLs, which also are loaded into memory. Hence, the executable application module relies on the presence of other, supplementary modules. Typically, the program cannot run in the absence of the required external, dynamically linked libraries.

Contrast this with the process of static linking, when the addresses of all subroutines are known beforehand, at compile-time. The compiler/linker can resolve appropriately any static references throughout the program and substitute actual addresses for symbolic names you used in the source code. Static linking results in a fully self-contained executable file.

Creating Custom DLLs

So far, you have been writing Windows programs. Now is the time to develop DLLs for use *by* programs. Many of the principles you have learned for writing Delphi programs also are applicable to writing Delphi DLLs, but there are some important differences.

As mentioned, DLLs enable you to more economically share code and resources among many applications. Although very important in the overall architecture of Windows, custom DLLs are not absolutely necessary for every Windows application. After all, you already have built a fair number of Delphi applications without worrying about the use of DLLs. The fact that every one of these applications relied on the access to Windows DLLs notwithstanding, you did not have to deal with the details of loading and binding to DLLs. This is about to change.

There are several distinctive advantages of DLLs that become increasingly important as your applications become larger, more sophisticated, and complex:

- DLLs enable you to share code and resources among many applications.
- You easily can customize your application for different purposes using DLLs.
- DLLs facilitate the development of complex, large applications by allowing a more strict separation of subsystems.
- DLLs enable you to streamline access to data and data-like resources, such as business-model infrastructures, as well as to hardware devices.

An important point to note is that you can use DLLs written in other language environments, and you can write your own DLLs in Delphi. The interfaces between a DLL and a program are for the most part transparent and totally independent of the implementation language.

Any program, therefore, potentially can call a subroutine in a Delphi-created DLL; whether that program is a C, C++, Visual BASIC, OPAL, dBASE, or any other kind of application; or whether it is an extension to an off-the-shelf application, including macro-language extensions written in Word for Windows or Excel.

Your Delphi programs also can call subroutines in DLLs written in other languages, such as C or C++. In fact, as mentioned, they do it continually, whether or not you are aware of that. Every Delphi program must interact with Windows, and that involves making calls to one, and typically more, of the three main Windows DLLs.

Declaring Libraries

Even though conceptually DLLs can be treated just as more autonomous units, from the perspective of a Pascal programmer, a DLL source code module looks a lot like a program module.

Syntax

Library Module

A dynamic link library (DLL) is defined just like a program, with the reserved word **library** replacing the word **program**:

```
library LibMane;
  <declarations and implementation>
begin
  <optional initialization code>
end.
```

Example:

```
library StrUtils;

  function UpperCaseStr(S: String): String; export;
    begin
      for I := 1 to Length(S) do
        S[I] := UpCase(S[I]);
      Result := S;
    end;

  exports
    UpperCaseStr;

begin
end.
```

A library module starts with a header, consisting of the reserved word **library**, followed by the library name, followed by a semicolon.

21

The library implementation follows much the same rules as the program implementation. You can insert uses clauses; declare types, constants, and variables; and declare and implement subroutines and classes—in other words, everything you could do inside a program.

Similar to how this appears in a program module, there is an executable block, enclosed within a pair of **begin** and **end** keywords, at the end of every library module. Its role is similar to the role of a unit-initialization block, rather than being similar to the role of a program's executable block: it is meant to initialize any local data and objects needed by the library.

The **begin-end** initialization block of a library module may, and often does, remain empty. Unlike the case with units, however, where you could omit the begin keyword of the initialization block when there was no initialization code, in a library, both the **begin** and the **end** keywords must be present even if there are no data structures to initialize.

Using the Exports Clause

One of the main reasons for actually having a library is to be able to reuse common subroutines across a number of different applications. This implies that you will have to implement the subroutines in the first place, in order to be able to use them.

Fortunately, the way you implement subroutines inside a DLL is not much different from the way in which you implement them inside a regular program. In fact, you can use the same source code units that implement subroutines in both programs and DLLs. The subroutines made public by being listed in the interface section of a unit can be used directly in a program by being linked statically to it via the **uses**-clause, or the subroutines can be linked into a DLL and made available to a greater number of applications simultaneously by being "exported" from the DLL.

The important point about building dynamically linked collections of subroutines, from the perspective of making the subroutines available outside the library, is that you must explicitly export those subroutines that you intend to be visible outside of the library by creating an exports clause.

Syntax

Exports Clause

The syntax for the **exports**-clause, in its simplest form, follows:

```
exports
  Subroutine1,
  Subroutine2,
  Subroutine3,
  ...
  SubroutineN;
```

Example:

```
exports
  FillStr,
  LTrimStr,
  RTrimStr;
```

The **exports**-clause begins with the reserved word **exports**, followed by a list of exported subroutines, separated by commas, and terminated by a semicolon.

Only one **exports**-clause may be present in a project. You cannot place an **exports** directive inside a unit belonging to a project, but only inside the main library or program module.

There may be any number of **exports**-clauses in a project's main source file. All the subroutines listed inside all the **exports**-clauses will be made visible to other modules "by name," and by other means, as you see later in this chapter.

When the module containing an **exports**-clause is compiled, the resulting executable file (EXE or DLL) contains special entries that enable Windows to dynamically link the exported subroutines at run-time to all other applications and modules that might need to use them.

The key to successfully exporting a subroutine from a DLL is to make the subroutine itself *exportable*. A subroutine cannot be exported unless you explicitly define it as exportable by placing the **export** directive at the end of the subroutine's declaration heading.

Syntax

Export Directive

The **export** directive makes a subroutine exportable and must be placed after the regular heading in the subroutine's declaration, as in the following example:

```
function Name(<Parameters>): ReturnType; export;
```

or

```
procedure Name(<Parameters>); export;
```

Examples:

```
function StripStr(S: String): String; export;
procedure RefreshBuffers; export;
```

The **export** directive instructs the compiler to create special code at the beginning and at the end of the compiled routine, which enables Windows to use it from another executable module.

Note: Remember that only subroutines that were explicitly exported may (but don't have to) be placed in an **exports** clause's list. A subroutine may be exportable (**export** directive) but not actually exported (**exports** clause).

21

In summary, to make a global subroutine inside a DLL project available to be used by other Windows executable modules, you must to ensure the following:

- The subroutine is declared with the **export** directive—it is *exportable.*
- The subroutine's name is listed inside an **exports** clause of the library module—it actually is *exported.*

Architecting DLLs

As a matter of principle, when building reusable DLLs, you should avoid implementing the subroutines being exported as part of the main library module.

The temptation is there to actually start creating the implementations of the exported subroutines directly inside the main library module: you just start writing code in the main library project file.

This approach, however, quickly leads to large and unmanageable library files. It is exactly for the same reason that you break up programs into separate units that you also should break up libraries into units. It is far easier to manage smaller units with well-defined interface sections, than to keep track of all the subroutines implemented in one place. Bear in mind that you may be implementing both the subroutines you intend to export from the library, and the auxiliary subroutines for the private use of the library itself that are not exported. By using separate units grouping closely related subroutines, you impose an additional layer of organization on the library's code.

An additional benefit to organizing your implementation code in units is that you leave yourself a choice whether to use dynamic linking, or to statically link the implementing unit into an application. On some occasions, you may decide that actually linking the code directly into the application is a better approach; on others, you will be content to use the services encapsulated by your DLL. In either case, it is better to have one unit source file that you can use in both scenarios.

Hence, a better approach to organizing a library's code is to have all the routines, both exported and private, implemented in a separate unit or in a collection of units. The main **`library`** module would have the units it incorporates listed in its **`uses`**-clause, and it would implement the **`exports`**-clause.

You see exactly how to organize your subroutines into separate units, yet make them exported from the library, in the following example.

A Simple Library Example

The best way to illustrate how a DLL is built is by showing you a practical example. You will see that the task of DLL writing has been made reasonably simple by Delphi: much simpler than in more traditional environments. You have to bear in mind, however, that writing DLLs is a traditional coding exercise, and that Delphi in its current incarnation does not support you in any special way beyond giving you the raw capabilities of creating and using DLLs.

You are going to build an example DLL implementing several useful string-handling subroutines.

Follow these steps to create the example project:

1. Create a new, blank Delphi project.
2. Close without saving the default form-unit file, `Unit1`, which Delphi created for you as part of the project. Right-click in the Code Editor window and choose Close Page from the pop-up menu that appears. Answer No when asked whether you want to save the unit.

   The Code Editor window closes because you have no files to edit.
3. Save the project at this point in a separate, empty directory that you created on your disk and called `DLLFIRST`, naming the project file `DLLFIRST.DPR`.

   Your entire project at this point consists of the main program file `DLLFIRST.DPR`.
4. Choose Project Source from the main Delphi View menu.

   The Code Editor reopens, showing you the `DllFirst` program file that looks like the following:

   ```
    1: program Dllfirst;
    2:
    3: uses
    4:   Forms;
    5:
    6: {$R *.RES}
    7:
    8: begin
    9:   Application.Run;
   10: end.
   ```

   You now convert this minimal Delphi program to an equally minimal dynamically linked library.
5. Replace the reserved word **`program`** on line 1 of the `DLLFIRST.DPR` file with the word **`library`**.
6. Remove the code in lines 3 through 6 of the file.
7. Remove line 9 with the `Application.Run` statement.

   Your main source code file now is reduced to the following:

   ```
   library Dllfirst;

   begin
   end.
   ```

   Congratulations. You have just created the world's simplest dynamically linked library! Don't forget to save the project.
8. Choose Compile from the main Delphi Compile menu.

It takes only a fraction of a second to compile this empty library, but you now can verify for yourself that instead of generating an executable program file (EXE) you have succeeded in creating your first DLL: `DLLFIRST.DLL`.

Of course, the library you have created is not particularly useful in its current state. It does not provide any services that a program might use. Soon, you will develop a set of simple character-string manipulation routines that will be made available from this DLL.

An interesting point to note, however, is that the library may be used almost as is to store various binary Windows resources, such as bitmaps, icons, and so on. In this context, the DLL is a repository of dynamically installable resources rather than a collection of subroutines.

Note: If, instead of Compile | Compile, you had chosen Run | Run in the preceding step, the DLL would have been compiled as well, but because it knows that DLLs are not directly executable, Delphi displays an error message: `Cannot run a DLL.`

Note: If you close the project at this point and attempt to open it later, Delphi opens the file but also displays an error message:

```
Error in module DllFirst: uses clause missing or incorrect.
```

What Delphi is telling you is that you don't have a **uses**-clause in your project file. Delphi needs the **uses**-clause to maintain the list of source files belonging to the project. Right now, however, your entire project consists of the single, main project file. Although there is no true need for the **uses**-clause at this point, you have to reintroduce one to keep Delphi code-generation facilities happy.

9. Add a **uses**-clause listing the standard WinTypes unit inside the library module, as follows:

```
uses
  WinTypes;
```

Listing `WinTypes` in the **uses**-clause of the library is "safe" because it does not introduce any real dependencies. `WinTypes` is a unit declaring various data types used by the Windows API. It does not implement any code, so you are not adding any overhead to your library. Also, you later can delete `WinTypes` from the **uses**-clause entirely. You cannot do that right now, because there are no other units in the project and this would eliminate the **uses**-clause altogether; you cannot leave the reserved word **uses** with no unit names listed afterward.

The resulting library module that you need to save to disk looks like the following:

```
library DllFirst;

uses
  WinTypes;

begin
end.
```

Make sure that you save your projects often. Save the project now.

Using *DLLFirst* String-Handling Functions

You now provide some useful functions for handling strings that you can put inside your dynamically linked library. You are going to implement a number of string-handling functions. Follow the directions given along with the explanation of each of the subroutines to create a reusable, dynamically linked library of string functions.

First, you create a separate unit, called `XString`, that implements all your string-handling subroutines.

- ☐ Create a new unit for the project by choosing New Unit from the main Delphi File menu. Save it under the name `XSTRING.PAS` by choosing Save File As from the main Delphi File menu.

The newly created unit is an empty shell that looks like the following:

```
unit XString;

interface

implementation

end.
```

You now are ready to provide the actual string-handling routines inside the `XString` unit.

You will implement the following subroutines:

- ☐ The `FillStr` function returns a string of a single, repeated character value.
- ☐ The `UpCaseFirstStr` function capitalizes the first letter of every word of the passed string argument.
- ☐ The `LTrimStr` function removes leading blanks from the passed string argument.
- ☐ The `RTrimStr` function removes trailing blanks from the passed string argument.
- ☐ The `StripStr` function removes all blanks, whether leading, trailing, or embedded, from the passed string argument.

Note in the following sections that the declarations of the string-handling subroutines to be put inside the interface section of the `XString` unit include the **`export`** directive, while the implementations no longer repeat and, in fact, must not repeat, the directive. The **`export`** directive, as noted earlier, makes these subroutines exportable across the Windows-module (DLL/EXE) boundaries.

FillStr Function

The first function to be included in your DLL's `XString` unit is the `FillStr` function. This classic library function returns a string of the specified length consisting of the indicated character, repeated throughout the entire string a specified number of times.

`FillStr` is declared as follows:

```
function FillStr (C: Char; N: Byte): String; export;
```

The function takes two parameters—first, the character to be repeated (`C`); second, the desired length of the string (`N`) or the number of times to repeat the character `C`.

Enter this declaration inside the interface section of the `XStrings` unit you previously created.

A suggested implementation for the `FillStr` function follows:

```
function FillStr(C : Char; N : Byte): String;
  {Returns a string with N characters of value C}
  begin
    FillChar(Result[1],N,C);
    Result[0] := Chr(N);
  end;
```

The implementation of the `FillStr` function uses a few tricks to get the job done more efficiently.

First, it uses the standard procedure `FillChar` to quickly fill the `Result` string with the desired character value. The alternative approach is to set up a **`for`** loop counting through the subsequent character positions in the result string and stuffing the character to be repeated in these character cells. The standard `FillChar` procedure accomplishes the same effect in a single step.

Second, the `FillStr` subroutine you are building forces the returned string to be of the desired length by setting explicitly the length byte. As you may recall, the length byte of a string variable is the first cell (byte) of the string's character array. `FillStr` sets the length byte directly to ensure that the returned string contains the desired number of characters.

Enter the code of the `FillStr` function inside the implementation section of the `XString` unit file you created.

You can use the `FillStr` function as in the following example:

```
var
  S1,
  S2: String;
begin
  ...
  S1 := FillStr(' ',12);
  S2 := FillStr('#',80);
  ...
end
```

`S1` will contain a string of 12 blanks, and `S2` receives a string of 80 number-sign (`'#'`) characters after execution of the two preceding statements.

UpCaseFirstStr Function

Another useful addition to the set of standard string-management routines already available in Delphi is `UpCaseFirstStr`. It complements the standard `UpperCase` and `LowerCase` string-handling functions from the `SysUtils` unit. `UpCaseFirstStr` provides support for changing the capitalization of the characters in its argument string to the title-like convention of capitalizing the first letter of every word.

`UpCaseFirstStr` is declared as follows:

```
function UpCaseFirstStr(const S: String): String; export;
```

The function takes a single string parameter and returns the same string with the title style of capitalization.

Enter this declaration inside the interface section of the `XStrings` unit.

`UpCaseFirstStr` is implemented as in the following example:

```
 1:   function UpCaseFirstStr(const s: String): String;
 2:     var
 3:       Index: Byte;
 4:       First: Boolean;
 5:     begin
 6:       Result := S;
 7:       First := True;
 8:       for Index := 1 to Length(s) do
 9:         begin
10:           if First then
11:             Result[Index] := UpCase(Result[Index]);
12:           if Result[Index] = ' ' then
13:             First := True
14:           else
15:             First := False;
16:         end;
17:     end;
```


The implementation of the `UpCaseFirstStr` function mainly consists of a **for** loop, in lines 8 through 16, that runs through all the characters in the string and, depending on whether the character is the first letter of a new word, capitalizes it or skips over it.

To keep track of whether the Index variable marks the position of the beginning of a word inside string S at any given point, the First variable is used. The First flag becomes True whenever the current Index corresponds to the first letter of a word inside the string S. The flag is set in lines 12 through 15. The new value of First to be used in the next iteration of the **for**-loop is True whenever the current location in the string S is occupied by a blank (ASCII 32 decimal or " "). This way, after a blank character is encountered, any nonblank after that is treated as the beginning of a new word.

The determination of whether to capitalize the current character is made in line 10 where the statement

```
if First then
```

checks to see whether the First flag is set—whether the *previous* character in the string was blank—and if so, attempts to capitalize the *current* character.

Note that the First flag initially is set to True in line 7, just before the loop begins execution. This implicitly assumes that the first nonblank character in a string also marks the beginning of a new word and forces it to be capitalized. Remember to always initialize your variables.

Enter the code of the UpCaseFirstStr function as shown inside the implementation section of the XString unit file you created.

UpCaseFirstStr is used as follows:

```
var
  S1: String;
begin
  ...
  S1 := UpCaseFirstStr('teach yourself delphi in 21 days.');
  ...
end
```

The string S1 contains

```
'Teach Yourself Delphi in 21 Days.'
```

after the assignment statement is executed.

LTrimStr Function

Often, there is a need to ensure that the string you are working with begins with a meaningful (a nonblank) character. If there are any leading blanks, you may need to remove them first. The standard procedure Val for converting strings of digits into their numeric representations, for example, requires that the first character of the argument string is a valid, nonblank digit. Before you can pass a string of digits to Val for conversion, you must trim the string's leading blanks.

The LTrimStr function is designed to perform the "trimming" of the leading blanks on the left-hand side of the passed string argument.

Enter the following declaration inside the interface section of the `XStrings` unit:

```
function LTrimStr(const S: String): String; export;
```

The only parameter `S` passed to this function is the string to be trimmed. The result returned is the same string, but without any leading blanks. If there are no leading blanks in the string `S` passed in the argument, the function returns the argument string unchanged.

`LTrimStr` is implemented as follows:

```
 1:  function LTrimStr(const S: String): String;
 2:    var
 3:      Index,
 4:      MaxIndex: Integer;
 5:    begin
 6:      Index := 1;
 7:      MaxIndex := Length(S);
 8:      while (Index <= MaxIndex)
 9:      and (S[Index] = ' ') do
10:        Inc(Index);
11:      Result := Copy(S,Index,MaxIndex-Index+1);
12:    end;
```

The implementation of the `LTrimStr` function relies on the **`while`**-loop in lines 8 through 10 to determine the position of the first nonblank character in the string. The loop terminates when a nonblank character is found or when the loop reaches the end of the string.

This last consideration is especially important to take care of if the function is to be a robust, production-quality subroutine that can be trusted at all times. It is necessary to ensure proper behavior in the case of the passed argument string containing no leading blanks, as well as in the case of the argument consisting of blanks only. In the former case, the argument string is returned unchanged; in the latter case, the result of trimming all leading blanks in a string consisting of blanks only is returned: a null (empty) string.

The loop counter `Index` is initialized in line 6 to point to the beginning of the argument string. To ensure that the loop does not run off past the end of the string, a guardian value `MaxIndex` is established in line 7. `MaxIndex` is the index of the last character of the string, and is equal to the original length of the string.

After the index of the first nonblank character of the argument string is determined, the portion of the argument string `S` containing the leading blanks is cut out, and the remainder is returned as the function result. Line 11 uses the standard string function `Copy` to select only the meaningful, nonblank portion of the original argument string `S`, leaving out the leading blanks from the function's result, as required.

Enter the code of the `LTrimStr` function as shown inside the implementation section of the `XString` unit.

`LTrimStr` is used as follows:

```
var
  S1: String;
begin
  ...
  S1 := LTrimStr('       Teach Yourself Delphi');
  S2 := LTrimStr('   123');
  S3 := LTrimStr('   456   ');
  ...
end
```

After the assignment statements executes,

- S1 contains `'Teach Yourself Delphi'`
- S1 contains `'123'`
- S1 contains `'456   '`

Note in this case that the function has no effect on any terminating or trailing blanks. This is the job for the next trimming function, `RTrimStr`.

RTrimStr Function

`RTrimStr` is very similar in concept to the `LTrimStr` function you implemented in the preceding section. Instead of removing the leading blanks, however, it removes any trailing blanks on the right-hand side of the string, thereby ensuring that the result is as short as possible. A typical use of the `RTrimStr` function is in preparation for converting the string to a number using the standard `Val` procedure.

Enter the following declaration inside the interface section of the `XStrings` unit:

```
function RTrimStr(const S: String): String; export;
```

As you can see, the declaration of `RTrimStr` is nearly identical to that of `LTrimStr`.

`RTrimStr` is implemented as follows:

```
1:   function RTrimStr(const S: String) : String;
2:     var
3:       Index: Integer;
4:     begin
5:       Index := Length(S);
6:       while (Index > 0) and (S[Index] = ' ') do
7:         Dec(Index);
8:       Result := Copy(S,1,Index)
9:     end;
```

The trick of implementing the `RTrimStr` function that makes it even simpler than the implementation of `LTrimStr` is that the **while**-loop in lines 6 and 7, which determines the position of the last nonblank character of the string argument, runs "backward," starting at the end of the string and proceeding toward the beginning. Once the loop counter `Index`, first initialized to mark the last character of the argument string, indicates a position of a nonblank character in the argument string, the loop has skipped all the trailing blanks and may terminate.

Just in case the argument string consists of blanks only, the loop condition checks whether the iteration reached the beginning of the string, indicated by the value of `Index` below 1, in which case it also terminates the **while**-loop.

After the **while**-loop is finished, the `Index` variable holds the position of the last nonblank character of the argument string. As before, the `Copy` function can be used to extract the nonblank leading portion of the string and to return it to the caller as the function result.

Enter the code of the `RTrimStr` function as shown inside the implementation section of the `XString` unit.

The `RTrimStr` function can be used as follows:

```
var
  S1,
  S2,
  S3: String;
begin
  ...
  S1 := RTrimStr('Teach Yourself Delphi        ');
  S2 := RTrimStr('123    ');
  S3 := RTrimStr('    456    ');
  ...
end
```

After the assignment statements execute,

- `S1` contains `'Teach Yourself Delphi'`
- `S2` contains `'123'`
- `S3` contains `'    456'`

`RTrimStr` removes the trailing blanks from the argument, but leaves the leading blanks still present.

StripStr Function

The last string-handling subroutine you implement inside your `DLLFirst` library is `StripStr`.

`StripStr` removes all blanks—whether they are leading, trailing, or embedded inside the argument string—and returns a result consisting of nonblank characters only.

The declaration of the `StripStr` function is similar to that of the previous string-trimming functions.

Enter the following declaration inside the interface section of the XStrings unit:

```
function StripStr(const S: String): String; export;
```

The implementation of the StripStr function makes use of a **for**-loop because the number of iterations is known in advance. The loop must run through all the characters in the argument string, removing any blanks as it visits the consecutive character locations.

The implementation of the StripStr function follows:

```
1:    function StripStr(const s: String): String;
2:      var
3:        Index : Integer;
4:      begin
5:        Result := '';
6:        for Index := 1 to Length(S) do
7:          if S[Index] <> ' ' then
8:            Result := Result + S[Index];
9:      end;
```

The **for**-loop in lines 6 through 8 visits every character position of the argument string S, and makes a determination in line 7 of whether the current character is a blank.

If the current character is a blank, it simply is skipped, and the loop continues with another iteration. Otherwise, the statement in line 8 appends the current character from the argument to the function's Result string. Thus, the resulting string is accumulated one character at a time, during the execution of the **for**-loop, skipping the blank characters in the process, and including only the nonblank characters.

The Result variable, which is an implicit variable of the same type as the return type of the function—String, in this case—and which automatically is available inside every function, is initialized in line 5 to be an empty string. This ensures that the result of the function is defined even if the argument received consists of blanks only, so that the assignment in line 8 never is executed. It also ensures that the Result is defined even if the argument string is empty and the **for**-loop itself never executes at all.

To use the StripStr function, write code similar to the following:

```
var
  S1,
  S2,
  S3: String;
begin
  ...
  S1 := StripStr('     Teach Yourself Delphi      ');
  S2 := StripStr('123   ');
  S3 := StripStr('   456   ');
  S4 := StripStr('   789');
  ...
end
```

After the assignment statements execute,

- S1 contains 'TeachYourselfDelphi' (a string with no embedded, leading, or trailing blanks)
- S2 contains '123'
- S3 contains '456' (RTrimStr removes both the trailing and the leading blanks from the argument)
- S4 contains '789'

You can use StripStr whenever you need to strip all blanks from the argument string.

Using the *XString* Unit

By now, you have completed the implementation of the XString unit containing the five useful string-handling functions.

To help you verify that the code you entered piece by piece is complete and valid, Listing 21.1 shows the XString unit in its entirety.

Listing 21.1. The XString unit.

```
unit XString;

{
A collection of String-handling routines complementing
the standard ones from the SysUtils unit.
}

interface

  function FillStr(C : Char; N : Byte): String; export;
    {Returns a string with N characters of value C}
  function UpCaseFirstStr(const s: String): String; export;
    {Capitalizes the first letter of every word}
  function LTrimStr(const S: String) : String; export;
    {Trims the leading blanks}
  function RTrimStr(const S: String) : String; export;
    {Trims the trailing blanks}
  function StripStr(const s: String): String; export;
    {Strips all blanks}

implementation

  function FillStr(C : Char; N : Byte): String;
    {Returns a string with N characters of value C}
    begin
      FillChar(Result[1],N,C);
      Result[0] := Chr(N);
    end;
```


continues

Listing 21.1. continued

```
function UpCaseFirstStr(const s: String): String;
  {Capitalizes the first letter of every word}
  var
    Index: Byte;
    First: Boolean;
  begin
    Result := S;
    First := True;
    for Index := 1 to Length(s) do
      begin
        if First then
          Result[Index] := UpCase(Result[Index]);
        if Result[Index] = ' ' then
          First := True
        else
          First := False;
      end;
  end;


function LTrimStr(const S: String): String;
  {Trims the leading blanks}
  var
    Index,
    MaxIndex: Integer;
  begin
    Index := 1;
    MaxIndex := Length(S);
    while (Index <= MaxIndex)
    and (S[Index] = ' ') do
      Inc(Index);
    Result := Copy(S,Index,MaxIndex-Index+1);
  end;


function RTrimStr(const S: String) : String;
  {Trims the trailing blanks}
  var
    Index: Integer;
  begin
    Index := Length(S);
    while (Index > 0) and (S[Index] = ' ') do
      Dec(Index);
    Result := Copy(S,1,Index)
  end;


function StripStr(const s: String): String;
  {Strips all blanks}
  var
    Index : Integer;
  begin
    Result := '';
```

```
84:       for Index := 1 to Length(S) do
85:         if S[Index] <> ' ' then
86:           Result := Result + S[Index];
87:     end;
88:
89: end.
```

The code in Listing 21.1 repeats the snippets of code you have entered based on the examples in the earlier sections. The `XString` unit comprises a collection of exportable string-handling functions. It is repeated here for completeness to help you get a general feeling for the unit's overall organization.

Some comments were added to make the code more readable. It is always a good idea to comment your code, even if you do not expect anyone else but yourself to use the code. You will be surprised how much you forget about the details of implementation of a particular subroutine or object after only a few weeks away from directly dealing with that code.

The unit implements five functions: `FillStr`, `UpCaseFirstStr`, `LTrimStr`, `RTrimStr`, and `StripStr`.

Each of the functions implemented inside the **`implementation`** section of the unit in lines 21 through 89 is listed in the **`interface`** section in lines 8 through 20. As explained earlier, each of the functions listed is made exportable by placing the **`export`** directive after the function declaration. This makes it possible to include the subroutines in an **`exports`** clause and to make them available outside the DLL.

You have just finished the implementation of the string-handling functions you want to make available from your DLL. Now is the time to complete the dynamically linked library project by actually exporting the functions so that they are visible and accessible from outside the DLLFIRST.DLL.

Exporting String Functions

As you recall from the discussion at the beginning of today's lesson, you must list the functions you want to make available to client applications inside an **`exports`** clause of your library source-code file.

Listing 21.2 shows you how to complete the library project by actually exporting the string-handling functions.

Enter the code as shown in Listing 21.2. Choose Project Source from the Delphi View menu, if necessary, to get back to the main library file.

Listing 21.2. Exporting the string-handling functions from the main library file.

```
 1: library DllFirst;
 2:
 3: uses
 4:   WinTypes,
 5:   XString in 'XSTRING.PAS';
 6:
 7: exports
 8:   FillStr,
 9:   UpCaseFirstStr,
10:   LTrimStr,
11:   RTrimStr,
12:   StripStr;
13:
14: begin
15: end.
```

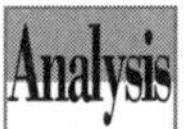

The code in Listing 21.2 shows you how to make the routines you implemented inside the `XString` unit visible to applications using the `DllFirst` DLL.

The unit `XString` is listed in the **`uses`**-clause of the **`library`**-module in line 5 in order to make its interface visible inside the library file. This is necessary so that you can reference the names of the subroutines you want to export.

Lines 7 through 12 list the exported subroutines.

As a result of your entering the **`exports`** clause as shown, the names of the five subroutines you listed will be available so that applications can use the services of the library.

Make sure that you recompile the `DLLFirst` project so that the executable DLL reflects all the latest changes you made.

You have successfully implemented a string-handling DLL that exports five functions. You now are going to look at the other side of the dynamic-linking equation: the application's side.

Using DLLs

You may be surprised to know that, whether directly or indirectly, you have been using dynamically linked libraries all the time when writing Delphi applications. You may have not realized it, but every Delphi applications uses, at the minimum, the Windows DLLs: KERNEL, USER, and GDI.

The key to being able to access externally implemented subroutines in DLLs is by creating import units that the application that wants to use the DLL's services must incorporate in its uses clauses.

The `WinProcs` unit, for example, imports the subroutines defined in the three Windows DLLs mentioned, comprising the Windows API. To be able to use the subroutines implemented inside the USER, KERNEL, or GDI module, you must include `WinProcs` in the uses clause of your application.

You now are going to create a corresponding import unit for the `DLLFirst` custom library you created earlier.

Creating the Import Unit

You are about to develop a test application that will use the subroutines implemented inside the `DllFirst` unit. Follow these steps:

1. If the `DllFirst` project you have been developing still is open, close it by choosing Close Project from the File menu.
2. Create a new, blank Delphi project and call it `DllTest` (`DLLTEST.DPR`). Save the main form unit of the new project (`Unit1` by default) as FrmFirst (`FRMFIRST.PAS`).
3. Choose New Unit from the File menu.

   A new, minimal unit file is created by Delphi. This will be the import unit enabling your application to use the subroutines encapsulated inside the DLLFIRST.DLL.
4. Save the new unit file under the name `First` (`FIRST.PAS`).

Interfacing the DLL

The interface section of the library import unit looks exactly like the interface section of any regular unit. It simply lists the subroutines available, which, in this case, are the subroutines exported by the DLL.

The difference between an import unit and a regular unit is in the implementation of each. Whereas the implementation section of a regular unit must provide the actual implementation code, the implementation section of a library import unit delegates the details of the implementation to the external library and merely binds the subroutine headings declared in the interface to the implementation provided elsewhere. Remember that you already have implemented the string-handling subroutines inside the `DllFirst` library. There is no point in repeating that code in the library import unit. The only missing link is to be able to tell the using application which of the subroutines listed in the interface of the unit correspond to which of the DLL's exported entry points.

To delegate the details of the implementation of a subroutine to an external module and to allow the program to compile without actually "seeing" the subroutine's implementation directly, use the **`external`** directive.

Syntax

External Directive

The **external** directive replaces the implementation of a subroutine, indicating that it is given outside the current project. The **external** directive is placed after the implementation heading of a subroutine as follows:

```
procedure Name1; external ModuleName;
function Name2; external ModuleName;
```

Examples:

```
procedure Clear; external 'CUSTOM';
function StripStr; external 'DLLFIRST';
```

The **external** directive completely replaces the implementation of a subroutine. Instead of the familiar **begin-end** pair of keywords and the implementation code inside the block they delimit, the **external** directive indicates that the actual implementation code is compiled and deployed separately, outside of the current project.

There are several possibilities regarding what comes after the **external** keyword. The simplest of these possibilities calls for the filename of the library, `DLLFIRST` in this case, to be included after the directive. This enables the compiler to bind the subroutine declared inside the import unit to its implementation residing in a DLL by the declared name.

When giving the name of the external library in this way, a filename extension of DLL is assumed (the library on disk actually must have the extension of DLL). It is possible to have DLLs with other extensions, but Windows is capable of automatically loading libraries only with the default extension of DLL.

When you run the program using this type of binding, after you make a call into the DLL, Windows attempts to resolve it by using the subroutine name declared in the import unit and searching for the same name inside the indicated DLL.

For example, a statement like

```
function StripStr; external 'DLLFIRST';
```

indicates that the implementation for the `StripStr` function resides in the external library `DLLFIRST.DLL`. Windows automatically loads `DLLFIRST.DLL` and searches for a subroutine `StripStr` matching the requested function by name to resolve the call.

You soon will learn about other ways of binding subroutines declared on the application (EXE) side to their DLL-based implementations. Right now, you continue with the `DllFirst` example, using the simplest possible binding: binding by the declared name.

Interfacing *DllFirst*

Based on the comments earlier in this chapter, you are ready to provide the interface unit for the `DllFirst` library.

The good news is that the declarative part of the unit (the subroutine headings that you need to list there) looks almost exactly like the one you already have entered inside the interface of the `XString` unit.

Listing 21.3 provides the complete import unit for the `DllFirst` library.

Listing 21.3. FIRST.PAS—an import unit for the `DllFirst` library.

```
unit First;

{
(Implicit) Library Import Unit for DLLFIRST.DLL.
This unit is to be listed in the uses-clauses
of applications wishing to use the services
of DLLFIRST.DLL.
}

interface

  function FillStr(C : Char; N : Byte): String;
  function UpCaseFirstStr(const s: String): String;
  function LTrimStr(const S: String): String;
  function RTrimStr(const S: String): String;
  function StripStr(const s: String): String;

implementation

  const
    LibName = 'DLLFIRST';

  function FillStr;        external LibName;
  function UpCaseFirstStr; external LibName;
  function LTrimStr;       external LibName;
  function RTrimStr;       external LibName;
  function StripStr;       external LibName;

end.
```

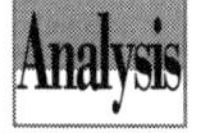

The code in Listing 21.3 implements a library import unit for the `DLLFIRST` library you implemented previously.

The interface section in lines 10 through 17 provides declarations of the subroutines imported from the external library. Note that the function headings are (and, in fact, must be) identical to those in `XSTRING.PAS`, with the exception of the **export** directive, which is missing in the import unit. The import unit does not implement these functions, but instead provides a way of importing their implementations from an external DLL. Hence, there is no need for an **export** directive here.

The implementation section of the unit in Listing 21.3, instead of providing the implementations of the functions listed in the unit's interface, provides their external bindings that enable Windows to find the appropriate implementation at run-time.

Lines 23 through 27 of the listing consist of the implementation headings for each of the imported subroutines, followed by the **external** directives indicating the library from which the functions are to be imported.

Note that you have a great deal of flexibility in how you can specify the library name. The name of the library is provided as a string constant in lines 20 and 21, so that the constant name is repeated with the external directives, and the constant itself is defined in line 21. This approach makes it easy to change the name of the external library, because the constant declaration in line 21 is the only place where you would need to change it before recompiling the import unit.

Remember that recompiling the import unit does not cause the DLL itself to be recompiled. The two entities are totally separate. In fact, it is possible to create discrepancies between the two entities. You can declare the same subroutines with different numbers of parameters on either side, for example, that lead to potentially serious and sometimes hard-to-find bugs. Be forewarned and always double-check whether the subroutine declarations inside the import unit correspond exactly to those declared in the DLL.

The import unit shown in Listing 21.3 is a typical example of a simple import unit, using the implicit binding. *Implicit* here means that you don't have to do anything special for the calls to any of the listed subroutines to be resolved automatically at run-time, beyond declaring them with the **external** directives as shown. Windows takes care of the details of when and how to load the external library and how to obtain the actual run-time addresses of the subroutines you are calling.

You already have taken the first step toward the creation of the unit shown in Listing 21.3. Namely, you have created the `FIRST.PAS` import unit, whose function is to import implicitly the subroutines from the `DLLFIRST` module.

Complete the library import unit `FIRST.PAS` by entering the code as shown in Listing 21.3. Make sure that you have saved the unit file before proceeding.

Creating the Example Program

You now are ready to actually try the external subroutines you have created and imported via the `FIRST.PAS` import unit.

In order to visualize the results returned by the various external functions, you are going to create a simple form-based Delphi application. Follow these steps:

1. Select the `FrmFirst` unit and bring the Form Designer window to the foreground.
2. Inside the Form Designer, place two copies of the `Edit` component from the "Standard" page of the Component Palette inside the form: `Edit1`, `Edit2`, as they are named by default, one below the other. Clear their `Text` property so that they appear blank on the form.
3. Change the `ReadOnly` property of the second edit box, `Edit2`, to `True`. Change its font's `Color` property to `clRed`.
4. Place a `Label` component, to become `Label1` by default, from the same Component Palette page on the form between the two edit boxes. Change the label's `AutoSize` property to `False`, and extend the enclosing box so that it accommodates the names of the external subroutines. Clear the `Caption` property of the label so that it initially appears blank.
5. Place several `Button` components on the form, one for each of the functions: `UpCaseStr`, `LTrimStr`, `RTrimStr`, and `StripStr`. Rename the buttons (named by default `Button1`, `Button2`, and so on) to `ButtonUpCase`, `ButtonLTrim`, `ButtonRTrim`, and `ButtonStrip`, respectively. Change the `Caption` property of the buttons to reflect the functions they represent: `UpCaseStr`, `LTrimStr`, and so on.

   The completed main form of the example program `DLLTest` is shown in Figure 21.1.

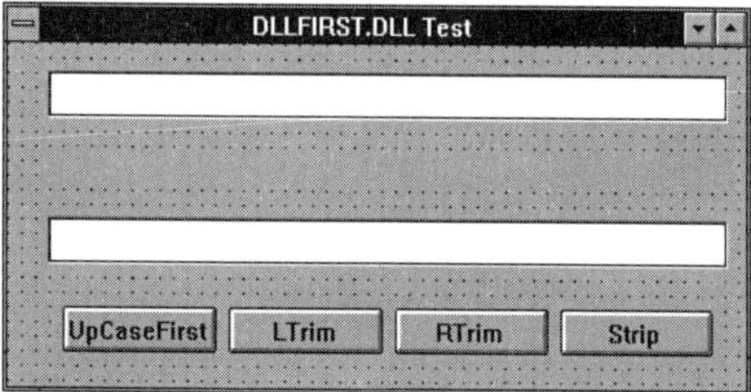

Figure 21.1.
The DLLTest program's main form.

6. Create the default empty shell event-handler form procedure method for the `ButtonUpCaseFirst` button. Enter the following code inside the created method:

```
procedure TForm1.ButtonUpCaseFirstClick(Sender: Tobject);
begin
  Edit2.Text := UpCaseFirstStr(Edit1.Text);
  Label1.Caption := (Sender as TButton).Caption;
end;
```

The first of the two statements exercises one of the subroutines you have implemented inside the external library: `UpCaseFirstStr`. After the user clicks the `UpCaseFirst` button, the contents of `Edit1` edit box are converted via a call to the external `UpCaseFirstStr` function and the result is displayed inside the `Edit2` box.

The second of the two statements inside the event handler updates the contents of the `Label1` component so that its `Caption` property reflects the function most recently applied. The label's caption is set to the caption of the sending button.

Note how the type of the argument to the `TForm1.ButtonUpCaseFirstClick` method is assumed to be a `TButton`. The **as** type conversion is used on the generic `TObject`-typed `Sender` argument to obtain the desired caption.

Complete the event-handling mechanism of the `FrmFirst` form unit by providing event handlers for the `OnClick` event of the remaining buttons. The resulting unit is shown in Listing 21.4. Be careful to copy everything shown in Listing 21.4 inside your own form unit, including the **uses**-clause in the implementation section, as discussed in the following text.

Listing 21.4. The completed form unit of the example DLLTest program.

```
unit FrmFirst;

interface

uses
  SysUtils, WinTypes, WinProcs, Messages, Classes,
  Graphics, Controls, Forms, Dialogs, StdCtrls;

type
  TForm1 = class(TForm)
    Edit1: TEdit;
    Edit2: TEdit;
    Label1: TLabel;
    ButtonUpCaseFirst: TButton;
    ButtonLTrim: TButton;
    ButtonRTrim: TButton;
    ButtonStrip: TButton;
    procedure ButtonUpCaseFirstClick(Sender: TObject);
    procedure ButtonLTrimClick(Sender: TObject);
    procedure ButtonRTrimClick(Sender: TObject);
    procedure ButtonStripClick(Sender: TObject);
  private
    { Private declarations }
  public
    { Public declarations }
  end;

var
  Form1: TForm1;

implementation
```

```
32:
33: uses
34:   First;
35:
36: {$R *.DFM}
37:
38: procedure TForm1.ButtonUpCaseFirstClick(Sender: TObject);
39: begin
40:   Edit2.Text := UpCaseFirstStr(Edit1.Text);
41:   Label1.Caption := (Sender as TButton).Caption;
42: end;
43:
44: procedure TForm1.ButtonLTrimClick(Sender: TObject);
45: begin
46:   Edit2.Text := LTrimStr(Edit1.Text);
47:   Label1.Caption := (Sender as TButton).Caption;
48: end;
49:
50: procedure TForm1.ButtonRTrimClick(Sender: TObject);
51: begin
52:   Edit2.Text := RTrimStr(Edit1.Text);
53:   Label1.Caption := (Sender as TButton).Caption;
54: end;
55:
56: procedure TForm1.ButtonStripClick(Sender: TObject);
57: begin
58:   Edit2.Text := StripStr(Edit1.Text);
59:   Label1.Caption := (Sender as TButton).Caption;
60: end;
61:
62: end.
```

Most of the skeleton code in Listing 21.4 has been generated by Delphi in response to your visually placing components on the form, and to your creating default `OnClick` handlers for the button components.

You have entered explicitly two executable statements for each of the event handlers created.

The first of these statements applies the appropriate external function; the second updates the visible label to give a visual clue to the user.

The code you have entered is listed in lines 40 and 41, 46 and 47, 52 and 53, and 58 and 59.

Note the **uses**-clause in lines 33 and 34. This is where you are making the imported, external subroutines visible to the code inside the `FormFirst` unit. Including `First` in the **uses**-clause makes it possible to call the external functions that are declared there. Without having the unit `First` listed in the **uses**-clause, attempting to call any of the imported subroutines would result in a compile-time error—"Unknown Identifier."

Compile and run the example program. The `DLLTest` example should appear as shown in Figure 21.2 and should enable you to enter a string value inside the top edit box (`Edit1` component).

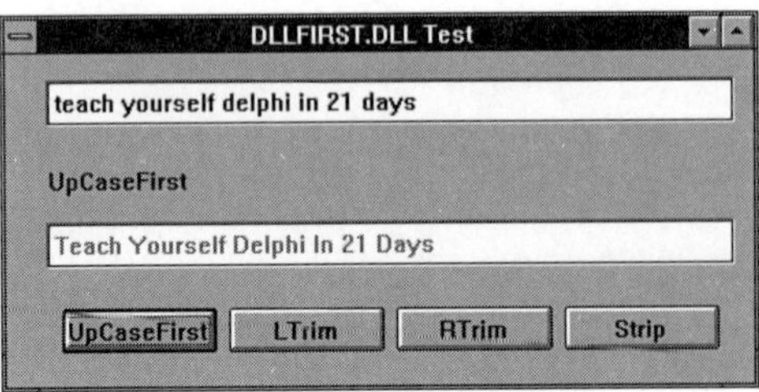

Figure 21.2.
The DLLTest program.

After you enter a text string inside the first edit box (`Edit1` component) and press one of the function buttons, the result of applying the external function appears inside the second edit box at the bottom (`Edit2` component).

The fact that you are calling external functions each time a button is pressed is completely transparent to the user, as well as to the application programmer. The functions just appear to work, regardless of where they were implemented. You call them in exactly the same way you would call functions implemented in a unit linked statically to the program.

Exporting by Ordinal

Consider a variation on the way in which you exported the string-handling functions from the `DllFirst` library.

Recall that the exports clause of the `DllFirst` library module looked like this:

```
exports
  FillStr,
  UpCaseFirstStr,
  LTrimStr,
  RTrimStr,
  StripStr;
```

In this case, the functions were exported simply by their names declared in Pascal code. There is another way of exporting subroutines from DLLs, however: by ordinal number.

Syntax

Exporting By Ordinal Number

The following is the general syntax for exporting subroutines by an ordinal number:

```
exports
  Subroutine1Name index <Number1>,
  Subroutine2Name index <Number2>,
  ...
  SubroutineNName index <NumberN>;
```

Example:

```
exports
  LTrimStr index 13,
  RTrimStr index 14;
```

To export a subroutine by an ordinal number, you must list it inside the **exports** clause of the library module with the additional **index** directive specifying the ordinal number by which the subroutine is to be known.

The ordinal number you specify after the **index** keyword must be a true constant expression evaluating to a 16-bit value (Word) at compile-time.

Remember that exporting a subroutine by ordinal number is always in addition to exporting it by name. The client application will have the capability to bind dynamically to the exported subroutine by ordinal number, in addition to being able to bind to it simply by the declared name, as before.

You now can change the **exports** clause of the `DLLFirst` library to the following:

```
exports
  FillStr index 11,
  UpCaseFirstStr index 12,
  LTrimStr index 13,
  RTrimStr index 14,
  StripStr index 15;
```

By doing so, you have introduced an explicit ordinal number by which each of the routines may be identified by Windows at run-time in addition to being identified by their names.

Importing by Ordinal

The client application has the capability to import the subroutines by their declared names, even if they were explicitly exported by an ordinal number. The client, however, also has the capability to import the subroutines by their ordinal numbers, if that's more convenient.

Importing subroutines by an ordinal results in programs running slightly faster; it is more efficient than doing so by name. In the latter case, Windows must exert extra effort to search for the name of the subroutine and to convert it into an actual callable address.

However, importing by ordinal runs a potentially greater risk of making an incorrect connection to the DLL. Importing by name is less error-prone.

Syntax

Importing Subroutines by Ordinal Number

The general syntax for importing subroutines by ordinal follows:

```
procedure Name1; external ModuleName index <Index1>;
function Name2; external ModuleName index <Index2>;
```

Examples:

```
procedure Clear; external 'CUSTOM' index $11;
function StripStr; external 'DLLFIRST' index 47;
```

To import a subroutine by a specific ordinal number, rather than by a name, place the index directive, followed by a number, after the external part of the subroutine external binding. The number after the index directive may be a decimal or hexadecimal constant, or a constant expression using symbolic names.

As an example of how to import subroutines by ordinal numbers rather than by their names, consider the modified `FIRST.PAS` library import unit, as shown in Listing 21.5, which utilizes the "import by ordinal" feature to rename the subroutines being imported.

Listing 21.5. A modified library import unit for the example `DllFirst` using the "import by ordinal" feature.

```
unit First;

{
Modified Library Import Unit for DLLFIRST.DLL.
This unit is to be listed in the uses clauses
of applications wishing to use the services
of DLLFIRST.DLL.
}

interface

  function XFillString(C : Char; N : Byte): String;
  function XTitleString(const s: String): String;
  function XLeftTrimString(const S: String): String;
  function XRightTrimString(const S: String): String;
  function XStripString(const s: String): String;

implementation

  const
    LibName = 'DLLFIRST';

  function XFillString;      external LibName index 11;
  function XTitleString;     external LibName index 12;
  function XLeftTrimString;  external LibName index 13;
  function XRightTrimString; external LibName index 14;
  function XStripString;     external LibName index 15;

end.
```

The library import unit shown in Listing 21.5 is functionally exactly equivalent to the import unit shown in Listing 21.3. The difference here is that this modified import unit renames the imported functions so that they are known to the using application under different names than their declared names inside the DLL that implements them.

This trick is possible thanks to the "import by ordinal" feature of Windows, which enables you to bind a subroutine prototype inside an import unit to an arbitrary external subroutine.

The **external** declarations in lines 23 through 27 assume that the subroutines were exported by the specified ordinal numbers from the DLL.

Note that the changes to the import unit do not affect the signatures of the imported functions: their parameter lists and return types remain identical to those in Listing 21.3. This is understandable once you realize that you are importing the exact same subroutines as before, implemented inside the `DLLFirst` library. The signatures of these subroutines did not change just because you chose to import them in a different way.

Exporting by Different Name

The flexibility of choosing a different name for an imported subroutine does not actually depend on it being exported by an ordinal number. It still is possible to import a subroutine by a name different than the export name specified within the DLL.

Correspondingly, it is possible to export a subroutine from a DLL under a different name than the name declared in the source code. Both these feats are accomplished with the **name** directive.

Syntax

Exporting by Different Name

The following is the general syntax for exporting subroutines by a name other than the original declared name:

```
exports
  Subroutine1Name name 'Name1',
  Subroutine2Name name 'Name2',
  ...
  SubroutineNName name 'NameN';
```

Example:

```
exports
  LTrimStr name 'TrimStringOnLeft',
  RTrimStr name 'TrimStringOnRight'';
```

The **name** directive is used much like the **index** directive inside the **exports** clause to make the exported subroutines known externally under their assumed names.

The **name** directive also can be used to import subroutines under different names than those under which they were exported.

Syntax

Importing Subroutines by a Different Name

The general syntax for importing subroutines by a name different than the name under which they were exported follows:

```
procedure Name1; external ModuleName name 'ExternalName1';
function Name2; external ModuleName name 'ExternalName2';
```

Examples:

```
procedure Clear; external 'CUSTOM' name 'CustomDLLClear';
function StripStr; external 'DLLFIRST' name 'XStripStr';
```

The **name** directive therefore can be used on both the exporting and the importing side to resolve naming conflicts, or simply to change the name of the subroutine being bound dynamically for convenience reasons.

Explicitly Loading Libraries

So far, you have learned the techniques involving import units where the subroutines to be imported are identified with the external directive. Import units enable the subroutines in DLLs to be imported implicitly; the process of loading the library and resolving the address of the subroutine at run-time is automatic and transparent to the programmer using the DLL, and it is the responsibility of Windows.

The implicitly loaded DLLs usually are loaded by Windows at the time the application starts. If any of the DLLs imported implicitly is missing or simply cannot be found, the application fails to load. The application never gets a chance to correct the problem by prompting the user to specify the location of the required files and changing to the indicated directory, for example. Windows prevents the application from loading before it even can respond to user events.

Another serious drawback to using an implicit import is that the name of the DLL has to be hard coded, or fully known at compile-time. As you may recall from the earlier sections, the name of the implicitly imported DLL must be a true string constant.

Fortunately, there is a way to gain an even greater control over the process of loading DLLs. Instead of importing the required subroutines implicitly via an external statement, you can take the responsibility for loading the DLL into memory and retrieving the addresses of the subroutines inside that DLL explicitly. This way, you can defer loading the library until you can determine at run-time what the name of the library is and where it is located.

Dynamically Loading a DLL

The key to explicitly loading a dynamically linked library is the pair of `LoadLibrary` and `GetProcAddress` functions that are part of the standard Windows API. The two functions always are used in conjunction.

To be able to explicitly load a DLL, you must issue a call to `LoadLibrary`. `LoadLibrary` is declared in the `WinProcs` unit, as follows:

```
function LoadLibrary(LibFileName: PChar): THandle;
```

You can use this function by passing it a string value as follows:

```
var
  ALibrary: THandle;
begin
  ...
  ALibrary := LoadLibrary('dllfirst.dll');
  ...
end
```

This example, however, hides a number of difficulties and issues that arise when you attempt to use the `LoadLibrary` function.

The first issue you must deal with is making sure that `WinProcs` unit is in the **uses** clause of the unit or module in which you intend to use `LoadLibrary`.

The second issue you must consider is that the function takes a single parameter, `LibFileName`, which is of type `PChar`. So far, you have avoided dealing with the non-Pascal string types, known as null-terminated strings. The standard string type was sufficient for most purposes. Note, however, that strings are limited to 255 characters, while null-terminated strings are not and may run up to 64KB characters. A `PChar` is essentially a null-terminated string (the issue of pointers deliberately is avoided here) for all intents and purposes.

Null-terminated strings are native to the Windows API, but Delphi shields you from them most of the time. When you need to make a direct call to an API subroutine, however, there is no "protection;" you are dealing with Windows directly and must use the data types that Windows expects.

NEW TERM A *null-terminated string* is an array of characters. Unlike Pascal strings, which have the length byte at the beginning, null-terminated strings do not explicitly store their lengths, but instead mark their ends with the null-character (ASCII 0)—hence, their name. A null-terminated string can be much longer than a Pascal string, up to the maximum limit of 64KB.

The `LoadLibrary` function expects you to pass the filename of the library in the form of a null-terminated string. The example in this section looks deceptively simple because it hides the fact that the string passed as the actual parameter is a null-terminated string:

```
'dllfirst.dll'
```

This line is treated by the compiler as the native Pascal string or a null-terminated string, depending on the context. In this case, because the function expects a null-terminated string, the compiler ensures that the literal constant is treated as such. This is possible only because the call uses a literal constant. Otherwise, without the additional information from the context in which the literal constant is used, you would not be able to tell whether

```
'dllfirst.dll'
```

refers to a Pascal string or a null-terminated string. Both look exactly the same when written as true constants.

Typically, however, you would not use literal constants for the filename with the `LoadLibrary` function. After all, you can import the library of interest implicitly using static constants. The advantage of using `LoadLibrary` is to be able to specify a variable as its parameter, thereby filling the actual value of the string at run-time. This is where the incompatibility problem between Pascal `Strings` and null-terminated Windows strings creeps in. The compiler does not accept a Pascal string variable in place of the actual parameter for the `LoadLibrary` function.

Warning: You must provide the complete filename in a call to the `LoadLibrary` function. At the minimum, this involves providing the filename and the extension. Because filename extensions other than the default DLL are possible, no default extension is assumed. You have to explicitly supply the extension, if any, even if it is DLL.

Fortunately, you don't have to worry too much about null-terminated strings to be able to make the `LoadLibrary` call. Just remember that it is not a straightforward string you are dealing with here. You typically need to go through a process of translation between a `String` variable, in which you likely will have the filename of the library stored, and what the `LoadLibrary` function requires.

Without getting into too much detail, Listing 21.6 illustrates the steps to issue the `LoadLibrary` call.

Listing 21.6. Explicitly loading a DLL via a `LoadLibrary` call.

```
uses
  ...
  WinTypes,
  WinProcs,
  SysUtils;

var
  AFileName: String;
  ABuffer: array[0..255] of Char;
  ALibrary: THandle;
begin
  ...
```

```
13:   AFileName := 'dllfirst.dll';
14:   ...
15:   StrPCopy(ABuffer,AFileName);
16:   ...
17:   ALibrary := LoadLibrary(ABuffer);
18:   ...
19:   if ALibrary <= HINSTANCE_ERROR then
20:     {There was a problem!}
21:   else
22:     {It is safe to use the library!}
23:   ...
24: end;
```

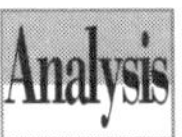

The code fragment in Listing 21.6 shows you how to use the `LoadLibrary` function in a generic situation, when the filename of the library to use for the call is stored as a Pascal string, as it typically would be.

First of all, the **`uses`** clause in lines 1 through 5 ensures that the required subroutines are visible. You need both `WinProcs` to access the `LoadLibrary` function and `SysUtils` to access `StrPCopy`, the conversion routine that translates between a Pascal string and a null-terminated string. You also need `WinTypes` to use the `HINSTANCE_ERROR` constant defined there when checking for the result of the `LoadLibrary` call.

Lines 7 through 10 declare the necessary variables.

`AFileName` is the string variable in which you store the filename originally. Here, for simplicity, the `AFileName` variable gets its value from a straightforward constant assignment in line 13, but in general, line 13 is replaced by a more elaborate scheme, such as getting the value from a user, reading it from an INI file, and so on.

After you have the name of the library file to load, you can proceed with the conversion to a null-terminated string. The `ABuffer` variable declared in line 9 serves as the storage for the filename string after the conversion in line 15. The `StrPCopy` subroutine converts between a Pascal string and a null-terminated string. The first parameter to `StrPCopy` is the destination buffer where the null-terminated equivalent will be stored. The second parameter is the Pascal string you want to convert.

After the conversion, you are ready to actually call `LoadLibrary`. This is done in line 17. The return value of the `LoadLibrary` function is assigned to the variable `ALibrary`, declared in line 9 as a `THandle`. The meaning of this handle is discussed later in this section. In a nutshell, it is a "token" through which you can refer to the library after it has been loaded.

You will need to check the value of the returned token, however, because a value below the predefined `HINSTANCE_ERROR` indicates an error condition. Lines 19 through 22 make the determination of whether the call to `LoadLibrary` was successful.

The result of the `LoadLibrary` function call is a value of type `THandle`. This value is a token, or an "abstract value," that enables you to identify the library to Windows after it has been loaded successfully. It is important to realize that, as long as the `LoadLibrary` call was successful, the numeric value of the handle it returns is of no importance to you directly. You simply supply whatever value `LoadLibrary` returned to other functions that require it, such as `GetProcAddress`.

The only time you need to actually look at the value returned by `LoadLibrary` is directly after the call, because the return value may indicate an error condition.

You can check whether a call to `LoadLibrary` was successful by comparing it with a predefined constant declared in the `WinTypes` unit: `HINSTANCE_ERROR`. If `LoadLibrary` returns a value that is less than or equal to this predefined constant, the call did succeed in actually loading the library, and it is not safe to use any of the functions that need the library to be loaded, such as `GetProcAddress`.

A call to `LoadLibrary` does not necessarily result in the library being loaded from disk. If the library already is loaded (it already is being used by another application or by another instance of the same application), the DLL's "usage counter" maintained by Windows is incremented. Only one copy of the library itself resides in memory at any time. This, after all, is the reason for having DLLs: to be able to *share* code.

Releasing a DLL

Assuming that the call to `LoadLibrary` was successful, you need to make sure that you free the library once you no longer need it. This is again different from the situation of implicitly importing the DLL, where Windows itself takes the responsibility for both loading and unloading the library when necessary. Once you have taken over the responsibility to explicitly load the library, you also must ensure that it is possible for Windows to unload it when it no longer is needed.

To indicate to Windows that your application no longer is interested in the library, you have to issue a call to the standard Windows `FreeLibrary` procedure.

`FreeLibrary` is declared inside `WinProcs` as follows:

```
procedure FreeLibrary(LibModule: THandle);
```

As you can see, `FreeLibrary` takes a single parameter, `LibModule`, of type `THandle`, which identifies the library to be released. This is the same "token" handle that `LoadLibrary` returns.

As it turns out, a call to `FreeLibrary` does not necessarily result in the library being unloaded immediately. It all depends on who else is using the same library at the time. If there are other applications also using the library in question, the call to `FreeLibrary` merely decrements a usage counter maintained by Windows. Only after the usage counter reaches zero (no application is using the DLL any longer) is the library actually unloaded.

The important thing to keep in mind is that if you used `LoadLibrary` to gain access to a DLL, you must use a corresponding `FreeLibrary` to release it, or otherwise the usage counter never is decremented to zero and the library remains loaded even if it no longer is being used.

DO	DON'T

DO match every call to `LoadLibrary` with a corresponding call to `FreeLibrary`.

DON'T forget to make sure that when your program terminates, normally or abnormally, it is still your responsibility to issue the `FreeLibrary` call, if you loaded the DLL with a call to `LoadLibrary`.

Using Dynamically Loaded DLLs

Again, assuming that the call to the `LoadLibrary` function was successful, you finally can take steps to retrieve the address or addresses of the subroutines you want to use from the library. The most convenient way of doing it is by declaring a subroutine-type variable, the value of which you fill at run-time with the address retrieved from a DLL via a call to `GetProcAddress`. You will see an illustration of this shortly.

`GetProcAddress` is declared in `WinProcs` as follows:

```
function GetProcAddress(Module: THandle; ProcName: PChar): TFarProc;
```

This declaration takes two parameters. The first parameter, `Module`, is the library handle previously returned to you from the call to `LoadLibrary`. The second parameter, `ProcName`, is a null-terminated string containing the name of the subroutine for which you want to obtain the address. As before, you may need to translate the Pascal string in which you stored the procedure name into a null-terminated string required by the `GetProcAddress` call.

Note: Windows does not give you any way of retrieving any information about the parameter lists and return types of the DLL subroutines you are accessing. In other words, you must know the *signature*, or the declaration of the subroutine you want to use beforehand. You can dynamically retrieve the run-time address of the subroutine in a DLL, but no run-time type information about it.

21

Now take a look at how you would go about dynamically loading and calling subroutines in the `DLLFirst` library you have developed earlier during today's lesson. Listing 21.7 provides you with a template for using any dynamically linked library. Just substitute the definitions and names specific to `DLLFirst` in the listing with ones pertaining to the specific library you want to access to use it in another context.

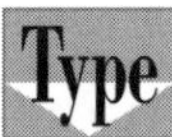

Listing 21.7. Dynamically loading the sample `DLLFirst` library.

```
uses
  WinTypes,
  WinProcs;

var
  TheLib: THandle;

  FillStr:        function (C : Char; N : Byte): String;
  UpCaseFirstStr: function (const s: String): String;
  LTrimStr:       function (const S: String): String;
  RTrimStr:       function (const S: String): String;
  StripStr:       function (const s: String): String;

begin
  ...
  {Initialize the variables}
  @FillStr       := nil;
  @UpCaseFirstStr:= nil;
  @LTrimStr      := nil;
  @RTrimStr      := nil;
  @StripStr      := nil;
  ...
  {Load the library dynamically}
  TheLib := LoadLibrary('DLLFIRST.DLL');
  if TheLib > HINSTANCE_ERROR then try
    ...
    {Retrieve the subroutine addresses}
    if TheLib > HINSTANCE_ERROR then begin
      @FillStr       := GetProcAddress(TheLib,'FillStr');
      @UpCaseFirstStr:= GetProcAddress(TheLib,'UpCaseFirstStr');
      @LTrimStr      := GetProcAddress(TheLib,'LTrimStr');
      @RTrimStr      := GetProcAddress(TheLib,'RTrimStr');
      @StripStr      := GetProcAddress(TheLib,'StripStr');
    end;
    ...
    {Use the routines here, almost the same as before. e.g.:}
    if Assigned(LTrimStr) then
      S := LTrimStr('   This is fun!   ');
      {S now equals 'This is fun!   '}
    S := StripStr(' Teach Yourself Delphi Now! ');
    {
    if StripStr = nil, an exception occurs and
    the control jumps to the finally block;
    if no exception has occurred,
    S now equals 'TeachYourselfDelphiNow!'
    }
    ...
  finally
    {Release the library once you are done}
    FreeLibrary(TheLib);
  end;
  ...
end.
```

Listing 21.7 gives you an idea of what is involved when using an explicitly loaded DLL. The example `DLLFIRST.DLL` is used here as an illustration of the steps needed.

The key to successfully using the subroutines in the library is to provide a set of variables capable of holding the values of run-time addresses of the library subroutines. Lines 8 through 12 of the listing declare a set of variables, conveniently named the same as the function addresses of which they will be storing.

The library handle `TheLib`, declared in line 6, is being retrieved via a call to `LoadLibrary` in line 24.

A **`try-finally`** exception-handling block is set up spanning lines 25 through 51 to protect the actual "working" code from the possibility that the code executed within the **`try`**-block may have failed. If an attempt to call a subroutine from the library within the **`try`**-block results in a failure, an exception is thrown. The **`finally`**-block is guaranteed to execute the `FreeLibrary` call, releasing the resources taken up by the library. In other words, after the initial determination that the library call was successful is made by the **`if`**-statement on line 25, the **`finally`**-clause of the **`try-finally`** block ensures that the library is unloaded properly, even if an exception occurs during the execution of the statements inside the **`try`** part.

Assuming that the `LoadLibrary` operation was successful, lines 29 through 33 retrieve the actual run-time addresses of the subroutines imported from the `DLLFirst` library module.

The `@` operator in front of the variable names is meant to deliberately circumvent the strong type-checking mechanism of Object Pascal and, for a short moment, to treat the procedural variables as if they were pointer variables (variables storing memory addresses of an unspecified type). Otherwise the compiler would complain about the incompatibility between the two sides of these assignment statements. Observe that `GetProcAddress` returns a `THandle`-type, while the left-hand-side variables are declared as function-typed variables.

The subroutine variables, after the address values are assigned to them, can be used to call the appropriate subroutines.

For example, line 38 looks exactly as if a call to a normal subroutine were being made. The function `LTrimStr` is being called and returns a value as before. The interesting point here is that `LTrimStr` is not a function *per se*, but a reference to a functional variable, the value of which was determined at run-time. The difference is that you must check the value of the variable for validity, because—unlike statically linked or implicitly imported subroutine addresses—the address of the subroutine may not be available. The determination as to whether it is safe to make the call is done in line 37. The **`if`**-statement in line 37 is an example of the traditional approach to error-checking. A run-time error is prevented by making sure that the functional variable contains a valid address.

A different approach to error-checking is taken in line 40. The new style of programming makes use of the exception-handling mechanism built into Delphi. Remember that the **`try-finally`** block you set up on lines 25 through 51 is in effect on line 40. If the call to `StripStr` on line 40 proves to be unsuccessful, such as when the value of `StripStr` is **`nil`**, a General Protection Fault (GPF) exception occurs. Instead of performing any useful action, the control of execution immediately jumps to the **`finally`**-block.

The **`finally`**-block on lines 48 through 51 traps the exception and, in this case, makes sure that the library is properly unloaded.

After you are done using the dynamic library that you have loaded explicitly, be sure to release it via a call to `FreeLibrary`. The sample code in Listing 21.7 ensures that the library eventually is unloaded by making a call to the `FreeLibrary` standard API procedure in line 50. Before the call is made, however, line 49 checks whether the library has been loaded successfully in the first place.

The discussion of DLLs presented here merely has scratched the surface of the issues involved. Be sure to consult other references when you are considering making heavy use of dynamic linking. There is much more to it than what was covered in today's lesson.

The remainder of today's lesson points out another important issue that makes using dynamic libraries different from using regular units: accessing data inside the library.

Accessing Data in a Library

An important point when you are considering implementing dynamically linked libraries is that there is no way of directly exporting data from them. Unlike in the case of a simple, statically linked unit, where a variable declared in the interface section is potentially visible to, and accessible from, any other unit or Pascal module in a project, variables declared inside a library remain "external" and private to that library. The only interface available to the users of the library is the subroutine interface: procedures and functions.

You are free to declare global variables inside a library module, and declaring them is just as easy as doing so in a program module. The variables you declare inside a DLL are private to that DLL, however. You must provide a procedural interface to allow the applications using the library to access the variable or variables declared inside it when needed.

Warning: Global variables in a DLL are shared across all clients of the DLL. If one client application using the DLL changes its value through a procedural interface to the DLL, all other clients will also see the new, changed value. (DLLs are shared resources, remember?) This may be useful sometimes, but often is unwanted, unexpected, and may be disastrous. Writing multi-user servers as DLLs is a tricky issue that has not been covered in this book at all.

The library presented in Listing 21.8 indirectly exports a string variable `AString` by providing two access subroutines: `GetValue` and `SetValue`.

Listing 21.8. Exporting a string variable from a DLL via a procedural interface.

```
 1: library ExtStr;
 2:
 3: var
 4:   AString: String;
 5:
 6: function GetValue: String; export;
 7:   begin
 8:     Result := AString;
 9:   end;
10:
11: procedure SetValue(AValue: String); export;
12:   begin
13:     AString := AValue;
14:   end;
15:
16: exports
17:   GetValue index 11,
18:   SetValue index 12;
19:
20: begin
21: end.
```

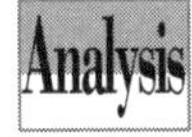

The code in Listing 21.8 accomplishes the goal of exporting a data element from a library module. The data element "exported" by the DLL, `AString`, is declared in line 4 of the listing.

The `AString` variable is not visible outside the module, however. To enable applications using the library to obtain and change the value of the variable, two access subroutines are defined:

- The `GetValue` function, to retrieve the current value of the variable.
- The `SetValue` procedure, to change the value of the variable.

These subroutines actually are exported via an `exports` clause, and the client applications can operate effectively on the value of the variable without "seeing" the variable directly. This is very similar to the concept of access methods for a class property, as you may recall. In both cases, the access subroutines shield the using code from directly manipulating the value and may introduce side effects, as well as validation and checking.

Summary

The focus of today's lesson was on dynamically linked libraries (DLLs). During the course of the lesson, you learned the following:

- DLLs are executable modules, as are application modules. DLLs are not directly executable, however.
- DLLs make it possible for many running applications, or many instances of the same application, to share code and binary resources.
- DLLs are created in Delphi by replacing the keyword **`program`** with the keyword **`library`** in the main Delphi project file, and by making some additional changes to the standard project file generated by Delphi.
- The **`export`** directive makes a subroutine *exportable*—capable of being exported by a DLL and used by an application external to that DLL.
- The **`exports`** clause lists the subroutines actually exported from a DLL. All the exported subroutines must have been declared with the **`export`** directive.
- The most convenient way of accessing the subroutines inside a DLL is by creating an implicit import unit, declaring the headers of the subroutines, and binding them to the corresponding routines inside a DLL via the **`external`** directive.
- There are many ways of binding the subroutines declared as **`external`** to the actual subroutines implemented inside a DLL. The subroutines can be bound by their declared or assumed name, or by an ordinal number.
- A `LoadLibrary` standard API function can be used to provide a greater degree of control over when a particular DLL is loaded. There must be a matching call to `FreeLibrary` for each invocation of the `LoadLibrary` function.
- Before you can use the subroutines inside a library explicitly loaded with a call to `LoadLibrary`, you must retrieve their addresses via a call to `GetProcAddress`.
- You can store the values retrieved by `GetProcAddress` in procedural-type variables, which later can be used to call the subroutines.
- You cannot export data elements directly from a DLL. To make data available to applications using a DLL, you must provide a procedural interface, consisting of a `GetXXXX` function and a `SetXXXX` procedure, to retrieve and change the value of a particular variable in question.

Q&A

Q Can I debug DLLs from within the Delphi Integrated Development Environment (IDE)?

A No. The IDE-based debugger does not give you access to the source code of the DLL to make symbolic debugging possible. You must use the external Turbo Debugger to debug the code inside a DLL. Of course, you *can* debug programs using DLLs from within the IDE; every Delphi program uses DLLs, after all. You just will not be able to step through the code inside a DLL you wrote in Delphi.

Q Can I export data types and constants from a DLL?

A Not really. If a DLL defines a custom data type, you can repeat the declaration of it inside the import unit for the DLL to make the type declarations and constant identifiers automatically visible and available to all users of the DLL, along with the DLL's subroutines.

Q Can a DLL import subroutines from another DLL? Can a DLL use its own exported subroutines? For example, can you write code inside a DLL that calls subroutines in that DLL?

A Yes, on both counts. DLLs can delegate all or part of their responsibilities for providing services to other DLLs. You also are free to use any subroutines defined in a DLL to accomplish a task within that DLL, subject to the normal rules of visibility and scope.

Q Can objects be exported from a DLL?

A Surprisingly, yes. Abstract classes can be implemented inside a DLL and made available to the requesting applications. This is precisely how the Component Library inside Delphi itself works. The technique, however, is considered advanced and has not been covered in this book.

Workshop

The Workshop provides quiz questions to help you solidify your understanding of the material covered, and exercises to provide you with experience in using what you have learned. Try to understand the quiz and exercise answers before continuing on to the next day's lesson. Answers are provided in Appendix B at the end of this book.

Quiz

1. True or False?

   There is a separate and distinct copy of each subroutine statically linked into an application present in memory for each instance of that Windows application.

2. True or False?

   It is possible to load more than one instance of a DLL by calling the standard `LoadLibrary` function repetitively.

3. True or False?

   There is no additional overhead involved in calling a subroutine implemented in a DLL, beyond the initial loading of the library, as compared to calling a normal, statically linked subroutine.

4. True or False?

   Different DLLs can be loaded and unloaded dynamically at run-time on demand, thereby creating the possibility of dynamically changing the meaning and behavior of a particular external subroutine.

5. True or False?

   It is possible to export the same subroutine under several different names.

6. True or False?

   It is possible to import the same subroutine implemented in a DLL several times, under different names.

7. True or False?

   An application can export subroutines in the same way that a DLL/library module can, by means of an **`exports`** clause.

Exercises

1. Implement a `TrimStr` function that combines the effect of the `LTrimStr` and `RTrimStr` functions you have implemented during today's lesson. `TrimStr` would eliminate all blanks on both sides of the string passed to it as the argument, but would *not* eliminate the blanks inside the string, the way `StripStr` does.
2. Build an example program similar to `DLLTEST`, in which you would exercise the `FillStr` function exported by the `DLLFIRST` library you developed during the course of today's lesson.

Bonus Day 1

DDE and OLE

by Tom Campbell

Previous chapters showed you how to build self-contained programs, and that's impressive enough. Delphi enables you to create small, fast, powerful applications easier than any other Windows language. But Windows isn't called a multitasking operating environment for nothing. This bonus chapter shows you how your program can communicate with and control other programs using Dynamic Data Exchange (DDE). Several examples show how you can use DDE to call Program Manager directly, creating program groups and querying them for information. Other examples use Microsoft Excel and Word for Windows. It's okay if you don't have them. You can still step through the text anyway. The output is shown in illustrations, and the principles work with any program that uses DDE. This chapter also shows how you can write your own programs to be controlled by other programs using DDE. Finally, you see how to use Object Linking and Embedding (OLE) to share data and to make other programs look like they're part of your program. Microsoft views OLE as the future and discourages use of DDE, but there are some things that can be done only by using DDE and no other way. In fact, large parts of OLE are currently written using DDE!

Today's chapter covers these interapplication communication topics:

- An overview of DDE
- Using the DDEClientConv component to control other applications
- Using the DDEServerConv component to let other applications control your application
- An overview of OLE
- Using the OLEContainer component to embed other applications in your application

This chapter contains several brief but complete DDE and OLE programs. The Delphi User's Guide has a couple of chapters covering virtually all the bases for a programmer who wants to use DDE and OLE. Borland's guide makes it seem like writing DDE and OLE applications requires hundreds of lines of code. Not true, although their examples are good ones. The programs presented in this chapter are all quite short, yet they all show how to get useful work done with minimal code. When you find out about DDE, you may be slightly overwhelmed by the jargon—*client*, *server*, *moniker*, and so on. Or, if you have had experience programming network applications, you will be pleasantly surprised. The client/server model used by both DDE and OLE to varying degrees is intentionally very much like network programming. Master one, and the other will fit like an old shoe.

Introduction to DDE

Have you ever wondered how installation programs create program groups and add icons to those groups to Program Manager? Or have you ever used Paste Link in Word for Windows to bring in some live cells from an Excel worksheet? Both of these disparate activities rely on DDE, a rudimentary communications protocol for Windows applications. You might think that there is a Windows API call named CreateProgramGroup in the first example, or an InsertPasteLink in the second, for example, but—logical though such guesses might be—you would be wrong.

Dynamic Data Exchange (DDE) provides a communications framework for Windows programs that enables *conversations* to be opened up between *client* and *server* applications. A DDE conversation is a session that is initiated and then closed between cooperating programs. Both programs must be running in order for the DDE conversation to occur, although there are provisions to start a program if it's not already executing.

The program that initiates the conversation and obtains assistance from another program is the *client*. The program that provides assistance to the client is the *server*. It's just as if you hired a catering service to help with a party: you're the client, so you call up the caterer (initiate the conversation) and ask for people to help dispense food. In this case, the caterer is the server. Eventually, the client closes the conversation, just as you would send away the caterer (server) when the party and cleanup were over. (Incidentally, if you have any old references to DDE lying around, you may be hopelessly confused at this point. You should be. Early Microsoft documentation reversed the meaning of client and server, but the definition given here is indeed the current one.)

A DDE conversation has topics, or categories, which are completely application-dependent. The most common example of a topic is a filename. Other topics might include the term *system*, which Microsoft applications use when you want to query them via DDE about such items as which Clipboard formats are supported. The data moved back and forth during the conversation is called the *item*. The most common example of an item is a row/column specification of a range in a spreadsheet. Another common example of an item is when you ask Program Manager to list what icons are listed in the Accessories group file. Here, *Group* is the topic and *Accessories* is the item. In DDE, the topics are represented as text strings, such as `Group` or `Progman`. Items also are represented as text strings; the value being discussed in this case is Accessories. Unfortunately, there is no systematic way to find out what topics an application supports. Your application must know in advance what topics the server application supports. A DDE *request* is just that—a query to a DDE server to find out about something. In the preceding example, the request would be finding out what icons are in the Accessories group.

One thing that has been glossed over is that your application also must know in advance the name used by the server program for contact via DDE. Interestingly, programs do not identify each other by the name of the executable file (for example, C:\MSOFFICE\EXCEL\EXCEL.EXE). Instead, programs use a moniker called a *service* or *application* name. (The term *moniker*, which simply means name or nickname, is widely used in OLE systems programming documentation in much the same context. I've purposely used the term *moniker* to get you accustomed to its use in OLE.) By convention, the service name is the name of the executable without the extension (for example, Excel, MSAccess, or WinWord), but it doesn't have to be. In Delphi, the service name is obtained from the ServerConv property of the DDEServerItem component, which works in with the DDEServerConv component. Service names are case-insensitive. *WinWord* is the same as *WINWORD* or *winword*, for example.

If you think about it, devising a means by which two programs running at the same time can communicate is not a simple task. One of the primary jobs of a multitasking operating system, in fact, is to put up a *firewall* between the task spaces of all running programs.

NEW TERM The term *firewall* comes from its real-life counterpart, which is a fireproof wall in a building that keeps fires "compartmentalized" so that they don't spread beyond the firewall. In computers it's a way to protect files or memory, normally with hardware assistance. For example, you probably know that all Intel processors that allow protected mode programming (the 80286 and above) have different levels of hardware protection for memory access and executable code. A real protected mode operating system, or OS/2, lets user applications run only at a lower level of protection than the operating system itself. That way, if the user-level program crashes, it won't violate memory in other processes or in the operating system code itself, as so often happens in the DOS and 16-bit Windows world.

One seemingly obvious technique is shared memory: just give two applications access to the same memory and let them deposit information there. On closer inspection, that raises the possibility of one application doing serious damage to another by virtue of this unrestricted access. If your application allocates memory dynamically, you don't want Delphi or Word for Windows taking over that space and overwriting its contents. If another program stops working correctly, you don't want its failure to corrupt the application you wrote. If your program opens a database and writes a record to it, you don't want another program altering that same record without authorization. In a multiuser environment, another set of problems arises revolving around security. It would be inconvenient for WinWord to knock out the Delphi program you were writing. It would be disastrous if a bank transaction being made by another user on the network could be derailed by a bug in your program.

Here's an illustration of DDE at work using popular Windows applications. Suppose that you are a loan officer writing a letter to a prospective customer. You want to embed part of an Excel worksheet in your letter. Because interest rates change frequently, you choose to embed that range of cells as *live data*; when you change values in the embedded cells, they're changed automatically in Excel. That way, if the customer calls again in a few weeks and interest rates

have changed, you can just type in new numbers and send the same letter. Figure BD1.1 shows what the letter might look like in Microsoft Word for Windows before you embed the cell range.

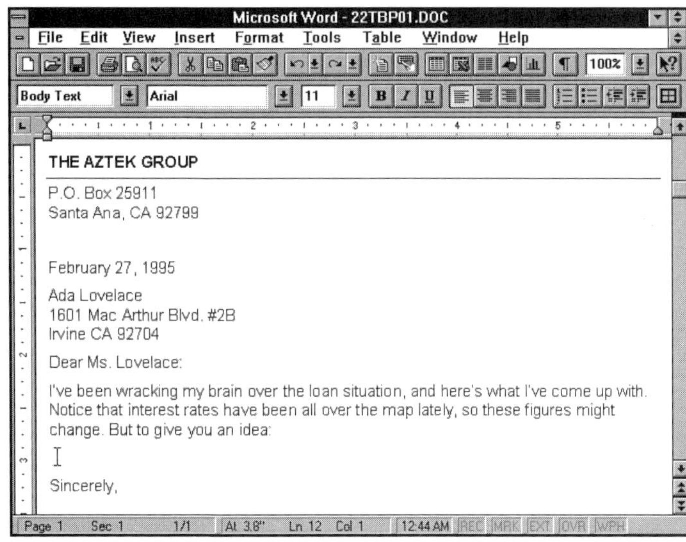

Figure BD1.1.
A Word for Windows document just before a range from Excel is inserted using a DDE link.

Microsoft Word is considered the DDE client in this case, because it's requesting for Excel to maintain the embedded data. (Word is just as capable of acting as a DDE server. It can respond to DDE commands from other applications.) Now you create a worksheet in Microsoft Excel, select the range in question (cells A1 to E4 in this example), and choose Copy from the Edit menu. This process copies the cells into the Clipboard in several formats simultaneously, enabling the recipient application—the client—to choose which format to use. Excel is the DDE server in this example, and it goes without saying that Excel also can act as a DDE client. Figure BD1.2 shows the cell range.

In order for DDE to work properly, the client and server must be active at the same time. You see later in this chapter what happens when they are not active at the same time. At this point, no DDE has occurred. Choose Paste Special from the Word menu. The dialog box shown in Figure BD1.3 appears.

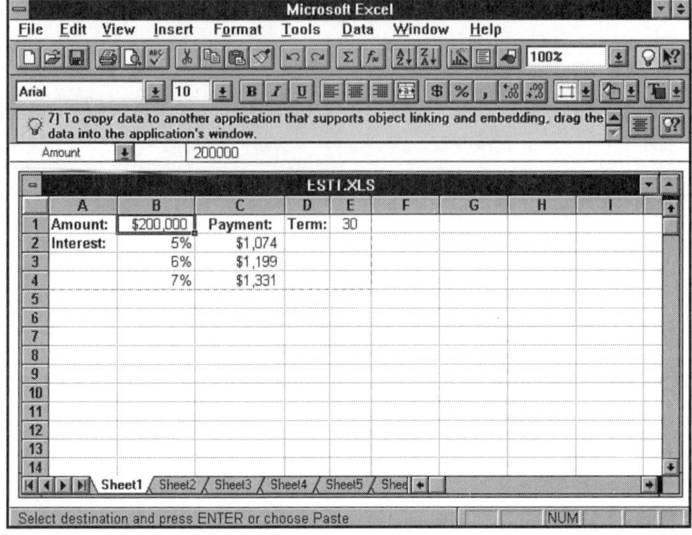

Figure BD1.2. *The Excel range to be inserted as a DDE link.*

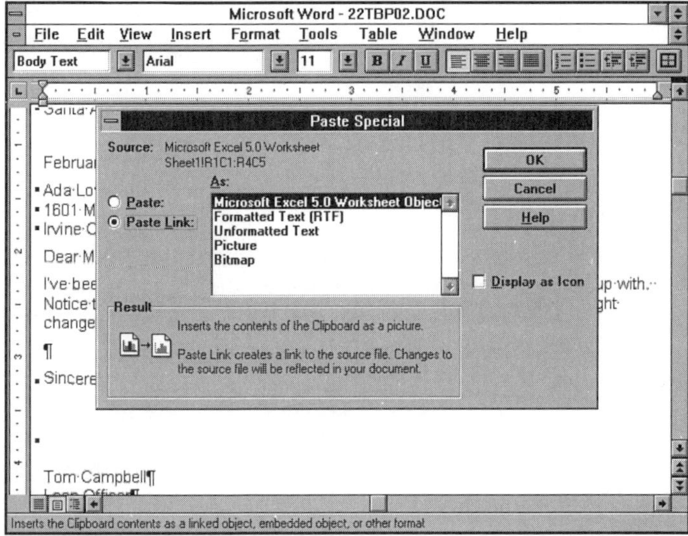

Figure BD1.3. *The Paste Special dialog box enables you to insert a portion of a document from a DDE server—in this case, Excel.*

Click the Paste Link radio button and select Microsoft Excel 5.0 Worksheet Object in the As column. If you had chosen Paste instead of Paste Link, the data would have come in statically. That is, it would look and feel like a table of numbers in Word with no connection to the spreadsheet file. If you changed a percentage in the interest rate, it would not recalculate the affected cells. Paste Link gives you a hot connection between the embedded spreadsheet cells and the word processing document. Change the cells in the spreadsheet, and the next time you load

this document into the word processor they'll have changed accordingly. Figure BD1.4 shows you how this connection appears on-screen.

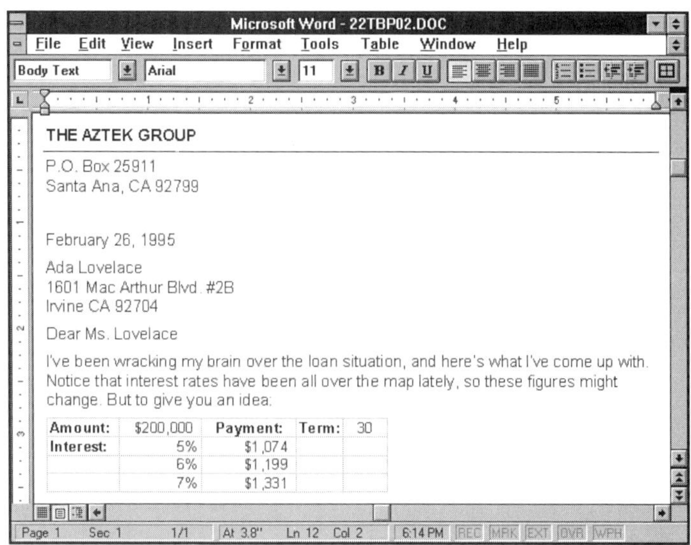

Figure BD1.4.
A link to an Excel file (the DDE server) to a Word document (the DDE client), which appears to be an integral part of the document, although it is actually a separate file.

As you can see, the cells are selectable as a single entity. If you click any of the cells with the mouse, it becomes selected as a single object. You can stretch, shrink, or delete the object at will. Double-clicking does something else entirely. It brings up Excel, as shown in Figure BD1.5.

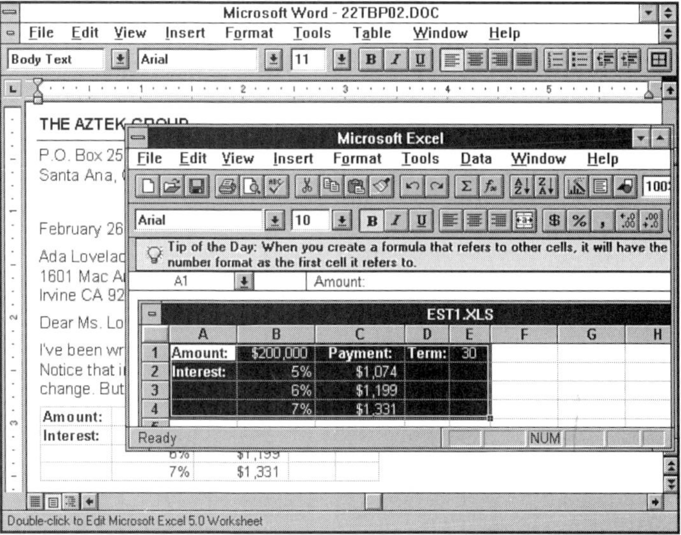

Figure BD1.5.
Double-clicking a link from the DDE client (Word, in this case) to bring up the linked DDE server (Excel).

You can edit the cells and then quit Excel, and the cells will be updated automatically in the word processing document. Suppose that you quit Excel after copying the cells, but before doing a Paste Special in Word. Remember that in DDE, the server (Excel, in this example) must be active when the connection is made. If you quit Excel before doing the Paste, you see the dialog box in Figure BD1.6.

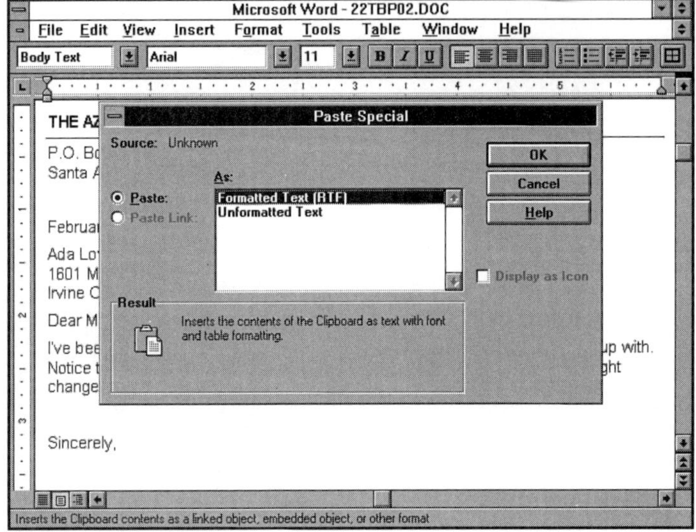

Figure BD1.6.
A link being made after the server application has been exited, showing how DDE requires a "live" document on each end.

As you can see, the Paste Link radio button is disabled and the application name at the upper left of the dialog box is `Unknown`.

You have seen that DDE can be done, and that it can be done well. You also have learned how much potential danger there is in possible implementations of DDE or any system like it. So how *do* you implement a communications channel?

Older operating systems simply allow properly flagged global memory to be shared between processes. Or, the systems can share text files, which is another primitive technique you can use. These methods are hardly elegant, and they certainly are error-prone. There is no built-in acknowledgment scheme, so you have to create one yourself. Nor is there any concept of security. In general, the systems lack an organizing principle.

DDE solves these problems. DDE generally is used to send textual data back and forth between communicating programs, although it also can be used for binary data. Because Windows knows about DDE, acknowledgment, error checking, and memory protection are built-in. The original DDE API calls originated in Windows 3.0, but they turned out to be too confusing and tedious even for Windows C hackers, who are notorious masochists. Windows 3.1 debuted the Dynamic Data Exchange Management Library (DDEML), which makes DDE a good deal easier to work with. Most DDE programming takes place via DDEML calls, but you don't need

to worry much. Delphi insulates you; the DDE components that come with Delphi take almost all the pain out of DDE. Incidentally, it turns out that DDE does end up using shared memory, among many other tricks. You can prove this by looking up GlobalAlloc in the Windows API reference, and you will see the little-known GMEM_DDESHARE flag. The explanation under GlobalAlloc makes its purpose clear.

Commands versus Requests

DDE clients often issue commands to the servers. Delphi demonstrates this concept by creating a Program Manager group and placing an icon inside it. The DDELAB program later in this chapter enables you to do this interactively.

Requesting data is a little trickier. The following section illustrates this technique.

Creating DDE Client Programs with DDEClientConv Components

The Delphi User's Guide has an extensive section on creating DDE clients, but it includes many extra steps that aren't necessary for many applications. Here's a very short program of surprising utility that gives you a fascinating glimpse into the inner workings of some major applications. DDEInfo enables you to make information requests of DDE servers such as Program Manager, Microsoft Excel, and Word for Windows. Here, DDEInfo is used to show information about topics in Excel and groups in Program Manager, and to discover that Word has an undocumented feature called a Woozle! (I still don't know what a Woozle is, but thanks to DDE requests, at least I know where to find one!) The Borland manuals do a great job describing how to create a DDE link at design-time. This section focuses on creating the link at run-time to give you maximum flexibility.

Here are the steps required to create DDE links from client to server at run-time. You use these steps in a complete, useful example program after this review. Follow these steps:

1. Add a DDEClientConv component to the form.
2. Set the DDEClientConv's ConnectMode property to Manual.
3. Call DDEClientConv's SetLink method, passing it two strings: the name of a service to contact and the topic of the conversation.
4. Call the DDEClientConv's OpenLink method to start the conversation.
5. Call the DDEClientConv's RequestData method, passing it a string naming the data to query. RequestData does two things you need to pay very close attention to. First, it returns a distinctly unPascal-like null-terminated buffer with the data you requested. Second, it allocates memory for that data—memory you now are responsible for and which you must deallocate at some point.

Warning: If you don't deallocate the memory passed to RequestData, your program probably will crash. The most common way to deallocate the memory is by using StrDispose. The example program here uses a little-known technique that hands over responsibility to the memo field and enables the TMemo object to deallocate it automatically. Delegating tasks always is fun.

6. End the conversation by calling the DDEClientConv's CloseLink method.

Note that the Delphi documentation uses DDEClientItems, but this example doesn't. It's not necessary to use DDEClientItems as shown here, because the link is being made at run-time. It turns out that making the link at run-time arguably is much simpler than doing it at design-time. Certainly, it affords you more flexibility.

Create a form using the data shown in Table BD1.1. Be sure to set properties for the controls as shown in Table BD1.1. Figure BD1.7 shows what the DDEInfo form should look like.

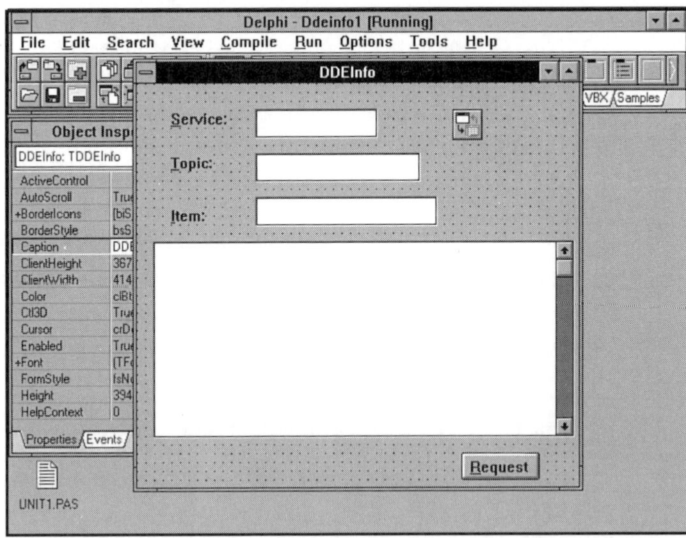

Figure BD1.7.
The DDEInfo form.

Table BD1.1. The DDEInfo project's form and its properties.

Component	Property	Value
Form	Name	DDEInfo
DEClientConv	Name	DDEClient
DDEClientConv	ConnectMode	Manual
Edit box	Name	txtService

Component	Property	Value
Edit box	Name	txtTopic
Edit box	Name	txtItem
Memo	Name	Memo1
Memo	ScrollBars	ssVertical
Button	Name	btnRequest

Create the Click event procedure for the button, which is named btnRequest. The code for this button is shown in Listing BD1.1.

Listing BD1.1. The code for the Request button.

```
procedure TDDEInfo.btnRequestClick(Sender: TObject);
var
  { Pointer to a null-terminated string. }
   pszInfo : PChar;
begin
     { Define link & topic for the DDE app named in txtService. }
     DDEClient.SetLink(txtService.Text,txtTopic.Text);
     { Because the ConnectMode is manual, this initiates }
     {the conversation. }
     DDEClient.OpenLink;
     { Ask server for Topic data. Write location to pszInfo. }
     pszInfo := DDEClient.RequestData(txtItem.Text);
     { The data comes back as a null terminated string with }
     { embedded newlines. This formats it directly into the }
     { memo object, handling memory allocation as well. }
     Memo1.SetTextBuf(pszInfo);
     { End the DDE conversation. }
     DDEClient.CloseLink;
end;
```

SetLink determines the service and topic of the DDE conversation. If the server is a Delphi application, the service name is the name of the executable file without the path and extension, and the topic is the name caption of the DDE server item component. If ConnectMode is automatic, SetLink tries to initiate the conversation.

That's all there is to it. An amazingly small amount of code for what you're about to do. One trick to note is that the TMemo's little-known SetTextBuf method is used to manage the memory returned by RequestData. If you check the help for TDDEClientConv's RequestData method, you will note that RequestData returns a dynamic, null-terminated PChar string of up to 64KB, for which you now are responsible. The traditional method is to call StrDispose on it later, but the solution lets you kill two birds with one stone. When you request the list of group names from Program Manager, as you're about to do, it comes back in a form that looks like this to a Pascal programmer:

```
Main#13#10Accessories#13#10Games#0
```

The group names are all returned in one null-terminated string, separated within by carriage return/linefeed sequences. This is an example of a minimal system. The result normally is much longer, far exceeding the 255 characters allowed in a Pascal string.

Somehow, these characters need to get into the memo control as separate lines of text. It would take only a few lines of code to parse this string into separate tokens, but why bother? TMemo's SetTextBuf is expecting the kind of string you just obtained from the DDE call to Program Manager. Such properties as Lines in a memo control or Text in an edit control expect Pascal strings, which cannot exceed 255 characters. SetTextBuf is a back door into the memo's full 64KB capacity for a string, and by using it you instruct the memo control to break the null-terminated string into lines.

Compile DDEInfo, run the program, and fill in the values shown in Table BD1.2.

Table BD1.2. Enter these values into DDEInfo to discover what groups you have in Program Manager.

In this text box	Enter this value
Service	progman
Topic	progman
Item	progman

Click the Request button. It performs the RequestData call, using the service and topic initialized by the SetLink, and using the item passed to RequestData as its sole parameter. RequestData returns the names of the program groups as a dynamically allocated PChar string. This example shows how you request the names of all groups from Program Manager, which is handy if you have an installation program that needs to see whether a group already exists. Otherwise, Program Manager can create duplicate group names if you request it.

After you click the Request button, you see the screen shown in Figure BD1.8.

Figure BD1.8 shows a listing of all program groups, conveniently displayed one per line. If you have more groups than fit in the memo field, just click the vertical scroll bar to see more. (What? No scroll bars? Then you forgot to set the memo control's ScrollBars property to ssVertical.) You can get information on any program group by using the group name as the topic (Accessories, for example). Just fill in this information, replacing Accessories with another group name if you want. Enter the values shown in Table BD1.3 into DDEInfo to find out what is in the Accessories Program Manager group.

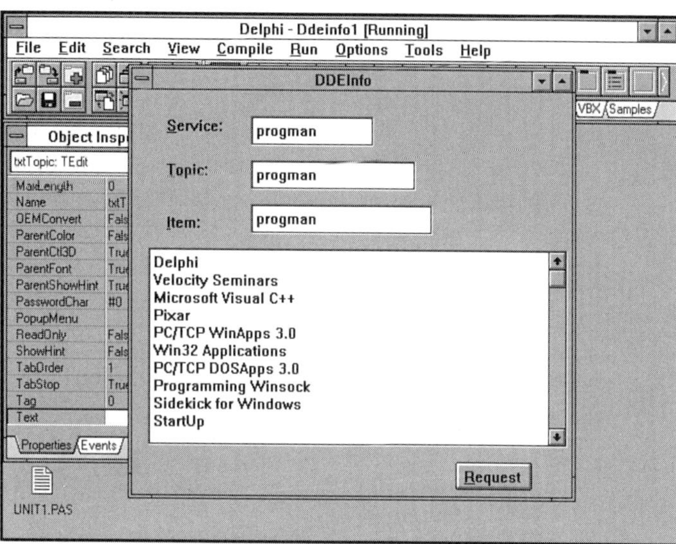

Figure BD1.8.
Example output from DDEInfo showing all Program Manager groups. Use the vertical scroll bar to see the remaining groups.

Table BD1.3. Entering values into DDEInfo to find out what's in the Accessories Program Manager group.

In this text box	Enter this value
Service	progman
Topic	progman
Item	accessories

Entering these values fills the memo field with a comma-delimited database of information on the Accessories group. The first line contains settings about the group itself: the name of the group, the path of the group file, the number of items in the group, and its order in the set of open group windows. Succeeding lines then list the icon description, the command line, the icon path (optional), the position in the group, the icon index, the shortcut keycode, and the minimize flag. The first few items should be very familiar. You can view or change them interactively when you select the icon and choose Properties from the Program Manager File menu.

Now try a DDE request with another program—Excel. Microsoft programs are useful in these DDE experiments for several reasons. First, they're ubiquitous. Microsoft Office is wildly popular. If you have bought a computer from a major vendor recently, the odds are very good that it has Office. Second, Microsoft applications are understandably considered the benchmarks for DDE and OLE compliance. Third, several of Microsoft's flagship applications respond to a common subset of topics. It's important to remember at this juncture that the DDE verbs supported by a server application aren't specified in any kind of a standards document, which might be a mistake. One program might use File | Open as its DDE macro command to open a file. Another program might use [OpenFile], and yet another might use a completely different command. DDE specifies a protocol, just as a terminal program might support XModem file downloads, but it knows nothing of the semantics of any server applications. It's just like the fact that terminal programs don't have any way of knowing whether you're logging onto CompuServe, a VAX mainframe computer, or the Internet. If you don't have Office or the individual Microsoft applications, don't worry. The results of the DDE queries are illustrated as the DDEInfo application you just wrote is demonstrated.

Try DDE with Excel, but first see what happens when you attempt a DDE communication link while the server (Excel, in this case) isn't running.

In the DDEInfo boxes, fill in the values shown in Table BD1.4 and click Request to see a list of DDE topics DDEInfo supports.

Table BD1.4. Entering values into DDEInfo while Excel is running.

In this text box	Enter this value
Service	excel
Topic	system
Item	topics

If Excel is running, exit it for now. Click the Request button. Nothing happens. There is no open application with which you can communicate. Now run Excel, switch back to DDEInfo, and do the request. You see, among other things, a list of all open worksheets, as shown in Figure BD1.9.

Your mileage may vary, depending on the version of Excel you're using. By convention, many applications—Excel and WinWord included—enable you to select a filename as a topic. That's why you see all the open worksheets as topics. Strangely, my version of PowerPoint, which came in the same Office suite as Access, WinWord, and Excel, does not support these DDE requests, even though the others do.

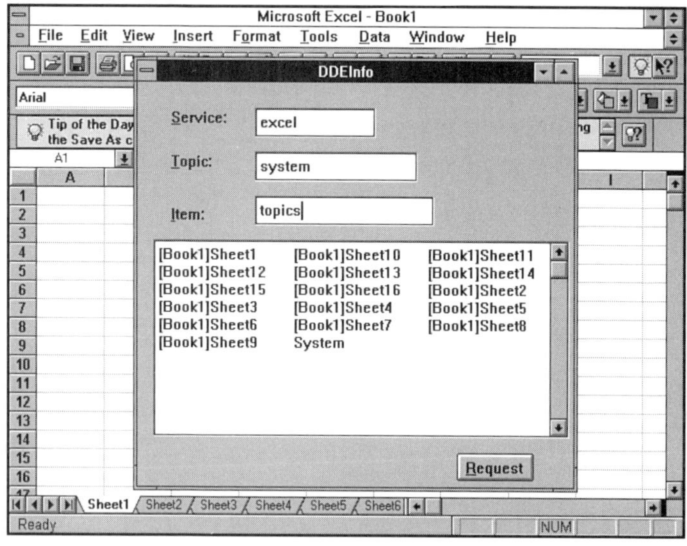

Figure BD1.9.
A list of all Excel System topics obtained through DDE.

Quit Excel and start Word. Enter the same old values for the topic and item into DDEInfo, as shown in Table BD1.5, while Word for Windows is running to get a list of system topics it supports.

Table BD1.5. Entering values into DDEInfo.

In this text box	Enter this value
Service	winword
Topic	system
Item	topics

You see a list of open documents and style sheets. Most Microsoft applications also respond to an item called Formats, which lists all Clipboard formats supported by that application. I was surprised, to say the least, when I saw one particular item in this list from Word for Windows 6.0a (see Fig. BD1.10).

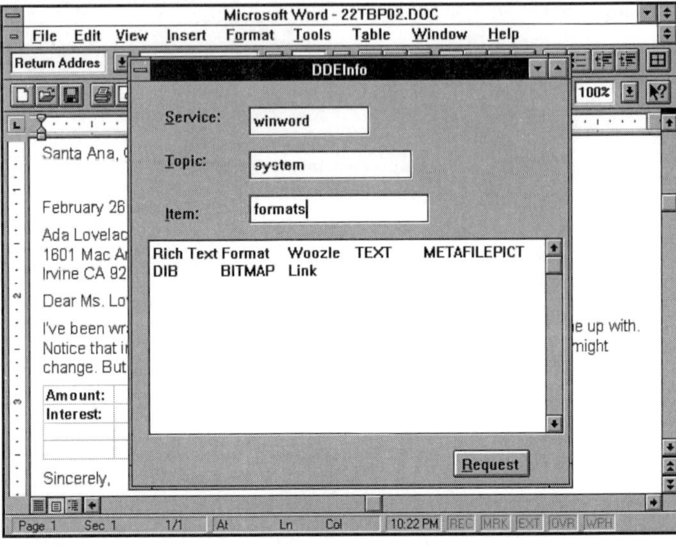

Figure BD1.10.
A list of all Clipboard formats Word for Windows 6.0a supports—including the all-important Woozle.

Now enter the values shown in Table BD1.6 while Word for Windows is running to get a list of Clipboard formats it supports.

Table BD1.6. Entering values into DDEInfo.

In this text box	Enter this value
Service	winword
Topic	system
Item	formats

I can't wait to see the next WinWord technical reference manual describing the Woozle format.

Creating DDE Server Programs with DDEServerConv Components

Just as DDE clients may control other programs and request data from them, DDE servers let programs push them around. The example in this section is a perpetual calendar program that enables you to use spin buttons or DDE commands to change the year or the month settings by one in either direction. (Spin buttons are the controls that show as a triangle pointing up,

stacked atop another triangle pointing down, with their bases meeting.) It's actually a handy little utility in its own right, DDE or not. A listing for a Delphi driver program that can control the calendar via a DDE connection follows.

Your program can use several techniques to receive commands. Because OnExecuteMacro is documented least well by Borland, it is used here. It also is the most convenient way to handle macros in the form of text strings.

Here are the steps required to create a DDE server that accepts macro commands, with the link established at run-time. They're illustrated in an example following this summary. Follow these steps:

1. Add a DDEServerConv component to the form.
2. Add a DDEServerItem component to the form.

   If your application doesn't need to accept macros, you don't need DDEServerItem.
3. Set the DDEServerItem ServerConv property to the name of the DDEServerConv component, if there is a DDEServerItem component.
4. Write an OnExecuteMacro event handler for the DDEServerConv component.

The text of the macro is passed to the handler. The format of the macro is up to you, so parse it as necessary and dispatch whatever actions are associated with it.

That's all. It's a simple process, in theory. Now try out that theory.

Create a form based on the items shown in Table BD1.7. The Calendar component is buried at the end of the component palette, under Samples. The two controls at the top center of the calendar are DDEServerConv and DDEServerItem components. Figure BD1.11 shows how the DDECAL form should look.

Table BD1.7. The DDECAL project's form and its properties.

Component	Property	Value
Form	Caption	DDE Calendar Server
DDEServerConv	Name	DDEServer
DDEServerItem	ServerConv	DDEServer

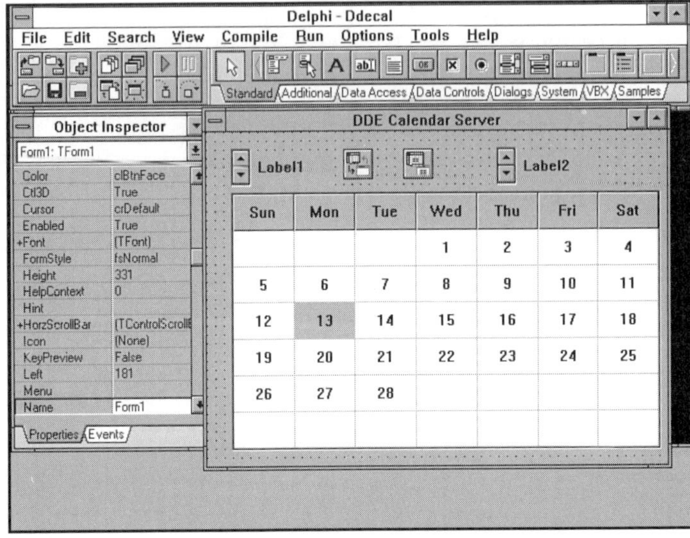

Figure BD1.11.
The DDECAL form.

Add the private declarations ChangeMonth, ChangeYear, and SetMonthLabel implementations to the form:

Listing BD1.2. Adding three private declarations.

```
TForm1 = class(TForm)
private
  { Private declarations }
  { Add the next 3 lines of code: }
  procedure ChangeMonth(NewMonth : Word);
  procedure ChangeYear(NewYear : Word);
  procedure SetMonthLabel(NewMonth: Word);
public
  { Public declarations }
end;
```

Add the implementations shown in Listing BD1.3 to the form.

Listing BD1.3. The ChangeMonth, ChangeYear, and SetMonthLabel implementations.

```
procedure TForm1.ChangeYear(NewYear : Word);
begin
     Calendar1.Year := NewYear;
     Label2.Caption := IntToStr(NewYear);
end;
```

```

procedure TForm1.ChangeMonth(NewMonth : Word);
begin
     { Reset the month and display it.
       If bumping up a month from the previous month and hitting
       the end of the year, wrap back to the beginning of the next
       year. }
     if NewMonth > 12 then
        begin
             { Move to January of the next year. }
             ChangeMonth(1);
             ChangeYear(Calendar1.Year + 1);
        end
     { If bumping back a month from the previous month and hitting
       the start of the year, wrap up to the end of the previous
       year. }
     else if NewMonth < 1 then
          begin
               { Move to December of the previous year }
               ChangeMonth(12);
               ChangeYear(Calendar1.Year [ms] 1);
          end
     else
         Calendar1.Month := NewMonth;
     { Redisplay the new month. }
     SetMonthLabel(Calendar1.Month);
end;

procedure TForm1.SetMonthLabel(NewMonth: Word);
const
     Months : array [1..12] of string[9] =
            ('January',
            'February',
            'March',
            'April',
            'May',
            'June',
            'July',
            'August',
            'September',
            'October',
            'November',
            'December');
begin
     { Convert the month from an ordinal number to a string. }
     Label1.Caption := Months[NewMonth];
end;
```

Add the event handler in Listing BD1.4 to the form activate event.

Listing BD1.4. The FormActivate event handler.

```
procedure TForm1.FormActivate(Sender: TObject);
var
   Present : TDateTime;
   Year, Month, Day : Word;
begin
     { Obtain the current time and date. }
     Present := Now;
     { Decompose the date into word values. }
     DecodeDate(Present, Year, Month, Day);
     { Display the current month next to the left spin button. }
     SetMonthLabel(Month);
     { Display the current year next to the right spin button. }
     ChangeYear(Year);
end;
```

Add the event handlers shown in Listing BD1.5 to the left spin button.

Listing BD1.5. The left spin button's event handlers.

```
procedure TForm1.SpinButton1DownClick(Sender: TObject);
begin
     { Count back a month, then redraw the month label. }
     ChangeMonth(Calendar1.Month [ms] 1)
end;

procedure TForm1.SpinButton1UpClick(Sender: TObject);
begin
     { Count forward a month, then redraw the month label. }
     ChangeMonth(Calendar1.Month + 1)
end;
```

And the event handlers shown in Listing BD1.6 to the right spin button.

Listing BD1.6. The right spin button's event handlers.

```
procedure TForm1.SpinButton2DownClick(Sender: TObject);
begin
     { Count back a year, then redisplay the year label. }
     ChangeYear(Calendar1.Year [ms] 1)
end;

procedure TForm1.SpinButton2UpClick(Sender: TObject);
begin
     { Count forward a year, then redisplay the year label. }
     ChangeYear(Calendar1.Year + 1)
end;
```

Finally, add DDEServerConv's OnExecuteMacro event handler, as shown in Listing BD1.7.

This code executes when the DDECAL DDE server receives a macro command from a DDE client application.

Listing BD1.7. The macro handler for DDECAL.

```
procedure TForm1.DdeServerConv1ExecuteMacro(Sender: TObject;
  Msg: TStrings);
var
   { Plucked off the Msg TStrings object for convenience. }
   Macro : String;
begin
     { Don't let a malformed command cause a runtime error. }
     if Msg.Count = 0 then
        begin
             ShowMessage(Application.Exename +
               ': Macro not received');
             exit;
        end;
     { Get the text of the macro in a good ol' string. }
     Macro := Msg.Strings[0];
     { Microsoft macros are usually surrounded by brackets,
       partly because of their complexity. These macros are
       much simpler and don't need brackets. It's strictly up the
       the programmer. }
     { If user clicked down arrow go forward a month. }
     if Macro = 'Month¦Next' then
        ChangeMonth(Calendar1.Month + 1)
     { If user clicked up arrow go back a month... }
     else if Macro = 'Month¦Prev' then
        ChangeMonth(Calendar1.Month [ms] 1)
     { And the same for years. }
     else if Macro = 'Year¦Prev' then
        ChangeYear(Calendar1.Year [ms] 1)
     { This is crying out for a CASE statement but it's impossible.
       Object Pascal doesn't allow case selectors to be strings. }
     else if Macro = 'Year¦Next' then
        ChangeYear(Calendar1.Year + 1)
end;
```

Save the project as DDECAL. You can compile and run this program as is, and you have a handy calendar that tells you at a glance what day March 11, 1962, fell on, or perhaps February 10, 1968. The real purpose of the exercise is to show its utility as a DDE server, however. Run DDECAL, and then create the next project, called DDELAB.

DDELAB is just that—a complete DDE laboratory. You will notice that it can do more things than just issue macros. These capabilities are explored after this first experiment, which attempts to open up a DDE channel between DDECAL and DDELAB and send a "show the next month" command from DDELAB (the client) to DDECAL (the server).

Table BD1.8 doesn't list all the controls; it lists only those whose names matter. Use the names you see here instead of the default names. It all will make sense when you see the code, which

helps make sense of the control names by matching them up with their DDE functions. Your DDELAB form should look like the form shown in Figure BD1.12.

Table BD1.8. The DDELAB project's form and its properties.

Component	Property	Value
DDEClientConv	Name	DDEClient
DDEClientConv	ConnectMode	ddeAutomatic
DDEClientItem	Name	DDEClientItem
DDEClientItem	DDEConv	DDEClient
Edit	Name	txtService
Edit	Name	txtTopic
Edit	Name	txtMacro
Button	Name	btnRequest
Button	Name	btnExecute

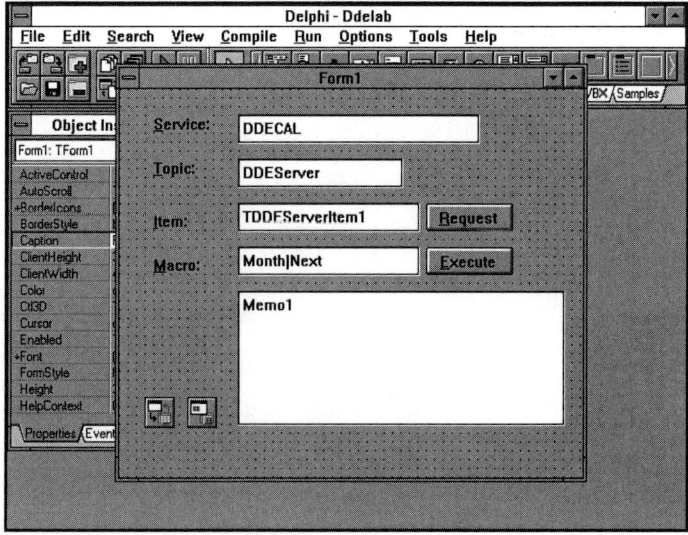

Figure BD1.12.
The DDELAB form.

Make the code shown in Listing BD1.8 the OnClick handler for btnExecute.

Listing BD1.8. The Execute button's OnClick handler.

```
procedure TForm1.btnExecuteClick(Sender: TObject);
var
   { Allocate plenty of space for a null-terminated buffer. }
   MacroCmd : array [0..80] of char;
begin
     DDEClient.SetLink(txtService.Text,txtTopic.Text);
     DDEClient.OpenLink;
     { This lets us use a program by its executable name instead
       of its application name.  If the Application field is
       nonblank, assign it to the DDEClient's ServeApplication
       field, which takes priority over the application name. }
     if txtApplication.Text <> '' then
       DDEClient.ServiceApplication := txtApplication.Text;
     { Convert the macro from a Pascal string to a null-terminated
       C string. }
     StrPCopy(MacroCmd, txtMacro.Text);
     { Pass the macro command to the server asynchronously.
       Come back as soon as it's been started, not after it's
       been executed. }
     if (DDEClient.ExecuteMacro(MacroCmd,False) = False) then
        ShowMessage('Unable to execute macro.');
     { Release conversation resources. }
     DDEClient.CloseLink;
end;
```

Add the code in Listing BD1.9 to the btnRequest's OnClick handler:

Listing BD1.9. The OnClick handler for the Request button.

```
procedure TForm1.btnRequestClick(Sender: TObject);
var
   szInfo : PChar;
begin
     { Define the DDE conversation, using the user-supplied topic.}
     DDEClient.SetLink(txtService.Text,txtTopic.Text);
     { Start the conversation. }
     DDEClient.OpenLink;
{ RequestData allocates a null-terminated string and returns it. }
     szInfo := DDEClient.RequestData(txtItem.Text);
     { Fill memo box with lines of text returned by RequestData}
     { The memo deallocates it automatically. }
     Memo1.SetTextBuf(szInfo);
     { Terminate the DDE conversation. }
     DDEClient.CloseLink;
end;
```

At this point, DDECAL should be running, as shown in Figure BD1.13. If it is not running, start it from Program Manager. Note the month DDECAL displays (it should be the current month, unless you have tweaked the spin buttons after starting it), because DDELAB is about to change the displayed month. Compile and run DDELAB. Switch to DDELAB, type `DDECAL` in the Service box, leave the Application box empty, type `DDEServer` in the Topic box, type `TDDEServerItem1` in the Item box, type `Month ¦ Next` in the Macro box, and then click the Macro button.

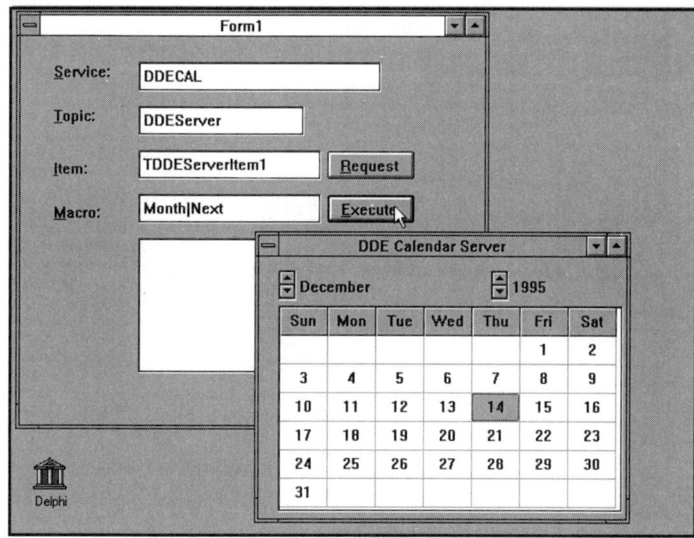

Figure BD1.13.
Using the DDELAB client to control the DDECAL server.

DDECAL receives the Month | Next macro command, and the month is bumped up one. If the current month is December, DDECAL's program logic also bumps up to the next year. Although this simple macro only moves DDECAL's month ahead one, you easily can add calls to use the other macros, such as Year | Prev. DDECAL already supports such code.

Getting Program Manager under Control

You can use DDELAB to explore the entire Program Manager DDE interface. This section contains a reference to all nine Program Manager commands and their parameters. Microsoft recommends that you explain the DDE interface to your server applications in your program documentation, but—surprise—this information can't be found in any of the Windows online help, README files, or manuals. Instead, you have to subscribe to the Microsoft Developer's Network CD. Just in case you don't have an extra few hundred bucks a year for MSDN, I have summarized the commands here. You can try them out in DDELAB.

In all cases, set Service to PROGMAN and Topic to PROGMAN. Type the command you want to issue in the Macro control, and then click the Execute button. Note that, as is the convention with many, but not all, Microsoft DDE servers, you need to surround the entire macro with square brackets. Many commands have optional parameters or comma-delimited lists of parameters. If there is a comma-delimited list, you can omit parameters as long as you leave the commas there as place markers and default values are used. Although as a programmer, you might expect string values to be delimited by single or double quotes, they aren't. The macro to create a group called EasySum would be [CreateGroup(EasySum)], not [CreateGroup("EasySum")]. The active group is the selected group; you can tell that it is active because its title bar is in a distinctive color if the group isn't minimized (iconized), and the text is shown in a distinctive color if it is minimized.

Figure BD1.14 shows an example that creates an empty program group called foo. If you already have a program group called foo, don't worry. It will just create a new one. You can use a different name, at any rate. Enter the values shown in Table BD1.9.

Table BD1.9. Entering values into DDELAB.

In this text box	Enter this value
Service	progman
Topic	progman
Macro	[CreateGroup(foo)]

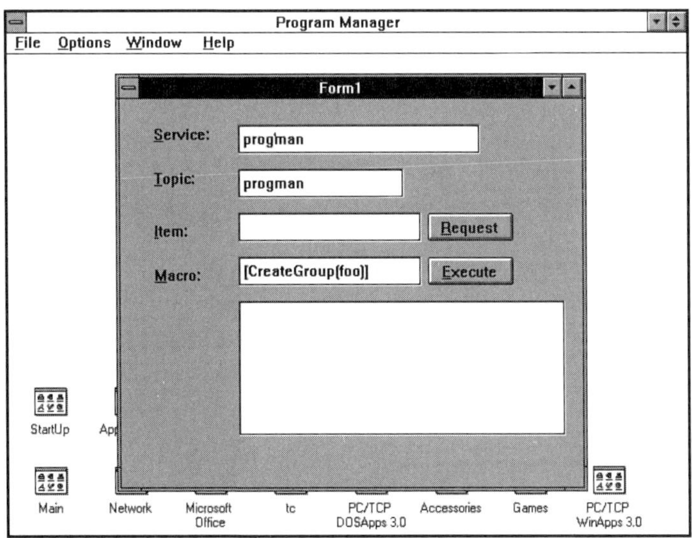

Figure BD1.14.
DDELAB after the values in Table BD1.9 are entered.

Click the Execute button. The new group appears, as shown in Figure BD1.15.

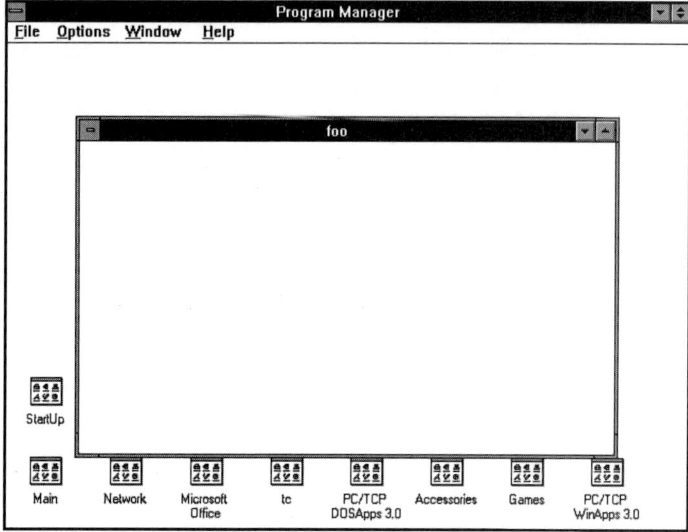

Figure BD1.15.
The group created using the [CreateGroup(foo)] DDE macro.

A Program Manager Macro Reference

The macros Program Manager can execute aren't well documented anywhere. This section contains reference information, examples, and some notes regarding experiments I ran. They were not always consistent with the Microsoft documentation, which could generously be described as sparse. As near as I can tell, this is the only reference of its kind.

AddItem

Format

```
[AddItem(CmdLine,Name,IconPath,IconIndex,XPos,YPos,DefaultDir,
HotKey,Minimize)]
```

Description

Adds an icon to a group. It must be an existing group. These are the same attributes you would set manually by clicking the icon in Program Manager and choosing Properties from the File menu.

All items except CmdLine are optional.

Parameters

CmdLine is the executable file. If it is on the path, you don't need to specify a drive or directory. If it is not on the path, it must be a fully qualified file name. You can use Windows associations. If you specify the file DELPHI.HLP, for example, WinHelp automatically runs on DELPHI.HLP. CmdLine also can use command-line parameters, as on a DOS command line (for example, NOTEPAD C:\T\ADA.TXT). When there is a command-line parameter like this, the title of the icon is given the root name of the parameter. The preceding example produces an icon named Ada, not NOTEPAD C:\T\ADA.TXT.

Name

The icon's title as it appears in the program group.

IconPath

The file from which to extract the icon itself. It can be an EXE, a DLL, an icon file, or even an associated file.

IconIndex

Many EXEs and DLLs have more than one icon in them. This is the icon's position in the file, starting with 1.

Xpos

An integer specifying the X coordinate of the icon's upper left corner in the program group.

Ypos

An integer specifying the Y coordinate of the icon's upper left corner in the program group.

If neither XPos nor YPos is specified, the icon appears in the next available slot. If ReplaceItem was used previously and XPos and YPos are left unspecified, the position is that of the icon that was removed with ReplaceItem (got that?).

DefaultDir

The working directory for the program named in the CmdLine parameter.

HotKey

Probably a virtual key code for the hotkey.

Minimize

If nonzero, the program is run minimized instead of in the normal position when it starts. If default (left empty) or 0, it does not minimize the program when it is run.

Examples

Add an icon called Notepad to the current group that runs Notepad:

```
[AddItem(notepad.exe)]
```

Add an icon called Log Calls to the current group that runs Notepad on the file C:\T\TIMELOG.TXT:

```
[AddItem(c:\windows\notepad.exe c:\t\timelog.txt,Log Calls)]
```

Add an icon called Minimized Notepad to the current group that runs Notepad minimized, using C:\ as the working directory:

```
[AddItem(c:\windows\notepad.exe,Minimized Notepad,,,,,c:\,,0)]
```

Add a shortcut to the Delphi Help system called Delphi Help. This displays the Help icon:

```
[AddItem(d:\delphi\bin\delphi.hlp,Delphi Help)]
```

Add an item called MyProg to the current program group. It starts Notepad, but it uses the Delphi icon. Place it in the next available space (no position was specified):

```
[AddItem(c:\windows\notepad.exe,MyProg,d:\delphi\bin\delphi.exe)]
```

Add an item called DOS Modem Program to the current program group. It actually starts Notepad, but it uses the fifth icon from PROGMAN.EXE, which is a picture of a telephone on a DOS screen. Place it in the next available space (no position was specified):

```
[AddItem(c:\windows\notepad.exe,DOS Modem Program,c:\windows\progman.exe,5)]
```

Add an item called Secondary DOS Shell to the current program group. It starts the DOS command shell in the root directory of drive C. It uses the MSDOS icon (the first one) from PROGMAN.EXE. It is positioned at position 4-3 in the current program group:

```
[AddItem(c:\command.com,Secondary DOS Shell,c:\windows\progman.exe,
1,4,3)]
```

CreateGroup

Format

```
[CreateGroup(Name,Path)]
```

Description

Creates an empty program group using the specified name. The Path parameter is optional.

Parameters

Name

The name of the program group to create. If it is the name of an existing group, that group is selected. You can include spaces and most punctuation marks in the name.

Path

The location for the GRP file, which contains information about the group and icons within it. If you omit it, a default name is generated and the file is placed in the Windows directory. A group name (the first parameter) can include punctuation marks and spaces, but filenames cannot. PROGMAN uses sophisticated algorithms to generate a legal filename from the group name. If you name a group A B C, for example, a group filename called ABC.GRP is generated. If you name a second group A B C, a group filename called ABC0.GRP is generated.

Examples

Create a program group named foo using the group filename foo.grp in the default Windows directory:

```
[CreateGroup(foo)]
```

Create a program group named foo using the group filename ada.grp in the \t directory instead of the Windows directory:

```
[CreateGroup(foo,c:\t\ada)]
```

Create a program group named foo with u.grp in the \t directory instead:

```
[CreateGroup(foo,c:\t\u.grp)]
```

DeleteGroup

Format

```
[DeleteGroup(Name)]
```

Description

Removes an existing group and all icons within it.

Parameter

Name

Name of the group (not the GRP filename).

Example

Remove the group named Regression Tests:

```
[DeleteGroup(Regression Tests)]
```

DeleteItem

Format

```
[DeleteItem(Name)]
```

Description

Removes an icon from the active group.

Parameter

Name

The title of the icon to delete.

Example

Remove the icon named New Minimized Notepad from the current group:

```
[DeleteItem(New Minimized Notepad)]
```

ExitProgman

Format

```
[ExitProgman(SaveGroups)]
```

Description

Quits Program Manager if it was started by another application. Does not work if you started Windows from the DOS prompt.

Parameter

SaveGroups

If nonzero, writes out all group and icon positions. Similar to choosing Save Settings on Exit from the Program Manager Options menu.

Example

Quit Windows. Do not save changed settings for program groups or icons.

```
[ExitProgman(0)]
```

Reload

Format

```
[Reload(Name)]
```

Description

Rereads the specified group file and updates the display accordingly. Name is optional. If omitted, rereads all group entries in PROGMAN.INI.

Parameter

Name

The name of the group file to regenerate.

Examples

Redisplay the Accessories group based on the most current group information:

```
[Reload(Accessories)]
```

Redisplay all of Program Manager's groups:

```
[Reload]
```

ReplaceItem

Format

```
[ReplaceItem(Name)]
```

Description

Deletes an icon from the current group and leaves that slot open for the next default AddItem. The next AddItem command without the XPos and YPos position coordinates given will place its icon in that position.

Parameter

Name

The name of the icon to delete.

Example

Leave a hole where the Notepad icon once resided:

```
[ReplaceItem(Notepad)]
```

ShowGroup

Format

```
ShowGroup(Name,WindowState)
```

Description

Displays or minimizes a group with the specified window state. I couldn't get all eight options to work in my experiments.

Parameters

Name

The name of the group to display.

WindowState

An integer from 1 to 8 inclusive. Here are the values and what they mean:

1. Activate specified group window and display in normal state.
2. Activate specified group window and display in minimized state.
3. Activate specified group window and display in maximized state.
4. Do not activate specified group window but display in most recent size and position.

Note: In my experiments, option 4 does indeed activate the group window. Therefore, it has the same effect as option 1.

5. Activate the specified group window, leaving its window state unchanged.

Note: In my experiments, option 5 simply does not work.

6. Minimize the specified group window.
7. Minimize the specified group window without activating it.
8. Display in current window state, without activating it.

Example

Restore the Accessories group and make it current:

```
Macro: [ShowGroup(Accessories,1)]
```

An Introduction to OLE

Although DDE can be used to share data between applications, it no longer is considered the preferred method to do so. OLE (Object Linking and Embedding) has subsumed DDE, in Microsoft's estimation. OLE is a much more sophisticated data model and provides a broader canvas to paint on, but it also represents a more complex set of programming issues. To a great extent, Delphi's OLEContainer makes OLE almost automatic. This section includes two complete programs that use OLE containers in typical scenarios, with far less code than you might expect.

OLE often is demonstrated by showing how you can insert a live Excel range into a Word document. Instead of using Paste Link, you use Insert Object; and you can use a file for the embedded data or start a new document. So far, this doesn't seem much different from DDE. The difference becomes more apparent when you double-click the Excel object. Excel does not pop up as a separate application, as it does with a DDE connection. Instead, it merges its toolbar and some of its menus with those of Word, giving you something closer to a seamless editing environment. This is called *in-place activation,* and it's considered one of OLE's coolest features—by those who don't know much about OLE.

Impressive as it is, in-place activation is trivial compared to some of the feats Microsoft already has demonstrated with OLE file systems. The overall effect is supposed to be that the document manages the applications that use it, instead of requiring the user to think in terms of what applications were used to create what parts of the document. If you look at the File menu of the server application (Excel, in this example) instead of Exit, you usually will see something like Exit and Update, although the application normally doesn't have Exit and Update on its File menu. Exit and Update silently saves the server's data in a file associated with the client document. As a user, you may not be aware of what's going on. All you did was insert a spreadsheet object; you didn't create a file, save it, and import that file into the word processor document. This is a stark difference from DDE, which provides a live link to an existing file, but which cannot duplicate the neat trick of essentially creating a new file with no user interaction at all, not even a name for the file.

You also can link files in OLE, and it's still slicker than DDE because of in-place activation. To emphasize what Microsoft so euphoniously calls this *document-centric* approach, the term *compound document* has been coined. It's a useful description for OLE's more transparent, automated approach to sharing data. Microsoft didn't get this slick menu-merging idea right the first time around, so OLE 1.0 applications still pop up the entire application in a window beside the one with the document, just like DDE, but they still can insert objects. Also, OLE 2.0 servers still cannot be guaranteed that the containing applications can do the menu-merging trick either. Chapter 15 of the Delphi User's Guide ably covers the issues of menus and in-place activation.

Tip: Chapter 15 of the Delphi User's Guide doesn't seem to know about the Form Gallery, where you can get a "canned" MDI application up and running fast. Use it to jump-start your in-place activation instead of following Chapter 15's remedial MDI instruction.

Future versions of Windows will go far, far beyond simple in-place activation, which is already a significant achievement. The new OLE file system will be completely object-oriented and distributed, and those aren't just buzzwords. Here's what that means in some future scenarios. Right now, Windows uses file extensions as a simple—and simplistic—mechanism for associating file "types" with an application. If you double-click a file ending in XLS in File Manager, for example, Windows runs Excel because there's an association between that file extension and Excel. Choosing Associate from Program Manager's File menu brings up a dialog box that gives you the illusion that an XLS file is a spreadsheet "type," although its only type attribute is a file extension.

It's easy to see the limitations of this approach. What happens if you have saved Excel data in a file that doesn't happen to end in XLS? Or, what if you have saved a text file, but have absentmindedly given it an XLS extension? An even more obvious problem is that applications sometimes battle for file extensions; there must have been four or five popular word processors over the years that used the extension DOC for their files. Because Associate is limited to one application for its association with DOC files, what would you do if someone wanted to install one of those other word processors on your Windows system for a writing project? Clearly, it would be useful to provide a less arbitrary and more reliable mechanism to associate file types with applications than to hope that the user happened to remember to suffix a filename with the

appropriate three letters, and to hope that all software manufacturers somehow will magically agree on this sharply limited set of file extensions (any bets on who gets to keep DAT, for example?). Along with the file extension, there are a few other small attribute bits and two date values that you can use to associate attributes with files, but calling these type information would be much more charitable than reality permits.

If you're an experienced Macintosh user, you immediately will recognize that a more sophisticated approach already has been in use for more than a decade. Macintosh files contain a 4-byte sequence called a *creator string*. Vendors register their creator strings with Apple and therefore are guaranteed uniqueness and a much stronger link between files and applications.

Much stronger, but still not strong enough. For one thing, 32 bits aren't necessarily enough to keep conflicts from arising, because for years Apple assigned blocks of creator IDs for vendors instead of just a single 32-bit signature at a time, and of course many smaller vendors never got around to registering or couldn't afford to register. If your company was named Telos Software Products, for example, Apple might in the early days have been generous enough to assign you all 256 possibilities starting with the 3 bytes T, S, and P, and ending with any number from 0 to 255. In those days, the creator string seemed to be more than enough for all eternity.

Fantasy aside, your application might need to associate a great deal more than 32 bits with its file. You might want to assign a separate, subfile of OLE data as an attribute to a file created by one of your applications, for example. Or, you might choose to associate not just an icon, but a moving 3-D picture with a few of your data files, but not all of them. Or, you might want as an attribute of the file a separate security application to prevent unauthorized users from using that file. None of these alternatives is possible with the Mac, Windows 3.1, or Windows 95, but a revision of Windows already is being demonstrated that offers virtually unlimited, object-oriented extensions to the Windows file system, and it's all implemented using OLE. But wait—there's more!

OLE-adherent applications will be expected to support a set of *verbs*, much like DDE topics. OLE server applications will perform more and more of their activity at the behest of other automated agents, so that users don't have to remember disparate command sets. A text-search program, for example, will be able to call on FoxPro to do SQL searches of a database, and Word for Windows to do a search, all without having to know each language syntax because it will be able to use an OLE verb such as Find, and the OLE server applications will map that verb to their own command sets.

If you think about it, this correlates very closely with the Object Pascal concept of a class. You provide a data structure (in this case, for example, a spreadsheet or a word processing document) and a set of methods that apply to that document. The methods will be OLE verbs supported by the application. All of these things and more will be possible with the OLE file system that will provide the underpinnings for later, non-DOS versions of Windows. But it doesn't end with rich attributes. The network will be implemented more like the Internet than NetWare.

In fact, future versions of Windows will be grafted onto OLE, not the other way around. Imagine storing a database in an OLE file. The OLE file system will be distributed completely and will allow portions of the same file to reside not only on different machines across a network, but on different networks across the world. To simplify only slightly, a single call to the traditional Pascal write or read routines could end up affecting databases in New York, Sri Lanka, and Shanghai without you, the programmer, being at all aware that this was happening.

Okay, you say, it's a whiz-bang vision of the future, but what benefits will all these features buy me? Quite a bit. At the moment, distributed file systems that need to coordinate in different parts of the world are much more common than you think, but network support is so primitive as to be useless in some cases and worse than useless in others. Suppose that a firm has branches in several countries. Where does the customer list reside? What happens if clerks in two offices want to update your customer profile at the same time? Right now, without operating system support for distributed file systems, it's a crapshoot. A good programmer will implement a necessarily complex semaphore/locking scheme that combines acknowledgment, time-outs, and handling of race conditions and deadlocks. This is hard to get right, but it doesn't mean that all applications running on the system have been equally well designed. Or what if a single database file—a huge Access MDB file, for example—needs to span two different disk media at two different locations? For now, that's a pipe dream. With distributed OLE, it will be a part of the OS, and you will need to do little more in the way of error checking than you now do with calls to Assign and Read.

At the moment, OLE is of slightly less interest than it might be for some utterly prosaic reasons. At the top of the list is the fact that OLE is so ungainly. RAM prices haven't dropped at all in the last few years, whereas hard disk prices have plummeted. Still, applications are being developed that seem to think RAM is unlimited. In order to get anything like acceptable performance from OLE compound documents on a Windows 3.1 or Windows 95 machine, you need at least 16MB of RAM, and that's only with two fairly large applications, such as Word and Excel. Another reason that OLE hasn't completely dominated application development in the four or five years it has been out is that it's hard enough for programmers to keep up with things like DDE; in fact, until Microsoft "simplified" DDE programming with the DDEML library, it languished. Much the same has happened with OLE, which is a couple of orders of magnitude more difficult to program. Even with shortcuts like Delphi's OLEContainer component or the BOCOLE library with Borland C++, there's a great deal to learn. If you want to create a fully formed, commercial-quality product, such as a drawing or word processing program that can handle compound documents as well as Word and Excel do, you will be in for some serious overtime.

Currently, Delphi has only OLE container components. That is, you can use the OLE container in your applications to make use of OLE services from other programs. Borland is working on support for OLE server components. If this whole container/server thing sounds hauntingly familiar, it's because it *is* familiar. OLE containers are very similar to DDE clients in concept,

and in implementation they *are* DDE clients. Server components enable your application to act as a service provider to OLE clients. There are a great many complications to be dealt with for whomever Borland assigns to writing server components, and almost no language environments at this point enable you to create servers, much less with the simplicity and convenience that are hallmarks of Delphi development.

One of the neat things about OLE currently is that much of it is visible. In order to graft a pseudo-object orientation on top of the staid old DOS, Microsoft has implemented *object registration*. This is a set of utilities and system calls that enable the operating environment (Windows, of course) to keep track of many object attributes, including their names and, to some extent, their file formats. The REGEDIT.EXE applet in your Accessories group is a good way to get an idea of how Windows registers OLE objects. Be sure to start it with the ill-documented /V command-line option using Program Manager's File|Run, which gives you full access to registration information.

Creating Applications with OLE Containers

The Delphi User's Guide does a yeoman's job of detailing all the considerations involved in the OLEContainer component. This has the unintended side effect of making it seem really complicated to whip together a simple container application, but it actually can be done in almost no time. Even the tiny example presented here, which does nothing but enable you to insert any OLE object into the single, provided container, has a direct counterpart in real life.

Some developers of vertical market (read: expensive and complicated) have applications that require a very large volume of online documentation. Instead of throwing massive amounts of development time at converting the word processor documents that comprise their manuals into Help files, they're using OLE containers like the one you're about to see as the "Help window" in their applications. The containers are linked to the original word processing documents, which therefore lose none of the formatting and style sheet information that have been so painstakingly built into the document, and which Help generators always seem to lose in translation. It's not limited to OLE server word processors like Word or Ami Pro from Lotus, either. You can use the same technique to embed database, spreadsheet, or any other kinds of data backed by OLE server applications. If you create your documentation in Microsoft Word for Windows, you even can get a free viewer program from Microsoft and use it as an OLE server to create a viewer for Word documents. That way, you don't have to buy a copy of WinWord for each copy of your application that you distribute.

OLE Container Quickstart

This section presents the steps required to create an OLE container application that can accept any OLE object from any OLE server at run-time. If you know in advance what OLE object you want to link to, you can make the connection at compile-time. Begin with the general-purpose case, in which you bring up an Insert Object dialog box to choose from all registered OLE objects on the system. After this summary, you will see an example.

To insert objects at run-time, follow these steps:

1. Add an OLEContainer component to the form.
2. Add a private InitializeOLEObject method to the form's class declaration to initialize the OLE mechanism. It must be passed a magic pointer value called Info.
3. Write an implementation of the InitializeOLEObject routine in your form class. This code must execute before any objects are inserted.
4. Make a call to InsertOLEObjectDlg. This routine alone is worth the price of admission, and represents a massive savings on the time it would take you to implement this feature yourself. This dialog box lists all registered OLE objects and gives you a chance to pick one. When you do, it is inserted on the OLEContainer and immediately becomes live data.
5. (Optional) Save the OLE data when your application terminates. The corollary is that you should load any existing OLE data on startup. Both of these cases are handled as an addendum to this section.

Now create a mini-application to see just how easy it is to add run-time OLE support to your application. Start a new project and choose the OLEContainer component from the System Palette. Drag until it fills most of the form.

Add this routine declaration to the private interface section of the form declaration (it doesn't have to use this name):

```
procedure InitializeOLEObject(Info: Pointer);
```

Your form declaration now should look like Listing BD1.10.

Listing BD1.10. The complete form declaration.

```
type
  TForm1 = class(TForm)
    OleContainer1: TOleContainer;
    procedure FormCreate(Sender: TObject);
  private
    { Private declarations }
    { ADD THIS DECLARATION }
    procedure InitializeOLEObject(Info: Pointer);
public
    { Public declarations }
  end;
```

Now add Listing BD1.11 to the implementation section of the form.

Listing BD1.11. Adding an InitializeOLEObject implementation to the form.

```
procedure TForm1.InitializeOLEObject(Info: Pointer);
begin
     OLEContainer1.PInitInfo := Info;
     ReleaseOLEInitInfo(Info)
end;
```

Select the OLEContainer component and add the OnDblClick handler for it shown in Listing BD1.12. Remember—this isn't the form's double-click handler, it's the OLEContainer's.

Listing BD1.12. Handling double-clicks for the OLE container.

```
procedure TForm1.OleContainer1DblClick(Sender: TObject);
var
   Info : Pointer;
begin
     if InsertOLEObjectDlg(Form1, 0, Info)then
        InitializeOLEObject(Info);
end;
```

That's all you have to do. Your program now is ready to accept OLE objects. Run the program. Double-click the OLE component, and the Insert Object dialog box appears, as shown in Figure BD1.16.

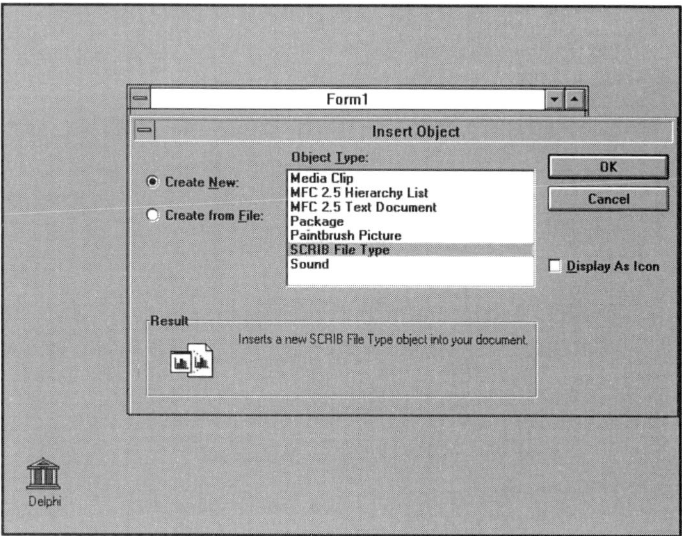

Figure BD1.16.
The Insert Object dialog box.

Choose Paintbrush Picture. Draw something, and then choose Exit & Return to Form1 from the File menu. Note that you're not asked for a filename, and that it doesn't say just Exit at the bottom of the File menu, as it does when Paintbrush is running normally.

This isn't the most flexible container application in the world, but it does okay and would be perfect if its job were simply to display data from an OLE server. If you double-click the picture again, you bring up the Insert Object dialog box again. You can click Cancel to exit that dialog box and replace the existing embedded object with another one. Or, you can reselect the Paintbrush object and edit the existing one. The main problem is that the program you just created doesn't know how to save documents.

Saving OLE Data

Although it was mentioned earlier that OLE container applications don't make the user save files explicitly, there is no magic to what happens. It turns out that you, the programmer, are responsible for saving that data, and it takes only a single line of code. Just call the SaveToFile method of the OLEContainer. You restore it by calling the component's LoadFromFile method, as in the following examples:

```
OLEContainer1.SaveToFile('\DATA\APP.OLE');
```

```
OLEContainer1.LoadFromFile('\DATA\APP.OLE');
```

You are expected to save the OLE data every time the user creates a file with OLE objects embedded in it. One convention for filenames is to use the root of the filename, but an extension of OLE, leaving it in the same directory as the data-containing file. This is somewhat limiting, because it only works on a per-container basis, meaning that if you have more than one container on a form, you will have a name conflict.

Now retrofit the following code to the OLE container program you just wrote. Your program will load existing OLE components from disk as soon as you open a form, and write them back to disk when the form is closed (the application is quit). Again, you should never ask the user for a filename when you're saving persistent OLE data.

The obvious place to start is the form's OnCreate() handler, which occurs when the form is loaded. Remember that the first time the program is invoked, there is no OLE file for it to load. Some sample code to read in the OLE data is shown in Listing BD1.13.

Listing BD1.13. The FormCreate code.

```
procedure TForm1.FormCreate(Sender: TObject);
begin
     if FileExists('foo.tmp') then
        OleContainer1.LoadFromFile('foo.tmp')
     else
          ShowMessage('No OLE data on first invocation.')
end;
```

Add the FormClose event to save any data that might have changed. It consists of a single line:

Listing BD1.14. The FormClose code.

```
procedure TForm1.FormClose(Sender: TObject;
  var Action: TCloseAction);
begin
     OleContainer1.SaveToFile('foo.tmp')
end;
```

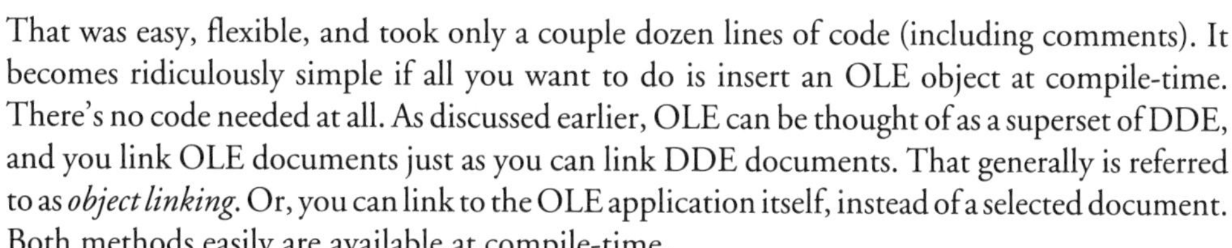

That was easy, flexible, and took only a couple dozen lines of code (including comments). It becomes ridiculously simple if all you want to do is insert an OLE object at compile-time. There's no code needed at all. As discussed earlier, OLE can be thought of as a superset of DDE, and you link OLE documents just as you can link DDE documents. That generally is referred to as *object linking*. Or, you can link to the OLE application itself, instead of a selected document. Both methods easily are available at compile-time.

To insert objects at compile-time, follow these steps:

1. Add an OLEContainer component to the form.
2. Select the OLEContainer and choose the ObjClass property if you want to link to an application.

   Alternatively, choose the ObjDoc property if you want to link to an OLE server application's document.
3. Double-click the value box and choose an object type from the list.

Alternatively, double-click the value box, click the File radio button in the Insert Object dialog box, choose an object type, and browse for a file to link to.

Try it with Paintbrush.

Summary

Today's bonus lesson opened up a whole new kind of programming: remote control of other applications through DDE and data sharing through OLE.

DDE is used primarily for interapplication communication, whereas OLE is used more for data sharing—most notably linking and embedding data into *compound documents*.

In DDE, the application requesting a service from another application is called the *client*. The application providing the service is called the *server*. Early Microsoft documentation (version 1.0 of DDE, originating with Windows 3.0) had the meanings of *client* and *server* reversed. They are now "corrected" to the meanings described here.

When contact is made, a DDE *conversation* has been initiated. The name used by one application to contact the other is the *service* or *application* name. The subject of the conversation is called its *topic*; very often, when data is being exchanged, the topic is a filename. The data that gets moved back and forth—the reason for the conversation—is called an *item*. In a spreadsheet, for example, the item might be a range of cells. In a word processor, it might be the selected text.

With some applications, you can use DDE to link "live" data from a server application into the client. When the data is changed in the server, it is reflected back in the client's document. If you double-click a DDE link, the server application executes and updates the file automatically.

OLE is seen by Microsoft as the successor to DDE, even though OLE is written using DDE. OLE follows the client-server model, but OLE clients now are called *container* applications. Embedded OLE 2.0 applications, if written correctly, can be made to merge menus with the client program while embedded values are being edited.

Q&A

Q Must a program be both a DDE client and a DDE server?

A No.

Q Can I write OLE server applications using Delphi?

A Not with version 1.0, the current version as of this printing. However, Borland plans to release a version with OLE server component support as soon as possible.

It's not entirely true that that you cannot write OLE server applications using Delphi. You could, if you were a Delphi wizard, but then you probably wouldn't be reading this book. In fact, you probably would be part of the Delphi development team—it's that challenging. Microsoft has documented the system calls required to create OLE server applications, but it's an enormously complex interface and requires numerous direct calls to the Windows API. It's best to wait for Borland to do it right.

Q Can I write OLE custom controls using Delphi?

A Okay, smarty pants, so you know about OLE custom controls. For the uninitiated, they will be explained in a bit. Anyway, as with the preceding answer, no, you cannot create OLE custom controls in a reasonable amount of time; but yes, you could do it if you were a genius and had a couple of years to devote to the process. OLE custom controls, sometimes called OCXs, are Microsoft's successor to VBXs. They cannot be termed wildly popular at the moment, but Borland also has pledged to add OCX development support to Delphi at some point in the future.

Q If Microsoft thinks DDE is becoming obsolete, why cover it at all in this book? Why not just stick to OLE?

A Because there are some things you just can't do any other way, like create program groups in an installation program. And as far as obsolescence goes, just fire up

WinSight and watch the blizzard of DDE messages when you do an Insert Object in an OLE container application. Microsoft has made it clear that it didn't *have* to use DDE to implement OLE, and that the DDE portion of it might go away, but I'd bet against it happening anytime soon. Too many applications rely on DDE, and with tens of millions of Windows installations, Microsoft no longer can be quite so cavalier about compatibility issues as new versions of Windows come out. There's even DDE support in Win32, Microsoft's "portable" version of the Windows API that runs on the Macintosh, DEC Alpha, PowerPC, and even some UNIX machines.

Workshop

The Workshop provides quiz questions to help you solidify your understanding of the material covered, and exercises to provide you with experience in using what you have learned. Answers are provided in Appendix B.

Quiz

1. True or False? Delphi has OLE server components, but no OLE client components.
2. True or False? An application cannot be both a DDE server and a DDE client.
3. True or False? It requires between 10 to 24 lines to add simple compile-time support for embedded OLE objects.
4. True or False? OLE is written using DDE.
5. Which of these statements is true?
    a. OLE takes less memory than DDE.
    b. OLE components use the LinkExecute method to send data.
    c. Some things can be done using DDE that cannot be done using OLE.

Exercises

1. Write a reusable procedure that enables you to determine information about a group. Pass all values in the procedure's parameter list so that the procedure can be recycled in any project.
2. Write a reusable procedure that allows the user to enter a service name, a topic, and an item, and then queries other applications using their root names to see whether they respond to any of Microsoft's standard DDE topics and items. Exit gracefully if they do not.

WEEK 3 IN REVIEW

15 16 17 18 19 20 21

Congratulations! You have completed the third week of training in Delphi and Object Pascal programming. Now that you have gained all that technical knowledge, you are ready to go back to Day 1 and work through the lessons and exercises of the entire three weeks with a full understanding of the issues involved…

More seriously, make sure that your education in Delphi development does not stop here. It is time for you to explore and discover. A single book could not have possibly answered all of your questions, but it surely should have raised many more. Hopefully it has helped you stand on your feet, to get you started at the point where starting is the most challenging task: at the very beginning. The knowledge you have gained throughout this book should give you enough courage and understanding to carry on with other books and with hands-on exploration.

The last week of study introduced you to a number of interesting areas of Object Pascal and Windows programming:

- You were taught the rules of visibility and scope in Object Pascal and how these rules allow you to access variables, object fields, and subroutines.
- You know how to display output under Windows, both on the screen and in the hardcopy format.
- You have an intimate familiarity with a number of built-in Delphi components, including all standard Windows controls.
- You know how to create your own components, thereby extending the capabilities of Delphi.
- You've learned how to create and use Dynamically Linked Libraries (DLLs), which enable you to take advantage of programming-language-independent development and to build a host of useful components and add-ons for other programs, all using Delphi.

Make sure you explore the more advanced issues of DDE and OLE programming in the bonus chapter that follows. Good luck!

Pascal Keywords

Pascal Keywords

Reserved Words

Object Pascal reserved words cannot be used as identifiers. The following is a list of 60 reserved words.

`and`	1. A logical operator. 2. A bitwise-manipulation operator.
`array`	Declares an array type, that is, a structured data type with many elements of the same kind.
`as`	Type-safe typecasting operator. Allows for type-safe polymorphism.
`asm`	The equivalent of begin in an assembly-language block.
`begin`	The beginning of an executable block of statements.
`case`	Introduces a multi-way conditional switch, allowing the selection of a particular path of execution depending on the value of a condition.
`class`	Declares a class type. Used in type-declarations to define new object-oriented classes.
`const`	Introduces a constant declaration block.
`constructor`	Appears in the header of a special method—a constructor—of an object; a constructor responsible for initializing an instance of an object.
`destructor`	Appears in the header of a special method—a destructor—of an object. A destructor is responsible for shutting down and de-initializing an instance of an object.
`div`	An integer division operator yielding an integer result.
`do`	1. An auxiliary keyword appearing in a header of a loop, such as **`while-do`**, **`for-to-do`**, **`for-downto-do`**. 2. Also appears in exception handling clauses, **`on-do`**.
`downto`	An auxiliary keyword used to define the direction of counting in a counted **`for`**-loop.
`else`	1. Introduces an alternate branch of an **`if-then-else`** statement. 2. Introduces a default clause in a **`case`** statement.
`end`	1. Ends a block of executable statements. Typically paired with a prior **`begin`**, also paired with a **`case`**. 2. End a structured data type declaration, such as a **`class`** or **`record`** declaration.
`except`	Introduces the exception-handling clause of a **`try-except`** block.
`exports`	Introduces a list of identifiers to be exported from an executable.

`file`	A built-in special data type handling input/output operations.
`finally`	The terminating part of the **`try-finally`** block guaranteed to be executed even in case of an exception.
`for`	Introduces a counted **`for`**-loop.
`function`	Appears in a subroutine header declaration indicating a subroutine returning a value.
`goto`	A mostly obsolete unconditional jump command indicating transfer of execution to a specified label.
`if`	Introduces a two-way conditional branch. Must be followed by a Boolean expression and paired with a **`then`** keyword.
`implementation`	Introduces one of the three possible sections of a source code unit (module). Implementation section is where all the subroutines are actually implemented in code.
`in`	A set membership operator. May appear as part of Boolean expressions to test whether a particular set member is present.
`inherited`	Indicates a call to a method inherited from an ancestor class. May only appear inside methods.
`initialization`	Introduces one of the three possible sections of a source code unit (module). Initialization is an executable block of statements executed at program start-up. May be replaced by a `begin`-keyword, except in units supporting visual forms, where such a replacement plays havoc with Delphi's automatic code generation facilities.
`inline`	A keyword introducing raw machine code.
`interface`	Introduces one of the three possible sections of a source code unit (module). Interface section is where you define types, constants, variables, and subroutines that are meant to be visible (exported) outside of the unit that declares them.
`is`	A class-type membership operator. Used to test whether or not a particular object is an instance of a given class.
`label`	Introduces a declaration of an identifier that can be a target of a **`goto`**-statement.
`library`	Designates a source-code file as the top-level module to be compiled into a DLL.
`mod`	An integer remainder operator.

Pascal Keywords

`nil`	A special value for a pointer or a class variable. Indicates "no reference".
`not`	1. A Boolean (logical) operator. 2. A bitwise manipulation operator.
`object`	Declares an old-style class type, now obsolete and replaced by the **`class`**-declarations. Used in type-declarations to define old-style object-oriented classes. Provided for compatibility with older versions of Borland Pascal.
`of`	An auxiliary keyword appearing in conjunction with other keywords in constructs like **`array-of`**, **`case-of`**, and so on.
`on`	Introduces a specialized branch of an exception-handling block, inside the **`except`**-clause of a **`try-except`** statement.
`or`	1. A Boolean (logical) operator. 2. A bitwise manipulation operator.
`packed`	A type-declaration modifier for structured types. Provided only for compatibility with other dialects of Pascal. Has no effect in Object Pascal.
`procedure`	Appears in a subroutine header declaration indicating a subroutine that does not directly return a value.
`program`	Designates a source-code file as the top-level module to be compiled into a Windows program (.EXE).
`property`	Appears inside class declarations defining a data attribute of a class.
`raise`	Appears inside executable blocks. Results in an exception being raised.
`record`	Declares a structured data type consisting of named fields.
`repeat`	Found inside executable blocks, introduces a loop that is executed at least once.
`set`	Declares a structured type known as a set (of ordinal values).
`shl`	A bitwise "shift-left" operator. Arithmetically performs the equivalent of raising an integer to a power of 2.
`shr`	A bitwise "shift-right" operator. Arithmetically performs the equivalent of dividing an integer by a power of 2.
`string`	Declares a Pascal-type of a character string, with the first byte designating the actual length of the string.
`then`	Must be matched with a preceding `if` keyword as part of a 2-way conditional branch statement.
`try`	1. As part of a **`try-finally`** block, introduces a "protected" executable section. If an exception occurs during the execution of the **`try`**-section, the `finally` section is guaranteed to execute the cleanup code.

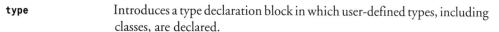

2. As part of a **try-except** block introduces a "protected" section during the execution of which any exception will cause the control to be transferred to the **except**-block.

A

`type`	Introduces a type declaration block in which user-defined types, including classes, are declared.
`unit`	Designates a source-code file as a non-top level module to be compiled into a Delphi binary unit, a .DCU file.
`until`	A closing clause of a **repeat-until** loop. Allows a Boolean test condition to be specified for loop termination.
`uses`	Introduces a **uses**-clause, in which names of other Object Pascal units are listed (imported).
`var`	Introduces a variable declaration block, in which actual storage is reserved for variables.
`while`	Introduces a **while-do** looping construct which may execute zero or more times, depending on the value of a Boolean condition preceding the **do**.
`with`	Introduces a context, or level of visibility, in which you may refer to instance variables or record fields without having to fully qualify them each time.
`xor`	1. An "exclusive-or" Boolean (logical) operator. 2. An "exclusive-or" bitwise manipulation operator.

Standard Directives

Standard directives are keywords that have special meaning in specific contexts. Outside of these contexts, these words are treated like regular identifiers. These are special words and their use to declare your own identifiers is discouraged, however. They are best treated as reserved words too.

`absolute`	Part of a variable's declaration, indicating a specific memory address for the variable.
`abstract`	Modifies a declaration of a method. An abstract method has no implementation and must be overriden in a descendant class.
`assembler`	Indicates that a particular subroutine is entirely written in the Built-In Assembler (BASM).
`cdecl`	Provides for compatibility with externally developed subroutines written in C and using the C calling conventions, which are different from Pascal's.

`default`	As part of a property declaration, indicates that a value other than the automatically initialized "zero-value" is to be treated as the default value for the property. Only values different than the default are persistently stored.
`dynamic`	Designates an object's method as a special virtual method, trading speed of execution for storage efficiency.
`export`	Designates an object's method as exportable, that is, capable of receiving calls from outside of the current Windows module (EXE, DLL).
`external`	Designates a subroutine as implemented externally. An external subroutine may be implemented in Assembler and statically linked into the application, or it may be implemented in a DLL.
`far`	Designates a subroutine as capable of being called from another segment, such as possibly another unit. All subroutines declared in a unit's interface are far by default.
`forward`	Allows a declaration of a subroutine to be given before its actual implementation, thus resolving a possible circular reference among subroutines in the same unit. All subroutines declared in the interface of a unit act as if **`forward`**-declared.
`index`	1. Designates the ordinal number by which an exported subroutine is to be known outside of the current Windows module (EXE, DLL). 2. Hard-codes an index in an indexed property.
`interrupt`	Designates a subroutine to be of a special kind: a DOS interrupt-handler. These are used for special low-level purposes like communicating with hardware.
`message`	Designates a method to be a Windows message handler: a special kind of dynamic method.
`name`	Allows for renaming of exported/externally imported subroutines from DLLs.
`near`	Designates a subroutine as local to the current code segment. The opposite of **`far`**.
`nodefault`	As part of a property declaration, reverses the effect of the **`default`** directive. Specifies that any value of the property diverging from the pre-initialized "zero" is stored persistently.
`override`	Designates a virtual method that will be called rather than the corresponding method of an ancestor in a polymorphic situation; the method called depends on the actual dynamic type of an object, not its static type.

`private`	Designates a section of a class declaration as visible only inside the unit defining the class, mostly to the methods of that class.
`protected`	Designates a section of a class declaration as visible only to the descendants of that class.
`public`	Designates a section of a class declaration as publicly visible.
`published`	Designates a section of a class declaration as publicly visible and exported in such a way that the Object Inspector can get access to the Run-Time Type Information about the class.
`read`	Optionally appears as part of a property declaration, specifying a means of obtaining a value for the property.
`resident`	Specifies that an external subroutine be cached permanently, that is, never unloaded or swapped to virtual memory.
`stored`	Explicitly designates a property as being persistently stored, even though the property was defined inside a section of the class declaration other than **`published`**.
`virtual`	Introduces a method that is meant to be overriden by descendant classes.
`write`	Optionally appears as part of a property declaration, specifying a means of setting a new value for the property.

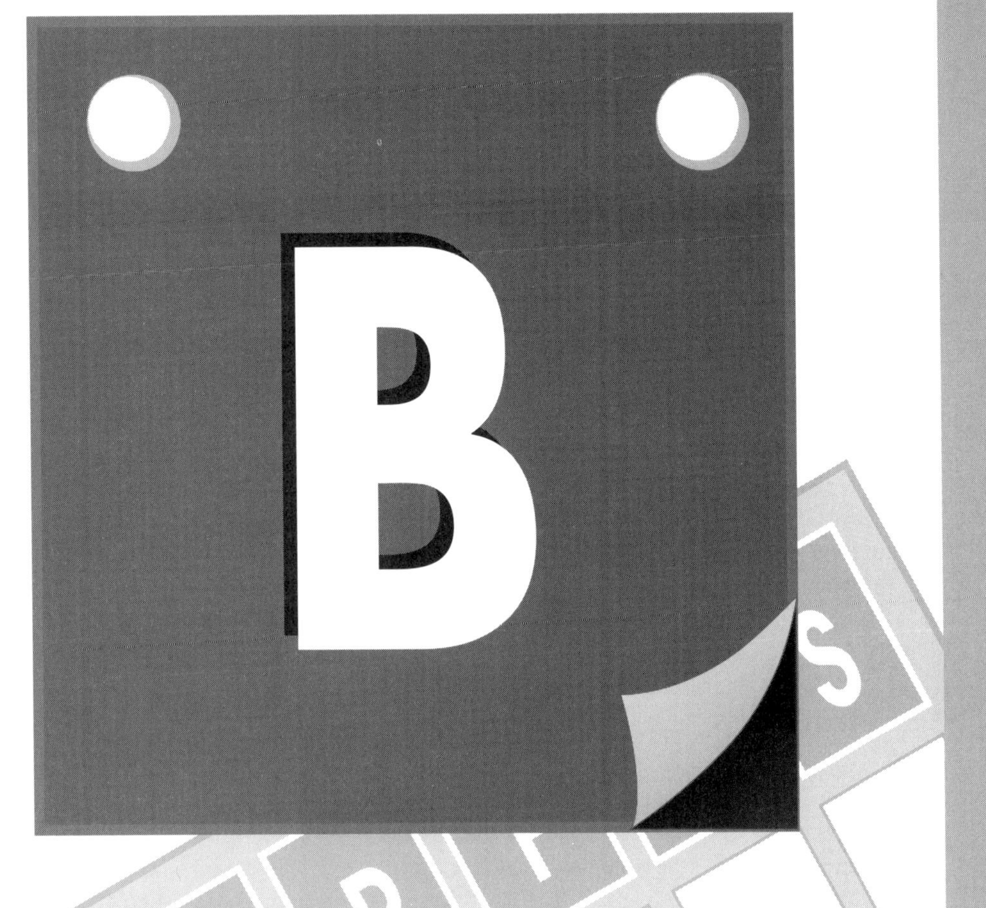

Answers to Exercises

Day 1

Quiz

1. Units traditionally have an extension of `.pas`; Delphi projects have an extension of `.dpr`.
2. This is not an easy question, since the overall productivity depends on many factors, the programming language being just one of them. There is no question, however, that measurable productivity improvement can be achieved by switching to a more readable language with an easier, more straightforward syntax like Object Pascal. Expect a productivity improvement by a factor of anywhere from 2 to 5. The improvement will be more dramatic with novice programmers than with experienced ones.
3. Yes, existing Turbo Pascal code can be compiled directly by Delphi, with only minor changes. Typically changes are localized to the `uses`-clause. For instance, the new unit `Messages` has taken some responsibilities over from the old `OWindows` and `ODialogs`.
4. Again, this is a fairly typical question that does not have a straightforward answer. It depends on your existing skills, your ability to learn, and your dedication. Learning a new programming language takes time. If you are also learning object-orientation and Windows at the same time, while you are exploring Delphi environment in the process, you can see that there is a lot to learn. Expect to invest anywhere from a year to two years of intense learning to truly master all of these areas of knowledge. Note that you become *productive* much earlier than that. (Hopefully after reading this book.)
5. There are many ways to align several visual components on a form all at once. One way would be to select all the components you wish to align by clicking on them inside the Form Designer while simultaneously holding down the Shift key. Once all the components of interest are selected, you can enter values for all the properties they have in common, including the Left or Top property in case of visual components. You can then enter the value of the property once, press the Enter key, and the value will be assigned to the corresponding property of each of the selected components.
6. The form's visible title is called its `Caption`.
7. In general, there is no relationship between the name of the form and the name of the form's unit. You are free to choose each one independently. Of course, if you choose a particular name for the unit, the form must not have the same name. This creates an identifier conflict and the compiler complains about it.

Exercises

1. Use the HELLO example you have developed during the course of today's lesson as the basis for this exercise. First, change the `Font` property of the label with the 'Hello World!' caption to display the text in white. Select the label by clicking on it with the left mouse button. The properties of the label become visible inside the Object Inspector. Double-click the right-hand column—the value column—of the `Font` property to open the standard Windows font selection dialog box. Inside the dialog box, select White for the color, then press the OK button.

   To center the 'Hello World!' message on the form, use the Alignment dialog box. First, select the label with the 'Hello World!' caption by clicking on it with the left mouse button. Click the right mouse button while the mouse cursor is over the form in the Form Designer. A local menu opens. Select "Align..." from the menu to open the Alignment dialog box. Select "Center in window" for both "Horizontal" and "Vertical" alignment. Press the OK button. The label is now centered within the form.

   Finally, change the background color of the form to Navy Blue. Click on the form outside the label to deselect the label. The Object Inspector now shows the form as the selected component. Click the `Color` property of the form inside the Object Inspector and then open the drop-down list of available `Color` values. Select clNavy for the color. The form is now navy blue and displays the Hello World! message centered in white. You can run your program to verify that the run-time appearance is indeed as desired.

   Note that the label is only centered if the form has not been resized at run-time. The label does not get centered automatically when you resize the form. This is because the Alignment dialog box you have used is a design-time aid only. At run-time, the label is in a fixed position within the form.

2. If you have worked your way through the previous exercise, you already know how to change the `Color` property of the form and how to make the text display in a specific color by changing the `Color` of the `Font` property of the label. While you have the font selection dialog box open, you are free to change the font itself by, for example, selecting Arial from the list of available fonts. Adjust the font's size to 18 points in the same dialog box, then press the OK button.

3. Create a new, blank project.

   Hold down the Shift key and click on the Edit component's icon inside the Standard page of the Component Palette to select in a "sticky" mode and be able to place several instances of this component on the form in short succession.

Place five instances of the Edit component on the form by clicking the Form Designer window roughly where you want them to appear, five times in succession.

Shift+Click the `Label` component's icon on the Standard page of the Component Palette. Place five labels, one in front of each of the edit boxes you placed on the form before.

Unselect `Label` from the Component Palette by clicking the regular arrow icon near the left edge of the Component Palette.

Select the Label components inside the Form Designer window one by one, and change their `Caption` properties to: `First Name`, `Last Name`, `Street Address`, `City`, and `Zip`, respectively.

Day 2

Quiz

1. No. A unit may never call a program.
2. True. An object can access its own (or inherited) protected fields from within its methods. However, one object cannot access the protected fields of another, unrelated object type.
3. The variable complex is defined before the definition of the type `TComplex`.
4. The class `TClass2` declares the field `X`, which is already declared in the parent class `TClass1`.
5. True, because Pascal is case-insensitive.
6. True, because the Pascal language allows multiple `var` and `type` clauses as long as they do not make references to undefined data types.

Exercises

1. Here is my modified version of unit `Ubutton`:

```
unit Ubutton;

interface

uses
  SysUtils, WinTypes, WinProcs, Messages, Classes,
  Graphics, Controls, Forms, Dialogs, StdCtrls, Buttons;

type
  TForm1 = class(TForm)
    CloseBtn: TBitBtn;
```

```
      procedure CloseBtnClick(Sender: Tobject);
    private
      { Private declarations }
    public
      { Public declarations }
    end;

var
  Form1: Tform1;

implementation
{$R *.DFM}
const MSG = 'I am a Pascal Programmer';

procedure TForm1.CloseBtnClick(Sender: Tobject);
begin
 MessageDlg(MSG, mtInformation, [mbOK], 0);
 Close;
end;

end.
```

2. Here is my version of file BTN2.DPR:

```
program Btn2;

uses
  Forms,
  Ubtn2 in 'UBTN2.PAS' {Form1};

{$R *.RES}

begin
  Application.CreateForm(TForm1, Form1);
  Application.Run;
end.
```

and here is my version of file UBTN2.PAS:

```
unit Ubtn2;

interface

uses
  SysUtils, WinTypes, WinProcs, Messages, Classes,
  Graphics, Controls, Forms, Dialogs, StdCtrls;

type
  TForm1 = class(TForm)
    Button1: Tbutton;
    procedure CloseBtnClick(Sender: Tobject);
  private
    { Private declarations }
  public
    { Public declarations }
  end;

var
```

```
  Form1: Tform1;

implementation

{$R *.DFM}

procedure TForm1.CloseBtnClick(Sender: Tobject);
begin
  MessageDlg('Close form', mtInformation, [mbOK], 0);
  Close;
end;

end.
```

Day 3

Quiz

1. False. Depending on the component, some properties might not be available at design-time.
2. False. You cannot resize a group of selected components, but you can move and delete such a group.
3. True.
4. True.
5. The Dialogs page tab contains the Color dialog box component.
6. The ComboBox component allows you to either select from a list or enter a new item.
7. True.
8. The TabbedNotebook component combines the effects of the Notebook and TabSet components.

Exercises

1. Here is my version of the source code for the UDLG21.PAS unit:

```
unit Udlg21;

interface

uses
  SysUtils, WinTypes, WinProcs, Messages, Classes,
  Graphics, Controls, Forms, Dialogs, StdCtrls,
  { manually inserted unit name }
  Udlg22;

type
```

```
  TForm1 = class(TForm)
    CloseBtn: Tbutton;
    ShowFormBtn: Tbutton;
    procedure ShowFormBtnClick(Sender: Tobject);
    procedure CloseBtnClick(Sender: Tobject);
  private
    { Private declarations }
  public
    { Public declarations }
  end;

var
  Form1: Tform1;

implementation

{$R *.DFM}

procedure TForm1.ShowFormBtnClick(Sender: Tobject);
begin
  BtnBottomDlg.Show;
end;

procedure TForm1.CloseBtnClick(Sender: Tobject);
begin
  Close;
end;

end.
```

2. Here is my version of the source code for the UDLG22.PAS unit:

```
unit Udlg22;

interface

uses WinTypes, WinProcs, Classes, Graphics, Forms,
  Controls, Buttons, StdCtrls, ExtCtrls;

type
  TBtnBottomDlg = class(TForm)
    OKBtn: TBitBtn;
    CancelBtn: TBitBtn;
    Bevel1: TBevel;
    ByeLbl: TLabel;
    procedure OKBtnClick(Sender: TObject);
    procedure CancelBtnClick(Sender: TObject);
  private
    { Private declarations }
  public
    { Public declarations }
  end;

var
  BtnBottomDlg: TBtnBottomDlg;

implementation
```

```

{$R *.DFM}

procedure TBtnBottomDlg.OKBtnClick(Sender: TObject);
begin
  Close;
end;

procedure TBtnBottomDlg.CancelBtnClick(Sender: TObject);
begin
  Close;
end;

end.
```

Day 4

Quiz

1. The second assignment statement, `I := L`, attempts to assign a value of `32768` to an `Integer` variable `I`. Since the largest possible `Integer` is 32767, the attempt generates a range-check error at run-time.
2. `_TotalCount`, `NumberOfHoursMinutesAndSecondsSinceMidnight`, `a`, and `PageNo___` are all valid. `1994Totals` is invalid because it starts with a digit. `AmountInUS$` is invalid because it contains a $-sign, which is an invalid character in Pascal identifiers. `Today'sDate` is invalid, because it contains an apostrophe.

Exercises

1. The modifications you need to make are localized to lines 15 and 17 of Listing 4.2.

   Swap the contents of lines 15 and 17 first. As a result, this program fragment should look like the following:

   ```
   15:   Fahrenheit := (9*Celsius) div 5 + 32;
   16:   Kelvin     := 273 + Celsius;
   17:   Celsius    := 100;
   ```

   Now, change line 17 to say:

   ```
   17:   Celsius := 5*(Fahrenheit - 32) div 9;
   ```

   Change line 15 to say

   ```
   15:   Fahrenheit := 212;
   ```

2. (a) Insert a constant declaration for the `DefaultHourly` right below line 15 of Listing 4.4 as follows:

   ```
   15:   DefaultHourly = 100.00;
   ```

   Swap lines 24 and 25 of Listing 4.4 as follows:

```
24:    Hourly    := Daily/8;
25:    Daily     := DefaultDaily;
```

Change the new line 24 to use the newly defined constant:

```
24:    Hourly    := DefaultHourly;
```

Change the new line 25 to perform the calculation based on the hourly rate given:

```
25:    Daily     := 8*Hourly;
```

(b) To express the annual income as a direct function of the daily rate, let us first assume that there are, on average, 240 working days in a year. Then, change line 27 of listing 4.4 as follows:

```
27:    Annually := 240*Daily;
```

Day 5

Quiz

1. The values are calculated as follows:

   (a) 2 + 3*4 - 5 **mod** 2 =
   2 + (3*4) - (5 **mod** 2) =
   2 + 12 - 1 = 13

   (b) 7 - 15 **div** 3 =
   7 - (15 **div** 3) =
   7 - 5 = 2

   (c) 15/3 = 5.0

   (d) (15/3) **mod** 3 is an invalid operation since the value on the left-hand side of the **mod** operator is a real number rather than the required integer. The compiler flags this as an error.

2. Assuming `A = True`, `B = False`, and `C = True`,

   (a) `A or B and C =`
   ```
   True or (False and True) =
   True or False = True
   ```

   (b) `A xor B xor C =`
   ```
   (True xor False) xor True =
   True xor (False xor True) =
   True xor True = False
   ```

   (c) `not (A or B) =`
   ```
   (not A) and (not B) =
   (not True) and (not False) =
   False and True = False
   ```

   (c) `not A or not (B and C) =`

```
(not A) or ( not (B and C) ) =
(not True) or (not (False and True) ) =
False or (not False) =
False or True = True
```

3. Assuming that `X = 2`, `Y = 1`, and `Z = 0`,

   (a) `(21 < 9) or (X <= Y) =`
   ```
   False or (2 <= 1) =
   False or False = False
   ```
   (b) `((X + Y) >= 3) and not ((Y mod 2) = 0) =`
   ```
   ((2 + 1) >= 3) and not ((1 mod 2) = 0) =
   (3 >= 3) and not (1 = 0) =
   True and not False = True
   ```

Exercises

1. To demonstrate `LongInt` overflow, change the `FormCreate` method of the overflow example program as follows:

   ```
   procedure TForm1.FormCreate(Sender: TObject);
   var
     i, j: LongInt;
   begin
     i := MaxLongInt;
     j := 1;
     i := i + j;
   end;
   ```

2. This question was a bit tricky. As it turns out, the calculator you have developed already supports `LongInt` operations.

   For example, the code inside the `BnSubtract` method looks like the following:

   ```
     EditResult.Text :=
       IntToStr( StrToInt(EditOperand1.Text) -
         StrToInt(EditOperand2.Text) );
   ```

   The calculation is performed using two results of the `StrToInt` function. `StrToInt` returns a `LongInt`, so that the whole expression is a `LongInt`-based calculation. No changes are required to satisfy the requirement of this question.

Day 6

Quiz

1. False. A **case**-statement allows ordinal expressions that include numbers, enumerated types, and subranges. A character type (`Char`) is also an ordinal and is allowed as a **case**-statement's selector.

2. There is a semicolon on the line just before the **else**-keyword. This would cause a compile-time syntax error.
3. False. If the value of the selector happens to be other than any of the listed values, the **case**-statement will not execute at all. Note, however, that when there is a default **else**-branch in a **case**-statement, the default branch will get executed if the selector's value does not match any of the listed values.
4. False. Every branch of a **case**-statement must contain at least one executable statement. The simplest case is when the executable statement is a so-called `null` statement: a semicolon by itself.
5. True. All values in a **case** statement must be unique. No overlap is allowed.

Exercises

1. You can implement the program using the standard `WinCrt` library. Create a new project based on the `WinCrt` template. Enter the program code as follows:

```
program Decide;

uses
  WinCrt;

var
  Ch: Char;
begin
  Write('Enter a single character or digit: ');
  ReadLn(Ch);
  case Ch of
    'a'..'z': WriteLn('CHARACTER');
    'A'..'Z': WriteLn('CAPITAL');
    '0'..'9': WriteLn('DIGIT');
  end;
end.
```

2. Create a blank, form-based project. Drop three edit boxes on the form and align their left edges vertically. Change the values of their `Text` properties to empty (null) strings. The edit boxes should be blank initially. Change the `ReadOnly` property of the bottom edit box to `True`, and its `Color` to `clSilver`. This will be the result box. Name the three edit boxes `EdHours`, `EdRate`, and `EdResult`, respectively.

   Drop three `Label` components on the form, and place them right in front of the corresponding edit boxes. Change their `Caption` properties to `Hours Worked`, `Hourly Rate`, and `Amount Earned`, respectively.

   Double-click the value of the `OnChange` property of the `EdHours` edit box. A new, blank `EdHoursChange` event handler gets created. Rename the event handler to `OnEdChange` by entering the new name in the value column of the object Inspector. Enter the following code inside the `OnEdChange` event handler:

```
 1: procedure TForm1.OnEdChange(Sender: TObject);
 2: var
 3:   Hours,
 4:   Rate,
 5:   Result,
 6:   Overtime: Real;
 7: begin
 8:   if EdHours.Text <> '' then
 9:     Hours := StrToFloat(EdHours.Text)
10:   else
11:     Hours := 0;
12:   if Hours > 37.5 then
13:     Overtime := Hours - 37.5
14:   else
15:     Overtime := 0;
16:   if EdRate.Text <> '' then
17:     Rate := StrToFloat(EdRate.Text)
18:   else
19:     Rate := 0;
20:   Result := Hours*Rate + 0.5*Overtime*Rate;
21:   EdResult.Text := FloatToStrF(Result,ffCurrency,10,2);
22: end;
```

The code you entered describes five major activities.

First, lines 8–11 retrieve the string value of the `EdHours` edit box and convert it to a `Real`-typed value suitable for calculations.

Second, overtime hours—if any—are calculated on lines 12 through 15.

Third, lines 16–19 convert the contents of the `EdRate` box to a `Real`. In both cases, if the corresponding edit box is empty, a default value of `0` is used for calculations.

Fourth, the resulting amount earned is calculated on line 20.

Fifth, the result of the calculation is converted back to a string and displayed inside the EdResult edit box. Note that the `FloatToStrF` standard subroutine from the `SysUtils` unit is used to format the resulting string into a currency-like appearance, with exactly two digits after the decimal point.

Now, assign the same `EdChange` event handler to the `OnClick` event of the `EdRate` edit box. Simply select the `EdRate` box inside the Object Inspector and, after clicking its `OnChange` event, select `EdChange` from the drop-down list.

This code calculates the result interactively, as soon as you enter some values in one of the editable edit boxes: `EdHours` and `EdRate`.

Day 7

Quiz

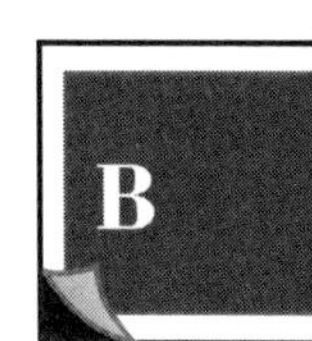

1. The loop never executes: `Statement1` is never called. Consider the loop condition:

   ```
   (Total < Max) and (Sum > Max) and (Sum < Total)
   ```

   It is equivalent to saying that both of the following conditions must be simultaneously satisfied:

   ```
   (i) Sum < Total < Max
   ```

   and

   ```
   (ii) Sum > Max
   ```

   which is impossible.
2. The loop's condition is equivalent to:

   ```
   (Sum <= Total) or (Sum > Total)
   ```

   which is always `True`. The loop is an infinite loop.
3. A **`while`**-loop may not execute its body at all, if the condition is `False` at the outset, which is equivalent to saying that the minimum number of repetitions is zero.
4. A **`repeat-until`** loop executes at least once.
5. The question is a little bit tricky. The maximum number of repetitions for a **`for`**-loop depends on the possible range of values for the loop counter, that is, on the type of the loop counter. For example, a `for` loop with an `Integer` counter can possibly iterate between the values of `-32768` and `32767` for the total of 65536 repetitions.

Exercises

1. The steps to create a new blank project with a form and to drop the necessary controls (`ListBox`, `Button`) from the Component Palette's Standard page should already be familiar to you now.

   The key to providing the required functionality rests in the `OnClick` event handler for the Go button. Create an `OnClick` event handler for the button and insert the following code in it:

```
procedure TForm1.BnGoClick(Sender: TObject);
var
  Counter: Char;
begin
  for Counter := 'A' to 'Z' do
    ListBox1.Items.Add(Counter);
end;
```

Note that the conversion from the character-typed Counter to a string is automatic, performed implicitly during the call to the `ListBox.Items.Add` method.

2. Here is a very simple Delphi program that counts the number of lines in an arbitrary text file:

```
program Count;

uses WinCrt;

var
  FileName: String;
  Count: LongInt;
begin
  Write('Enter filename: ');
  ReadLn(FileName);
  if FileName = '' then
    Halt;
  Assign(F,FileName);
  Reset(F);
  Count := 0;
  while not Eof(F) do begin
    ReadLn(F);
    Inc(Count);
  end;
  Close(F);
  WriteLn(FileName,' has ',Count,' lines.');
end.
```

Day 8

Quiz

1. False. Set members don't have any particular order.
2. False. The fields in a record are accessed by name. There is no index describing their position in the record declaration.
3. False. A real number cannot be used to index an array. Only ordinal types can be used as array indices.
4. True. The `Ord` built-in function can be used with any ordinal type, including a character.
5. False. Real numbers cannot be used to define subranges. A subrange-type can only be defined using ordinal types for its base.

6. `[100,102,104,105,106] + [100, 101, 102, 103, 104] =`

   `[100, 101, 102, 103, 104, 105, 106] =`

   `[100..106]`

   b. `[One, Two, Three, Four] - [Five, Four, Six]`

   `= [One, Two, Three]`

   c. `['a','b','c','D','E','F'] * ['A', 'B', 'c', 'd']`

   `= ['c']`

Exercises

1. `type Age = (0..120);`
2. `type Gender = (gUnknown, gFemale, gMale);`
3. Here is the postulated record declaration:

```
type
  RBook = record
    Title: String;
    Author: String;
    Publisher: String;
    ISBN: String[15];
    Pages: LongInt;
    Price: Real;
    Edition: Integer;
  end;
```

   To use this definition, create the following `WinCrt` program:

```
program Books;

uses WinCrt;

type
  RBook = record
    Title: String;
    Author: String;
    Publisher: String;
    ISBN: String[15];
    Pages: LongInt;
    Price: Real;
    Edition: LongInt;
  end;

var
  ABook: RBook;
  Buffer: String;
  Count: LongInt;
  Price: Real;
begin
  {Obtain input}
  Write('Enter Title: ');
  ReadLn(Buffer);
```

```
    ABook.Title := Buffer;
    Write('Enter Author: ');
    ReadLn(Buffer);
    ABook.Author := Buffer;
    Write('Enter Publisher: ');
    ReadLn(Buffer);
    ABook.Publisher := Buffer;
    Write('Enter ISBN: ');
    ReadLn(Buffer);
    ABook.ISBN := Buffer;
    Write('Enter Page Count: ');
    ReadLn(Count);
    ABook.Pages := Count;
    Write('Enter Price: ');
    ReadLn(Price);
    ABook.Price := Price;
    Write('Enter Edition: ');
    ReadLn(Count);
    ABook.Edition := Count;

    {Produce output}
    WriteLn;
    WriteLn;
    with ABook do begin
      WriteLn('Title     = ',Title);
      WriteLn('Author    = ',Author);
      WriteLn('Publisher = ',Publisher);
      WriteLn('ISBN      = ',ISBN);
      WriteLn('Pages     = ',Pages);
      WriteLn('Price     = ',Price:1:2);
      WriteLn('Edition   = ',Edition);
    end;
  end.
```

Day 9

Quiz

1. There are three ways of passing parameters to subroutines in Object Pascal: by reference (**var**-parameters), by value, and by constant-reference (**const**-parameters).
2. Value parameters are like local variables. They can be used within subroutines, assigned values to, and so on. There is no modifier in front of a value-parameter in a subroutine declaration.
3. Of course a variable can be an actual parameter corresponding to all of the following: a formal value parameter, a reference parameter, and a constant parameter of a subroutine.

Exercises

1. A suggested implementation for the string-utility function unit follows:

```
unit StrUtils;

interface

  function LeftJustify(const S: String; Len: Byte): String;
    {Left-justifies S within a blank string of length Len}
  function RightJustify(const S: String; Len: Byte): String;
    {Right-justifies S within a blank string of length Len}
  function Center(const S: String; Len: Byte): String;
    {Centers S within a blank string of length Len}
  function FillStr (C: Char; N: Byte): String;
    {Returns a string with N characters of value C}

implementation


  function FillStr;
    begin
      FillChar(Result[1],N,C);
      Result[0] := Chr(N);
    end;


  function LeftJustify;
    var
      Margin: Byte;
    begin
      Margin := Len - Length(S);
      Result := S + FillStr(' ',Margin);
    end;


  function RightJustify;
    var
      Margin: Byte;
    begin
      Margin := Len - Length(S);
      Result := FillStr(' ',Margin) + S;
    end;


  function Center;
    var
      Margin: Byte;
    begin
      Margin := (Len - Length(S)) div 2;
      Result := FillStr(' ',Margin) + S + FillStr(' ',Margin);
      if Length(Result) < Len then
        Result := Result + FillStr(' ',Len - Length(Result));
    end;

end.
```

2. A suggested implementation for the reusable array-manipulation unit follows:

```
unit IntArr;

{
Generic integer array manipulation subroutines.
}

interface

  function Average(const A: array of Integer): Real;
  function Sum(const A: array of Integer): Real;
  function Minimum(const A: array of Integer): Integer;
  function Maximum(const A: array of Integer): Integer;
  procedure CopyArray(
    const Src: array of Integer;
    SrcIndex, NumElements: Integer;
    var Dest: array of Integer;
    DestIndex: Integer);


implementation


  function Average;
    {
    The arithmetic average of the
    values in the array A.
    }
    var
      Count,
      Index: Integer;
    begin
      Count := High(A) - Low(A);
      Result := Sum(A) / Count;
    end;


  function Sum;
    {
    The sum of all the values
    in the array A.
    }
    var
      Index: Integer;
    begin
      Result := 0;
      for Index := Low(A) to High(A) do
        Result := Result + A[Index];
    end;


  function Minimum;
```

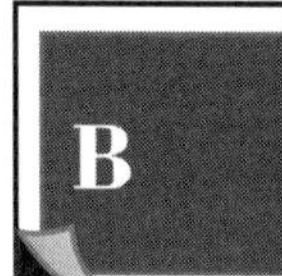


```
    {
    The value of the smallest element
    in the array A. All elements must be
    examined since no particular order
    of elements is assumed.
    }
    var
      Index: Integer;
    begin
      Result := A[Low(A)];
      for Index := Succ(Low(A)) to High(A) do
        if A[Index] < Result then
          Result := A[Index];
    end;


  function Maximum;
    {
    The value of the largest element
    in the array A. All elements must be
    examined since no particular order
    of elements is assumed.
    }
    var
      Index: Integer;
    begin
      Result := A[Low(A)];
      for Index := Succ(Low(A)) to High(A) do
        if A[Index] > Result then
          Result := A[Index];
    end;


  procedure CopyArray;
    {
    Copies NumElements from the Src array starting
    at position SrcIndex into the Dest array,
    starting at position DestIndex.
    No check is made for validity of indexes
    or array bounds.
    }
    begin
      while SrcIndex < (SrcIndex + NumElements) do
        begin
          Dest[DestIndex] := Src[SrcIndex];
          Inc(SrcIndex);
          Inc(DestIndex);
        end;
    end;


end.
```

Day 10

Quiz

1. False. No variables are automatically initialized in Pascal. To initialize a variable of class-type, you must create an instance of the class—via a call to a constructor—and assign the resulting reference to the variable.
2. False. Polymorphism allows for substitution of a descendant type for an ancestor type.
3. True. The object state is determined by the collective values of all its fields, and all the other objects it refers to.
4. True. Just list more than one variable in a single **with**-statement, separating consecutive variable identifiers with commas.
5. True. A **with**-statement is a shorthand for a dot notation and works as well with records as it does with instances.

Exercises

1. Here is a suggested interface for the `TDate` class:

```
uses
  SysUtils;

type
  TDate = class
    private
      FYear,
      FMonth,
      FDay: Word;
    protected
      procedure SetYear(ANumber: Word);
      procedure SetMonth(ANumber: Word);
      procedure SetDay(ANumber: Word);
    public
      constructor Today;
      constructor Create(ADate: TDateTime);
      function LeapYear: Boolean;
      property Year: Word
        read FYear write SetYear;
      property Month: Word
        read FMonth write SetMonth;
      property Day: Word
        read FDay write SetDay;
    end;
```

2. Here is a suggested interface for the `TInvoice` class:

```
uses
  Customer;
```

```
type
  TInvoice = class
  private
    FNumber: String[12];
    FCustomer: TCustomer;
    FItems: TStrings;
    FTotal: Real;
  protected
    procedure SetNumber(ANumber: String);
  public
    property Number: String
      read FNumber write SetNumber;
    property Customer: TCustomer
      read FCustomer write FCustomer;
    property Items: TStrings
      read FItems;
    property Total: Real
      read FTotal;
  end;
```

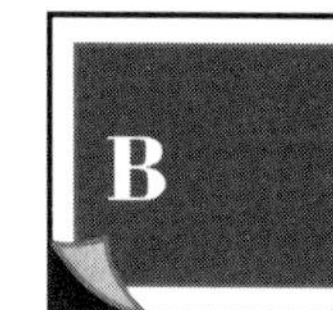

Day 11

Quiz

1. True. Constructors are functions in disguise. They return a valid instance or **`nil`**.
2. True. Class methods do work exactly like stand-alone subroutines.
3. All statements are true, except (d): constructors cannot be invoked through a valid instance of a class, because they are meant to create an instance of a class. Where would the first instance of a class come from otherwise?
4. The only exception is (e), private fields and methods that are inherited, but cannot be used by a descendant, unless that descendant is defined in the same unit as the ancestor class.

Exercises

1. Following is the complete implementation of the `TDate` class you defined as part of Exercise 1 on Day 10.

```
unit Dates;

interface

  uses
    SysUtils;
```

```
    type
      TDate = class
        private
          FYear,
          FMonth,
          FDay: Word;
        protected
          procedure SetYear(ANumber: Word);
          procedure SetMonth(ANumber: Word);
          procedure SetDay(ANumber: Word);
        public
          constructor Today;
          constructor Create(ADate: TDateTime);
          function LeapYear: Boolean;
          property Year: Word
            read FYear write SetYear;
          property Month: Word
            read FMonth write SetMonth;
          property Day: Word
            read FDay write SetDay;
        end;

  implementation

    constructor TDate.Create;
      begin
        DecodeDate(ADate,FYear,FMonth,FDay);
      end;

    constructor TDate.Today;
      begin
        Create(SysUtils.Now);
      end;

    procedure TDate.SetYear;
      begin
        FYear := ANumber;
      end;

    procedure TDate.SetMonth;
      begin
        if ANumber in [1..12] then
          FMonth := ANumber;
      end;

    procedure TDate.SetDay;
      begin
        if (ANumber < 1) or (ANumber > 31) then
          Exit;
        case FMonth of
          2: begin
            if (ANumber > 29) then
```

```
          Exit;
        if (ANumber = 29) and not LeapYear then
          Exit;
      end;
      4, 6, 9, 11: begin
        if (ANumber > 30) then
          Exit;
      end;
    end;
    FDay := ANumber;
  end;


function TDate.LeapYear;
  begin
    Result := False;
    if (FYear mod 4) <> 0 then
      Exit;
    if ((FYear mod 100) = 0)
    and ((FYear mod 400) <> 0) then
      Exit;
    Result := True;
  end;

end.
```

2. Here is a suggested implementation for the `TCustomer` class:

```
unit Customer;

interface

  type
    TCustomer = class
    private
      FirstName: String[25];
      LastName : String[40];
      Street   : String[80];
      City     : String[20];
      State    : String[2];
      Zip      : String[10];
      LastOrder: String[10];
    public
      constructor Create(const First, Last: String);
      function GetFirstName: String;
      procedure SetFirstName(const AText: String);
      function GetLastName: String;
      procedure SetLastName(const AText: String);
      function GetStreet: String;
      procedure SetStreet(const AText: String);
      function GetCity: String;
      procedure SetCity(const AText: String);
      function GetState: String;
      procedure SetState(const AText: String);
      function GetZip: String;
      procedure SetZip(const AText: String);
      function GetLastOrder: String;
      procedure SetLastOrder(const AText: String);
    end;
```

```
implementation

  constructor TCustomer.Create;
    begin
      FirstName := First;
      LastName := Last;
    end;


  function TCustomer.GetFirstName: String;
    begin
      Result := FirstName;
    end;


  procedure TCustomer.SetFirstName(const AText: String);
    begin
      FirstName := AText;
    end;


  function TCustomer.GetLastName: String;
    begin
      Result := LastName;
    end;


  procedure TCustomer.SetLastName(const AText: String);
    begin
      LastName := AText;
    end;


  function TCustomer.GetStreet: String;
    begin
      Result := Street;
    end;


  procedure TCustomer.SetStreet(const AText: String);
    begin
      Street := AText;
    end;


  function TCustomer.GetCity: String;
    begin
      Result := City;
    end;


  procedure TCustomer.SetCity(const AText: String);
    begin
      City := AText;
    end;
```

```
  function TCustomer.GetState: String;
    begin
      Result := State;
    end;


  procedure TCustomer.SetState(const AText: String);
    begin
      State := AText;
    end;


  function TCustomer.GetZip: String;
    begin
      Result := Zip;
    end;


  procedure TCustomer.SetZip(const AText: String);
    begin
      Zip := AText;
    end;


  function TCustomer.GetLastOrder: String;
    begin
      Result := LastOrder;
    end;


  procedure TCustomer.SetLastOrder(const AText: String);
    begin
      LastOrder := AText;
    end;

end.
```

3. A complete implementation of the `TInvoice` class is given below:

```
unit Invoice;

interface

uses
  Classes,
  Customer;

type
  TInvoice = class
  private
    FNumber: String;
    FCustomer: TCustomer;
    FItems: TStrings;
    FTotal: Real;
  public
    constructor Create(ACustomer: TCustomer);
    destructor Destroy; override;
    function GetNumber: String;
```

```
    procedure SetNumber(const ANumber: String);
    function GetCustomer: TCustomer;
    procedure SetCustomer(ACust: TCustomer);
    function GetItems: TStrings;
    function GetTotal: Real;
    procedure SetTotal(AnAmount: Real);
  end;


implementation


constructor TInvoice.Create;
  begin
    inherited Create;
    FCustomer := ACustomer;
    FItems := TStringList.Create;
  end;


destructor TInvoice.Destroy;
  begin
    FItems.Free;
    inherited Destroy;
  end;


function TInvoice.GetNumber: String;
  begin
    Result := FNumber;
  end;


procedure TInvoice.SetNumber(const ANumber: String);
  begin
    FNumber := ANumber;
  end;


function TInvoice.GetCustomer: TCustomer;
  begin
    Result := FCustomer;
  end;


procedure TInvoice.SetCustomer(ACust: TCustomer);
  begin
    FCustomer := ACust;
  end;


function TInvoice.GetItems: TStrings;
  begin
    Result := FItems;
  end;
```

```
function TInvoice.GetTotal: Real;
  begin
    Result := FTotal;
  end;


procedure TInvoice.SetTotal(AnAmount: Real);
  begin
    FTotal := AnAmount;
  end;

end.
```

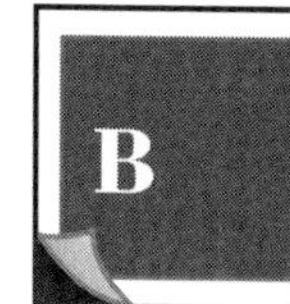

Day 12

Quiz

1. True. The ultimate ancestor of all Object Pascal classes is `TObject`.
2. The parent of the specified `TJournal` class is not given explicitly, hence—by default—it is `TObject`.
3. False. Polymorphism allows for type substitution, not dynamic type changes.
4. False. There is no notion of a default constructor or destructor in Object Pascal. Every object descending from `TObject` already inherits a constructor `Create`, and a virtual destructor `Destroy`. Unless there is a good reason, you don't have to define constructors and destructors for any descendant classes.
5. False. You don't need to define any constructors even if the class you are defining contains virtual methods. The constructor inherited from `TObject` will work fine. The only reason to actually have a constructor, is to initialize the instance of a descendant beyond what default initialization does.

Exercise

1. Following is a minimal skeleton class with a constructor and a destructor:

```
type
  TAnyClass = class
  public
    constructor Create;
    destructor destroy; override;
  end;
```

Day 13

Quiz

1. True. You need to use the `read` and `write` clauses to specify how to access the property value.
2. False. This scheme leads to corrupt property values.
3. Zero for a simple property and one for an array property.
4. One for a simple property and two for an array property.
5. Graphics Device Interface (GDI) functions perform device-independent graphics operations for Windows applications.
6. The System services interface functions handles sound.
7. The Windows-management messages group includes the WM_CLOSE message.

Day 14

Quiz

1. The resource recuperation statements are executed only if an exception is raised.
2. True, because the `on-do` handlers are checked in a top-down order for a matching handler.
3. True. The expression yields `True` because object B is an instance of class `ClassB` and which is a descendant of the parent class `ClassA`.
4. Here is the general code that implements the effect of the operator `as` using the operator `is`.

```
if AnObject is TObjectType then
  ATypeCastObject := TObjectType(AnObject);
else
  raise EInvalidCast.Create;
```

Exercise

1. Here is my version of the UCALC2.PAS unit (the bold lines show the new and modified code from UCALC1.PAS):

```
unit Ucalc1;

interface

```

```
uses
 SysUtils, WinTypes, WinProcs, Messages, Classes,
 Graphics, Controls, Forms, Dialogs, StdCtrls;

type
 TForm1 = class(TForm)
  Operand1Box: TEdit;
  Operand1Lbl: TLabel;
  OperatorLbl: TLabel;
  OperatorBox: TEdit;
  Operand2Lbl: TLabel;
  Operand2Box: TEdit;
  ResultBox: TEdit;
  ExecuteBtn: TButton;
  CloseBtn: TButton;
  ResultLbl: TLabel;
  procedure CloseBtnClick(Sender: TObject);
  procedure ExecuteBtnClick(Sender: TObject);
 private
  { Private declarations }
 public
  { Public declarations }
 end;

 EOperatorErr = class(Exception);

var
 Form1: TForm1;

implementation

{$R *.DFM}

procedure TForm1.CloseBtnClick(Sender: TObject);
begin
 Close;
end;

procedure TForm1.ExecuteBtnClick(Sender: TObject);

var
 x, y, z : real;

begin
  { clear result box }
  ResultBox.Text := '';
  { obtain the first operand }
  x := StrToFloat(OperandBox1.Text);
  { obtain the second operand }
  y := StrToFloat(OperandBox2.Text);
  { execute the operation }
  case OperatorBox.Text[1] of
   '+': z := x + y;
   '-': z := x - y;
   '*': z := x * y;
   '/': z := x / y;
```

```
      '^': z := exp(y * ln(x));
     else
      raise EOperatorError.CreateFmt(
          'Invalid operator: "%s"',[OperatorBox.Text[1]]);
     end;
     { display the result }
     ResultBox.Text := FloatToStr(z)

  end;

end.
```

Day 15

Quiz

1. The call to procedure `WriteReal` is ambiguous and should be qualified by either unit name.
2. The routines use the data type `ArrayType` before it is declared. In other words, the array type is not in scope for these routines.
3. True.
4. The value of the global variable `i` is `1` at the end of the program.
5. The open array is passed by reference (using `var`) and therefore cannot accept on-the-fly array arguments.
6. The procedure relies on the parameter `numElems` to accurately report the number of elements in the open array. If the argument for the parameter `numElems` is inaccurate, you get a run-time error. The procedure should use the function `High` instead. Whenever you have the choice of programmer-generated information or compiler-generated information (such as `SizeOf` and `High`), go with the compiler-generated solution.

Exercises

1. Here is my version of the `toLoCaseStr` procedure:

```
procedure toLoCaseStr(var aStr : array of char);

var i, asciiShift : Integer;

begin
  asciiShift := ord('a') - ord('A');
  i := 0;
  while (aStr[i] <> #0) and
        (i <= High(aStr)) do begin
    if aStr[i] in ['A'..'Z'] then
```

```
      aStr[i] := chr(ord(aStr[i]) + asciiShift);
    inc(i);
  end;
end;
```

2. Here is my version of the procedure `MinMax`:

```
procedure MinMax(arr : array of real;
                 var small, big : real);
var i : word;
begin
  small := arr[0];
big := arr[0];
  { access rest of the array elements }
  for i := 1 to High(arr) do begin
     if small > arr[i] then small := arr[i];
   if big < arr[i] then big := arr[i]
  end;
end;
```

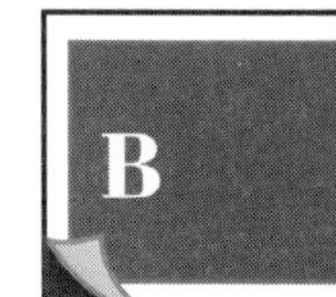

Day 16

Quiz

1. False. Yes, you can change the visual appearance of control that has a Windows handle. This can for example be accomplished through the process known as subclassing, that is, replacing the default controls' handler for Windows messages with one of your own. This, however is an advanced technique, not covered in this book.
2. True. You can have almost as many pens as you wish, instantiated and ready. Of course you draw with one of those pens at a time, but you may switch them at will by copying their characteristics to the `Canvas.Pen` through a call to `Canvas.Pen.Assign(AnotherPen);`.
3. True, in principle, but the existing methods provide a lot of shortcuts and allow you to concentrate on more important details of your application.
4. False. Very often only a small portion of the control needs redrawing. You can speed a lot of graphics-intense applications up by avoiding unnecessary redraws. `ClipRect` is a property of a `Canvas` which allows you to look at what area needs actually be redrawn.
5. True, if you insist. However, for most routine operations the encapsulation provided by `Canvas` is more than adequate, and a lot easier to deal with than calling Windows API directly.

Exercises

1. Create a new, blank project BMPRNT.DPR. Place an `Image` component from the "Additional" page of the Component Palette on the form. Change its `Align` property to `alClient`.

Place a `Menu` component from the Standard page on the form. Double-click its icon on the form to open the Menu Designer. Right-click in the Menu Designer to display a local menu. Choose "Insert From Template." In the dialog box, select "File Menu" from the list of templates. Close the Menu Designer.

Place an `OpenDialog` component from the "Dialogs" page of the Component Palette on the form. Change its `Filter` property to `Bitmaps (*.bmp)¦*.bmp¦Metafiles (*.wmf)¦*.wmf`.

Create an event handler for the `OnClick` event of the File|Open menu selection. Insert the following code inside the event handler:

```
procedure TForm1.Open1Click(Sender: TObject);
begin
  if not OpenDialog1.Execute then
    Exit;
  Image1.Picture.LoadFromFile(OpenDialog1.FileName);
end;
```

The code you have entered loads and displays an image file.

Create an event handler for the `OnClick` event of the File|Print menu. Insert the following code inside the event handler:

```
procedure TForm1.Print1Click(Sender: TObject);
begin
  Printer.BeginDoc;
  Printer.Canvas.Draw(100,100,Image1.Picture.Graphic);
  Printer.EndDoc;
end;
```

The code you have entered prepares the printer driver, renders the current graphic, and sends the job to the printer. You have to make sure that the Printers unit is in the **uses**-clause of the form unit. Manually add `Printers` to the **uses**-clause of the form unit.

The finished form unit, called Bmp1, follows:

```
unit Bmp1;

interface

uses
  SysUtils, WinTypes, WinProcs,
  Messages, Classes, Graphics, Controls,
  Forms, Dialogs, Menus, ExtCtrls, Printers;

type
  TForm1 = class(TForm)
    Image1: TImage;
    MainMenu1: TMainMenu;
    File1: TMenuItem;
    Exit1: TMenuItem;
    N1: TMenuItem;
    PrintSetup1: TMenuItem;
    Print1: TMenuItem;
```

B

```
    N2: TMenuItem;
    SaveAs1: TMenuItem;
    Save1: TMenuItem;
    Open1: TMenuItem;
    New1: TMenuItem;
    OpenDialog1: TOpenDialog;
    procedure Open1Click(Sender: TObject);
    procedure Print1Click(Sender: TObject);
  private
    { Private declarations }
  public
    { Public declarations }
  end;

var
  Form1: TForm1;

implementation

{$R *.DFM}

procedure TForm1.Open1Click(Sender: TObject);
begin
  if not OpenDialog1.Execute then
    Exit;
  Image1.Picture.LoadFromFile(OpenDialog1.FileName);
end;

procedure TForm1.Print1Click(Sender: TObject);
begin
  Printer.BeginDoc;
  Printer.Canvas.Draw(100,100,Image1.Picture.Graphic);
  Printer.EndDoc;
end;

end.
```

The form you created supported by the `Bmp1` unit is capable of displaying graphic images. When the user selects Print from the File menu, the graphic is printed on the default printer.

2. The changes you need to make to the `NotePrnt` project to support the Printing dialog box with a Cancel button are minor.

   Create a new, blank form, called `FormPrinting`. Place a button on the form. Give it a `Caption` of `Cancel`, and change its `ModalResult` property to `mrCancel`.

   Create an `OnClick` handler for the `Cancel` button. Insert the following code inside the handler:

```
procedure TFormPrinting.Button1Click(Sender: TObject);
begin
  Printer.Abort;
end;
```

   Change the main body of the `PrintCurrentFile` method of the main form (inside `Note1` unit) as follows:

```
 1:   begin
 2:     if Memo1.Lines.Count = 0 then
 3:       Exit;
 4:     Printer.Title := Caption;
 5:     Printer.BeginDoc;
 6:     FormPrinting.Show;
 7:     StartDoc;
 8:     while MorePages do begin
 9:       StartPage;
10:       while MoreLines do begin
11:         PrintLine;
12:         NextLine;
13:         Application.ProcessMessages;
14:       end;
15:       NextPage;
16:     end;
17:     FormPrinting.Close;
18:     Printer.EndDoc;
19:   end;
```

The changes you need to make involve inserting lines 6 and 17 with calls to `FormPrinting.Show`, and `FormPrinting.Close`, respectively.

Finally, you need to ensure that when the user presses the Cancel button, the action will be recognized by the printing logic and will cause the main printing loop to terminate. Add an additional check to the implementation of the `MorePages` local function inside `PrintCurrentFile` as follows:

```
function MorePages: Boolean;
  begin
    Result := (CurrentLine < Memo1.Lines.Count)
      and not Printer.Aborted;
  end;
```

Day 17

Quiz

1. True. The standard `Edit` component is a single-line editor control. You must use `Memo` that defines an `Alignment` property for this purpose. This is simply the behavior of the standard Windows EDIT control.
2. False. Delphi gives you a `Cursor` property to change the cursor, and a number of mouse-related events, such as `OnClick`, to respond to mouse movements and clicking.
3. True. You can only owner-draw a combo box in its drop-down list version.
4. True. You can create very complex custom components by combining functionality of almost any number of visual controls.

Exercises

1. To simulate a `ComboBox` you need to support the interaction between an `Edit` box and a `ListBox` on a form. Place `Edit` and `ListBox` components on the form.

   Create an `OnClick` event handler for the `ListBox`, and insert the following code:

```
procedure TForm1.ListBox1Click(Sender: TObject);
begin
  Edit1.Text := ListBox1.Items[ListBox1.ItemIndex];
end;
```

   Create an `OnChange` event handler for the `Edit` box, with the following code:

```
procedure TForm1.Edit1Change(Sender: TObject);
var
  I: Integer;
begin
  I := ListBox1.Items.IndexOf(Edit1.Text);
  if I <= 0 then
    Exit;
  ListBox1.ItemIndex := I;
end;
```

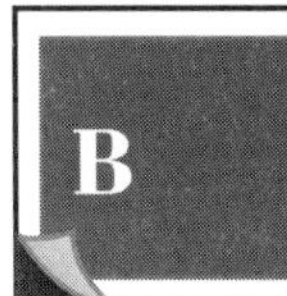

2. Create a new project called `MiniFM` with the main form `Form1` and the supporting unit called `MiniFM1`.

   Place a `ListBox` component on the form and change its `Align` property to `alClient`. Drop an `OpenDialog` on the form and change its `Filter` property to `Programs¦*.exe;*.com;*.pif`. Drop a `Menu` component on the form and create a single menu item: `Run`. Double-click the item to create an empty `OnClick` event handler. Insert the following code inside this newly created event handler:

```
procedure TForm1.Run1Click(Sender: TObject);
var
  S: String;
begin
  if not OpenDialog1.Execute then
    Exit;
  ListBox1.Items.Add(OpenDialog1.FileName);
  S := OpenDialog1.FileName + #0;
  WinExec(@S[1],SW_NORMAL);
end;
```

   Create an `OnClick` event handler for the `ListBox`. Insert the following code:

```
procedure TForm1.ListBox1DblClick(Sender: TObject);
var
  S: String;
begin
  S := ListBox1.Items[ListBox1.ItemIndex] + #0;
  WinExec(@S[1],SW_NORMAL);
end;
```

Day 18

Quiz

1. The string that contains the file extension has an unneeded dot.
2. True.
3. The `Options` property needs to include the value `ofAllowMultiSelect` in order to support multiple files.
4. The limit is 255 characters.
5. You separate the wildcard with semicolons.
6. The `*.txt` file filter appears, because when the value for the `FilterIndex` property exceeds the number of actual filters, the dialog box selects the first file filter.
7. The properties `MinFontSize`, `MaxFontSize`, and `fdLimitSize` define the range of font sizes.
8. The property `Copies` controls the maximum number of copies.
9. Use the `MinPage` and `MaxPage` properties to define the range of printed pages.

Day 19

Quiz

1. True, a single table is not a database, although a database may consist of just a single table. Conceptually, however, a database is a collection of any number of tables.
2. True. You can use the standard triplet: `Table+DataSource+`Data-aware Control to access database tables individually. You can use a `Query` component`+DataSource+`Data-aware Control to access multiple tables simultaneously.
3. False. The ability to connect more than one `DataSource` to a single `DataSet` is one of the main reasons for `DataSource`'s existence.
4. True. The triplet of `DataSet+DataSource+DBControl` is a standard combination to gain access to the database data.
5. False. "Calculated" here means that the values of those fields are created on the fly, not that they are numerically computed. The value may well turn out to be a string, for example.

Exercises

1. See the answer to Exercise 2.
2. Open the Table Browser project. Make sure that you have a generic version of the project, for example, one without any field components defined on the main form.

   Create a new form, `Form2`, with its supporting unit `Unit2`. Insert the following **uses**-clause into the implementation section of the `Unit1` form unit:

   ```
   uses
     Unit2;
   ```

   Similarly, insert the following **uses**-clause into the implementation section of the `Form2` unit:

   ```
   uses
     Unit1;
   ```

   Drop a `ComboBox` component on the new form. Call it `CbTables`. Drop another `ComboBox` and call it `CbDatabases`.

   Drop a `BitBtn` component onto `Form2`. Change its `Kind` property to `bkOK`. Drop another `BitBtn` onto `Form2` and change its `Kind` property to `bkCancel`.

   Create a new `OnShow` event handler attached to `Form2` by double-clicking the value of the `Form2.OnShow` event inside the Object Inspector. Insert the following code inside this newly created event:

   ```
   procedure TForm2.FormShow(Sender: TObject);
   begin
     Session.GetDatabaseNames(CbDatabases.Items);
     CbDatabases.Text := Form1.Table1.DatabaseName;
   end;
   ```

   Create a new `OnChange` event handler attached to the `CbDatabases` combo box. Insert the following code inside this event handler:

   ```
   procedure TForm2.CbDatabasesChange(Sender: TObject);
   begin
     Form1.Table1.DatabaseName := CbDatabases.Text;
     Session.GetTableNames(Form1.Table1.DatabaseName,
       '',True,True,CbTables.Items);
     CbTables.Text := Form1.Table1.TableName;
   end;
   ```

   Drop a `Menu` component on the main form, `Form1`. Create a menu item labeled `Open`. Create an `OnClick` handler for this menu item and insert the following code inside it:

   ```
   procedure TForm1.Open1Click(Sender: TObject);
   begin
     if Form2.ShowModal <> mrOK then
       Exit;
     Table1.Close;
     Table1.TableName := Form2.CbTables.Text;
     Table1.Open;
   end;
   ```

3. Create a new, blank project, called `OneToM`.

   Drop three `Table` components on the main form, calling them `TblCustomers`, `TblOrders`, `TblItems`, respectively. Change their `Database` property to `DBDEMOS`, their `TableName` property to CUSTOMER.DB, ORDERS.DB, and ITEMS.DB, respectively. Change their `Active` property to `True`.

   Drop three `DataSource` components on the form, naming them `SrcCustomers`, `SrcOrders`, and `SrcItems`, and attach them to their respective `Table` components by setting their `DataSet` property.

   Drop and visually place three `DataGrid` components on the form: `GridCustomers`, `GridOrders`, and `GridItems`. Attach the grids to the respective `DataSource` components: `GridCustomers` to `SrcCustomers`, and so on.

   Change the `MasterSource` property of `TblOrders` to `SrcCustomers`. Change both the `MasterFields` property of `TblOrders` and its `IndexFieldNames` property to `CustNo`.

   Similarly, change the `MasterSource` property of `TblItems` to `SrcOrders`, and its `MasterFields` and `IndexFieldNames` properties to `OrderNo`.

Day 20

Quiz

1. True. You can publish a public property. You cannot "unpublish" a property that has already been published by an ancestor class.
2. True. Initialization of object's fields and properties is the responsibility of a constructor.
3. False. The **`default`** directive you may place after the property declaration has to do with persistent storage of objects, such as forms, and specifies which particular value of a property is treated as "default" that is not stored.
4. False. Typically constructors and destructors are declared **`public`**, but declaring them **`protected`** or even **`private`** is perfectly valid, and may sometimes be useful.
5. False. Side effects may be dangerous if used haphazardly. Property access methods are an example of a good use of side effects.
6. True. All Delphi components are—direct or indirect—descendants of `TComponent`.

Exercises

1. The full implementation of the extended `TPointDiagram` would take up too much space for explanation, also depending on how sophisticated the extension you develop. Consider the following hints on how you may approach this task:

Define an additional array/indexed property, `Labels`, based on a private field declared as `FLabels: TStrings`, which manages a list of string labels and that is defined as follows:

```
property Labels: TStrings read FLabels;
```

You can use the string-values of the individual items to store and maintain the actual labels. Furthermore, you can use the associated Object values to store the coordinates at which the label itself is to be drawn. You would therefore be able to control the position of individual labels to fine tune the diagram's appearance. For example, you are able to ensure that one label does not obscure another point's label.

2. Change the definition of the `Points` property as follows:

```
property Points[Layer, Index: Integer]: TPoint
  read GetPoint write SetPoint;
```

Corresponding to this change, you need to modify the access methods and the underlying data structure, as follows:

```
private
  FPoints: array[0..2,0..MaxTPoints-1] of TPoint;
protected
  function GetPoint(Layer, Index: Integer): TPoint; virtual;
  procedure SetPoint(Layer, Index: Integer;
    APoint: TPoint); virtual;
```

The implementations of `GetPoint` and `SetPoint` now refer to a two-dimensional array of points:

```
function TPointDiagram.GetPoint;
begin
  Result := Point(-1,-1);
  if (Index >= MaxTPoints) or (Index < 0) then
    Exit;
  if (Layer < 0) or (Layer > 2) then
    Exit;
  Result := FPoints[Layer,Index]
end;


procedure TPointDiagram.SetPoint;
begin
  if (Index >= MaxTPoints) or (Index < 0) then
    Exit;
  if (Layer < 0) or (Layer > 2) then
    Exit;
  FPoints[Layer,Index] := APoint;
  Invalidate;
end;
```

Similarly, the `DataPen` and `DataBrush` properties should be converted to arrays of pens and brushes, respectively, one pen and one brush for each supported layer.

3. Simply add the following to the **`published`** section of the class declaration, for example:

```
property OnDragDrop;
property OnDragOver;
property OnMouseDown;
property OnMouseMove;
property OnMouseUp;
```

The events you listed are already defined by the `TPointDiagram`'s ancestors. Here you are just making them visible to the Object Inspector by listing them inside the **published** section.

Day 21

Quiz

1. False. All instances of an application running under Windows share the same code. There is only one copy loaded per application, not per instance.
2. False. Only one instance of a DLL is ever loaded. Calling the `LoadLibrary` function repetitively merely increments the internal usage count that Windows maintains about the DLL.
3. False. There is some very small overhead involved related to loading segment registers every time a subroutine implemented in a DLL is called.
4. True. Loading and unloading DLLs dynamically at run-time can be a basis for a truly user-extensible application, allowing its components to be dynamically installed on demand.
5. True. It is possible to export the same subroutine under several different names by using the `name` directive and listing the same subroutine within the **exports**-clause multiply, each time with a different name after the **name**-directive.
6. True. The **name**-directive allows you to rename an imported subroutine.
7. True. An application can list exportable subroutines in its `exports` clause and other modules, such as DLLs, can in turn retrieve the addresses of such subroutines by means of the now-familiar `GetProcAddress` function.

Exercises

1. Here is an implementation of a `TrimStr` function:

```
function TrimStr(const S: String): String;
  begin
    Result := LTrimStr(RTrimStr(S));
  end;
```

2. A very simple, `WinCrt`-based implementation exercising the `FillStr` function follows.

```
program Ex2Day21;

uses
  First,
  WinCrt;

begin
  WriteLn('A row of 20 dashes:');
  WriteLn('"',FillStr('-',20),'"');
  WriteLn('A row of 20 spaces:');
  WriteLn('"',FillStr(' ',20),'"');
  WriteLn('A row of 20 asterisks:');
  WriteLn('"',FillStr('*',20),'"');
end.
```

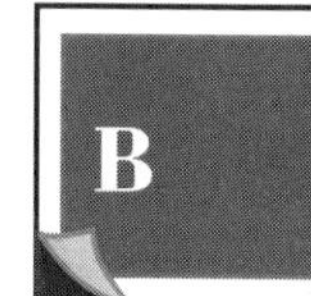

Bonus Day 1

Quiz

1. False.
2. False.
3. False. It takes no code at all to add rudimentary compile-time support for embedded OLE objects.
4. True, although in the future that may change.
5. Answer: c.

Exercises

1. The most notable trick to this one is that you have to pass in a `TDdEClientConv` object as one of the parameters. That way you don't have to use the name of the `TDdEClientConv` object directly, as if it were a global variable. Here's the whole function; a button click procedure using it follows.

```
{ Given the name of a TDdeClientConv component and a
  Program Manager group, such as 'Accessories' or
  'Main' (the search is case-insensitive)
  retrieve the exact caption, the name of the .GRP file,
  the number of items in the group, and the group
  icon's Z-order position. Return TRUE if there is
  a program group by the specified name, or FALSE
  and all VAR parameters unchanged if not. }
function GetGroupInfo(DdeClientConv: TDdeClientConv;
      GroupName: string;
      var GroupCaption : string;
      var GroupFile: string;
      var ItemsInGroup: integer;
      var ZOrder: integer) : boolean;
```

```
var
   { TDdeClientConv.RequestData allocates a PChar string
     dynamically, leaving it up to you to delete its
     contents with StrDispose. }
   Info : PChar;
   { Index tracks the current position in the PChar string
     returned by TDdeClientConv.RequestData. }
   Index : integer;
   { StrNum is a temporary variable to track the text
     value of a number; the numbers returned by
     TDdeClientConv.RequestData are in string format.
     StrNum is then converted into an integer. }
   var StrNum : String;
begin
     { Hardcode the service and topic because they're
       always the same: all we want is information
       about program groups. }
     DdeClientConv.SetLink('PROGMAN', 'PROGMAN');
     { Initiate the DDE conversation with Program
       Manager. }
     DDEClientConv.OpenLink;
     { Get information about the specified group. }
     Info := DDEClientConv.RequestData(GroupName);
     { A NIL return value means there's no group
       by that name. }
     if Info = NIL then
        begin
             { Return failure code. }
             GetGroupInfo := FALSE;
             { Leave this routine. }
             Exit;
        end;

     { Info is a string containing a "database" full
       of "records." The first "record" contains the
       information about the specified group. That's
       what this function wants to know about. Remaining
       "records" contain information about icons in
       the group, which are of no interest here. The
       "records" are delimited by newlines (carriage
       return/linefeed pairs).  "Field" information
       within the records is comma-delimited.
       1. The group name in quotes, e.g. "Accessories".
       2. The filename of the group, e.g.
       C:\WINDOWS\ACCESSOR.GRP. Not quoted.
       3. The number of items in the group as text.
       4. The Z-order of the group window (its position in the
       "stack" of group icons) as text.
       This record ends with a newline. }

     { Skip the first character in the string, which is
       a double quote. }
     Index := 1;
     GroupCaption := '';
     { Search for the next double quote. }
     while Info[Index] <> '"' do
```

B

```
    begin
        { As long as it's not found, add each
          character encountered to the caption
          name return value. }
        GroupCaption := GroupCaption + Info[Index];
        { GroupName is case insensitive: If you pass
        in 'FOO' as the group to query it
        will find the group even if its caption
        is 'Foo' or 'foo'. That's why the caption
        is returned; you may want to know exact
        capitalization. }
        Inc(Index);
    end;

    { Skip to the group filename. }
    Index := Index + 2;
    GroupFile := '';
    { Search for the next comma. }
    while Info[Index] <> ',' do
    begin
        { Accumulate the pathname of the .GRP file. }
        GroupFile := GroupFile + Info[Index];
        Inc(Index);
    end;

    { Skip past the comma. }
    Inc(Index);
    StrNum := '';
    { Search for the next comma. }
    while Info[Index] <> ',' do
    begin
        { Accumulate the number of items in the
          group as a text value. }
        StrNum := StrNum + Info[Index];
        Inc(Index);
    end;
    { Convert the text value, such as '14', to
      binary and write to the return value parameter. }
    ItemsInGroup := StrToInt(StrNum);

    StrNum := '';
    { Skip past the comma. }
    Inc(Index);
    { Search for the newline that ends this record. }
    while Info[Index] <> #13 do
    begin
        { Accumulate the last item, the group icon's
          Z order. }
        StrNum := StrNum + Info[Index];
        Inc(Index);
    end;
    { Convert the text value to binary. }
    ZOrder := StrToInt(StrNum);
    { The group was found, so return a success code. }
    GetGroupInfo := TRUE;
    { Reclaim memory allocated by the RequestData
      method. }
    StrDispose(Info);
end;
```

Here's an example of its use. Add a `TDdeClientConv` control, a button, and an edit control to a form. Set the `ConnectMode` property of `TDdeClientConv` to `ddeManual`. Add the routine above to the form.
When you run the program, you'll type the name of the group you want to find out about in this edit control, then click the button. Leave its default name of Edit1. The code for the button would look like this:

```
procedure TForm1.Button1Click(Sender: TObject);
const
   NL = #13#10;
var
   Info : String;
   var GroupFile: string;
   var GroupCaption : string;
   var ItemsInGroup: integer;
   var ZOrder: integer;
begin
     if GetGroupInfo(DdeClientConv1, Edit1.Text, GroupFile,
         GroupCaption, ItemsInGroup, ZOrder) = TRUE then
         begin
              ShowMessage('Group: ' + GroupCaption + NL +
              'Filename: ' + GroupFile + NL +
              '# of items in group: ' + IntToStr(ItemsInGroup) + NL +
              'Z order: ' + IntToStr(ZOrder));
         end
     else
         begin
              ShowMessage('Can''t find this group.');
         end;
end;
```

2. What's interesting about this solution is that it doesn't use any of the data returned by RequestData. It just returns `TRUE` if there was a response; that's enough to tell you whether the application responded to the DDE request, which is all you wanted to know.

```
{ Returns TRUE if the specified topic and item (typically,
  'SYSTEM' and 'TOPICS' or 'SYSTEM' and 'FORMATS' are
  supported by the application.  This is an informal
  Microsoft standard, although not all Microsoft
  applications support it.  Service is the
  DDE service name of the application; for example,
  'EXCEL' or 'WINWORD'.}
function RespondsToDDEReq(DdeClientConv: TDdeClientConv;
     Service: string;
     Topic: string;
     Item: string) : boolean;

var
   { TDdeClientConv.RequestData allocates a PChar string
     dynamically, leaving it up to you to delete its
     contents with StrDispose. }
   Info: PChar;
```

```
begin
     { Service is the DDE program name.
       Topic is usually 'SYSTEM', but it
       might be 'FORMATS'. }
     DdeClientConv.SetLink(Service, Topic);
     { Initiate the DDE conversation with Program
       Manager. }
     DDEClientConv.OpenLink;
     { Get information about the specified topic. }
     Info := DDEClientConv.RequestData(Item);
     { The information itself doesn't matter.
       But if RequestData returned a non-null
       value, it means that the application
       specified by Service supports the
       topic. }
     if Info <> NIL then
        RespondsToDDEReq := TRUE
     else
         RespondsToDDEReq := FALSE;
     { Reclaim memory allocated by the RequestData
       method. }
     StrDispose(Info);
end;
```

Here's an example of its use. Add a `TDdeClientConv` control, a button, and an edit control to a form. Set the `ConnectMode` property of `TDdeClientConv` to `ddeManual`. Add the routine above to the form.

When you run the program, you'll type the name of the group you want to find out about in this edit control, then click the button. The code for the button is shown below. Before running the program, start Microsoft Excel. Type `Excel` into the edit control. If you have Word for Windows, type `Winword` into the edit control. If you have neither program, don't worry—that's just as relevant; it exits gracefully returning a `FALSE` condition. The same would happen if you had Excel or Winword but didn't choose to run either of them.

```
procedure TForm1.Button1Click(Sender: TObject);
begin
    if RespondsToDDEReq(DdeClientConv1,
     Edit1.Text, 'System', 'Topics') = TRUE then
        ShowMessage('Supports standard Microsoft DDE topics')
    else
        ShowMessage('Does not supports standard DDE topics');
end;
```

If you had Excel or Word for Windows running, `RespondsToDDEReq` returned `TRUE` and displayed the message "Supports standard Microsoft DDE topics." If you don't have Excel or Word for Windows, or if you didn't have them running, the message "Does not supports standard DDE topics" is displayed.

Index

Symbols

A

B

C

D

E

F

G

H

I

J-K

L

M

N

O

Q

R

S

T

U

V

W-X-Y-Z

g and
nately
k and

ervice

0470-8

ers...)

umber

on Date

ignature

countries

riptions

da

co

her countries